The UNIX® Operating System

Operating System

Third Edition

Kaare Christian
Susan Richter

QA76.8
U65C554
c.5

John Wiley & Sons, Inc.
New York ■ Chichester ■ Brisbane ■ Toronto ■ Singapore

ISBN 0-471-58683-8 (cloth)
ISBN 0-471-58684-6 (paper)

Printed in the United States of America

10 9 8 7 6 5 4

For Edward Josiah Bunker

Preface

It's been more than 12 years since I wrote to four publishers, suggesting a book on the UNIX system. Two declined, possibly because they had never heard of the UNIX system. One of the better-known publishers in the field, noted for its early books on C, declined. They told me that if they were to publish a book on the UNIX system, they would prefer an author they had worked with previously. It now sounds quaint, a large publisher imagining just a single book on the UNIX system. Luckily for me, Jim Gaughan at John Wiley & Sons had heard of UNIX and thought it might be a well-received topic.

In the first edition, I tried to create a book that novices could read easily but that could also be useful to more advanced users. The first edition of this book covered many of the topics addressed in this current edition, plus it contained coverage of the UNIX typesetting tools, a glossary of UNIX terms, and an abridged system manual. These three large subjects eventually became separate books during the revisions that led to the second edition.

Both the first and the second editions of this book were notable for the cover, a single frame from the movie *Star Trek II, The Wrath of Khan*. The image was created by Ed Catmull, Alvy Ray Smith, and others at LucasFilm Ltd., and at the time it was the state of the art in computer graphics.

I labored to make the second edition of this book more focused than the first. By the time of the second edition, the continuing blizzard of UNIX titles was in full force, and it was apparent to me that I could best weather the storm by specializing. I strengthened coverage of the shell and other programmable tools that could be used by nonprogrammers, and I improved and extended the introductory material. The second edition, like this third edition, is a book for professionals, not necessarily programmers, who need to get the most out of their computer system.

As part of the process of preparing the second edition, I advertised on the USENET for reviewers. There were many people who responded and proved helpful, but none was so helpful as the person who replied in bold caps, "Pick Me! Pick Me!" That reviewer, Susan Richter, always stepped in with an apt phrase or illuminating paragraph whenever her radar detected something amiss, and her "something amiss" radar showed blips very often!

Susan became my co-author for the first time during the preparation of the *Xenix Command Reference Guide,* and now we are again working together on this third edition. So before switching from "I" to "we," let me say that working with Susan is a rare privilege. Her criticism of my work is ever on target, her own writing is uniformly first-rate, and her position as a UNIX systems programmer at The Rand Corporation gives her just the right perspective for this book.

We've made this third edition a book for would-be power users. More than other books, we talk about the why and when, and we always try to give some of the background. We try to show you that while the UNIX system isn't perfectly consistent, overall it makes sense. The more you know, the easier it is to extend that knowledge because the pieces fit together.

We start at the beginning, and don't assume very much. If you're already a UNIX user, you can surely skip the first three chapters, which cover the historical development of the UNIX system and the basics of using the UNIX system. Even if you've used the UNIX system in the past, you'll probably find something new in Chapter 4, which discusses interactive use of the UNIX shell, and Chapter 5, which discusses the UNIX file system.

The most important UNIX utilities are discussed in Chapters 6 through 8. Chapter 6 focuses on file management commands, Chapter 7 talks about miscellaneous utilities that let you manage your interaction with the UNIX system, and Chapter 8 introduces all of the renowned utilities for working with text files. In these three chapters, and in other places where utilities are discussed, we've included complete tables of command-line options and often other reference tables, so that this book serves both as a tutorial introduction and a long-lasting reference.

Chapters 9 and 10 cover the vi text editor. Vi is sleek, terse, and powerful, but most importantly it is available on all UNIX systems. Chapter 9 starts with the basics, but then manages to present enough of vi for casual users. If becoming a vi expert is your goal, then tackle Chapter 10. For those who want or need even more, there are three appendices on vi. Yes, it's complete.

Starting with Chapter 11, you may want to pick and choose your topics. If you are interested in automating routine chores, you'll find a wealth of shell programming information in Chapters 11 and 12. Chapter 11 presents most of the shell's programming features while 12 shows some longer shell programming examples. If you're interested in shell programming, you will probably also be interested in sed and awk, which are discussed in Chapters 13 and 14. Sed is a script-based text editor, while awk is a small but powerful programming language that is excellent for working with text files.

Why a workstation instead of a PC? Read Chapter 15, which discusses the criteria that are used to evaluate UNIX systems, and which compares the major hardware platforms that now run the UNIX system.

If you're a newcomer to the X Window System scene, Chapter 16 will give you some terminology, a look at the pieces of this client-server technology, and an understanding of how everything ties together. UNIX without a network is like a fish out of water—Chapter 17 gives a broad overview of computer networking concepts. Chapter 18 focuses on UNIX LAN utilities, and Chapter 19 talks about UNIX telecommunications capabilities.

Once you know how to use the UNIX system, you may want to have your own. Whether you opt for a high-end workstation or an economical-yet-speedy PC, you'll need to know the fundamentals of system management. Chapter 20 talks about basic system management principles, while Chapter 21 covers the most often used utilities for doing system management chores.

Security is a hot item today, with the computing world exploding with new networking capabilities and the accompanying threats of intrusion. Chapter 22 presents practical advice on how to assess the security needs of your system, some pointers on how to put security measures to work, and where to look for help.

After all this, there's some light reading to fill your Sunday afternoon! Chapter 23 dissects the kernel, so you can begin to understand what happens inside the system. Based on the idea that an ounce of understanding is worth a pound of how-tos, Chapter 23 helps you tie it all together.

Kaare Christian
Susan Richter

Acknowledgments

We would like to thank Terri Hudson, our editor at Wiley, for her able help and encouragement throughout this revision. Kaare would like to thank his family, Robin, Kari, Arli, and Reed, whose help and understanding made this book possible. Susan would like to thank Wilson H. Bent, Jr., for his constant encouragement as well as constructive and insightful comments on parts of the manuscript; and Laura Pearlman and Bob Schwartzkopf for lively and enlightening discussions on how things really work.

We would also like to thank those people whose help, encouragement, and constructive criticism made the first two editions of this book possible. For the second edition, these people include Maria Taylor and Diane Cerra at John Wiley & Sons, Inc.; Torsten Wiesel, Charles Gilbert, Dan Ts'o, and Owen Smith at the Rockefeller University; Jürgen Bolz at the Max Planck Institute in Tübingen, West Germany; Bruce Steinberg and Bridget Fuller at the Santa Cruz Operation; and Jan Heissinger and Julie Dollinger. For the first edition, these people include Robert Schoenfeld, Owen Smith, Edward Gershey, and Paul Rosen at the Rockefeller University; Tom Krausz and Eric Rosenthal of IMI Systems; Ed Catmull and Alvy Ray Smith of LucasFilm Ltd.; and Jim Gaughan and Jenet McIver at John Wiley & Sons, Inc.

Contents

21   System Management Utilities

1

The History of the UNIX System

The UNIX system is one of the major advances in the progression of computers from the esoteric realm of high technology into the mainstream of people's daily activities. It has demonstrated that a powerful operating system can be largely machine independent, and it has shown that powerful software tools can be used effectively by people in the course of using a computer to solve problems.

The UNIX system provides essentially the same services as those provided by all operating systems: it allows you to run programs, it provides a convenient and consistent interface to the wide variety of peripheral devices (printers, tapes, disks, terminals, etc.) that are connected to most computers, and it provides a file system for information management. The UNIX system's uniqueness is largely due to the way it evolved. We can best understand the system's growing popularity by adopting a historical perspective.

1.1 Modest Beginnings

Ironically, the UNIX system emerged from the attic of one of the world's strongest and most powerful corporate monoliths: Bell Laboratories, the research lab of AT&T. Most operating systems have been developed by computer manufacturers in order to sell computers. AT&T was not in the business of selling computers during the first decade of UNIX development, and the UNIX system was not originally envisioned as a commercial product. The UNIX system has only become a commercial venture in response to the demand that has developed.

In the late 1960s Bell Laboratories participated in the development of an operating system called Multics. Multics is a multiuser interactive system using a GE mainframe computer. Bell Labs withdrew from the Multics project in 1969, but Multics had a major influence on the UNIX system. In fact, the name UNIX is a play on the word Multics. One of the most striking differences between the UNIX system and Multics is complexity—the UNIX operating system is relatively simple while Multics is extremely complex.

At about the same time as Bell's withdrawal from Multics, the "grand-daddy of the UNIX system," Ken Thompson, began tinkering on a reject Digital Equipment Corporation PDP-7 minicomputer. Ostensibly, Thompson sought to create an operating system that could support the coordinated efforts of a team of programmers in a programming research environment. In retrospect this objective has been successfully accomplished. Also, in order to appease management, Thompson proposed that further UNIX system development be supported by Bell Labs in order to provide a document preparation tool for the Bell Labs patent organization. An early version of the UNIX system using a PDP-11/20 was actually delivered to the Bell Laboratories patent organization in 1971.

From the very beginning two seemingly incompatible disciplines, programming and document preparation, have been the cornerstones of the UNIX system. In practice the UNIX system has demonstrated that text management is central to many disciplines, including programming. While there are applications that require operating systems other than the UNIX system, the focus on text manipulation has served to make it an extremely general purpose operating system. Text is an accepted medium for communication, a key feature for a general purpose interactive operating system. And now that graphics have become increasingly important to many document preparation and other personal productivity applications, the UNIX system has proven its ability to expand into that area with graphics workstations combined with software such as the X Window System.

Ken Thompson's original efforts culminated in the creation of an operating system, a PDP-7 assembler, and several assembly-language utility programs. In 1973 Dennis Ritchie rewrote the UNIX system in the C programming language. C is a general purpose high-level programming language that was developed by Ritchie. It has proven to be adaptable to many different types of computer architecture. If the UNIX system had not been rewritten in a high-level language, it would have been chained to the machine (the outdated PDP-7) upon which it was developed. Once the original assembly-language programs were rewritten in C, it was suddenly possible to move the entire UNIX system from one environment to another with a minimum of difficulty.

Operating systems have traditionally been tied to one computer or family of computers because they were written in assembly language. Although the UNIX system was not originally intended to be a portable operating system, once it was coded in C, everything was in place to move it to other computer systems. The first move to a different type of computer was accomplished by Ritchie and Stephen Johnson in 1976 when they transported the UNIX system to the Interdata 8/32. Since then, the UNIX system has been ported, which means changed as necessary to work on a different type of computer, to virtually every popular computer architecture.

1.2 The Seventies

As Thompson gained acceptance from his colleagues and management during the early 1970s, the UNIX system began to be used internally throughout the Bell system. As word of the operating system spread, it generated interest at numerous universities. In 1975 Western Electric started licensing the UNIX system. The fee was nominal for academic institutions, encouraging many of them to use and further develop the UNIX system.

Even though the UNIX system was looked upon favorably by the academic high-technology research communities, it was initially met with skepticism by the business community. The UNIX system gained a reputation as a user-hostile, business-hostile system. Its strong adherents in the academic communities had little success in introducing it into mainstream businesses, although a few high-tech industries—aerospace, oil and gas exploration, financial services—recognized that UNIX gave them a competitive technological advantage.

1.3 The Eighties

During the eighties UNIX became accepted as a workhorse for high-tech applications, especially engineering and computer-aided design. The UNIX system gradually attained flexible and powerful networking capabilities, workstations became commonplace, and dumb terminals headed for the scrap heap. The mid-eighties introduction of workstation technology, pioneered by Sun, Apollo, Hewlett Packard (HP), and others, led to a glut of software windowing systems. But by the end of the decade only the X Window System remained on its feet.

The X Window System, like UNIX itself, was first husbanded in academia, and its success was largely due to its availability in source code form and its easy licensing. The X Window System is now accepted as the standard windowing system, also known as a graphical user interface (GUI), for computers running UNIX. The X Window System is extensible, it operates easily over a network, and its appearance and operation can be customized. The X Window System gives the UNIX system ease of use that matches the Apple Macintosh and the PC's Windows environment without forsaking the UNIX system's legendary prowess.

The main event during the eighties was the UNIX system's continuing internal struggle to define itself. AT&T is a formidable telephone company, but it has never been able to fully shape the future of UNIX. When AT&T was strong, other companies with an interest in UNIX, such as IBM, Sun, NCR, Apollo, HP, the Santa Cruz Operation (SCO), Microsoft, and others, complained bitterly that AT&T was competing unfairly. When AT&T faltered, these other companies developed competing versions and alternative technologies, further muddying the already murky waters.

For much of the decade there were two main factions: AT&T, which eventually settled on a strategy dubbed System V, and Berkeley, which produced the BSD (Berkeley Software Distribution) version of UNIX. Somewhat less contentious but extremely important because of its high sales volume was the Santa Cruz Operation. SCO first produced a UNIX version called Xenix that ran on the IBM PC architecture, but SCO switched to System V toward the end of the decade. During the eighties BSD UNIX's cause was gradually taken over by Sun Microsystems. Thus by the end of the decade the two main camps were AT&T and Sun.

Sun Microsystem's first innovation was the workstation. They created an industry around the idea of a personal workstation, equipped with a graphics display, a pointer, and networking, running the UNIX system. Sun's original workstations were based on CISC (complex instruction set computing) processors. CISC processor chips, which include the Intel 80x86 series of chips and the Motorola MC680x0 series of chips, are modeled after mainframe computers but made at a lower cost that enables manufacturers to build computers for individuals.

Sun's next innovation was use of a new CPU chip architecture called RISC (reduced instruction set computing). RISC tries to make CPU chips faster by making them simpler. Sun's own RISC implementation is called SPARC, but there are many competing RISC implementations, including IBM's PowerPC, and Digital Equipment's Alpha. In the late eighties the fastest workstations were all based on RISC chips, but the old-style CISC architecture, which is still used in most desktop PCs, has nearly caught up.

During the UNIX system's fractious eighties, tens of millions of PCs and Macintoshes were deployed on desktops around the world. These machines became ubiquitous tools for personal productivity software, which means word processors, spreadsheets, drawing packages, and other single-user applications. During the eighties UNIX remained a technological marvel, with impressive networking and communications' capabilities, but it never managed to crack the mainstream business market.

1.4   Into the Nineties

The nineties started in much the same manner as the eighties, with control of the UNIX system contested by a cacophony of contentious companies. But AT&T recognized that it had a hardware culture, not a software culture, and it recognized that UNIX needed room to grow. AT&T's first move was to transfer the UNIX operation to a new company called Unix Software Labs (USL). USL was independent, although it was owned primarily by AT&T.

In a similarly sensible style, Sun Microsystems modified its Sun OS 4 system to create Solaris, which is compatible with System V. Sun's move, coupled with SCO's earlier move to System V, legitimized System V as the major definition of UNIX. Variants will remain forever, but System V is now the undeniable center of the UNIX universe.

In late 1992 USL was purchased by Novell, which owns the lion's share of the PC networking business. This remarkable development stripped AT&T of its influence over UNIX, something that few observers had expected. And it gave full control of UNIX's destiny to a company whose roots, interests, and successes had all been in the PC marketplace. The results of Novell's stewardship of the UNIX system haven't yet been felt, but the 1990s promise to be a remarkable period.

Another development in 1992 was the announcement at Summer Use-NIX, a meeting of UNIX users, that Berkeley UNIX would conclude its contribution to the UNIX community with Release 4.4. Several of the people involved in BSD UNIX systems have formed small companies to support and extend the system but in a much smaller scale than when the project was supported by both Berkeley and ARPA, the Department of Defense's Advanced Research Projects Agency.

1.5 Versions of UNIX

In July of 1974 Ken Thompson and Dennis Ritchie published their classic paper, "The Unix Time-Sharing System," in the Communications of the ACM (Association for Computing Machinery). That paper led to widespread interest in UNIX, especially when people learned that copies of the Version 5 system, as described in the paper, could be acquired for just $150, unsupported but with complete source code.

By 1976 Version 6 of the UNIX system was distributed, both within the Bell system and to universities throughout the world. Version 6 featured a primitive shell, the ed text editor, and a set of about one hundred utilities strikingly similar to those supplied with the latest UNIX systems. The programming features of the Version 6 shell were rudimentary—it contained a goto statement for flow of control, variables named A-Z, and simple expression testing. However, its interactive features were similar in form and function to those found on today's shells; there was I/O redirection, pipelines, and background processing.

Version 6 served as a basis for development of several variants of UNIX, including the MERT real-time UNIX derivative, the PWB (programmers workbench) systems, and the early work on UNIX at Berkeley. Version 6 also gained the distinction of being the first UNIX to be copied by a commercial firm when Whitesmiths Inc. produced its Version 6 work-alike called Idris. Version 6 is also remembered as the system that was featured in John Lions' revealing book, A Commentary on the UNIX Operating System. Lions' sometimes-suppressed book was the first independent discussion of UNIX; other books were not forthcoming until this, and one or two other books appeared in 1983.

In 1978 Version 7 UNIX was released by Bell Laboratories. Version 7 UNIX is clearly recognizable to anyone who is accustomed to the more modern systems. Version 7 is important for many reasons. It featured the first release of the Bourne shell, the first shell to combine a powerful interpretive programming language with flexible features for interactive command entry. Version 7 had an important influence on the PWB systems, and it was the basis for the UNIX 32V system for Digital Equipment VAX computers. Many of UNIX's important subsystems attained their nearly final form in Version 7. Some UNIX veterans have a nostalgic feeling for Version 7; it was the last of the small, clean UNIX systems, yet it was certainly a "modern" UNIX system.

Inside the Bell system, the PWB UNIX system became Release 3.0, then 4.0, and finally in 1982 it evolved to 5.0. In the early 1980s, as Bell regained its interest in the UNIX system, they prepared commercial releases of UNIX. The name was changed from Release 5.0 to System V, a few additional documents were prepared, and then System V was proclaimed to be a standard. The original version of System V still contained the ed line editor, although later releases of System V contain the vi editor adopted from Berkeley.

During the late seventies and early eighties, when the UNIX system was nurtured but little at Bell Laboratories, it was being aggressively supported and improved by gifted graduate students at the University of California at Berkeley. Starting with the 32V system, Berkeley created 3 BSD and 4 BSD for the VAX series of computers. Berkeley UNIX enhancements include the C shell, the vi visual editor, the Franz Lisp programming language, the Pascal programming language, networking support, improved inter-process communication via sockets and pseudo-ttys, virtual memory support, and many significant performance enhancements. This stunning string of technical achievements has made Berkeley UNIX systems very popular, especially with the most demanding users.

Toward the end of the eighties, Berkeley reduced its UNIX development activities, and stewardship of most features known as "Berkeley" features passed to Sun Microsystems, who produced SunOS 3 and then SunOS 4. Sun's UNIX extended the Berkeley networking tools with a network file system (NFS) that became an industry standard. Sun also did early work in windowing software for UNIX workstations, although it eventually lost those battles to the X consortium, and its X Window System. In 1993 Sun moved to Solaris, which is essentially System V Release 4 plus some value-added features carried over from both BSD UNIX and SunOS UNIX systems.

While the UNIX system's early roots are on minicomputers, and its middle age was hosted on powerful workstations, the numbers point to increasing importance on personal computers. On the Macintosh, Apple's A/UX gives Macintosh users the benefit of the UNIX system without losing the benefits of the supportive Macintosh environment.

On the PC, which means personal computers that are broadly compatible with the architecture offered originally by the IBM PC, there are many versions of UNIX. For many years the PC market leader has been the Santa Cruz Operation, which originally offered Xenix. Currently SCO is actively promoting their version of System V, which retains compatibility with their older Xenix product line. The new player is Univel, which is a Novell spinoff, that is selling a System V implementation for the PC called UnixWare. Univel promises to be a major supplier, because of Novell's ownership of UNIX System Laboratories, the prime developer of the UNIX system.

1.6 UNIX Innovations

The UNIX system has pioneered several important ideas, both technical and philosophical. Let's first look at a few of the technical innovations, many of which come from the very early history of the UNIX system.

Perhaps the UNIX system's most important technical innovation is its portability. Portability, which is closely related to the idea of "open systems," decouples the once close relationship between software and hardware. Portability means that UNIX can run on many different hardware platforms. This enables applications software that was developed for UNIX to be portable, which promotes competition and gives users more choices. Portability means that software can evolve alongside hardware; it makes software longer lived and more economical.

Another important innovation is the pipe, which is a connection between the output of one program and the input of a second program. This has led to the idea that complicated operations can be managed by a set of programs working together. Solving a complicated problem using a group of cooperating processes has proven to be convenient for both program developers and program users, and it is a feature of UNIX that has been copied and extended in other environments.

Another idea that has pervaded the UNIX system is the notion of a software tool. A software tool is a program that addresses a single function. It does one thing well. In addition, a software tool is able to cooperate with other tools, usually using pipe connections, to perform more complex tasks. This contrasts with the style of desktop personal productivity software that developed on both the PC and the Macintosh, which emphasizes large do-it-all applications.

Another trailblazing aspect of the UNIX system is its use of a command-line user interface that is also a complete programming language. Version 6 of UNIX contained a primitive command-line interface called the shell, but in Version 7 and beyond the shell has been both a user interface and a sophisticated programming language. Understanding the shell is a key to getting the most from the UNIX system, and it is covered extensively in this book.

Another innovation of the UNIX system is its modularity. The earliest example was the removal of the user interface from the the UNIX system kernel. This was innovative at the time but is now standard for all operating systems. Similarly, the UNIX system evolved to support multiple, installable file systems, networking became a modular component, and many other subsystems became configurable options, so that UNIX systems could be delivered with a wide range of functionality. The ultimate expression of this trend is the Mach kernel, which provides minimal basic functionality. Mach provides only a rudimentary operating system substrate. Specific operating systems enhance the substrate by adding file systems, process structures, networking, and all the other features that we expect from a modern operating system. Mach is now being used as a basis for UNIX systems and for operating systems other than the UNIX system, and its ideas are influencing other current operating system designs.

The preceding paragraphs detail an impressive set of technical accomplishments, but they skirt the true importance of the UNIX system. I think that empowerment is the UNIX system's most important contribution. The UNIX system started the trend away from the glass house, away from the mainframe mentality. Ken Thompson was, in the best sense, selfish. He wanted a computer to meet his needs, an individual's needs. He wasn't interested in corporate goals or strategies, but rather he was interested in utility, in getting the most use out of a computer.

Empowerment is the heart of the UNIX system's early appeal, but empowerment nearly got lost during the eighties. The next logical step for the UNIX system, bringing the power of computers to everybody, not just the technically elite, stalled. Instead the makers of personal computers, primarily PCs and Macintoshes, learned how to create software that's universally usable. The UNIX system has come a long way in attaining the same ease of use as PCs and Macintoshes, but it has lost the first-round fight to occupy the desktop, and it remains to be seen if it will be a more prominent desktop player in the future.

The mid-nineties versions of the UNIX system take empowerment to a new level. They combine easy-to-use graphical interfaces with the UNIX system's traditional set of powerful utilities. Today the UNIX system lets you use a graphical calendar for setting up group meetings, a powerful CAD program for designs, or a modern spreadsheet for financial analysis, and then you can move into a command-line interface and use the traditional tools for the chores at which they still excel.

2

Fundamentals

As a first step in understanding the UNIX system, or any other operating system, you should have a general understanding of the building blocks that underlie a computer. This chapter presents some of these fundamentals. It starts with a brief hardware tour, and then talks about some of the major features of the UNIX software.

One of the major functions of an operating system is to disguise the building blocks of computers. You don't have to understand motors and circuit theory to operate an electric appliance, and you shouldn't have to understand computer architecture to use a computer. However, a basic understanding of the fundamentals will make it easier to understand some of the ebb and flow of ideas in the following chapters. If you have some experience with computers, then you should probably skip to Chapter 3.

2.1 The Old Way—Minicomputers

The UNIX system started out on minicomputers, which are often called *minis,* and it still has many features that don't make much sense while sitting in front of a modern workstation. But the UNIX system is still used to operate minis, especially in universities, and much of the generality forced upon the UNIX system by its heritage remains important today.

There are a few things that distinguish a minicomputer from a PC or workstation. Minis usually are shared by more than one user, they usually are accessed using dumb terminals, and they usually are operated by specially trained staffs. Minis are an evolutionary half-step. Their technology is a refinement of mainframe technology, and much of their culture looked backward to mainframes.

But minis also anticipated the PC revolution of the eighties. To some hidebound manufacturers, minis were just less costly, less capable mainframes. But to savvy programmers and to aggressive start-up companies, minis were an early and important step in the long march to a computer on every desktop.

Like other computers, minis are simply machines that follow a sequence of instructions. The instructions perform operations such as adding two numbers, moving some information from one location to another, making comparisons, or changing the sequence of instructions. The part of the computer that executes the instructions is called the *processor* (the central processing unit, abbreviated CPU), and the place where the instructions are stored is called the *memory*. Each storage location in the memory is assigned a unique number, called an *address*.

The major advantage of main memory is speed. Information can be retrieved very rapidly from the main memory of a computer. The disadvantages of the computer's main memory are that it has a limited capacity, it is relatively expensive, and on most computers the information in main memory is lost when the computer is turned off.

Secondary storage complements the abilities and drawbacks of the primary storage. The secondary storage has a relatively large capacity, it is relatively inexpensive, and it doesn't lose information when the computer is turned off. On minis the secondary storage devices (also called *mass storage devices*) are usually disks and tapes. Disks and tapes store data magnetically, as do audiocassette tapes. Disks are used for rapid access, which is sometimes called *on-line access*, while tapes are generally used for archival storage of information. (See Figure 2.1.)

You usually interact with a minicomputer using a terminal, which is often called a *video display terminal* or *VDT*. A terminal is a relatively inexpensive device that consists of a keyboard for data entry and a video screen for information display. The video display screen is often 80 characters wide by 24 or 25 lines tall, although several other sizes have been used. Historically most terminals have been limited to display of text, or perhaps text plus horizontal and vertical lines for grouping, although now there are graphics terminals that allow display of graphical information.

Computer terminals can be connected to a computer over telephone lines or by direct connections. Direct connections are preferable because they are faster and simpler but they work only when the computer terminal and the computer are physically close, which usually means within a few hundred yards. Terminals are relatively slow; typical terminals can receive a few thousand characters per second. It usually takes a second or more to completely rewrite the information on the screen of a terminal.

Terminals can be connected to computers via the telephone system. The key is to use a modem, which is a device that translates the terminal's electrical signals into audible chirps and squeals that can be sent through the telephone network. When you initiate a modem call, the modem often keeps its speaker on for the first second or two of the call, giving you a chance to eavesdrop on the static sound of data moving back and forth.

Terminals

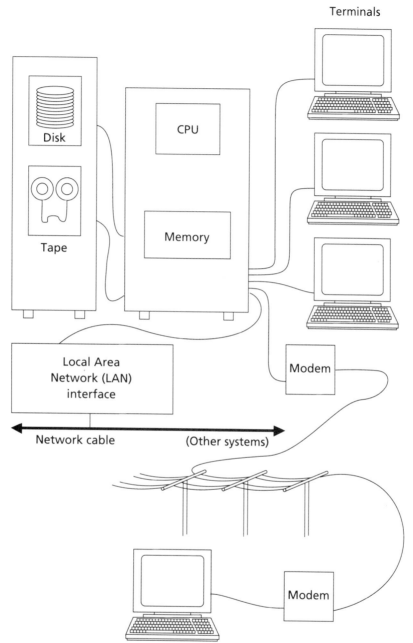

Figure 2.1 ■ A Typical Minicomputer

Today minicomputers are invariably connected to a network so that computers can communicate at high speed. All modern versions of the UNIX system support networking, most often the TCP/IP protocol suite using the Ethernet transport mechanism. Much more information on networking is in Chapters 17 and 18.

In the past most terminals were connected directly to a computer, but today many terminals connect to a terminal server, which then connects the terminals to a computer via the network. This adds flexibility for terminal users, since they can access any mini on the network once connected to the terminal server. It also makes it much easier to upgrade computer systems without touching the expensive (and sometimes delicate!) wiring connections to the terminals.

2.2   And the New Way—PCs and Workstations

PCs and workstations use the same sorts of components as minis, but they put the whole kit in a package small enough to sit on (or next to) your desk. The most important improvement, besides the packaging, is the integration of the display electronics into the main system unit. This provides vastly higher speed for display update operations, which is a key feature that is heavily used by most modern software packages.

Most PCs and workstations include a mouse or other pointing device, and many contain various specialized devices, such as CD-ROM drives for vast read-only storage, and floppy disk drives for access to diskettes. Some workstations omit the fixed disk drive, and instead rely upon larger machines for file services, using the network as a transport. These machines, known as diskless workstations, are very cost effective and reliable, because the disk is one of the most expensive and failure-prone parts of a computer. (See Figure 2.2.)

It has gotten very hard to tell the difference between a workstation and a PC, and it's also become less important. In the late eighties, workstations were partly derived from minicomputer technology, and they usually had high performance and a large display. At that time, PCs usually had less costly technology, lower performance, and poor video displays. Today the two technologies have converged. Machines that follow the standard originally set by IBM for PCs are usually called PCs, while machines from the traditional workstation vendors are called workstations. Most workstations use RISC CPU chips, while most PCs use Intel architecture (or Motorola architecture for the Macintosh) CPU chips.

2.3   Operating Systems

An operating system is a program that manages the resources of a computer. It serves both the application's software, which performs tasks that people usually find interesting and important, and the hardware, which has its own

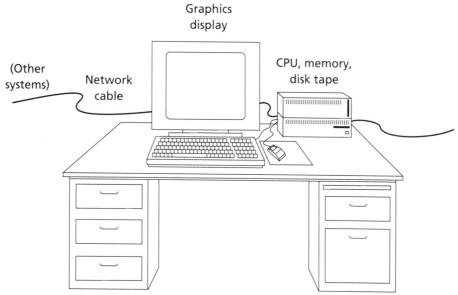

Figure 2.2 ■ A Typical Workstation or PC

set of needs and requirements. Operating systems send information to the communication devices, manage the storage space on mass storage devices, load information and programs into memory, and so on. In computer systems that support multitasking, such as the UNIX system, the operating system arbitrates the various requests in order to distribute the computer's resources fairly and effectively.

Operating systems first gain control when a computer is turned on, either by loading from disk or loading from the network. This process is called booting because it is analogous to pulling on your boots in the morning. On most machines that have attached disk drives, booting relies on the disk. Most computers that boot from a disk contain simple built-in software that loads the first few blocks on a disk, and then those blocks usually contain a simple loader that pulls in the remaining part of the operating system from the disk.

On diskless machines the built-in software places a message on the network asking for assistance booting. The request is answered by a machine known as a boot server that uses the network to download a copy of the operating system to the diskless machine. In either case, at the conclusion of the boot process the operating system is in charge and ready to serve applications.

A collection of information on a disk or a tape is called a *file,* and files are usually identified by names. One of the most intricate and important tasks of an operating system is managing the storage of files on disks. The way that files are organized is one of the central features of an operating system; the UNIX system's file storage scheme is discussed in Chapter 5.

2.4   Multitasking

Multitasking is a technique that allows a computer to work on several tasks seemingly at once. In practice the computer attends to one task for a brief period, then switches to the next, and so on. But if the switching is rapid, the computer creates the impression that all tasks are being processed simultaneously. Multitasking can be used to serve the needs of an individual, or it can be used to meet the needs of several people.

There are two forms of multitasking, cooperative and preemptive. In cooperative multitasking each process operates for as long as it wants, and then it voluntarily yields control, allowing the system to switch to some other task. This type of multitasking is used in the Microsoft Windows environment. In preemptive multitasking, which is found in all versions of the UNIX system, the operating system switches from one task to another at will. The benefit is that a single task can't hog all the execution time; each application operates independently. Also, the UNIX system is smart enough to skip over tasks that aren't ready to run, which increases efficiency.

2.5   Networking

When computers were rare, each could be utilized fully in isolation. However, today, with the ever-increasing numbers of computers, it is increasingly important to be able to move information easily between computers. A network is a group of computers that have hardware and software that enables them to communicate.

A wide area network (WAN) is a network consisting of computers that are far apart. Machines in a WAN typically communicate using the public telephone system, higher-speed leased telephone lines, microwaves or other high-speed terrestrial data links, or satellites. One of the earliest, and probably the most famous, WAN is the Advanced Research Projects Agency (ARPA) network developed to support defense industry projects. Over time the ARPA network became less a research network, and more a practical interconnection of most major computing sites in the country. Consequently it's now called the Internet, to reflect its role as an international backbone of computer communication.

In the UNIX community there is a UUCP (UNIX to UNIX Copy) network connecting, mostly via ordinary dial-up telephone lines, many UNIX systems. The UUCP network is not formally administered; rather each site makes individual agreements with nearby sites for access. The UUCP network is still in use, but its importance has been greatly reduced because of widespread use of the Internet, which has much higher speed than the UUCP network and many more capabilities.

When computer systems are physically close, high performance, cost-effective local area networks (LANs) are feasible. A LAN requires special cabling and interfaces, and typical LANs are limited to a distance of about a mile. Usually the term LAN is reserved for high-speed communications (at least one million bits per second). For example, two computers in a building might be connected by a serial data line operated at ten thousand bits per second. Such a connection wouldn't usually be called a LAN, even though it might perform many LAN functions. The two most common LAN transport standards in the UNIX environment are Ethernet and Token-Ring.

Communications on a LAN are governed by protocols, which are descriptions of the format of messages on the LAN. The first widely used LAN protocol on UNIX LANs is TCP/IP, which was originally developed by ARPA for use on the ARPA-net. Novell network protocols are often used on UNIX systems used in environments where PCs are common, and AppleTalk is often used on UNIX systems that are connected to Macintosh computers.

2.6   The Kernel

Certain operating system functions are required many times each second. For example, the part of the UNIX system that is involved in switching from one program to another (multitasking) is needed many times each second, as are the part that reads files from disks, the part that manages the keyboard, and the part that manages the display screen. In the UNIX system all the functions that are needed immediately are constantly kept in a memory resident part of the operating system that is called the *kernel*.

Other operating system functions are needed only occasionally, such as the capability to move a file from one place to another. These types of function are provided by utilities, standard programs that are invoked upon demand by the computer users. In the UNIX system it is easy for people to add to the stock of utilities simply by writing a new and useful program, often by combining and connecting existing utility programs.

In many operating systems the kernel contains a great many features. The UNIX system attempts to endow the kernel with relatively few features so that most operating system functions can be provided by utility programs. If you are curious about the kernel you should read Chapter 23, which explains the general organization of the kernel. The UNIX system kernel is simple enough to be understood in principle by most users.

2.7   Programs and Processes

A program is a sequence of instructions that the computer follows in order to achieve a certain result; it's what a programmer creates. When a program is not being executed, the sequence of instructions is stored in a file on the disk. To run the program, a copy of the instructions must be loaded into memory. While a program is running a UNIX system, it is called a *process*. If more than one copy of the program is running at the same time, then there are several processes but only one program.

Well-designed programs work flexibly. It would be foolish to write a program that changed the name of a file called alex to alicia. The program would be used once and then discarded. Instead there is a program that renames a file, and it is your responsibility when you run the program to supply the two names.

Although well-designed programs work flexibly, all programs have limits. Sometimes the limits seem arbitrary. For example, you can't use the program that changes the names of files to change other types of names in the system, such as the name that you use in your dialogs with the UNIX system (your login name). When you use a program, it is important to know what information the program requires from you, what the program can do, and what it cannot do.

Most UNIX system programs perform just one function. A complicated operation such as using the computer to write and distribute a memo may require a sequence of programs. It is usually up to you to decompose complicated operations (e.g., writing a memo) into a series of steps that correspond to the available set of programs. As you become proficient with the UNIX system you will realize that there are usually several different approaches to most complicated operations. Over time, operations that once required many steps are often automated. For example, in primeval UNIX systems the mail program didn't include text editing capabilities; most modern mail programs have a full set of text editing functions so that you only need to learn a single program to handle all aspects of electronic mail.

Programs can be divided into two general classes: utility programs and application programs. Utility programs usually perform general functions while application programs are designed for more specific purposes. For example, a program that an accounting firm runs to automate its bookkeeping would be classified as an application program, whereas a program that displays the time would usually be considered a utility. Utilities are usually supplied with an operating system while application programs are often acquired separately. Admittedly, the boundary is both shifting and blurry.

One purpose of this book is to acquaint you with the most useful UNIX system utility programs. Chapters 6, 7, and 8 present many of the most common and useful of the UNIX system utility programs. The majority of these programs are simple, effective tools for performing simple functions. The presentation of the programs in these three chapters shows typical applications. The idea is to acquaint you with these programs, not to present an exhaustive treatment of each program. After reading the general descriptions in this book, you should be able to learn the details of the utilities that you rely on from the documents supplied with your system.

2.8   The Vi Text Editor

An editor is a program that allows you to create and modify text files. You control the editor program by entering commands. All editor programs contain commands to display lines of a file, commands to add text to a file, and commands to change text that has already been entered.

UNIX systems contain several different text editor programs. The original editor was ed, a simple but effective program. Ed is important because it is universally available and because the style of operation pioneered by ed has been adopted by many other programs. However, for interactive use, better editors are now available. Ed's successor, ex, is discussed in Appendix III.

Today there are a handful of good editing programs for UNIX systems. In this book we focus on vi, a descendant of ed developed at Berkeley. Vi is powerful, flexible, and almost universally available. Hence, it is the program best able to claim to be the "standard" UNIX systems editor.

You can acquire a basic working knowledge of the vi editor in Chapter 9. A basic understanding will allow you to use vi but if you plan to use it extensively, you should also become familiar with the advanced functions discussed in Chapter 10 and the reference material in Appendixes I, II, and III. All versions of vi contain several features that are not mentioned in this book so you should probably examine the manuals for your system in addition to Chapters 9 and 10.

Text editors shouldn't be confused with word processors. In a text editor, the focus is on content, on creating a file containing text. A word processor also allows you to enter text, but the focus in a word processor is form, the visual appearance of the text. Word processors usually offer printer support, a choice of fonts, and other formatting options so that you can create a document that has an attractive appearance.

There are many word processors available for UNIX systems, but they aren't covered here because they don't relate directly to the goal of this book, which is showing you how to tap the native power of the UNIX system. Most commercial word processors are very easy to use, and most are documented and supported well by the manufacturer.

2.9 The UNIX Shell

The shell is one of the most important programs in the UNIX system. The shell is an interactive program, plus an interpreter for executing command scripts. You can control the shell by entering commands which the shell interprets (decodes) and executes. Therefore, the technical name for the shell is *command interpreter*. You can also control the shell by creating a script and then having the shell execute the script.

The function of a command interpreter is to execute the commands that you enter. For instance, if you want to run the program that prints the date and time on your screen, you enter the command *date* and the shell then arranges for that program to be executed by the UNIX system.

On many systems the command interpreter is a part of the internal structure of the operating system. However, in the UNIX system the shell is just an ordinary program, similar to the date program or any other program. The only thing that is special about the shell is the fact that it is central to most of your interactions with the UNIX system. If you are a typical user, then you will spend much of your time entering commands. The shell has many features that can increase your effectiveness.

The UNIX system is primarily a tool for information management. The power of the UNIX system stems from its ability to let programs work together to produce the information that you need. On most computer systems each program is a world unto itself. In the UNIX system, most programs are simple tools that can be combined with other programs to produce more powerful tools.

The shell is the key to coordinating and combining UNIX system programs. Several chapters present the features of the shell. About half of Chapter 3 is a very simple introduction to the shell. Chapter 4 focuses entirely on the shell as an interactive command interpreter. The information in Chapter 4 may seem dry on first reading; try to work through it a second time after you have some experience with the UNIX system.

Besides being an interactive command interpreter, the shell is also a very sophisticated programming language. Most users ignore the programming language features of the shell simply because most users are not computer programmers. However, if you want to use the shell as a programming language, read Chapter 11 and work through the examples given in Chapter 12.

3
UNIX System Basics

Learning about a new computer system is like visiting a foreign country—the experience may be intimidating at first. You may be using the UNIX system on a graphical workstation, which means that you already have point-and-click access to many functions, such as electronic mail and word processing. The goal of this chapter is to introduce you to some of the traditional UNIX tools, which is a first step in learning to harness the power of the UNIX system.

Some people want to read a short paragraph that will tell them everything they need to know in order to use the UNIX system. Perhaps a typewriter or a toaster can be described that briefly but a computer operating system cannot. To use the UNIX system effectively you have to master a fairly large body of knowledge. However, most of the ideas are straightforward and if you are patient, you will soon be an effective UNIX system user.

3.1 Logging In

The first thing that you have to do to use the UNIX system is to log in. The purpose of logging in is twofold: to let the UNIX system verify your right to use the system and to let the UNIX system set up your environment. In computer systems that allow access over the telephone, it is very important to restrict use to authorized people; and in computer systems where the users are charged, it is important to know who is using the computer so that the billing can accurately reflect use. One of the functions of the UNIX system is to manage the computer resource so that several people can share the computer. In order to do this, the UNIX system maintains a separate environment for each user. The UNIX system remembers who each user is, when each logged in, how much computer time each has used, what files each owns, what files are immediately accessible, what type of a terminal is being used, and so on.

In most single-user computer systems (e.g., PCs, Macintoshes), there is no login procedure because physical access to the hardware confirms your right to use the system. In some mainframe operating systems, there is no formal login process; instead each submitted job is identified for billing and scheduling purposes. In the UNIX system, once you have completed the login process, you don't have to identify yourself each time you run a program.

Before you can log in for the first time, you must have an account. In many organizations there is a system administrator who will create your account. It is usually simple to set up an account at a UNIX system that doesn't charge the users for computer time. Setting up an account at installations that charge for computer time is more difficult because the system administrator will ask you to provide information about billing and money. See Chapter 20 for more information.

From your point of view, the major issue in setting up an account is deciding on your login name. Your login name is the name that you want to use during your interactions with the UNIX system. Short, lowercase names are usually easiest. Many people use their initials, nickname, or first name. The names betsy, kc, and m are all acceptable. Some organizations have guidelines for login names. The two most common guidelines are to use your first name (or possibly your shortened first name) followed by the initial of your last name, or your first initial followed by your last name. You should check with the system administrator to make sure that your name follows the local guidelines and that it isn't already in use in your organization.

3.1.1   Logging in Using a Terminal or PC

Once you have an account, you can try logging in. If you are using a local terminal or workstation, your first chore is to activate the login message. On a terminal you sometimes need to strike **Enter** or **Carriage Return** once or twice (striking **Ctrl-D** may also help) to get a fresh login message.

If you're using a PC or Macintosh, run your communications program, specify the phone number and connection speed, and follow the instructions provided with your communication software. If you are using a dial-up terminal, you should set the full-duplex/half-duplex switch to full, and you should set the speed of the terminal and/or modem to the correct speed. Dial the number of the computer and wait for the beep. When you hear the beep you should place the handset in the acoustic coupler or hit Hold on a multiline phone or Online on a data phone. The exact scheme depends on what telephone hardware you have.

Once you have established a connection, the computer will type something on the screen. If the message is

```
login:
```

or something similar, then the communication speeds (of the terminal and the computer) are synchronized and you can go ahead and enter your login name. If the message on your screen is garbled, then hit the break key on your terminal, or instruct your communication software to send a break. The break causes the UNIX system to change its communication speed in an attempt to synchronize with your terminal. The UNIX system will type a fresh message. If the message is garbled, try hitting the break key again. The UNIX system usually cycles through a list of four or five speeds in order to synchronize speed with your terminal. If after four or five attempts you can't get the UNIX system to print a clear `login:` message on your terminal, you should seek the help of an expert.

Eventually you should see the `login:` message. Enter your login name and hit return. After a brief pause, the UNIX system will ask for your password. A password is a secret word that you enter in order to confirm your identity. Enter your password and hit return.

During most of your interactions with the UNIX system, you will see each character that you type. However, while you are entering your password, the UNIX system will try to maintain the privacy of your password by not echoing the characters that you are typing. The UNIX system is listening, but not echoing. You must type your password very carefully because you will not see it as it is entered. If you make a typing mistake, you will probably have to restart the login process from the beginning.

Once you have entered your password, the system checks it. If it passes inspection, then the login process will continue. If the password or login name is incorrect, you will be asked to enter your login name and password again. On some systems the password system is not used. Some systems have an additional layer of security—they require you to enter a dial-up password before you are asked to enter your login name and personal password.

The UNIX system may print several messages at the end of the login process. These messages, which are usually called the *message of the day* or *motd,* may divulge news about system scheduling, new programs, users' meetings, and so forth. After the messages, the UNIX system will print a prompt to indicate that the system is ready to accept your commands. The default prompt is usually a currency symbol ($). Here's what it looks like:

```
login: kc
Password:
                NOTICE
The system will be down from tonight at 8:00
until 6:00 tomorrow morning for routine maintenance.
** Remember, monthly users meeting this Weds at 8 pm. **
$
```

3.1.2 Logging in Using a Workstation

Logging in using a workstation is very similar. The first task is to get to the login screen. On a workstation that is already running a window system, you sometimes need to move the mouse to restore the screen. (When a workstation is idle for a few minutes, a screen blanker usually turns off the display to reduce the wear and tear on the monitor.) A typical login screen is shown in Figure 3.1.

Once you have the login prompt displayed on the screen, enter your login name, press **Return** or **Enter**, and then enter your password. Your password won't be displayed, to protect its privacy. After the password has been entered, press **Return** or **Enter** again and the system will start to display your desktop. The initial desktop on my PC running UnixWare is shown in Figure 3.2.

On a graphics workstation, you typically access many UNIX system functions using icons and menus. This is a great simplifier, and it's wonderful for many chores. But it doesn't really unlock the power of the UNIX system; instead it makes it easy to do routine tasks. In this book the focus is on using all the UNIX system facilities, which means you need to enter commands directly.

If you want to use the command-line interface on a workstation, you need to run a virtual terminal program. Usually there's an icon somewhere on your desktop or in one of your folders that will start up the terminal program. Double-click on the terminal icon and the terminal program will start to execute.

A virtual terminal program is simply a graphical application that mimics an ordinary video display terminal. The text that you type is displayed on the screen, interwoven with the responses generated by the system. However,

Figure 3.1 ■ A Typical Workstation Login Screen

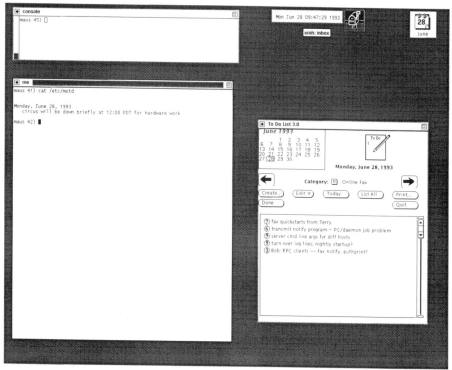

Figure 3.2 ■ Initial Desktop Screen on a Workstation

there are several big advantages to running a virtual terminal program on a workstation, instead of using a real terminal. The first is speed. Because the virtual terminal is just that, virtual, it can operate very rapidly, usually far faster than a real VDT. The second advantage is that you can have several virtual terminal windows open at once. This is great when you want to work on several tasks at once because you can switch easily from one virtual terminal to another.

3.2   Some Simple Commands

The best way to learn about the UNIX system is to use it. Try the date command.

```
$ date
Weds Jan 21 16:32:39 EST 1993
$
```

In this dialog, things that you type are shown in bold type and responses from the computer are plain. The currency symbol is UNIX's prompt. (The prompt may be different on your system.) To enter the date command, type the letters *d*, *a*, *t*, and *e* followed by a carriage return. The carriage return says to the computer, "I've finished typing the command, now it's your turn." Don't forget to press carriage return or Enter at the end of every entry.

Next try the who command. Here's what is displayed on my personal workstation:

```
$ who
kc        pst000    Jan 21 16:04
$
```

On a multiuser machine, you'll get a whole list of names of users:

```
$ who
td        tty10 Jan 20 15:37
kc        tty18 Jan 21  9:17
alvy      tty11 Jan 21 10:49
karl      tty03 Jan 19 12:40
$
```

The output lists people who are currently using the system along with the time they first logged in and the identification name of the terminal they are using. Notice that my own login name, kc, is in the list.

Now let's explore the echo command.

```
$ echo hello
hello
$
```

In this dialog the word echo is the name of the command and the word hello is an argument to the command. Arguments are used to supply additional information to a command. The echo command simply repeats its arguments. Several uses for the echo command will be seen later in this book. In the UNIX system, commands and their arguments (there can be several arguments) are separated by spaces or tabs. The white space (spaces or tabs) is extremely important. If you omit the white space, the system will not understand your command.

```
$ echohello
UX:sh: ERROR: echohello: Not found
$
```

Capitalization is also extremely important. The UNIX system understands that lowercase letters are different from uppercase letters. The names of most UNIX system commands are written in lowercase. If you type in the wrong case, the system will not understand your command.

```
$ Echo Hello
UX:sh: ERROR: Echo: Not found
$
```

3.3   Files and Directories

A file is a named collection of information. You will use numerous files in your interactions with the UNIX system. The computer term *file* is extremely well chosen. A computer file is completely analogous to a paper file stored in a filing cabinet. Computer files have names, they have lengths, they can get bigger and smaller, they can be created and discarded, and they can be examined.

It is impossible to exaggerate the importance of files in the UNIX system. Every time you run a program, you are accessing a file. Most of the programs that you run then access more files, often files that you have mentioned on the command line.

While there may be thousands of files in a UNIX system, only a few of the files are visible at one time. In the UNIX system, files are clustered into groups called *directories*. Each directory has a name; for example, the full name of the directory that contains most of my files is /home/kc. The file system is discussed in detail in Chapter 5 and the utility programs for managing files are discussed in Chapter 6.

One of the reasons for the login process is to establish your initial environment. One element of your environment is the name of your current directory. When you first log in, the system makes the current directory your home directory. Each user usually has his or her own home directory. If your account has just been created for you, then your home directory is probably empty except for a few administrative files. On a graphical workstation, your home directory will probably contain files that relate to the choices and folders that appear on your electronic desktop.

The pwd (print working directory) command prints the name of the current directory. The current directory is your location in the large set of files found on most systems; it's the place in the library stack where you are "sitting" right now. Since different files are available in different directories, you should always be aware of the name of the current directory.

```
$ pwd
/home/kc
$
```

On my system, the pathname /home/kc is displayed on the terminal when I run the pwd command just after logging in. On your system, the name of your own home directory will be displayed. The organization of the UNIX file system and the use of pathnames (e.g., /home/kc) are discussed in the next chapter. The remainder of this chapter only requires you to understand that files are grouped into units called *directories*. (In a graphical environment, directories are often called *folders*.)

Besides knowing the name of the current directory, you often want to know what files are in the current directory. The ls (list) command is used to list the files in a directory. Here's the output from ls just after my account was created on my PC running UnixWare:

```
$ ls
Accessories    Folder_Map    Preferences    Utilities      mailbox
Applications   Games         Shutdown       Wastebasket    netware
Disks-etc      Help_Desk     System_Setup
$
```

There are certain standard directories on most UNIX systems. For example, the directory /bin usually contains many of the programs that you use. Enter the following command to see a list of the files in the /bin directory:

```
$ ls /bin
```

When you supply the name of a directory as an argument to the ls command, all of the files in that directory are listed.

The UNIX system allows you to move from one directory to another, which means that a new directory becomes the current directory. The cd command is used to move to a new directory. (Cd stands for change directory.)

```
$ cd /bin
$
```

If nothing is printed by cd, it means the change was okay. It's common for UNIX system commands to say nothing when things work. You'll get used to it. When there are failures, UNIX commands almost always display error messages, although the usefulness of those messages varies.

Now try the pwd command to verify that you are in a new directory.

```
$ pwd
/bin
$
```

When you are in the /bin directory, you can use the ls command to list all of the files in /bin. Remember that when you were in your home directory you had to use the argument /bin with the ls command to get this same list of files.

As you can see, the operation of some commands varies according to what directory you are in. Many people are very confused by the rather changeable UNIX system environment. Operations that work in one directory often don't work in another. You should always be aware of the name of the current directory. Once you understand the UNIX system directory structure, you will see that directories are an asset, not an impediment.

3.4   UNIX System Dialogs

Users engage in dialogs with the UNIX system. Typically you enter a command and then the UNIX system replies. For simple commands, the reply usually occurs in a second or less. Complicated commands can take much longer, and even simple commands can take forever when a UNIX system is seriously overloaded. The dialog rules are discussed in some detail because the dialog is central to working effectively with the UNIX system.

Entering a UNIX system command is analogous to submitting a job on certain other computer systems. When you enter a command you ask the computer to do something for you. For now you can imagine that the phrase "entering a command" means that the computer runs a program for you. As you learn more about the UNIX system, you will realize that entering a command often involves more than just running a program, and you will begin to understand how the UNIX system environment makes the whole greater than the sum of its parts.

As a beginner you should enter just one command on a line. Later chapters will show you how to enter several commands on one line or to run several commands at once. You enter a line of input by typing a string of characters and then hitting the Enter (sometimes labeled carriage return) key. Enter specifies the end of a line of input. When you are entering commands, it usually specifies the end of a command and it tells the UNIX system to execute the command.

One difference between the computer and human listeners is that the computer virtually ignores your sentence (command) until you press Enter. It is easier to talk to human listeners because they give you feedback as you talk. Another difference between computers and human listeners is that the computer is extremely picky about what you say (type). People will usually understand what you are saying even if your grammar or pronunciation is poor, but the dumb computer is stopped cold by the simplest typo. You have to be careful as you type your commands or you will spend too much time reentering them.

Once you hit the Enter key, the UNIX system suddenly becomes interested in what you have typed. The UNIX system immediately attempts to figure out what you want. The first word of the command is always the command name and a program called the shell attempts to locate that particular command. Let's suppose that you want to run the echo program but by mistake you type the word Echo. We saw earlier that you get a message similar to `UX:sh: ERROR Echo: not found` because there is no command named Echo.

If the UNIX system can find the command, it hands over control of your terminal to that program. Each particular command has its own format for telling you about errors in your input. For example, you might want to list the files in the /bin directory but by mistake you type `/bum`.

```
$  ls /bum
UX:sh: ERROR: Cannot access /bum: no such file or directory
$
```

When you make a mistake in entering the argument to a command, it is the command itself that prints an error message. In the example above, it is ls that complains about the missing /bum directory. As you can see, the message is quite clear and informative. Although an attempt has been made to make the UNIX system error messages uniform, you will certainly encounter some misleading messages.

It is important to understand that the characters that you type are not sent directly from the keyboard to the screen. Instead, the characters are sent first to the UNIX system and then back to your screen. This rather complicated arrangement is for flexibility. The UNIX system gets each character before it is printed on your screen so that it can perform any necessary transformations. As an example, the UNIX system can translate a tab character into an appropriate number of space characters. Or the UNIX system can refrain from returning characters to you at certain times such as when you are entering a private password.

As you type in your line of input, the UNIX system is spending most of its time attending to other matters. However, two special characters are attended to immediately: the erase character and the kill character. The erase character will erase the already entered characters one at a time and the kill character will erase the whole line so that you can start over.

You can specify which key on your keyboard should be used for the erase character and which should be used for the kill character. For historical reasons, many UNIX systems initially assign the erase character to the sharp key (#) and the kill character to the commercial at sign (@). The # and the @ are used because they are present on most terminals and they are seldom used otherwise. If your keyboard has more suitable characters, the erase and kill should be reassigned. On many terminals, the Ctrl-H key or the rubout key is used instead of the # as the erase character, and the Ctrl-U key is often used in place of the commercial @ sign as the kill character. (A control character is formed by holding down the Ctrl button and then hitting the specified character.)

On some systems the only way to correct errors during the entry of your login name and password is to use the # and the commercial @ because the reassignment doesn't occur until near the end of the internal login procedure.

Here is an example of using the erase character (assigned in this case to the default #, which is a good character to use in a book because it is easily visible):

```
$ qgi###wgo##ho
kc            pts000      Jan 21 23:03
$ ▮
```

If you follow the character sequence shown, you will see that the user actually specified the who command.

Here is an example of using the kill character (assigned in this example to the commercial @ sign) to erase a mangled input line so that it can be completely retyped:

```
$ echohello@
echo hello
hello
$ ▮
```

The exact appearance of a line following the entry of the kill character varies from system to system. On some systems the kill character erases the input line if you are using a display terminal. This is very hard to show in a book. On other systems the kill character automatically advances you to the next line (as shown in this example), while on some older systems the kill character logically erases the line but there is no acknowledgment on the screen.

While you are typing a line you can use the erase character to erase portions of the line or the kill character to erase the whole line and start over. However, once you press the Enter key, your input is interpreted as a command.

Many commands perform one function and then stop. For example, a program to type a file will type the file and then be finished. Other commands work interactively. One example of an interactive command is a text editor. The text editor interactively accepts commands from the user using a dialog similar to the UNIX system command dialog that we are describing in this chapter.

While you are executing an interactive program, only the commands of that program are directly available. When the interactive program terminates, you return to command level and a prompt is printed to tell you that the UNIX system is ready to accept your commands. You always have to remember the context while using a computer. Once you become familiar with the system, this context switching will become a reflex. When things don't work as you expect, you should explicitly think about the context of the situation. Perhaps you are entering editor commands while you are in the UNIX system command mode or perhaps you are entering UNIX system commands while you are in the editor.

Occasionally you will run a program that you will want to stop. In the UNIX system you stop a running program by striking the interrupt character. The interrupt character is similar to the erase and kill characters because it leads to immediate action by the system. The interrupt character is usually assigned to the delete key (often labeled ''DEL'') or to Ctrl-C. The interrupt character can be assigned to any key on your terminal.

Because certain programs must not be halted during critical sections of their operation, the UNIX system allows programs to disable the interrupt function. If a program has disabled the interrupt function, then the interrupt key will have no effect. For example, the text editor disables interrupts during most of its operation because you don't want to lose the file that you are working on by accidentally striking the interrupt key. (Those of you who understand the internal working of computer hardware should be careful not to confuse the UNIX system interrupt function with hardware interrupts.)

3.5   Logging Out

It is much easier to log out than to log in. When you are finished using the system, you should log out. Logging out informs the system that you are not going to place any further demands upon the system. In a system where you are billed by the minute, it is very important to log out as soon as you finish your work.

Logging out also has security and reliability considerations. In a business or academic setting you might want to log out before going to lunch or leaving your work area for a long period of time. That's because your files are accessible to anyone wandering by while your workstation is logged in but unattended. Once you've logged out, it's far harder for other people to access your files. This is less important for people with private offices or for people who don't store private information on the computer. Similarly, when you're logged out, all your current files are closed and in a very stable state. You're much less likely to lose files during a power outage or hardware failure if you're logged out.

When you are using an ordinary terminal, you can log out by running the exit command. Another way to log out is to strike a Ctrl-D at the beginning of a line. The Ctrl-D is the UNIX system's end-of-file character. Typing an end-of-file character tells the UNIX system that there are no further commands to process. If you are connected to the system by a dial-up line, an alternate way to log out is to hang up the phone.

On a workstation you should log out by pulling down the system menu, which is usually in the top left corner of your desktop window, and then select Exit. Note that if you're using a virtual terminal and you enter the exit command (or you strike Ctrl-D at the beginning of a line), all you will do is shut down that virtual terminal—you'll still be logged in.

On either a terminal or a graphics workstation, you know that you're logged out when the login message appears. If you don't get a login message, you haven't successfully logged out (except when you log out of a phone connection; on many systems logging out hangs up the phone, which makes it impossible to see the subsequent login message).

3.6   The UNIX User's Reference

One of the major reference documents for anyone who is using the UNIX system is the *User's Reference Manual* (URM). (Some editions use the title, *The UNIX User's Manual*.) The *User's Reference Manual* contains information about most of the commands that are available on your system. Make sure that you have the manual that is appropriate for the version of the UNIX system that you are using. Obsolete manuals frequently are more readily available than the latest manuals.

This book is not a replacement for the references that are supplied with your system. They contain specific information for your system, and they contain information for many obscure commands and features that aren't discussed in this book. The strength and the weakness of the standard references is that they are specific. In contrast, this book attempts to present general information that pertains to all UNIX systems. Another function of this book is to distinguish the common and useful programs from the obscure. Naturally, the *User's Reference Manual* gives full coverage to all programs.

The manual is designed by and for people who are familiar with the basic operation and services of the UNIX system. If you are a novice user, you might find that some of the descriptions in the manual are too terse to be very helpful. As you become a more advanced user, you might find that the terse style of the manual makes it easier to use than a verbose manual.

Most simple commands are described adequately in the manual. For example, the reference for the *pwd* command in our UNIX manual states clearly: "Pwd prints the pathname of the working (current) directory."

However, the manual entries for many of the more complicated commands are much less useful for most people. Some of the more complicated commands are described in separate documents, often in papers published in academic journals. These accounts usually are adequate descriptions for computer scientists, but sometimes they are indecipherable to casual users.

The user's manual is divided into eight sections. The first section describes most of the commands that are available on the system. Sections 2 through 8 describe aspects of the system that programmers are interested in. For most nonprogrammers, Sections 2 through 8 are mere curiosities (except for Section 6, Games).

Section 1 of the manual contains an alphabetized list of citations for the UNIX system commands. There should be a citation in Section 1 for most commands that are available at your installation. Commands that are unique to your installation, such as graphics commands at a graphics laboratory, are often described in a locally distributed addendum to the manual.

Closely related commands are occasionally discussed in a single citation. In our URM, the *mv* (move), *cp* (copy), and *ln* (link) commands are all discussed in a single citation because they all shuffle files. If you can't remember the exact name of a command, you should try looking up any related word in the permuted index, which usually is printed at the beginning of the manual. For example, you could look up the word move in the permuted index in order to discover that the *cp* citation describes how to "copy, link, or move files." The permuted index in the *User's Reference Manual* is similar to the keyword in context index used by some abstracting services and scholarly journals.

Each citation in Section 1 of the URM follows a uniform format. The top of the citation shows the name and a brief description followed by a synopsis of the command. For the *ls* command, the top of the citation looks like

```
NAME
     ls - list contents of directories
SYNOPSIS
     ls [ -ltasdriu ] names
```

The synopsis gives you an indication of how you would enter the command. The synopsis for *ls* indicates that you enter the word ls optionally followed by a list of options (one or more of the characters ltasdriu) followed by a list of names of directories or files. Square brackets in the synopsis indicate that the bracketed item is optional.

The description of the command usually follows the synopsis. For the *ls* command, the description is a little more than a page long. The description of a command usually describes the basic operation of the command and how you can alter the basic operation by using various options. For example, the *ls* command has options that allow you to display additional information, such as file dates and sizes, along with the list of file names.

After the description are several brief paragraphs: the FILES paragraph names any files that are used by the program, the SEE ALSO paragraph lists related commands whose citations might contain useful information, the BUGS paragraph might contain some useful caveats, and the DIAGNOSTICS paragraph might help you decipher error messages. Any or all of these four paragraphs may be omitted, and additional paragraphs may be present. The entire citation for most commands is about a page long.

The citations in Sections 2 through 8 follow a similar format that should be understandable by anyone who needs to use these sections. They will not be discussed here. Remember that as a novice you will usually use Section 1 of the manual. Beware that Sections 2 through 8 occasionally contain citations with the same names as citations in Section 1.

4
Entering Commands Using the Shell

Computers can perform operations at great speed, but they have no sense of value. The computer cannot distinguish between useful work and idle cycling. Since computers have no initiative, they must be told exactly what they should do. Occasionally someone writes a program that makes it appear that a computer has initiative but in reality the computer is a sloth.

People have developed command languages to make it easier to control a computer. Most command languages are designed so that there are easy commands to specify common operations. Commands specify exactly what programs the computer should execute.

Computers do not have an innate ability to decipher the commands that you type at the terminal. Most operating systems provide a command interpreter to perform this function. The standard UNIX command interpreter is called the *shell*. The term shell was coined after the notion that the command interpreter program, like the shell of a sea creature, surrounds the messiness of the operating system's innards and provides you with something firm and easy to grasp.

To use the UNIX system effectively you have to know how to enter shell commands. The shell provides a wealth of features that make it possible to specify very powerful commands. It is possible to use the UNIX system with only a slight knowledge of the shell; however, your work will be more rewarding and efficient if you learn about the shell. For those of you who want to learn more about the shell, later chapters discuss shell programming and other advanced features. This chapter presents the shell at a level that can benefit most users.

4.1   Unix System Shells

Today there are three common shell programs: Steven Bourne's Bourne shell (also known as sh and often pronounced by spelling it out), Bill Joy's C shell (also known as csh), and Dave Korn's Korn shell (also known as ksh). Let me start with the Bourne shell and Joy's C shell, because they came first.

Steven Bourne's shell features a powerful command programming language. It was developed while Bourne worked at AT&T, and it has long been a standard component of all UNIX systems. Bill Joy's shell is known for its interactive features. Joy developed C shell while he was a graduate student at Berkeley, and it was a standard component of all BSD UNIX releases. But the BSD versions of UNIX also included the Bourne shell, which is why it can claim to be the most "standard" UNIX system shell.

In some areas these two shell programs are very similar. Their basic features, syntax, and notation are extremely close because both designs were heavily influenced by the obsolete Version 6 shell. However, the areas of difference are deep. Both shells contain many of the features of a programming language, such as variables, if statements, and loop statements. However, the syntax for these programming language features is totally different between the two shells. Another incompatibility concerns the C shell features for interactive command entry, aliases, and a history mechanism that are not found in the Bourne shell. The C shell introduced features for job control, which provide an easy way for you to interact with several tasks using a single terminal. These features are now also found in some versions of the Bourne shell. However, job control features are now less important than in the past because graphical windowing systems let you have multiple terminal sessions on a single screen.

Many advisers recommend the C shell for interactive use, and the Bourne shell for writing shell command scripts. The obvious disadvantage of this method is that one must learn two separate systems where ideally one system should suffice. However, most people prefer the C shell amenities for interactive use, and the Bourne shell is the best choice for writing portable shell scripts because it is the most widely available.

The Korn shell is Dave Korn's attempt to solve the dilemma of what shell to use. The Korn shell is fully compatible with the Bourne shell, but it also contains additional components that improve on the interactive functionality of the C shell. Even better, the Korn shell is extremely efficient. Thus, the Korn shell is a hybrid that contains the best of the Bourne shell and the C shell, and then some. But there is a catch—the Korn shell isn't universally available. In a move that has baffled many observers, AT&T tried to make some pocket change by selling the Korn shell separately, instead of bundling it with all systems.

In this book we are emphasizing the features of the Bourne shell because of its universal appeal. Most of the shell dialogs shown in this book are based upon the Bourne shell, as signified by the use of the currency symbol ($) as the standard shell prompt. In a few cases where the C shell is substantially different, we have shown an equivalent C shell dialog. The occasional C shell dialogs use the percent sign (%) as a prompt. Regarding most features discussed in this chapter, the two shells have equivalent syntax and operation so only the Bourne shell dialogs are shown.

4.2   Simple Shell Commands

A simple command is a sequence of (one or more) words separated by blanks or tabs. The first word of the command is the command's name. Subsequent words are the command's arguments. (You should remember from Chapter 3 that arguments are used to pass additional information to a command.) The simplest simple command is a single word. For example, the *pwd* command prints the name of the current directory.

You can enter several commands on one line by separating the commands with semicolons, which serve as statement terminators. This feature is useful when you know in advance the sequence of programs that you are going to run. If you wanted to know the name of the current directory and what files are in the current directory, you might run the pwd program followed by the ls program:

```
$ pwd ; ls
/home/kc
Accessories    Folder_Map    Preferences    Utilities      mailbox
Applications   Games         Shutdown       Wastebasket    netware
Disks-etc      Help_Desk     System_Setup
$ ▓
```

When you enter two commands on a single line, separated by a semicolon, the shell runs the programs in quick succession. In the previous example, pwd runs first and then ls runs.

In general, the shell ignores all "white space" (spaces or tabs) except white space that is needed to separate one word from another. Thus the spaces surrounding the semicolon may be omitted.

```
$ pwd;ls
/home/kc
Accessories    Folder_Map    Preferences    Utilities      mailbox
Applications   Games         Shutdown       Wastebasket    netware
Disks-etc      Help_Desk     System_Setup
$ ▓
```

4.3   Command Arguments

In Chapter 3 arguments to commands were discussed. Arguments are used to pass additional information to a program. It would be silly to write a program that performed some function (e.g., displaying a file on your terminal) for only one particular file. Instead, programs are written to provide general services, and arguments are used to provide the specific information, such as a file name, each time you use that service.

We didn't supply any arguments to the *ls* command that we used in the first example in this chapter since we wanted to use its standard function. You can control the operation of *ls* by supplying an argument specifying a long format listing. A long listing prints more information about each file. Arguments that alter the operation of a command are often called *flags* or *options*. (On some other operating systems, these arguments are called *switches* or *controls*.) You can get a long format list of your files by using the option argument l (letter ell) with *ls*:

```
$ ls -l
-rw-r--r--   1 kc       other    234 Jan 20 15:11 arli
-rw-r--r--   1 kc       other    528 Feb 14 17:02 kari
-rw-r--r--   1 kc       other    396 Mar 26 14:33 reed1
-rw-r--r--   1 kc       other    985 May 17 13:01 reed2
-rw-r--r--   1 kc       other    185 Sep 21 16:20 susan1
-rw-r--r--   1 kc       other    894 Nov 12  7:30 susan2
-rw-r--r--   1 kc       other     74 Dec 29 12:56 susan3
$
```

The name of the command and the argument must be separated by one or more spaces or tabs. (If you omit the white space then you will get an error message similar to "UX:sh: ERROR: ls-l: Not found.") The *ls* command and its options are discussed further in Chapters 5 and 6.

In the UNIX system it is customary to insert a hyphen in front of option arguments, and it's customary for each option to be designated by a single letter. Since option arguments (actually, all arguments) are interpreted by individual commands, there are a few commands that ignore these customs. The UNIX system has been heavily criticized for its use of single characters to designate command options. The advantage is that they are terse, and it's easy to supply several options to a single command. The longer, more descriptive full-word options used on some operating systems are great for use in canned scripts because they are self-documenting, but they require too much typing when you're working interactively.

Arguments to commands often specify file names. For example, if you supply a file name argument to ls, then it will confine its report to just that file.

```
$ ls -l arli
-rw-r--r--   1 kc       other    234 Jan 20 15:11 arli
$
```

Ordinarily, arguments don't contain spaces or tabs because spaces and tabs are used to separate one argument from the next. However, a quoted word can contain spaces or tabs. For example, "the end" is a single argument consisting of the seven characters t through d (including one space). Quoting is discussed in Section 11.3.

The shell knows nothing about the particular arguments that specific programs need. In the example given previously, the shell doesn't make sure that the word arli references a file. However, the ls program expects that its arguments do in fact reference files, and ls considers it an error if one of its arguments, other than the option arguments, doesn't refer to a file.

```
$ ls -l arles
US:ls: ERROR: Cannot access arles: No such file or directory
$ ▮
```

The shell is responsible for passing the argument list to the program, but each program is responsible for making sure that the arguments are reasonable.

4.4 Background Processes

Sometimes you need to run programs that take a long time to finish. If the program doesn't require input from the terminal, then you can run it unattended. There are two ways to run something unattended, depending upon whether you are using a multiwindow graphical user interface, or whether you are using a dumb terminal. On a terminal you have to use the traditional approach to put the task in the background, while if you're using a multiwindow interface, you can simply open a second virtual terminal window and run the unattended process in that second window. We want to focus on the traditional method, background execution.

The shell has a special feature that enables you to start a program and then let it run unattended while you continue to enter additional commands. The program that is running unattended is said to be running in the background, while the subsequent commands that you enter are running in the foreground. Because the UNIX system is a multitasking system, the background processes and the foreground process are able to run simultaneously. You direct the shell to run a program in the background by placing an ampersand at the end of the command line. After you strike Enter, the shell will start the requested command, and then immediately prompt you to enter another command.

Suppose you want to run a time-consuming program called acctxx. Presumably the acctxx program takes a long time to run, so you might prefer to do something else while it is working. The exact function of acctxx is not important for this example. Here's how you can run acctxx in the background using the Bourne shell:

```
$ acctxx &
15388
$ ▮
```

The number printed after the command is started is the process ID number of the background acctxx process.

The process looks slightly different when you're using the C shell:

```
% acctxx &
[1] 15388
% ▮
```

The number in the square brackets, 1, is the job number, and you can use it to refer to the background process when you use the C shell commands to manipulate jobs, such as *fg*, to bring a background job to the foreground, and *bg*, to move a job to the background. The second number is the process ID number of the background process.

If acctxx produces output that is sent to the terminal, then there will be ample evidence that acctxx is really running. However, if acctxx places its output in a file, then you might prefer to see some evidence that it is actually running. You can use the ps (process status) program to print a list of all the processes on your terminal.

```
$ ps
PID      TTY      TIME     COMD
15388    pts001   0:14     acctxx
15390    pts001   0:01     ps
$
```

Notice that two programs are running, acctxx and ps. From the ordinary output of the *ps* command, there is no way to distinguish the background process from the foreground process.

You shouldn't run a program in the background if it requires input from the terminal because both the background program and the shell will be fighting for access to the terminal. It is possible to run a background program that sends voluminous output to the terminal, but it is very awkward because the output is interspersed with the normal foreground output messages. Normally you would redirect such output to a file for later examination. Both of these limitations illustrate why it's better to run secondary processes on a second virtual terminal (in a windowing environment) rather than run them in the background (on a standard terminal).

This brings up an interesting point. While you are entering a command, the shell is clearly running in the foreground. What happens to the shell while your command is running? In the UNIX system it is possible for a program to go to sleep while waiting for a certain event. When you enter a normal foreground command, the shell sleeps during the execution of the command. When the command completes, the shell is activated and prompts you for another command. The sleeping shell and the executing command don't fight over the terminal because the shell sleeps while the command executes. (Incidentally, the terms *sleep, wait,* and *wake up* are all standard terms. UNIX system jargon is often quite descriptive.) Also, you might wonder why the sleeping shell isn't in the ps report. By default, ps only reports active processes; Section 7.4 shows how you can ask ps to produce a report on all processes, including sleepers.

Here is another way to start the acctxx program in the background and then run the ps command in the foreground. Note that the & serves as a command terminator, just as the ; does.

```
$ actxx & ps
15790
  PID      TTY      TIME        CMD
```

```
15790    pts001    0:02    acctxx
15794    pts001    0:01    ps
$
```

After ps finishes, the shell prompts you for a command. Acctxx will still be running in the background. There is usually a limit to the number (often 20) of background processes that you can have running simultaneously.

4.5   The Standard Output and the Standard Input

Today there are three sorts of application programs that run on UNIX systems:

- GUI programs, which are programs specifically written for a graphical environment, usually the X Window environment. All input and output is performed using functions from the GUI library.

- Screen I/O model programs, which are programs written to create a simple user interface using the text positioning, highlighting, and other capabilities of video display terminals. All input and output is performed using a screen I/O library; curses was the first such library but termcap is used today on System V UNIX versions. Screen programs offer a relatively simple user interface, but they are highly portable to various systems and environments. Vi is probably the best known screen I/O model program in the UNIX environment.

- Teletype (simple ASCII) model programs, which are programs whose output consists of a series of lines of text. All input and output is performed using the C standard I/O library. These programs offer only a primitive command-line-based user interface, but they can be easily interconnected to perform more sophisticated tasks. Much of this book focuses on teletype model programs because they comprise the UNIX system's powerhouse utilities that are the key to making the UNIX system work for you. (The term teletype refers to the archaic teletype line printer, whose only formatting ability was to move to the next line of the paper. ASCII is the American Standard Code for Information Interchange, which is a standard way to represent text in a computer.)

A few programs straddle the border between the screen I/O model and the teletype I/O model. For example, the Korn shell is mostly a teletype model program, but it also contains a tiny command-line editor that bears some similarity to the screen I/O model.

When a teletype model program outputs something on your terminal, the program is (usually) performing output operations to what is called the *standard output* or *stdout* (pronounced stid-out). When you type at your terminal, a program is (usually) reading your typed characters from what is called the *standard input* or *stdin* (pronounced stid-in), as sketched in Figure 4.1. For error and diagnostic messages, there's a separate output connection called *standard error* or *stderr* (pronounced stid-err).

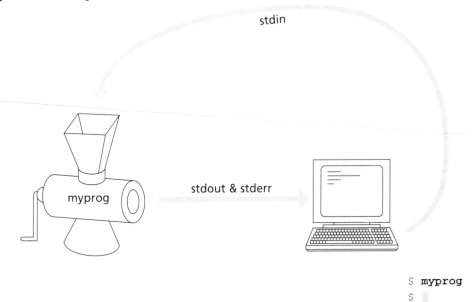

stdin

stdout & stderr

myprog

$ **myprog**
$

Figure 4.1 ■ The Standard I/O Connections
A program's standard input, output, and error are usually connected to the terminal.

The standard input and the standard output are UNIX system conventions that simplify programs. They make it possible for programs to work with each other by connecting one program's output to another program's input. (The qualifier "usually" is used in definitions of the standard input and output because it is possible to access the terminal without using the standard input and output. However, the great majority of utility programs do use the standard input and output.)

For example, programs such as ps, ls, who, date, pwd, and echo use the standard output to deliver their information to you. Many other programs, including some interactive programs (e.g., the shell and the line editor), read from the standard input and write their responses on the standard output.

4.5.1   Output Redirection

The standard input and output are normally attached to the computer terminal; stdin to the keyboard and stdout to the screen. However, the standard input, output, and error connections are performed by the shell, which makes it possible for them to be reassigned by the shell. This is one of the UNIX system's most powerful features. (See Figure 4.2.)

Let's suppose that you want to save the output of the *ps* command in a file. If you enter the command as shown previously, the process status program will write its information on the standard output—your screen. However, the UNIX system's notation for *output redirection* enables you to place the ps program's output into a file:

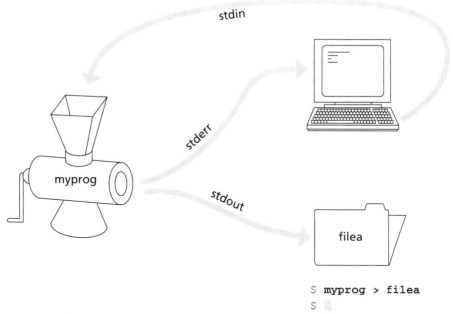

$ **myprog > filea**
$ ▮

Figure 4.2 ■ Output Redirection
Output redirection connects a program's standard output to a file. Note that redirecting the stdout connection doesn't alter the stderr connection.

```
$ ps > posterity
$ ▮
```

The process status program will still write its information to the standard output, but because of the special notation ''> posterity'' the shell will connect the ps program's standard output to the ordinary file named posterity. As you can tell from the preceding session, you won't see the output on your screen. The > is a special shell character specifying that the standard output of the preceding command should be directed to the file named by the next word of the command. (Note that the spaces surrounding the > are optional.)

You can see that the file named posterity actually contains the output of ps using the cat program:

```
$ cat posterity
   PID    TTY    TIME  COMD
  16004    53    0:03  ps
$ ▮
```

4.5.2   Appending Output Redirection

Normal output redirection completely overwrites the output file. In the example previously given, the file posterity would be overwritten and any previous contents would be lost. Occasionally you want to direct output to a file, but you want the output to be appended to the end of the file. Here's how you can invoke the appending form of output redirection to append the output of ps to the existing file named ps.logfile:

```
$ ps >> ps.logfile
$ 
```

You could also achieve the same results with a series of commands. Here's the equivalent operation performed using the rewriting form of output redirection:

```
$ ps > temp1
$ cat ps.logfile temp1 > temp2
$ mv temp2 ps.logfile
$ rm temp1
$ 
```

Obviously, it is much simpler to enter the command using the >> operator to append the output to the file.

4.5.3   Redirecting the Standard Error

The UNIX system usually opens two output streams for each program, the standard output, which is the usual output channel, and the standard error output, which is used for error and diagnostic messages. When both output streams are connected to the terminal, it doesn't matter much which is used because both go to the same place.

Having two separate streams becomes important when redirection is used. For example, suppose you redirect the output of a program to a file. If an error occurs, you'd probably like to see that message on your terminal instead of having it vanish into the output file. In the following dialog, an illegal option is specified for ls, which makes it output a diagnostic message.

```
$ ls -z > filelist
UX:ls: ERROR: Illegal option.
$ 
```

Even though output redirection is used, the error message appears on the terminal because the standard error isn't redirected.

If you are running a program that produces voluminous output, you might want to direct error messages into a file so that you can examine that file separately to see any error messages. (See Figure 4.3.) You can redirect the standard output by writing a 2, which is the connection number of the standard output, in front of the > symbol that forces redirection.

```
$ ls -z 2> msgfile
$ cat msgfile
UX:ls: ERROR: Illegal option.
$ 
```

In the preceding dialog, the standard error output of ls is redirected to msgfile. In the dialog, the cat program shows the contents of msgfile.

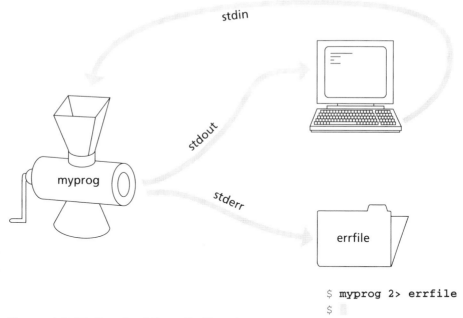

Figure 4.3 ■ Standard Error Redirection
The standard error connection can be redirected to a file. If it is not redirected explicitly, the standard error connection remains connected to the terminal.

4.5.4   Input Redirection

The standard input can also be redirected. (See Figure 4.4.) Thus far, the only program we have encountered that reads information from the standard input is the shell. The other programs we have used (ls, who, ps, date, echo, and pwd) all produce output without reading from the standard input. The shell normally reads commands from the standard input; that is, the shell reads commands that you type at the terminal. Since the standard input can be redirected, it is possible to have the shell acquire its commands from an ordinary file. The commands in a file can be executed by a shell by using input redirection, as shown in the following dialog:

```
$ cat whoops
who
ps
$ sh < whoops
gilbert   tty17    Dec  1 15:41
gilbert   ttyh1    Dec  1 15:31
kc        ttyh3    Dec  1 15:28
  PID TT STAT   TIME COMMAND
  954 p0 S      0:00 sh
  956 p0 R      0:01 ps
$
```

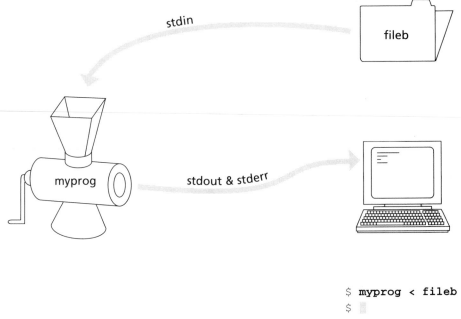

```
$ myprog < fileb
$ 
```

Figure 4.4 ■ Input Redirection
Input redirection connects a program's standard input to a file.

In this dialog, the cat command is used to display the contents of the whoops file, and then the shell program sh is invoked to execute the commands in the whoops file by making that file the shell's standard input. (The file whoops can be created using a text editor; see Chapter 9.)

The file whoops contains two familiar shell commands that you could enter at the terminal. If you often need to run these two commands, rather than typing the commands each time, it might be easier to put the commands in a file and let the shell read the commands from the file. Obviously the example shown here isn't a compelling argument for shell command scripts; rather, it is a demonstration of input redirection.

The shell is just an ordinary program that reads commands from its standard input. If we type the command sh, we will execute another copy of the shell that reads commands from the standard input, the terminal. However, if we redirect the input of the new shell, we can force it to read commands from a file rather than from the terminal. In the previous dialog, the < notation is used to connect sh's standard input to the whoops file. The output of this new shell, and the output of all of the commands that it runs, is connected to the stdout, which is the terminal's screen, because the output is not redirected.

The first command in whoops is who, so the shell runs the who command, which prints a list of the active users. (Notice that the user named gilbert is logged on twice.) Next the shell runs the ps command, which prints a list of the active processes. Notice that sh and ps are listed because both are active. Who is not listed because it has finished by the time ps starts to run. When the new shell reaches the end of the whoops file, it exits and returns control to the login shell. (Other methods for executing a shell command file are discussed in Section 11.1. However, these alternate methods reflect specific capabilities that are built into the shell rather than the general ability to redirect input and output.)

It is also possible to redirect the standard input and standard output simultaneously. When this happens, as shown in Figure 4.5, the only role of the terminal is to enter the command line that starts the process. Once the program starts to execute, neither its input nor its output is attached to the terminal.

4.5.5   Pipes

A pipe connects the standard output of one program to the standard input of another program, as depicted in Figure 4.6. A pipe is different from I/O redirection. Output redirection sends a program's output to a file, and input redirection connects a program's input to a file, whereas a pipe connects the output of one program directly to the input of another program.

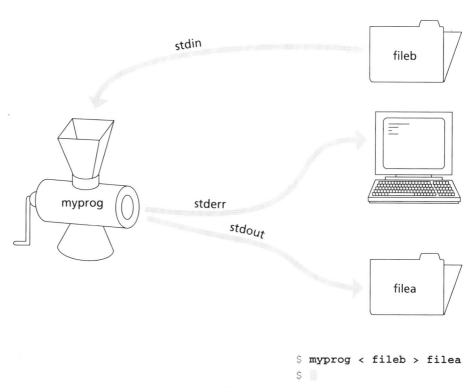

```
$ myprog < fileb > filea
$
```

Figure 4.5 ■ Input and Output Redirection
Both the input and the output can be redirected simultaneously.

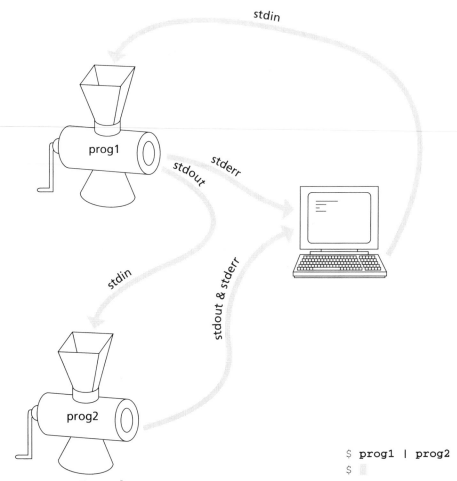

stdin

prog1

stdout   stderr

stdin

stdout & stderr

```
$ prog1 | prog2
$ ▊
```

Figure 4.6 ■ Pipelines
A pipeline connects the standard output of one program to the standard input of another program.

I/O redirection and pipelines can be used in a single command. You can pipe the output of one program to the input of another, while simultaneously redirecting the first program's input, or the second program's output, or both. This type of connection is shown in Figure 4.7.

Let's suppose we want to know how many files are in my home directory (/home/kc). Perhaps the most obvious method would be to run the ls command and count the number of files that are listed on the terminal. For a directory with only a handful of files, this might work, but for a crowded directory, the simple method is unattractive. Fortunately, there is a command for counting words (and lines and characters) called *wc* (see Section 8.6). Using ls we can generate a list of files in the /home/kc directory, and using

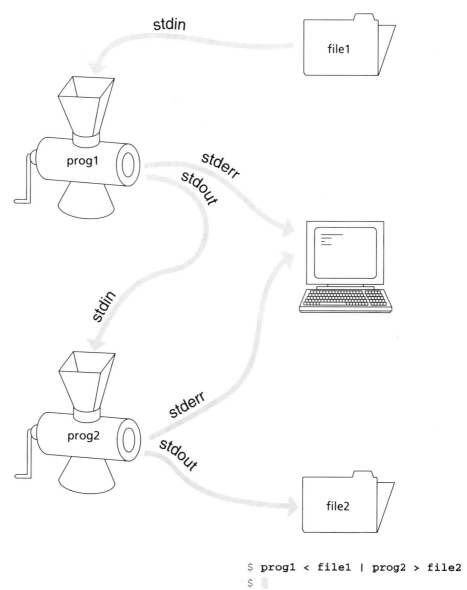

```
$ prog1 < file1 | prog2 > file2
$
```

Figure 4.7 ■ I/O Redirection and Pipelines
I/O redirection can be used with a pipeline.

wc we can count the number of words in a list. It seems we have the basic tools for discovering how many files are in our home directory, but how can we combine these tools to work together? As with most work in the UNIX system, there are at least two reasonable methods. Let's explore both methods. The first method uses the I/O redirection technique of the previous section and the second method uses a pipeline.

1. I/O Redirection Method: Redirect the output of ls so that the list of files is saved in a temporary file. Then use wc to count the number of lines in the temporary file. (The -l option makes wc count lines.) Finally remove the temporary file. These actions are performed by the following three commands.

```
$ ls /home/kc > tempfile
$ wc -l tempfile
17
$ rm tempfile
$
```

2. Pipeline Method: Pipe the output of ls to wc. The special shell notation for a pipeline connection is a vertical bar (|). Like ; and &, the | symbol is a command terminator. (In the distant past the caret symbol was also allowed to indicate a pipe connection, which explains why you have to quote the caret when it is used for other purposes.) The following command pipes the output of ls to the input of wc:

```
$ ls /home/kc | wc -l
16
$
```

As you see, the pipeline method looks simpler. Although the I/O redirection method works, it has some unpleasant side effects. If you don't have permission to create files in the current directory, you won't be able to execute the command

```
ls /home/kc > tempfile
```

because it creates and writes to tempfile. Another problem is that the shell has to create tempfile and redirect the standard output to it before the ls program can run. Thus tempfile will be one of the files in the list if the current directory is /home/kc. Therefore, the count of files may be one too large (as shown in the previous example). And finally, it's easy to forget to remove tiny temporary files, which can quickly clutter your directories.

Pipelines make many procedures conceptually easier. Since each program in a pipeline can concentrate on one aspect of a task, it is possible to write coherent, unified programs. It would be very awkward to write the ls program so that it could perform all conceivable operations on its output, although if you read the ls man pages, you'll see that its authors gave it a good try. The ls program concentrates on listing files and the wc program concentrates on counting. In the UNIX system, you can create a new function by using pipelines to connect existing tools.

Many of the text file utilities (Chapter 8) can be used in a pipeline with ls in order to augment the capabilities of the ls command. It would not be reasonable to build all of these capabilities into the ls program, but all of these capabilities are built into the UNIX system via the pipe mechanism. You should note that if ls is part of a pipeline, then it is always the first element. Since ls does not acquire information from the standard input, there is no way to deliver information to ls via a pipe.

Wc is a typical example of a text manipulation program that can perform processing on files named as arguments (the command "wc -l tempfile" in the first dialog in this section) or on text supplied via the standard input (the command "ls | wc -l" in the previous dialog). This flexibility is one of the most powerful features of the UNIX system.

4.6   Metacharacters and File Name Generation

Most of the command-line arguments that you supply to programs are file names. It is very common to name files so that related files have related names. For example, C-language program file names conventionally end with the suffix .c. All of the chapters of a book might be stored in a series of files named chap1, chap2, and so on. If you wanted to perform some operation on all of the C-language programs in a directory, it would be very tedious to type in all of the names as arguments on a command line.

In order to avoid tedium, the UNIX system allows you to specify sets of file names automatically by using file name generation or so-called wildcard characters. When you enter the arguments to a command, the shell examines your arguments to see if you are using the file name generation shorthand. You control file name generation facility by specifying a model for the file names. The shell compares your model to all of the file names in the current directory. If any of the file names match the model, then the alphabetized list of matching file names is delivered to the program. If none of the file names in the directory matches the model, then the unchanged model is delivered to the program. (When the C shell notices that a model doesn't match any file names, it displays the diagnostic message, "No match," and then refuses to execute the command.)

A model consists of ordinary characters and metacharacters, which are also called wildcards. The ordinary characters stand for themselves while the metacharacters have special meanings. A model that consists entirely of ordinary characters (e.g., myfile) doesn't invoke file name generation.

You need to learn about the file name generation process because it can occur every time you enter a command. The least that you can safely know is the fact that file name generation occurs and that you should not use the metacharacters *, ?, and the square brackets in your file names. As a next step, you should master the metacharacters * and ? because they are really quite simple to use, and you should know how to turn off the special meanings of the metacharacters. If you want to master the UNIX system, then learn about character classes, which are specified using square brackets.

Some of the UNIX system documents use the phrase *regular expression* to refer to what we are calling a model. We prefer the term *model* because it lends a more intuitive perception to the confusing topic of file name generation.

The following metacharacters are used to control file name generation:

*	Matches any character string
?	Matches any single character
[	Introduces a character class
]	Terminates a character class
–	Indicates a character range in a character class

Table 4.1 contains a full list of Bourne shell metacharacters.

The asterisk and question mark metacharacters are very easy to use. An asterisk will match any string of characters, including the null string. Thus the model *.c will match a file named .c or a.c or abcdefg.c, but not a file named a.ca or A.C (UNIX file names are case sensitive).

A question mark will match any single character. Thus the model ??.c will match a file named ab.c or 77.c but not a.c or abc.c or bc.cc.

Square brackets and hyphens are used to form models for groups of characters. The characters in the group are enclosed by the brackets. The model abc[aeiou] will match any file name that starts with the string abc and ends with a single vowel. The hyphen can be used inside a pair of square brackets to indicate a range of characters. The model def[0-9] will match any file name whose first three characters are def and whose fourth and final character is a numeral. The range is inclusive (both zero and nine are included in the previous example) and is defined by the numerical sequence of the ASCII character set. To give another example, the range [a-zA-Z] matches any single alphabetic character, either lower- or uppercase.

The hyphen loses its role as a metacharacter when it is used outside of the square brackets. Conversely, the asterisk and the question mark lose their power as metacharacters when they are used within the square brackets. In the model [*?]a-bc, only the square brackets are active metacharacters. Thus the model [*?]a-bc matches exactly two file names: *a-bc and ?a-bc. To make your life simpler, avoid creating file names that contain file name generation metacharacters. Always avoid * and ? because they are so commonly used for file name generation. Avoid - at the beginning of a file name because a file name that starts with a hyphen looks like a command-line option.

The role of metacharacters is not the only thing you should understand about the shell's file name generation procedure. When the shell compares the model strings to the file names, any leading period in a file name must be matched explicitly. The original designers of the UNIX system deliberately chose to make files beginning with a period (also called a dot) be invisible by default. This is because many programs look for setup and configuration commands in dot files, such as .login and .profile. The designers wanted to keep these mundane and ubiquitous files from cluttering up directory listings. So if you have a file named .invisible, the model *visible will not match. Use the model .*visible to match the file named .invisible. The model name .* will match all of the file names that begin with a period.

Another aspect of file name generation that many people find confusing is the fact that slash characters in a pathname must be matched explicitly. A pathname is a path from directory to directory that leads to a file. The name

Table 4.1 ■ Bourne Shell Metacharacters

Metacharacters	Usage	Command Terminator?	See Section
`cmd ;`	Command terminator.	Yes	4.2
`cmd &`	Run preceding command in the background.	Yes	4.4
`> file`	Output redirection.	No	4.5.1
`>> file`	Appending output redirection.	No	4.5.1
`< file`	Input redirection.	No	4.5.2
`<< word`	Input from a "here" document.	Yes	11.16
`cmd	cmd`	Form a pipeline between the preceding command and the following command (^ is also allowed but is archaic).	Yes	4.5.3
`*`	The * is used in file name generation to match any sequence of characters.	No	4.6
`?`	The ? is used in file name generation to match any single character in a file name.	No	4.6
`[set]`	The [introduces a character set for file name generation and] closes the set. Within the square brackets, a hyphen is used to specify a character range.	No	4.6
`$word`	The word following the $ will be treated as a parameter (variable) and will be replaced by its value.	No	11.2
`\c`	The character following the backslash will be quoted.	No	11.3
`'txt'`	The text between the forward single quotes is strongly quoted. No substitutions will occur.	No	11.3
`"txt"`	The text between the double quotes is weakly quoted. Parameter (variable) and command substitution occur, but most other substitutions are prevented.	No	11.3
`` `cmd` ``	Command substitution. The output of the command specified between the back single quotes is used as part of the command line.	No	11.14
`( list )`	Execute a command list in a subshell.	No	11.6
`{ list; }`	Execute a command list in the current shell.	No	11.6
`cmd && cmd`	Execute the second command only if the first completes with a zero exit status.	Yes	11.6
`cmd || cmd`	Execute the second command only if the first completes with a non-zero exit status.	Yes	11.6
`:`	Do nothing.	No	11.23
`. file`	Read shell input from a file.	No	11.23
`# txt`	Quote the rest of the line.	Yes	11.7

/etc/motd is a simple pathname that leads from the /etc directory to the file motd. Pathnames will be discussed in detail in Section 5.3.

The metacharacters are used only to generate file names within a directory. The model /etc*.c will not match the files with the .c suffix in the /etc directory, but rather it will match files in the root directory that start with the letters etc and end with the suffix .c. However, the model /etc/*.c will match files in the /etc directory that end with the suffix .c. This restriction on explicitly matching the slash characters in a pathname is basically sensible because the current directory is the default environment unless you explicitly state otherwise.

Here are a few examples. Let's suppose that the current directory contains the following files:

```
ch1    ch2    ch3    ch4
abc    ab.c   ch3.a  33.doc
```

The command ls ch* will list the following files: ch1, ch2, ch3, ch3.a, and ch4. Notice that the list is alphabetized because file name generation occurs alphabetically.

The command ls *3* will list the following files: 33.doc, ch3, and ch3.a. Notice that the asterisk can stand for a sequence of zero or more characters.

The command ls ch? will list the following files: ch1, ch2, ch3, and ch4. Since a question mark always matches exactly one character, ch3.a is omitted.

The command ls ch[2-9] will list the following files: ch2, ch3, and ch4. The file ch1 is omitted because 1 isn't in the range 2-9 and ch3.a is omitted because of the trailing .a.

Here's one for the masters. The command ls ch[0-15] will list the file ch1. Although the character class appears to include the numerals 0 to 15, it actually contains just three characters: 0 through 1, and 5. You should remember that a character class is formed from a group of characters. The sequence 15 looks like the number fifteen but in a character class it is simply two characters, the 1 and the 5.

4.7   Disabling Special Characters

Sometimes the power of the shell is a valuable asset and you want to use its special features such as metacharacters, I/O redirection, pipelines, and background execution. However, at other times the special shell characters used to control these functions are needed for more mundane operations. If you explicitly want any one of the special shell characters to lose its power, you can precede it with a backslash character. Here's how you could get a list of all the files whose names end with an asterisk (bear in mind, you shouldn't create file names that include special characters):

```
$  ls *\*
dark*    death*    tel*
$
```

In this ls command, the first asterisk is a metacharacter and the second asterisk is an ordinary character because it is preceded by a backslash. During file name generation, the first asterisk matches anything while the second asterisk matches only an asterisk.

If the current directory also contained a file named death*logo, the ls command in the dialog above wouldn't list it because death*logo doesn't end with an asterisk. However, multiple metacharacters can be used in a model.

```
$ ls *\**
dark*      death*  death*logo  tel*      *tled
$ ▌
```

The first and third asterisks are used as metacharacters; the middle asterisk is a plain asterisk.

Another way to remove the power from special shell characters is quoting. When there is only one special character that needs to be escaped, it is easier to escape it with a backslash, but when there are several, then quoting is usually easier. Quoting is discussed more thoroughly in Section 11.3.

4.8   Conclusions

Using the UNIX system effectively is closely tied to understanding the basic operation of the shell. You should know how to run a normal foreground process and how to run a background process, and you should understand the idea of command-line arguments. I/O redirection and pipelines are essential for everyone—why use the UNIX system without using its strongest features? Every command-line user should at least be aware of file name generation. Learn to use file name generation if you want to get the most out of the UNIX system.

These few topics are just a small fraction of the power of the shell. However, for people who use the shell as an interactive command interpreter, the topics presented in this chapter are enough to use the UNIX system productively. The shell is one of the most impressive features of the UNIX system, so for those of you who want to know more, there are several more chapters on the shell.

5
The UNIX File System

Let's start with two simple definitions:

1. An ordinary file is a named collection of information stored on a mass storage device, which almost always means a disk. Ordinary files store documents, spreadsheets, executable programs, e-mail messages, and so on.

2. A file system is the organizational framework that specifies how a mass storage device is organized. File systems usually contain a map, which is called the *i-node table* on the UNIX system, that is used to locate a file, given its name.

On many computer systems, files are organized by lumping them together into one big heap, which is sometimes called a *flat file system*. As long as there are only a few dozen files, a flat file system works fine. Unfortunately, a flat file system is inappropriate for a multiuser computer system with large modern disks that can store several hundred thousand files.

Because placing thousands of files into one big heap is an obvious nightmare, the early UNIX designers searched for a more flexible approach. They decided to create a hierarchical file system. Each node in the hierarchy is a directory, and directories can contain both files and directories. Directories can be created easily and used easily, which encourages people to create a storage organization that meets their needs. Each file in the file system occupies a specific place in a hierarchy, just like each leaf occupies a specific place in a tree. (Unlike tree leaves, files can be moved from one place to another!)

File access restrictions are an essential aspect of a file system on a multiuser computer. Without file security, few people would put private information in a computer and nobody could vouch for the safety and reliability of the operating system's own files and tables. Access modes are a necessary nuisance of shared computer systems. You need to be aware of file access modes even if you have your own workstation that isn't shared with others. For example, if your workstation is connected to a network, your file access modes are your first defense against snoopers from the net. Also, file access modes are important for performing routine administration of your system, as shown in Chapter 20.

All of these aspects of the UNIX file system are discussed in the remainder of this chapter. You should have a working knowledge of these ideas in order to use the UNIX system effectively. A few advanced file system topics are presented in Sections 20.8 and 20.9, but these sections are not required reading for most users. Some of the data structures that underlie the UNIX system file system are discussed in Section 23.5.

5.1 UNIX File Types

One of the early innovations of the Unix system was its nontraditional use of the file system. All operating systems use the file system to store ordinary files. That's unremarkable. But the early UNIX designers realized that they could get even more use out of the file system model by building in the capability to support various file types.

Of course, the UNIX system contains ordinary files. They will be discussed in more detail in the following section. Directory files are the second type of file in the UNIX system. Directories are places in the file system; they are collections of files. A directory file stores the names of the files it contains plus information that is used to locate and access the files. Thus directory files are partly like ordinary files because they contain information, but they are also somewhat special, because that information is organized and structured by the UNIX system.

The third type of UNIX file is the device file, which is also called a special device file. A device file is a means of accessing a hardware device, usually an I/O device. Examples of I/O hardware include the keyboard, the video adapter, network adapters, disk controllers, tape drives, and mouse interfaces. Each I/O device (printer, terminal, disk, etc.) is associated with at least one special file. A UNIX program accesses a special device file in order to access the I/O hardware. Although this sounds complicated, it is actually a great simplification compared to most other computer systems. The UNIX system's special device files are customarily stored in the /dev directory, or in subdirectories of the /dev directory.

Many special device files don't reference real devices but instead they simulate devices. These simulated devices are usually called *pseudo devices*. For example, a true terminal interface is often called a *tty device* (named archaically after the long defunct TTY [or teletype] type of terminal), and a device that simulates a tty device is usually called a *pseudo-tty*. Pseudo devices have become increasingly important in the UNIX system. For example, when you log into a UNIX system via a network, or when you use a virtual terminal in a windowing system, you are working with pseudo-tty devices. In either case, you aren't interacting with the system using a real terminal but rather with a cobbled-up terminal that is implemented using a pseudo-tty.

The fourth type of special file is the symbolic link file. A symbolic link is a way to make a new name for an existing file. This odd-sounding feature actually proves very useful, because it makes it easy to place "copies" of things wherever they are needed, without the overhead (and duplication) of truly making copies. Symbolic links were developed first for Berkeley UNIX systems but they were soon picked up by AT&T and now they are widely used in System V.

Some versions of the UNIX system have additional types of files, such as the named pipe found on System V, but they are less important than the four types already mentioned.

Having different file types is important because it provides a uniform interface to a wide variety of resources and functions. All of the file types mentioned above have many things in common, but most importantly they are all governed by standard UNIX file access rules. This provides flexibility because it lets you specify how and when the files should be accessed. Much of this relates directly to system administration, and it will be discussed more in Chapter 20.

The uniformity of the UNIX system's file system also adds power to some of the utilities. For example, utilities that display and modify files can work with ordinary files, and they can operate on memory regions or on raw disks using special device files. These tasks aren't often performed by casual users but they are sometimes important for system administration, system development, and other important tasks.

The UNIX system maintains a variety of information that describes each file. The information includes the file access privileges, the file type, the important dates for the file, the size of the file, and the physical location of the file on the disk. (This information is stored in a file system structure called an *i-node*, which is discussed further in Chapter 23.)

5.1.1 Ordinary Files

An ordinary file is used to store information. An ordinary file might contain a program that you can execute, the text of a document, the records of a company, or any other type of information that can be stored in a computer. During a session with the UNIX system you will encounter dozens of ordinary files. Ordinary files are a vital part of a computer system because they allow information to be stored permanently. Without long-term information storage, the information processing ability of computers would be much less useful.

You can use whatever characters you want for file names, although file names that contain unprintable characters, space characters, tabs, and shell metacharacters (*, ?, [, $, #, |, &, ^, \, ', ", <, >) are difficult to use. Every

UNIX system directory has the file names . and .. built in, so you cannot ever use these names for your own files. A file name may not contain the / character because it is used to separate the elements in pathnames.

The UNIX system does not impose any naming conventions on files. However, many UNIX system programs expect files to be named with certain suffixes. For example, files with the suffix .sh (such as bakup.sh) are usually shell programs, files with the suffix .bas (such as aster.bas) are usually BASIC programs, and files with the suffix .c (such as xrefer.c) are usually C-language source files. Files created by the compress (file compression) program consist of the original name followed by .Z so the compressed version of xrefer.c would be xrefer.c.Z. Files that contain executable programs (such as who) customarily have no suffixes.

There are two forms of ordinary file: text files and binary files. Text files contain lines of plain text. In the United States this means that each element in the file is either a printable character (a letter, a digit, a common punctuation mark) or a space or a tab or an end-of-line marker. Many European languages contain accented characters, or characters in addition to the standard English character set.

Text files are simple, and they are an ideal format for information storage when the information might need to be processed by many of the UNIX system's standard utilities. Shell scripts are text files, C and other program source files are text files, and most of the input and output files used by standard UNIX utilities are text files.

Files that contain codes that are not part of the ASCII character set are called binary files. Since binary files use the full range of possible values for the bytes in the file, binary files are a slightly more efficient way to store information. A binary file cannot be directly typed on your terminal because most of the 256 possible values for each byte are not printable ASCII characters.

Binary files are more compact than text files and can often be processed more rapidly. They are often used to store word processor documents (documents containing text interspersed with formatting instructions), spreadsheets, drawings, databases, font files, and executable programs. Binary files often have a format that is understood only by the program that created the file, which makes it hard to use binary files in different applications. However, many applications programs, such as word processors, have an option that allows you to output a text file. Unfortunately, something is usually lost in the conversion to text. For example, the text version of a word processor document usually doesn't contain the format information, such as the font information, the margin settings, and so on.

You can display text files by using the cat utility or by using a text editor. Here's how you could use cat to display the /etc/motd file, which often contains the message of the day:

```
$ cat /etc/motd
NOTICE - The system will be down
from 17:00 to 19:00 tomorrow
for routine maintenance.
```

```
Remember, monthly users' meeting
this Weds at 5 pm.
$ ▊
```

You can inspect the contents of any binary file by using the octal dump (od) program. Unfortunately, od cannot represent a document or spreadsheet the same way as the application that created the file; all it can do is display the individual values in the file as printable characters. (See Section 6.13.)

```
$ od -x /bin/ls
0000000   010b 0000 3800 0000 0800 0000 a864 0000
0000020   093c 0000 0000 0000 0000 0000 0000 0000
0000040   0000 0000 0000 0000 0000 0000 0000 0000
*
0002000   0f00 3d11 5ed0 c15a 5a04 d050 5950 59d0
0002020   d558 1389 1102 d1fa 6859 0319 04c2 d059
0002040   ef59 37de 0000 efdd 37d8 0000 58dd 6add
^C
$ ▊
```

The od command is not supplied with some versions of the UNIX system.

Four commands are especially important for controlling your collection of ordinary files: mv (move), cp (copy), ln (link), and rm (remove). These four commands are discussed in Chapter 6.

5.1.2 Directory Files

Directories are files that contain lists of files. The UNIX system maintains the directory system. The content of directory files can only be changed by the operating system; they can't be modified with a text editor or other user utility. Executing programs can read directory files but the operating system prevents programs from writing directly to directory files to guarantee the integrity of the file system. A UNIX program can add a new file to a directory but it can only make that happen by invoking a UNIX system call that causes the operating system to make the necessary changes. Similarly, a file entry can be removed from a directory by using another system call.

Each user has a special directory called the *home directory*. When you log into the system, you are placed in your home directory. During the course of your session with the UNIX system, you are free to move from one directory to another using the cd command.

```
$ pwd
/home/kc
$ cd /bin
$ pwd
/bin
$ ▊
```

The argument to cd (/bin in the dialog above) specifies the directory to which you want to move. The directory that you are in is called the *current directory* or the *working directory*. The default destination directory for cd is your home directory, so you can always return to your home directory easily.

```
$ pwd
/bin
$ cd
$ pwd
/home/kc
$
```

The name of the current directory will be printed if you enter the pwd command. Cd and pwd are discussed in Section 6.1.

The mkdir (make directory) command is used to create a directory and the rmdir command is used to remove a directory. Directories are created empty except for the standard files . (dot) and .. (dot dot). (The standard entries . and .. are discussed in the following text.) You can only remove a directory that is empty (except for the files . and ..). Mkdir and rmdir are discussed in Section 6.7.

Utilities that expect to work with directory files usually won't work with ordinary files, and vice versa. For example, the cd command expects its argument to specify a directory because you can't change directory to an ordinary file.

```
$ cd /home/kc/report.1
UX:cd: ERROR: /home/kc/report.1: Not a directory
$
```

The error occurs because /home/kc/report.1 is not a directory but an ordinary file containing a document. Similarly, utilities that work with ordinary files often can't do the same thing with data files. The following command will produce gibberish because /home/kc is a directory, not a text file.

```
$ cat /home/kc
```

There are many situations in which ordinary files, special device files, and symbolic link files can be used interchangeably, but directory files are different and must be used carefully.

5.2 The Hierarchical File System

Files in the UNIX system are grouped into directories and the directories are organized into a hierarchy. The top of the hierarchy is a special directory called the root directory, which is notated with a / character. The root directory contains a variety of system-related files and it usually contains standard directories such as /bin, /usr, /dev, /etc. /tmp, and /lib. A typical but very simplified view of a file system hierarchy is shown in Figure 5.1.

The advantage of a hierarchical file system is organization. Let's use the corporate analogy. In a corporation you could allow every worker to report directly to the president. This type of organization works well for a small ma-and-pa grocery but it would be disastrous for a huge organization such

60

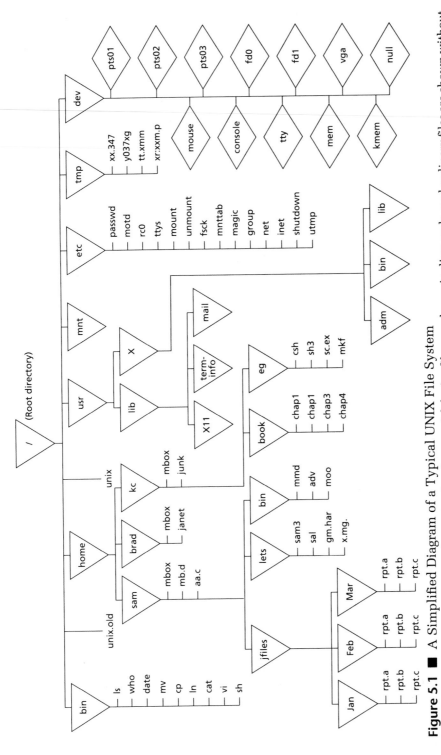

Figure 5.1 ■ A Simplified Diagram of a Typical UNIX File System

In this diagram, directory files are shown in triangles, special device files are shown in diamonds, and ordinary files are shown without borders.

as General Motors. Similarly, in the UNIX system it is a great advantage to organize the system by allowing multiple directory levels.

The UNIX file system is often called tree-structured because diagrams of it resemble an upside-down tree, with the root directory shown at the top. The current subtree is that part of the file system that is at a lower level in the hierarchy than the current directory. If the /usr directory were the current directory, then all of the /usr subdirectories, and so forth, would be the current subtree—see Figure 5.2. Most UNIX system commands work with files in the current directory unless you specify another directory. A few UNIX system commands work with the current subtree.

5.3 Pathnames

The files in the current directory are directly accessible; they can be referenced by simply entering their name. Files that are not in the current directory must be referenced using a pathname. A pathname specifies a path through the file system that leads to the desired file. Paths through the file system can only start in one of two places: your current directory or the root

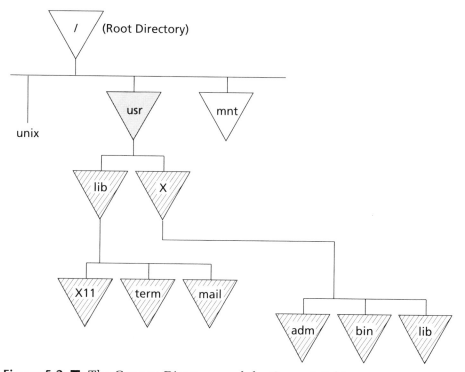

Figure 5.2 ■ The Current Directory and the Current Subtree
In this diagram, the current directory is /usr, which is shown shaded. The current subtree consists of all of the directories and files below /usr in the file system hierarchy, which are shown hatched.

directory. Pathnames that start with the / character are absolute pathnames, specifying a path starting in the root directory. All other pathnames are relative pathnames, and they specify a path starting in your current directory.

Every directory contains entries for the names . and .. . These two entries are the glue that holds the file system together. The entry . is a pseudonym for the name of the current directory. Programs that want to read the current directory file can use the name . rather than scrounge around to determine the name that was given to the directory when it was created.

The name .. is a pseudonym for the parent directory of the current directory, which means the directory one level higher in the tree. The entry .. in each directory allows you to specify a pathname that ascends the file system. Note that each directory has only one parent, so there is only one path from any given directory back toward the root directory. Also notice that all of the other entries in a pathname specify files that are at a lower level in the file system hierarchy. You need to be comfortable with the ideas behind the names . and .. because you will use these names very often in your interactions with the UNIX system.

A few simple rules apply to all pathnames:

- If the pathname starts with a slash, then the path starts in the root directory. All other paths start in the current directory.

- A pathname is either a list of names separated by slashes or a single name. The initial names in the list (if there are any) are directories. The final name in the list is the target file, which may be a file of any type.

- You can ascend the file system hierarchy by specifying the name .. in a pathname. All other names in a pathname descend the hierarchy.

Here are a few examples of pathnames. The pathname /home/kc is an absolute pathname specifying the file kc. Since the pathname starts with a slash, it is an absolute pathname that starts in the root directory. Obviously the directory home is a subdirectory of the root directory (see Figure 5.3).

The pathname jfiles/Jan/rpt.a is a relative pathname because it doesn't start with a slash. Hence the path starts from the current directory, which is /home/sam for this example (see Figure 5.4). The directory jfiles is a subdirectory of the current directory, Jan is a subdirectory of jfiles, and rpt.a is a file in Jan.

The pathname ../../brad/janet is harder to understand. The path starts in the current directory, which is /home/kc/eg for this example (see Figure 5.5). The first .. in the path leads to the parent of /home/kc/eg, which is /home/kc. The next .. in the path then ascends further to /home, and then descends to the directory brad. The target file is janet in the brad directory. Long pathnames are very hard to use. It is usually safer and simpler to change the directory to the scene of the action.

5.4   File Access Modes

Each time you access a file, the system checks your right to perform that access. The privileges normally are set so that you have fairly free reign over

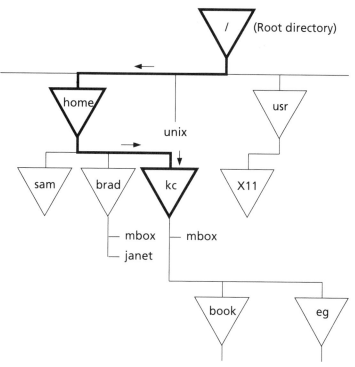

Figure 5.3 ■ The Absolute Pathname /home/kc

your own files, much more limited access to your neighbor's files, and little or no access to critical operating system files. Some of the more cryptic UNIX system error messages are simply trying to tell you that you are unable to access a certain file because of the file access protection system.

In the UNIX system there are three operations that can be performed on a file: reading, writing, and executing. Reading and writing are just what they sound like. Reading a file means the contents of the file are made available. Writing a file means the contents of the file are changed. Execution is a bit trickier. For an ordinary file, executing either means loading the file into main memory and performing the machine instructions that are stored in the file, or it means reading shell commands from the file and executing those commands. However, execute permission for a directory file means that you can search the directory (informally, search means browse through it) in the course of resolving a pathname.

Each UNIX system file is owned by a particular user and each file is also associated with a particular group. In the UNIX system, a group is a set of users—groups are typically users from one department, students in a particular class, people working together on a project, etc. Ordinarily the group associated with a file will be one of the groups to which the file's owner belongs.

The UNIX system's file access protection scheme depends on the type of access that is desired (read, write, or execute) and who is doing the access.

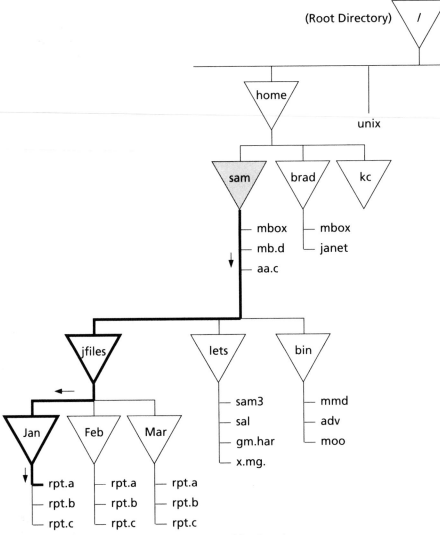

Figure 5.4 ■ The Relative Pathname jfiles/Jan/rpt.a
The path starts in the current directory, which is /home/sam.

There is a set of privileges for the file's owner (the "user" privileges), another set for members of the file's group (the "group privileges"), and a third set for everyone else (the "other" privileges). The privileges for a file can be displayed using the ls command. Several examples are shown in Figure 6.2 in Section 6.2.

The owner of a file is able to control the permissions of that file by using the chmod (change mode) command (discussed in Section 6.5). The ownership and the group association can also be changed by using the chown (change owner) and chgrp (change group) commands (also discussed in Sec-

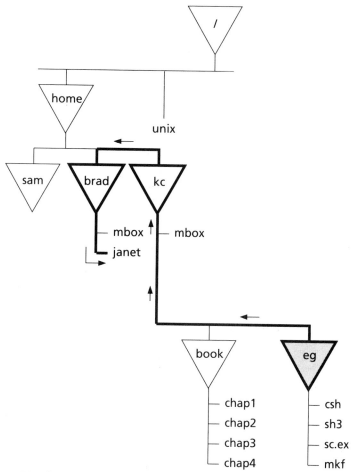

Figure 5.5 ■ The Relative Pathname ../../brad/janet
The path starts in the current directory, which is /home/kc/eg.

tion 6.5). The superuser (the system manager uses the superuser privilege to perform operations that are denied to ordinary users) is also able to change the modes of your files, although in most systems this is not likely to happen unless you request some help.

Many UNIX system files are known by several names. The number of names that a file has is also called the *number of hard links* because each pseudonym is a link from a directory entry to the system's internal book-keeping system for the files. (The UNIX system also supports symbolic links, which don't operate at the low level described here.)

Every directory, even an empty one, has at least two links because of the . entry, the automatically created pseudonym for itself. A directory's link count goes up by one for each subdirectory it contains because each subdirectory's (automatically created) .. entry is another link to the parent directory. It is also possible to explicitly create several names for a given file by using the ln (link) command, as discussed in Section 6.4.

5.5   Directory Access Modes

Directories have the standard read, write, and execute permissions for user (the owner), group, and other. However, in a directory these permissions are interpreted differently from ordinary files.

The read permission for a directory means that standard utility programs are allowed to open and read the information in the directory. For example, the ls program reads directories to discover their contents. If the read privilege is denied, then it is impossible to discover (until the read privilege is restored) what files are contained in the directory.

It is possible to operate in directories where you are denied read permission. As an example, on one of the UNIX systems that we often use, all of the directories containing the operating system source code have the read permission denied, which means we couldn't use the ls program to see the names of the files stored there. However, since we already know the names of many of the source files, we had no problem examining them—the lack of read permission on the directory didn't stop us from looking at the files. Restricting read privileges of directories keeps the uninformed away but it isn't real protection—it is an annoyance.

The write privilege for a directory means that you are allowed to create or remove files in that directory. You do not have to have the read privilege to create files or remove files in a directory. Making the write privilege control the creation and deletion rights makes intuitive sense when you consider that creating a file in a given directory means that the system writes the name of the created file into the directory file. Similarly, in deleting a file the system must erase the entry for the vanishing file from the directory file.

Write permission for a directory does not mean that you are allowed to modify files in that directory. It's the write privilege on each individual file that controls your ability to modify that file. Modification of a file can include truncating it to zero length, which is just as effective as deletion to someone with bad intent. Denying write privilege in a directory provides limited protection of that directory's files because certain changes can't be made. But denying write privilege for a directory, like denying read privilege, isn't real protection—it is an annoyance.

The execute permission for a directory means that the system will search the directory in the course of resolving a file name. When you specify a pathname in place of a simple file name, each of the directories in the pathname is searched for the name of the next directory in the sequence. If you ask the system to

```
$ cat /usr/bin/source/README
```

then you must have execute (search) permission for the directories usr, bin, and source. Denying a directory's search permission is the strongest protection against people using files in that directory. You cannot change directory to a directory where execute permission is denied. However, you can list the files in a directory where execute permission is denied, provided the directory's parent directory is accessible.

6
Managing Your Files

The UNIX Operating System is a tool for managing information stored in files. This chapter describes the UNIX system utility programs that allow you to manage your files. All of these programs perform very simple functions, usually functions that are analogous to the functions that you might perform while you are organizing your house or while you are doing spring cleaning. Periodically during your interactions with the UNIX system, you have to remove old information, make room for new information, adjust the file access privileges for certain files, and occasionally acquire files from other users.

While there are some areas where information management occurs automatically, in most cases you have to supply the management talent. The unit of information in the UNIX system is the ordinary file. Most operating systems, including the UNIX system, contain programs to create ordinary files, to move ordinary files from one location to another, to rename files, to make copies of files, and to remove files. You need to perform these functions as necessary on your collection of files.

In a multiuser operating system, all files are owned by someone and it is necessary to have a security system so that owners can protect their files from unwanted access by others. Therefore, the UNIX system has programs to control the access rights of files and to change the ownership of files.

The UNIX file system is more than a big bunch of files. In the UNIX system, files are grouped into directories and directories are arranged in a logical hierarchy. The hierarchy makes it easier to organize and arrange your collection of files. Because of this, the UNIX system contains several programs to maintain the directory system. One of the major aspects of your information management task is to decide how you are going to organize your directories. A well-organized set of directories makes it easier to use the UNIX system, especially if you use it for several different functions.

6.1 Pwd and Cd—The Current Directory

The name of the current directory is probably the most basic piece of information about your current environment. The pwd command reveals the name of the current directory, which is also called the *working directory.*

All files are stored in directories (see Chapter 5). At any given time, just one of these directories is your current directory. If you're not sure where you are, you can use the pwd command to print the name of the current directory:

```
$ pwd
/home/kc
$ ▚
```

Immediately after logging in, you are in your home directory, the directory assigned to you by the system manager. My home directory is /home/ kc. If I execute the pwd command immediately after logging in, then /home/ kc is printed on my screen, as previously shown. If expected files are not present, or if things are not working as you expect, use pwd to make sure you are where you think you are.

The remedy for being in the wrong directory is to change directory to the correct directory. The cd command will change the current working directory to the named directory.

```
$ cd /home/kc/source
$ pwd
/home/kc/source
$ ▚
```

If you don't specify a directory name when you enter the cd command, the new directory will be your home directory.

```
$ cd
$ pwd
/home/kc
$ ▚
```

The pathname argument to cd may either be an absolute pathname, as shown in the preceding first example, or a relative pathname, as shown in the following dialog:

```
$ cd ../../source
$ pwd
/home/kc/source
$ cd junk/programs
$ pwd
/home/kc/source/junk/programs
$ ▚
```

The first command makes the current directory the child directory named "source" of the parent of the current directory's parent. You might think as follows as you read the directory name: "Go up two levels, then down into the directory named source." The second cd command makes the current directory the child directory named "programs" of the child directory named "junk." Note that the second cd path starts where the first one finished because it is a relative pathname.

6.2   Ls—List Files

The ls command is used to list the contents of directories and to print information about files. The ls command uses many options, most of which are not discussed here. See Table 6.1 for a complete list of ls options.

Each argument to the ls command is either the name of a file (either an ordinary file or a special file), the name of a directory, or an option (option list). The options are used to control the ordering of the list of files and the information that is printed for each file. For each file argument, the requested information is printed. For each directory argument, the requested information is printed for all of the files in the directory (unless the -d option is used).

The following four ls options are used very frequently:

-l   (letter ell) The long list option is used to print detailed information about each listed file. Without the -l option, only the file names are shown.

-t   The time sort option sorts the list of files according to the file's modification dates. The most recently modified files are shown first.

-d   The directory option is used to force ls to simply print the requested information for each directory in the argument list. Normally any directory named in the argument list is searched and the requested information is printed for all of the files in that directory.

-a   Files whose names begin with a period are normally omitted from the list. However, when the -a option is used, even files whose names begin with a period (such as the standard entries . and ..) are shown.

For ordinary files in the argument list, only the file name and the requested information is printed. However, for each directory named in the argument list, all files contained in that directory are listed. If you don't specify a file or directory, then the contents of the current directory are listed.

```
$ ls
README     megaa.c        megab.c    todo
makefile   megaa.c.orig   megab.c    zsrc
$
```

Table 6.1 ■ Ls Command-line Options

-1	Display output in single column format. (Numeral one.)
-a	List all files, including those whose names begin with a period.
-b	Display nontext characters in file names using octal \ddd notation.
-c	Use i-node modification time, both for sorting and for long format display. An i-node is modified, for example, when you change a file's mode.
-C	Display output using multiple columns.
-d	For directories mentioned on the command line, list information for the directory file. (The default is to list information for the files in that directory.)
-f	Force arguments to be interpreted as directories. (Mostly used for system management.)
-F	Display file names according to usage: directory file names will be suffixed with a /, symbolic links will be suffixed with @, executable file names will be suffixed with a *.
-g	Display a long format listing, like -l, but omit the owner field.
-i	Display i-node numbers in the first column. (Mostly used for system management.)
-l	Display a long format listing. The display contains the file type and mode field, the number of links, the file's owner, the file's group, the size of the file in bytes, the time and date stamp, and the file name. (Letter ell)
-L	For a symbolic link, list information for the referenced file. (The default is to list information for the symbolic link itself.)
-m	Display information in a comma-separated format.
-n	Display a long format listing, like -l, except that the owner and group columns contain ID numbers instead of names.
-o	Display a long format listing, like -l, except omit the group field.
-p	Display directory names suffixed by a /. (Use -F for a more informative display.)
-q	Display nontext characters in file names as ?. (See -b.)
-r	Reverse the sort order. (See -t.)
-R	List subdirectories recursively.
-s	Display file sizes in 512-byte blocks.
-t	Sort by file time, showing the latest first, instead of sorting alphabetically. The default time is the file's modification time: -c changes this to the file's i-node modification time; -u changes this to the file's access time.
-u	Use time of last access, both for sorting and for long format display.
-x	List files in columns sorted left to right. (The default columnar display is to sort from top to bottom, and then left to right.)

Notice that the list of files is alphabetized. You can also use ls to detail groups of files, using the shell's file name generation capability:

```
$ ls *.c
megaa.c    megab.c   megaxy.c
$ ▮
```

In this dialog, ls lists, in alphabetical order, every file in the current directory whose names ends in .c .

The -t option can be used to order the files according to modification dates rather than alphabetic ordering.

```
$ ls -t *.c
megaxy.c    megaa.c    megab.c
$
```

The dialog shows a list of the files in the current directory whose names contain the pattern .c, sorted according to the modification dates of the files.

One thing that confuses many UNIX system users is the difference between the ls command and the ls * command. The ls command has no arguments so a simple list of the files and directories in the current directory is produced (see the first dialog in this section). The ls * command uses the metacharacter * to match the names of all entries in the current directory. Therefore, the shell provides the second command with one argument for every file and directory in the current directory. If only ordinary files are present, the two commands produce the same output. But when subdirectories are present, the first command lists only the subdirectory name, whereas the second command lists the subdirectory's contents (because the subdirectories are explicitly mentioned in the argument list). Here's an example of the ls * command:

```
$ ls *
README       megaa.c        megab.c     todo
makefile     megaa.c.orig   megaxy.c
zsrc:
zeands.c     ikonas.c       zmega.c     ztek.e
$
```

Note that ls * lists the files in the zsrc subdirectory. A different example showing the difference between ls and ls * is shown in Figure 6.1.

When you need more detailed information about a file, use the -l (letter ell) option to ls. Using the long format option allows you to see the mode (permissions) of each file, the number of links, the owner, the group, the size, and the modification time. For special files, the major and minor device numbers are printed in place of the file size. Figure 6.2 shows some typical outputs of the ls command using the -l option.

Understanding the output of the long format output of ls is very important because interacting with the UNIX system involves accessing files. The long format output of ls is the only way to discover the key information for each file (file type, mode, ownership, and size).

The first field in the long format listing is the mode field. It consists of ten characters, the first character indicating the file type and the next nine characters indicating the file access privileges. The coding for the file type is given as follows:

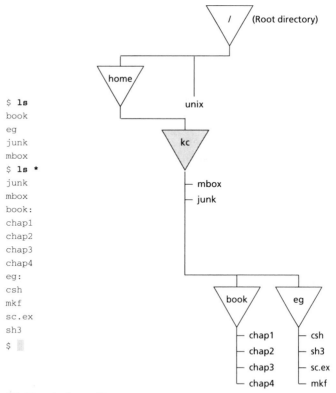

```
$ ls
book
eg
junk
mbox
$ ls *
junk
mbox
book:
chap1
chap2
chap3
chap4
eg:
csh
mkf
sc.ex
sh3
$ ▓
```

Figure 6.1 ■ Examples of Ls

The command ls and the command ls * act very differently when the current directory contains subdirectories, which are book and eg in this example. Without arguments, the ls command will print a list of the files in the current directory, which is shown by the first command in this figure. However, when the ls command receives the name of a directory as an argument, the requested information is displayed for each file in that directory. In this case, the command $ **ls *** is expanded by the shell to the command $ **ls book eg junk mbox** Therefore, the files in the subdirectories book and eg appear in the list, which is shown in the second command in this figure.

Code	Meaning
–	Ordinary file
d	Directory file
c	Character special file
b	Block special file
l	Symbolic link
p	Fifo (named pipe) file

The file type is the most basic characteristic of a file. After a short while you will automatically interpret the first character in a long listing.

In Section 5.4, we discussed the three operations that can be performed on a UNIX system file: reading, writing, and executing. We also discussed

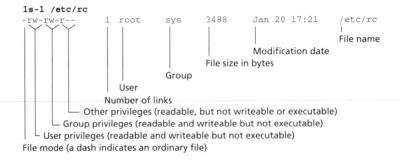

```
ls-l /etc/rc
-rw-rw-r--    1 root      sys      3488      Jan 20 17:21    /etc/rc
```

File name

Modification date

File size in bytes

Group

User

Number of links

Other privileges (readable, but not writeable or executable)

Group privileges (readable and writeable but not executable)

User privileges (readable and writeable but not executable)

File mode (a dash indicates an ordinary file)

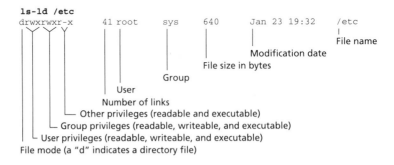

```
ls-ld /etc
drwxrwxr-x   41 root      sys       640      Jan 23 19:32    /etc
```

File name

Modification date

File size in bytes

Group

User

Number of links

Other privileges (readable and executable)

Group privileges (readable, writeable, and executable)

User privileges (readable, writeable, and executable)

File mode (a "d" indicates a directory file)

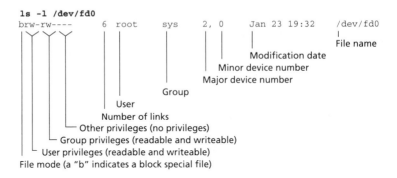

```
ls -l /dev/fd0
brw-rw----    6 root      sys      2, 0      Jan 23 19:32    /dev/fd0
```

File name

Modification date

Minor device number

Major device number

Group

User

Number of links

Other privileges (no privileges)

Group privileges (readable and writeable)

User privileges (readable and writeable)

File mode (a "b" indicates a block special file)

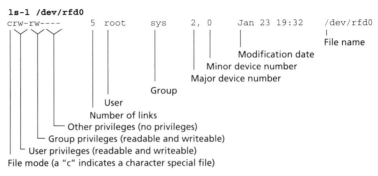

```
ls-l /dev/rfd0
crw-rw----    5 root      sys      2, 0      Jan 23 19:32    /dev/rfd0
```

File name

Modification date

Minor device number

Major device number

Group

User

Number of links

Other privileges (no privileges)

Group privileges (readable and writeable)

User privileges (readable and writeable)

File mode (a "c" indicates a character special file)

Figure 6.2 ■ The Long Format Output of the Ls Command

the three tiers of access privilege, the user's (owner's) privileges, the group's privileges, and the others' privileges. Since there are three access operations (read, write, and execute) and three tiers of protection (user, group, and others) there are nine (three times three) access permissions associated with each file. The first three characters of the permissions show the read, write, and execute privileges of the owner, the second set of three characters shows the read, write, and execute privileges of members of the group, and the third set of three characters shows the read, write, and execute privileges of all others. If a privilege is allowed, the appropriate letter (r, w, or x) is shown. If the privilege is denied, a hyphen is shown. The access privileges for the first example in Figure 6.2 are shown as follows:

```
-rw-rw-r--
```
Others' privileges
(r-- means readable, but not writeable or executable)
Group's privileges
(rw- means readable and writeable but not executable)
User's (owner) privileges
(rw- means readable and writeable but not executable)
File mode
(- indicates an ordinary file)

If a privilege is denied and you attempt to exercise the privilege, your attempt will be thwarted by the operating system. In many UNIX system environments, the read and write privileges associated with files are almost immaterial because everyone customarily allows everyone else free access. In some other UNIX system installations, file access modes are carefully controlled to ensure security and system integrity.

Occasionally you need to know the access modes or some other information about a directory file. The simpleminded approach doesn't work.

```
$ ls -l zsrc
-rw-r--r--  1  kc      1804  Feb 13 11:03  zeands.c
-rw-r--r--  1  kc       272  Oct 12 19:54  zikonas.c
-rw-r--r--  1  kc       500  May 14 19:54  zmeg.c
-rw-r--r--  1  kc      2702  Jan  1  7:36  ztek.c
$
```

The output shows information about all the files in zsrc but nothing about the directory itself. As I mentioned above, using a directory name as an argument to ls will produce a long format listing of all of the files in the named directory. When you need information about a directory, use the -d option to suppress ls's normal behavior and force it to simply list the required information for the named directory.

```
$ ls -ld zsrc
drwxr-xr-x  2  kc       512  Dec  7 12:45  zsrc
$
```

Another example of the difference between

```
$ ls -l dirname
```

and

```
$ ls -ld dirname
```

is shown in Figure 6.3.

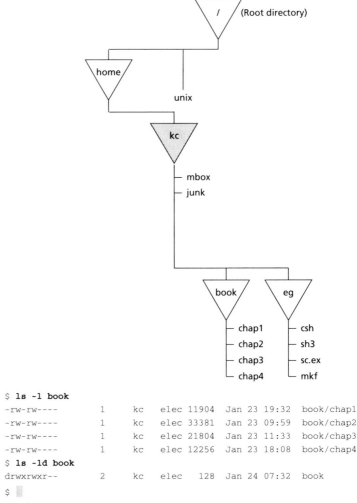

```
$ ls -l book
-rw-rw----      1    kc    elec 11904   Jan 23 19:32   book/chap1
-rw-rw----      1    kc    elec 33381   Jan 23 09:59   book/chap2
-rw-rw----      1    kc    elec 21804   Jan 23 11:33   book/chap3
-rw-rw----      1    kc    elec 12256   Jan 23 18:08   book/chap4
$ ls -ld book
drwxrwxr--      2    kc    elec   128   Jan 24 07:32   book
$
```

Figure 6.3 ■ Listing Directory Contents

When ls is passed the name of a directory, its usual response is to list the requested information for every file in that directory. The first command in this figure shows the ls long format listing of the files in the directory book. The -d option to ls prevents it from listing the contents of the directory, forcing it instead to list information about the directory file. In the second command shown in this figure, ls lists information about the book directory file.

6.3 Rm—Remove Files

The rm command allows you to delete ordinary files. (The rmdir command is used to remove directories. See Section 6.7). To remove a file you must have write permission in the directory containing that file but you need neither read nor write permission for the file itself. However, if you don't have write permission for that file, then rm may, as a precaution, ask you if you really want to remove that file.

```
$ ls -l dnaseq*
-rw-rw-rw-   1  kc      41087  Dec 16 19:40  dnaseq
-r--r--r--   1  kc      47153  Dec  2  8:31  dnaseq.bak
$ rm dnaseq dnaseq.bak
rm: override protection 444 for dnaseq.bak? y
$
```

Notice that rm verifies your request to remove dnaseq.bak because its write privilege is denied. Notice also that the file access privilege is displayed in octal notation rather than the symbolic notation used by ls. The -f (force) option of rm will suppress the verification query. (See Table 6.2 for a full list of rm options.) Be very careful when you use rm because removed files really are gone. The only way to recover a removed file is to ask the system administrator to recover a copy of the file from a recent backup tape. Whenever you are in doubt, refrain from removing files.

File naming conventions are useful for organizing groups of related files. However, you should be very careful, because using wildcard file name specifications with rm can remove too many files if unrelated files are named similarly. The command rm * will remove all of the ordinary files in the current directory. Don't use this command unless you want to entirely clean out a directory.

The remove command contains two additional options. If the -i (interactive) flag is present, then rm will interactively ask you if you really want to remove every mentioned file.

```
$ rm -i dnaseq dnaseq.bak
rm: remove dnaseq? y
rm: remove dnaseq.bak? y
$
```

Replies starting with a y or yes will cause the file to be removed. Any other reply will cause the file to be retained.

Table 6.2 ■ Rm Command-line Options

-f	Force removal of write protected files, without prompting for confirmation.
-i	Interactive operation; ask permission to remove each file. Responses starting with y or Y are affirmative; all other responses are negative.
-r	Recursive operation; remove files and subdirectories, all the way down the tree.

The interactive remove is especially useful if files with untypeable names appear in your directory. Any file name containing control characters can be difficult or impossible to type. Weird, unnameable files are occasionally produced by errant programs or by other transient problems. If you want to remove a file with an unprintable name, enter the command

```
$ rm -i *
```

and then reply no for each file except for the one with the unprintable name.

Another very useful rm option is -r (recursive), which is used to remove a directory, all of its contents, and all of the files and directories in that directory's subtree. Enter the command

```
$ rm -r bookdir
```

to remove the directory bookdir and all of its files, subdirectories, etc. The recursive option obliterates the whole tree below the mentioned point. Naturally you should be extremely careful when using the -r option. It is safer (but slower) to remove ordinary files using rm and then remove directories using rmdir.

6.4   Managing Files with Mv, Cp, and Ln

The commands mv (move), cp (copy), and ln (link), together with ls and rm, are the major commands for managing your files. Mv and cp are used to move files from one place to another; the main difference is that cp doesn't alter the original files whereas mv deletes the original. The ln command is used to make links, pseudonyms, for files.

6.4.1   Mv—Move Files

The mv command moves a file from one location to another. If both locations are on the same file system, then the movement is essentially a renaming operation since the data in the file don't have to be relocated. If the locations are on different file systems, then the data in the file must be relocated from one device to another; it's essentially a copy followed by a delete.

```
$ ls chapt*
chapt3
$ mv chapt3 chapt3.save
$ ls chapt*
chapt3.save
$ ▒
```

The old name is chapt3 and the new name is chapt3.save. After the operation there is not a file named chapt3. The first file (chapt3) is called the source file and the second file (chapt3.save) is called the target or destination. In general, you can't use mv to rename directories across file systems.

If the source file is an ordinary file and the target file is a directory file, then mv will move the source file into the target directory. If wkfile is an ordinary file and mydir is a subdirectory of the current directory, then you can use the following command to move wkfile into the mydir directory. (It's a good idea to verify the operation by using the ls command.)

```
$ ls wkfile mydir/wkfile
ls: mydir/wkfile not found
wkfile
$ mv wkfile mydir
$ ls wkfile mydir/wkfile
mydir/wkfile
ls: wkfile not found
$ ▓
```

You can move several source files if (and only if) the target file is a directory. For example, the following command will move three source files into the (already existing) mydir directory.

```
$ mv wkfile1 wkfile2 wkfile3 mydir
$ ▓
```

Mv's command-line options are listed in Table 6.3.

6.4.2 Cp—Copy Files

The cp command makes a copy of a file. The difference between mv and cp is that mv removes the source file, whereas cp leaves the source file alone. As the name implies, after the copy you have two copies of the file.

```
$ ls chapt4*
chapt4
$ cp chapt4 chapt4.archive
$ ls chapt4*
chapt4
chapt4.archive
$ ▓
```

Notice that the file chapt4 is not changed by the operation. The cp command doesn't allow the source file to be a directory.

If the target of a cp operation is a directory, then the copy operation will copy the source file to that directory, using the same file name. The target directory must exist before the operation. For example, we have a directory named bkpdir where we often keep copies of important files.

```
$ ls chapt4 bkpdir/chapt4
ls: bkpdir/chapt4 not found
chapt4
```

Table 6.3 ■ Mv Command-line Options

-i	Interactive operation; prompt for confirmation if the destination file already exists.

```
$ cp chapt4 bkpdir
$ ls chapt4 bkpdir/chapt4
bkpdir/chapt4
chapt4
$ ▊
```

Cp, like mv, lets you have several source files when the target file is an existing directory. For example, the following command copies several files into the bkpdir directory:

```
$ cp chapt* bkpdir
$ ▊
```

Cp's command-line options are listed in Table 6.4.

6.4.3 Ln—Create Links

The ln (link) command is used to establish a pseudonym, which in the UNIX system is often called a link. System V supports two types of links, the traditional form, which are sometimes called *hard links,* and symbolic links. Let's first talk about traditional links.

The ln command (see Table 6.5 for a list of command-line options) creates a new name which references the original file. No new copies of the actual data in the file are produced by the ln command. Think about this for a second; ln creates a new name, but it does not make any new copies of the data. The new name and the old both refer to the same file—the same data in the same physical location on the disk.

```
$ ls -l chapt8
-rw-rw-rw-   1  kc  other     17935  Dec 12 18:07   chapt8
$ ln chapt8 introcmds
$ ▊
```

In the above dialog, a pseudonym (introcmds) is created for the chapt8 file. Both names are equally valid and either name can be used to reference

Table 6.4 ■ Cp Command-line Options

-i	Interactive operation; prompt for confirmation if the destination file already exists.
-p	Preserve file modification time.
-r	Recursive operation; copy subdirectories and their contents.

Table 6.5 ■ Ln Command-line Options

-f	Force operation; don't prompt for confirmation if the second file already exists.
-n	Don't create the link if the target already exists.
-s	Create a symbolic link.

the file. No matter which name you use, if you change the file, you've changed the file—only one copy exists although it has two names.

The difference between ln and cp is important. When you use the copy command, you create a second file, with its own name. Changes to one copy of the file will not alter the other copy. Clearly this differs from ln, which creates a new name for the file but doesn't make a copy of the data.

There are several reasons for wanting two names for a file. The reason in the preceding example is that we want one naming system that reflects the number of the chapter, chapt8, and one system that reflects the contents of the chapter, introcmds.

You can discover the number of links that a file has using the long format option of the ls command. The number of links is shown in the second column.

```
$ ls -l chapt8 introcmds
-rw-rw-rw-   2  kc   other    17935  Dec 12 18:07   chapt8
-rw-rw-rw-   2  kc   other    17935  Dec 12 18:07   introcmds
$
```

You can tell that the two names are actually links to just one file by using the i-node option -i of the ls command. (An i-node is an entry in a data table that the system uses to define the characteristics of a single file. See Section 23.5.) If two names reference the same file, then both names will be associated with the same i-node number.

```
$ ls -i chapt8 introcmds
1321   chapt8
1321   introcmds
$
```

If the names are actually links to one file, as in this case, then the i-node numbers (displayed in the first column) will be identical. If the names refer to different files, then the i-node numbers will be different.

One place where hard links are important is in the directory hierarchy. The name .. always references the parent directory. When a directory is created, the system links the name .. to the parent directory and it links the name . to the current directory. The whole directory hierarchy is maintained with links between directory files. You cannot use the ln command to change the linking that binds the file system together; those links are made automatically when the system creates directories.

6.4.4 Hard Links Versus Symbolic Links

Traditional hard links are vital to the operation of the UNIX system because they are the glue that binds the hierarchical file structure. But they aren't the best way to create pseudonyms. Let me briefly show you why you shouldn't usually use hard links and then discuss the better (for most users) form of linkage, symbolic linkage.

The first problem with hard links is that they only work within a file system because they are based on i-nodes, which are assigned within a file system. You can't create a hard link between a file in one file system and a file in another. If you're only creating links in your own home directory or its subdirectories, then this restriction won't bother you. But say you want to create a new name in your home directory, e.g., dir, for the ls command. On most systems this won't work because the ls command is usually stored in a different file system than your home directory.

The second problem with hard links is that they can be very transitory because they operate at such a low level in the UNIX file system. In the preceding UNIX dialog, we showed how you can make a new name called introcmds to refer to an existing file called chapt8. If you use either name to modify the file, both names will refer to the modified file. But many applications don't really modify files, which technically means making changes to the file in place. Instead they make a new copy of the file that contains the modifications. This is an important but subtle distinction, and it varies from one program to another.

For example, if you edit the chapt8 file, the editor may make its own copy of the file's text. While editing, you'll work with this internal copy. Then when you save your work, the editor might remove (technically, it will unlink) the old file, and then create a new file using the text stored in its internal buffer. This new copy won't be linked to the name introcmds; instead introcmds will refer to the original data. For all intents, the linkage has been lost. From a technical perspective, everything has operated according to plan, but from most users' perspectives, the system has failed to deliver what was expected. This sequence of events is shown in the following dialog:

```
$ ls -l chapt8
-rw-rw-rw-   1   kc   other      17935   Dec 12 18:07   chapt8
$ ls -i chapt8
1321   chapt8
$ ln chapt8 introcmds
$ ls -l chapt8 introcmds
-rw-rw-rw-   2   kc   other      17935   Dec 12 18:07   chapt8
-rw-rw-rw-   2   kc   other      17935   Dec 12 18:07   introcmds
$ ls -i chapt8 introcmds
1321   chapt8
1321   introcmds
$ emacs chapt8
# . . . the file is modified and then saved . . .
$ ls -l chapt8 introcmds
-rw-rw-rw-   1   kc   other      17990   Dec 12 19:11   chapt8
-rw-rw-rw-   1   kc   other      17935   Dec 12 18:07   introcmds
$ ls -i chapt8 introcmds
1899   chapt8
1321   introcmds
$ ▊
```

The beginning of the dialog shows the creation of a hard link called introcmds for the existing file called chapt8. Then in the middle of the dialog, the file is edited and saved, which as we've already described will create a totally new file whose name is chapt8. At this point, as shown in the end of the dialog, chapt8 and introcmds refer to two separate files, which is almost always undesirable from a user's perspective.

The solution to both these problems with hard links (the inability to link across file systems and the impermanence of hard links) is to use symbolic links. A symbolic link operates at a higher level than a hard link because a symbolic link refers to a file by name, not through the i-node table. This difference is shown in Figures 6.4 and 6.5. Figure 6.4 shows a hard link between chapt8 and introcmds, which operates via the i-node table. Figure 6.5 shows a symbolic link, in which introcmds refers to the file name chapt8, and then the name chapt8 refers to the file in the usual way, via the i-node table.

6.4.5 Creating Symbolic Links with Ln

You create symbolic links using the -s option of ln:

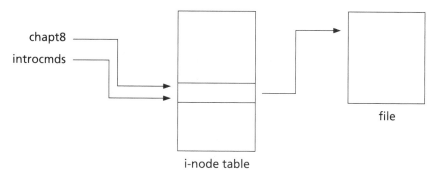

Figure 6.4 ■ A Hard Link Between introcmds and chapt8

A hard link operates at the level of the i-node table. In this example, the file names introcmds and chapt8 both refer to the same i-node, hence both are links to the same file.

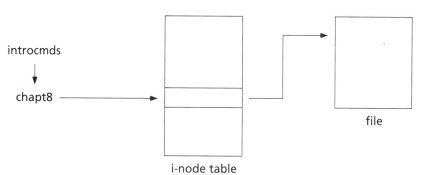

Figure 6.5 ■ A Symbolic Link Between introcmds and chapt8

Symbolic links make one file name refer to another. In this example, the file name introcmds is a symbolic link to the file chapt8. The file chapt8 may be modified in any way, but so long as the name chapt8 exists, the symbolic link will remain valid.

```
$ ls -l chapt8
-rw-rw-rw-  1  kc   other   17935   Dec 12 18:07   chapt8
$ ls -i chapt8
1321  chapt8
$ ln -s chapt8 introcmds
$ ls -i chapt8 introcmds
1321  chapt8
1467  introcmds
$ ls -l chapt8 introcmds
-rw-rw-rw-  1  kc   other   17935   Dec 12 18:07   chapt8
lrwxrwxrwx  1  kc   other       6   Dec 14 19:17   introcmds -> chapt8
$
```

In the preceding dialog, you should notice that after the creation of the symbolic link, the two file names' i-node numbers are different. Also notice that in the long format listing of ls, the file type of the symbolic link file, introcmds, is l and its name field shows the file to which it refers. The -L option of ls will direct ls to show the file referred to by the symbolic link.

```
$ ls -lL chapt8 introcmds
-rw-rw-rw-  1  kc   other   17935   Dec 12 18:07   chapt8
-rw-rw-rw-  1  kc   other   17935   Dec 12 18:07   introcmds
$
```

If you edit chapt8 or introcmds and then save your work, the linkage will be preserved. The only way to break the linkage is to delete introcmds, which will delete the symbolic link but won't delete the data, or to rename (or delete) chapt8. If you rename chapt8, you'll turn introcmds into a dangling symbolic link, one which refers to nothing. This isn't a problem until you try to use it. If you move a symbolic link file to a new directory, you'll also break the linkage unless the symbolic link used an absolute pathname.

6.5   Chmod—Change File Modes

The chmod (change mode), chown (change owner), and chgrp (change group) commands are used to control the access rights to files. The ability to fine-tune the file system for flexible and protected access to files is one of the strengths of the UNIX system. All of these commands are operable only by the owner of a file or by the superuser.

The three operations that can be performed on a file are reading, writing, and execution. There are three levels of privilege associated with each file: the owner's privileges, the group's privileges, and the others' privileges. For each level of privilege, each of the three basic operations may either be allowed or denied. (The set ID modes and the sticky mode can also be allowed or denied, but they are not discussed here because they are system programming attributes. See Sections 20.7 and 20.8.)

You are allowed to determine the modes (access privileges) of the files that you own. For example, you can make a file unreadable and unwriteable to anyone but yourself.

```
$ ls -l  swampdata
-rw-rw-rw-   1  kc   other    3109  May 13 11:51  swampdata
$ chmod go-rw swampdata
$ ls -l  swampdata
-rw-------   1  kc   other    3109  May 13 11:51  swampdata
$ ▒
```

The word go-rw is the option that specifies the new mode for the file. The letters g and o indicate that you want to change the group and others' permissions, the character - indicates that you want to deny privileges, and the letters r and w indicate the read and write privileges.

The mode of a symbolic link file is always rwx for owner, group, and other. When you use chmod and specify a symbolic link file, you'll change the mode of the file to which the symbolic link refers. If the symbolic links are to your own files, you'll encounter few surprises, but if your links are to system files or to other users' files, you'll probably be denied permission to change their modes.

It's usually the case that members of the group have the same or less access than the file's owner, and that others have the same or less privilege than those in the file's group. But the UNIX system doesn't impose any restrictions; you can easily make a file unreadable to its owner but readable to group and others.

The chmod command's single command-line option is detailed in Table 6.6, and the two ways of specifying a new file mode, symbolically or in octal notation, are discussed in the following two sections.

6.5.1 Symbolic File Access Modes

A symbolic mode control word (go-rw in the preceding example) consists of three parts: who, operator, and permission. In the example, the who was go, to indicate group and others; the op was -, to remove permission; and the permission was rw, to indicate read and write. The characters used in constructing the symbolic mode control word are summarized in Table 6.7.

Here are some examples of chmod.

Make myfile readable and writeable for the user (owner), members of the file's group, and everybody else:

```
$ ls -l myfile
----------   1  kc   other   13109  May 13 11:51  myfile
$ chmod a=rw myfile
$ ls -l myfile
-rw-rw-rw-   1  kc   other   13109  May 13 11:51  myfile
$ ▒
```

Table 6.6 ■ Chmod Command-line Options

-R	Recursive operation.

Table 6.7 ■ Forming the Chmod Mode Control Word

Who		Operator	
u	User	–	Remove permission
g	Group	+	Add permission
o	Other	=	Set permission
a	All (ugo)		

Permissions	
r	Read
w	Write
x	Execute
l	Set locking privilege
s	Set user or group ID mode
t	Set save text (sticky bit) mode
u	User's current permissions
g	Group's current permissions
o	Others' current permissions

Add the group execute permission for the file myfile (the user's and the others' permissions won't be affected):

```
$ ls -l myfile
-rw-rw-rw-   1  kc   other    13109  May 13 11:51  myfile
$ chmod g+x myfile
$ ls -l myfile
-rw-rwxrw-   1  kc   other    13109  May 13 11:51  myfile
$
```

Make myfile inaccessible to members of the group:

```
$ ls -l myfile
-rw-rwxrw-   1  kc   other    13109  May 13 11:51  myfile
$ chmod g-rwx myfile
$ ls -l myfile
-rw----rw-   1  kc   other    13109  May 13 11:51  myfile
$
```

Make myfile's group privileges match its user (owner) privileges:

```
$ ls -l myfile
-rw----rw-   1  kc   other    13109  May 13 11:51  myfile
$ chmod g=u myfile
$ ls -l myfile
-rw-rw-rw-   1  kc   other    13109  May 13 11:51  myfile
$
```

6.5.2   Octal File Access Modes

Most people prefer to specify file access modes symbolically, using the notation described in the preceding section. But chmod also allows a numeric specification. Even if you don't plan to use a numeric file access mode when you use chmod, it is a good thing to understand octal notation. For example, the umask command of the shell requires a numeric file access mode (Section 11.23), as does the -perm option of the find command (Section 6.8). And when mv, cp, ln, or rm are unsure if you really want to perform an operation, usually because you don't have write permission for the file, they will display the file's current access mode in octal and then prompt you for confirmation. Thus there are many reasons to understand octal file access modes.

Octal numbers are in base eight, which means that in octal the digits are zero through seven. Each octal digit is represented by three binary digits. Octal's reliance on three binary digits makes octal notation good for representing things that come in trios, because a single octal digit can represent all the possiblities.

For example, a single octal digit can store one set of read/write/execute permissions:

Octal Digit	Read Privilege	Write Privilege	Execute Privilege
0	no	no	no
1	no	no	yes
2	no	yes	no
3	no	yes	yes
4	yes	no	no
5	yes	no	yes
6	yes	yes	no
7	yes	yes	yes

Since a single digit can only store one set of read/write/execute permissions, we need three digits to store the permissions for the file's owner, the file's group, and other. The UNIX convention is to use the far right (first) digit for others' permissions, the next (second) digit for the group's permissions, and the third digit for the owner's permissions.

When you use octal permission specification with chmod, you need to fully specify the mode. You can't add and subtract permissions as you can with symbolic modes.

Here are some of the symbolic mode setting examples, redone to use octal mode specifications.

Make myfile readable and writeable for the user (owner), members of the file's group, and everybody else:

```
$ chmod 666 myfile
$ ls -l myfile
-rw-rw-rw-   1  kc   other     13109  May 13 11:51  myfile
$ ▊
```

Make myfile readable, writeable, and executable to the owner, readable and executable to members of the group, and executable by others:

```
$ chmod 751 myfile
$ ls -l myfile
-rwxr-x--x   1  kc   other    13109  May 13 11:51   myfile
$ ▒
```

Make myfile inaccessible:

```
$ chmod 000 myfile
$ ls -l myfile
----------   1  kc   other    13109  May 13 11:51   myfile
$ ▒
```

Octal notation can be used to specify the set user ID, set group ID, and sticky bit modes for executable files.

4000	Set user ID mode
2000	Set group ID mode
1000	Set sticky bit (save text mode)

These three values may be used in combination with each other and with the file access modes discussed already.

Here's how you could make a file have the set user ID mode, plus be read/write/execute for owner, and executable for group and others:

```
$ chmod 4711 myfile
$ ls -l myfile
-rws--x--x   1  kc   other    13109  May 13 11:51   myfile
$ ▒
```

6.6 Chown and Chgrp—Change File Owner and Group

The commands chown and chgrp change the owner and group associated with a file. These commands usually are used when one user inherits another user's files or when one user gets copies of files from another user. The following command will transfer ownership of all of the files in the current directory to the user named kc:

```
$ chown kc *
$ ▒
```

The name of the new owner must be either a valid login name or a user identification number (UID). The login names and the corresponding UIDs are found in the /etc/passwd file. (Chown is not permitted to anyone but the superuser in some versions of the UNIX system, and System V can be configured so that chown is restricted to the superuser.)

The following command will associate the group staff with the file named corelist:

```
$ chgrp staff corelist
$ ▒
```

The groups mentioned in the chgrp command can either be group names or numbers from the /etc/group file. Some systems make very little use of the

UNIX system group feature. Chown and chgrp command-line options are shown in Table 6.8.

6.7   Mkdir and Rmdir—Create and Remove Directories

The mkdir (make directory) command is used to create a new directory. When the system creates a directory, it automatically inserts entries for the names . and .. . The name . is a pseudonym for the directory, and the name .. is a pseudonym for its parent directory. All directories contain these entries and ordinary users are prohibited from removing these entries. A directory that contains only the entries for . and .. is considered empty. Mkdir and rmdir command-line options are listed in Tables 6.9 and 6.10.

Here's how you can use mkdir to create a directory:

```
$ mkdir morestuff
$ 
```

You can use the ls command to verify that the directory is empty:

```
$ ls morestuff
$ 
```

But all directories contain entries for . and .. , which is easily seen using the -a option of ls:

```
$ ls -a morestuff
.          ..
$ 
```

Table 6.8 ■ Chown and Chgrp Command-line Options

-R	Recursive operation.
-h	Change the ownership or group of the symbolic link file itself, not the file to which it refers.

Table 6.9 ■ Mkdir Command-line Options

-m mode	Specify the mode, in octal, for the new directory.
-p	Create both the directory, and any parent directories that don't already exist.

Table 6.10 ■ Rmdir Command-line Options

-p	Remove the directory and any empty parent directories.
-s	Suppress warning messages.

The -i and -d options to ls can help you to understand how hard links glue the file system together:

```
$ ls -id .
 9319   .
$ ls -id morestuff
10041  morestuff
$ ls -ia morestuff
10041  .
 9319  ..
$ ▊
```

The first two commands in the preceding dialog reveal that the current directory and the morestuff subdirectory use i-nodes 9319 and 10041, respectively. Then the third command reveals that the entries . and .. in morestuff refer to i-nodes 10041 and 9319, respectively. This is a bit confusing at first, but well worth understanding.

If you want to remove the directory morestuff, you first have to remove all of its contents. If morestuff contains just ordinary files, then it is easy to clear it out using rm and then remove the directory using rmdir:

```
$ rm morestuff/*
$ rmdir morestuff
$ ▊
```

If morestuff contains subdirectories, emptying it will require more work, or it will require the -r (recursive) option of rm.

6.8   Find—Search for Files

The find command is an aid for locating misplaced files. Find examines a file system subtree, not just a single directory, looking for files that match a set of criteria. Find is one of those curious UNIX programs that is used by both beginners and black belts. Programmers and system administrators often use find almost as if it were a programming language, invoking one option after another to search for a file based on complex criteria. Instead of explaining find in all its glory, I am going to present a few of its capabilities—capabilities that most UNIX users will find useful. If you want to delve further, consult Table 6.11, which lists all of find's command-line options.

Probably the most common use of find is to find a file whose name, or part of whose name, is known. This capability is useful because it is easy to misplace a file when you are using several directories and subdirectories. Remember that find, unlike most programs, will search through an entire file system subtree. This means that find will start in one directory, search its subdirectories, its sub-subdirectories, and so on.

Find's first argument is a pathname that specifies where the search should start, and then the subsequent arguments specify the search criteria and the actions. Here's a simple example of using find to search through the current subtree for a file named checklist:

Table 6.11 ■ Find Command-line Options

Searching

`-atime` *n*	Find files accessed n days ago. -n means less than n days, n means exactly n days, while +n means more than n days.
`-ctime` *n*	Find files whose i-node was modified n days ago. -n means less than n days, n means exactly n days, while +n means more than n days.
`-depth`	Perform a depth first search, which means examine a directory's subdirectories before examining the files in the directory. Always true.
`-follow`	Follow symbolic links. Always true.
`-fstype` *type*	Confine the search to file systems of the specified type. Common file system types are rfs, nfs, and s5. Always true.
`-group` *groupnm*	Search for files belonging to the specified group.
`-inum` *num*	Search for files that have the specified inum.
`-links` *n*	Search for files with n links.
`-local`	Search only for files on local file systems.
`-mount`	Search for files within a single file system.
`-mtime` *n*	Search for files that have been modified in n days. -n means less than n days, n means exactly n days, while +n means more than n days.
`-name` *file*	Search for files with the specified name. The name may contain shell metacharacters, but they must usually be quoted.
`-newer` *file*	Search for files newer than the specified file.
`-nogroup`	Search for files without a group, meaning files whose group ID number doesn't appear in /etc/group.
`-nouser`	Search for files without an owner, meaning files whose owner ID number doesn't appear in /etc/passwd.
`-perm` *perms*	Search for files whose permissions exactly match the specified perms, which are the file access modes in octal. If perms is preceded by a -, all permission bits (sticky, set UID, set GID) are included.
`-prune`	Stops a search from proceeding beyond the specified point.
`-size` *n*	Searches for files that are n blocks large. -n means less than n blocks, n means exactly n blocks, while +n means more than n blocks.
`-type` *x*	Searches for files whose type is x: f for regular files, b for block special files, c for character special files, d for directory files, p for fifo (pipe) files, l for symbolic link files.
`-user` *name*	Search for files owned by the specified user.
`( ` *expr* ` )`	Parentheses for grouping.
`!`	NOT
`-o`	OR
`-a`	AND (Not needed, because search criteria are ANDed left to right by default.)

Actions

`-exec` *cmds*	Execute the specified command, which may be many words. The command must be terminated by an escaped semicolon. In the command, the word {} will be replaced by the name of the matched file.
`-ok` *cmds*	Same as -exec, except that it will operate interactively. For each found file, find will print the first word of the command, the name of the file, and then a question mark. You can type y to execute the command or anything else to skip the command.
`-print`	Print the name of each found file.

```
$ find . -name checklist -print
m2book/checklist
m2book/rev1/checklist
yaccsrc/checklist
$ ▐
```

Let's examine each argument to find. The first argument always specifies the subtree to be searched. In this case, it is a . , which means start the search in the current directory. Any directory name could have been supplied in place of the . (such as /home/kc or /bin). The second argument is -name, which tells find to search for files whose names match the following argument, which is checklist in this example. Instead of specifying the name explicitly, shell matching characters (which would need to be quoted) could have been used to specify a group of names. The last argument is -print, which tells find to print the names of all found files. This is probably the most common thing for find to do, and -print is the most common last argument for find (just as . is probably the most common first argument).

Let's graduate to a more complicated example. This one is similar to the first, because it looks for files by name, but in this case the file names start with a v and end with a digit. The search is confined to the /usr subtree.

```
$ find /usr -name 'v*[0-9]' -print
/usr/share/lib/terminfo/v/vt100
/usr/share/lib/terminfo/v/vt52
$ ▐
```

Another common use of find is to search for files that are larger or smaller than a certain size. Instead of the -name option, the -size option is used. But other than that, the syntax is similar to the first two examples. Following the -size is a number that represents the size of the file in blocks (512 bytes). A plus sign in front of the number means files larger than that many blocks, and a minus sign in front means files smaller than that many blocks. Here is an example that shows a search for large files:

```
$ find /usr -size +1000 -print
/usr/X/lib/lib0lit.so
/usr/X/lib/lib0lit.so.t
$ ▐
```

The dialog reveals that the only files in our /usr file system subtree larger than 1,000 blocks are in the /usr/X/lib directory.

The last use of find that we are going to mention here is to find files that have been recently modified. For this, find recognizes the -mtime option. The option must be followed by a signed number to find files that have been modified within that many days. The following command searches for files in the /usr directory that have been modified within the last day (24 hours):

```
$ find /usr -mtime -1 -print
/usr/lib/merge/console.disp
/usr/merge/console.disp
$ ▐
```

If you place + before the -mtime number, find will find files older than that many days. This is very useful when you want to generate a list of old files.

System administrators often use find to search for dangerous or wasteful uses of the file system. For example, when UNIX programs fail, they sometimes leave behind a (usually huge) file named core that can be used for postmortem debugging. On a system used for software development, these core files can be very helpful, but on most other systems they have no value and should be periodically purged. Here's a find command that will search the entire file system for files named core and remove them.

```
$ find / -name core -exec rm {} \;
$
```

The -exec argument, like -print, is a request for action. The -exec argument is used to execute any UNIX command. After -exec you place the UNIX command and its arguments, followed by an escaped semicolon (\;). You can use a pair of curly braces to stand in for the file name supplied by find, but the braces must stand alone, as in the preceding example. The command will be executed once for each file that is found, which can impose a heavy burden on a system if your find criteria matches many files.

Find takes a long time to search through a large (many megabytes) subtree; it is best to make the subtree as small as possible. You should probably run find during times of light usage if you are routinely searching through a huge file system.

Many other uses of find, including many that are much more complicated than those shown, are possible. You should refer to Table 6.11 for a list of find's criteria and action keyword arguments.

6.9 Pack and Compress—Save Space

Disks are constantly getting cheaper, but our appetite for disk storage is ever increasing. The balance is constantly shifting, but for many users there is an ongoing tension between keeping needed information on line and staying within reasonable disk usage limits. If you have 20 megabytes of information but you only have a megabyte of storage for personal use (this is a common situation for students at a university), then you have no choice but to keep most of your data off line, probably on tape, erasable optical disks, or floppy. But if you have 20 megabytes of information that you need to stuff into 10 or 15 megabytes of personal storage, then you should consider another option—compression.

Compression reduces the space occupied by files by eliminating redundancy. There are two basic types of compression, lossy and lossless. Lossy compression doesn't allow you to make a perfect restoration of the compressed file. If you take an original file, perform lossy compression, and then uncompress the file, the uncompressed file won't be identical to the original file. This isn't a problem for some types of data, such as image data and sound data, provided that the difference between the original and the restoration is small. The advantage of lossy compression is that it can usually produce much smaller files than lossless compression.

Lossless compression guarantees that you can compress a file, and then restore it, without any change. When you are working with files where every bit is critical, such as documents, data bases, and executable programs, your only choice is lossless compression. Unfortunately, lossless compression can't reduce files in size as much as lossy compression.

There are two lossless compression programs that are commonly supplied with System V: pack and compress. Pack uses the Huffman compression technique, whereas compress uses Lempel-Ziv. Both programs operate similarly. When you compress a file, the programs create a new program of the same name but with a .z (pack) or .Z (compress) suffix, and then delete the original. Both programs can reverse the compression, and both have a reader utility (similar to the UNIX cat utility) that can perform an on-the-fly decompression without disturbing the compressed file. Both programs will preserve the file's time stamp, so that configuration and other systems that rely on a file's time stamp will continue to operate properly. The command-line options for pack, compress and uncompress are listed in Tables 6.12, 6.13, and 6.14.

To demonstrate both pack and compress, we copied several executable files into a directory and used both pack and compress to compress them.

Table 6.12 ■ Pack Command-line Options

–	Display extensive statistics during compression. By default, only the compression ratio is displayed.
-f	Force file compression. By default, pack won't compress a file if it won't save space.

Note that unpack and pcat don't have any command-line options.

Table 6.13 ■ Compress Command-line Options

-b *bits*	Specify the number of bits to use for coding. The value of bits must be between 9 and 16. The default is 16, which allows the highest compression. If you are going to uncompress the files on another computer system, such as a PC or a Macintosh, you might want to specify fewer than 16 bits, because not all programs can handle 16-bit coding. Twelve is a good choice, because it allows relatively high levels of compression but is also widely supported.
-c	Write to standard output and don't alter the original file.
-f	Force output. It will overwrite existing files and will produce a compressed output file even if no space is saved.
-v	Verbose output. The compression ratio will be displayed.

Note that zcat doesn't have any command-line options.

Table 6.14 ■ Uncompress Command-line Options

-c	Like zcat; write to standard output and don't alter original file. Uncompress -c is equivalent to zcat.
-v	Verbose output.

Here's the dialog for packing the files:

```
$ ls -l
total 478
-r-xr-xr-x    1 kc        other       18292 Feb   4 21:53 ls
-r-xr-xr-x    1 kc        other      161260 Feb   4 21:53 vi
-r-xr-xr-x    1 kc        other       64148 Feb   4 21:54 who
$ pack *
UX:pack: INFO: ls: 24.7% Compression
UX:pack: INFO: vi: 17.9% Compression
UX:pack: INFO: who: 19.6% Compression
$ ls -l
total 390
-r-xr-xr-x    1 kc        other       13775 Feb   4 21:53 ls.z
-r-xr-xr-x    1 kc        other      132403 Feb   4 21:53 vi.z
-r-xr-xr-x    1 kc        other       51581 Feb   4 21:54 who.z
$
```

Now here's the same task performed by compress:

```
$ ls -l
total 478
-r-xr-xr-x    1 kc        other       18292 Feb   4 21:53 ls
-r-xr-xr-x    1 kc        other      161260 Feb   4 21:53 vi
-r-xr-xr-x    1 kc        other       64148 Feb   4 21:54 who
$ compress -v *
ls: Compression: 34.22% -- replaced with ls.Z
vi: Compression: 34.43% -- replaced with vi.Z
who: Compression: 30.90% -- replaced with who.Z
$ ls -l
total 320
-r-xr-xr-x    1 kc        other       12032 Feb   4 21:53 ls.Z
-r-xr-xr-x    1 kc        other      105729 Feb   4 21:53 vi.Z
-r-xr-xr-x    1 kc        other       44323 Feb   4 21:54 who.Z
$
```

As you can see, compress does significantly better on this set of binary files.

Let's also see how they do on text files, which are often much more compressable. As a sample text file, we decided to compress the file containing the text of the first six chapters of this book. Here's how the two programs fared:

```
$ ls -l
total 880
-rw-r--r--    1 kc        other      241942 Feb   4 22:32 part1.doc
```

```
$ pack *
UX:pack: INFO: part1.doc: 40.0% Compression
$ ls -l
total 284
-rw-r--r--   1 kc        other       145090 Feb  4 22:32 part1.doc.z
$ unpack *
UX:unpack: INFO: part1.doc: Unpacked
$ compress -v *
part1.doc: Compression: 61.35% -- replaced with part1.doc.Z
$ ls -l
total 184
-rw-r--r--   1 kc        other        93487 Feb  4 22:32 part1.doc.Z
$ ▮
```

Again, compress did better, attaining 61 percent size reduction instead of pack's 40 percent.

The reader utilities, pcat for pack and zcat for compress, are used to uncompress a file without altering or deleting the compressed version on disk. Both of these utilities read in the specified compressed file and write the uncompressed version to the standard output. Here's a dialog showing how zcat might be used:

```
$ ls -l
total 880
-rw-r--r--   1 kc        other       241942 Feb  4 22:32 part1.doc
$ wc part1.doc
    2430     39588     241942  part1.doc
$ compress -v *
part1.doc: Compression: 61.35% -- replaced with part1.doc.Z
$ zcat part1.doc.Z | wc
    2430     39588     241942
$ ls -l
total 184
-rw-r--r--   1 kc        other        93487 Feb  4 22:32 part1.doc.Z
$ ▮
```

In the dialog, wc (the UNIX word count program, which counts words, lines, and characters in a text file) is used to analyze the uncompressed document. It discovers that part1.doc contains 2430 lines, 39,588 words, and 241,942 characters. Then the file is compressed. Finally, zcat is used to perform an on-the-fly decompression, and its output is piped to wc, which produces the same result as before. The final ls command in the above dialog shows that the compressed file hasn't been altered by zcat. The pcat utility, for packed files, works similarly to zcat, which can only be used with compressed files.

6.10   Tar—Collect Files

Pack and compress are great for squeezing space from large files, but they don't do much for small files. First and most obviously, small files are small, and compressing them doesn't bring much benefit. But there's also a technical difficulty that you should understand. In most UNIX file systems, space is allocated not a single block at a time but usually in clusters of two, four, or even eight 512-byte blocks. Cluster sizes vary, but larger disks usually have larger cluster sizes. If you create a file containing just a single character, the UNIX system will typically allocate either two or four 512-byte blocks to store that file.

The obvious implication of clustering is that compressing a 500-byte file down to 256 bytes won't save any space because it will still be stored in several (often two or four) 512-byte blocks. Another difficulty with small files is that you may have many of them. For example, e-mail messages are often small but abundant. If you've got a few 1K files, they don't add up to much, but if you have 500 or 1,000 of them, that's real storage.

The tar program addresses these and other problems. Tar was originally designed as a program for writing files on tape; its name stands for tape archive. Tapes are usually treated as a single large file, and tar was designed to be adept at packaging sets of files into a single file that could be stored on a tape. Tar continues to be used for archiving files onto tape, but it's also very useful for archiving a large set of files into a disk file, which is usually called an archive or more specifically a tar archive.

Like on-line compressed files, on-line archived files are somewhat harder to access than ordinary files but they may take less space. If your storage needs wildly exceed your actual storage, on-line tar archives won't help much. But if you want to free some space and reduce clutter, but still keep things on line, tar archives are a good solution.

Tar can save space because it stuffs files into an archive without the overhead of a fixed cluster size. In a tar archive, files are placed back to back (separated by a 512-byte header). If your system uses two-block clusters, you won't save any space in a tar archive, but on disks that use four- and eight-block clusters, there will be space savings. Perhaps more importantly, a group of small files in a tar archive can easily be compressed, even though compression of the individual files won't help (because of clustering).

Tar isn't the easiest program to use, but it's not too hard once you get the idea. The first argument to tar specifies what you want it to do. There are five basic choices:

-c   Create an archive.
-r   Replace files, by adding to the end of the archive.
-u   Update files, by writing newer or missing files to the end of the archive.
-t   Tabulate (list) files on an existing archive.
-x   Extract files from an existing archive.

Usually you just use the create, tabulate, and extract options. Also remember that tar can work on trees of files, not just on files in the current directory.

When you are working with an on-line archive, you need to use the -f filename option, which specifies the name of the on-line archive. Be careful to supply the archive file name in the argument immediately following the -f flag. Usually you should also use the -v (verbose) option so tar will tell you what it's doing. Here's a dialog that shows how you can put a group of files into a tar archive:

```
$ ls -l
total 454
-rw-r--r--    1 kc         other        19036 Feb  5 09:18 don.ltr
-rw-r--r--    1 kc         other        36337 Feb  5 09:18 don2.ltr
-rw-r--r--    1 kc         other         4213 Feb  5 09:18 don3.ltr
-rw-r--r--    1 kc         other       102436 Feb  5 09:17 jane.ltr
-rw-r--r--    1 kc         other        45060 Feb  5 09:17 sam.ltr
-rw-r--r--    1 kc         other        21110 Feb  5 09:18 sam1.ltr
$ tar -cvf letters.tar *.ltr
a don.ltr 38 tape blocks
a don2.ltr 71 tape blocks
a don3.ltr 9 tape blocks
a jane.ltr 201 tape blocks
a sam.ltr 89 tape blocks
a sam1.ltr 42 tape blocks
$ ls -l *.tar
-rw-r--r--    1 kc         other       245760 Feb  5 09:19 letters.tar
$
```

The messages from tar indicate what it is doing. In the preceding dialog, a stands for add; then the name of the file appears, followed by the size of the file in blocks. Tar doesn't remove the original files, which makes sense when you consider that tar was designed to perform backups to tape. But if you are creating an on-line archive, you'll probably want to delete the original files.

```
$ tar -tfv letters.tar
-rw-r--r--101/1      19036 Feb  5 09:18 1993 don.ltr
-rw-r--r--101/1      36337 Feb  5 09:18 1993 don2.ltr
-rw-r--r--101/1       4213 Feb  5 09:18 1993 don3.ltr
-rw-r--r--101/1     102436 Feb  5 09:17 1993 jane.ltr
-rw-r--r--101/1      45060 Feb  5 09:17 1993 sam.ltr
-rw-r--r--101/1      21110 Feb  5 09:18 1993 sam1.ltr
$ rm *.ltr
$
```

Note that before deletion, we used the -t (tabulate) option of tar to verify that the archive was okay. As usual, be very careful with rm. If you plan to create an on-line archive, a good first step would be to make sure you already have a reliable tape backup. Don't delete the original files until you are certain that they are backed up reliably and you're also certain that they are stored on line in a tar archive. Be very careful, because mistakes in these sorts of operations can be very difficult to undo.

When you have a tar archive, you can extract files either individually or en masse. Here's how you can extract an individual file:

```
$ tar -xvf letters.tar sam1.ltr
x sam1.ltr, 21110 bytes, 42 tape blocks
$
```

To extract all the files in an archive, simply specify the extract operation without mentioning any file names:

```
$ tar -xvf letters.tar
x don.ltr, 19036 bytes, 38 tape blocks
x don2.ltr, 36337 bytes, 71 tape blocks
x don3.ltr, 4213 bytes, 9 tape blocks
x jane.ltr, 102436 bytes, 201 tape blocks
x sam.ltr, 45060 bytes, 89 tape blocks
x sam1.ltr, 21110 bytes, 42 tape blocks
$
```

When a directory is specified on the tar command line, then tar can work recursively and archive or extract entire trees of the file system. This is a useful and powerful capability, but it can also be surprising. When you are extracting files, you can't use wildcards, but you can extract whole directories by mentioning the directory name.

You should always try to use relative pathnames with tar. For example, instead of archiving /home/kc, change directory to /home/kc and then archive . (the current directory). Relative pathnames make it possible to extract the files to someplace other than their original location, which is an important capability. Table 6.15 shows the tar command-line options.

6.11 File—Deduce File Types

The file command attempts to determine what type of information is stored in the files named as arguments. Whereas the ls command prints hard facts about files, the file command makes an educated guess concerning the files' contents. The file command makes its guess by examining the first 1,000 bytes or so of the file, so it can be fooled by files whose beginning differs from the end.

The most important use of the file command is probably to determine whether a file contains text or binary information. Text files can be displayed on your terminal; binary files cannot. (Attempting to display a binary file on your terminal may make your terminal freeze because some of the binary values in the file may be interpreted as control codes by either your terminal or modem.)

If a file contains binary information, the file program will attempt to determine whether the information is an executable program or binary data. If the file contains text, file will attempt to discern the language. On most systems, the file program knows about languages such as the shell, C, nroff/troff, PostScript, as well as English. The classification for recognized binary files is reliable because it is based on magic numbers and other firm criteria. However, the classification of text files is more speculative and may be wrong.

```
$ ls
Readme          megaa.c.orig      zsrc
makefile        megaxy.c
megaa.c         todo
$ file *
Readme:         ascii text
makefile:       ascii text
megaa.c:        c program text
megaa.c.orig:   c program text
megaxy.c.:      c program text
todo:           English text
zsrc:           directory
$
```

Table 6.15 ■ Tar Command-line Options

Major Functions
(One of the following functions must always be specified.)

-c	Create an archive.
-r	Replace files, by adding to the end of the archive.
-u	Update files, by writing newer or missing files to the end of the archive.
-t	Tabulate (list) files on an existing archive.
-x	Extract files from an existing archive.

Secondary Functions

-b *blk*	Use the next argument as the blocking factor. The default is 20.
-f *fil*	Use the next argument as the archive file. The argument - means the standard output.
-l	Complain about links that cannot be resolved, i.e., dangling symbolic links. The default is silence for unresolvable links.
-L	Follow symbolic links. The default is to archive the link itself.
-m	Don't restore the file modification time; the modification time will be the time of the extraction. By default, the file's modification time is restored.
-o	During extraction, use the user ID and group ID of the person doing the extraction for all files. The default is to preserve the ownership recorded in the archive.
-w	During archival or extraction, prompt for permission to perform each action. Responses starting with y are affirmative.
-v	Verbose.
#s	Specify which tape unit. # is a number indicating which drive, and s is either l, m, or h indicating speed.

Note: All tar command-line options must be specified in the first command-line argument. Thus you must write
```
$ tar -cv
```
and not
```
$ tar -c -v
```
The -b and -f options require subsequent arguments to specify the blocking and the archive file. If both are used, two arguments must be provided, in the order of the -b and -f options, as follows:
```
$ tar -cbf 10 letters.tar
```
If a file name is not provided, . is assumed.

The file command uses a configuration file named /etc/magic to help determine many file types. You can add entries to /etc/magic for file types that are specific to your own installation. File's command-line options are listed in Table 6.16.

6.12   Du—Disk Usage

You can use the du (disk usage) command to see how much disk storage your files are occupying:

```
$ du
728      ./originals
31       ./rev1/mycu
3        ./rev1/m4
37       ./rev1/demo
309      ./rev1
253      ./jan
1286     .
$
```

The summary shows the number of 512-byte blocks of disk storage used in every directory in the current subtree. (The current subtree consists of all files in the current directory, all files in any subdirectories, etc.)

You can also specify which subtree should be examined:

```
$ du /etc/fs
446      /etc/fs/s5
270      /etc/fs/bfs
468      /etc/fs/ufs
562      /etc/fs/sfs
570      /etc/fs/vxfs
232      /etc/fs/cdfs
0        /etc/fs/fd
70       /etc/fs/fdfs
70       /etc/fs/proc
0        /etc/fs/rfs
60       /etc/fs/XENIX
2750     /etc/fs
$
```

Table 6.16 ■ File Command-line Options

-c	Check the magic file for errors.
-h	Don't follow symbolic links.
-f *listfile*	Use listfile for the list of files to examine.
-m *mfile*	Use mfile as the magic number file.

The summary details disk usage in the /etc/fs subtree, which contains system management utilities for the supported file systems. The last line shows the total storage in the /etc/fs subtree.

If you're just interested in the total, you can specify -s on the command line:

```
$ du -s /etc/fs
2750    /etc/fs
$
```

One of the maxims of the UNIX system is that "users' disk storage requirements expand to fill the available space." Periodic removal of old files is necessary to keep your storage charges down and to keep free space on the system. People often use du when they are cleaning their directories in order to concentrate on the directories that consume the most space. Table 6.17 lists du's command-line options.

The df (disk free) command can be used to see how much free space exists on a particular storage volume. System managers often run df periodically to keep track of free space. When the free space diminishes to a certain point, most administrators ask the users to prune their directories.

6.13   Od—Dump Files

Occasionally you want to know exactly what binary codes are contained in a file. The od octal dump program is used to produce octal, decimal, ASCII, and hexadecimal format dumps of a file. The various formats can be produced together or separately.

The term *dump* originated many years ago when program debugging was usually performed by producing a printout of all of the values in memory following a program failure. Since the quantity of information was large and the programmer's deciphering job was unpleasant, the printout was called a dump. Today much debugging is done more intelligently, although dumps are still used. Most program failure dumps are examined today with the help of programs that make interpreting the information much easier. Whenever a UNIX system program fails inexplicably, a dump is performed into the file named core in the working directory of the program and the mysterious message "core dumped" is produced.

The octal dump program is often used to search for control characters embedded in text files. For example, suppose you want to know whether a

Table 6.17 ■ Du Command-line Options

-a	Specify the disk usage of each file, not just of each directory.
-r	Complain about directories and files that can't be accessed.
-s	Output only the grand total for the files and directories mentioned on the command line.

certain file contains tab characters. If you were to cat the file onto your screen, the UNIX terminal handler or your terminal would automatically expand the tabs into the correct number of spaces. However, if you use the od program to dump the file, you can examine the output for the notation \t, which indicates a tab. During a dump in ASCII format, printable characters are displayed normally, and unprintable control characters are printed in octal except for a few very standard characters, which are represented as follows:

Backspace	\b	Carriage return	\r
Tab	\t	Null	\0
New line	\n	Form feed	\f

Here is how od is used to dump a file called spices in ASCII (the -c flag) format:

```
$ cat spices
thyme     nutmeg
sage      cumin
salt      pepper
$ od -c spices
000000   t   h   y   m   e  \t   n   u   t   m   e   g  \n   s   a   g
000020   e  \t   c   u   m   i   n  \n   s   a   l   t  \t   p   e   p
000040   p   e   r  \n
000044
$ ▓
```

The numbers in the left column are byte addresses within the file, in octal.

Table 6.18 ■ Od Command-line Options

-b	Display bytes in octal.
-c	Display bytes as ASCII characters.
-d	Display words in unsigned decimal.
-D	Display long words in unsigned decimal.
-f	Display long words in floating point.
-F	Display double-long words in floating point.
-o	Display short words in octal (the default).
-O	Display long words in octal.
-s	Display words in signed decimal.
-S	Display long words in signed decimal.
-v	Display all data. (By default, identical lines are omitted and replaced with an asterisk.)
-x	Display words in hexadecimal.
-X	Display long words in hexadecimal.
+offset	The offset specifies how far to skip past the start of the file before dumping. The numeric value is interpreted in octal unless it contains a period, and it is interpreted as bytes unless you use the suffix b to indicate 512-byte blocks.

Od can dump special or directory files as well as ordinary files. The superuser can use od to examine (in the octal radix) the information stored on a floppy disk by entering the command

```
$ od /dev/rfd0
```

Od also allows you to examine a file starting in the middle by specifying an offset, which should appear after the file name. The floppy disk could be examined starting at byte 1024 by using the command

```
$ od /dev/rfd0 +1024.
```

The argument +1024. indicates that you should start dumping 1,024 bytes past the start of the file. The + indicates that the argument specifies an offset, the 1024 is the value, and it is interpreted in decimal (octal is the default) because of the period. The same offset could be specified in terms of blocks (a block is 512 bytes) by entering the command

```
$ od /dev/rfd0 +2b.
```

The b suffix stands for blocks. Od's command-line options are listed in Table 6.18.

7
What's Going On Utilities

One of the strengths of the UNIX Operating System is its large set of utility programs. This chapter focuses on the utilities that allow you to observe and control your interactions with the UNIX system. Utilities for text files are covered in Chapter 8 and utilities for file management are covered in Chapter 6. Utilities that relate to networking are in Chapters 18 and 19 and utilities for the system manager are covered in Chapter 21.

The idea of these chapters is to describe a set of programs which form a useful and powerful nucleus of UNIX system knowledge. Anyone who seriously uses the UNIX system will be very familiar with most of these programs; less serious users will probably use at least half of them. Large, complicated programs (e.g., the shell, vi) are discussed individually elsewhere in this book (the shell—Chapters 11, 12; vi—Chapters 10, 11).

One of the things that novices often find confusing is the fact that the UNIX system environment is variable. As an example, consider the fact that two different users would usually have different home directories and different access rights to files. They might have different types of terminals, and they might need to use very different sets of programs. One of the strengths of the UNIX system is its ability to support many environments. The utilities in the "What's Going On" category help you understand the current environment.

7.1   Date—Display the Date and Time

The date command prints the current date and time:

```
$ date
Thu Feb  3 22:30:48  EST   1993
$
```

You can specify a different format on the command line using the + format option, as described in Table 7.1.

```
$ date '+%a %d:%m:19%y'
Thu 03:02:1993
$ date '+It is now exactly %H:%M and %S seconds.'
It is now exactly 16:06 and 16 seconds.
$
```

In addition, the superuser can use the date command to set the date. Date's command-line options are listed in Table 7.1.

7.2   Who and Finger—List Logged-in Users

The who command prints a list of the people who are currently using the system.

```
$ who
nuucp      tty01    Dec 15  22:24
gilbert    tty17    Dec 15  15:34
dan        ttyh0    Dec 15  17:37
kc         ttyh3    Dec 15  21:02
$
```

Table 7.1 ■ Date Command-line Options

+ format	The + format option lets you specify your own output format. The format should be quoted, and it can contain ordinary text plus the following codes to output specific fields:

%H	Hours (2 digits)	%m	Month (2 digits)
%M	Minutes (2 digits)	%d	Day (2 digits)
%S	Seconds (2 digits)	%y	Year (2 digits)
%a	Abbreviated weekday (Sun, Mon, Tue, Wed, Thu, Fri, Sat)	%h	Abbreviated month (Jan, Feb, Mar, Apr, May, Jun, Jul, Aug, Sep, Oct, Nov, Dec) .
%j	Julian day of the year (001..366)	%w	Day of the week (0..6, 0 is Sunday)
%r	Time in 12-hour notation (HH:MM:SS AM|PM)	%T	Time in 24-hour notation (HH:MM:SS)
%n	A new line		

mmddhhnn[yy]	Set the date to the specified time. This may only be done by the superuser. Mm is the month (01..12), dd is the day (01..31), hh is the hour in 24-hour format (00..23), nn is the minute (00..59), and yy is the optional year (00..99). The format is inflexible—you must enter exactly eight (or ten, if you specify the year) digits.

When you run who, your login name should be in the list. Some of the older systems were adept at difficult philosophical questions such as "who are you," "who am i" ("whoami" on some systems), and "who is god." Perhaps your system still knows the answers. Who accepts numerous command-line options that are useful for system administration; they are not discussed here.

The finger command is similar to who, but it provides more information. Its command-line options are listed in Table 7.2. If you enter the finger command without arguments, it acts like who, listing logged-in users, but provides more information.

```
$ finger
Login       Name           TTY Idle     When            Office
kc          Kaare Christian  01         Mon 10:34   425 Tower      x-7669
kc          Kaare Christian  13      2d Wed 14:12   425 Tower      x-7669
jjones      Jennifer Jones   B4      18 Thu 16:49   423            x-8052
clay        Clay Reid        E1     12: Mon 16:51   405            x-7665
gilbert     Charles Gilbert  h7         Sun 16:22   423 Tower      x-7670
$
```

The name and office fields are taken from the password file, and the when field indicates the time of the login. The idle time field obeys the following conventions: a plain number indicates minutes; a number followed by a : indicates hours, and a number followed by d indicates days. The preceding dialog shows that my second login session has been idle for two days, Clay has been idle for about 12 hours, and Jennifer for just 18 minutes.

If you finger specific users, it will provide even more information, even if the users aren't logged in.

Finger also works remotely (across a network), which allows you to find out about people on other machines. (Some systems disallow remote finger,

Table 7.2 ■ Finger Command-line Options

-b	Suppress display of the user's home directory and shell in a long format listing.
-f	Suppress display of the header in a non-long format listing.
-h	Suppress display of the .project file in a long format listing.
-i	Use the idle format, which shows the login name, terminal, login time, and idle time.
-l	Use the long format, which is the default when you finger individual users. The -l option is usually used when you don't specify people on the command line, to force long format output fingering of all the current users.
-m	Match user names exactly; don't match on first or last name.
-p	Suppress display of the .plan file in a long format listing.
-q	Use the quick format, which shows the login name, terminal, and login time.
-s	Use the short format, which is the default when you don't specify individual users. The -s option is usually used when you're fingering an individual, to force the more compact output.
-w	Suppress display of the full name in the short format listing.

because of security considerations.) One common use of finger is to find people's login names, so that you can send mail to them. For example, you might use finger if you know that Kari Reed has an account on a machine called rocksun, but you don't know her login name.

```
$ finger Kari@rocksun
[rocksun]
Login name: kr                          In real life: Kari Reed
Directory: /vh/home/kr                  Shell: /bin/csh
Last login Sat Feb  6 09:13 on ttyp2 from fs1
New mail received Mon Feb  8 10:30:55 1993;
  unread since Mon Feb  8 10:35:06 1993
Project:
Plan:
$ 
```

The information about mail would be helpful after sending mail, to know if the person had read mail since the last mail arrived. The Project: and Plan: lines refer to Kari's .plan and .project files. If information is present in those files, it will be displayed in the finger output. For example, you might place the following schedule information in your .plan file so that others could easily discover your schedule:

```
Coding standards meeting 12-2; dentist 3-4
```

The .project file is similar, but it usually indicates your role in an organization and it usually isn't changed very often. Many people place humorous or whimsical remarks in their .project files; other people make no use of these files.

7.3   Passwd—Change Login Password

The passwd command is used to change your login password. Some people change their passwords periodically (some system managers insist) to maintain security. The passwd command first prompts you to enter your current password, and then it twice asks you to enter your new password. None of the passwords are echoed to the screen to enhance password security.

```
$ passwd
Old password:
New password:
Retype new password:
$ 
```

Password makes you enter the new password twice, to make sure that you entered it correctly. Imagine the confusion that would result if you entered your new password wrong and the system accepted it, and then you tried to log in with the new password.

A good password contains both uppercase and lowercase letters, does not appear in the dictionary, and is longer than five or six letters. If your password is too skimpy, the system might ask you to choose another. If you forget your password, the system administrator can remove your old password and give you another one. System V UNIX systems can be administered so that passwords age periodically. You will be forced to choose a new password the first time you login after your password expires. The superuser can set anyone's password, while ordinary users can only change their own passwords.

7.4 Ps—List Processes

The ps command prints a list of your processes, which are the programs that you are running. The ps command often is used by systems programmers (and occasionally by nosy administrators) to determine what is happening on an entire system. You are most likely to need the ps program to determine the process identification (PID) numbers of errant processes so that you can kill them. For a list of your most important processes, you can use ps without options:

```
$ ps
   PID    TTY        TIME    COMD
26344    pts002     0:14    -sh
29313    pts002     0:01    -ps
$ 
```

The command name, process identification (PID) number, controlling tty (terminal name), and the execution time are displayed. PIDs are assigned sequentially as each new UNIX process starts, and they cycle around to the beginning when they reach about 32,767.

If you are executing a process in the background, you can use the ps command to monitor that process. For example, if the PID number of a background process is 2150, then you can restrict the ps display to that one process:

```
$ ps -p 2150
   PID    TT     TIME    COMMAND
  2150   01     0:43    tu58 -s9600
$ 
```

As process 2150 progresses, you can repeatedly use the ps command to watch the cumulative execution time increase. At some point, process 2150 will complete and then the command ps will print a message similar to "2150: no such process."

Ps contains numerous command-line arguments, but most are highly technical and used only by systems programmers or systems administrators. A few that are useful to most people are shown in Table 7.3.

7.5 Kill—Abort Background Processes

When a program is running in the foreground, you can usually stop it by striking the interrupt character (usually Ctrl-C or DEL). However, you cannot

Table 7.3 ■ Ps Command-line Options

-e	List all process.
-f	Display a full set of information, which additionally includes the start time of the process, the ID of the process's parent, the user ID associated with the process, and a full listing of the command name and arguments (if possible).
-p *pid*	Display information about the specified process.
-t *tty*	Display information about processes associated with the specified terminal.
-u *uid*	Display information about processes associated with the specifed user.

Note 1: This is only a partial list.
Note 2: PID, UID, and tty can be a single identifier, or a comma-separated list of identifiers. If a list is used, it must be quoted if it contains spaces.

stop a background process by striking the interrupt character because it is detached from the terminal. Instead, the UNIX system has a special command called kill for killing your own background processes. Other people's processes can also be killed, but only by the superuser.

When you run a command in the background, the shell automatically prints its process identification number. You can kill a background process by entering the kill command followed by the PID. For example, you can kill process 1284 using the following command.

```
$ kill 1284
$
```

If you have forgotten the process ID number, use the ps command. Process 1284 will be killed only if it exists and if it is your process and if it does not catch or ignore the kill signal. If the process that you are trying to kill is a fairly ordinary command, such as a text processing job, then the kill will probably work. Many interactive processes, such as text editors and spreadsheets, catch and ignore the kill signal, so that users won't lose work accidentally. The kill command's command-line options are listed in Table 7.4.

A process that catches or ignores the ordinary kill signal can definitely be killed (unless there is an unusual failure) by sending signal number nine.

Table 7.4 ■ Kill Command-line Options

-*n*	Send signal n. The default is 3 (QUIT).
-*SIG*	Send signal SIG, where SIG is one of the standard signal names.
-l	List the names of all signals. The following signals are available on my personal UnixWare system:

HUP	INT	QUIT	ILL	TRAP	ABRT	EMT	FPE	KILL	BUS
SEGV	SYS	PIPE	ALRM	TERM	USR1	USR2	CLD	PWR	WINCH
URG	POLL	STOP	TSTP	CONT	TTIN	TTOU	VTALRM	PROF	XCPU
KFSZ									

-p*n*	Send the signal to process n.

There's no good mnemonic for remembering nine, but it is an important signal to remember.

```
$ kill -9 1284
$ ▊
```

Using the -9 option with kill is the surest way to stop a command, but you should be careful because it can cause loss of data in interactive applications.

You can also use names to specify signals. Here's how to send the kill signal by using its name:

```
$ kill -KILL 1284
$ ▊
```

On a workstation you can use one window to send signals to a process running in another window. This is occasionally necessary if you run a command in one window that gets really stuck. The advantage of sending signals using the kill command, instead of typing the keyboard equivalents, is more precise control. (Most people know what key generates the interrupt character—usually Ctrl-C or DEL—but few know what key to strike for the other possible signals.)

Processes are killed by sending them a signal. Signals are simply flags that a process examines each time its time-slice comes around. Signals always arrive during a process's waiting (for a time-slice) period. Some of the common signals are SIGHUP (the modem connection has been broken), SIGINT (the user has struck the interrupt key), SIGQUIT (the process should stop and produce a coredump file as a debugging aid), SIGKILL (signal nine, the surest kill), and SIGTERM (the default termination signal sent by kill). Processes have some ability to control what happens when a signal arrives; they may have their own routine to do some special processing when a particular signal arrives.

A process that is sleeping or waiting for some event will not react immediately when a signal arrives. Processes that are waiting for events that will never happen can never die. The point of this discussion is that the kill program can only kill reasonable processes that are still communicating with the UNIX system. Really aberrant processes live on until the computer is rebooted.

When you log out of the system, any processes that are still running in the background will be sent the SIGHUP signal, which will terminate them unless you have used the nohup command or unless the process has arranged to ignore the SIGHUP signal. When things get uncontrollable, log out (or hang up the phone) and start from the beginning.

7.6 Nohup—Run Programs While Logged Off

The nohup command allows you to run a command that will continue to run after you hang up or log off the system. This isn't much value if you're using a workstation or some other personal UNIX system that lets you stay logged in indefinitely. But it's a very useful capability on systems where you log in over the phone lines or on systems that discourage long login connections.

Nohup is usually used to run large jobs, such as big text processing commands, sorts of very large files, and major program recompilations that don't need interaction. Usually you use nohup to start a background job.

In the following example, there is a shell command file called nroffbook that formats and prints a book manuscript.

```
$ nohup nroffbook &
13972
Sending output to 'nohup.out'
$
```

You can log off the system immediately after entering the command and the work will proceed in your absence. If you don't use nohup, the processing will cease when you log off because when you log off, all of your active processes receive the SIGHUP signal. As noted in the preceding dialog, any output of the command that nohup executes will be sent to the file 'nohup.out' unless you make other arrangements. Nohup is not supplied on some systems.

7.7   Nice—Run Processes at Low Priority

The nice command is usually used to reduce the priority of a command. You should use nice whenever you are doing intensive processing and you want to reduce the demands on the system. Programs started by nice may take significantly longer than programs run at the usual priority, but they let other work go on with minimal interference. On a workstation, you might use one window to run long-term, compute-intensive chores at reduced priority, while using the other window for tasks running at ordinary priority. On systems accessed via terminals, nice often is used in conjunction with background tasks, and often with tasks that are run using nohup.

Nice essentially reduces the size of the time slice allocated to a process, but the process is bound to consume some CPU time under all conditions. Unfortunately, there is no method in the UNIX system for running a job that only executes when the system has absolutely nothing else to do. On busy multiuser systems, very demanding jobs that can wait till the early hours of the morning or the weekend should be run at those times in order to completely minimize interference with the normal processing on the system.

The following dialog shows how to run a large job (the same one as in the previous section) in the background at reduced priority.

```
$ nice nroffbook &
14920
$
```

If you want to log off while the processing is proceeding, then you can combine nohup with nice:

```
$ nice nohup nroffbook &
15072
Sending output to 'nohup-out'
$ ▓
```

Nice values should be in the range from 1 to 19, and the default nice value is 10. This means that a process's priority without using nice is 0, but if you run it with nice, its priority is 10. Yes, higher numbers mean lower priority.

You can explicitly specify the priority. For example, specifying a nice value 5 will run the process at a lower priority than usual, but not as low as the default nice value of 10:

```
$ nice -5 nroffbook &
14920
$ ▓
```

The superuser can increase a process's priority by specifying a negative nice value:

```
$ nice --5 nroffbook &
14920
$ ▓
```

The first dash means argument follows and the second dash indicates a negative number.

7.8 Time—Time Processes

The time command is used to time processes. You might want to time a process in order to compare two different methods or you might just want to know how long something takes. For example, you might want to time the print job mentioned in the previous sections.

```
$ time nroffbook
338.8  213.7  26.5
$ ▓
```

After the nroffbook command completes, the time command prints three key timing statistics. The first number is the total elapsed time for executing the command, the second number is the user time spent executing the command, and the third number is the time spent by the system on behalf of the command. All three times are reported in seconds. On most systems, the total elapsed time is measured differently than the user time and the system time. Thus it is possible for the sum of user and system time to exceed elapsed time. Ordinarily, the sum of user and system time is much less than total elapsed time because the system spends some time performing other people's work.

In the preceding example, user time plus system time is about 70 percent of total time. This is indicative of a very lightly loaded system.

The reported times can vary depending on load conditions and other random influences. Timing a command several times in quick succession is likely to generate consistent data; timing a command at several different times of the day may generate less consistent data because of load variations. The ratio of system time to execution time indicates the relative importance of system calls during the execution of the process. (See Section 23.2.3.)

7.9   Echo—Repeat Command-line Arguments

The echo command repeats its arguments. When the arguments are simple words, the echo command is useful for printing messages on the terminal, especially when it is used in shell program files.

```
$ echo tum de dum dum dumnnn
tum de dum dum dumnnn
$ 
```

The echo command can also be used to investigate the shell's argument processing capabilities. Arguments that you supply to programs are scanned by the shell to discover whether you have used any of the shell's special characters. The special characters are used to control various substitutions that the shell performs. For example, the shell maintains a system of variables. The word $PATH is a reference to a shell variable named $PATH which codes the current search string. (Shell variables are discussed in Section 11.2 and the search string is discussed in Section 11.2.6.) You can discover the current value of the $PATH variable by using the echo command

```
$ echo $PATH
:/bin:/usr/bin:/usr/local/bin:/home/kc/bin:/graphics/bin
$ 
```

File name generation is another form of argument substitution that the shell performs. The shell metacharacters ?, *, and [provide mechanisms for generating lists of files. You can use the echo command to discover what argument lists are passed to programs when you specify arguments containing shell metacharacters.

```
$ ls
c1    c2    c3    c3.1
$ echo c?
c1  c2  c3
$ echo d?
d?
$ 
```

As shown in the preceding dialog, the user's current directory contains four files. The first echo command uses the shell ? metacharacter. When the c? pattern is expanded by the shell, it becomes c1 c2 c3, as shown in the output of the first echo command. In the second echo command, the Bourne shell attempts to expand the d? pattern. When the expansion fails (because there aren't any two character file names beginning with d) the original pattern is passed to echo, as shown by the output of the second echo command.

The C shell works differently when you specify a file name pattern that doesn't match any files—it refuses to run the program:

```
% echo d?
No match.
%
```

You can reverse this standard behavior by setting the C shell's nonomatch variable:

```
% echo d?
No match.
% set nonomatch
% echo d?
d?
%
```

File name generation is a powerful technique for focusing the attention of certain commands on groups of appropriately named files—use the echo command when you want to know exactly what argument lists are being generated.

The echo command treats each word as a separate argument and then displays those arguments on the output separated by a single space. Echo, like all UNIX commands, will ignore the amount of white space that you place between arguments.

```
$ echo A B       C
A B C
$
```

If exact spacing is important to you, you must quote the arguments.

```
$ echo 'A B       C'
A B       C
$
```

The echo command recognizes one command-line option, and it recognizes nine escape codes, as detailed in Table 7.5. Here's an example of using those features:

```
$ echo 'A\nB\n\07\tC'
A
B
         C
$
```

The \n advances to the next line, the \t advances to the next tab stop, and the \07 is the ASCII code for the bell character, which sounds a beep. As you can see in this example, the escape codes may appear anywhere in the input, and the backslashes in the escape codes must be escaped from the shell, which is done by the single quotes in the preceding example.

Table 7.5 ■ Echo Command-line Options and Escape Conventions

Command-line Options	
-n	Don't output a trailing new line.
Escape Conventions	
\b	Output a backspace character.
\c	Output the line immediately, without the final new line. (Should be the last item in the argument list.)
\f	Output a form feed character.
\n	Output a new line character.
\r	Output a carriage return character.
\t	Output a tab character.
\v	Output a vertical tab character.
\\	Output a backslash.
\0n \0nn \0nnn	Output the ASCII character whose code is specified by the one-, two-, or three-digit octal number. If the number is followed by a non-numeric character, then you can use the one- or two-digit forms, but if the following character is numeric, then you must use the three-digit form.

7.10 Write and Talk—Communicating with Other Users

The write and talk commands are used to establish typed communication between two logged-in users. Using a telephone, an intercom, or two tin cans and a string is usually a better way to communicate. Since someone may unexpectedly write to you someday, you should prepare by learning how to use these two commands.

The write command is the simpler of the two. When two people write to each other, what each types appears on both terminals. This transcript is confusing for a third party to examine but it usually is clear to the two people who had the conversation. The main limitation of write is that it only works within a single machine, which makes it useless for communicating from one workstation to another. Talk is the more sophisticated utility. Unlike write, talk divides the screen into two regions, so that each person's contribution to the conversation is shown separately. And unlike write, talk supports conversations over a network.

Let's first look at write. When someone writes to you, the message, "Message from harry on tty33" (or similar), will appear on your terminal. You should respond by stopping whatever task you are engaged in and running the write command

```
$ write harry
```

Once both parties have executed the write command, anything that either party types will appear on both terminals. Therefore, it is best if only one person types at a time. The person who initiates the conversation usually types a few lines and then types a line containing a single o which stands for over. The other person is now free to respond with a few lines and then type o for over. The conversation continues until someone types a line containing oo for over and out. You can terminate the conversation by striking the EOF (Ctrl-D) character. If both people type simultaneously, the outputs are intermixed and it is almost impossible to sort it all out. The following dialog shows Kari's terminal following a conversation between Kari and Sally, the system administrator. Kari starts the write conversation because she is having trouble with a printer.

```
$ write sally
Message from sally on tty9.
Hi Sally, is the fast line printer working today?
o
No, the printhead burned out.
It will be fixed by Friday.
o
Ok, thanks.
oo
oo
^D
$ ▒
```

In the preceding dialog, the line, "Message from sally on tty9," is printed on Kari's terminal when Sally, responding to Kari's write sally command, issues the command

```
$ write kari
```

If Sally were not at her terminal, then Kari would not receive Sally's reply. In this case, after waiting a short time, Kari would strike Ctrl-D to abandon her attempt to write to Sally. The conversation shown above is a typical use of write; more complex conversations require a more sophisticated medium, like a telephone.

Using talk is similar to using write—one party starts the conversation by entering the command talk *username*. A message is printed on the recipient's terminal that indicates a conversation has been requested, and then the recipient replies. Talk splits the screen so that each half of the conversation appears in its own window. This makes it easier to follow, and it makes it possible for both people to talk (type) at once without garbling the screen. Write's o and oo conventions aren't necessary with talk. Either party can end a conversation by striking the interrupt character (often ^C or DEL).

Perhaps the most important advantage of talk is that it works over a network. Thus users on different machines can have a conversation. Although a user name can be a simple login name of someone on your own machine, it can also be of the form user@host, where the @ indicates that the user should be contacted on the machine host.

Permission for others to access your screen is granted or denied using the mesg command. Use the argument -y to allow messages, such as those from talk and write, or use -n to deny messages.

```
$ mesg -n
$ ▒
```

When used without arguments, mesg will display the current setting without changing it. If you're using a window system, you can use mesg to control input to each of your windows independently.

7.11   Stty and Tty—Your Terminal Handler

The tty command is used to print UNIX's name for the communications port or virtual terminal port that your terminal is using. If you use a single hard-wired terminal, your communication port will remain the same, but if you use dial-up ports or virtual terminals, your port may vary. One common situation where your terminal's name is important is restoring order when one of your jobs hangs. You can use the ps command to find out what jobs are running on a given port and then use kill to remove those jobs.

You also might want to know the name of your communication line for system administration purposes. For example, names are important if communication lines need to be reconfigured or repaired.

```
$ tty
/dev/pts002
$
```

The dialog above indicates that the login session is using the /dev/pts002 character special file.

```
$ ls -l /dev/pts002
crw--w----  2 kc        tty    35,   2 Jan 20 23:31 /dev/pts002
$
```

The tty command is also used in shell programs to determine whether the standard input is a terminal. The exit status of tty is true if the standard input is a terminal and false otherwise. (See Section 11.5.)

The stty (set terminal options) command allows you to control the way the system treats your terminal. Stty is very important because there are many different types of terminals and because users have different preferences, habits, and expectations. On most systems, you should include any necessary stty commands in the file .profile (.login, for C shell users) to set the modes appropriately at the beginning of each login session.

The part of the UNIX system that performs the conversions to adapt to a particular type of terminal is called the *terminal handler* (also called the *tty handler*). The stty command was created when video display terminals had just been invented, to provide a way for people to interact with the terminal handler. Thus stty was originally concerned with specifying low-level characteristics of the serial communications protocol, such as the transmission speed, terminal-dependent delays, parity, and the like. The original UNIX terminal handler also was concerned with things like tab settings, the interrupt and quit characters, and other primitive aspects of the user interface. Thus stty was also used to specify these user dialog settings.

Today the stty command is still an important part of the UNIX system, although now many people use workstations or network connections. Thus, for most people, stty is used for setting their interrupt and erase characters, not for specifying their terminal's speed or their transmission parity.

This section discusses just a few of the options that can be enabled in the tty handler using the stty command. A complete discussion of all of the possibilities is beyond the scope of this book, partly because there are so many options and partly because some options are system, version, and hardware dependent.

The stty command (without options) displays the settings of a few key modes:

```
$ stty
speed 9600 baud; -parity hupcl
rows = 25; columns = 40; ypixels = 331; xpixels = 300;
erase = ^h; swtch = <undef>; rprnt = <undef>; flush = <undef>;
werase = <undef>; lnext = <undef>;
-inpck -istrip icrnl -ixany onlcr tab3
echo echoe echok
$ 
```

The output shows you a lot of information, including many things that are irrelevant. For example, the preceding dialog shows the communication speed is 9,600 baud even though we ran the above stty command on a virtual terminal on a workstation. The reason for the chaff in the display of stty is compatibility; those few programs that expect to be able to set the communication speed expect that such a setting will exist. This is, in our opinion, the sort of technical tunnel vision that continues to hinder acceptance of the UNIX system. Stty should be aware of what type of terminal is in use, and act accordingly.

The three most important characters in a typed dialog with the UNIX system are the erase, kill, and interrupt characters:

■ The erase character is used to erase the previously entered character.

■ The kill character is used to erase the entire current line.

■ The interrupt character is used to abort the currently executing program.

The standard erase and kill characters are # and @. These are universal characters because they are present on all keyboards, but they are very awkward to use and nearly all users make alternate choices. For example, Ctrl-H (backspace) and Ctrl-U are much more often used for erase and kill, respectively. Here's how that can be specified using stty:

```
$ stty erase \^h kill \^u
$ 
```

The notation of a caret followed by a letter indicates a control character to stty; the backslash is used to escape the caret because the caret has a special meaning to some versions of the shell. You could verify that the assignments have actually changed by using the stty command.

Striking the interrupt character sends an interrupt signal to the currently executing foreground process. Some programs such as the shell and the editor choose to ignore the interrupt but most other programs, such as cat and grep, halt when they receive the interrupt. Many people prefer to use Ctrl-C as the interrupt key rather than the default DEL key.

```
$ stty intr \^c
$
```

You could use the stty command to verify the reassignment.

If your terminal handler settings get corrupted, you can sometimes recover by specifying sane as an argument to stty:

```
$ stty sane
$
```

This doesn't always work, because you won't be able to enter commands in some situations. For example, you won't have any luck typing commands when the baud rate is wrong. When you're trying to reset your terminal handler to a sane configuration, don't be surprised if your typed input isn't echoed. You can try typing Ctrl-M (or Ctrl-J) instead of Enter, and try newlines immediately before and after typing stty sane. If your terminal handler settings are totally wrong, go to another terminal and kill all the processes on your first terminal so that you can start over from a fresh login prompt.

Stty contains many other options you can use to adapt the system to individual terminals. You need to know a lot about terminals, computers, and serial communication to use most of the options of the stty command. On many systems, the system administrator will place the appropriate commands into your login script and you won't need to use the obscure options of the stty command.

8
Text File Utilities

Many people use the UNIX system because of its excellent set of utilities for processing text files. It is not surprising that many programmers love the UNIX system because much of the work of programming is manipulating text. But the text file utilities are also heavily used by scientists, engineers, students, system administrators, and many other people who have found that the UNIX system's text facilities can increase their productivity.

Naturally the UNIX system contains programs to type files on the terminal or to print files on a printer. The UNIX system also contains programs to sort files, to search through files for text patterns, to count lines, words, and columns in files, and to check for spelling errors in document files. These programs are described in this chapter.

Text files are often created by using a text editor such as vi. A text editor allows you to enter and change text in a file. Many UNIX systems have several text editors, including EMACS, ed, the Rand editor, and ex/vi. Ex/vi is a multipersona text editor; ex is the line-oriented interface, while vi is the visual, full-screen interface. Vi is described in Chapter 9, and some of its advanced features are described in Chapter 10. Ex is described in Appendix III.

The UNIX system contains two programmable text manipulation programs: awk and sed. Awk implements a simple programming language that combines standard modern programming language features with special features for text pattern matching and text manipulation. The sed editor is a text editor designed expressly for use in editing scripts; that is for noninteractive use. Its command syntax is close to that of ex or ed. Awk is described in Chapter 13 and sed is described in Chapter 14.

8.1   Cat—Type Files

The cat (concatenate) program is one of UNIX's most versatile text manipulation programs. Its command-line options are listed in Table 8.1. The standard use of the cat program is to display files on your terminal:

```
$ cat /etc/motd
System will be down all
weekend for equipment
installation.
$ ▊
```

Since cat is an abbreviation for concatenate, it is reasonable to expect cat to concatenate files.

```
$ cat /etc/greeting
Welcome to RNA UNIX 4.3
$ cat /etc/greeting /etc/motd
Welcome to RNA UNIX 4.3
System will be down all
weekend for equipment
installation.
$ ▊
```

The ability of cat to concatenate files is also useful in the following way:

```
$ cat chapt1 chapt2 chapt3 chapt4 chapt5 > book
$ ▊
```

This command concatenates five chapters of a book into a single file called book using output redirection. The command could have been entered more elegantly:

Table 8.1 ■ Cat Command-line Options

-	Read from the standard input.
-e	Display a $ at the end of every line. (-e may only be used with -v; it is ignored if -v is not present.)
-s	Silence. Cat doesn't complain about missing input files.
-t	Display ^I for each tab in the input, and ^L for each form feed. (-t may only be used with -v; it is ignored if -v is not present.)
-u	Unbuffered. Don't buffer output.
-v	Visibility. Make all characters in the file visible, except for tabs and new lines: ■ Characters in the range 0–037 (octal), which are often called control characters, will be displayed as ^n where n is the corresponding ASCII character in the range 0100–0137 (@, A, B, C, …, X, Y, Z, [, \,], ^, _). ■ Characters in the range 040–0176, the normal alphanumeric and punctuation characters, are displayed literally. ■ DEL (0177) is displayed as ^?. ■ Characters in the range 0200–0377 are displayed as M-X where X is the value in the lower seven bits, displayed according to the three previous rules.

```
$ cat chapt[12345] > book
$ ▒
```

This works identically because file name generation occurs alphabetically. (Single-digit numbers are alphabetized as you would expect, 1, 2, etc.) If there were only five numbered chapters in the directory, the command could also have been entered as

```
$ cat chapt? > book
$ ▒
```

or it could have been entered as

```
$ cat chapt* > book
$ ▒
```

However, you should note that the command

```
$ cat chapt3 chapt1 > newchapters
$ ▒
```

is not equivalent to the command

```
$ cat chapt[31] > newchapters
$ ▒
```

The second case relies on the shell's file name generation process to generate the argument list for the cat program. File name generation always produces an alphabetized list, so if you are relying upon file name generation when you are concatenating files, remember the alphabetization. You can use the echo command to see the difference:

```
$ echo chapt3 chapt1
chapt3 chapt1
$ echo chapt[31]
chapt1 chapt3
$ ▒
```

Another use of the cat command is to create empty files:

```
$ cat /dev/null > empty
$ ls -l empty
-rw-rw-rw-  1 kc     other        0  Jan 7 13:01  empty
$ ▒
```

The UNIX system "bit bucket" is a special file named /dev/null. If you direct output to the null device, it is discarded. If you read input from the null device, you immediately encounter an end of file. Therefore, performing a cat of the null device will produce a zero length output (which was directed above to the file named empty).

Another way to create an empty file for Bourne shell users is as follows:

```
$ > naught
$ ls -l naught
-rw-rw-rw-  1 kc     other        0  Jan 7 13:01  naught
$ ▒
```

When you enter a command that consists solely of an output redirection, the shell creates the named file.

Another use of the cat program is to place a few lines of text in a file without the bother of using a text editor. If you execute cat without arguments, it reads from the standard input until an end of file is encountered.

```
$ cat > msgforbob
Victor from IBM called.
New machine will arrive on
Tuesday. He will try to
call you tomorrow.
^D
$ ▊
```

Since cat is not an editor, you cannot back up a few lines and fix errors, but it is useful for simple one- or two-line inputs. When you strike Ctrl-D, cat receives the end-of-file indication, closes the output file, and exits.

Many UNIX system text file utilities read their input from the standard input if you don't explicitly mention an input file on the command line. When used intentionally, this is a powerful technique because it enables the utility to be used in a pipeline. But when you accidentally fail to mention an input file, most programs are willing to sit there all day waiting for input from the terminal while you sit there all day waiting for them to complete their chores.

8.2   Pr—Title and Paginate Files

The pr command is used to paginate and title text files. The most common use of the pr command is to prepare a text file for printing on a line printer. Pr is also used to produce multicolumn output, compress tabs to spaces or spaces to tabs, number lines, and perform other simple reformatting tasks. Its command-line options are listed in Table 8.2.

If you don't supply any command-line options, pr will paginate its input, produce single-column output, and supply a five-line header for each page, a five-line trailer for each page, and pages that are 66 lines long. The header will consist of two blank lines, a line containing the file name, date, and the page number, and then two more blank lines. The page trailer will be five blank lines.

Let's first see what pr does by default, using a five-line file that contains some sentences that a first-grader used as a penmanship exercise.

```
$ cat verse
Birds can fly.
Cats are fun.
Dogs sniff.
Fish can swim.
I like monkeys.
$ ▊
```

Table 8.2 ■ Pr Command-line Options

`-`	Read from the standard input.
`-cols`	Produce *cols* columns, filling each column before starting the next. (Use this option with -a to produce multicolumn output filled across the page.)
`+pg`	Start output at page *pg*. By default, start output at page 1.
`-a`	Fill columns across the page.
`-d`	Double space.
`-eck`	Expand input tabs. *c* is the input tab character, which defaults to a tab, and *k* is the tab width.
`-f`	Separate pages with a form feed, instead of inserting blank lines.
`-F`	Fold input lines. This option is used to avoid truncating long lines in multicolumn output.
`-h hdr`	Use *hdr* as the text line in the header. Note that a space is required between -h and the header, and note that the header must be a single word, or a quoted group of words.
`-ick`	Use tabs in the output. *c* is the output tab character, which defaults to a tab, and *k* is the tab width.
`-llen`	Set the page length to *len* lines. When *len* is ten or less, the header size is reduced to allow for text to appear on each page.
`-m`	Merge multiple input files, one per column. This option is incompatible with the *-cols* option. Up to eight files may be merged.
`-nck`	Number the input lines. *c* is the character that follows the number, which by default is a tab. *k* is the width of the number, which by default is 5.
`-ooffs`	Offset the output by *offs* columns.
`-p`	Pause before every page of output, and wait for the user to strike Enter to advance to the next line. This option only works if the output is to a terminal. (Note that the pg program provides more flexible pagination on a video terminal. Pr's -p option is primarily used when the output device is a printer that needs to have each page loaded manually.)
`-r`	Ignore files that can't be opened, instead of printing error messages.
`-ssep`	Use *sep* to separate columns, instead of the default behavior of using spaces and tabs. This option prevents truncation of long lines, except when -w is specified.
`-t`	Omit the header and trailers, and stop output after the last data has been output. The default is to output headers and trailers, and to pad all output to a multiple of the page length. The -t option produces continuous output with no visible page breaks and is primarily used when pr is used only for putting the input into columns or changing the tab characteristics.
`-wwid`	Set the line width for multicolumn output to *wid*, which defaults to 72. There is no fixed width for single column output.

Here is what pr output for this file. The only option being used is -l15 (letter ell, fifteen), which will set the page length to 15 lines instead of the default 66. Making pr use a shorter page makes it easier to see the output in a book.

```
-        $ pr -115 verse
-
-
-        Feb  8 17:00 1993   verse Page 1
-
-
-        Birds can fly.
-        Cats are fun.
-        Dogs sniff.
-        Fish can swim.
-        I like monkeys.
-
-
-
-
-
-        $
```

So that you can see the line-by-line output, we put a short dash to the left of each line.

Pr is often used to produce multicolumn output. The number of columns is specified by the -n option, where n is the number of columns. Here's how the verse can be displayed in three columns:

```
-        $ pr -3 -112 verse
-
-
-        Feb  8 17:13 1993   verse Page 1
-
-
-        Birds can fly.       Dogs sniff.       I like monkeys.
-        Cats are fun.        Fish can swim.
-
-
-
-
-        $
```

As you can see, the default is to fill one column before turning to the next. The opposite strategy, filling primarily across the page, is produced using the -a option:

```
-        $ pr -3 -a -112 verse
-
-
-        Feb  8 17:13 1993   verse Page 1
-
-
-        Birds can fly.       Cats are fun.       Dogs sniff.
-        Fish can swim.       I like monkeys.
-
```

```
$
```

Pr also contains options for line numbering (-n) and double spacing (-d):

```
$ pr -d -n -l19 verse


Feb  8 17:00 1993   verse Page 1


     1   Birds can fly.

     2   Cats are fun.

     3   Dogs sniff.

     4   Fish can swim.

     5   I like monkeys.




$
```

8.3   Fmt—Justify Lines

The fmt command is a simple text formatter. It's often used to smooth margins of e-mail messages or perform other very simple formatting tasks. Fmt takes a text file and rearranges the lines so that they are all about the same length. It does this by changing the location of the line breaks. Keep in mind that fmt is a very simple formatting program; it doesn't insert any control codes into a file, it knows nothing about bold or italics, it can't underline, and it doesn't hyphenate. Its command-line options are listed in Table 8.3.

Table 8.3 ■ Fmt Command-line Options

-c	Crown margin mode. Use the indentation of the first two lines of each paragraph. The first line's indentation is retained, then all subsequent lines use the second line's indentation.
-s	Split long lines but don't join short lines.
-w *wid*	Use *wid* as the width of the output, instead of the default of 72.

Here's a very simple example of fmt. In the following dialog, cat is used to show you what's in the hammy file, and then fmt is used to reformat the file.

```
$ cat hammy
He?s a happy hamster who howls hungrily.
He?s a happy hamster who howls hungrily.
He?s a happy hamster who howls hungrily.
He?s a happy hamster who howls hungrily.
He?s a happy hamster who howls hungrily.
He?s a happy hamster who howls hungrily.
$ fmt -w 65 hammy
He?s a happy hamster who howls hungrily.  He?s a happy hamster
who howls hungrily.  He?s a happy hamster who howls hungrily.
He?s a happy hamster who howls hungrily.  He?s a happy hamster
who howls hungrily.  He?s a happy hamster who howls hungrily.
$
```

Note that fmt always writes to the standard output. If you want to save fmt's output in a file, you need to use output redirection. Also note that fmt will read from the standard input if you don't mention files on the command line.

Fmt usually works by splitting long lines and joining short lines to balance the lines in each paragraph. To fmt, a paragraph is a group of lines followed by a blank line. Sometimes you don't want fmt to join short lines but only to split long lines. That's shown in the following dialog, which uses the -s (split only) option, as well as the width option (-w 40) to produce a narrower output than the default width of 72.

```
$ cat hammy2
He?s a happy hamster who howls hungrily.
a
b
c
He?s a happy hamster who howls hungrily.
$ fmt -w 40 -s hammy2
He?s a happy hamster who howls
hungrily.
a
b
c
He?s a happy hamster who howls
hungrily.
$
```

The split option is useful with text from many word processing programs, which often follow the convention of storing paragraphs in a single line of text. Fmt doesn't work very well with lines that don't contain blanks, such as program input data, or lines of decorative dashes or stars.

Fmt's only other trick is its ability to indent paragraphs according to your specification. If you use the -c option, format will honor the indentation of the paragraph's first line and then make all subsequent lines follow the indentation of the second line.

```
$ cat hammy3
He?s a happy hamster who howls hungrily.
   He?s a happy hamster who howls hungrily.
He?s a happy hamster who howls hungrily.
He?s a happy hamster who howls hungrily.
He?s a happy hamster who howls hungrily.
He?s a happy hamster who howls hungrily.
$ fmt -c -w 66 hammy3
He?s a happy hamster who howls hungrily.  He?s a happy hamster who
   howls hungrily.  He?s a happy hamster who howls hungrily.
   He?s a happy hamster who howls hungrily.  He?s a happy hamster
   who howls hungrily.  He?s a happy hamster who howls hungrily.
$ ▉
```

The preceding dialog shows how to make a hanging indent, but of course you can also make a more traditional indented paragraph using fmt:

```
$ cat hammy4
   He?s a happy hamster who howls hungrily.
He?s a happy hamster who howls hungrily.
He?s a happy hamster who howls hungrily.
He?s a happy hamster who howls hungrily.
He?s a happy hamster who howls hungrily.
$ fmt -c -w 66 hammy4
   He?s a happy hamster who howls hungrily.  He?s a happy hamster
who howls hungrily.  He?s a happy hamster who howls hungrily.
He?s a happy hamster who howls hungrily.  He?s a happy hamster who
howls hungrily.
$ ▉
```

In Chapter 10, we'll show how you can use fmt while editing with vi to produced formatted paragraphs.

8.4 Lp—Print Files

Printer sharing allows a single printer to serve several people. The basic task is managed by lp. It queues the print requests so that each can be printed individually. The lp command's command-line options are listed in Table 8.4. The main role of the lp command is to synchronize requests for the line printer. If the line printer is busy when you enter the lp command, your files will be placed in a queue and then printed when the printer is free. The printer may be on your own machine, or on a remote machine that is accessible using the network. Lp will return control to you as soon as the print files are placed in the queue.

Lp does not insert blank lines at the top and bottom of pages or number pages or perform any of the other formatting actions. If you want to paginate or title contents of the file, you should use the pr command first.

Table 8.4 ■ Common Lp Command-line Options

`-c`	Copy files. By default, lp makes a link to each file, which means that you can't modify or delete the original file until after it is printed. If lp copies the file, you can do anything to the original as soon as lp finishes its part of the printing process.
`-d dest`	Specify *dest* as the print destination. *dest* may be either a class of printers or a specific printer. The default destination is specified in the LPDEST environment variable.
`-m`	Send mail when the printing is complete.
`-n num`	Print *num* copies.
`-o opt`	Print using the specified option:
	`nobanner`
	Don't print the banner page.
	`nofilebreak`
	Don't skip pages between input files. This allows several short files to print on a single page.
	`length=len`
	Set the page length to *len*. You may use the *i* suffix to indicate inches, or *c* for centimeters; the default unit is lines.
	`width=wid`
	Set the page width to *wid*. You may use the *i* suffix to indicate inches, or *c* for centimeters; the default unit is characters.
	`lpi=n`
	Set the lines per inch to *n*. You may use the *c* suffix to indicate centimeters; *lpi=5c* specifies five lines per centimeter.
	`cpi=n`
	Set the horizontal characters per inch to *n*. You may use the *c* suffix to indicate centimeters; *cpi=8c* specifies eight characters per centimeter.
	`stty=opts`
	Use the specified stty options during output to the printer.
`-P pglist`	Print the specified pages. The *pglist* may be a single number (e.g., *-P 1*), a page range (e.g., *-P 5-10*), or a comma-separated list of page numbers and page ranges (e.g., *-P 1,5-10,20,30*).
`-t title`	Print *title* on the banner page instead of the file name. This option is often used to provide a name for a print job when lp is used at the end of a pipe.
`-w`	Write a message to the user's terminal when the printing is complete. If the user is no longer logged in, send mail when printing is complete.

```
$ ls -l /bin /usr | pr | lp
$ ▌
```

When you are using lp, it's your responsibility to make sure that what you are sending to the printer is compatible with that printer. In particular, the preceding lp command assumes that the printer is capable of printing text. Traditional daisy wheel and dot matrix printers can print text, as can laser printers that use Hewlett Packard's PCL printer language. But laser printers that use Adobe's PostScript printer language need some assistance to print a text file. In the following example, the postprint filter is invoked to translate the text output of pr into PostScript, which is then sent to lp, which arranges to have it printed.

```
$ ls -l /bin /usr | pr | postprint | lp -d ps
$ 
```

The preceding dialog shows lp using the -d ps command-line option to specify the print destination. The word following -d is the destination, which may either refer to a class of printers or to a specific printer. Printer class names and specific printer names are site dependent. Typical printer class names are pcl for PCL language printers, ps for PostScript language printers, plt for plotters, tek for Tektronix printers, and so on. In the preceding example, ps implies PostScript, meaning "print this job on the next available PostScript printer." The default destination for print requests should be specified in the LPDEST environment variable.

8.5 Pg—Browse Through a Text File

The pg program lets you browse through a text file. If you simply start pg, it will display the first screenful of the file. You can then hit Enter to display the next screenful, and Enter again for the next, and so on until you've seen the entire file. At any point you can type q to quit.

Pg lies between using cat to output a file to the terminal and using a full text editor (e.g., vi, emacs) to display the file. Pg gives you more control than cat but is easier to use and more convenient than a text editor. Some systems may have a similar utility called more. I'm not going to describe more, but it is essentially similar to pg and isn't hard to master.

Like most text editors, pg uses scrolling and other capabilities of the terminal. You should specify the terminal type in the environment variable $TERM. On most workstations, when using a virtual terminal window, the terminal type will be xterm. If pg's output isn't connected to a terminal, then it will behave similarly to cat, except that if there is more than one file, a header will be printed before each file. Pg's command-line options are listed in Table 8.5, and its interactive commands are listed in Table 8.6.

8.6 Wc—Count Lines, Words, and Characters

The wc (word count) program will tally a count of characters, words, and lines in a text file.

```
$ wc chapt?
   408   2007  12093  chapt1
   684   7921  32313  chapt2
  1071  11040  45818  chapt3
   509   7210  29398  chapt4
```

Table 8.5 ■ Pg Command-line Options

-	Read from the standard input.
-n	Make the window n lines high. (The default is the whole screen.)
+n	Start the display at line n of the file.
+/pat/	Start the display at the first line that contains the pattern pat.
-c	Clear the screen, if possible, before each page.
-e	Don't pause at the end of each file.
-f	Don't fold long lines.
-n	Don't require a new line to terminate interactive commands.
-p prmpt	Use prmpt as the prompt. The prompt may contain a %d which will be replaced by the page number.
-r	Restricted. Don't allow the interactive shell escape.
-s	Standout. Use reverse video, if possible, for prompts.

```
 606    7680   30910   chapt5
3278   35858  150532   total
$
```

Flag arguments detailed in Table 8.7 can be used to direct word count to count only characters, words, or lines; the default is to count all three.

8.7 Diff—Compare Files

The diff program is used to show which lines are different in two text files. Diff's command-line options are listed in Table 8.8. Diff supports several output formats, which we'd like to discuss individually. For all the formats, we're going to refer to the files arlinote and arlinote2, which are shown in the left and right columns of the following table:

```
Arli, Kari, and Reed,          Arli, Kari, and Reed,
Here is the list of            Here is the list of
people who might want           people who might want
to help set up the              to help setup the
ice rink.                       ice skating rink.
Good luck, and call             Good luck, and call
me when you have a              me when you have a
specific date.                  specific date.
Martine - 383-2201             Martine - 383-2201
Philippe - 787-0990            Philippe - 787-0990
                               Susan - 586-1234
```

The traditional output of diff consists of a line that resembles an ed editor command followed by the relevant lines from the two files. Lines from the first file are preceded by a < and lines from the second file are preceded by a >.

The traditional diff output uses three types of editor pseudo-command

Table 8.6 ■ Pg Interactive Options

`<Enter>`	Display the next page of the file. With a signed numeric prefix, skip that many pages back (-) or forward (+). E.g., *-1<Enter>* displays the previous page. With an absolute numeric prefix, display that specific page. E.g., *3<Enter>* displays page 3.
`<space>`	Same as <Enter>, but often used with the -n command-line option.
`z`	Display the next page of the file. If a numeric prefix is present, that value becomes the page size.
`l`	Display the next line. With a signed numeric prefix, skip that many lines back (-) or forward (+). E.g., *-1l* scrolls back one line. With an absolute numeric prefix, display that specific line. E.g., *3l* places line 3 at the display point, which by default is the top of the page. (See */pat/* for description of the display point.)
`d`	Display the next half screen. Numeric prefixes are ignored, but the - prefix will scroll back a half screenful.
`f`	Skip a page. Numeric prefixes specify how many pages to skip.
`.`	Redraw the current page.
`^L`	Redraw the current page.
`$`	Skip to the last page.
`/pat/`	Search forward, with wraparound from the end of file to the beginning if necessary, for *pat*. With a numeric prefix *i*, search for the *i*th occurrence of the pattern. Suffixes control the placement on the screen of the matched line. The suffix *t* means place the matched line at the top of the screen (the default), *m* means place the matched line in the middle of the screen, and *b* means the bottom of the screen. The */pat/* command must be terminated by striking Enter, even when the -n command-line option is used.
`^pat^`	Search backward for *pat*. Otherwise the same as */pat/*.
`?pat?`	Search backward for *pat*. Otherwise the same as */pat/*.
`n`	Skip to the next file mentioned on the command line. A numeric prefix *i* specifies the *i*th next file.
`p`	Skip to the previous file mentioned on the command line. A numeric prefix *i* specifies the *i*th previous file.
`w`	Display the next window of text. If a numeric prefix is present, it becomes the window size.
`s file`	Save the input in *file*.
`h`	Print a help message.
`q`	Quit.
`Q`	Quit.
`! cmd`	Send *cmd* to the UNIX shell for execution. You can spawn a new interactive shell with the command *! sh*.

Table 8.7 ■ Wc Command-line Options

`-l`	Count lines.
`-w`	Count words.
`-c`	Count characters.

Table 8.8 ■ Diff Command-line Options

-b	Ignore trailing blanks and collapse other series of blanks to a single blank. This allows diff to ignore trivial differences.
-c	Produce a context diff using three lines of context.
-C *num*	Produce a context diff using *num* lines of context.
-D *str'ag*	Produce a C preprocessor style difference, controlled by the *string* identifier.
-e	Produce an ed script that can create file 2 from file1.
-f	Produce an ed script, similar to the -e script, but in the opposite order. Note that this script cannot be used to reproduce file 2 from file 1.
-h	Do a half-hearted job. (Fast!)
-i	Ignore case.
-l	When comparing directories, use a long format output. This means each text file is piped through pr for pagination, and files not present in one or the other directory are summarized at the end.
-n	Similar to -f, except a count of changed lines is specified for each command.
-r	When comparing directories, recursively descend the hierarchy.
-s	When comparing directories, mention identical files, instead of seemingly ignoring them.
-S *name*	When comparing directories, start with file *name*.
-t	Expand tabs in output lines.
-w	Ignore all blanks.

lines. *n1* and *n2* are line numbers from the first file, while *n3* and *n4* are line numbers from the second file.

n1 a *n3, n4*
> Lines *n3* through *n4* in the second file are absent from the first file after *n1*.

n1, n2 c *n3, n4*
> Lines *n1* through *n2* in the first file are different from lines *n3* through *n4* in the second file.

n1, n2 d *n3*
> Lines *n1* through *n2* are missing from the second file after *n3*.

Here's an example that demonstrates the traditional diff output format.

```
$ diff arlinote arlinote2
5c5
< ice rink.
---
> ice skating rink.
10a11
> Susan - 586-1234
$
```

The output indicates that the two files will be identical if the fifth line is changed from ice rink. to ice skating rink. and if the line Susan - 586-1234, which is line 11 in arlinote2, is appended after line 10 of arlinote.

When you use the -e option of diff, the output is modified slightly to produce an actual ed script:

```
$ diff -e arlinote arlinote2
10a
Susan - 586-1234
.
5c
ice skating rink.
.
$ 
```

You might notice that the changes start from the end of the file and work forward. That's because all the line numbers in the script refer to the original, unchanged file. If you work from the end back to the beginning, these line numbers will be correct, but if you work forward through the file, your initial edits might alter the numbering, which would lead to serious problems.

Here's how you could create a file called arlinote3 from arlinote using the preceding script.

```
$ diff -e arlinote arlinote2 > script
$ (cat script; echo 'w arlinote3') | ed - arlinote
$ diff arlinote2 arlinote3
$ 
```

However, for human readers, it's often better to produce the ed script in the forward order, which is what diff produces when you use the -f option.

```
$ diff -f arlinote arlinote2
c5
ice skating rink.
.
a10
Susan - 586-1234
.
$ 
```

Note carefully that the script produced using diff's -f option cannot be used to recreate the file; all it does is document the differences in a form that makes sense to most people.

Diff's most legible format is called a context diff. It's the format that we usually prefer both because it shows some context and because it's the format that makes it easiest for us to understand the differences. In a context diff, there are a few lines of context, followed by the changed lines. Lines in file1 are marked with a - if they are omitted from file2, and lines in file2 are marked with a + if they are not present in file1. Lines that simply changed are marked in both files by a ! character.

Diff's -c option produces the standard context diff, using three lines of context. For easier display in this book, we've chosen the alternate -C option to produce the context diff because it allows us to specify that we want two lines of context:

```
$ diff -C 2 arlinote arlinote2
*** arlinote Tue Feb  9 14:08:42 1993
--- arlinote2 Tue Feb  9 13:59:56 1993
```

```
* * * * * * * * * * * * * *
*** 3,7 ****
  people who might want
  to help set up the
! ice rink.
  Good luck, and call
  me when you have a
--- 3,7 ----
  people who might want
  to help set up the
! ice skating rink.
  Good luck, and call
  me when you have a
* * * * * * * * * * * * * *
*** 9,10 ****
--- 9,11 ----
  Martine - 383-2201
  Philippe - 787-0990
+ Susan - 586-1234
$
```

Diff's last format is most often used by programmers. It produces a merged file in which C language #ifdef lines are used to identify the two versions. An identifier (a preprocessor identifier in C jargon) controls which version is produced when the file is processed using the standard C preprocessor. The first version of the file will be produced if the given identifier is not defined; the second version will be produced if the identifier is defined.

```
$ diff -D VER2 arlinote arlinote2
Arli, Kari, and Reed,
Here is the list of
people who might want
to help set up the
#ifndef VER2
ice rink.
#else VER2
ice skating rink.
#endif VER2
Good luck, and call
me when you have a
specific date.
Martine - 383-2201
Philippe - 787-0990
#ifdef VER2
Susan - 586-1234
#endif VER2
$
```

Diff may also be used to compare all of the files in a pair of directories. The two directories should be specified on the command line, and any of the -e, -f, -c, -C, -D, and -n options can be used to specify what type of diff will be performed for files that appear in both directories. Diff will print messages for files that only appear in one of the two directories.

There are several other programs that look for differences between files:

- Cmp tests to see if two files are identical. It works on both binary and text files.

- Bdiff lets diff work on huge files by partitioning the file into chunks small enough to work with diff.

- Diff3 works with three files at a time, instead of two.

- Comm compares sorted files using a columnar format.

These programs are easy to learn if you know diff.

8.8   Sort—Order Files

The sort command is used to sort and/or merge text files. Its command-line options are listed in Table 8.9. Sort rearranges the lines in a file according to your command-line specifications. Unless you make other arrangements, the sorted output will appear on the terminal. Naturally you can place the output in a file if you want a permanent copy of the sorted output.

Each line of the input can contain several fields. The fields are delimited by a field separator, which is usually a tab or space but may be assigned to some other character. The portion of the input line that sort examines to determine an ordering for the file is called the *sort key*. The sort key can be one or more fields, or parts of fields, or the entire line.

As an example, let's sort a file containing a list of people's telephone numbers and initials. To sort a file, you must have a file with a regular structure and you must know the details of that structure. In our example, let's suppose that each line of the file contains a person's initials, a tab character, and that person's telephone number, in that order. For simplicity, let's consider a file named telnos containing some phone numbers:

```
$ cat telnos
kc      362-4993
gmk     245-3209
arm     333-3903
$
```

In telnos a tab separates the initials from the phone numbers.

It's easy to sort according to the people's initials, since sort defaults to sorting the entire line:

```
$ sort telnos
arm     333-3903
gmk     245-3209
kc      362-4993
$
```

Table 8.9 ■ Sort Command-line Options

`+m.n`	The sort key starts at character *n* of field *m*. The *.n* is optional; *n* defaults to zero. May be followed by the suffixes b, d, f, i, n, or r to specify an ordering for the individual field. When *b* is in effect, *n* is counted from the first nonblank (zero means the first nonblank).
`-m.n`	The sort key ends before character *n* of field *m*. The *.n* is optional; *n* defaults to zero. When *b* is in effect, *n* is counted from the first nonblank.
`-b`	Ignore leading blanks in a sort key.
`-c`	Check that the input is sorted. Issue an error message if the file(s) aren't sorted.
`-d`	Dictionary ordering. Only letters, digits, and blanks are significant; punctuation is ignored.
`-f`	Fold lowercase into uppercase.
`-i`	Ignore nonprintable characters.
`-m`	Merge sort, which is only used with multiple input files. The input files are assumed to contain sorted data. Sort merges the input files, producing an ordered output.
`-M`	Compare month names. Jan < Feb < Mar and so on.
`-n`	Compare numbers.
`-ooutfile`	Send the output to *outfile,* which may be one of the input files.
`-r`	Reverse the ordering.
`-tfs`	Use *fs* as the field separator, to determine the meanings of the +*m.n* or -*m.n* sort keys. The default field separator is white space.
`-u`	Unique. Only output one of a series of lines whose sort keys compare equal.
`-ymem`	Use *mem* kilobytes of memory for the sort. If *mem* is zero, sort starts out with minimal memory. If *mem* is missing, sort starts out with maximal memory. For some sorts, it's much faster to start with a large block of memory rather than ratchet up to a large buffer as records are read in.
`-zrecsiz`	Use *recsize* bytes as the size of the input buffer. This option doesn't need to be specified for ordinary sorts but may need to be specified for merges (-m) or checks (-c).

If we wanted the file sorted according to the telephone numbers, we would have to specify that the primary sort key is the second field. You can specify individual fields using a field identifier. Field 0 is the first (leftmost) field, field 1 is the second, and so on. The notation +*n* indicates a key starting at field *n*, and the notation -*n* indicates that the sort key stops just before field *n*.

```
$ sort +1 telnos
gmk      245-3209
arm      333-3903
kc       362-4993
$
```

The +1 argument informs the sort program that we want to start the sort key to start at field 1, the phone numbers field. If two lines compared equally using the specified sort key, then sort would start over comparing the whole line.

It's often necessary to sort a file in place. Given, say, the telnos file, you're more likely to want it sorted than you are to want a new sorted file of telephone numbers. First, the *wrong way*—output redirection:

```
$ sort telnos > telnos
$ 
```

If you enter the preceding mistake, the output redirection will truncate the telnos file to zero length before sort has a chance to sort it. This will destroy your input.

Second, the laborious way:

```
$ sort telnos > telnos.tmp
$ mv telnos.tmp telnos
$ 
```

This approach will work fine, but it involves an extra step.

Third, the preferred way to sort a file in place, sort's -o option:

```
$ sort -o telnos telnos
$ 
```

As a general rule, you should be skeptical about sending any UNIX command's output to one of its input files. But sort is an exception; the need for in-situ sorting is so common that sort was built with this capability in mind.

Sort usually orders lines according to a simple comparison of the bytes in the line according to their (machine dependent) values. This usually works fine for text, but numbers should be converted to binary numeric values before they are compared. Consider the following example:

```
$ cat numbs
5
2000
40
10000
300
$ sort numbs
10000
2000
300
40
5
$ 
```

Sort gets the answer exactly wrong in this contrived example because it's looking at the numbers as plain text, which in this example means it only looks at the first digit. Instead, we need to use the -n option with sort so that it looks at each number, well, numerically:

```
$ sort -n numbs
5
40
300
```

```
2000
10000
$ ▮
```

Let's talk a bit more about the field notation used in sort. In the earlier example, we used the notation +1 to refer to field one. Actually, field notation can also refer to a specific character in that field by following the field number with a period and then an offset in characters. Thus the field identifier 1.3 refers to character three in field one. The numbering of character offsets, like the numbering of fields, starts at zero. 0.0 is character zero of field zero.

Here's a short data file in which each line consists of a four-digit number followed by a single character code, followed by a name.

```
$ cat names
0991M Christian, Kaare
0732M Raskin, Robin
0654C Smith, George
0220P Aldrige, Ricky
0739C Kitay, Ken
0184C Duffin, Pat
$ ▮
```

We can make the primary sort key the single character code (C, M, and P in this example), which is the last character of field zero:

```
$ sort +0.4 -0.5 names
0184C Duffin, Pat
0654C Smith, George
0739C Kitay, Ken
0732M Raskin, Robin
0991M Christian, Kaare
0220P Aldrige, Ricky
$ ▮
```

The +0.4 indicates that the sort key starts at character four of field zero, and the -0.5 indicates that the sort key stops before character five of field zero. (Another way to indicate the end of the sort key would be -1, meaning before the start of field one.) When the primary sort key doesn't indicate an ordering, then the sort will restart the comparison using the whole line, which in this example means that the numbers in field zero will be the secondary control of the ordering.

It's easy to make the names be the secondary sort key, by adding a second field indicator:

```
$ sort +0.4 -0.5 +1 names
0184C Duffin, Pat
0739C Kitay, Ken
0654C Smith, George
0991M Christian, Kaare
0732M Raskin, Robin
0220P Aldrige, Ricky
$ ▮
```

Field indicators can be followed by the option flags b, d, f, i, n, or r to indicate the ordering strategy for that particular field. When you use any of these options before the first field indicator, it indicates a default sorting strategy for all the fields.

8.9 Grep—Search for Text Patterns in Files

The grep program (and its relatives fgrep and egrep) searches for text patterns in files. Whenever the text pattern is recognized on a line, that line of the file is presented on the standard output. You can think of the grep program as performing a horizontal slice through a file based on a text matching criterion. One common bit of UNIX trivia is the derivation of the word grep—it comes from the phrase "global regular expression print," which is ed (the early UNIX text editor) syntax for the operation performed by grep.

The first argument to the grep command is the text pattern, and the following arguments specify the files that should be examined. Grep's command-line options are listed in Table 8.10. The text pattern for grep can use most of the regular expression syntax of the ed text editor. The text patterns for egrep can be more complicated, while the text patterns for fgrep are limited to fixed strings. Grep and egrep can only search for a group of strings if the group can be specified by a regular expression.

Suppose you want a long format list of the symbolic link files in the root directory. If you enter the command

Table 8.10 ■ Egrep, Fgrep, and Grep Command-line Options

-b	EFG	Precede each line with its block number. (Occasional system administration applications.)
-c	EFG	Print only a count of the number of lines containing the pattern.
-e *strng*	EF	Use *strng* as the pattern. This option is useful for patterns that begin with a hyphen, which would otherwise be interpreted as a command-line option.
-f *file*	EF	Take the regular expressions (egrep) or fixed strings (fgrep) from *file*.
-h	EFG	Don't print matching file names when searching through multiple files. Usually, when you are searching through multiple files, each file name is printed in front of the matched lines.
-i	EFG	Ignore case distinctions.
-l	EFG	Print only the name of each file containing a match; don't print the matched lines.
-n	EFG	Print line numbers.
-s	G	Don't complain about missing input files.
-v	EFG	Print only lines that don't match the pattern.
-x	F	Print only lines matched entirely. (In egrep and grep, this capability can be attained by making ^ the first character of the pattern and $ the last character of the pattern.)

Note: The second column of the table shows the usage of the command-line options in the three programs: E indicates the option is used by egrep; F indicates the option is used by fgrep; and G indicates the option is used by grep.

```
$ ls -1 /
```

you will produce the desired list intertwined with a list of all of the other files contained in the root directory. The grep command can be used to filter out all of the unwanted information. If no files are supplied as arguments to grep, then like other text filters it reads from the standard input. Thus grep can be used in a pipeline as follows:

```
$ ls -l / | grep \^l
lrwxrwxrwx   1 root      root       8 Feb   4 04:12 bin -> /usr/bin
lrwxrwxrwx   1 root      root       8 Feb   4 04:13 lib -> /usr/lib
lrwxrwxrwx   1 root      root       8 Feb   4 04:13 shlib -> /usr/lib
lrwxrwxrwx   1 root      root      11 Feb   4 04:19 unix -> /stand/unix
$
```

The text pattern for grep is quoted (by a \) because it contains a caret, a meaningful character to the shell. The editor regular expression ^l matches all lines that begin with the letter l. Thus only symbolic links are listed, since symbolic lines in a long listing start with an l while ordinary file lines start with a - and directory files start with a d.

The standard use of grep is to find all occurrences of some word in a document. For example, you may have a bad habit of typing teh when you mean the:

```
$ grep teh chapt*
chapt3: In one of teh drosophila experiments James
chapt3: until teh ether is evaporated
chapt5: another day. Then teh result can be explained
$
```

Of course you could do the search using the editor, but it is easier to use grep to identify those files that contain errors before using the editor to fix the errors.

Fgrep is the easiest way to look for one of several fixed strings, and it's also the fastest member of the grep family because it doesn't include regular expression logic. For example, you can look for the words Darwin or Malthus in a set of files with the following commands:

```
$ echo 'Darwin\nMalthus' > names
$ cat names
Darwin
Malthus
$ fgrep -f names ch*
ch21: If Darwin relied on metaphors
ch21: crucial. Darwin, at least, claimed
ch21: his reading of Thomas Malthus's essay on
$ rm names
$
```

The egrep command expands the regular expression language accepted by grep. The additions are the ability to group regular expressions using parentheses and metacharacters (similar to the * metacharacter) to apply a regular expression zero or one times (?), or to apply it once or more than once (+). These additions are summarized in Table 8.11.

8.10 Cut and Paste—Rearrange Columns of Files

Cut and paste are used to manipulate vertical slices of files. Their command-line options are listed in Tables 8.12 and 8.13. Cut and paste are most useful for files that contain tabular text data. The cut program is used to cut a vertical section from a file, whereas the paste program merges several vertical sections into one file. Both cut and paste manipulate input files and produce their output on the standard output. Usually you will want to redirect their output to a file.

To use cut and paste, you need to know how the columns (fields) of the files are separated. The easiest field separator is a tab, although other characters can be used.

Table 8.11 ■ Egrep and Grep Regular Expression Metacharacters

^	EG	Anchors a pattern to the beginning of the line.
$	EG	Anchors a pattern to the end of the line.
\<	EG	Anchors a pattern to the beginning of a word.
\>	EG	Anchors a pattern to the end of a word.
.	EG	Matches any single character.
*	EG	Matches any zero, one, or more occurrences of the preceding single character (grep) or full (egrep) regular expression.
?	E	Matches zero or one occurrences of the preceding full regular expression.
+	E	Matches one or more occurrences of the preceding full regular expression.
\{m\}	EG	Matches exactly m occurrences of the preceding single character regular expression.
\{m,\}	EG	Matches m or more occurrences of the preceding single character regular expression.
\{m,n\}	EG	Matches between m and n occurrences of the preceding single character regular expression.
[ ]	EG	A character set, which will match any one of the characters in the set. Character sets contain single characters and character ranges, such as a-m. A leading caret means match characters not in the set. For example, [0-9a-fA-F] is a character set that will match any of the digits or a lower- or uppercase letter in the range A through F; [^0-9] is a character set that will match any character that's not a digit.
|	E	The logical OR of two (usually parenthesized) full regular expressions. It's usually easier to place a set of regular expressions in a file, one per line, to produce the same effect.
( )	E	Parentheses for grouping. (Usually used with ?, + and | metacharacters.)

Note: The second column of the table shows the usage of the metacharacters in the two programs: E indicates the metacharacter is used by egrep; G indicates the metacharacter is used by grep.

Table 8.12 ■ Cut Command-line Options

-c*list*	Cut according to character positions, as specified in *list*. The list may indicate individual characters or character ranges. For example, the list 1,3,5-9 specifies characters 1, 3, and 5 through 9. An initial -*n* is short for characters 1 through *n*, and a trailing *m*- is short for characters *m* through the end of the line.
-d*fs*	The character *fs* is the field delimiter for the -f option; the default is a tab.
-f*list*	Cut specific fields, as specified in *list*. The list may indicate individual fields or field ranges. For example, the list 1,3,5-9 specifies fields 1, 3, and 5 through 9. An initial -*n* is short for fields 1 through *n*, and a trailing *m*- is short for fields *m* through the end of the line.
-s	Suppress lines that don't contain the field delimiter. (Only used with the -f option.) Ordinarily these lines are passed through unchanged.

Note: Either the -f or the -c option must be specified.

Table 8.13 ■ Paste Command-line Options

-	Used in place of a file name to indicate the standard input.
-d *list*	A list of field separators. Usually each column is followed by a tab, except for the last column which is followed by a new line. The *list* allows you to specify an alternate strategy. The list may contain the special characters \n (new line), \t (tab), \\ (backslash), and \0 (the empty string; not a null character). For example, the list ": \t" might be used in a four-column paste operation to specify a colon between the first two fields, a space between the next two, and a tab between the next to last and last. In a parallel merge, which occurs when the -s option is not used, each line is always terminated by a new line, which isn't taken from *list*. In a serial merge, *list* should contain a new line, unless you want output that doesn't contain any new lines.
-s	Serial merge. Merge subsequent lines from the files, instead of taking one line from each in turn (a parallel merge). This option is almost always used with the -d option. (If the -d option is not present, a single line of output will be produced.) The end of the output is always terminated by a new line.

Let's suppose that we need to separate the initials from the telephone numbers in the telnos file described above. As you remember, the telnos file contained a few phone numbers:

```
$ cat telnos
kc      362-4993
gmk     245-3209
arm     333-3903
$
```

The -f option of cut tells it which field you want to cut:

```
$ cut -f1 telnos
kc
gmk
arm
$
```

We can use the paste command to combine vertical slices. Let's create a new file called newtelnos where the numbers come before the initials on each line. Paste will automatically separate the two columns with a tab character.

```
$ cut -f1 telnos > names
$ cut -f2 telnos > numbers
$ paste numbers names > newtelnos
$ cat newtelnos
362-4993    kc
245-3209    gmk
333-3903    arm
$ rm names numbers
$ ▓
```

8.11 Tr—Translate Characters

The tr program translates individual characters. It can do things like change lowercase letters to uppercase or delete punctuation. Unlike most programs that work with text files, tr only works via the standard input and output; it can't operate on files named on the command line. Its command-line options are listed in Table 8.14.

Here's a simple example of tr, in which it changes commas to periods and periods to commas.

```
$ cat numbs
    1,300.50
      900.35
1,333,545.80
$ tr ., ,. < numbs
    1.300,50
      900,35
1.333.545,80
$ ▓
```

As shown above, tr usually requires two string arguments. The first string specifies characters that will be replaced, and the second specifies the replacements. If the second character of the first string is present in the input, it will be replaced by the second character of the replacement string in the output.

Table 8.14 ■ Tr Command-line Options

-c	Complement the characters in the first string, which means form the first string from all characters not specifically mentioned.
-d	Delete all characters in the first string.
-s	Squeeze repeated characters output from the second string into a single character.

In the preceding example, the first string contains a period and a comma, while the second contains a comma and a period. Each time a period occurs in the input, it is replaced by a comma in the output, and vice versa.

The two strings supplied to tr can contain character groups, which are shortcuts for specifying groups of characters. There are two conventions: character ranges and character repetitions. Groups are always enclosed in square brackets.

- A set of characters separated by a hyphen stands in for that entire range of characters. Thus [a-z] is the set of lowercase letters.

- A set of characters followed by a * and then a number is repeated that many times. If n is zero or is missing, then the character is repeated forever, or thereabouts. Thus the group [a*5] is five lowercase a's. For example, the following tr command will replace all digits with zeros:

```
$ tr [0-9] [0*]
```

The preceding command is equivalent to the following, more verbose command:

```
$ tr [0-9] 0000000000
```

You can also specify characters in octal. The common octal characters are shown in the following table:

\010	Backspace	\011	Tab
\012	New line	\014	Form feed
\015	Carriage return	\033	Escape

Here is a tr command that will capitalize its input files:

```
$ echo Hello World | tr [a-z] [A-Z]
HELLO WORLD
$
```

The following tr command uses the -d option, which means delete all characters found in the string, to delete all carriage returns from a file. This meets a common need when MS-DOS format files, in which lines are usually terminated by a carriage return and a line feed, are transferred to a UNIX system, in which lines are usually terminated solely by a line feed:

```
$ tr -d \\015 < file > file2
$
```

The pair of backslashes are necessary because \ is a special character to the shell. To pass a single backslash argument to a command, you need to write two backslashes, otherwise a single backslash will quote the following character. The argument could have been specified equivalently using quoting as "\015" or '\015'.

The -c option of tr allows you to form a string from all characters not mentioned in a string. For example, suppose you want to remove everything but numeric digits from the numbs file used in the earlier example.

```
$ cat numbs
   1,300.50
     900.35
1,333,545.80
$ tr -cd [0-9] < numbs
13005090035133354580$ ▮
```

In all likelihood, the result is not quite what you wanted, because even the line separators have been deleted, including the last, which explains why the shell prompt isn't on its own line. More likely, the following was intended:

```
$ tr -cd \\012[0-9] < numbs
130050
90035
133354580
$ ▮
```

In this command, a new line is included in the list of characters so that it doesn't appear in the complement list and thus isn't deleted.

8.12 Spell—Find Spelling Errors

The UNIX system spell program checks a text file for possible spelling errors. Spell uses a dictionary of common words. Each word in the input text is looked up in the dictionary. Spell is rarely fooled by prefixes, suffixes, and inflections, and spell is able to ignore most nroff/troff formatting commands. Its command-line options are listed in Table 8.15.

If "frequent" is in the dictionary, then spell will accept "frequents," "frequently," "frequenting," and other variants. This policy makes the list relatively compact, but it also means that the speller may accept nonsense words formed by incorrectly adding suffixes. Because some words don't follow the normal rules for prefixes and suffixes, there is a separate dictionary listing all of the exceptions. Words from this dictionary (called the *stop list*) must be matched exactly.

Table 8.15 ■ Spell Command-line Options

-b	Check British spelling instead of U.S. spelling.
-l	Follow all files included using the nroff/troff .so, .nx constructs. Ordinarily, spell only follows include requests that don't originate in the /usr/lib directory.
-v	Verbose. Print all words not literally in the spelling list. This sometimes helps explain irregularities, but it is usually too voluminous for ordinary usage.
-x	Show all plausible stems for each word.
+*file*	Use *file* as a list of acceptable words. You can place your personal collection of correctly-spelled-but-nevertheless-flagged words into *file* so that they won't appear in spell's output. The *file* should be sorted after each addition (sort -o wdfile wdfile).

There are many many possible spelling errors that spell is incapable of finding. Spell also complains about many correct words because its dictionary can't possibly contain every word, especially proper names or technical terms. Spell is a valuable proofreading aid but it is not a substitute for careful proofreading.

```
$ spell chapt5
arthropod
Darwin
Mendel
teh
vicorously
$
```

Spell will find hundreds of problems in a moderately large document, so you should usually collect the words in a file using output redirection.

If no files are mentioned on the command line, then spell reads from the standard input. This is useful for checking spellings interactively or for using spell in a pipeline.

8.13   Crypt—Encode Files

The crypt program encrypts files, which is the most secure protection of information that is available in standard UNIX systems. Crypt is much more secure than relying on the UNIX file protection mechanism. An encrypted file can be decoded only if you know the key or if you are very good at cryptanalysis and you have substantial computer time to devote to the decoding. Your encrypted files will remain secure even if your system's root password is compromised, unless the intruder is the CIA, NSA, KGB, or similar organization with the rumored power to decrypt such files. (Remember that the UNIX file access system is simply a sturdy fence; it's easily breached by the superuser, by any electronic intruder who attains superuser privilege, by anyone with access to the computer console, or by anyone with access to backup tapes.) On the negative side, don't expect your system administrator to be able to recover the contents of an encrypted file if you forget the key. Crypt's command-line options are listed in Table 8.16.

The crypt program reads from the standard input and writes to the standard output. Unlike most utilities, it doesn't accept file names on the command line.

Table 8.16   ■ Crypt Command-line Options

-k	Use the key stored in the environment variable CRYPTKEY. To maintain security, do not set the CRYPTKEY variable in one of your dot files. Using -k is advised if you want to encrypt many files using a single key and you want to avoid the bother of typing the key many times, and the attendant possiblity that you will type it incorrectly.

```
$ crypt xyZZy321 < chaptn.doc > chaptn.cry
$ rm chaptn.doc
$ ▉
```

In the example, the file chaptn.doc is encrypted using the key xyZZy321. The result is placed in the file chaptn.cry. Then the rm command is used to delete the original copy of the document, leaving only the encrypted copy on the system.

Putting the key on the command line is somewhat insecure because there are utilities that allow anyone to see the command lines that other UNIX users are using. So, instead of supplying the key as an argument to crypt, you can enter it interactively:

```
$ crypt < chaptn.doc > chaptn.cry
Password:
$ rm chaptn.doc
$ ▉
```

Echoing is turned off during your response just like when you enter your login password. This is one of the relatively rare cases where a program needs to read input from the controlling terminal, not from the standard input.

The original file can be recovered using the same key:

```
$ crypt xyZZy321 < chaptn.cry > chaptn.new
$ ▉
```

The file chaptn.new should be identical to the file chaptn.doc. We usually decrypt encrypted files before deleting the original, just to make sure that the key is correctly typed.

In most installations the key is the weakest link. You should choose keys that are memorable, that have mixed case, and that are six or more characters long. Keys should not be stored on your computer because the security of the encryption is limited by the security of the keys.

Crypt is not available in most versions of UNIX exported from the United States because of restrictions on the export of cryptanalysis software. This seems to make little sense because the algorithm used by crypt is well known and simple enough that its implementation holds no secrets.

8.14 Tee—Duplicate Output

The tee program reads the standard input and diverts it both to the standard output and to one or more named files. It is analogous to the tee pipefitting that plumbers use to split one pipe into two. The command-line options are listed in Table 8.17. Tee is usually used when you want to divert a program's output to a file and also see it on your terminal.

```
$ spell chapt5 | tee errwords
arthropod
Darwin
Mendel
```

Table 8.17 ■ Tee Command-line Options

-a	Append to the output files instead of overwriting them.
-i	Ignore interrupts.

```
teh
vicorously
$ cat errwords
arthropod
Darwin
Mendel
teh
vicorously
$ ▋
```

Tee can also be used to collect intermediate results in a pipeline. If you want to print a five-column titled document showing the contents of a directory, you might use the following command:

```
$ ls | pr -5 | lp
$ ▋
```

You could save the two intermediate stages of the pipeline by inserting the tee command in the the pipeline:

```
$ ls | tee .stage1 | pr -5 | tee .stage2 | lp
$ ▋
```

The file .stage1 will contain the original output of the ls command and the file .stage2 will contain the five-column titled version of the ls output. We chose to name tee's output files using a leading period so that they aren't listed by ls.

8.15 Head and Tail—Print the Beginning and End of a File

The head and tail programs are used to print the beginning and end of a file. This allows you to see part of a large file without sitting through a tedious display of the entire file.

The following example shows how head and tail might be used to look at the beginning and end of a large file called grt_am_novel. (Both head and tail show ten lines by default, but we're only showing seven in this example to keep it brief.)

```
$ head grt_am_novel
Chapter 1
    Five years ago I was introduced by my father to a man
named Savitsky. He was small and dapper, a hound-like figure
who radiated charm and intelligence. At first our relationship
was trivial, but then the DeJean murders occurred, and our
```

```
paths were linked for a time.
    Herewith the story of those times.
$ tail grt_am_novel
''So,'' remarked Savitsky, ''there remains but one suspect.
As we have all agreed, the evidence rules out the family members,
the maids, and the cook. Only James, the butler, knew the safe
contained ten thousand dollars on the night of the third.''
    ''But it didn't! It was empty,'' blurted out James.
    ''Exactly!'' triumphed Savitsky. ''And only the murderer could
have known that fact. Sergeant, take him away!''
$ ▓
```

The command-line options listed in Tables 8.18 and 8.19 let you control just how much of the start or end of a file is printed:

```
$ head -3 grt_am_novel
Chapter 1
    Five years ago I was introduced by my father to a man
named Savitsky. He was small and dapper, a hound-like figure
$ tail -3 grt_am_novel
    ''But it didn't! It was empty,'' blurted out James.
    ''Exactly!'' triumphed Savitsky. ''And only the murderer could
have known that fact. Sergeant, take him away!''
$ ▓
```

As you see in this example, a number preceded by a hyphen tells head or tail to show that many lines from the beginning, or to start that many lines from the end of the file.

Tail has a number of additional options. First, by specifying $+n$ (instead of $-n$), tail will skip to line n of the file, and then print from that line to the end.

Table 8.18 ■ Head Command-line Options

$-n$	Display the first n lines of a file.

Table 8.19 ■ Tail Command-line Options

$-n$	Display the last n lines (default), blocks, or characters of a file. The default n is ten lines. The optional suffixes l, b, and c can be used to indicate lines, 512-byte blocks, and characters.
$+n$	Skip to line n and then print the rest. You can also specify the skip amount in blocks or characters, using the b and c suffixes mentioned in the -n option description.
$-f$	Follow. Continue reading and displaying new data until killed.
$-r$	Output lines in reverse order; may not be used with the b or c suffixes. The default region to reverse is the entire file. The -r option may not be used with -f.

```
$ wc chapt3
    266    3018   19036   chapt3
$ tail +67 chapt3 > chapt3.end
$ wc chapt3.end
    200    1922   12403   chapt3.end
$
```

The default units for tail are lines, but you can also move by characters using the c suffix, or 512-byte blocks using the b suffix:

```
$ tail -256c chapt3 | wc
    5     40    256
$ tail -1b chapt3 | wc
    7     80    512
$
```

You can also use the l (letter ell) suffix to specify the default lines.

Tail can be used to monitor a growing file by using the -f option. When you run tail with the -f option, it will immediately print the end of the file, and then it will wait for the file to grow. As it grows, the new information will be printed. Tail -f is often used to observe long-running processes that provide output in text status files, such as large compilations, backups, and the like. To stop tail when the -f option is used, you have to use the interrupt key, which is often ^C or DEL, or you must send it the SIGINT signal.

Tail's remaining option is -r, to print lines in reverse order. If no other options are provided, tail will print the entire file in reverse order. With other options, the -r option will just print the end of the file in reverse order.

```
$ echo "one\ntwo\nthree\nfour\nfive" > num
$ cat num
one
two
three
four
five
$ tail -r num
five
four
three
two
one
$ tail -3r num
five
four
three
$ rm num
$
```

Both head and tail can be used in pipelines:

```
$ ls /usr/bin | tail -5
xrestor
xrestore
xtract
yes
zcat
$
```

9
Basic Text Editing with Vi

Vi is a text editing program that was originally conceived as a programmer's editor. University of California at Berkeley graduate student Bill Joy enhanced ed, the original UNIX text editor, to create vi. Although vi contains some features that are only used when you are writing programs, its flexibility and power are useful for many users.

All UNIX systems contain the vi editor, which makes it a lingua franca in the UNIX community. There are more powerful text editors that are preferred by some programmers, there are simpler editors that are preferred by many administrators and occasional users, and there are word processors which are preferred for most document preparation. But vi is universal, and all people who know the UNIX system have at least a rudimentary knowledge of vi.

Vi is actually the full-screen, display-oriented persona of a family of text editors. The other members of the family are edit, a simple line-oriented editor; ex, a powerful line-oriented editor; and view, a browsing (no changes) visual editor. A display editor such as vi uses the screen of your display terminal to portray a portion of the document. (A line editor shows you the lines in your document, but the lines displayed on your screen may not be in the same order as those in your document.) Most people find visual editing more convenient than line editing, and the focus of these vi chapters is on visual mode commands. The ex line-editing commands are described in Appendix III.

You needn't master vi to use it successfully; in fact, enough basic vi is presented in this chapter for realistic use. However, if you are planning to work with it extensively, you should learn most of the more advanced features that are discussed in Chapter 10. If you already know vi, you can skip this chapter and possibly Chapter 10.

154

The original vi document is *An Introduction to Display Editing with Vi* by William Joy, with revisions by Mark Horton. A related document is *Ex Reference Manual,* also by William Joy, and also containing revisions by Mark Horton. The ex manual describes the line-oriented command set of vi. People who want to master line editing can read any of the original UNIX ed documents or the extensive ex material in Appendix III.

9.1 UNIX Text Editors

Throughout the UNIX system's history there have been several common programs for editing text. The UNIX system's first text editor was ed. Ed is a powerful program but it is best used by programmers or other technically inclined people. Because it was the original text editor, ed has had a major impact on the entire UNIX system. Many UNIX programs contain a syntax or command language that has many similarities to ed's. Some examples are sed (a stream editor), lex (a programmer's utility), awk (a programmable text manipulation language), grep (a text searching program), and the edit/ex/vi family of text editors. Because of ed's enduring legacy, most serious UNIX users learn its use. However, both System V and Berkeley UNIX contain the vi program, and it is recommended as a better general purpose editing program.

Another common UNIX text editor is Emacs. First developed at MIT by Richard Stallman, Emacs is a flexible and powerful text editing program. Most versions of Emacs support windowing so that several documents can be displayed and edited simultaneously. Emacs can be programmed to behave one way for one user and in another way for someone else. This is Emacs's strength and weakness—there are many versions, all slightly different, and then once customized, the many versions become a dense forest of different editors. If you want to program your editor so that it behaves as you think an editor should, then Emacs is for you. Many versions of Emacs are available for the UNIX system including Warren Montgomery's version, Jove (Jonathan's Own Version of Emacs), Gosling's Emacs, and GNU Emacs (a recent version produced by Stallman for his GNU project).

Some editors are touted as "modeless," meaning that all commands are accessible at all times. Emacs is a good example. You don't need to go into a text entry mode to enter text, you just need to start typing. The drawback is that all of Emacs's commands are control sequences, which some people find hard to type. Bill Joy had more freedom to design vi's command structure because of its different modes of operation. (Perhaps more importantly, vi was based on the ed text editor, which has always had two basic modes of operation. Vi has, by our count, five modes of operation if you don't count the shell escape as a separate mode.)

It's important to keep in mind the difference between a text editor and a word processor. Text editors work on text files, which are commonly used for electronic mail, programming, system configuration, and other common chores. Word processing deals with textual information, too, but in word processing the focus is also on appearance. Most word processors allow you to specify fonts and font styles, such as italics, to insert graphics in a document and to specify headers, footers, and margins. There is no standard word processor that is delivered with UNIX systems, although many commercial word processors are available including Word and WordPerfect.

Of course, there is a fuzzy middle ground between text editors and word processors. First, most word processors have a "plain text" mode of operation that allows them to function as a plain text editor. If you ever need to modify a plain text file but you feel more comfortable with your word processor than with vi, simply switch to your word processor's plain text mode and use it instead of vi. The second reason for the fuzzy distinction is that text editors can be used for word processing. In brief, you use the text editor to place format codes into a document, and then you use a separate text formatting program that obeys the embedded commands to produce an attractive printed version. In UNIX systems, the nroff/troff formatter is often used, although Donald Knuth's T_EX program is also widely used.

9.2   Checking Your Terminal Type

Vi is called a *visual* (or screen-oriented) editor because it portrays, on your terminal's screen, a picture of part of the file being edited. Because there are a multitude of different terminals, each with their own rules for moving the cursor, vi must know what model of terminal you are using. It is possible to start vi and then specify the terminal, but it is much better to specify the terminal type in your login script so that you can use vi conveniently.

Vi learns the name of your terminal from the $TERM environment variable. Ordinarily your system administrator will make sure that $TERM is set correctly when your account is created. On many windowing systems, the $TERM variable should be set to xterm. You can check to see if $TERM is set correctly by entering the command

```
$ echo $TERM
vt100
$
```

In this example, the word vt100 is the name of the terminal. If the answer had been a blank line, or if the answer had been wrong, then you would have to go through the procedure specified in the following section to tell the UNIX system the name of your terminal. If the $TERM variable is set correctly, skip the following section and proceed to Section 9.4.

9.3   Setting the Terminal Type

Each time you log into the UNIX system, your shell executes a login script. If your standard shell is the Bourne or Korn shell, the login script is a file in your home directory named .profile; if you are using the C shell, the login script file name is .login. For your convenience, you should put the commands to set $TERM in your login script so that the terminal type is set correctly each time you log in. You can do that with vi once you learn to use it, but for now you can set $TERM using simple UNIX commands.

You should enter the following command to set the $TERM variable. Ideally this command should be placed in your login script so that you can forget about this messy side of the UNIX system. You needn't understand all of the following right now; it will become clearer when you learn more about the shell.

Each model of terminal has been assigned a short name. Like your login name, terminal names are generally in lowercase, they never contain spaces, and they don't usually contain punctuation other than a hyphen or underscore. Typically a terminal's UNIX name consists of a few identifying characters followed by a model number. The easiest way to find the UNIX name for your terminal is to ask your system administrator.

Here is the Bourne shell command to tell the UNIX system that your terminal is an ADM model 3A:

```
$ TERM=adm3a ; export TERM
$
```

If you are using the Berkeley csh command interpreter, the command would be

```
% setenv TERM adm3a
%
```

Once you have learned to use vi, you can place the command in your login script.

9.4   Starting Vi

Once the name of your terminal is stored in the $TERM environment variable, you can start vi. Enter the command *vi*. The screen should clear, vi will print the message ''[new file]'' at the bottom of the screen, and the cursor will be left flashing at the top left corner of the screen. This event is portrayed in the following pictures:

```
$
$
$ echo $TERM          <CR>     ~
xterm                          ~
$ vi                           ~
                               [new file]
```

The picture on the left shows a portrayal of a miniterminal (five short lines) before a <CR> has been struck to tell the UNIX system to start the vi text editor. The screen on the right portrays the screen once vi has started. The <CR> between the screens indicates that a carriage return was struck to advance from the situation on the left to the situation on the right. The ▓ in each screen symbolizes the cursor. The tildes (~) below the cursor on the right screen are vi's indication that there is no text on those lines.

If your result is a garbled screen, or if vi prints a warning message and then prompts you with a colon, your $TERM variable is unset, or set to an unrecognized name. Section 9.3 shows how to set $TERM correctly.

Another possibility is that $TERM is set, but it is set to something other than the terminal that you are using. If the terminal vi thinks you are using has very different control codes than those for the terminal you actually are using, the screen will display an obvious mishmash of control codes. This problem is easy to diagnose, and the fix is obvious: get $TERM set correctly. However, there are only a few families of terminals, and within a family, the members usually have similar control sequences. This makes it possible for the name of your terminal to be slightly wrong, so that vi won't send an improper code except in some obscure situation. This problem is subtle, but the remedy is, as before, obvious. Get the $TERM environment variable set correctly.

The hard part of portraying vi in a book is the fact that most commands have an effect, but the command characters that you type aren't displayed on the screen. Another problem is that most commands are carried out as you enter each keystroke. This is very different than your line-at-a-time interactions with the shell, where you have time to review and correct your command before you strike Enter to have it executed. You must be very careful while entering vi commands because the keyboard is live—each keystroke is acted on immediately and there is no way to take back an erroneous keystroke, short of typing <ESC>, which usually lets you restart a command entry from the beginning. This immediacy of execution coupled with vi's refusal to echo your keystrokes on the screen makes for an interesting dialog. You must (correctly) remember your keystrokes to deduce what went wrong when some command produces an unexpected result.

Of course you could proceed to edit text, but instead let's see how you depart from vi. For example, the command to write the file (if it's been modified) and quit vi is *ZZ* (capital *Z* struck twice).

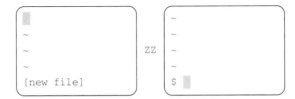

In these diagrams, vi is running in the left picture, and the *ZZ* command is entered, causing the user to return to the shell command level of the UNIX system, as portrayed in the right-hand picture. Notice that the *ZZ* isn't displayed on the screen. You can see that you have returned to the shell by the characteristic shell prompt in the lower left-hand corner of the screen.

If you had added some text to the file, the *ZZ* command would have written the file before exiting and a write status message would be visible above the shell prompt. This step doesn't occur in this example because nothing is added to the file.

In the following section, you will learn several vi commands for moving from one place to another in a file. For that exercise you need to have a file for practicing. Here's how to make your practice file using vi. Carefully perform these simple steps:

1. Enter the following shell command to create a file called ex1 and edit it using vi:

    ```
    $ vi ex1
    ```

    The screen should clear and the cursor will move to the upper left-hand corner of the screen.

2. Enter the vi command *a* to enter text entry mode. There will be no response on the screen. Only type the *a* once, and remember that there won't be any visual feedback.

3. Type the following list of words, one per line. While you are entering a word, you can use the backspace key to fix a typo but don't bother to fix mistakes on any previous line. Remember that for the following section you only need a list of words; it doesn't matter if the words are spelled correctly. At the end of each word, hit return (enter) to advance to the next line.

    ```
    John
    has
    seen
    some
    mice
    and
    men.
    ```

4. Strike the ESC key to return to vi command mode. Text entry will be explained in more detail in Section 9.6.

5. Strike *ZZ* to save your work and return to the shell. Vi should print a message about the size of the ex1 file and then a shell prompt should appear on the bottom left of the screen.

Just as a check, you might want to display your newly created file using the UNIX cat command, a simple program that can display a file on your terminal. (See Section 8.1.)

```
$ cat ex1
John
has
seen
some
mice
and
men.
$
```

9.5   Moving from Here to There

Now you are ready to use the ex1 file that you created in the previous section to learn the vi cursor movement commands.

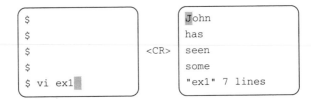

Note that the ex1 file is too large to fit on the screen of these little diagrams, but it will certainly fit onto the screen of your terminal. On our diagram screen, the name of the file is shown on the bottom row, whereas the name and file length would be shown on a full-size screen.

Since most files are too large to be displayed on your terminal screen, vi actually presents a window that shows just a part of the file. For the mini-screen in our vi diagrams, the active part of the window is only four lines tall. Thus just four lines of this seven-line file are visible. When vi is used with a standard terminal connected directly to a computer, the entire screen, which is normally 24 or 25 lines, is used. However, when your connection is via a telephone link, vi attempts to compensate for the slower communication speed by using a smaller window. This can improve the speed of screen updates, although the smaller viewing region is a drawback. When you edit the example file on your terminal, the entire file will probably be visible.

On some terminals vi uses the terminal's arrow keys to move around in the file. However, some terminals don't have arrow keys, and even some that include arrow keys don't always use them with vi. Therefore, vi has adopted the convention of using the *hjkl* keys for moving the cursor. Notice that on a standard keyboard layout, the *hjkl* keys are next to each other. The *h* key moves one character left, *j* moves one line down, *k* moves one line up, and *l* moves one character right. Here is a picture of that region on the keyboard showing how these four keys move the cursor:

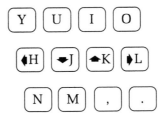

The *hjkl* keys work on any terminal, and they are easy to use because your right hand doesn't need to leave the main part of the keyboard. On keyboards where the arrow keys also work, you can use them if you prefer.

Here is an example showing simple cursor movement:

Many commands can be performed repeatedly by supplying numeric prefixes. For example, the command *4j* will move the cursor down four lines.

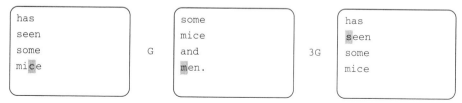

On these miniscreens, moving down four lines causes the text on the screen to scroll up one line so that the line containing the cursor will be visible. Note that the status line at the bottom of the screen is cleared when the screen scrolls. Because your screen is larger than four lines, you won't see it scroll if you enter the *4j* command.

Another way to move around is the *G* command. You can go to a specific line by typing the line number followed by *G*. Typing the command *G* without out a numeric prefix will move to the end of the file. Note that the line number is not echoed on the screen as it is typed.

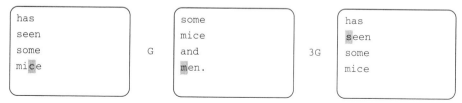

Another way to navigate in a text file is to use vi's page forward command and page backward command. These commands move through a file in larger chunks, making them very useful for browsing. However, these commands are easier to demonstrate with a large file. So if you are still editing the ex1 file, use the *ZZ* command to exit from vi. On most systems there is a large dictionary of words in a file called /usr/dict/words. (If you don't have a copy of /usr/dict/words on your system, ask your system administrator for the name of a large file to use for this exercise.) To make sure that you don't accidentally modify your practice file, you should use vi's -R "read-only" command-line option. The read-only option makes it impossible to accidentally modify the file.

Starting from a shell prompt, execute the following command:

```
$ vi -R /usr/dict/words
```

As usual, the screen will clear and then the first few lines of the /usr/dict/words file will appear on your screen. The commands to move forward and backward by screen-sized chunks are control characters. You must hold down the Ctrl key and then strike the given letter. For example, the ^F command (the caret F notation means Ctrl-F) scrolls forward one screen and ^B scrolls back one screen. Variants on these commands are ^D to scroll forward (down) about a half screen and ^U to scroll up about a half screen.

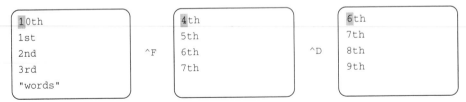

Two additional commands for moving around in a text file are w to move forward one word and b to move backward one word.

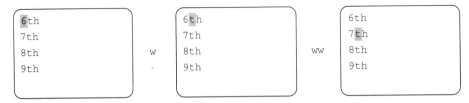

Vi considers a word to be any string of letters, a string of digits, or punctuation. Thus vi thinks of 6th as two words, the 6 and the th. That's why the first w command shown moves the cursor from the 6 to the th instead of all the way to the following line. The W command, a variant of w, also moves a word forward, but when you use W, a word is considered a chunk of text delimited by white space.

The commands e and E move to the end of a word. Similar to the w and W commands, the e command considers words to end at any boundary between letters and digits or digits and punctuation, while the E command considers a word to be any text delimited by white space.

Table 9.1 summarizes the movement commands that have been presented in this section plus those that will be covered in the next few sections.

9.6 Adding and Inserting Text

Although moving from one place to another in a document is an important part of text editing, actually adding (and deleting—see next section) text is really the heart of the matter. In this section, we are going to show commands that are used to enter and leave vi's visual text entry mode.

To understand what happens when you insert text into a document, you must understand that the vi editor has several distinct modes, including a visual command mode (several of its commands were discussed above) and a visual text entry mode. In command mode, you can move the cursor, delete

Table 9.1 ■ Basic Vi Commands

Cursor Movement Commands

h	Left		^F	Forward screenful
j	Down		^B	Backward screenful
k	Up		^D	Down half screenful
l	Right		^U	Up half screenful
w	Forward one word		nG	Go to line n, or to the end
b	Backward one word			of the file if n is omitted

Text Entry Commands

Text Deletion and Undo Commands

a	Append text following current cursor position		x	Delete character
i	Insert text before the current cursor position		dw	Delete word
o	Open up a new line following the current line and add text there		db	Delete word backward
			dd	Delete line
O	Open up a new line in front of the current line and add text there		d$	Delete to end of line
			d^	Delete to beginning of line
<ESC>	Return to visual command mode		u	Undo last change
			U	Restore line

File Manipulation Commands

:w<CR>	Write workspace to original file
:w file<CR>	Write workspace to *file*
:e file<CR>	Edit new *file*
:r file<CR>	Read contents of *file* into workspace after the current line
:q<CR>	Quit (a warning is printed if a modified file hasn't been saved)
:q!<CR>	Quit (no warning)
ZZ	Save workspace and quit

text, scroll through your document, and so on. Everything that you type in command mode is interpreted as a command. (The two vi modes mentioned here aren't its only modes. There is also a line-oriented command mode similar to the ed editor and an open-line editing mode that lets you edit (somewhat) conveniently on a single line. These two vi modes are less used by most people and they aren't discussed here.)

Although there are several ways to get into visual text entry mode, there is only one way out—the escape key (often labeled ESC). In the diagrams that follow, the escape key will be indicated using the <ESC> notation. When you see <ESC>, it means that you strike the escape key (without the angle brackets).

One simple way to add text to a document is with vi's append command. From visual mode, striking the *a* key places you into visual append mode. From that point forward, everything you type will be added to the document as text, until you strike <ESC>.

Here is a simple example:

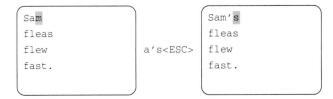

In the command illustrated here—a's<ESC>—the *a* is used to enter visual append mode, the apostrophe and the *s* are the added text, and the <ESC> is the terminator for visual text entry mode. Notice that the appended text was placed after the position of the cursor.

A similar command allows you to insert text in front of the cursor. The *i* command puts you in text entry mode. Then everything that you type will be inserted into the file in front of the cursor position, until you strike <ESC> to return to visual command mode. When you use append or insert with the cursor positioned in the middle of the line, any existing text that follows the cursor will be "pushed along" as you type.

In this example, the added text is the letters *er* followed by a carriage return (or Enter) followed by the word *still*. Note that the screen scrolls up as necessary.

Both *a* and *i* modify text starting at the current position in the current line. However, sometimes you want to open up a new line and start there, for which you would use the *o* command.

The *o* (lowercase) command opens up the line following the current line, but there is also an *O* (uppercase) command to open up the preceding line, as shown in the following:

Whenever you are in one of vi's visual text entry modes, the only way back to command mode is by entering <ESC>. You should especially note the fact that the cursor movement commands discussed in the preceding section don't work while you are in text entry mode. If you want to move the cursor, you must first return to command mode, and then you can use any visual mode command. When in doubt, strike <ESC> to return to the ordinary command mode. If you are already in visual command mode, the terminal's bell will sound after about a second; but if you are in a text entry mode, you will be returned to visual command mode.

9.7   Deleting Text

Some people can enter text once, correctly, and be done with it. However, most of us need to revise our work, delete the worst, add new material, and change existing material. In this section we are going to cover the most useful of vi's numerous text deletion commands.

The simplest vi text deletion command is *x*. The *x* command will delete text one character at a time. When you strike *x*, whatever is under the cursor is deleted, and material to the right of the cursor shifts left to fill in.

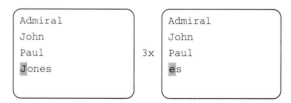

Remember that you can type a number before a command to make the command repeat that many times.

Now that you can make deletions, you should know about vi's *u* (undo) command. By striking *u*, you can undo the last change to the edit buffer. (More sophisticated methods of recovering deletions are discussed in Chapter 10.)

Notice that there are two deletions, first four characters and then three characters. When vi executes the *u* command, it merely undoes the most recent deletion; thus, in the example here, only the last three letters are recovered.

A variant undo command is executed when *U* (uppercase) is struck. Unlike *u*, which undoes the last change, the *U* command undoes all the recent changes to a given line. (Recent means since you last moved to the line. Once you move away from the line, the *U* command won't work.) Here is the preceding example, redone using the *U* command.

Vi's general purpose text deletion command is *d*. The *d* command can be used to delete any unit of text. For example, the command *dw* will delete the following word, *db* will delete the previous word, *d$* will delete to the end of the line, *d^* will delete to the beginning of the line, and *dd* will delete the entire line. Several other modifiers are available to instruct the *d* command how much to delete. In our work, we use *dw* (delete word), *d$* (delete to end of line), and *dd* (delete line) more frequently than the other variants.

You should remember that commands for deleting single characters and words can't delete lines. In the preceding example, the *dw* command erased the word Admiral, leaving a blank line. If you want to get rid of the line itself, you must use *dd*.

The . command lets you redo the most recent buffer modification. For example, if you type *dw* to delete a word, then you can type . to delete the next, and so on. If you type *4dd* to delete four lines, then . will delete the next four. And, of course, the redo can be redone; you may type . as many times as you like.

9.8   Managing Files

One way to tell vi which file you want to edit is to supply that file name as an argument when you start vi. Thus, the following UNIX shell command tells the system that you want to use vi to edit the file ch8.t:

```
$ vi ch8.t
```

If the file doesn't exist, vi will print "[New file]," and then create it when you first save your work (perhaps using the *:w* command, or when you save and exit, perhaps using the *ZZ* command).

The simplest way to manage files with vi is to edit a file, make your changes, and then exit using the *ZZ* command. This method is fine if all you want to do is edit a single file and then do something else, but it is clumsy if your needs are more complicated. Vi contains several other file manipulation possibilities that you should know about.

9.8.1 Saving Without Exiting

If you are working with a single file for an extended period of time, you should occasionally save your work. This helps to prevent a loss of data in the unlikely event that the machine should crash. More realistically, periodic saving will help you if you make an editing mistake. The reason that periodic saves are a good idea is that while editing a file with vi, you are actually working with a copy of the original file. The working copy is contained in vi's edit buffer, an internal storage area that vi uses when you are working on the file. If you've worked for five or ten minutes, you should probably copy your changes back to the original file using the :w (write) command. When you invoke the :w command, the command itself is displayed on the bottom of the screen, and then when the write is complete, the size of your file is printed on the bottom line of the screen.

All vi commands that require the : prefix are more like ordinary UNIX shell commands than the vi commands that have previously been discussed. Unlike other vi commands, the : commands are echoed on the bottom of the screen, they must be completed with a carriage return, and you can use the backspace or rubout key to correct typing errors.

The following dialog shows the :w command in action. (Not shown is the beginning of the editing session, when vi was invoked to edit a file named f1. Vi remembers the name of the file being edited, and when you issue a :w command without explicitly specifying a file name, you will write the edit buffer to the original file. Unlike some editors, vi will not keep a backup copy of your original file using a different name. Once you perform the write operation, your original file will be replaced by the updated copy.)

```
My first              My first
file.                 file.
~            :w<CR>   ~
~                     ~
                      "f1" 2 lines
```

The :w command also allows you to specify a file name when you write the file. This allows you to make copies of your text in several different files.

```
My first              My first
file.                 file.
~            :w kc<CR> ~
~                     ~
                      "kc" 2 lines
```

9.8.2   Quitting Without Saving

Occasionally while editing, you make a mess of the file. Your mistake might be an accidental deletion, an addition that you don't like, or some other change that is too pervasive to repair with the undo command. In these cases it is sometimes better to abandon the changes without updating the original copy. The *:q!* command quits an editing session without saving the work. The exclamation point in the command says to vi "yes, I know what I'm doing" so vi won't question your action or print a warning message. Without the exclamation point, vi will warn you if the file has been modified and it will refuse to quit.

You should be very careful when you quit without saving your work. As a safety precaution, you might save your work in a file with a different name, so that you have the original copy and the copy that you are abandoning.

9.8.3   Editing a Different File

It isn't necessary to leave vi to start working on a completely different file. All you need to do is to save your work (*:w*) and then tell vi that you want to edit a new file using the *:e* command. You must supply the name of the new file following the *:e*. If the file doesn't exist, it will be created; otherwise, it will be read in so that it can be edited. (If you don't specify a file name with *:e*, you'll start a new editing session with the current file.)

If you haven't saved your previous work, the *:e* command will cause vi to print an error message because the new file will overwrite the file you have been working on. If you really want to start working on a new file without saving the changes to your previous file, you must use the *:e!* command to tell vi that you know what you are doing.

You can abandon changes you've made to your file and start over from the beginning by entering the command *:e!* without using a file name.

9.8.4   Adding One File to Another

The last file manipulation command in this section lets you take one file and insert it into the file that you are working on. Unlike the :e command, which starts a new editing session, the :r command takes the text from a UNIX file and merges it into the file that you are editing The text is added following the current line. One common use of the :r command is to add boilerplate text to a document.

Notice that the new text is added after the current line of the file and that the status line tells you how many lines were added to the file. If you were to move the cursor down to the end of the added text, you would then see the lines *in* and *Spain,* which are the lines that originally followed the line *rain* (the original current line).

9.9   Making Sense of Vi's Command Syntax

At first glance, the vi command set appears to be a hopeless jumble. There are 128 separate codes in the ASCII character set, and vi has assigned a specific meaning to about 100 of them. Although few people master all 100 commands, many people know most of them. The goal of this section is not to teach any particular commands but rather to help you understand how it is organized.

The overriding goal in the design of the vi commands was to make them mnemonic. With just a few exceptions, each command letter or symbol is reminiscent of the command name: *a* for append, *i* for insert, <ESC> to escape from text entry mode. Some of the exceptions have other organizing principles; for example, the *hjkl* keys have a layout on the keyboard that makes them easy to remember and the < shift operator looks like what it does.

Another principle is that for many lowercase commands, there is an uppercase variant. For example, the *w* command moves forward one word (meaning any sequence of letters), but *W* moves forward one larger word (meaning any chunk of text surrounded by white space). Another example is that both *a* and *A* lead into text entry mode—*a* adds text after the cursor position while *A* adds text at the end of the current line. Once you have learned the lowercase commands, it is easy to remember their uppercase variants.

Many vi commands accept numeric prefixes. For most commands, a numeric prefix means repeat the command that many times. For example, if you type *50j*, you will move the cursor down 50 lines. You must be careful when you type numeric prefixes because they are not echoed on the screen. A few commands interpret the numeric prefix uniquely. For example, the unadorned *G* command goes to the end of the file, whereas *50G* goes to line 50. (It would be pointless to go to the end of the file 50 times!) You should be careful, because not all commands accept a numeric prefix. For example, the intra-line search commands (*f* and variations) can be repeated with a prefix, but the full search command (/ and variations) cannot be repeated. Even stranger are commands where the ordinary form (e.g., *d*) can be repeated but the uppercase variant (*D*) can't. Commands that accept a numeric prefix are marked in Appendix I with a bullet.

There are six vi commands that are called *operators*. These six commands must be followed by a suffix that indicates a region of text in which to work. The suffix can be any of the cursor movement commands, text search commands, or the go to marked place command (Sections 1, 2, and 3 of Appendix I). But again you must be careful—the <, >, and ! operators can only take a suffix that indicates a range of lines, while the *c*, *y*, and *d* operators can take any suffix. One of the initially confusing aspects of operators is that each operator can be doubled to operate on whole lines. For example, the command *dd* will delete the current line, *cc* will change the current line, and *yy* will yank the current line.

10
Advanced Text Editing with Vi

Although vi has over 100 commands, you can get by with just a handful. In Chapter 9, we presented our personal selection of introductory commands, the commands that we usually show to someone starting to learn vi. Now in this chapter, we present a second handful, a group of commands that will enable you to do more sophisticated text editing with vi. But even this chapter isn't a full description of vi. Consult Appendix I for a summary of vi's visual mode commands, and see Appendix II for a full list of vi's option settings.

10.1   Escaping to the Shell

Interruptions are a fact of life. The phone rings, and you need to look up a telephone number stored on the system. A coworker wants to see the latest draft of an important business letter. Or perhaps lunchtime is approaching and you want the computer to display the time.

Of course you could save your vi file, exit from vi, and then attend to the interruption. However, it is usually easier to escape temporarily to a UNIX shell, do what needs to be done, and then resume your vi session where you left off.

There are two ways to escape to the UNIX command interpreter without leaving vi. The first method is used if you simply want to run a single UNIX command, such as the date command or the ls command. From the vi visual command mode, enter :! followed by the UNIX command, followed by a carriage return. Vi takes the UNIX command, hands it to a shell (command interpreter), the shell executes the command, and then vi continues. Escaping to the shell doesn't alter your file.

In the example pictured here, the *ls* command is executed from within vi. When *ls* has finished listing the four files in the current directory, vi regains control, prompting the user to strike return to continue. When the carriage return is entered, vi erases the screen and redraws the display of the file being edited, and returns the cursor to the original position.

The second method of escaping to a shell from within vi is used when you are likely to want to execute several commands. From visual mode, the command *:sh*<CR> starts a new shell that can be used as long as you want.

```
┌──────────────┐              ┌──────────────┐              ┌──────────────┐
│ Flying       │              │ Flying       │              │ Roaches      │
│ Roaches      │              │ Roaches      │              │ Tonight at   │
│ Tonight at   │    :sh       │ Tonight at   │    <CR>       │ Roseland.    │
│ Roseland.    │              │ Roseland.    │              │ :sh          │
│              │              │ :sh          │              │ $            │
└──────────────┘              └──────────────┘              └──────────────┘
```

The shell prompt in the right-hand frame indicates that a shell is running, waiting for commands. You can enter as many UNIX shell commands as you want, and then you can resume your original editing session by terminating the shell, either by entering the exit command or by striking ^D at the beginning of a line.

One common mistake in this situation is to attempt to resume the original vi editing session by entering the *vi* command. The problem with this is that you will be starting a fresh vi session, not returning to the original vi session. Because the UNIX system has multitasking, you can have multiple vi programs running concurrently. Sometimes you want to let one vi session lay dormant while temporarily using another vi session to do something else, but usually you want to use just one copy of vi. If you become confused about how many copies of vi are running, use the *ps* command. (If you are really confused, type exit to each shell prompt, and quit from each vi session, until you get back to a login prompt!)

10.2   Searching for Text

Vi has several ways to search for text patterns in your file. Vi has a single character search for moving from one place to another place on the same line, and it has a more sophisticated search command for locating a text pattern anywhere in the file. Let's first look at the command for searching for individual characters on the current line.

The single character search command, the *f* command, is a speedy way to maneuver on the current line. After the *f* you type a single character, the search target. The cursor will move right to the next occurrence of the target on the current line. For example, *fa* will move the cursor to the next *a* on the line. The *F* command is the same, except that it will search to the left from the cursor position. If the target isn't found, the cursor stays where it is and the terminal beeps. The last *f* or *F* search can be repeated using the *;* command (or it can be repeated in the reverse direction using the *,* command).

Now let's look at the general text search capability, which is invoked by the */* command. Following the */* you enter the search target, and then a carriage return. Vi then moves the cursor forward (down) to the target or beeps to indicate that the target isn't found.

You can direct the search to start from the current location and proceed toward the top of the file (backward search) by using the *?* command. The last search can be repeated by using the *n* (next occurrence) command, or it can be repeated in the opposite direction by using the *N* command:

Notice that the *n* command performs a reverse search if the previous search was a reverse search. In the dialog shown here, the *N* command would have performed a forward search.

In a forward search, if the search target isn't found between the cursor location and the end of the file, vi restarts the search from the top of the file and searches down to the current location. Similarly, in a reverse search, if the target isn't found before the start of the file is encountered, the search continues from the end of the file and stops only when the current line is reached. (See the wrapscan setting in Table 10.2 to see how this behavior can be modified.) In long files you can save time by searching in the correct direction, and if there are multiple search targets, it is of course important to search in the correct direction.

Besides the literal searches described here, vi also can perform searches using a pattern matching language. This lets you find text that meets some criteria. For example, you might search for the word *The* only if it appears at the beginning of a line, or you could search for a word in its capitalized or uncapitalized form, and so on. You specify these powerful searches using pattern matching (magic) characters, which are described in Table 10.1.

You can avoid this capability by avoiding the characters *, [, ^, $, \, and . (period) in your target strings, or you can set the nomagic mode (see Table 10.2). Another way to make a special character lose its meaning inside a search target is to precede it with a backslash. You must use a backslash in front of a literal / in a forward search (and you must use a backslash in front of a literal ? in a reverse search). There are examples of editor search strings in Appendix III.

Table 10.1 ■ Vi's Pattern Matching Characters

^	A caret anchors a search target to the beginning of a line. Thus the pattern ^*the* will match the letters "the" at the beginning of a line. The caret is only magic when used as the first character of a target (or when used in a character set).
$	A currency symbol anchors a search target to the end of a line. Thus the pattern *PP$* will match the letters "PP" only when they occur at the end of a line.
.	A period matches any character. Thus the pattern *b.d* will match "bed", "bid", "bad", etc.
[	A left square bracket introduces a character set. The end of the set is indicated by a right bracket. A character set matches any one of the characters in the set; e.g., *[aeiou]* matches any single vowel. A hyphen may separate two characters to indicate that range of characters; e.g., *[0-9]* indicates any one of the numerals. A caret as the first character of a character set means "the character set consists of all characters not explicitly mentioned." Thus the character set *[^A-Z]* matches anything other than a capital letter.
*	An asterisk matches zero or more repetitions of the previous single character matching expression. The asterisk is often used after a period, to match anything, or after a character set, to match any number of occurrences of that set. Thus the pattern *[aeiou][aeiou]** will match any sequence of one or more vowels.
\<	The pair of characters, backslash and less-than, anchors a pattern to the beginning of a word.
\>	The pair of characters, backslash and greater-than, anchors a pattern to the end of a word.
\	A backslash is used to escape the next character.

10.3   Fine-tuning Your Screen Display

Sometimes you want the current line to appear at a given point on the screen. Perhaps you want the first line of a paragraph to rest on the top line of the screen, or you might want one line in a list to appear in mid-screen so that you can see what comes before and after. Vi has the z command to let you position your screen exactly as you wish. The z command requires one of three suffixes that specifies where (on the screen) the current line should be displayed:

z<CR>	Move the current line to the top of the screen.
z.	Move the current line to the middle of the screen.
z-	Move the current line to the bottom of the screen.

Here is an example:

Another way to move your window to exactly where you want it is with the ^E and ^Y commands. The ^E command moves the window down one line (the text on the screen moves up one line, while the cursor stays at the same point in the text). ^E is similar to the ^D command that scrolls down a half screenful, except ^E moves just one line. The ^Y command is the opposite. It moves the window up one line (the text moves down on the screen). The ^Y command is a relative of the ^U command that moves up a half screenful. Of course, both the ^E and ^Y commands accept a numeric prefix to direct them to scroll just that many lines.

You can move the cursor to the top of the screen with the *H* (home) command, to the middle line using the *M* (middle) command, or to the bottom line using the *L* (last) command. If the cursor is on the bottom line, it's easier to use the *H* command to move to the top rather than strike 22 *k* commands, or enter the command *22k*.

On some terminals, vi would have to redraw a large part of the screen whenever a line was deleted. Fortunately, most newer display terminals are more sophisticated, and vi can insert or delete lines without redrawing from the cursor to the bottom of the screen. On terminals without modern screen-redraw capabilities, vi often places an @ on the left end of a blank line to indicate that the display is not quite up-to-date. This is especially common when you are logged in over a phone line and are operating at speeds of 1200 baud or less. The @ isn't part of the file; it merely means that particular line of the screen should be disregarded. At some point vi may close up the gap, but you can force a screen update by entering the ^R command. Vi lets you choose when you want the screen update so that your typing isn't disrupted by slow screen redraws. If your screen begins to appear sloppy because of several @ lines, use the ^R command. (Vi also places an @ in the left margin when a line that is longer than the screen width would be partially displayed at the bottom of the screen. Such lines aren't cleared up by the ^R command.)

Occasionally your editing screen is disrupted without vi's knowledge. For example, you might receive a broadcast message, or transmission line (phone line) problems might cause a display irregularity. In any case, you can tell vi to completely redraw the screen by entering the ^L command. The ^L command is a more powerful but slightly slower screen update command than ^R.

10.4   More Ways to Modify Text

In Chapter 9, we presented the basic commands for appending and inserting text (the *a* and *i* commands) and for opening lines (the *o* and *O* commands). Vi has several similar commands that are very useful for more specialized situations.

You often need to change one letter to another. One approach is to use the *x* command to delete the incorrect character, and then use the *i* command to go into insert mode, then enter the replacement character, and then hit <ESC> to get out of insert mode.

That process can be simplified using the *r* (replace) command. Following the *r* you must type the replacement character. The easiest way to split a long line into two is to move the cursor to a space and then enter the command *r*<CR> to replace the space with a line separator.

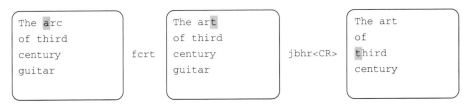

The first command shown here moves the cursor to the c (the *fc* command) and then replaces the *c* with a *t* (the *rt* command). The second command moves the cursor to the blank on the second line (the *jbh* command) and then replaces that blank with a line separator (the *r<CR>* command).

The *R* command is a variant of *r*. After entering the *R* command, each character you type replaces the character under the cursor, and then the cursor moves right. This feature is called *overtype mode*. Overtype mode ends when you press <ESC>.

A similar command is the *s* (substitute) command. The *s* command replaces the character under the cursor with whatever is typed in. An <ESC> terminates the input. The *s* command is often used to form the plural of a word or other simple chores where one letter is replaced by a few letters.

In the dialog shown here, the *e* moves to the end of the word, the *s* starts the substitute command, the *th* is the replacement text, and <ESC> terminates the substitute command.

An even more powerful editing command is the *c* (change) operator. The *c* operator, like the delete operator, requires a suffix that indicates how much text should be changed. For example, the command *cw* will change a word, *cb* will change the preceding word, *c$* will change to the end of the line, *c^* will change to the beginning of the line, and *cc* will change the entire line. Numeric prefixes make the change affect that many text objects. We use *cw* and *cc* most often. After the change command is initiated, you type in replacement text, and then you hit the <ESC> key to terminate the change.

In the dialog shown here, the cursor is moved to the beginning of the word *units* (the *b* command) and then the word is changed to *members* (the *cwmembers*<ESC> command). (In this particular situation, the change command could have been *cc*, because the entire line is changed.)

Lines can be joined using the *J* command. Put the cursor on a line, and then strike *J*. The following line will be glued onto the first, with an intervening space, and the cursor will be placed between the two parts. If you want to delete the (vi-inserted) space, you can immediately strike the *x* command. Any trailing white space on the top line, or leading white space on the following line, will be lost.

When you are in text entry mode, a control character can be entered into the document using the *^V* prefix. For example, you can enter a form-feed character into a document by striking *^V^L* when you are in insert mode. (*^L* is the ASCII code for a form-feed.)

The *^V* prefix is also useful when you are setting up macros or abbreviations. Note that *^V* isn't a command. Striking *^V* while in command mode has no effect. It is only used in text insert mode.

10.5   Selecting Your Preferences

Vi can adapt to your needs and preferences. Many of its features are controlled by internal options that can be enabled and disabled using the set command. You can see a list of the settings that differ from the defaults by entering the set command:

```
:set<CR>
```

You can see the complete list of settings using the all option of set:

```
:set all<CR>
```

Also note that many of the setting names have abbreviations.

Many of vi's settings are either on or off. For those settings, the mode is enabled by specifying the mode name as the argument to set. For example, here's how you can set the autoindent mode:

```
:set autoindent<CR>
```

You can unset a mode by prefixing a *no* to the mode name:

```
:set noautoindent<CR>
```

The other options have values, which are set by specifying a value. For example, here's how you can set the wrapmargin to eight:

```
:set wrapmargin=8<CR>
```

Table 10.2 lists the most common vi options. You should consult Appendix II for more information about all vi options.

Although any of these option settings (except for term, which can only be set outside of visual mode) can be changed while in visual mode, you might want to place your customary vi options into a .exrc start-up file so that they will be engaged each time you use the editor. Each time vi starts to execute, it reads and executes the commands stored in the .exrc file. The .exrc file can be in your home directory, or in your current directory, or both. Alternatively you can place a :set command in the shell environment variable $EXINIT. Most people set environment variables in their login session start-up file, either .profile for Bourne shell users or .login for C-shell users.

10.6 Marking Text

Vi has numerous ways to identify lines of text. As in ed, you can identify a line with a text pattern or with line numbers. Line numbers are easy to use if you set the number option (see Section 10.5). You can always find out what line you are on using the ^G command.

Notice in this example that the top line visible on the screen is actually the fifth line of the document.

Another method for identifying lines is the *m* (mark) command. Vi can remember up to 26 marked lines, each identified by one of the letters *a* through *z*. For example, you can identify the current line with the label *a* using the *ma* command. There is no visible feedback when you enter the mark command.

Marks can make it easy to move from one place in the file to another, or they can mark regions of text so it can be deleted or moved. When a mark is placed, the particular marked line can be referenced using the ' command (a ' is a single quote), or the particular marked character location can be referenced using the ' command (a ' is a reverse single quote, which is sometimes

Table 10.2 ■ Common Vi Option Settings

autoindent is often used for editing programs and other work in which many lines contain leading white space. When autoindent is set, each newly added line of text has the same indentation (i.e., the same amount of leading white space) as the preceding line. You can add additional white space to the beginning of a line, thus causing all following lines to be similarly indented. Striking ^D at the beginning of a line will cause the indentation level to retreat to the left. The special input character sequence ^^D (a caret followed by a Ctrl-D) will reset the indent to zero for a single line, while the special input sequence 0^D will reset the indent to zero. (The default is noautoindent, and the abbreviation is ai.)

ignorecase causes vi to ignore case distinctions in searches and substitutions. (The default is noignorecase, and the abbreviation is ic.)

list causes vi to display tabs and end-of-line markers explicitly. Tabs are displayed as ^I and end of line is shown as $. List mode is useful in cases where the distinction between a tab and an equivalent number of spaces is important, and it is the easiest way to discover white space dangling at the end of lines. (The default is nolist, and the abbreviation is li.)

magic mode enables the vi regular expression characters. When nomagic mode is turned on, only ^ and $ are magic. Nomagic mode is often more convenient than using a backslash to escape the special characters. (The default is magic.)

number mode makes vi display the line number at the beginning of each line. (The default is nonumber, and the abbreviation is nu.)

shell contains the name of the shell to use for the :! and :sh commands. The value of this option is taken, if possible, from the shell environment variable $SHELL when vi starts to run. Setting shell to /bin/csh will make the C-shell your default shell. (The abbreviation is sh.)

shiftwidth specifies the width of vi's software tab stop. This value is used by the shift commands and when autoindent mode is on. (The default is 8, and the abbreviation is sw.)

term is the name of the terminal. This setting may only be changed from ex line-editing mode. The value of the term option is taken, if possible, from the $TERM shell environment variable when vi starts to execute. The following commands change to line-editing mode, set term for a C.Itoh 500 terminal, and then change back to visual editing.

```
Q
:set term=cit500<CR>
:vi<CR>
```

wrapscan mode affects vi's text search strategy. Setting wrapscan forces vi to search the entire file before giving up. When nowrapscan mode is set, searches proceed from the current location to the end (or beginning) of the file and then stop. (The default is wrapscan, and the abbreviation is ws.)

wrapmargin sets the boundary at which vi automatically inserts a new line when you are entering text. When you get within wrapmargin characters of the right screen column during a text insertion, vi will attempt to break your line at a space character and continue on the next line. This mode is very useful when you are entering ordinary text because you don't need to strike the Enter key at the end of every line. Some people find the wrapmargin-induced cursor movement disconcerting. Another hazard is that the new lines inserted by wrapmargin mode occasionally make it hard to use the delete key to erase the last few input characters (because the erase can't back up to the previous line). You can disable wrapmargin by setting it to zero. When enabled, wrapmargin is often set to eight so that vi will wrap your lines when you get to about eight characters from the right edge of the screen. (The default is 0, and the abbreviation is wm.)

called a *backquote* or an *accent grave*). Both the single quote and the reverse single quote must be followed with a letter indicating the given mark. By itself, the command '*a* will move to the line marked *a*.

The ' command shown here interprets the given location as a line location and returns to the beginning of that line. A similar feature, the ' command, interprets the given location as a character position and moves to that exact character.

Marks can be used with the *d* (delete) command to delete regions of text. In Chapter 9, we mentioned some of the variants of the *d* command, including *d$*, *dw*, and *d^*. In all of these commands the *d* is followed by an indicator of the region of text to be deleted. This feature also works with the ' indicator; thus *d'a* will delete from the current line to the line marked *a* (in either direction), inclusive. The command *d'a* will delete from the current cursor position to the character position marked *a*, inclusive.

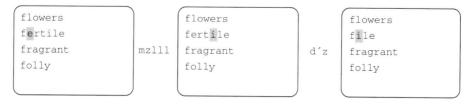

The marks in a file only last during your current editing session. When you start a new session, all the marks are unset. A mark also disappears when you modify the line on which it is placed.

10.7   Moving Blocks of Text Using Native Vi Commands

Editing text with a computer is more efficient than working with a typewriter because the revisions are easier. Some revisions are local: fixing the spelling of a word, revising a sentence, adding or deleting snippets of text. However, the greatest benefit of text processing is making those much harder global changes, moving paragraphs from one place to another, or moving text from one file to another.

Vi's text movement capability works with several internal buffers. To move text from one place in a file to another, you delete the text into a buffer, move to the destination, and then put the text back in the file (to move text from one file to another, see Section 10.9). You can't see what's in a vi buffer without putting the text in the file, but since vi has an undo command, you can always put the contents of a buffer into your file, look at it, and then undo the operation if necessary. The best rule for working with buffers is "Keep it simple." Although it is possible to load up a dozen buffers and keep track mentally (or on paper) of what's in each, it is usually better to use just one or two buffers at a time.

Vi contains three sets of buffers:

1. The unnamed buffer (it doesn't have a nicer name)

2. Nine numbered buffers that contain the nine most recent largish deletions

3. Twenty-six buffers identified by *a* through *z*

The easiest way to move a chunk of text from one place in a file to another is to use the unnamed buffer. There are two ways to put something into the unnamed buffer: you can perform a deletion or you can use the yank command. If you want to move text from one place to another, the easiest way is to delete it from one place, move to the destination, and then put the text back. However, you must be careful. Once you make a deletion, the text is in the unnamed buffer, but it vanishes from the unnamed buffer when you make another deletion or when you switch to another file. Thus, a common mistake is to delete something that you want to recover, then delete something trivial, thereby making it harder (but not impossible) to retrieve the original text.

Any of the text deletion commands, *x, dw, d$, dd,* and so on, will place the deleted text into the unnamed buffer. You can then move the cursor to somewhere else in the file, and then put the text in the unnamed buffer back into the text using the *p* (put) command, which places the buffer text after the cursor. Alternatively, you can use the *P* command to put the text in front of the cursor. When the deletion was a sequence of characters or words, the text is put back relative to the current cursor location in the file. When the deletion was a group of lines, the text is put back relative to the current line, and the position of the cursor within the line doesn't matter. Both of these situations are shown in the following two examples:

dwjh

P

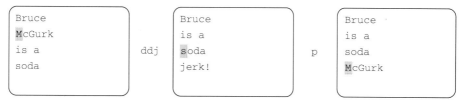

In the first example, a word is deleted on one line (*dw*) and then put back (uppercase *P*) on the following line. Since the original deletion wasn't a full line (or group of lines), the put-back text was inserted in front of the cursor. In the second example, the deleted line (*dd*) is put back (lowercase *p*) following the current line, and the position of the cursor within that line is irrelevant.

It's easy to fix transposed characters by using the *x* command to delete a single character followed by the *p* command to put it back following the cursor:

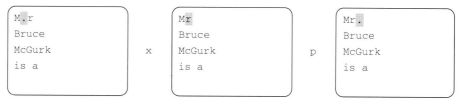

Yanking text into a buffer is somewhat safer than deleting text into a buffer because yanking leaves the original text in the document. The *y* (yank) command is similar to the *d* (delete) command; following the *y*, there must be an indication of how much text to yank. The suffixes *w, $, ^, 'a, 'b*, and *y* mean yank word, yank to end of line, yank to beginning of line, yank to the line marked *a*, yank to the character position marked *b*, and yank the full line, respectively.

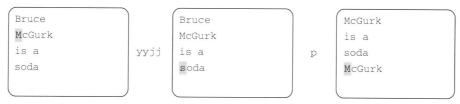

Notice that in this example the cursor must be moved down one more line (*jj*) than in the previous example to get to the line containing *soda* because the line *McGurk* is yanked (*yy*), not deleted. With the cursor on the bottom line of the screen, puting the McGurk line into the text (lowercase *p*) causes the screen to scroll up.

10.8   Moving Blocks of Text Aided by a Windowing System

Vi was created long before a mouse was a standard peripheral, and it continues to operate without the aid of a mouse. But most modern windowing systems use a mouse (or some other pointing device, such as a trackball). Even though vi itself can't make direct use of a mouse, it can cooperate with a windowing system that does use a mouse.

When you're using a workstation with a graphical user interface, you use vi from within a virtual terminal program, which is usually xterm. Details vary slightly, but in most xterm sessions you can cut and paste text using a mouse. For example, using the Motif window manager on a UnixWare system, the procedure for copying a block of text within a document would be as follows:

1. Edit the file with vi.

2. Scroll to the beginning of the text that you want to move.

3. Use the mouse to select all of the text in the block to be moved.

4. Cut the text into the windowing system's own buffer. Using the Motif interface, you can access the edit menu by holding down the Ctrl and Shift keys, then striking the left mouse button, and then selecting Edit on the pop-up Terminal menu. This step will likely vary, depending on the window manager and the number of buttons on your mouse. Then select Copy on the Edit menu. This will copy the text into the window manager's own buffer, without disturbing vi.

5. Move vi's text cursor to the insertion point, using ordinary vi commands. Then specify one of the text entry modes, using the *a, A, i, I, o, O, s,* or *c* commands.

6. Again access the edit menu and select paste. The selected text will be pasted into the document as if you had entered it at the keyboard.

7. Type <ESC> to terminate vi's text entry mode.

This seems like a lot of work, but it's very natural and straightforward once you get past the details. You should realize that what we've described is a copy operation. If you want to delete the text from its original position, then you need to go back to that position and perform the deletion, all with vi commands. Also, you should realize that the preceding process can easily transfer text from one file to another, or from any source of text in one window to a vi session in another window.

10.9   Moving Text from One File to Another Using Native Vi Commands

There are two basic methods for using vi to move blocks of text from one file to another. The overall procedure is the same for both methods: the first file is edited with vi, the text is saved somewhere, the second file is edited, and then the saved text is inserted. The difference between the two methods is where the text is saved. In the first method shown in the following, the text is saved in a named buffer, whereas in the second, it is saved in an intermediate file.

Since a previous section talked about buffers, let's start with that technique. Once you understand moving text with the unnamed buffer, it's easy to extend your understanding to moving text from one file to another. First we need to talk about named buffers. Whenever a delete or yank command is prefixed with a "*c* command, where *c* represents any letter *a .. z*, the indicated text is deleted or yanked into the named buffer. Thus the command "*fdw* will delete a word (*dw*) into the *f* buffer (the "*f* part). Vi has 26 named buffers, but use of more than two or three at once is error-prone. Similarly, whenever the put command is prefixed with the "*c* command, the extracted text will come from buffer *c*, where *c* is any letter *a .. z*. Thus the command "*fp* will put the contents of the *f* buffer into the text.

Whenever you start to edit a new file, vi clears the unnamed buffer. Thus it cannot be used to transfer text from one file to another. However, the named buffers are preserved when you switch from one file to another, so they are ideal for moving text from one file to another. You should be careful here, because the named buffers are only maintained during your current session with vi. Their contents are lost if you exit from vi and then restart vi to start another editing session.

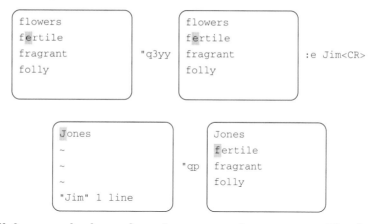

All four panels shown here form a complete sequence. The first command, "*q3yy*, tells vi to yank three lines (*3yy*) into the buffer named *q* ("*q*). The second command, *:e Jim*<CR>, tells vi to switch to the file named Jim. As you can see from the screen's status line in the fourth panel, the file Jim has just one line. In the final command, "*qp*, the *q* buffer is put into Jim.

The second method for moving text from one file to another uses an intermediate file to contain the text. If you are familiar with ed, this technique will seem natural because ed uses the same method for moving text. If you don't feel confident of your ability with buffers, use this intermediate file method.

The vi write command will write the entire workspace to a file by default, but by supplying line addresses you can write a portion of the workspace to a file. The simplest line addresses are line numbers, which can be obtained by the ^G command (to learn the number of the current line), or by turning on the line numbers option. (See the number setting in Section 10.5). In either case, a command of the form *:n1,n2w filename*<CR> will write lines *n1* through *n2* to the named file. Once the text to be transferred has been copied to an intermediate file, you can edit the second document file and use the read file command (see Section 9.8) to load in the intermediate file.

The following panels show how an intermediate file can be used to transfer text from one file to another. The write command shown assumes that the first line on the screen is actually the first line of the file. In practice you will have to determine line numbers as previously discussed.

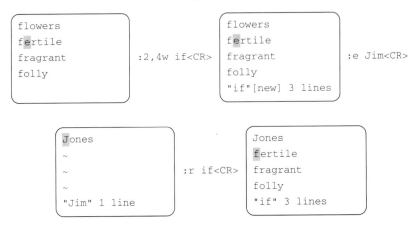

The first command in these panels, *:2,4w if*<CR>, tells vi to write lines 2 through 4 to an intermediate file named if. The message on the screen's status line in the second panel confirms the write and mentions the fact that three lines were written. In the next command, *:e Jim*<CR>, the file named Jim is edited. The final command *:r if*<CR> uses the vi read command to read in the intermediate file and place it after the current line. The intermediate file will remain in your directory until it is removed, so you should plan to perform frequent housecleaning if you commonly use intermediate files to transfer text from one document to another.

Vi will complain if you attempt to use the *:w* command to overwrite an existing file. If you really want to overwrite an existing file, use the *:w!* variant to tell vi that you know what you are doing and you really want to overwrite the file.

10.10   Recovering Accidental Deletions

Vi is an austere, stern program. We've used it for more than a decade, but we occasionally make mistakes while editing. In many areas vi is unforgiving, but it does save your last nine deletions, which makes it possible to recover from most errors.

Each time you delete or change text (in visual editing mode), it is saved in buffer 1; the previous contents of buffer 1 is moved to buffer 2, and so on.

Thus to recover the most recent deletion, all you need to do is to put buffer 1 back into the text.

This isn't especially useful, because buffer 1 usually contains the same thing as the unnamed buffer. The second command shown above could have simply been p, and the unnamed buffer would have been put into the text to produce the same result.

Here's a more complex example in which the third most recent deletion is recovered:

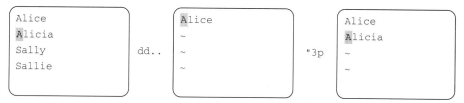

The first command performs three deletions. The *dd* deletes the current line, then the . (redo) command repeats the previous modification command (the *dd*), which again deletes the current line, and then the second . again deletes the current line. After these three deletions, buffer 1 contains *Sallie* (the most recent deletion), buffer 2 contains *Sally* (the previous deletion), and buffer 3 contains *Alicia*. In the second command, buffer 3 is put back into the file to produce the result shown in the third panel.

It's common to delete something, and then to perform some more deletions before realizing that you want to retrieve the original deletion. In a few cases you might be able to remember or deduce the number of the buffer you want, but usually it's easier to simply put all (or several of) the buffers back into the text. That's easy if you first enter "1p to put the first buffer back, and then enter . to repeat the command. When the previous command has used a numeric buffer, the . command will increment the buffer number before repeating the command. Thus "1p..... will put the first six buffers back into the file. Here's an example of repeating a "put numbered buffer" command:

In this example, the "1p command puts the contents of buffer 1, the line *Sallie,* back into the buffer. Then the first . puts back buffer 2, and then the second . puts back buffer 3. This reverses the lines, but it also returns everything to the file, which lets you recover your deletions.

When we realize that we have accidentally deleted something, we often go to the end of the file and append a few blank lines to serve as a divider between the end of the true text and the buffer scraps that we're about to insert. Then we type "1p to put in the most recent deletion, and then we type . repeatedly, until the missing deletion appears or we run out of buffers. This technique has served us well; the only times we've ever lost something using vi was when we exited before realizing that we had made an accidental deletion.

10.11   Filtering the Buffer

Vi allows you to filter a portion of the edit buffer. Text from the edit buffer is routed into a UNIX pipeline, it is transformed by the pipeline, and then the output of the pipeline replaces the original text. The operation of a vi filter is shown schematically in Figure 10.1.

Filters have numerous applications. Programmers sometimes filter their work through cb, a C-language formatting program. You can enter commands using vi and then send them to a command processor such as the shell or the bc arithmetic program. If you want to include the output of a UNIX command in a document, you can filter a single line of the buffer into that command. But for us, the most common reason for filtering parts of the vi buffer is to send a paragraph through the fmt formatter (see Section 8.3) to roughly balance the line lengths.

There are two approaches to filtering the vi edit buffer: you can use commands in visual command mode or you can use ordinary line editing commands. In either case, the exclamation point is the command character. In

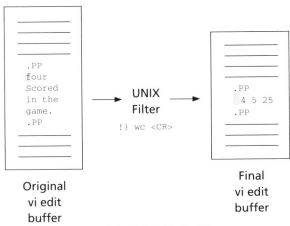

Figure 10.1 ■ Filtering Part of the Vi Edit Buffer.
In this example, a paragraph is being filtered by the *wc* command.

visual command mode, you enter the *!* operator followed by a suffix that selects a region of text. The suffixes must select whole lines; for example, suffixes such as *w* (word) are not accepted (see Section 9.7). The usual visual mode filter commands are *!!* to send one line into the pipeline, *!}* to send the remainder of the paragraph into the pipeline, *!G* to send the remainder of the file (from the current line to the last line) into the pipeline, and *!]]* to send the remainder of the section into the pipeline. Any of these suffixes (except *G*) may be preceded by a number, meaning send that many items into the pipeline.

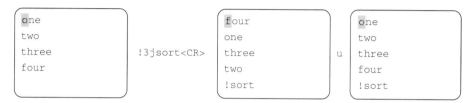

These three panels show how to filter four lines of the buffer using sort. The first command is *!3jsort*<CR>, which specifies filtering of the current line and the next three lines through sort. As soon as the *3j* is entered, the cursor moves to the bottom line of the screen for entry of the name of the filter program, which is sort in this example. After the sort command executes, its standard output replaces the original four lines, producing the sorted output shown in the middle panel. If you want to undo the whole operation, you can use the *u* command to return to the original state, as shown in the third panel.

In line-editing mode, you filter the buffer using the *!* command:

```
:n1,n2! command
```

Lines *n1* through *n2* will be sent to the pipeline specified by *command*, and its output will then replace those lines.

For example, you might suspect that one of the words on the current input line is misspelled. In visual mode you can enter the command *!!spell*<CR>. The output of the spell program, a list of possibly misspelled words (see Section 8.12), will replace the current line. Carefully examine the output for misspellings, then enter the command *u* to undo the buffer change and then fix any incorrectly spelled words. This style of interaction with vi is more dangerous than any presented so far because you don't really want to discard your original text and replace it with a list of incorrectly spelled words. Timely use of the undo command is essential; don't be too adventurous until you are confident of your abilities.

The same technique can be used to check spelling of an entire paragraph or an entire document. Occasionally you might want to pipe all (or part) of a document to wc for a word count, and so on.

You can also use vi buffer filters with commands that don't read the standard input. For example, you might want to include today's date in a document. Open up a blank line, type the vi command *!!date*<CR>, and the date will appear on the given line. This technique is often used with ls, who, and so on to include their output in a file.

Be careful not to confuse *!!date*<CR>, which pipes the output of date into the current line, with *:!date*<CR>, which simply runs the date command and displays the output on the screen. Remember that *!* is an operator, while *:* is the prefix for line-editing commands.

10.12   Vi Macros

A macro is a short phrase of text that is expanded into something else, usually into something larger than the macro itself. Vi macros let you expand one or two keystrokes into a more complicated chain of keystrokes. Vi has four types of macros that are discussed in the following text.

10.12.1   Buffer Macros

Buffer macros allow you to place a series of vi commands into one of vi's 26 named buffers. Table 10.3 shows advanced vi commands. To create a buffer macro, you type the desired vi command into your file and then you delete that text into a named buffer. To use a buffer macro, you enter the command @*b* to execute the macro stored in buffer *b*, where *b* is any of the letters of the alphabet. Here is an example:

As a typical task, consider the job of entering the troff command to italicize a given word. Any word in a troff document can be presented in italics (underline in nroff) by preceding it with *fI* and following it with *fP*. If you have a document that needs to have keywords italicized, it will save time to automate the process. But first, let's see how the task would be done manually. To begin, you would move the cursor to the beginning of the word, then you would use the *i* command to enter insert mode, then you would type *fI*, then you would escape from insert mode, then you would move to the end of the word, and then you would go into append mode to add the text *fP*, and finally you would return to command mode—a simple series of commands for a vi expert, but a grand total of 11 keystrokes.

To create an italicizing macro in vi, you open up a blank line in your input file and then type the following 13 characters:

```
i \ f I ^V <ESC> E a \ f P ^V <ESC>
```

(A ^*V* stands for Ctrl-V and <ESC> is the escape key.) In the macro, the *i* enters insert mode, the *fI* is the inserted text, the ^*V* allows a literal escape to be entered into the buffer, <ESC> terminates insert mode, the *E* moves to the end of the word, the *a* appends the text *fP* to the end of the word, and the ^*V* and <ESC> terminate the append mode.

On your screen it will look like this when it is completely typed because vi displays the escape code on screen as ^[:

```
i\fI^[Ea\fP^[
```

Table 10.3 ■ Advanced Vi Commands

Shell Escapes

`:!`*cmd*`<CR>`	Escape to perform one command.
`:sh<CR>`	Start a subshell. You may enter commands, then exit from the subshell to return to vi.

Text Searches

`f`*c*	Intra-line search forward for character *c*.
`F`*c*	Intra-line search backward for character *c*.
`;`	Repeat last intra-line search.
`,`	Repeat last intra-line search in opposite direction.
`/`*pat*`<CR>`	Forward search for pattern *pat*.
`?`*pat*`<CR>`	Reverse search for pattern *pat*.
`n`	Repeat last search.
`N`	Repeat last search in opposite direction.

Window and Cursor Movement

`z<CR>`	Current line to top of screen.
`z.`	Current line to middle of screen.
`z-`	Current line to bottom of screen.
`^Y`	Scroll down one line.
`^E`	Scroll up one line.
`H`	Move cursor to top line of screen (home).
`M`	Move cursor to middle line of screen.
`L`	Move cursor to lowest line of screen.

Text Entry

`r`	Replace character under cursor.
`R`	Enter overtype mode; <ESC> terminates overtyping.
`s`	Substitute the following text entry for character under cursor; <ESC> terminates text entry mode.
`c`*x*	Change the given object. *x* is a cursor movement suffix, which is commonly c, w, b, <sp>, $ or ^. <ESC> terminates text entry mode.

Marked Text

`m`*a*	Mark text with mark named *a*.
`'`*a*	Go to line marked *a*.
`` ` ``*a*	Go to character position marked *a*.
`^G`	Report current line number.

Buffers

`y`*x*	Yank (copy) text into buffer. *x* is a cursor movement suffix, which is commonly y, w, b, <sp>, $, or ^. (Delete also saves text in a buffer.)
`p`	Put back text from buffer and place it after current line or character position.
`P`	Put back text from buffer and place it before current line or character position.
`"`*a*	A prefix to yank, delete, or put to indicate that buffer named *a* should be used. *a* should be *a .. z* or *0 .. 9*.

To put that text into a named buffer, you move the cursor to the beginning of the line and enter the vi command

```
"iD
```

which deletes text up to the end of the line into the buffer named *i*. It's important to use *D* and not *dd* because the macro should contain only the macro text, not the macro text plus the trailing new line.

To insert italics codes around a word, you move the cursor to the word's beginning and type the command *@i*. The troff italics codes should instantly bracket the given word. Here's what it looks like when you use the *i* buffer macro just described:

You can see what's in a buffer macro by simply putting the buffer into the text.

In the preceding example, the *o*<ESC> opens up a blank line, and then the *"ip* command puts the contents of buffer *i* onto that line. (You need to open a blank line first because the buffer macro is a chunk of text, not a complete line. If you don't open up a blank line, the buffer macro will be put in the midst of the current line, which is probably not what you want.)

10.12.2 Maps

Vi's maps allow you to assign a given command string to a given key on the keyboard. You enter a map using the map command:

```
:map lhs rhs<CR>
```

The *lhs* (left-hand side) is replaced by the *rhs* (right-hand side) as soon as it is typed. The *lhs* must be one of the following:

- A single keystroke

- The character sequence produced by a function key

- The notation #*n* to mean function key *n* (0-9)

Remember that ^*V* can be used to quote the next character, so that control characters, escapes, carriage returns, and so on can appear in the *rhs*. You can put a ^V itself into the *rhs* by typing it twice. This lets you quote spaces or tabs.

You can see a complete list of the current maps by entering the map command without arguments:

```
:map<CR>
```

Here's an example of how you might use a map. On a model VT100 terminal, function key one (labeled PF1) normally sends the three-character sequence <ESC>OP. You can assign it the italicizing macro described in the previous section by typing any of the three following vi commands:

```
:map #1 i\fI^V<ESC>Ea\fP^V<ESC><CR>
:map ^V<ESC>OP i\fI^V<ESC>Ea\fP^V<ESC><CR>
:map ^V<PF1> i\fI^V<ESC>Ea\fP^V<ESC><CR>
```

The *lhs* of the second command was formed by typing Ctrl-V, and then the exact character code that's transmitted by the PF1 key, whereas the *lhs* of the third command was formed by striking Ctrl-V, and then the <PF1> key.

On your screen, these three commands will look like the following:

```
:map #1 i\fI^[Ea\fP^[
:map ^[OP i\fI^[Ea\fP^[
:map ^[OP i\fI^[Ea\fP^[
```

You can use any of these commands; they all produce the same result. In a .exrc vi start-up file, the *#n* notation is preferred because it will work for any terminal's function keys. During an editing session, simply hitting ^V and then the given function key is probably the simplest. You can assign a macro to any key, including the common vi command keys.

If your terminal doesn't have function keys, you have two choices: you can assign a macro to an ordinary key (including control keys) or you can assign a macro to a function key using the *#n* notation and then activate that macro by entering the two-character sequence *#n*. (On terminals that have function keys, the *#n* notation can be used to enter a map but it can't be used to activate a map.)

Given any one of the preceding map definitions, you can enter the troff codes to italicize a word by moving the cursor to the beginning of the word and then hitting the first function key.

```
Cozette is a                    Cozette is a
very fine                       \fIvery\fP fine
feline,          <PF1>          feline,
he mused.                       he mused.
```

A map can be disabled with the :unmap command.

10.12.3   Insert-mode Maps

Maps are also possible during insert mode, although the command used is map! instead of map. An ordinary map is not active while you are in text insert mode, and a text insert mode map isn't active while you are in visual command mode, although it is active while in line-oriented command mode. Like ordinary maps, insert-mode maps should be assigned to a single keystroke, or to a function key.

Let's set up two insert mode maps to make it easier to enter text containing troff italicizing commands. The plan will be to hit a function key to enter the start italics command, then type in the word or phrase to be italicized, and then hit another function key to enter the code that cancels italics. Here are the two vi commands that you would type to set up the two insert mode maps:

```
:map! #1 \fI<CR>
:map! #2 \fP<CR>
```

Pressing the given function keys while in insert mode will make the replacement text appear in your document.

10.12.4   Abbreviations

Abbreviations are vi's fourth type of macro. An abbreviation is a word that, when it is recognized during insert mode, is replaced by some other character sequence. For example, you could make *ux* an abbreviation for the word *Unix(tm)* with the following command:

```
:ab ux Unix(tm)<CR>
```

When *ux* is typed as a word, it is replaced by the full phrase. However, typing a word such as *flux* will not trigger the replacement, and if the word *ux* already exists in the document, it won't be replaced; an abbreviation is only active during text entry.

You can cancel an abbreviation using the :una command, and you can list the current abbreviations using the :ab command without specifying arguments.

You must avoid using the abbreviation in the replacement text. For example, the following command is a disaster—whenever you type Unix, the system will repeatedly try to substitute the whole phrase each time it encounters the word Unix inside the phrase.

```
:ab Unix The Unix Operating System<CR>
```

You should avoid self-referential abbreviations.

10.13 Line-editing Commands

Vi has multiple personalities, a feature or a fault depending on your preference. The easiest vi personality to use is visual mode, and most of the commands discussed in this chapter and in Chapter 9 are visual mode commands. In addition, vi has a line-editing command set similar to (but somewhat more powerful than) the command set of ed. The line-editing command set is harder to learn than the visual command set, but it is much more powerful.

As shown in many of the examples in this chapter (and Chapter 9), you can temporarily dip into the line-editing command set by prefixing a line-editing command with a : (colon). When you enter such a command, the cursor is immediately moved down to the bottom line of the screen (the status/command line) where you enter the remainder of the command. When you dip into the line-editing command set, you are immediately returned to visual mode when the command is completed.

If you are going to perform a sequence of line-editing commands, you can use the Q command to move from visual mode to line-editing mode. Once you have moved from visual mode to line-editing mode, the screen will scroll upward as lines are displayed on the screen, as if you were using ex. While in line-editing mode in vi, you can prefix your line-editing commands with a : as if you were in visual mode. The redundant : is allowed in line-editing mode because old habits die hard. When you are through entering line-editing commands, the command *vi<CR>* will return you to visual editing mode.

Other than the file reading and writing commands, the line-editing commands aren't discussed extensively in this book. However, Appendix III provides a summary of ex. The ultimate reference for ex is *Ex Reference Manual* by William Joy, with revisions by Mark Horton.

10.14 Open-line Editing

Besides the ability to work on a full screen, vi can perform most of its commands on a single line, much as if the window were just a single-line tall. This feature is useful on primitive terminals that don't have cursor-addressing capability, and it can even be used reasonably on a printer terminal. If you start vi without first setting the TERM environment variable, it will complain that it doesn't know what terminal you are using and proceed to enter line-editing command mode. You won't be able to enter visual mode until you tell vi what kind of terminal you are using, but you can enter open-line editing mode immediately because vi doesn't need to know anything about your terminal to use open-line mode.

Open-line editing can be invoked from line-editing mode by entering the command *open*<CR>. In open-line mode, your cursor will always be on the bottom line of the screen (or on the only line of the printer). All of the vi visual commands will work, although only one line at a time will be visible. For example, if you enter the *j* command to move down one line, the screen will scroll up to make room, and then the next line will be displayed. When you enter the *k* command, the screen will also scroll up and then the preceding line will be displayed. Thus the commands work, but the text displayed on the screen is a record of your previous line selections, not a window into the file.

While in open-line mode, you can use the : prefix to escape temporarily to line-editing mode. You can return to simple line-editing mode from open-line mode using the *Q* command.

11
The Bourne Shell
Programming Language

The Bourne shell is the principal UNIX system utility program; it's the force that shapes and directs your interactions with the UNIX system. The shell is the best sign that UNIX is an empowering computer system. The shell tries to provide an environment that helps you do whatever you need to do. That's why the shell is both an interactive command interpreter and a powerful programming language.

Unfortunately, this duality is a barrier to understanding the shell. We realize that many, perhaps most, UNIX users don't need to understand shell programming. For example, you don't need to learn shell programming if you start a word processor or mail program each morning, and then use it all day as your major application. But for many others, the reason for using the UNIX system is access to flexible computing power, which is why all UNIX power users are, first and foremost, shell power users.

We have already discussed the shell (Chapter 4), and you should have already used the shell interactively. Most interactive users exercise only a few of the shell's capabilities. Typical interactive use of the shell involves:

- entering simple commands (e.g., ls)

- using the shell's file name generation facilities (e.g., ls *.doc)

- specifying I/O redirection (e.g., ls > myfile)

- specifying pipelines (e.g., ls | wc -l)

These techniques are powerful and extremely useful but they are only a small part of the shell's capabilities.

Choosing an interactive shell is really a matter of personal taste and local availability. Many people prefer the C-shell for interactive use. It was the first shell to implement a history list so that already-entered commands could easily be modified and reentered. It also was the first shell to implement job control, which lets you manage tasks running in the background. (As mentioned earlier, job control was important historically but it is less important today because multiple-window user interfaces provide a better way to interact with multiple tasks.)

Choosing a shell for writing shell scripts is a somewhat easier task. If you are already knowledgeable in the C-shell, and your shell script needs are modest, then you should probably use the C-shell even for your scripts. But most people are best served by writing shell scripts using the Bourne shell. The Bourne shell is the only shell that is found on all UNIX systems. It also was designed from the outset for use as a programming language, which explains the breadth of its programming features. But perhaps most importantly, it's the accepted language for shell programming in the UNIX community.

The first third of this chapter is useful for most UNIX system users. This part of the chapter, which extends through Section 11.8, presents features that are useful both interactively and in shell scripts. After reading these sections, you will understand the transformations made to each command that you enter. You should read the remainder of the chapter if you intend to write shell programs or if you really want to know more about the shell. Read Chapter 12 to see some examples of shell programs.

11.1   Executing a Shell Program

Any command or sequence of UNIX system commands stored in a text file is called a *shell program,* a *command file,* or simply a *script.* Usually the term command file or script is used when the file contains a simple sequence of commands; the term shell program usually identifies a file containing a more complicated arrangement of commands (often using the shell's conditional commands and other advanced features).

There are three ways to get the shell to execute a command file. For example, let's see the three ways that we can execute a short script called lsdir. We'll explain how lsdir works in a moment, but for now let's just see how we can get the shell to run it. Here's what is in the lsdir script:

```
$ cat lsdir
if [ $# -eq 0 ]
then
  dir=.
else
  dir=$1
fi
find $dir -type d -print
$
```

The first method of executing a shell script is very simple. Since the shell normally reads commands interactively, you can use input redirection to get the shell to read commands from a file.

```
$ sh < lsdir
./bin
./bkpdir
./corr
./corr/zsrc
$ 
```

The shell is an interactive program, which means it's built to read its commands from the standard input, as shown in the preceding dialog. But using this feature for executing a script is a bit clumsy. First, you need to use the < symbol to specify input redirection. For an accomplished UNIX user, it's straightforward, but try explaining this to a novice. A second disadvantage is that you can't supply command-line arguments to a script that you execute via input redirection.

The second way to execute a shell script is to supply the script name as an argument to the sh command. This reflects a special capability that's built into the shell. However, it's common for utilities (such as the shell) that are built to read input from the standard input to also allow an input file to be specified on the command line.

```
$ sh lsdir
./bin
./bkpdir
./corr
./corr/zsrc
$ 
```

One big advantage of specifying a shell script as a command-line argument is that you can also supply arguments to the script. As we explain in the following text, the lsdir script will list the subdirectories of any directory that you mention on the command line. We haven't tapped this capability yet, so let's see how it's done:

```
$ sh lsdir /home/kc/projects
/home/projects/bin
/home/projects/bkpdir
/home/projects/corr
/home/projects/corr/zsrc
$ 
```

One drawback of the two methods already shown is that you need to explicitly run the shell to execute your script. You can't avoid using the shell to execute a script—these are shell scripts—but you can have the shell executed automatically if you set the execute privilege of your script. When you use a text editor to create a shell script or any other text file, the execute privilege is initially turned off. This makes sense because most of the files you edit aren't executable scripts. But if you turn on the execute privilege for a shell script, you can execute it simply by typing its name:

```
$ ls -l lsdir
-rw-r--r--   1   kc    other    68   Dec 2 11:15 lsdir
$ lsdir
UX:sh: ERROR: lsdir: not found
$ chmod a+x lsdir
$ ls -l lsdir
-rwxr-xr-x   1   kc    other    68   Dec 2 11:15 lsdir
$ lsdir
./bin
./bkpdir
./corr
./corr/zsrc
$
```

The main advantage of this third method is the one already mentioned: You can execute a shell program by merely entering its name as a command. You don't have to treat shell programs differently from any other programs. But there is one other important advantage. When you execute a command using the first two methods (e.g., *sh lsdir* or *sh < lsdir*), the shell script must reside in the current directory or it must be specified using a path name. However, the shell searches for executable commands in a set of directories that you specify (see Section 11.2.6). Thus, if you make your scripts executable, you can store them in a standard executables directory, which is both convenient (because the scripts needn't reside in the current directory) and organized (because the scripts are all in one place).

When you make a script executable, it must be located somewhere in your search path. Many people's search paths are constructed to look for executable commands in the current directory. If yours isn't, then you need to provide an explicit path when you execute a file in the current directory. The previous dialog assumed that the search path included the current directory. Here's what happens when the current directory isn't part of the search path:

```
$ ls -l lsdir
-rwxr-xr-x   1   kc    other    68   Dec 2 11:15 lsdir
$ lsdir
UX:sh: ERROR: lsdir: not found
$ ./lsdir
./bin
./bkpdir
./corr
./corr/zsrc
$
```

Even though lsdir was in the current directory and was executable, it wasn't executed because the search path didn't specify the current directory. This will be explained further in Section 11.2.6. The remedy, shown in the preceding dialog, is to use the relative path ./lsdir to execute the lsdir script. Specifying the path bypasses the shell's search strategy and ensures that the script will be executed.

You can pass arguments to executable shell programs the same way that you pass arguments to ordinary programs:

```
$ lsdir /home/kc/projects
/home/projects/bin
/home/projects/bkpdir
/home/projects/corr
/home/projects/corr/zsrc
$ ▊
```

Shell programs that are going to be used frequently or by many users should be made executable and placed in a standard executables directory (such as /bin) so that users can execute them easily. Many users create a bin directory in their home directory, where they store scripts and programs that they have created for their own use.

11.2   Shell Variables

A programming language uses variables to store values. The name variable suggests that the stored values can change during the course of execution. The UNIX system shell variables can store strings of text. Numbers are stored in shell variables as text strings rather than in a binary format that would be more appropriate for a more computationally-oriented language.

A variable can be set by entering an assignment command:

```
$ kc=Kaare
$ echo $kc
Kaare
$ ▊
```

The assignment command listed above assigns the value Kaare to the shell variable named kc. The name of a shell variable must start with a letter and it may contain letters, digits, and underscores. Be careful to put the = symbol immediately after the name of the variable; this is one of the few instances where white space isn't allowed. If you use the white space, the system thinks you are trying to run a command, as shown here:

```
$ kc = Kaare
UX:sh: ERROR: kc: not found.
$ ▊
```

When you assign a value to a variable, you use the name of the variable. However, when you use the value stored in a variable, you have to place a currency symbol before the name of the variable. The currency symbol informs the shell that the following name refers to a variable, not a file or literal. In the preceding example, the argument $kc to the echo command used the currency symbol to indicate that kc was a variable. As you can also see from that example, the echo command is often used to display the values of variables.

Since $kc is a variable, its value can be changed by using another assignment statement:

```
$ echo $kc
Kaare
$ kc=KChristian
$ echo $kc
KChristian
$
```

If you want to assign a value that contains internal spaces, tabs, or new lines, you need to quote the value:

```
$ kc="Kaare Christian"
$ echo $kc
Kaare Christian
$
```

The shell has a very cavalier attitude toward variables that haven't been assigned a value. It is not an error to refer to a variable that has not been assigned a value. The result is merely an empty string, which is sometimes called the *null string*.

```
$ echo $pn butter is yummy
butter is yummy
$ pn=peanut
$ echo $pn butter is yummy
peanut butter is yummy
$
```

You need to use curly braces to surround the name of a variable when the name is immediately followed by characters that are not part of the name:

```
$ ux=UNIX
$ echo ${ux}tm
UNIXtm
$
```

Another way to separate variable names from surrounding characters is by using double quotes:

```
$ echo "$ux"tm
UNIXtm
$
```

See Section 11.3 for an explanation of quoting to understand why this works.

11.2.1   Read-only Shell Variables

The read-only command allows you to mark a variable so that its value cannot be changed:

```
$ flower=tulip
$ readonly flower
$ flower=rose
UX:sh: ERROR: flower: read only
$ echo $flower
tulip
$ ▓
```

When used without arguments, the read-only command is used to list the variables that are read-only.

```
$ readonly
flower
$ ▓
```

Once you've made a variable read-only, there's no way to make it write-able again. Thus, you should use read-only judiciously.

11.2.2 Exporting Shell Variables

The variables that you create are local to the current shell unless you mark them for export. Variables marked for export will be made available to any commands that the shell creates. The following command marks the variable kc for export:

```
$ export kc
$ ▓
```

The export mark sticks until the shell terminates. You can get a list of the variables that you have marked for export by entering the export command without arguments:

```
$ export
kc
$ ▓
```

Note that export only lists variables that have been exported from the current shell. It doesn't list variables that have been inherited from parent shells, which are also exported.

Here is a longer example showing how the export command lets you pass the value of a variable from your login (interactive) shell to a subshell. It uses a one-line script called foodilike that refers to a shell variable called $pn.

```
$ cat foodilike
echo $pn butter is yummy
$ pn=peanut
$ foodilike
butter is yummy
$ export pn
$ foodilike
peanut butter is yummy
$ ▓
```

11.2.3 Using Shell Variables Interactively

Besides their obvious value in shell programs, shell variables can also be very useful interactively. They can be used to store any chunk of text that you might need to type during interactive command entry.

Suppose that there is a certain directory (we'll use /home/td/c/mon/src/ doc) containing some files that you are using, but for some good reason you decide to remain in your current directory and reference the files in the /home/ td/c/mon/src/doc directory using absolute pathnames. It is clumsy to enter commands that reference the /home/td/c/mon/src/doc directory because they are so hard to type. You can simplify matters by storing the directory name in a variable and typing the variable name instead of the full directory name.

```
$ doc=/home/td/c/mon/src/doc
$ echo $doc
/home/td/c/mon/src/doc
$ ls $doc
mon.doc1    mon.doc2    sema.txt    tmonprint
$ ls -i $doc/*.txt
13801    /home/td/c/mon/src/doc/sema.txt
$ ▓
```

If you need to run a program called tmonprint that resides in the $doc directory, you might want to create a new variable to store the absolute pathname of tmonprint. Here's one way:

```
$ tmonprint=/home/td/c/mon/src/doc/tmonprint
$ ▓
```

But because the $doc variable already contains most of what you want, here's a shorter way to create the $tmonprint variable:

```
$ tmonprint=$doc/tmonprint
$ ▓
```

Here's how you might use these two variables:

```
$ $tmonprint $doc/sema.txt
$ ▓
```

Shell variables are a convenient shorthand for simplifying common interactive tasks.

11.2.4 Automatic Shell Variables

The following shell variables are automatically set by the shell:

$?   contains the exit value returned by the last executed command.

$$ contains the process ID number of the shell.

$!   contains the process number of the last background process that the shell invoked.

$-   contains the flags that were passed to the shell when it was invoked or flags that were set using the set command.

$# contains the number of arguments (positional parameters) to the shell (see Section 11.8).

$* contains the current argument list. By itself $* is equivalent to $1, $2, and so on up to the number of arguments. The construct "$*" is equivalent to "$1, $2 ..." which glues all the arguments into a single argument (see Section 11.8).

$@ contains the current argument list. By itself $@ is equivalent to $1, $2, and so on up to the number of arguments. The construct "$@" is equivalent to "$1" "$2" ..., which preserves the argument list. Without the quotes, $@ divides arguments containing spaces into separate arguments (see Section 11.8).

These automatic variables can be used the same way as user-created variables. For example the following prints the process ID number of the shell:

```
$ ps
   PID TTY      TIME COMD
   322 pts002   0:00 sh
   338 pts002   0:00 ps
$ echo $$
322
$
```

11.2.5 Standard Shell Variables

The meanings of a handful of shell variables have been standardized over time. These variables are no different than any other variables, except that they have conventional meanings that you should understand.

You can produce a full list of all your current variables using the set command. The set command, when invoked without arguments, will print a list of the current variables. (The set command, which is discussed further in Section 11.18, is used for several other tasks.) Here's the output of the set command on our UnixWare system:

```
$ set
CODEPAGE=pc437
CONSEM=no
COUNTRY=1
DESKTOPDIR=/home/kc
DISPLAY=unix:0.0
DT=yes
HOME=/home/kc
HZ=100
IFS=

KEYB=us
LANG=C
LC_CTYPE=C
LC_MESSAGES=C
LC_NUMERIC=C
```

```
LC_TIME=C
LD_LIBRARY_PATH=:/usr/X/lib
LOGNAME=kc
MAIL=/var/mail/kc
MAILCHECK=600
OLSETUP=yes
OPTIND=1
PATH=/usr/bin:/usr/dbin:/usr/ldbin:/usr/X/bin
PS1=$
PS2=>
SHELL=/usr/bin/sh
TERM=xterm
TERMCAP=/etc/termcap
TFADMIN=
TIMEOUT=0
TZ=:US/Eastern
WINDOWID=20971554
XDM_LOGIN=yes
XGUI=MOTIF
XMODIFIERS=@im=Local
XNLSPATH=/usr/X/lib/nls/elsXsi
XWINHOME=/usr/X
$
```

These variables are created during the login process, and they are an important part of the system's functionality. Note that the automatic variables $$, $?, $!, $#, and $- are not listed by the set command, and also note that any variables created by you would also appear in the list.

Many of the variables in the preceding list are used only by one or two programs and aren't of general interest. We don't want to talk about each of these variables, but we do want to touch on several that are very important to many aspects of your dialog with the UNIX system. Also, there are a few important standard variables that aren't in the preceding list that are important and worth understanding.

$HOME contains the name of your home directory. It is set during login and it is used by programs that need to access files stored in your part of the UNIX file system. For example, programs that read initialization information from configuration files in your home directory (typically the so-called dot files such as .profile, .login, and .Xdefaults) usually access these files using the $HOME variable.

$PATH contains the name of the search path (search string) that the shell uses when it searches for your commands. The search string is discussed in Section 11.2.6.

$CDPATH is a list of directories that is searched when you use the cd command. It is analogous to $PATH, but is used for switching directories.

$IFS contains the internal field separators, which are usually space, tab, and new line. The internal field separators separate the words of commands. (The blank line following IFS in the output of set in the preceding dialog is the new line that is part of its value.)

$LOGNAME is your login name. (The alternate name $USER is used on some systems.)

$MAIL or $MAILPATH are used if you want to be notified of the arrival of mail. Only one should be set. If $MAIL is set, it should be set to the name of the file in which your mail is placed. If $MAILPATH is set, it should be a colon-separated list of mail files. Note that these variables don't specify where the mail programs should place your e-mail but instead specify where the shell should look to see if new mail has arrived.

$MAILCHECK is the interval, in seconds, between checks of your mail files.

$SHELL is the name of the login shell. It is used by programs, such as the vi text editor, that want to spawn another interactive shell for use without exiting from the program.

$SHACCT is the name of a file into which accounting information will be placed. If it is not set, the accounting information will not be generated.

$PS1 is the primary prompt string used by the shell. Its default is a $.

$PS2 is the secondary prompt string. It is used when commands are obviously incomplete and the shell is prompting for additional lines of input. Its default is >.

$TERM contains the brand name of your terminal. Some commands such as vi need to know what type of terminal you are using in order to produce correct output.

When an interactive Bourne shell first starts executing, it reads and executes the commands in the file .profile in your home directory. Typically the commands in .profile adjust the system's treatment of your terminal using the stty command and adjust some of these variables to suit your preferences. For example, if the .profile file contains the assignment

```
PS1="Yes boss ->"
```

then the system will address you with the "Yes boss ->" prompt rather than the standard prompt. Of course, you can also reassign $PS1 interactively.

11.2.6 The Search Path

When you enter a command, the first thing that the shell does is search for the program. But where does it look? Many UNIX system installations contain thousands of directories and it would be too time-consuming to look everywhere. To focus the search, the UNIX system shell maintains a *search path*, which is also called a *search string*. The search path is a list of directories where the shell looks for your commands.

Most search paths include the current directory, the /bin directory, and the /usr/bin directory, where most of the standard software is located. (Directories containing executable files are conventionally named bin because executable programs are stored in binary files.) Large applications that consist of many executable programs usually are installed into their own bin directory. For example, systems running the X Window system often place the X Window software in /usr/X/bin. In Berkeley UNIX systems, commands are also stored in /usr/ucb.

The search path can be modified so that additional directories are searched whenever you enter a command. If the command is not found in any of the directories in the search string, then the shell prints a message complaining that the program was not located. Each executing shell has its own search path, which is usually initialized in your .profile login script. Thus different users may have access to different sets of commands.

You can display the current search path by using the echo command:

```
$ echo $PATH
/usr/bin:/usr/dbin:/usr/X/bin
$
```

This search path specifies searches of the /bin directory, then the /usr/dbin directory, and finally the /usr/X/bin directory. The directories in the search string are separated by colons. The order of the directories in a search string is important. The shell will execute a command as soon as it is found. When different commands with the same name exist in several directories, the order of the search string decides which will be executed.

Any null directories (two colons in a row or a leading or trailing colon) in the search string are taken to mean the current directory. The preceding search string won't search the current directory because it doesn't specify a null directory. Here's how we could change that behavior:

```
$ echo $PATH
/usr/bin:/usr/dbin:/usr/X/bin
$ PATH=:$PATH
$ echo $PATH
:/usr/bin:/usr/dbin:/usr/X/bin
$
```

The path in the preceding dialog specifies that the shell should search for commands in the current directory, then in /usr/bin, next in /usr/dbin, and then, finally, in /usr/X/bin. Changes to the search string take effect immediately.

If your login directory contains a file called .profile, then the shell commands in that directory will be executed when you log in. The commands in .profile are usually used to adjust the terminal handler to your terminal, initialize variables such as $PATH, and execute any commands that you want executed. If you want a unique search string, you should place the appropriate command in .profile.

It is important to search as few places as possible and to search them in the optimal order. Historically, large search paths were frowned upon because they hurt response time; they forced the shell to spend too much time searching. Today both the Bourne and C-shell operate more efficiently; they remember where commands are located and thus only search once no matter how many times you use a command. Similarly, it is important to keep the sizes of bin directories manageable. It takes much less time to search a directory containing just a few files than a swollen directory that contains hundreds of files.

Search strings are very important when a group of people all need access to a body of programs. For example, if a group of people all use a set of word processor programs, then all of the word processor programs should be put in a directory (perhaps /usr/wp/bin). Everyone who uses the programs should modify their search string to include the /usr/wp/bin directory. If instead the wp programs were placed in /bin or /usr/bin, then every user on the system would constantly be penalized because it would take longer to search through the standard directories; hence, it would take longer to execute each command. This is an example of the system manager's ability to create a more efficient, organized environment.

11.2.7 Handling Null and Unset Variables

As mentioned earlier, the shell has a cavalier attitude toward variables that haven't been set. This feature is sometimes used to advantage in shell scripts, and it's an aspect of the shell that seems natural after a time. But there are other alternatives that you should understand and that you may occasionally find useful.

The easiest way to detect and react to unwitting usage of unset variables is to use the -u option of the set command. When the -u option is in force, the shell will complain whenever you use an unset variable:

```
$ echo $hi sam
sam
$ set -u
$ echo $hi sam
UX:sh: ERROR: hi: Parameter not set
$
```

The versatile set command is covered in Section 11.18, where all of its options are explained.

Using the -u option of set is a blunt instrument; it forces an error on every use of an unset variable. Here are some more selective solutions that let you specify what to do about unset variables and that let you exert control for specific variables:

${*var*:-*word*}   If *var* is set and is non-null, its value will be used. Otherwise the value *word* will be used. *Var* won't be changed.

${*var*:=*word*}   If *var* is set and is non-null, its value will be used. Otherwise the value *word* will be assigned to *var,* and then this new value will be used.

$\{var:?word\}$ If *var* is set and is non-null, its value will be used. Otherwise print *word,* which should be an error message, and exit from the shell script. If *word* is omitted, the message "Parameter null or not set" will be printed before the shell script terminates. This is an extreme solution and should be used carefully. Note that this substitution won't terminate a login shell.

$\{var:+word\}$ If *var* is set and is non-null, substitute *word.* Otherwise substitute nothing.

Here is an example of using these features. First the ${var:-word} substitution, which replaces *var* with *word* when *var* is not set:

```
$ echo $name Spade
Spade
$ echo ${name:-Sam} Spade
Sam Spade
$ echo $name Spade
Spade
$
```

Note that the unset variable $name isn't altered. By contrast, the ${var:=word} substitution alters the parameter, if it's found to be unset or null:

```
$ echo $name Spade
Spade
$ echo ${name:=Sam} Spade
Sam Spade
$ echo $name Spade
Sam Spade
$
```

11.3   Quoting Special Characters

Unfortunately, most of the special characters used by the shell are also used by other programs. There just aren't enough characters and symbols to go around. When you enter commands interactively, or when you place commands in a file and execute the file, the shell is the first program to acquire the text that you've typed. If the command text contains any of the shell's special characters, then you can expect the shell to alter the information unless it is quoted.

Some of the special characters that we have already encountered are > and < to symbolize input/output redirection, | to symbolize a pipeline, and $ to indicate a shell variable. When you want to send these symbols to a program, they must be quoted. Without quotes, the special symbols will be gobbled up by the shell and interpreted as shell metacharacters, instead of being passed as arguments to programs.

There are three methods of quoting in the UNIX system shell:

1. A \ (backslash) quotes the immediately following character.

2. Characters enclosed by single quote marks (') are quoted. No interpretations occur.

3. Characters enclosed by double quote marks (") are quoted except for backslash, accent grave, double quote, and currency symbol. Command and parameter variable substitution occur within double quotes.

When a single character has to be quoted, it is usually easiest to use a backslash. When a group of characters must be quoted and you don't want any interpretations to occur, then it is easiest to use the single quotes, the strongest form of quoting in the UNIX system shell. The double quote marks are a weaker form of quoting. Command and parameter substitution occur within double quote marks; therefore, the characters that control command and parameter substitution (', $) need to be quoted if you want to suppress these substitutions. Backslash and, of course, the double quote are also special within double quotes.

Here's a short example that shows each form of quoting:

```
$ echo $HOME
/home/kc
$ echo '$HOME'
$HOME
$ echo \$HOME
$HOME
$ echo "$HOME"
/home/kc
$ 
```

In the second and third commands, the $ is strongly quoted, so its shell meaning, "This is a variable," is suppressed. In the third command, the weaker " quotes are used. Shell variables are active within " quotes, so the value of the $HOME variable is substituted.

Here is an example where the double quotes are strong enough to change the meaning of the enclosed characters:

```
$ echo Howdy | wc
1 1 6
$ echo Howdy \| wc
Howdy | wc
$ echo 'Howdy | wc'
Howdy | wc
$ echo "Howdy | wc"
Howdy | wc
$ 
```

In the first command, the echo program pipes its output to the wc program because the | isn't quoted. In the second, third, and fourth commands, the pipe character is quoted, which suppresses its meaning, so it and the word wc are printed by echo.

However, you should note that there is a subtle difference between the second command and the third and fourth. In the second command, the \ quotes the following | character, so echo receives three arguments. In the third and fourth commands, the quotes effectively combine all three words into a single argument.

Here is an example of quoting that shows how white space is treated:

```
$ echo    one    two    three
one two three
$ echo "   one    two    three"
   one    two    three
$
```

In the first command, the multiple spaces separating the arguments are just field separators. The shell passes three arguments (with no spaces) to echo. In the second command, all the spaces are quoted. The shell passes a single argument to echo, containing embedded spaces. The difference is visible in the output.

Quoting is also used to assign values that contain spaces to variables:

```
$ macedonian=Alexander the Great
UX:sh: ERROR: the: Not found
$ echo $macedonian
Alexander
$
```

In this example, $macedonian is assigned the value Alexander and then the shell reports an error in locating a program called the. Instead, you could enter any of the following commands:

```
$ macedonian='Alexander the Great'
$ macedonian="Alexander the Great"
$ macedonian=Alexander\ the\ Great
$ echo $macedonian
Alexander the Great
$
```

All three commands assign the value Alexander the Great to the shell variable $macedonian.

Another example that shows the differences between the three forms of quoting can be found at the end of Section 11.20.

11.4   Command Exit Status

The primitives of a system are the lowest level operations that are built into the system. In computer programming languages such as BASIC and C, the primitives are operations on binary quantities. The control flow in a BASIC or C program is based on the results of the primitive operations. The shell doesn't operate primarily on binary values, but instead its main task is to execute programs. Therefore, in the shell command programming language the control flow is based on the success or failure of the executing programs. The exit status of a pipeline is the exit status of the last command in the pipeline.

When a UNIX system program executes successfully, it returns a zero exit status. By convention, if an executing program encounters serious problems, it returns a non-zero exit status. If we enter the following command on our system, the exit status of ls will be zero because our computer contains a /home/kc directory:

```
$ ls -d /home/kc
/home/kc
$ █
```

However, if you enter the same command on your system, the ls program will probably print an error message, because there is no /home/kc directory on your system, and the exit status of ls will be a small number, often one or two.

The shell's built-in $? variable contains the exit status of the last command executed by the shell. You can echo the $? variable if you want to see the exit status of a command:

```
$ ls -d /home/kc
/home/kc
$ echo $?
0
$ ls -d /home/John
UX:ls: ERROR: Cannot access /home/John: No such file or directory
$ echo $?
2
$ echo $?
0
$ █
```

Note that $? only reflects that exit status of the last command, not the last erroneous command. That's shown at the end of the preceding dialog. After trying to list a nonexistent directory, echo shows that the exit status of ls was 2. But when we display $? a second time, its value is zero because the preceding command was echo, which exited without error.

11.5   Simple Conditionals

The ability to make a decision is the hallmark of intelligence. Decisions imply a choice among options, a selection of one path in preference to others. When a decision is made in a program, one sequence of commands is executed and the other possible execution sequence is ignored. The statements that enact decisions in a programming language are called *conditionals.*

The Bourne shell has several conditional operators that are used to control the flow of execution in a shell program. The simplest conditional is the double ampersand (&&) operator. When two commands are separated by a double ampersand, the second command will execute only if the first command returns a zero exit status (an indication of successful completion).

```
$ ls -d /home/kc > /dev/null && echo FOUND
FOUND
$
```

On our system, the message "FOUND" is printed because the exit status of ls is true. The result would probably be different on your system because you don't have a /home/kc directory. (Note that the test program is a better way to determine the existence of files. See Section 11.19.)

The opposite of the double ampersand is the double bar operator (| |). When two commands are separated by the double bar operator, the second command will only execute if the first command returns a non-zero exit status (indicating failure).

```
$ ls -d /usr/xyz || echo No /usr/xyz
UX:ls: ERROR: Cannot access /usr/xyz: No such file or directory
No /usr/xyz
$
```

Most systems contain the special programs true and false. The only function of the program true is to return a true (zero) exit status. Similarly, the only function of the false program is to return a false (non-zero) exit status.

```
$ true && echo True
True
$ false || echo False
False
$
```

True and false are often used in the shell's if and while conditionals, which will be covered in Sections 11.7 and 11.9.

11.6   Simple Commands, Pipelines, Lists

We have already defined a simple command to be a command and its arguments. There are two other command types in the UNIX system shell: pipelines and lists. You need to be familiar with pipelines and lists because they are used in shell control statements, which we're about to encounter.

A pipeline is a simple command or group of simple commands connected by pipe fittings, which are symbolized by the vertical bar character (|). Each of the following lines is a pipeline:

```
ls -l /bin /usr/bin
who | wc -l
a|b|c|d
ps
```

In the UNIX system, a list is a sequence of pipelines; therefore, the four pipelines just mentioned form one list. In the preceding list, the list elements (the pipelines) are on separate lines. (In UNIX system jargon, we say that the pipelines are separated by the newline character.) The following list is equivalent to the first:

```
ls -l /bin /usr/bin ; who|wc -l ; a|b|c|d ; ps
```

The only difference is that the elements are separated by semicolons. The following characters are used to separate the elements of a list:

;	or the newline character indicates sequential execution.
&&	indicates conditional true execution of the following pipeline.
||	indicates conditional false execution of the following pipeline.
&	indicates background (asynchronous) execution of the preceding pipeline.

The list is a basic structure in the UNIX system. A list can be as simple as a single command or as complicated as you choose to make it. The value returned by a list is the exit status of the last pipeline in the list. It is important to understand the differences between a command, a pipeline, and a list:

- A simple command executes one program.

- A pipeline is a sequence of simple commands joined by pipe fittings. The simplest pipeline is a simple command.

- A list is a sequence of pipelines. The simplest list is a single pipeline (which may be a simple command).

You can surround a group of statements with curly braces if you need to use a list in place of a single command.

```
$ ls -d /home/kc > /dev/null && { echo '/HOME/KC:'; ls /home/kc; }
/HOME/KC:
Accessories    Games         System_Setup   errfile    stopfile
Applications   Help_Desk     Utilities      lsdir      tmp
Disks-etc      Preferences   Wastebasket    mailbox
Folder_Map     Shutdown      comp           netware
$
```

You can also surround a list of commands in parentheses, if you want that list executed by a subshell. In a subshell, a new shell is spawned to execute the group of commands. Because of this, only the exported variables are passed along to the subshell, I/O is redirected from the shell as a whole, and changes to the operating environment, such as changes to variables or changes to the current directory, don't alter the environment of the parent (original) shell.

11.7 The If Conditional

The double ampersand conditional and the double bar conditional are useful for creating very simple conditional statements. However, the shell has many much more sophisticated conditional statements. One of the most important shell features is the Bourne shell if conditional.

The syntax of the if conditional is:

```
if condition-list
  then list
elif condition-list
  then list
else list
fi
```

The words if, then, elif, else, and fi are keywords, and the parts of the if statement that vary are shown in italic. Keywords are words that the shell (or any programming language) uses to indicate built-in structures such as the if conditional statement. Keywords are only recognized when they appear in expected positions; the word *if* at the beginning of a line is treated as a keyword, but the word *if* used as an argument to a command is simply text that's passed to a command.

The conditions and lists in the if conditional are lists of UNIX system commands. The "elif...then..." part is optional, the "else" part is optional, and there can be as many "elif...then..." parts as necessary. Therefore, the simplest if conditional is:

```
if condition-list
  then list
fi
```

The Bourne shell's if conditional behaves similarly to the if statement in many programming languages. Let's use a simple example to show how the if statement works. Imagine there are four programs—winter, spring, summer, and fall—that return a true exit status during their season and false otherwise. Also imagine a set of programs which print the chores that should be performed during each season. Here's our shell program to print chore reminders:

```
$ cat chores
if winter
    then
        # winter chores
        snowremoval
        weatherstrip
elif spring
    then
        # spring chores
        startgarden
        mowlawn
elif summer
    then
        # summer chores
        tendgarden
        painthouse
```

```
        mowlawn
        waterlawn
elif fall
    then
        # fall chores
        harvest
        mowlawn
else
        echo Something is wrong.
        echo Check the 4 season programs.
fi
$ ▓
```

During the spring season, the spring command will be true and the start-garden and mowlawn programs will be executed. During the fall season, the fall command will return a true status and the harvest and mowlawn commands will be executed. If none of the season programs exit with a true status, then the else part of the conditional will be executed causing an error message to be printed. This short example also shows that the # character introduces shell comments, which extend to the end of the line. Comments can be used both in scripts and interactively.

Now let's show a more realistic example. Suppose some continuously running program writes a diagnostic to an error file each time it encounters errors during an operation. Another program runs once each hour to log the errors. If the error file exists, then this second program should print and then delete the error file. If the error file doesn't exist (because no errors occurred), then the second program should print an "all is well" message. The following shell command file performs this simple task:

```
$ cat errmonitor
if test -r errorfile
    then
        lp errorfile
        rm errorfile
else
        echo "\n\n\nError Monitor\n\nNo errors this hour." | lp
fi
$ ▓
```

You can make the errmonitor program run once each hour using the UNIX system's cron facility; we'll talk more about the test command in Section 11.19.

11.8 Shell Program Arguments

We have already seen the importance of writing programs that perform general functions. Most programs that perform general functions can be directed to perform more specific functions by supplying them with command-line arguments.

For example, the ls command's default operation is to list all the files in the current directory:

```
$ ls
corr    corr.c    corr.c.1    corr.doc
$ ▊
```

If you want a more specific list, such as a list of all of the files in the /home/kc/bin directory, you have to enter a more specific command:

```
$ ls /home/kc/bin
checkit    mycw    printit.qms
$ ▊
```

The argument /home/kc/bin is used by the ls program to direct its attention to the /home/kc/bin directory.

In shell programs, the command-line arguments are made available in a series of numbered variables. $1 is the variable that contains the first command-line argument, $2 contains the second argument, and so on. The numbered variables are often called *positional parameters* because $1 refers to the argument in the first position, and so on. The special variable name $0 always refers to argument 0, which is the name of the executing shell program. An additional feature is the special variable $#, which refers to the number of arguments to the command (see Section 11.2.5).

Suppose you need a program that takes four arguments and then echoes those arguments in the reverse order. It's easy to do in the shell using positional parameters and the echo command. However, there's one small complication: You should probably check to make sure that four arguments are supplied. Here is the program, called rev-4, that prints four arguments in reverse order. It checks the number of arguments and prints an error message if there are too few or too many.

```
$ cat rev-4
if test $# -eq 4
then
   echo $4 $3 $2 $1
else
   echo Usage: $0 arg1 arg2 arg3 arg4
$ ▊
```

In rev-4, we use the test command (see Section 11.19) to see if the automatic variable $# indicates that the script was executed with four arguments. If it was invoked correctly, we use the positional parameters $1, $2, $3, and $4 to output the arguments in reverse order.

Here is how rev-4 is used:

```
$ rev-4 20 30 40 50
50 40 30 20
$ ▊
```

As a convenience, the UNIX system allows any expression enclosed in square brackets to be evaluated by the test command. Using the square bracket notation, the preceding example could have been written equivalently as follows:

```
$ cat rev-4a
if [ $# -eq 4 ]
  then
    echo $4 $3 $2 $1
else
    echo Usage: $0 arg1 arg2 arg3 arg4
fi
$
```

If you invoke the test program using its pseudonym, [, then the last argument must be a], so that the brackets look balanced. The square bracket notation is used to make things more readable, but you should keep in mind that in either case the test program is actually performing the operations. Note that the UNIX system expr command can also be used to perform arithmetic comparisons, and the for conditional (see Section 11.11) provides a more flexible method for working with positional parameters. Also note that you should avoid using standard UNIX system names for your own work. For example, many people have used the name test for short, experimental shell scripts. Later, when they use test in other scripts, they end up mistakenly accessing their own test script instead of the standard test command.

Some shell scripts can accept a list of arguments, even though they like to work with just one argument at a time. The easiest way to do this is to use the first argument, then execute the shift command to move all the arguments down to the next lower number. When you shift the arguments, the first argument is discarded, the second becomes the first, the third becomes the second, and so on. This simple script shows how it works:

```
$ cat shiftdemo
echo $# : $1 $2 $3 $4 $5 $6 $7 $8 $9
shift
[ $# -gt 0 ] && shiftdemo $1 $2 $3 $4 $5 $6 $7 $8 $9
$ shiftdemo a b c d
4 : a b c d
3 : b c d
2 : c d
1 : d
$
```

The intriguing shiftdemo script shows how shift works, but it also shows that a shell script can call itself, which is called *recursion*. There are occasions when recursion is a useful approach to solving a problem, but you have to be careful that the depth of recursion doesn't go too far.

The shell lets you work with only nine arguments at a time in a shell script. It doesn't discard arguments 10 and higher, but there isn't a shell variable to let you reference these arguments. The only solution is to use shift to discard already processed arguments, which lets you access the higher arguments.

Even though you can't access arguments 10 and higher individually, they are part of the $@ shell variable, which stores the current list of arguments. As mentioned in Section 11.2.4, you should usually quote $@ so that arguments containing internal spaces aren't split apart. Here's a rewrite of the shiftdemo program that handles more than ten arguments:

```
$ cat shiftdemo1
echo $# : $1 $2 $3 $4 $5 $6 $7 $8 $9
shift
[ $# -gt 0 ] && shiftdemo1 "$@"
$ shiftdemo1 a b c d e f g h i j k l
12 : a b c d e f g h i j k l
11 : b c d e f g h i j k l
10 : c d e f g h i j k l
9 : d e f g h i j k l
8 : e f g h i j k l
7 : f g h i j k l
6 : g h i j k l
5 : h i j k l
4 : i j k l
3 : j k l
2 : k l
1 : l
$
```

The importance of writing "$@" instead of $@ in shiftdemo1 is illustrated by the following:

```
$ shiftdemo1 a "x y z" b
3 : a x y z b
2 : x y z b
1 : b
$
```

If shiftdemo had been written using $@, not "$@", the ouput would have been the following:

```
3 : a x y z b
4 : x y z b
3 : y z b
2 : z b
1 : b
```

As you can see, when the quotes are absent the argument that contains internal spaces is split apart.

A better way to write the shiftdemo script would be to use a while loop, which is discussed in the following section.

11.9 The While and Until Conditional Loops

The while and until conditionals allow you to repeat a group of commands. Let's first examine the while conditional. Here is its syntax:

```
while condition-list
   do list
done
```

The keywords here are while, do, and done; they must always appear first on a line or immediately following a semicolon. First, the condition-list is executed. If it returns a true exit status, then the do list is executed and the operation restarts from the beginning. If the condition-list returns a false exit status, then the conditional is complete.

Suppose that you must write a shell program that waits for a certain file to be removed. (Some other program is responsible for removing the file.) The while command can wait for a condition to become true. Since we want other UNIX system users and tasks to get some processing time, we should delay a few seconds between tests rather than test continuously. The following shell program waits for a file named lockfile to vanish:

```
$ cat waitlock
while test -r lockfile
    do sleep 5
done
$ ▊
```

This program tests to see if the file named lockfile is readable. If it is, then the command sleep 5 suspends execution for five seconds. When lockfile is removed, the test fails and the command completes.

Notice that the foregoing shell program separates the command lists by placing them on separate lines. We could also enter the program on a single line and use semicolons to separate the lists.

```
$ cat waitlock1
while test -r lockfile ; do sleep 5 ; done
$ ▊
```

The until conditional is a variant of the while statement. Whereas the while statement repeats as long as the condition returns a true value, the until statement repeats each time the condition returns a false value.

The syntax of the until statement is:

```
until condition-list
  do list
done
```

The only new keyword is until.

Suppose you have to write a shell program that waits until a certain file is created. One method would be to use the while statement and negate the test:

```
$ cat waitgo
while test ! -r proceedfile ; do sleep 1 ; done
$ ▊
```

The exclamation point argument to the test program negates the readability test so that the test returns a true indication if the file is not readable. Another method uses the until statement:

```
$ cat waitgo1
until test -r proceedfile ; do sleep 1 ; done
$ ▌
```

Using this method, the loop will continue until the test command returns a true value (until the file proceedfile is created).

11.10   Structured Commands

Conditional structures such as while and until are executed by the shell almost as if they are a single command. The entire structure is scanned by the shell before any part of it is executed. Try entering the following line interactively on your system:

```
$ until test -r stopfile ; do
> ▌
```

The command is obviously incomplete so the shell prompts you for further input (usually with a >, the secondary prompt that is stored in the $PS2 variable). Complete the command by typing

```
$ until test -r stopfile ; do
> sleep 2 ; echo Hello ; done &
$ ▌
```

The final ampersand indicates that the entire until command should run in the background. The command will type Hello every two seconds until you create the stopfile. Since your command is running in the background, the shell should be ready to accept another command. When you tire of seeing the greeting on your terminal, type the command > stopfile to create a file called stopfile. Here's what it might look like if you can type quickly:

```
Hello
Hello
Hello
> stopfile
$ ▌
```

Since it might take you longer than two seconds to enter the command, you will probably be interrupted in midstroke by a greeting or two. Just remember that the shell is keeping track of the characters that you are typing even while your loop in the background is periodically typing the Hello greeting. As soon as you successfully create stopfile, the background greeting process will terminate. The command that creates stopfile is simply a > (greater than symbol) followed by the file name. This is a well-known Bourne shell shortcut for creating an empty file; it's a null command followed by output redirection. (Don't forget to remove stopfile so that your directory doesn't become cluttered.)

All Bourne shell conditionals are structured commands. In a structure, all of the alternative processing paths are part of the structure; control flow is local to the structure. The converse of a structure is the goto construct. In a goto statement, the alternative processing paths are not part of the statement; control flows to a nonlocal statement.

Modern programming languages favor control structures over the goto construct. Goto's are out of favor because their nonlocal control transfers can lead to incomprehensible programs. The Bourne shell doesn't include the goto statement because it would violate the convention of processing one command (or structured command) at a time.

11.11   The For Statement

The UNIX system shell contains a for statement, which allows a list of commands to be executed once for each word in a list of words. Note that the Bourne shell's for statement is very different from the for statements in numeric programming languages, such as C and BASIC. In the Bourne shell, the for statement iterates once for each word in a list of words. In most other languages, the for statement iterates once for each numeric value in a sequence of numeric values.

Here is the general form of the Bourne shell for statement:

```
for name in word1 word2 . . .
do
  do-list
done
```

The commands in the do-list will be executed once for each word in the list of words (word1, word2, etc.). The current word in the word list will be assigned to the shell variable $name. The keywords are for and in, plus the familiar do and done.

The following example shows a simple use of the for statement:

```
$ cat fruits
for fruit in apples pears oranges mangoes
  do
    echo $fruit are fruits
 done
$ fruits
apples are fruits
pears are fruits
oranges are fruits
mangoes are fruits
$ 
```

The for statement can also be used without the keyword "in," followed by the list of words. When used without an explicit word list, the word list is the list of positional parameters (i.e., the command-line arguments):

```
for name
do
  do-list
done
```

This form of the for statement meets a common need, stepping through the arguments to a shell program. Here's a simple example that simply prints its arguments one per line:

```
$ cat echoecho
for arg
do
    echo $arg
done
$ echoecho spot likes jane
spot
likes
jane
$
```

We can use the second form of the for statement to rewrite the reverse argument's shell program:

```
$ cat revargs1
list=""
for arg
  do
    list="$arg $list"
  done
echo $list
$ revargs1 spot likes jane
jane likes spot
$
```

In revargs1, the for statement sequences through the arguments to the shell, placing each argument in front of the previous arguments that have already been stored in the variable $list. The reversed list is printed in the last line of the program. If you want to see more graphically how this script is working, move the statement echo $list into the body of the loop. You'll see how the variable $list is built up one argument at a time.

11.12   The Case Statement

The shell's case statement is a multiway branch based upon pattern matching. The general form of the case statement is

```
case word in
  pattern1) pat1-list ;;
  pattern2) pat2-list ;;
  ...
esac
```

The word is compared with all of the patterns, in order. The first match causes the corresponding pattern-list to be executed, and execution of the statement is complete. At most, one pattern-list will be executed.

The patterns can be composed of the usual shell metacharacters: * to match any sequence of characters, ? to match any single character, and square brackets to delimit a class of characters. Several distinct patterns can be included in one pattern-list by using the vertical bar to indicate or. The usual meaning of the vertical bar (pipe connection) is suppressed during a case statement.

The following shell program attempts to determine the breed of the animals whose names are specified in the argument list. It illustrates simple usage of the case statement, but it also illustrates how case statements are often used in conjunction with the for statement to process a script's argument list:

```
$ cat breeds
for breed
do
  case $breed in
    arabian|palomino|clydesdale)    echo $breed is a horse ;;
    jersey|guernsey|holstein)       echo $breed is a cow ;;
    husky|shepherd|setter|labrador) echo $breed is a dog ;;
    siamese|persian|angora)         echo $breed is a cat ;;
    *) echo $breed is not in our catalog ;;
  esac
done
$
```

Notice that the final pattern is *, which is a catchall condition that will match everything. If you want a catchall condition in a case statement, make sure it's the last condition. Since the pattern * matches anything, placing it before the end will prevent following conditions from matching. Remember that only one of the pattern-lists can be executed on a single pass through the case statement.

```
$ breeds husky holstein terrier
husky is a dog
holstein is a cow
terrier is not in our catalog
$
```

11.13   Break and Continue

The shell's break and continue statements are used to alter the action of for loops, while loops, and until loops. The break statement causes the shell to break out of the enclosing loop, while the continue statement causes the shell to branch to the beginning of the enclosing loop and start another iteration.

As a first example, let's rewrite the waitlock script that we presented in Section 11.9. Here's the original version of waitlock:

```
$ cat waitlock
while test -r lockfile
do
```

```
      sleep 5
done
$ ▓
```

The program could be written equivalently using a break statement:

```
$ cat waitlock2
while true
do
  test -r lockfile || break
  sleep 5
done
$ ▓
```

In this program a break statement offers little advantage because there is only one loop exit criterion and only one exit point. Break is a good solution when a loop has several exit points or when the exit criterion is quite involved.

The continue statement initiates the next iteration of the enclosing loop. It's a clean way of skipping the tail end of a loop. For example, here is a variant of the breeds script that shows typical usage of the continue statement:

```
$ cat breeds1
for breed
do
  case $breed in
    arabian|palomino|clydesdale)     animal=horse ;;
    jersey|guernsey|holstein)        animal=cow ;;
    husky|shepherd|setter|labrador)  animal=dog ;;
    siamese|persian|angora)          animal=cat ;;
    *)
        echo $breed is not in our catalog
        continue
        ;;
  esac
  echo $breed is a $animal
done
$ ▓
```

In the breeds1 script, the case statement looks at each argument and sets the variable $animal to indicate what type of animal has been specified. Following the case statement is an echo statement that displays the information about each animal. The catchall case condition, *, prints an error message, and then uses the continue statement to start the next iteration of the loop, bypassing the echo statement that follows the case statement.

11.14   Command Substitution

The shell allows you to capture the standard output of a command and use it within a shell procedure. When a command is surrounded by ' marks (accent graves), that command is executed by the shell and the resulting text is substituted in place of the command. For example, you could deposit the current date and time into a variable called now by executing the following command:

```
$ now=`date`
$
```

It might help to think of this process in two stages. In the first stage, the date program is executed and the resulting text is substituted. Conceptually this leaves us with the following shell command:

```
now="Mon Mar  1 09:30:14 EST 1993"
```

This command is executed causing the text to be stored in the variable $now. We can see what was stored in $now using the echo command:

```
$ echo $now
Mon Mar  1 09:30:14 EST 1993
$
```

Command substitution is often used to perform arithmetic on shell variables. The expr command, which will be covered in Section 11.20, can perform arithmetic operations on its arguments. For example, here's how you could use expr to add two numbers:

```
$ expr 5 + 13
18
$
```

Many of the operators that you use in arithmetic expressions (parentheses, asterisks, ampersands, etc.) are special characters to the shell, and you have to be very careful to escape them (see Section 11.3) when you use expr. Adding command substitution lets us store the result in a variable:

```
$ sum=`expr 5 + 13`
$ echo $sum
18
$
```

If a shell variable is assigned a numeric value, then the value can be increased by one by using command substitution:

```
$ count=10
$ echo $count
10
$ count=`expr $count + 1`
$ echo $count
11
$
```

The expr command will receive the arguments 10, +, and 1. The result is 11, which is stored in the shell variable $count.

11.15   Shell Substitutions

Thus far we have discussed all of the substitutions that the shell performs. Let's summarize all of the substitutions in the order in which they occur. The order becomes very important in situations where one word undergoes several substitutions.

Command substitution. Commands that are surrounded by accent graves are executed and the resulting text is substituted in place of the command, as discussed in Section 11.14.

Parameter (or variable) substitution. The words in the command line that begin with a "$" are replaced by their values, as discussed in Section 11.2.

Blank interpretation. The results of the preceding substitutions are scanned for field separators. The usual field separators are blanks, tabs, and new lines. Any word that contains a field separator is divided into multiple words. Field separators in quoted words are ignored, and null words (except for explicitly quoted null words) are discarded.

File name generation. The shell examines each word for the metacharacters *, ?, and [. If any of the words contain these metacharacters, that word is replaced by an alphabetically sorted list of file names that match the pattern or by the original word if there are no matches. File name generation is discussed in Section 4.6.

Much of the shell's power lies in its ability to perform these text substitutions. However, the technique is confusing for people who are used to programming languages such as FORTRAN and BASIC, which are oriented toward numbers. The substitutions that occur in the shell are more similar to the general text handling capabilities that are built into programming languages such as LISP and SNOBOL.

11.16   Here Documents

Here documents are used to temporarily redirect the standard input within a shell program. They are useful when you want a script to contain multiline text that is routed to the standard input of a command. Here documents let you keep things all in one place; they let you take the data that would normally be placed in an external file and instead place it within the script.

The notation for a here document resembles standard input redirection:

```
cmd args <<symbol
. . . the here document . . .
symbol
```

The start of the here document is indicated by the << notation. The symbol after the << is remembered and is used to indicate the end of the here document. The here document can be as long as necessary. A line that contains only the symbol indicates the end of the here document.

Consider the problem of handling errors in a large shell program that runs unattended each morning. You could have the shell program write an error message to a file and give someone the responsibility of looking at the file every day, but a better method is to send mail to the responsible person so that error notification is automatic.

Let's first look at the old-fashioned way of handling this problem. The solution requires two files: the script that runs each morning plus an external file containing the message to mail to someone when an error is detected. First, let's look at the file containing the message:

```
$ cat midnight.errmsg
************* PROBLEMS AGAIN ***************
The midnight error has struck again!
Tdata file missing - all processing stopped.
$
```

We don't want to show the processing script in full detail, but let's look at the line in the script that mails the message when an error is detected:

```
mail opsmanager < midnight.errmsg
```

This old-fashioned approach uses too many files. When you look at the shell script, you can't see what message is being sent when the error is detected. When you look at the message file, you can't see how it is being used.

The better approach is to fold the error message into the script by using a here document. Again, I don't want to show the whole script but instead just focus on the part of the script that mails the error message when a problem is detected:

```
mail opsmanager <<!
************* PROBLEMS AGAIN ***************
The midnight error has struck again!
Tdata file missing - all processing stopped.
!
```

The here document solution is cleaner and clearer; everything is in one place.

An alternative to a here document is to use the echo command to pipe multiline text into a command. Here's the preceding script fragment written using the echo command to pipe the error message into the mail command:

```
echo '************* PROBLEMS AGAIN ***************
The midnight error has struck again!
Tdata file missing - all processing stopped.' | mail opsmanager
```

Our objection to using echo is that it obscures the intent of the script. The mail command is easy to miss because of where it is placed in the script. What's important is the mail command, but what's most visible is the echo command, which argues for here documents instead of using echo to pipe multiline text into a command.

11.17   Shell Functions

The Bourne shell is touted here and elsewhere as a powerful programming language. It is, but as critics have pointed out, the original Bourne shell lacks one of the major components of a modern programming language—functions. A function is a bundle of statements that are executed as a group. For example, a group of statements that performs a useful operation, such as computing the trigonometric sine of a number, is usually programmed as a function.

Some people have noted that functions in a shell program can be provided by other shell programs. This is true, but at what cost? One shell script can invoke another, thereby making the second a function from the point of view of the first. One problem is the overhead; a second copy of the Bourne shell has to be executed to process the commands in the function script. Another practical consideration is that storing functions in individual script files can quickly lead to a lot of files.

The obvious omission of functions from early versions of the Bourne shell has been rectified starting with System V, Release 2. By now, shell functions are available in most systems, but if you're using an archaic version of the UNIX system you might not be able to use shell functions. If your version of the Bourne shell doesn't support shell functions, think seriously about updating your software.

Shell functions have a very simple syntax:

```
name()
{
    statements
}
```

Shell functions must be defined before they are used. In most shell scripts, the functions are defined at the top of the script, before the main body of the script.

You can pass arguments to a shell function using the familiar UNIX notation. Within a shell function, the values of the arguments are accessed using the notation $1, $2, and so on, just like the arguments to the script itself. Note that within a shell function, the command-line arguments to the script are not directly available.

There is only one pool of variables in a shell script. Within a shell function, you can access the variables of the surrounding shell script, and the surrounding script can access any variables created within a shell function. A shell function can return an exit value using the return keyword.

Here is an example shell program that contains two shell functions. The first shell function, called errexit, is used to exit from the program when an error is encountered. The reason for using a shell function is to make it easy to perform a standard set of chores before exiting. In this example, errexit deletes temporary files, logs the error in a log file, and prints a message. The other shell function is called ok. It reads in a line from the standard input, and then returns a true or false indication, depending on whether the user response starts with a y or an n.

The body of the shell program simply asks if you want to test the errexit function. The errexit function will be invoked if the response is y, and skipped if the response is n.

```
$ cat fna
#files
TMP=/tmp
PIDLOG=${TMP}/pidlog$$
DATEFILE=${TMP}/date$$
ERRLOG=${TMP}/errlog
#shell function to clean up and exit after an error
errexit()
{
  echo $1
  date >> $ERRLOG
  echo $1 >> $ERRLOG
  rm -f $PIDLOG $DATEFILE
  exit
}
# read a y/n response
ok()
{
  while true
  do
    read ans
    case $ans in
      [yY]*) return 0 ;;
      [nN]*) return 1 ;;
      *) echo please answer y or n ;;
    esac
  done
}
echo $$ > $PIDLOG
date > $DATEFILE
echo -n "Test errexit function [y/n] "
ok && errexit "Testing the errexit function"
echo Normal termination
echo Please remove $PIDLOG and $DATEFILE
$ 
```

Here's how the fna script can be used:

```
$ fna
Test errexit function [y/n] y
Testing the errexit function
$ fna
Test errexit function [y/n] n
Normal termination
Please remove /tmp/pidlog313 and /tmp/date313
$ 
```

11.18   Set—Display Variables and Specify Shell Operating Modes

The set command is used for several purposes. We've already seen that the set command by itself (without arguments) will display a list of the current variables. When arguments are supplied, two other tasks can be performed: you can control the settings of the shell's internal options, or you can load values into the shell's positional parameters.

Some shell options, which are listed in Table 11.1, can only be supplied on the sh command line. Other options, which are listed in Table 11.2, can be supplied on the sh command line, or they can be controlled using the set command. For example, the following command will set the -v flag (verbose), which makes the shell print commands as they are read in:

```
$ set -v
$ echo Hello from $LOGNAME
echo Hello from $LOGNAME
Hello from kc
$
```

Verbose mode can be turned off by using +v instead of -v:

```
$ set +v
set +v
$ echo hi
hi
$
```

In this dialog the set +v command is echoed because verbose is still enabled, but subsequent commands aren't echoed.

Another useful debugging flag is -x, which makes the shell display commands, preceded by +, as they are executed. Setting this is good for debugging, because it shows you exactly what arguments are being passed to commands, unlike -v which shows you exactly what arguments you've specified.

Table 11.1   ■   Sh Command-line Options

-c *str*	Execute the commands in the *str* string.
-i	Run an interactive shell: (1) The TERMINATE signal is ignored. (2) The INTERRUPT signal is caught and then ignored, which allows wait to be interrupted.
-p	Don't set the effective user and group IDs to the real user and group IDs.
-r	Run a restricted shell: (1) Cd is not allowed. (2) Changing $PATH is not allowed. (3) Command names may not contain a /. (4) Output redirection is not allowed.
-s	Specifies the start of the positional parameters.

Note: The options specified in Table 11.2 are also available.

Table 11.2 ■ Set and Sh Command-line Options

-a	Automatically export variables that are modified or created.
-e	Exit immediately if a command fails. This option must be used with extreme caution because some UNIX programs don't properly set their exit status, and thus may appear to fail when everything is fine.
-f	Disable file name generation.
-h	Locate and remember functions as they are defined.
-k	Place keyword arguments, which means any argument that looks like an assignment statement, into the environment of the given command. When this option is set, it is hard to pass an argument to a program that contains an embedded hyphen (minus sign), but this option does make the notation for passing environment variables more attractive. This option is most often set in an interactive shell to make it easier to run shell scripts that make heavy use of environment variables.
-n	Read commands without executing them. It is useful when you want to test the syntax of a shell script without actually running it. -n is often used together with -v for syntactic debugging.
-t	Exit after executing one command.
-u	Makes it an error to reference an unset variable. Ordinarily an unset variable expands to nothing.
-v	Print the input as it is read. Note that the shell reads structured commands (loops, conditionals) in a single gulp. This option is useful as a debugging tool to trace shell scripts.
-x	Print each command, preceded by a +, as it is executed. This option is probably the most commonly used shell script debugging tool.
-	Disable the -v and -x debugging flags.
--	No-op; none of the flag options will be changed. The -- option is useful when some of the true arguments have leading hyphens. If arguments with leading hyphens aren't preceded by the -- option, the set command will interpret those arguments as its own options, and havoc will ensue.

```
$ set -x
$ echo Hello from $LOGNAME
+ echo Hello from kc
Hello from kc
$
```

The flag arguments that can be controlled using the set command can also be supplied as command-line arguments when you are invoking the shell to execute a script:

```
$ cat lsdir
if [ $# -eq 0 ]
then
  dir=.
else
  dir=$1
fi
find $dir -type d -print
```

```
$ sh -x lsdir
+ [ 0 -eq 0 ]
dir=.
+ find . -type d -print
./bin
./bkpdir
./corr
./corr/zsrc
$
```

The effect of invoking the shell with the command-line option -x is the same as if the command *set -x* were the first command in the script.

Once the options have been attended to, set takes the remaining arguments and assigns them to the positional parameters $1, $2, and so on. If this feature of set is used in a shell script, then the original values of the positional parameters are lost. If only flags are supplied, then set doesn't alter the positional arguments.

The following example shows how set can give you access to the individual words of a string by assigning them to the positional parameters. When you use set to assign values to the positional parameters, you should place the option -- (two hyphens) in front of the parameters, to tell set explicitly where the options stop and the arguments start:

```
$ set -- The Quick Brown Fox Jumped
$ echo $1 $2 $4 $5 Mr. ${3}.
The Quick Fox Jumped Mr. Brown.
$ date
Mon Aug 11 22:40:08 EDT 1993
$ set -- `date`
$ echo $6
1993
$ echo "$@"
Mon Aug 11 22:40:10 EDT 1993
$ ls -l /etc/motd
-rw-r--r-- 1   root   staff   270 Aug 11 00:00 /etc/motd
$ set -- `ls -l /etc/motd`
$ echo $9 : $5 $1
/etc/motd : 270 -rw-r--r--
$
```

Once you have used set to divide a line into individual words, the original arguments are unavailable. In a shell script this technique must be performed after argument processing, unless the arguments can be ignored.

In case you don't understand the necessity of the -- option of set, here is the last part of the previous example repeated, without using the -- option.

```
$ ls -l /etc/motd
-rw-r--r-- 1   root   staff   270 Aug 11 00:00 /etc/motd
$ set `ls -l /etc/motd`
sh: -rw-r--r--: bad option(s)
$
```

The set command in this example fails because the first word of the ls -l output starts with a hyphen. This makes set think that you are trying to set an option.

Some shell scripts use the following technique to duplicate the facility provided by the -- option:

```
$ set X `ls -l /etc/motd`
$ shift # discards X, moves other options to their usual position
$ echo $9 : $5 $1
/etc/motd : 270 -rw-r--r--
$ ▋
```

Many shell scripts have debugging facilities that are activated by command-line options. Here is the prototype for such a script. Its command-line options -U, -V, and -X control the shell's corresponding options:

```
$ cat opts
#
# skeleton script
#    to set sh debugging options from command line flags
#
while test $# -gt 0
do
  case $1 in
    -U) set -u
        ;;
    -V) set -v
        ;;
    -X) set -x
        ;;
    #
    # other option handling goes here
    #
  esac
  shift
done
#
echo The body of the shell script goes here.
#
$ opts
The body of the shell script goes here.
$ opts -X
+ shift
+ test 0 -gt 0
+ echo The body of the shell script goes here.
The body of the shell script goes here.
$ ▋
```

The preceding script could be written more compactly as follows, using the tr program to translate the script's uppercase option flags into the low-ercase flags that set requires:

```
$ cat opts
#
# skeleton script
#    to set sh debugging options from command line flags
#
while test $# -gt 0
do
        case $1 in
            -U|-V|-X)  set `echo $1 | tr UVX uvx`
                ;;
            #
            # other option handling goes here
            #
        esac
        shift
done
#
echo The body of the shell script goes here.
#
$
```

Variable assignments that appear before the command name on the command line are automatically exported into the environment of that command. Here's a brief example in which a small script named myname uses a variable called $name. If a value is assigned to name at the beginning of the myname command line, then $name will be exported into myname's environment:

```
$ cat myname
echo My name is $name and my argument is $1
$ name=george myname john
My name is george and my argument is john
$
```

The assignment must be written in front of the command; otherwise the intended assignment will simply be used as an argument. Here's what happens when the assignment is placed after the start of the myname command:

```
$ myname name=george john
My name is and my argument is name=george
$
```

As you can see, the variable $name isn't in the environment passed to myname; instead, the first argument seen by myname is the text name = george.

If you are using shell scripts in which you control options using environment variables, you may want to enable keyword arguments using the -k flag. This means that arguments that look like assignment statements (arguments that contain an equal sign) will be treated as environment variable assignments.

```
$ set -k
$ myname name=george john
My name is george and my argument is john
$
```

The advantage is the freedom, as usual, to place the name of the command first on the command line. The disadvantage is that it is hard to use arguments that contain equal signs once you've enabled keyword arguments.

11.19   Test—Evaluate Conditions

The test command is commonly used in shell scripts to perform various tests and to determine if certain files and directories exist. For efficiency, the test command is built into most versions of the Bourne shell.

The test program performs three different types of tests:

1. It can test files for certain characteristics.

2. It can perform string comparisons.

3. It can make numeric comparisons.

Test indicates the success or failure of its testing by its exit status. Thus it is almost always used as the conditional part of an if, while, until, or conditional (&&, ||) statement. Each flag and operator used by test must be passed as a separate command-line argument.

The name [is a recognized synonym for test. When the [alias is used, the last argument to test must be a]. Some people find the [ ] form of test more readable, but in either case the test program is doing the work. All of test's command-line options are specified in Table 11.3.

Here are two simple examples of test demonstrating the -r (is readable) and -d (is directory) tests:

```
$ if test -r /etc/motd
> then
> echo Readable
> fi
Readable
$ [ -d /bin ] && echo /bin is a directory
/bin is a directory
$ 
```

The test program can also compare strings for equality or inequality, and it can look for zero-length strings:

```
$ pwd
/home/kc/src
$ echo $HOME
/home/kc
$ [ $HOME = `pwd` ] || echo we are not home now
we are not home now
$ 
```

Here is an example of performing a numeric comparison, which is performed in a directory that contains about 80 files:

Table 11.3 ■ Test Command-line Options

File Access Tests

-b *file*	Returns true if *file* is a block special file.
-c *file*	Returns true if *file* is a character special file.
-d *file*	Returns true if *file* is a directory file.
-f *file*	Returns true if *file* is an ordinary file.
-g *file*	Returns true if *file* has the set-group-ID privilege.
-h *file*	Returns true if *file* is a symbolic link.
-k *file*	Returns true if *file* has its sticky bit set.
-L *file*	Returns true if *file* is a symbolic link.
-p *file*	Returns true if *file* is a named pipe (fifo).
-r *file*	Returns true if *file* is readable.
-s *file*	Returns true if *file* is one or more bytes long.
-t [*n*]	Returns true if file descriptor *n* (assumed to have the value one if *n* isn't supplied) refers to a terminal.
-u *file*	Returns true if *file* has the set-user-ID privilege.
-w *file*	Returns true if *file* is writeable.
-x *file*	Returns true if *file* is executable.

String Comparisons

-n *s1*	Returns true if string *s1* has length greater than zero.
s1	Returns true if string *s1* is non-null.
-z *s1*	Returns true if string *s1* has zero length.
s1 = *s2*	Returns true if the two strings are equal.
s1 != *s2*	Returns true if the two strings are unequal.

Numeric Comparisons

-eq	Equal	-gt	Greater than	-ge	Greater or equal
-ne	Not equal	-lt	Less than	-le	Less or equal

Logical Operations

!	NOT	-a	AND	-o	OR

Note: The precedence of OR is lower than AND. Parentheses (which must be escaped from the shell) may be used for grouping.

```
$ [ 40 -lt `ls | wc -l` ] && echo too many files here
too many files here
$ 
```

Test also allows you to combine tests using the Boolean operators shown in Table 11.3.

11.20 Expr—Evaluate Expressions

The expr command is a simple, general purpose integer arithmetic program. The expression that is evaluated is supplied on the command line, and expr produces its answers on the standard output. You must use command substitution if you want to capture the output in a shell variable. Expr yields a true exit status when the result is non-zero, and a false exit status otherwise.

Each of expr's arguments should be either a number (integers only) or an operator, except when you use the : or the comparison operators, which allow text arguments. The operators are listed in Table 11.4. Because most operators are shell metacharacters, they need to be quoted. But be careful to make each element of the expression a separate argument. You can't simply quote the entire expression, thereby forming a single argument. In Table 11.4, the operators that need to be quoted are shown quoted by a backslash, which is common usage.

We've already encountered examples that use expr for performing arithmetic on shell variables. Here's a script that counts up to the number specified on the command line:

Table 11.4 ■ Expr Command-line Operators, In Order of Increasing Precedence

`expr | expr`	Return the left *expr* if it is non-null and non-zero; otherwise return the right *expr*.
`expr \& expr`	Return the left *expr* if both *exprs* are non-null and non-zero; otherwise return zero.

`expr cmp-op expr`	Return one if the comparison is true, and zero otherwise. The comparison will be a numeric comparison if both *exprs* are numeric; otherwise it will be a text comparison. The following operators can be used:
	
	`\>` `=` `\>=`
	`\<` `!=` `\<=`

`expr add-op expr`	Add or subtract the two *exprs.* The following two operators can be used: `+` `-`
`expr mul-op expr`	Multiply, divide, or compute a remainder. The following operators can be used: `\*` `/` `%`
`expr : regexp`	Compare *expr,* which must be a fixed string, with *regexp,* which may be a regular expression that may contain the following metacharacters: `.` Match any single character. `$` Anchor a search to the end of the string. (The metacharacter `^`, which in ed and ex matches a search to the beginning of a line, isn't needed because all patterns are anchored to the beginning of the string.) `[list]` Match any single character in the list. `*` Match zero or more occurrences of the preceding single-character regular expression. `\(` `\)` Return the enclosed portion of the match. When this option is not present, the result is the length of the match, or zero to indicate no match.

Note: This table shows the operators quoted using a leading backslash, e.g., \>. Alternatively you could surround the operators with single quotes, e.g. '>'. The regular expression metacharacters aren't shown quoted. Regular expressions are usually quoted as a group, often using single quotes.

```
$ cat countto
count=0
[ $# -ne 1 ] && { echo "usage: countto val"; exit; }
while [ $1 -gt $count ]
do
   count=`expr $count + 1`
   echo $count
done
$ countto 5
1
2
3
4
5
$
```

One of expr's most useful capabilities is string extraction, which uses the : operator. The left operand of the : operator is a fixed string, and the right operand is a regular expression which may contain ordinary text plus all the metacharacters mentioned in the : citation in Table 11.4.

Here's how you can use the : operator to get the last three digits of your tty port number:

```
$ tty
/dev/pts002
$ expr `tty` : ".*\(...\)\$"
002
$
```

The regular expression consists of .*, which matches anything, followed by \(, which indicates the start of the match region (the part of the match text to be output), followed by ..., which matches any three characters, followed by \), which terminates the match region, followed by \$, which anchors the match to the end of the line. We put the regular expression (the third argument) inside double quotes to suppress the shell meaning of the * and \ characters. Since double quotes don't suppress the meaning of $ (parameter substitution), we explicitly quoted the $ with a backslash. (The most frustrating part of expr often is getting the quoting right. To help you get it right, use the -x option of set so you can see exactly what is happening to your arguments.)

Here's how we could have written the same expression without using double quotes. To make sure everything is right, we are using the -x set option to see exactly what is happening to our regular expression.

```
$ set -x
$ expr `tty` : .\*\\\(...\\\)\$
+ tty
+ expr /dev/pts002 : .*\(...\)$
002
$
```

Because the regular expression isn't inside double quotes, you must type two backslashes to get a single backslash, and you must quote *, (,), and $ with a single backslash, as shown in the preceding dialog.

If we had used the stronger single quotes, we would have had to omit the backslash in front of the $ because single quotes quote everything:

```
$ expr `tty` : ´.*\(...\)$´
+ tty
+ expr /dev/pts002 : .*\(...\)$
002
$ 
```

In this dialog, the -x option remains in effect.

11.21   Ulimit—Set and Display Resource Limits

The ulimit command lets you specify various resource limits. There are usually two limits for each resource, a soft limit and a hard limit. You can usually exceed the soft limit, although a warning message will be printed. You are prohibited from exceeding hard limits. You can print a list of all the current soft limits using the -a (equivalent to -Sa) option, or -Ha to print the hard limits.

```
$ ulimit -a
time(seconds) unlimited
file(blocks) 16384
data(kbytes) 16384
stack(kbytes) 16384
coredump(blocks) 2048
nofiles(descriptors) 64
memory(kbytes) 16384
$ 
```

Table 11.5 lists the ulimit options that are used to control individual limits.

Table 11.5 ■ Ulimit Command-line Options

-a	List limits.
-H	Set hard limits.
-S	Set soft limits, which is the default.
-c	Maximum core dump file size, in 512-byte blocks.
-d	Maximum data segment size, in kilobytes.
-f	Maximum file creation size, in kilobytes.
-n	Maximum number of file descriptors.
-s	Maximum size of stack segment, in kilobytes.
-t	Maximum CPU time, in seconds.
-v	Maximum size of virtual memory, in kilobytes.

11.22   Getopts—Manage Options in Scripts

The getopts command helps you build shell scripts that follow the System V standards for option flags. Without getopts, it is hard to create shell scripts that have standard option flag usage because it is otherwise hard in a shell script to divide a single word (such as -abc) into individual option flags (a, b, and c). Getopts supersedes an older facility called getopt that operated differently; use getopts in all new development and convert existing code that uses getopt to getopts.

The getopts command requires two arguments: a list of option flags and a variable into which the current option flag will be stored. Each time it is called, getopts will peel off one of the option characters from the command line and store it in the variable. When there are no more options to process, getopts will return with a False status. The list of option flags should be the individual option letters that are acceptable. Each option that requires an argument should be followed in the list by a :. When an argument-taking option flag is detected, its argument will be stored in the shell variable $OPTARG. The index of the first nonoption argument (the first true argument) is stored in the $OPTIND variable. Both $OPTIND and $OPTARG should be treated as read-only in your script.

Here's a remake of the opts script from Section 11.18. In this version, getopts is used to make the option syntax much more flexible. In the original version, each option (-U, -V, -X) had to be specified separately. In this getopts version, the option flags can be written separately or placed in a single word (-UVX).

```
$ cat opts2
#
# skeleton script
#    to set sh debugging options from command line flags
#
while getopts UVX op
do
  case $op in
    U) set -u
       ;;
    V) set -v
       ;;
    X) set -x
       ;;
    #
    # other option handling goes here
    #
  esac
done
shift `expr $OPTIND - 1`
#
echo The body of the shell script goes here.
#
$ opts2 -VX
```

```
+ getopts UVX opt
echo The body of the shell script goes here.
+ echo The body of the shell script goes here.
The body of the shell script goes here.
$ ▊
```

Options that take arguments are handled in two parts. In the option list passed to getopts, the flag character for an argument-taking option should be followed by a colon. Then in the option handling part of the script, the option argument is picked up from the $OPTARG variable. Here is an example script that accepts an optional -o file option, along with options flags a, b, and c, plus ordinary arguments:

```
$ cat opts3
#
# skeleton script
#   to demonstrate getopts
#
filename=
oOption=0
aOption=0
bOption=0
cOption=0
while getopts abco: op
do
 case $op in
  a) aOption=1 ;;
  b) bOption=1 ;;
  c) cOption=1 ;;
  o) oOption=1 ; filename=$OPTARG ;;
 esac
done
shift `expr $OPTIND - 1`
[ $aOption -eq 1 ] && echo '-a option'
[ $bOption -eq 1 ] && echo '-b option'
[ $cOption -eq 1 ] && echo '-c option'
[ $oOption -eq 1 ] && echo '-o option:' $filename
[ $# -gt 0 ] && echo arguments: $@
$ opts3 -ab -o myname arg1 arg2 arg3
-a option
-b option
-o option: myname
arguments: arg1 arg2 arg3
$ ▊
```

Any shell script that uses more than one option flag should use getopts to parse the command-line options so that the script will follow the standard syntax for option specification.

11.23   The Bourne Shell's Built-in Commands

The Bourne shell has many built-in commands. The most important ones have already been presented; the goal of this section is to cover the remainder so that this chapter is a complete guide to the shell. Table 11.6 lists the Bourne shell's built-in commands.

Some commands are built in because they are central to the role of the shell. Examples include cd, the conditional and loop commands, and the commands that relate to shell variables. Other commands are built in for efficiency. Examples of these programs include echo and test. Note that both echo and test have external versions that can always be activated by prepending /bin/ to the name.

Table 11.6 ■ The Shell's Built-in Commands

:	Do nothing. Note that the remainder of the line following : is evaluated normally, which may have side effects. (Historically the : was used as a poor-person's comment. It is a poor choice for comments; use # instead.)
. *file*	Read commands in the current shell from *file;* it's the same as if you were typing the commands at the terminal. The . command allows you to change the environment of the current shell. For example, people often enter the command . .profile after changing PATH and other variable settings in their .profile file. (If you simply execute .profile after making changes, those changes will affect the subshell that executes .profile but it won't alter anything in your login shell.)
break [*n*]	Break out of the enclosing for or while loop; break *n* levels if *n* is specified.
continue [*n*]	Continue the enclosing for or while loop; continue the nth outer loop if *n* is specified.
cd [*dir*]	Change to your home directory, or to *dir* if it is specified.
echo [*arg* ...]	Echo arguments. Use /bin/echo to use the stand-alone version of echo.
eval *cmd* ...	Reevaluate the arguments in *cmd*. This forces the shell to take another substitution pass through the argument list.
exec *cmd* ...	Execute *cmd* in place of the currently executing shell. This lets you substitute a new process for the current shell, which might be desirable if you want to switch to a different shell or to an alternate user interface.
exit [*n*]	Exit, with exit status *n* if *n* is specified.
export [*var* ...]	With no arguments, print the new environment variables. With arguments, specify that those variables should be exported.
getopts *args*	Get option flags. See Section 11.22.
hash [-r] [*cmd* ...]	Using $PATH, determine and remember the location of each *cmd* so they can be more rapidly found and executed. The -r clears the remembered list. With no arguments, print the list of remembered commands, showing the number of hits and the cost of each access.
newgrp [*arg*]	Equivalent to exec newgrp *arg*, which runs the newgrp program to log you into a new group, which results in execution of a new shell.
pwd	Print the name of the current (working) directory.

Table 11.6 ■ The Shell's Built-in Commands (*continued*)

read *var* ...	Read a line of input from the standard input. The first word is assigned to the first variable, and so on. Any excess is assigned to the last variable. If only one variable is supplied, it gets the whole line. The return is true (0) unless end of file is encountered.
readonly [*var* ...]	Without arguments, print the list of read-only variables. With arguments, mark those variables as read-only.
return [*n*]	Exit from a function, returning exit status *n* if supplied.
set [-*op*] [*arg* ...]	Set a shell option. See Section 11.18.
shift [*n*]	Shift the arguments down one position, or down *n* positions if *n* is specified.
test *args* ...	Test an expression. See Section 11.19.
times	Print execution times.
trap [*cmd*] [*n*]...	Execute *cmd* when signal *n* arrives. The *cmd* text is scanned twice. The best signal handlers are shell functions. If *cmd* is absent, then signal *n* is reset to default. If *cmd* is null, then signal *n* is ignored. If *n* is zero then *cmd* is executed on exit from the script. With no arguments, a list of traps and actions is printed.
type [*name* ...]	Print how *name* would be used as a command. The command type ls would print ls is /usr/bin/ls while the command type cd would print cd is a shell builtin.
ulimit *args*	Set resource limits. See Section 11.21.
umask [*nnn*]	Set the file creation bitmask to *nnn* if *nnn* is supplied; otherwise print the current mask. *Nnn* is in octal. Bits that are set in the mask are turned off in the permissions of newly created files and directories. Setting umask to 22 will disallow writes by group and others; setting umask to 777 will disallow all access to newly created files.
unset [*name* ...]	Unset the specified variables or functions.
wait [*n*]	Wait for the background process whose PID is *n* to complete; or wait for all background processes to complete.

12

A Few Shell Programs

One of the most interesting features of the UNIX system is the shell, a powerful interactive command interpreter entwined within a sophisticated high-level programming language. The primitive operations in the shell programming language are the UNIX system commands. Hence the entire power of the UNIX system can be used in a shell program.

Programmers usually are trained to work with conventional programming languages, which often are designed for numeric computation. Shell programming requires a different mind-set, because shell programs make use of UNIX utilities and because text transformation is heavily used. Since the shell is so important to the UNIX system, we next consider a few examples of shell programs. All of these examples are designed to work on the Bourne shell, which is available on all modern UNIX systems.

A simple shell program can be written by nonprogrammers, which is one of its key advantages. The first section of this chapter examines some of the issues that you should consider when you are thinking about using the shell language for a given application. Simple shell programs are commonly used UNIX system commands conveniently stored in a file. One example is shown in Section 12.2. Other shell programs are conceptually simple but involve more commands, such as the examples shown in the last sections of this chapter.

12.1 When Do You Use the Shell Programming Language?

There are no firm rules for deciding when to use the shell programming language to write a program. When program execution speed is important, more efficient languages should be used because there is a large execution speed penalty for using the high-level features of the shell. But even when execution speed is important, the shell is often a good prototyping language. Write your speed-critical application first using the shell, to get the kinks out, and then rewrite the final version in another language for greater speed.

The shell programming language should be considered when the problem solution involves many operations that are standard UNIX system commands. There are UNIX commands to search through files, sort files, transform files, create files, move files, and so on. If the problem can be expressed in terms of the operations that are already part of the UNIX system tool chest, then a strong case can be made to use the shell programming language.

Once you are fluent in shell programming, you begin to view problems in terms of their potential for shell language solutions. Many problems that don't appear at first to be amenable to shell language solutions actually can be performed elegantly by shell scripts.

Another way to evaluate the suitability of the shell programming language is to examine the basic data items that are involved in the problem. If the basic data items are either lines of text or files, then the shell may represent a good solution. If the basic data are numbers or single characters, then the shell may not be a good solution.

Shell programs invariably have a command-line user interface. If you want to create a GUI-style program for managing mail messages, then C or some other compiled language is the best choice. However, if you want to build a program to compute the fraction of your mail messages that originated in Europe, or one to tally how many memos you sent to your boss, then the shell is probably the best choice.

12.2   How Many Users Are Logged In?

Although the who command will tell you who is on the system, it won't tell you how many. However, the who command combined with wc, the word count program, will work nicely:

```
$ cat nusers
who | wc -l
$ who
nuucp      tty01     Dec 15 22:24
gilbert    tty17     Dec 15 15:34
dan        ttyh0     Dec 15 17:37
kc         ttyh3     Dec 15 21:02
$ nusers
4
$ 
```

The -l option to wc specifies that wc should count only lines; normally wc counts lines, words, and characters. If you want to be fancier, you can embed the summary in a message:

```
$ cat > nusers1
echo `who | wc -l` users are on the system
$ nusers1
4 users are on the system
$
```

Why would you want a one-line summary of the number of users? Many systems keep track of system usage for management purposes. For example, a graph of daily usage would provide a visual display that might be useful for your management reports. Here is a variant of nusers that will keep a log of system usage in files named Sun, Mon, and so on. Given a day's worth of info, a separate program can be used to produce the actual graph.

```
$ cat logusers
while true
do
  set -- `date`
  day=$1
  who | wc -l >> /usr/adm/$day
  sleep 600
done
$
```

The $day shell variable contains the name of the day. The name of the day is obtained using set to put the date components into the positional parameters, and then using the first argument. Notice in the fourth line that >> style output appends the number of users information onto the usage file. Sleep 600 is a ten-minute (60 sec * 10) delay.

As written here, there is one thing missing from loguser. For the first week, everything will be fine, but when the eighth day arrives the new data will be tacked onto the end of the previous, instead of truncating the old data and starting fresh. Cleaning up the old files could be handled by cron but instead let's see how it would be handled in this program:

```
$ cat logusers1
lastday=never
while true
do
  set -- `date`
  day=$1
  [ $day != $lastday ] && > /usr/adm/$day
  who | wc -l >> /usr/adm/$day
  lastday=$day
  sleep 600
done
$
```

In this version of logusers, the shell variable $day contains the days of the week, and $lastday contains the day that logusers last updated a usage file. The line that ends > /usr/adm/$day clears out the new day's usage file each time the $day variable changes. The > output redirection symbol usually follows a command to redirect the command's output. Without a command, the > symbol tells the shell to create an empty file with the given name. This version of logusers could be run in the background to provide continual monitoring of system usage. Notice that logusers expects to run continuously; if it were started fresh every ten minutes by cron, it would wipe out its log file each time; and since logusers never exits, the process table would soon fill up. (However, cron could be used to run the earlier nusers every ten minutes.)

How would you solve this problem using the C language? A C solution to this problem would be difficult because you would have to be able to decipher the contents of the file /etc/utmp (the file where logins are recorded) to find out how many people are using the system. Since the who command already knows how to examine /etc/utmp, this is an example of a problem that is solved trivially using existing UNIX system tools but is much harder to solve using C.

12.3   Listing Subdirectories

The UNIX Operating System contains the ls command to list all of the files in a directory, but it lacks the built-in capability to list only the directory files in a directory. Whenever you are poking around in an unfamiliar part of the file system, you are likely to want to know the names of the subdirectories of the current directory.

Section 8.9 explained that the following command will list all of the directory files in the root directory (we've piped the result to head so that only the first ten lines are shown):

```
$ ls -l / | grep '^d' | head
drwxrwxrwx    2 root       root            96 Feb   4 17:09 Disk_A
drwxrwxrwx    2 root       root            96 Feb   4 17:10 Disk_B
drwxrwxrwx    2 root       root            96 Feb   5 08:11 Disks-etc
drwxrwxr-x    2 root       sys             96 Feb   4 04:12 bck
drwxrwxrwx    2 root       root            96 Feb   4 17:09 cdrom1
drwxrwxr-x    2 root       bin             96 Feb   4 04:12 config
drwxr-xr-x   20 bin        bin           6144 Mar   8 08:08 dev
drwxr-xr-x    2 bin        bin             96 Feb   4 10:24 els
drwxrwxr-x   41 root       sys           3072 Mar   8 08:09 etc
drwxrwxr-x    2 root       sys             96 Feb   4 04:13 export
$
```

This works because the lines describing directories in a long format ls listing start with the letter d. We can make this simple command line into a useful utility by placing it in its own file and by using arguments so that we can list the subdirectories of any directory, not just the root directory:

```
$ cat lsdir
ls -l $1 | grep '^d'
$ lsdir / | head -5
drwxrwxrwx    2 root       root            96 Feb   4 17:09 Disk_A
```

```
drwxrwxrwx    2 root      root        96 Feb  4 17:10 Disk_B
drwxrwxrwx    2 root      root        96 Feb  5 08:11 Disks-etc
drwxrwxr-x    2 root      sys         96 Feb  4 04:12 bck
drwxrwxrwx    2 root      root        96 Feb  4 17:09 cdrom1
$
```

If no arguments are supplied, then the positional parameter $1 will be unset and the ls program won't receive any directory names as arguments, which means that subdirectories in the current directory will be listed. This is very nice behavior, because it makes lsdir behave like ls.

In its current form, the lsdir command expects just one argument. If you supply two arguments, only the first is used:

```
$ lsdir /home /
drwxr-xr-x  12 kc        other      1024 Mar  8 08:24 kc
$
```

Probably the easiest way to fix this is to change $1 to $@ in the lsdir script. Then ls will get all of the arguments instead of just the first. However, instead, let's use a for loop so that the shell arguments can be managed individually:

```
$ cat lsdir2
for i
do
  ls -l $i | grep '^d'
done
$
```

This improved version will work with one or more arguments. But, think about what happens when no arguments are supplied. With no arguments, the for loop will never execute and no output will be generated. In order to correct this deficiency, we need to put a test at the beginning of the script to make sure that there is at least one argument. Here is one way to do it:

```
$ cat lsdir3
[ $# -eq 0 ] && set -- .
for i
do
  ls -l $i | grep '^d'
done
$
```

The first line of lsdir3 detects that it has been called with no arguments. When this problem occurs, lsdir3 solves the problem by using set to supply a single argument, a period, which is the name of the current directory. You could also use an if statement instead of the && conditional to solve this problem, or you could solve it by calling lsdir3 recursively with a period as the argument.

An alternative way to list subdirectories is to use the test program. As described in Section 11.19, test can perform many tests on UNIX files. Here's how we can use test in a script that lists subdirectories:

```
$ cat lsdir4
for i in $1/*
do
  [ -d $i ] && echo $i
done
$ lsdir4 /home
/home/kc
$ ▓
```

The list of words in the for statement is created by file name generation. The pattern $1/* expands to a list of all the files (whose names don't start with a period) in the $1 directory. This is a common construct for writing a for loop that processes each file in a directory. The -d option of test means "Test to see if the named file is a directory." The names of all of the files that pass the test are printed using the echo command.

One problem with lsdir4 is that it will list files in the root directory if you don't supply arguments! This happens because the phrase $1/* in the for statement becomes /* if the variable $1 isn't set.

```
$ pwd
/home
$ lsdir4 | head -5
/Disk_A
/Disk_B
/Disks-etc
/bck
/bin
$ lsdir4 .
./kc
$ ▓
```

One solution is to use the ${var:-word} construct (see Section 11.2.7) for handling the case of $1 being unset:

```
$ cat lsdir5
for i in ${1:-"."}/*
do
  [ -d $i ] && echo $i
done
$ pwd
/home
$ lsdir5
./kc
$ ▓
```

The lsdir5 script could be enhanced to use a for loop so it could handle multiple command-line arguments. That task is left as an exercise for the reader.

Can you think of any alternative methods for generating a list of the subdirectories of a given directory? Of the two approaches shown, which is more efficient, and why? Which approach is more general? Compared to these simple shell scripts, how hard would it be to write a C program to list subdirectories?

12.4   Listing Files in the Current Subtree

Everyone who uses the UNIX system occasionally misplaces a file. Perhaps you can't remember the exact name of the file, or you put it in some unknown directory. In any case, the file is missing and you want to find it. Very often you will know that the file is in a certain part of the file system but you don't know exactly where. Typically the file is in some unknown subdirectory of your home directory.

If there aren't too many files in the current subtree, then perhaps you can find the missing file simply by listing all the files. The simplest way is to use the -R option of ls:

```
$ ls -R
LTR          cr           file2        lines        numbs        script
arlinote     dlg1         file3        logusers     op           shft
arlinote2    don.ltr      fna          lsdir        opts         t.fil
arlinote3    don1.ltr     hammy        lsdir4       opts1        val.dat
breeds       don2.ltr     jane.ltr     names        revargs      verse
comp2        don3.ltr     junk         nocr         sam.ltr
count        file         letters.tar  num          sam1.ltr
./comp2:
dlg1      don.ltr    don2.ltr    don3.ltr
$
```

The find command is another way to list the files in the current subtree. You can use arguments to find files with certain names, to find files that have been modified more recently than a certain date, to find files with certain privileges, and so on. If you don't use any of the special options, then find will find all of the files in the subtree.

Here is the simplest form of the find command:

```
find . -print
```

This will print all of the files in the current subtree. The dot indicates that the search should start in the current directory (remember that dot is always the name of the current directory) and the option -print indicates that the file names should be printed. (See Section 6.8 for a complete explanation of the find command and all of its options.) To be more useful, you should probably sort the output of find and also print it in a multicolumn format (pr's -4 option produces 4-column output, and -t omits headers and trailers). Here's how you might use find to list the files in the current subtree.

```
$ find . -print | sort | pr -4t
.              ./cr          ./jane.ltr     ./op
./LTR          ./dlg1        ./junk         ./opts
./arlinote     ./don.ltr     ./letters.tar  ./opts1
./arlinote2    ./don1.ltr    ./lines        ./revargs
```

```
./arlinote3        ./don2.ltr      ./logusers       ./sam.ltr
./breeds           ./don3.ltr      ./lsdir          ./sam1.ltr
./comp2            ./file          ./lsdir4         ./script
./comp2/dlg1       ./file2         ./names          ./shft
./comp2/don.ltr    ./file3         ./nocr           ./t.fil
./comp2/don2.ltr ./fna            ./num            ./val.dat
./comp2/don3.ltr ./hammy          ./numbs          ./verse
./count
$
```

You could memorize the syntax for the preceding find-sort-pr command, or you could put the command in a shell command file that we will call lstree. Whenever you want a list of all of the files in the current subtree, you can enter the command

lstree

instead of the command

find . -print | sort | pr -4t

Many shell programs are this simple; they are just a useful but complicated command placed in a file.

A variant on this problem is the problem of listing all of the directories in the current subtree. As a first solution, let's use the find command. The find command contains a test for directories. The following command will find and print all of the directories in the current subtree:

```
$ find . -type d -print
.
./comp2
$
```

The argument -type indicates that we are trying to find certain types of files—directories, in this case, as indicated by the d argument. We could place this command in a file and enter the name of the file whenever we want a list of the directories in the current subtree.

Let's look at another way to list the subdirectories in the current subtree. We can use the shell's for loop to perform tests on each file in a directory:

```
$ for i in *
> do
> [ -d $i ] && echo $i
> done
comp2
$
```

In order to list all of the directories in the current subtree, we can extend this concept using recursion. We can modify the preceding command so that it descends into each directory and then calls itself to list the directories in that directory, and descend still further, and so on.

```
$ cat lstree1
[ $# -eq 0 ] && set -- .
for i in $1/*
```

```
do
   [ -d $i ] && { echo $i ; sh lstree1 $i; }
done
$ lstree1
./comp2
$ █
```

The argument to lstree1 is used to keep track of the pathname leading to the directory being examined. When lstree1 is invoked without arguments, then set is used to set $1 to the value ".". When a directory is found, lstree1 is called to list its subdirectories.

Let's look at yet another method. Instead of a for loop to generate a list of all of the files in the current directory, we can use the ls command in combination with the read command in a subshell:

```
$ cat lstree2
[ $# -eq 1 ] && cd $1
ls | (
   while read i
   do
      [ -d $i ] && { echo $i ; lstree2 $i ; }
   done
)
$ █
```

In lstree2, we generate a list of the files in the current directory using the ls command. The list is piped to the list of commands enclosed in parentheses, which are executed in a subshell. The read command reads individual lines from the pipe and places them in the variable $i. When the pipe is drained, read will return a false exit status, which will terminate the while loop.

None of these scripts has directly addressed the problem posed at the beginning of this section: finding a lost file. Probably the easiest way to address that specific need is to use find:

```
$ cat findbyname
[ $# -ne 1 ] && { echo Usage: $0 filename ; exit ; }
find . -name "$1" -print
$ findbyname '*.ltr'
./sam1.ltr
./don.ltr
./don2.ltr
./don3.ltr
./jane.ltr
./sam.ltr
./don1.ltr
./comp2/don.ltr
./comp2/don2.ltr
./comp2/don3.ltr
$ █
```

The argument passed to the findbyname script must be quoted so that it won't be expanded by your login shell. If the argument is expanded by the interactive shell, the findbyname script will receive a list of the .ltr files in the current directory instead of the '*.ltr' specification to be used throughout the current subtree. Inside the script, the $1 variable is quoted because the argument must be passed directly to find instead of being used by the subshell executing the script. If $1 weren't quoted in the script, then the subshell executing the script would pass a list of the .ltr files in the current directory to find, which isn't what we need.

12.5 Using Eval to Reevaluate Command Lines

In Chapter 11 we played with a short program to print a shell program's arguments in reverse order. The task is very simple if you know how many arguments you are going to receive, but it is harder to create a solution that works for any number of arguments.

In the following example, we want to show you how to make a more general reverse arguments program, and we also want to show you how you can build up and then execute shell command lines. This is very different from all the scripts we've shown so far in which the commands are initially present in the script.

In its simplest form, you can build up a shell command line interactively:

```
$ cmd=echo
$ cmd=$cmd hi
$ cmd=$cmd there
$ $cmd
hi there
$
```

This same idea is used in the revargs script, which reverses any number of arguments:

```
$ cat revargs
count=$#
while test $count -gt 0
do
    eval echo -n \$$count
    echo -n " "
    count=`expr $count - 1`
done
echo
$ revargs A B C
C B A
$ revargs  Q W E R T Y U I O P
P O I U Y T R E W Q
$
```

This revargs program is a bit difficult because it uses many of the facilities of the shell. The program consists of a while conditional loop that executes once for each argument, starting at the final argument and sequencing down to the first argument. The argument being processed is indicated by the variable $count; its initial value is the number of the last argument and then its value is decreased by one each time through the loop.

The easiest way to understand revargs is to take it apart. First, let's look at the general structure, using a stripped down version of revargs. The only change is the omission of the eval construct, which will be explained shortly.

```
$ cat revargsA
count=$#
while test $count -gt 0
do
    echo -n \$$count
    echo -n " "
    count=`expr $count - 1`
done
echo
$ revargsA  A B C
$3 $2 $1
$ revargsA A B C D E F
$6 $5 $4 $3 $2 $1
$
```

What's happening in the first echo command is the heart of the matter. The echo command is passed the -n flag, which directs it to produce its output without a trailing new line, plus the word \$$count. The first $ is quoted by the \, so it is output literally, followed by the value of $count. Because of the logic in the while loop, the $count variable starts at the number of arguments and then is decreased by one each time through the loop. Thus, if you give revargsA three arguments, $count is 3, then 2, and then finally 1, and echo outputs $3 the first time through, $2 next, and then finally $1, as shown in the preceding dialog. (The second echo command puts the spaces in the output, and the third echo prints the trailing new line.)

This is close to what we want, but not quite. We don't want echo to literally print "$3 $2 $1," rather we want it to print the values of those positional parameters. Remember that by the time we've constructed the $3, $2, and $1 strings, the shell has already processed the command line once. It won't normally reprocess it to substitute their values. The key tactic is to use eval, which makes the shell take a second pass through the command line.

Now let's return to the first version of revargs, the one that uses eval. After the shell's first pass through the eval/echo command line, that line will look like this (assuming $count has the value 3):

```
eval echo $3
```

Yes, we're in confusing territory here. If you typed in the command echo $3, then the third positional parameter would be printed. But we've constructed the text string $3 by using the shell's parameter substitution process, and ordinarily you only get one pass through the substitution process. That's why revargsA prints $3, and that's why eval is used in revargs, so that the line will be reevaluated, thereby printing the value of the third parameter.

Constructing commands within shell scripts is a powerful and flexible technique. Understanding the technique requires a thorough understanding of the shell and how it works, and it is one of the hallmarks of a sophisticated UNIX user. People who've worked with AI languages such as Lisp and Prolog have a head start; people with more conventional backgrounds take longer to understand eval and the notion of command-line reevaluation.

13

The AWK
Programming Language

Awk is a programmable filter for text files. Like grep, awk can search for patterns in a text file. Like sed, awk can replace one text pattern with another. Like expr, awk has arithmetic capabilities. And like the shell or C, awk is programmable. These characteristics make awk a valuable tool for manipulating text files.

Awk is an appropriate tool for jobs too complicated for less programmable filters like sed or tr. However, if speed is essential, you might need to consider a C-language solution, because awk is not as fast as a custom C solution. But even where speed is essential, awk may be useful for prototyping. Although awk and the shell are both programmable, they are specialized for different applications. Awk is best at manipulating text files, whereas the shell is best at managing UNIX commands.

There are two common versions of awk. The first is the original awk, which is available on virtually all UNIX systems. All of the examples in this chapter are written to be compliant with the original awk, so that they will be as portable as possible. The newer version of awk, which is called nawk on many systems, has a few additional features but is remarkably faithful to the original. We've detailed the features of nawk in the tables and mentioned several in the body of the text.

Awk is suitable both for very simple chores, such as extracting one of the words printed by the date command, and for more complex chores, such as serving as a simple data-base manager or statistics package. Here is an example of a simple awk application, a program that prints the day of the month:

```
$ cat dayofmonth
date | awk '{ print $3 }'
$ date
```

```
Wed Mar 10 20:15:43 EST 1993
$ dayofmonth
10
$
```

More complicated awk programs will be shown later in this chapter. Awk's command-line options are shown in Table 13.1.

Awk was developed by Alfred V. Aho, Peter J. Weinberger, and Brian W. Kernighan. They also wrote the manual for awk, *Awk—A Pattern Scanning and Processing Language.* Brian Kernighan has pointed out that "naming a language after its authors . . . shows a certain poverty of imagination." Although awk's name lacks the conciseness and mystique of some of UNIX's more renowned names (e.g., C), nonetheless it is a fitting name for a useful UNIX tool.

13.1   Simple Scripts

An awk script consists of two components, patterns and actions. The patterns are similar to ed's regular expressions, and the actions bear some resemblance to the C language. In an awk program there are patterns followed by actions, with curly braces surrounding each action. An action is performed if the pattern matches something in the input line. For example, if the pattern is Jan, then the action will be performed on all lines of the file that contain the text Jan.

Either the pattern or the action can be omitted. If the pattern is omitted, the action is performed for each line in the file. If the action is absent, the default action is to print the line. A few simple cases should make some of these ideas clear.

One easy task is to write an awk script that mimics UNIX's grep command. The goal is to print each line of a file that matches the given pattern. Later in the chapter we'll show how you can generalize this to handle multiple arguments. However, for now, let's look at an awk program called find-paris that simply looks for the text pattern paris in its standard input. Each line containing the pattern is output.

Table 13.1 ■ Awk Command-line Options

`-f scriptfile`	Execute the script in *scriptfile.* If this option isn't given, the script is executed from the first (nonoption) command-line argument, which should usually be strongly quoted.
`-F re`	Specify *re,* which may be a regular expression, as the field separator. The default field separator is any sequence of blanks and/or tabs. (In the original awk, *re* was limited to a single character.)
`-v var=val`	Assign *val* to *var* before execution of the script. (In the original awk, the -v was not necessary; any arguments containing an = were considered to be assignments to awk variables.)

```
$ cat findparis
awk /paris/
$ echo an american in georgia | findparis
$ echo an american in paris | findparis
an american in paris
$ ▮
```

The findparis awk program consists of a single pattern, /paris/. Since there is no action specified for the pattern, the default action, print the entire line each time there is a match, is performed.

Here is an equivalent program, with the action clearly spelled out:

```
$ cat findparis
awk '/paris/ { print }'
$ echo an american in georgia | findparis
$ echo an american in paris | findparis
an american in paris
$ ▮
```

The quotes surrounding the awk script are necessary because the script contains blanks. Either single or double quotes would suffice. The script itself must be a single argument.

The print statement in the findparis program doesn't have any parameters, so the entire line is printed. It is also possible to print constants, words from the input line, and so on by supplying them as arguments to print. An example of print with arguments appears in the next example.

In an awk program, the words $1, $2, and so on refer to the words of the current input line. So if the current line in an awk script is "The rain in Spain," then $1 in the awk script has the value *The*, $2 has the value *rain*, and so on. The special variable $0 contains the entire input line. This is similar to the meanings of $1, $2, and so on in a shell program, but different enough to cause problems, especially when an awk command is a part of a shell program using positional parameters.

Here is an awk script that computes the average position of a series of x, y, z points. The input contains x, y, z values on each line; the desired output should contain the average of the x, y, and z values. A final version, also shown, will simply print the final result, but in this first-cut version, let's produce all of the intermediate answers. Here is a first-cut awk script to average a series of x, y, z coordinates:

```
$ cat ave
awk '{
    n = n + 1
    X = X + $1
    Y = Y + $2
    Z = Z + $3
    print X/n, Y/n, Z/n
    }'
$ cat test
1 2 3
4 5 6
```

```
7 8 9
0 1 2
$ ave < test
1 2 3
2.5 3.5 4.5
4 5 6
3 4 5
$ █
```

This awk script is several lines long, so it must be quoted using the powerful single (') quotes. The single quotes also are good because the shell's parameter substitution doesn't occur within single quotes. Because $1 and so on in this program are awk variables, not shell positional parameters, they must be strongly quoted; double quotes won't do. Even a one-line awk script containing $1 and so on must be quoted with single quotes (or backslashes) to suppress parameter substitution. (Note that the ave script in the preceding example was executed simply by typing its name. This works only if you have made the script executable using the chmod command, and if you include the current directory in your search path.)

Besides its use of the field variables $1, $2, and $3, this program shows that a variable in an awk program is created automatically, simply by mentioning its name. In this program the variables are named n, X, Y, and Z. In awk you can count on a variable to start out initialized to zero (or blank, if it is used as a text variable), although it is good style to initialize variables explicitly. In a language designed for larger projects, awk's relaxed attitude toward variable declarations would be a fault, but in a language designed for short projects, awk's lack of rigor seems acceptable. You should also notice that the default pattern is missing for the action in this script, which explains why the action is performed for every line of the input.

Our average program would be more useful if the average position were only printed after all of the input had been exhausted. As a first attempt the program is useful; in fact, an overly verbose first attempt is usually better than a silent, mysterious first attempt. However, consider the overhead of running this program with an input of 10,000 lines. The resulting output would clutter the screen for a very long time.

Awk has the built-in patterns BEGIN and END that are used for specifying actions that should be performed before or after the data is read. BEGIN and END must be the first and last patterns respectively, if they are present. In the following variation on the preceding program, the BEGIN pattern is used to explicitly (but somewhat needlessly) initialize all of the variables, and the END pattern is used to print the result. Although the initialization is, in a strict sense, not necessary, I think it is useful as a form of documentation. It draws the reader's attention to the assumed initial values of the variables.

```
$ cat ave2
awk '
BEGIN { n = 0 ; X = 0 ; Y = 0 ; Z = 0 }
     {
         n = n + 1
```

```
                        X = X + $1
                        Y = Y + $2
                        Z = Z + $3
                }
END     { print X/n, Y/n, Z/n }'
$ cat test
1 2 3
4 5 6
7 8 9
0 1 2
$ ave2 < test
3 4 5
$ █
```

The ave2 awk program has three actions, two that have patterns and one that, because it doesn't have a pattern, is executed for every line of the input. (Notice that if the input file for this program is empty, then n will have the value 0 when the END pattern is encountered. This will lead to a "divide by 0" message, which can in this case be ignored. In Section 13.2, the if statement is introduced; it could easily solve this problem.)

Awk patterns are more flexible than simple ed-style regular expressions. One extra feature was shown in the preceding text, the special patterns BEGIN and END. Another awk feature is the built-in awk variable NR (number of records), which is the input line counter. (All of the built-in variables are listed in Table 13.4.) For example, the pattern "NR == 5" will print line 5. More complicated patterns using NR are possible, such as those in the following script, hcut1, which prints lines between 3 and 5.

```
$ cat hcut1
awk 'NR >= 3 && NR <= 5'
$ echo 'A\nB\nC\nD\nE\nF\n' | hcut1
C
D
E
$ █
```

This version of the program relies on a logical expression to determine which lines are output. It is also possible to use patterns like those in ed to indicate a range of lines. For example, the ed command 100,200p prints lines 100 through 200. Here is the awk analog of this:

```
$ cat hcut2
awk 'NR == 3, NR == 5'
$ echo 'A\nB\nC\nD\nE\nF\n' | hcut2
C
D
E
$ █
```

In both hcut1 and hcut2, the awk program consists of a single pattern without an action, meaning the input will be printed for every line matched by the pattern. The first line matched by the pattern is line 3, the last is 5, so the range of lines from 3 to 5 is printed.

Obviously this program is much too specialized. It would be more useful if it accepted a command-line specification of which lines to print. This requirement leads directly into confusing territory; the shell uses the notation $1 to indicate the first command-line parameter, while awk uses the same symbol to refer to the first word on the current input line. If we are to supply command-line parameters to hcut, we need to let the shell perform its parameter substitution without interfering with the awk script. One way to do this is to leave the shell positional parameters outside of the protection of the single quotes. Another approach, shown in the following example, is to store the shell's positional parameters in named variables. This avoids the issue of the dual meanings of $1 and eliminates the need for fancy quoting strategies. We have arbitrarily decided that if no line numbers are supplied as parameters, the entire input should be printed, and if just one line number is supplied, then just that line should be printed.

```
$ cat hcut3
case $# in
    0) first=1 ; last=1000000000 ;;
    1) first=$1 ; last=$1 ;;
    2) first=$1 ; last=$2 ;;
    *) echo "Usage: $0 [line1 [line2]]" ; exit ;;
esac
awk "NR == $first, NR == $last"
$ echo 'A\nB\nC\nD\nE\nF\n' | hcut3
A
B
C
D
E
F
$ echo 'A\nB\nC\nD\nE\nF\n' | hcut3 2
B
$ echo 'A\nB\nC\nD\nE\nF\n' | hcut3 2 3
B
C
$ 
```

Remember that the built-in shell variable $# is the number of parameters that have been supplied to the script. We used double quotes around the awk script so that the shell variables $first and $last would be substituted inside the quotes.

When a program is needed once and then thrown away, anything that works is probably good enough. However, a program that is used more frequently needs more attention. Hcut is a potentially useful program, but as written above it doesn't follow UNIX system conventions. Wherever possible programs (especially filters) should read their input either from the standard input or from named files. Hcut can't do the latter. Also, program options are traditionally marked by placing a hyphen in front of an option key letter.

The version of hcut shown above doesn't follow this convention. All these faults are remedied in the following version of hcut. It accepts two options, *-f first* and *-l last*, to specify the range of lines. We've used getopts to process the command line, which produces a compact and elegant script.

```
$ cat hcut4
first=1
last=1000000
while getopts f:l: op
do
 case $op in
  f) first=$OPTARG ;;
  l) last=$OPTARG ;;
 esac
done
shift `expr $OPTIND - 1`
#
awk "NR == $first, NR == $last" "$@"
$ echo 'A\nB\nC\nD\nE\nF\n' | hcut4
A
B
C
D
E
F
$ echo 'A\nB\nC\nD\nE\nF\n' | hcut4 -f 4
D
E
F
$ echo 'A\nB\nC\nD\nE\nF\n' | hcut4 -f 4 -l 5
D
E
$
```

Notice that the awk command line is passed a list of files in the $@ shell variable. If this list is empty, awk will read from the standard input.

We've already seen that the awk script can be supplied as the first argument on the command line:

```
$ date | awk '{ print $3 }'
25
$
```

But what we haven't seen yet is that the awk script can also be supplied in a separate file. To use a script in a separate file, you use awk's -f command-line option. The word after the -f must be the name of the file that contains the awk script.

```
$ cat prarg3.awk
{ print $3 }
$ date | awk -f prarg3.awk
25
$
```

In either form of the command, file names can be mentioned on the tail end of the command line if you want awk to read its input from named files instead of from the standard input.

13.2 Flow of Control Statements

The preceding awk scripts exhibit some intelligence, but much more powerful scripts are possible using awk's flow of control primitives. Like many common programming languages, awk has if statements, and while and for loops. As in C, curly braces can be used to group statements together. All of awk's flow of control statements are listed in Table 13.2.

13.2.1 The If Statement

An if statement is used to select between alternatives. An if statement contains an expression that is tested. If the expression is true, the associated statement (or statements) is executed. If the expression is false, the alternate else statement, if supplied, is executed.

Here is a simple example that uses an if statement to process graphics data. It comes from a 3-D computer graphics system for making line drawings. In this system a line drawing consists of just two elements: lines and points. The lines can be visible or dark. You could draw a dashed line by alternating dark and visible segments. The data files for this system are plain text files with one point or line specified on each line of text. They follow these conventions:

■ Dark vectors are represented by x, y, z coordinates followed by a zero.

■ Visible vectors contain x, y, z coordinates followed by a one.

■ Points are represented by x, y, z coordinates followed by a two.

The coordinates are the end points of the vectors, the starting point of each is the end point of the previous vector, with the starting point of the first vector assumed to be zero. For example, here's a data file that draws a square with a point in the center (see Figure 13.1):

```
$ cat sdata
100 100 0 0
100 200 0 1
200 200 0 1
200 100 0 1
100 100 0 1
150 150 0 2
$
```

When printed versions are made of these line drawings, the points are often much harder to see than on the interactive display. That's why we wrote an awk script to convert points into small triangles that are easier to see. Here

Table 13.2 ■ Awk Flow of Control Statements

```
{ statement ; statement . . . }
```
A list of statements in curly brackets is treated as a single statement.
```
if ( expression ) statement [ else statement ]
```
An if conditional will execute the given statement if the expression is true. Otherwise the optional else clause's statement, if present, will be executed.
```
while ( expression ) statement
```
A while loop will first test *expression*. If it is true, it will execute *statement* and then repeat. Execution stops when the expression becomes false. The *statement* won't be executed if the *expression* is initially false.
```
do statement while ( expression )
```
A do loop will first execute *statement*, and then it will test *expression*. If *expression* is true, the statement will be executed again, and so on, until *expression* becomes false. The *statement* of a do loop will always be executed at least once, even if the *expression* is initially false.
```
for ( expr1; expr2; expr3 ) statement
```
This form of the for loop is usually used to step a control variable through a sequence of values. It is closely equivalent to the following while loop:
```
expr1 ; while ( expr2 ) { statement ; expr3 }
```
The only difference is that a continue statement in the body of the loop will branch to the beginning of *expr3*. (A continue in a true while loop would skip to the end of *expr3*.) *Expr1* is often called the initialization expression, *expr2* is commonly called the test expression, and *expr3* is commonly called the increment expression.
```
for ( var in array ) statement
```
This form of the for statement does the following for each element of the array: It assigns *var* the value of an index of the array, and then executes statement.
```
break
```
A break statement terminates the enclosing while, do, or for loop.
```
continue
```
A continue statement starts the next iteration of the enclosing while, do, or for loop.
```
next
```
A next statement reads in the next line of input, and starts the script from the beginning. (From the beginning of the ordinary part of the script; the BEGIN section is not reexecuted.)
```
exit [ n ]
return [ n ]
```
Stop execution of the script immediately. The program's exit status will be *n*, if it is supplied.

---

is a simple awk program that converts the point commands in a display list into vector commands to draw a small triangle centered at the point's location:

```
$ cat tri.awk
awk ' {
        if ($4 != "2")
            print $0
        else {
```

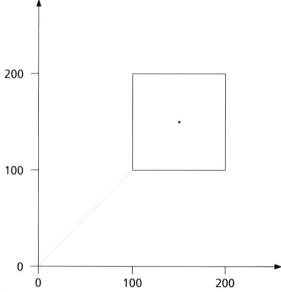

Figure 13.1 ■
The drawing produced by the display list commands in the file sdata, which is shown in the body of the text. The light gray line represents the dark vector at the beginning of the display list; it is shown for clarity and normally isn't visible.

```
            print $1, $2+12, $3, "0"
            print $1+10, $2-6, $3, "1"
            print $1-10, $2-6, $3, "1"
            print $1, $2+12, $3, "1"

        }
}' $*
$ tri.awk sdata
100 100 0 0
100 200 0 1
200 200 0 1
200 100 0 1
100 100 0 1
150 162 0 0
160 144 0 1
140 144 0 1
150 162 0 1
$
```

Notice that the four statements in the else part of the if are enclosed in braces so that they are executed as a group. The result is shown in Figure 13.2.

13.2.2 The While and Do Statements

A while loop is a repetitive flow of control statement. It executes either one statement or a block of statements repeatedly, so long as a control condition

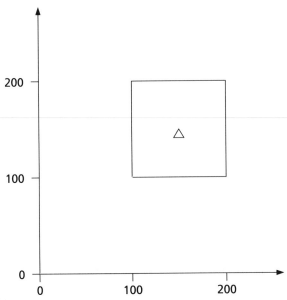

Figure 13.2 ■
The drawing produced when the tri.awk script processes the sdata file. Note that there are two dark vectors in this drawing; the first is the initial vector in the file, while the second is the dark vector that moves to the starting position of the triangle marker.

is satisfied. The following example produces a line-by-line average of the numbers stored in a file. For each line of the file, the program adds all of the numbers on the line and prints their average.

```
$ cat aveline
awk '
    {
        if (NF > 0) {
            sum = 0
            n = 1
            while (n <= NF) {
                sum = sum + $n
                n = n + 1
            }
            print sum/NF
        }
        else
            print
    }' $*
$ cat hits
11 3 44 10
13 -7
20 30
18 -18
$ aveline hits
```

```
17
3
25
0
$ █
```

The do loop is similar to a while loop, except that the test occurs at the end of the loop instead of at the beginning. This assures that the loop will always be executed at least once, even if the control condition is initially false. In a while loop, the body of the loop won't be executed at all if the condition is initially false.

13.2.3 The For Statement

There are two types of for loops in awk. In this section, we discuss the more traditional form, which steps a control variable through a predictable sequence of values. Then in Section 13.4, we discuss the second type of awk for loop, which steps through the indices of an associative array.

For a traditional for loop, there are three separate conditions that must be specified: the starting value, the final value, and the increment. Awk for loops follow the mysterious syntax pioneered by C. The word for is followed by three expressions: the first is an initialization expression that usually initializes the control variable, the second is a test whose failure signals the end of the loop, and the third is an expression that is performed at the end of each trip through the loop, usually an increment expression. The expressions are separated by semicolons, and any or all may be absent. Any introductory book on C can provide more information on the form of awk for loops—they are the same as C for loops.

Here's a simple for loop that sequences the variable i from 1 to 10:

```
for(i=1; i<=10; i++)
    print i
```

The expression $i=1$ is the initialization, the expression $i<=10$ is the test, and the expression $i++$ is the increment.

Let's move to a more interesting awk program that uses a for loop to print a table of the first ten values of N! (N factorial). Unlike the previous awk programs, this one doesn't read any input. The special BEGIN pattern takes over before any input is read, and the exit statement at the end of the BEGIN action terminates the program. Thus awk is more than a programmable text filter, it is a rudimentary stand-alone programming language.

```
$ cat nfact
awk '
BEGIN {
        prev=1
        print "N N!"
        for(i=1; i<=10; i++) {
            fact = i * prev
            prev = fact
```

```
                    print i, fact
            }
            exit
        }'
$ nfact
N N!
1 1
2 2
3 6
4 24
5 120
6 720
7 5040
8 40320
9 362880
10 3628800
$ ▮
```

The i++ expression in the for loop increments i by one. The ++ increment operator is discussed in Section 13.3 and is listed with the other awk operators in Table 13.3.

The break and continue statements are used to alter the operation of awk's looping statements. When break is encountered, the immediately enclosing for or while is terminated and control resumes at the statement following the loop. When the continue statement is encountered, it causes the next iteration of the loop to start immediately. The effect of continue is that the part of the loop below the continue statement is skipped.

13.3   AWK Patterns and Expressions

The key feature of awk is the way it combines a traditional, C-like programming language, with a powerful grep-like pattern matching language. The operators that can be used in an awk expression are listed in Table 13.3. Most of these operators are familiar. Perhaps the least familiar are the two operators for pattern matching: ~ and !~.

The ~ and !~ operators are binary string comparison operators (binary means they require two operands). Their left operand is a fixed string, which is compared to the right operand, which may be a regular expression. The ~ operator produces a True result if the match succeeds, while !~ is True if there is no match. Here's a simple example that demonstrates these operators:

```
$ cat match
awk '
/[0-9]/             { print "a digit is on line", NR }
$1 ~ /[0-9]/        { print "a digit is in field 1 of line", NR }' $*
$ echo 'a b
> a 1
> 1 a' | match
a digit is on line 2
```

Table 13.3 ■ Awk's Operators

++ - -	The autoincrement and autodecrement operators are a shorthand for adding one to (or subtracting one from) a numeric variable. Thus the expression x = x-1 is equivalent to x--. To a person used to the C language, this shorthand is clear and concise, but persons used to other languages may find it to be peculiar.
* / %	These conventional operators signal the operations multiplication, division, and remainder.
+ -	Addition and subtraction. Note that awk has three classes of arithmetic operators, all having higher precedence than awk's other operators.
nothing	When two strings appear side by side, without any separator other than white space, they are concatenated. That's why the statement "print 1 2 3" will print 123, whereas the statement "print 1, 2, 3" will print 1 2 3. Because of the precedence of arithmetic over string concatenation, the statement print 1 + 1 3 will print 23.
< > <= >= == !=	Awk relational operators can compare either strings or numbers, whichever is appropriate. If both operands are numbers, then a numeric comparison is performed; otherwise a string comparison is performed.
~ !~	The two tilde operators are used to compare a string (the left operand) with a regular expression (the right operand). The regular expression must be delimited by a pair of slash characters.
!	The exclamation point complements the value of an expression.
&&	A pair of ampersands denotes the logical AND operation.
||	A pair of vertical bars denotes the logical OR operation.
= += -= *= /= %=	Assignment operators take the value to their right and assign it to the variable on their left. The *op=* forms of the assignment statement are equivalent to *var = var op (expr)*. Thus the expression x + = 10 is equivalent to x = x + 10. The *op=* notation is a gift from C; while C cognoscenti may appreciate its brevity, others often find it too terse.

Note: This table is in order of precedence, from highest to lowest.

```
a digit is on line 3
a digit is in field 1 of line 3
$
```

The precedence of an operator dictates which operation should be performed first when several are present in an expression. For example, the expression 5 + 2 * 3 should be interpreted as "add five to the result of multiplying two times three" because multiplication customarily has precedence over addition. In Table 13.3, the operators are listed from high precedence to low precedence.

13.4 Arrays

Like most programming languages, awk has arrays. An array is a list. The list as a whole has a name, and individual elements of the list are accessed using the name plus an index. In a traditional programming language, such as C, the indices of an array are numbers. For example, if X is an array of three elements, in C those elements would be X[0], X[1], and X[2]. Awk is more flexible; the indices of an array can be any awk data type, including strings. Thus an awk array named scores might have the elements scores["mary"], scores["rich"], scores["redteam"] and scores["champ"]. (The quotes are necessary; scores[mary] will evaluate the variable named mary, and then use the value of mary to locate an item in the scores array.)

Another convenience of awk arrays is that the array elements are created as necessary, while the awk script executes. You don't have to tell awk how big an array you want or what indices you plan to use. Instead the whole business is taken care of as you actually use the elements of an array. Each time you refer to an array element, it is created if it doesn't already exist. The only limitation is that sometimes awk needs a nudge to understand that a given name refers to an array, not an ordinary variable.

Here is an example program that removes duplicate lines from a text file. Each time the program reads a line from the file, it compares that line with all of the lines it has read previously. If the line hasn't been encountered before, it is added to the list and then ouput. If the line has been previously encountered, it is skipped and the next input line is examined. This filter is a more powerful form of the standard uniq utility, which will only remove duplicate lines if they are adjacent. The drawback of rmdups is that it can only handle files small enough to fit in memory, because eventually the entire input is stored in the awk array. (Uniq will handle any size of input file.) Many current UNIX machines support virtual memory, and on those machines rmdups can handle large files, albeit very slowly.

```
$ cat rmdups
awk '{
    found = 0
    for ( i=0; i<nlines; i++ )
        if ( lines[i] == $0) {
            found = 1
            break
        }
    if (!found) {
        lines[nlines++] = $0
        print
    }
}' $@
$ cat dups
A quick brown fox
Jumped super-fast over
A quick brown fox
$ rmdups dups
A quick brown fox
Jumped super-fast over
$
```

Notice that the lines array has as many elements as there are unique lines in the input file.

Awk has a special form of the for statement that is used to examine all of the elements of an array. If you have an array such as that in the previous example where the indices are a numeric sequence, then you can use the usual (C-like) form of the for statement to examine the entire array. However, when your indices are more eclectic, the alternative form of the for statement is useful. Here is the syntax:

```
for ( var in arrayname )
    statement
```

The var will successively take on the value of each index in the named array. The order in which the indices appear is completely arbitrary. The for loop in the preceding rmdups program could have been replaced with the following for statement, and the operation of the program would be unchanged:

```
for ( i in lines )
```

However, in this case, awk might need to be warned that lines was an array by including a BEGIN pattern whose action simply stuck an empty string into an element of the lines array.

Here is an awk script that prints a list of how many times each person is logged in. This script derives its basic input from the who command, and an array called nlogins keeps track of how many times each person is logged in. This script relies on the fact that when an array element is created, it is automatically set to zero if it is used in a numeric context. The indices of the nlogins array are the names of the people who are logged in.

```
$ cat nlogins
who | awk '{
    nlogins[$1] = nlogins[$1] + 1
    }
END   {
    for (i in nlogins)
        print i, nlogins[i]
    }'
$ who
kc        pts000        Mar 15, 16:00
joe       pts002        Mar 12, 10:19
sam       pts010        Mar 16,  9:15
kc        pts001        Mar 18, 15:15
joe       tty01         Mar 18, 16:05
$ nlogins
kc 2
joe 2
sam 1
$
```

When the data has been tabulated, the END pattern's action prints the results in an unpredictable order. If you want a predictable order, you can pipe the output to sort.

It is possible to construct multidimensional arrays in awk by using string concatenation. For example, 5 "." 8 concatenates a 5, a period, and an 8, forming the string 5.8. X[5 "." 8] is a valid array expression. Any character could be used in place of the period. Or, you could use more of a row/column notation. For example, you could concatenate "R" 5 "C" 8 to form "R5C8", an equally good array index.

The new version of awk allows you to specify a comma-separated list of indices. For example, in new awk X[5,8] is a valid array expression. This provides a slightly better syntax than string concatenation. But at root, the two techniques are the same—only the syntax differs.

Here is an example that uses two-dimensional arrays. The task is to reverse the rows and columns of a matrix.

```
$ cat revtable
awk '{
    for(i=1; i <= NF; i++)
        x[NR "." i] = $i
    if (maxfields < NF)
        maxfields = NF
}
END {
    for(i=1; i <= maxfields; i++) {
        for(j=1; j <= NR; j++)
            printf "%s%s", x[j "." i], OFS
        printf "\n"
    }
}' $@
$ cat data
A B C D
E F G H
I J K L
M N O P
$ revtable data
A E I M
B F J N
C G K O
D H L P
$
```

13.5   Built-in Variables

Awk has several built-in variables. We have already encountered NF, the number of fields in a record, and NR, the number of records encountered. Table 13.4 is a complete list of awk's built-in variables.

You can tell if you are using the traditional awk or the new awk by printing one of the built-in variables that only exists in new awk. For example, new awk has a variable called FNR that contains the line number within the current file. FNR is not present in traditional awk.

Table 13.4 ■ Awk Built-in Variables

ARGC	The number of command-line arguments. (Only available in nawk.)
ARGV	An array of the command-line arguments. (Only available in nawk.)
ENVIRON	An array containing the environment variables. The indices are the environment variable names. (Only available in nawk.)
FILENAME	The name of the current file.
FNR	The number of the current record (line) in the current file. (Only available in nawk.)
FS	The input field separator character. The default is white space, which is either a space or a tab. Other common choices are commas, colons, and semicolons. You can assign a value to FS to change the field separator in your awk script, or you can use the -F *re* (-F*c* in old awk) command-line argument to set FS to *re* (or *c* in old awk). (FS may be a regular expression in new awk; it may only be changed to a single character in the traditional awk.)
NF	The total number of fields in the current input record.
NR	The number of input records that have been encountered. This total is cumulative across multiple files. If you want a count of records in the current file, you can use FNR (in new awk), or you can reset NR each time a new file is encountered using the following awk code: `FILENAME != prev { NR = 1; prev = FILENAME }`
OFMT	The output format for numbers. The default is %.6g, which will print most numbers reasonably. You can change OFMT to any of the numeric format specifications recognized by the printf function. OFMT applies to numbers printed by the print statement, not to numbers printed by the printf function, which is discussed in Section 13.6.
OFS	The output field separator. The default is a space. The output field separator is placed after each field printed by the print statement. For example, *print a, b* will print the value of *a*, followed by the OFS character, followed by the value of *b*. If the input is simply echoed, or printed by *print $0*, then the original FS will be preserved. (OFS may be a string in new awk; it must be a single character in the original awk.)
ORS	The output record separator. The default is a new line. It works the same as OFS.
RS	The input record separator. The default is a new line. You can assign any single character to RS in an awk script. As a special case, if RS is empty, a blank line will be used as the record separator.
SUBSEP	The separator character used in multidimensional array indices. The default is 034, an ASCII field-separator code. (Only available in nawk.)

```
$ awk 'BEGIN { print FNR; exit }'
0
$ 
```

We've shown the response from new awk, a zero indicating that no lines have yet been processed. As FNR doesn't exist in traditional awk, its output will be a blank line because variables that haven't been set are treated as null strings.

13.6   Built-in Functions

Awk contains functions for performing arithmetic and for managing text strings. These functions can be used in expressions, almost as if they were variables. Awk's mathematical functions are listed in Table 13.5, the functions related to text are in Table 13.6, while those related to input and output are in Table 13.7.

Here is an awk script that prints a small table of the powers of Euler's transcendental number e:

```
$ cat exp.awk
awk 'BEGIN {
        print "i e**i"
        for(i=0;i<10;i++)
                print i, exp(i)
        exit
        }'
$ exp.awk
i e**i
0 1
1 2.71828
2 7.38906
3 20.0855
4 54.5981
5 148.413
6 403.429
7 1096.63
8 2980.96
9 8103.08
$
```

Awk has a flexible and easy-to-use set of functions for managing strings, as you might expect from its use for text file processing. The index function can search one string to see if it contains a second string.

```
$ cat index.awk
awk 'BEGIN {
        print "substr", "sub", index("substr", "sub")
```

Table 13.5 ■ Awk Built-in Math Functions

atan2(y, x)	Returns the trigonometric arctangent of the ratio of its arguments. (Only available in nawk.)
cos(n)	Returns the trigonometric cosine of its argument. (Only available in nawk.)
exp(n)	Calculates the exponential of its argument.
int(n)	Returns the integer part of its argument.
log(n)	Returns the natural logarithm of its argument.
rand	Provides a random number in the range 0..1. (Only available in nawk.)
sin(n)	Returns the trigonometric sine of its argument. (Only available in nawk.)
sqrt(n)	Returns the square root of its argument.
srand(s)	Seeds the random number generator. (Only available in nawk.)

Table 13.6 ■ Awk's Built-in String Functions

gsub(*orig, repl, s*)	Same as sub, except that all occurrences of *orig* are replaced. (Only available in nawk.)
index(*s1, s2*)	Used to search string *s1* for an occurrence of string *s2*. If *s2* is found, its location is returned. If it is not found, the value 0 is returned. The index of the first character of a string is 1.
length(*s*)	Returns the length of string *s*.
match(*s, re*)	Return the index of the first occurrence of *re*, which may be a regular expression, in *s*, or return 0 if it does not occur. Match is the same as index, except that the second argument of match may be a regular expression. (Only available in nawk.)
split(*s, array, sep*)	Divides the string *s* into fields. Each field will be placed into an element of the array, using the indices 1, 2, and so on. If the *sep* parameter is supplied, it is used as the input field separator, instead of using the default FS. This function is useful when you want to separate an input into fields based upon several different criteria, when you want to access subfields, and so on.
sprintf(*f, arg1, arg2, ...*)	Returns a string formatted according to its arguments. The format string *f* follows the conventions of the printf statement. See Section 13.7.
sub(*orig, repl, s*)	Substitute *repl* for the first occurrence of *orig*, which may be a regular expression, in *s*. If *s* is omitted, the string $0 is used. (Only available in nawk.)
substr(*s, n1, n2*)	Used to extract a string from *s*. The extraction starts at position *n1*, and continues to position *n2*. If *n2* isn't given, the extraction continues to the end of *s*.

Table 13.7 ■ Awk Built-in Input/Output Functions

close(*file*)	Close the file or pipe connection. (Only available in nawk.)
getline	Read in the next line from the input and store it in $0. Getline's return value is 0 for end of file and 1 for success. Following a successful getline, the built-in variables NR and NF reflect the latest line of input, and the execution of the script continues at the statement following getline.
getline < *file*	Get a line from *file*. (Only available in nawk.)
getline *x*	Get a line and store it in *x*. (Only available in nawk.)
getline *x* < *file*	Get a line from *file* and store it in *x*. (Only available in nawk.)
"*cmd*" | getline	Run a UNIX command and route its standard output to getline. Each successive call to getline will return the next line of the output. This form of getline is commonly used in a while loop. (Only available in nawk.)
system("*cmd*")	Execute a UNIX command and return its exit status. (Only available in nawk.)

```
        print "sub", "substr", index("sub", "substr")
        print "substr", "str", index("substr", "str")
        exit
        }'
$ index.awk
substr sub 1
sub substr 0
substr str 4
$ ▓
```

Awk's split function can split the words in a string into separate pieces, much like awk's input strings are split into fields named $1, $2, and so on. The first argument for split is the input string, the second is an array in which split puts the fields of the input string, and the third, optional, argument is the field separator character.

```
$ cat split.awk
awk 'BEGIN {
        v = "This:is:a split demo"
        n = split(v, words, ":")
        for(i=1; i<=n; i++)
              print i, words[i]
        exit
        }'
$ split.awk
1 This
2 is
3 a split demo
$ ▓
```

13.7   Print and Printf

Awk's print and printf statements are used for output. The print statement is the simplest. It prints its arguments to the output connection. Print's arguments may be separated by commas, so that on output they will be printed as separate fields. By default the output field separator (OFS) is a space. If you don't separate print's arguments with commas, string concatenation will occur before they reach print, which means they will output together.

You should use printf when you need more control over output format. Unlike print, printf can output without appending a trailing new line, which allows an output line to be built up in phases. Printf also allows you to control numeric formats and to specify field widths.

The print and printf statements have several options that let you control the destination of the output. Ordinarily the output from the print and printf statements is directed to the standard output. However, the output can be directed into a named file using a notation similar to the shell's output redirection syntax.

For example, you can follow the print or printf statement with > *file* to direct output to a specific file:

```
print "Hello, world" > greeting
```

Similarly, you can write >> *file* to append output to a file, and you can use | *cmd* to pipe output into a UNIX command. The output connections are created only once, no matter how many times each print command is executed.

The following awk script is a blend of UNIX's col and split commands. It takes each column of the input file and writes it to a separate output file. If the input is in a file named data, column 1 is output to data.1, column 2 is output to data.2, and so on. A production version of col.awk would allow you to specify the field separator character; this version uses the awk default.

```
$ cat col.awk
awk '{
     for(i=1; i <= NF; i++)
          print $i > FILENAME "." i
     }' $*
$ cat data
1 2 3
4 5 6
7 8 9
10 11 12
$ col.awk data
$ ls data.*
data   data.1   data.2   data.3
$ cat data.2
2
5
8
11
$
```

Awk's printf statement provides more control than the standard print statement. Awk's printf, like the C-language printf, has a format string as the first argument. The format string specifies exactly what the output will look like, but it is left to the following arguments to specify the content of the output. The format string contains plain text that is output directly, plus format control codes that specify how the following items will be output. The format codes all start with %: %d to output a decimal number, %s for a string, %e for a floating point number in scientific (exponential) notation, and so on. The format codes are listed in Table 13.8.

Format strings can also contain special character codes, such as \n to output a new line and \t to output a tab. Printf doesn't automatically tack on a new line to the end of the string. Place a \n at the end of your format string to output a new line sequence, so the next output will be on the next line.

The following printf statement specifies that the variables x and y should be printed in decimal format, and that the variable named count should be printed as a string.

```
printf "x %d, y %d %s\n", x, y, count
```

Table 13.8 ■ AWK Printf's Format Strings

String Output

% *flag width .prec* s

> *flag* may be − to specify left justification. The default is right justification.
>
> *width* specifies the minimum field width. If it is not given, the field is the same width as the string. If the string is longer than *width*, the full string is printed, unless *.prec* is used.
>
> *.prec* is the maximum field width. No more than *.prec* characters will be printed.

Whole Number Output

% *flag width .prec* dox

> *flag* may be any combination of the following:
>
>> − specifies left justification. The default is right justification.
>>
>> + specifies a leading + for positive numbers. The default is no leading character for positive numbers.
>>
>> *space* specifies a leading space for positive numbers. (Negative numbers are always preceded by a − sign.)
>>
>> # specifies a leading 0 for octal radix, or a leading 0x for the hexadecimal radix.
>
> *width* specifies the minimum field width. If it is not given, the field is the same width as the number of digits in the number, plus one if the number is negative.
>
> *.prec* is the minimum number of digits to print, by left padding with 0.
>
> *dox* is either d for the decimal radix (base 10), o for the octal radix (base 8), or x for the hexadecimal radix (base 16).

d.ddde[+/−]nn Floating Point Output (%e)

% *flag width .prec* e

> *flag* may be any combination of the following:
>
>> − specifies left justification. The default is right justification.
>>
>> + specifies a leading + for positive numbers.
>>
>> *space* specifies a leading space for positive numbers.
>>
>> (Negative numbers are always preceded by a − sign.)
>>
>> # specifies that the number will always contain a decimal point. By default, the decimal point is only present if there are following digits.
>
> *width* is the field width. The width should be at least the precision plus seven (one for a leading + or −, two for the leading digit and period, plus four for the trailing exponent). Thus if the precision is four, width should be at least 10. (For exponents over 99, you'll need an additional digit, and for numbers that are positive and don't need a leading + you may need one less digit.)
>
> *.prec* is the number of digits following the decimal point. The default is 6.

The %e format prints numbers in scientific notation. The number may start with a sign character (−, +, or *space*). Then there will be a single digit, followed by a period, followed by *prec* digits, followed by an exponent. The exponent will be e followed by + or − followed by at least two digits.

ddd.ddd Floating Point Output (%f)

% *flag width .prec* f

> *flag* is the same as for the %f format.
>
> *width* is the field width.
>
> *.prec* is the number of digits following the decimal point.

The %f format prints numbers in fixed point notation.

Table 13.8 ■ AWK Printf's Format Strings (*continued*)

Variable Floating Point Output (%g)

`% flag width .prec g`

> *flag* is the same as for the %f format.
> *width* is the field width.
> *.prec* is the number of significant digits to be printed.

The %g format prints numbers in either fixed or scientific notation, depending on which representation is best. Style f (fixed point) will be used unless the exponent is less than −4, or unless the exponent of the number is greater than or equal to the precision (*prec*). If precision is set to the default of 6, then fixed point will be used for numbers with exponents in the range −4..5, and scientific notation will be used for numbers outside this range.

Here is an example showing some of the possible format codes. This example reads lines of input containing a format string and arguments, and then calls printf to output the arguments according to the format string.

```
$ cat printf.awk
awk 'BEGIN { FS="\t" }
    {
        printf $1 "\n", $2, $3, $4, $5
    }' $*
$ ▨
```

In this script, we set the field separator (FS) to a tab so that the format string can contain blanks. The result is that you have to type a tab in between each argument. Here's an example of entering some format codes by hand to demonstrate printf and the printf.awk script. (In the following listing, we've indicated each tab character with a small box.)

```
$ printf.awk
%s□Hi
hi
%5s□Hi
   Hi
%5s□abcdefg
abcdefg
%5.5s□abcdefg
abcde
<%10s> <%-10s>□arg1□arg2
<      arg1> <arg2      >
%5d %+5d□10□20
   10 +20
%.4g %.4g %.4g %.4g□1e4□1e3□1e-4□1e-5
1e+04 1000 0.0001 1e-05
$ ▨
```

If you try running printf.awk, be careful to use a tab to separate each argument; only use spaces within the format string.

13.8 Perl: Successor to Awk

In the late eighties, Larry Wall wrote an awk-like language called perl. It combined the features of the shell, sed, and numerous other UNIX utilities into a single interpreted programming language. Since its inception, perl has become one of the hottest tools for UNIX power users, and many people use it to do all the tasks they once performed with the original utilities.

The beauty of perl is that functions such as string operations, file operations, arithmetic, and so on, are all built into the language. This is more efficient than traditional shell programming, which relies heavily on spawning UNIX processes to perform most chores.

Perl is widely used and widely admired, but it is not covered in this book for several reasons. Most importantly, perl isn't a standard part of System V, which is our major guideline for making decisions about what to cover. In addition, the complexity of perl makes it hard to cover in a book of this size. To learn more about perl, read *Programming Perl* by Larry Wall and Randall Schwartz.

14
The Sed Text Editor

Sed is a noninteractive text editor. It is a powerful tool for performing routine modifications of text files, provided that the modifications can be keyed to textual contents in the files and provided that the operations can be done while reading forward through the file. For example, sed can delete all lines that contain a given text pattern, replace one text pattern with another on certain lines, read one file into another at certain places, or disseminate parts of the input file to output files. Sed cannot perform chores such as adding a column of figures in a file, performing sophisticated file reformatting, or storing parts of a file for later use. Those more sophisticated operations are ideal chores for awk, which is more programmable than sed. Sed's command-line options are listed in Table 14.1.

Sed is similar to ed, which correctly implies that it is also similar to ex, the line-editing flavor of vi. But there's also an important difference: sed is designed to be controlled by a script rather than by a person. This difference in philosophy has led to a difference in how sed operates internally. Whereas

Table 14.1 ■ Sed Command-line Options

`-n`	Don't output the pattern space at the end of each cycle. When -n is given, output is only produced when one of the print commands is encountered.
`-e` *script*	The -e argument specifies that the following argument is an editing script. Multiple editing scripts may be specified on a single command line. You can omit the -e flag if there is just a single script specified on the command line and no scripts in auxiliary files.
`-f` *scriptfile*	The -f argument specifies that the following argument is the name of a file that contains an editing script.

ed may course through the edit buffer each time a command is entered, sed browses through the command script each time a new line of text is read from the input file.

There are a few simple concepts that must be mastered to use sed. First, sed operates cyclically. A cycle usually consists of (1) reading a line of input into the pattern space, (2) executing the edit script, which may possibly alter the contents of the pattern space, and (3) copying the pattern space to the output. Note that this is simply the usual cycle; some of the commands in the edit script can produce alternate cycles.

Sed, like ed, has an edit buffer to hold the text that is being edited. The difference is that the sed edit buffer, called the *pattern space,* typically contains just one line of text, whereas the ed edit buffer contains the entire file. Although there are sed commands that let you stuff more than a single line into the pattern space, conceptually it is a single-line buffer that can hold lines containing embedded new lines.

Besides the pattern space, sed contains a hold buffer. Several commands exist to swap text back and forth between the pattern space and the hold buffer.

Sed addresses lines in the style of ed. An address may be:

n	An absolute line number *n*. The line counter is not reset each time a new file is processed. Thus, if the first file has 20 lines, line 21 is the first line of the second file.
$	The last line of the input.
/pat/	A context address matches any line containing the *pat* regular expression. Ed-style regular expressions are allowed: . (period) will match any single character except a trailing new line, ^ will match the beginning of the pattern space, $ will match the end of the pattern space, [*abc*] will match any one of the enclosed characters, * will match zero or more repetitions of the previous single character regular expression, and anything else will match itself. In sed, \n will match a new line embedded in the pattern space.

One of the hardest aspects of sed for experienced ed users is its inability to address lines using ed-style relative addresses. For example, the following relative addresses are not allowed:

```
+++
/sam/--
```

This limitation results from sed's forward-only journey through a file. Relative addresses sometimes need to back up.

Sed also doesn't allow the character . to name the current line. This limitation doesn't hurt, because sed always works with the current line, without use of special notation.

Most sed commands accept zero, one, or two addresses. Zero addresses means perform the command on every line, one address means perform the command on all lines that match that address, and two addresses means perform the command on that range of lines (inclusive). If the second address is less than the first, then the command is performed only on the first line. An address may be specified either by a line number or by a search pattern.

Any command may be preceded by a ! so that the command will be executed on lines that don't match the given address. You can surround a group of commands with { } to make them execute as a group. The syntax is one or two addresses followed by the { command, then commands on the following lines, and then a final } to delimit the end of the group.

The following example prints every 10,000th word from the on-line dictionary, which stores words one per line. In this example, the command script is stored in the file pr10k.

```
$ wc /usr/dict/words
   93371    93371   906255    /usr/dict/words
$ cat pr10k
10000p
20000p
30000p
40000p
50000p
60000p
70000p
80000p
90000p
$ sed -n -f pr10k /usr/dict/words
brazilwood
delusions
finance
incineration
miffed
photophobia
savior
suspensory
vermivorous
$ 
```

The /usr/dict/words file is not present on all systems.

14.1 Text Modification

Sed's text modification commands, which are listed in Table 14.2, resemble ed's. You can append, insert, or delete lines of text, change one group of lines to another, substitute one text pattern for another, or translate one group of characters into another.

Note that the append and insert commands allow only one address, while delete, change lines, substitute text patterns, and translate allow one or two addresses. You should also notice that the transfer and move commands from ed are not present in sed because they might entail reverse motion through the file.

Table 14.2 ■ Sed Text Modification Commands

```
addr a\
text\
text
```
    The append command places *text* on the output before the next input line is read. All but
    the last line of text must have a \ at the end to escape the following newline.

```
addr1,addr2 c\
text\
text
```
    The change command deletes each addressed pattern space, then outputs the *text*, and
    then starts a new cycle. All but the last line of *text* must have a \ at the end to escape the
    following newline. The difference between this command and the substitute command is
    that the change command changes whole lines while the substitute command can operate
    on parts of a line.

```
addr1,addr2 d
```
    The delete command deletes the pattern space, and then starts a new cycle.

```
addr1,addr2 D
```
    The variant delete command deletes the initial segment of the pattern space, which
    extends from the beginning of the pattern space to the first newline, and then starts a new
    cycle. D is equivalent to d if the pattern space contains just one line.

```
addr i\
text\
text
```
    The insert command immediately places *text* on the output, followed by the pattern
    space. All but the last line of *text* must have a \ at the end of the line to escape the
    newline.

```
addr1,addr2 s/expr/repl/f
```
    Substitute *repl* for *expr* on all of the addressed lines. The text of *expr* may contain regular
    expression characters: . will match any single character except a trailing newline, ^ will
    match the beginning of the pattern space, $ will match the end of the pattern space, [abc]
    will match any one of the enclosed characters, * will match zero or more repetitions of
    the previous single character regular expression, and anything else will match itself. The
    optional flags *f* may be: g (global) to make all possible substitutions on each line, rather
    than just the far left; p to print the pattern space if a substitution is made; and w *wfile* to
    append the pattern space to the named file.

```
addr1,addr2 y/string1/string2/
```
    Translate each occurrence of a character in *string1* into the corresponding character from
    string2. *String1* and *string2* must be the same length. This is similar to the tr utility.

Here is a simple example of sed editing commands.

```
$ cat remind
Janet today at 4.
Call DEC
add serial line for Brad
Home at five sharp
$ cat script
s/DEC/Dept. Environ. Cons./
/Janet/s/today/tomorrow/
```

```
1i\
Werner and Raquel this weekend\
Feed polly for adam
4d
$ sed -f script remind
Werner and Raquel this weekend
Feed polly for adam
Janet tomorrow at 4.
Call Dept. Environ. Cons.
add serial line for Brad
$ ▓
```

The sed script changes the abbreviation DEC into the more complete name, it changes the word *today* into *tomorrow* on the line containing the text pattern *Janet*, it inserts two lines in the beginning of the script, and it deletes the original line 4 of the file.

Here's another example of using simple editing commands to alter the remind file. In this example, the two commands in the script are supplied as command-line arguments.

```
$ cat remind
Janet today at 4.
Call DEC
add serial line for Brad
Home at five sharp
$ sed -e /DEC/d -e s/five/four/ remind
Janet today at 4.
add serial line for Brad
Home at four sharp
$ ▓
```

In this example, the script deletes the line containing the text DEC, and it changes the word *five* to *four* throughout the input file.

14.2 Control Flow

Sed has two kinds of control flow primitives. The most familiar is the branch, which changes the point of execution in the command script. Branches move the point of execution to a label, or to the end of the script if you don't specify a label. Sed has two kinds of branches: unconditional branches, which always branch, and conditional branches, which branch if a substitution has been performed.

Sed's other way to control the flow of execution is to change the ordinary operation of its cycle. Again there are two variations: you can either append another line of input to the pattern space, or you can prematurely start another cycle without completing the current cycle. Both types of control flow commands are listed in Table 14.3.

The following example demonstrates some of the flow of control statements. The sed script searches for the text .DS and prints an error message

Table 14.3 ■ Sed Control Flow Commands

: *label*
  Make *label* a symbolic name for this location in the script.
addr1,addr2 b *label*
  Branch to the given *label*, or to the end of the script if *label* is absent.
addr1,addr2 n
  Write the pattern space to the output and then read in the next line of input. Note that the next line of the script to be executed will be the following line, not the first line of the script (which would be executed if a new cycle were started).
addr1,addr2 N
  Append the next line of input to the pattern space. The boundary between the previous end of the pattern space and the start of the newly added line will be marked with an embedded new line.
addr q
  Quit writes the pattern space to the output and then halts processing.
addr1,addr2 t *label*
  Branch to *label* if any substitutions have been made since the last t or since the previous input line. If *label* is missing the branch will go to the end of the script.

if it occurs in the input. At the same time, the script will print all text between lines containing the text .EQ and .EN.

```
$ cat f1
.CX 3
.DS
Twas Sol and solstice
Ad and Astra
Til Hic saw Sum
In Corporate
.DE
$ cat script
/\.DS/b fail
/\.EQ/,/\.EN/p
b
: fail
s/.*/No displays allowed/p
q
$ sed -n -f script f1
No displays allowed
$ sed -e 's/\.DS/\.EQ/' -e 's/\.DE/\.EN/' -f script f1
.CX 3
.EQ
Twas Sol and solstice
Ad and Astra
Til Hic saw Sum
In Corporate
.EN
$ █
```

14.3   Input and Output

The input and output commands, which are listed in Table 14.4, let you control which parts of the input are printed and which parts are copied to other files.

The following script prints the nth line of its input.

```
$ cat line_n
if [ $# -eq 0 ]
then
     echo usage: $0 n [ files ]
     exit -1
fi
n=$1
shift
case $n in
     [0-9] ) ;;
     [0-9][0-9]   ) ;;
     [0-9][0-9][0-9]   ) ;;
     [0-9][0-9][0-9][0-9] ) ;;
     [0-9][0-9][0-9][0-9][0-9] ) ;;
     *)   echo usage: $0 n [ files ]
          echo n must be a number
          exit -1
          ;;
esac
sed -n -e ${n}p $*
$ echo 'one\ntwo\nthree\nfour\nfive' | line_n 3
three
$ 
```

The sed command in this script will completely read all of its input, which might be undesirable when you print an early line of a long file. The

Table 14.4 ■ Sed Input and Output Commands

addr1, addr2 p
  Print the addressed lines. An explicit print command isn't suppressed by the -n command-line flag, which only stops the default output at the end of each cycle.
addr1, addr2 P
  Print the initial segment of the pattern space. (The initial segment is from the beginning to the first embedded new line.)
addr1, addr2 r *file*
  Read the named file, and place its contents on the output before reading the next input line. The entire file will be copied to the output each time this command is encountered.
addr1, addr2 w *file*
  Append the pattern space to the named file. Each file mentioned in a w command is created before the script starts to execute, and there can only be ten output files used in a script.
addr1 =
  Print the line number on the standard output.

script could be updated to make sed exit immediately after printing the desired line.

14.4 The Sed Hold Space

Sed's hold space is its only extra storage space; you can copy text from the hold space to the pattern space and back. Unfortunately, this primitive storage scheme makes it difficult to write editing scripts that need more storage. Sed's hold-space commands are listed in Table 14.5.

The following script double spaces a file by printing each input line, copying the empty hold space into the pattern space, and then printing the blank pattern space.

```
$ cat lines
10
20
30
$ sed -n -e 'p
> g
> p' lines
10

20

30

$ 
```

The following script shows a practical application of sed, a script to insert cross reference numbers into documents. Managing cross references is difficult when you are writing large documents because document organization changes during the writing process. If you insert cross-reference numbers into your document too early in the process, they will probably need to be

Table 14.5 ■ Sed Hold-space Commands

addr1, addr2 g
  Load the pattern space with the contents of the hold space. The original contents of the pattern space are lost.
addr1, addr2 G
  Append the hold space to the end of the pattern space.
addr1, addr2 h
  Load the hold space with the contents of the pattern space. The original contents of the hold space are lost.
addr1, addr2 H
  Append the pattern space to the end of the hold space.
addr1, addr2 x
  Exchange the pattern space and the hold space.

changed later, to match the evolving organization. However, it's also bad to delay too long, because you tend to forget exactly what should be cross-referenced. One solution is to create symbolic names as you write each section in a document, and then use a sed filter during final document printing to replace the names with the correct references.

```
$ cat script
s/CABCBASIC/3/g
s/SCMDARGS/CSHONE.2/g
s/SMETA/CSHONE.8/g
s/CSHONE/4/g
$ cat doc
Chapter CABCBASIC covers the fundamental
features of the ABC language. However two
important features -- arguments and meta-
arguments -- aren't discussed until
Section SCMDARGS and Section SMETA.
$ sed -f script doc
Chapter 3 covers the fundamental
features of the ABC language. However two
important features -- arguments and meta-
arguments -- aren't discussed until
Section 4.2 and Section 4.8.
$ 
```

Notice that two substitutions are made to create section numbers. The first substitution replaces the section name with a chapter name and a section number, and then the second substitution replaces the chapter name with its number. This minimizes the changes to the script when entire chapters are moved. However, you need to be careful to write the script in the correct order, so that chapter numbers are substituted after all of the section substitutions in which they are used.

A related script of ours helps you to find all of the cross-references that have not yet been inserted into the cross-reference script. It is a simple shell script that turns the input into a list of words, performs the substitutions in the cross-reference script, and then prints any word that contains three or more adjacent capital letters.

```
$ cat capsfind
deroff -w $* | \
  sed -n -f sedscript -e '/[A-Z][A-Z][A-Z]/p' | \
  sort -u
$ capsfind doc
ABC
$ 
```

The output happens not to be a cross-reference; rather it is a fully capitalized acronym. (Deroff -w separates the input into words, sort -u sorts the list of words and removes duplicates.)

15
UNIX Platforms

One of the UNIX system's major advantages is its adaptability. The UNIX system was first used on computers that, seen from today's perspective, were slow, primitive, and restrictive. But over time, the UNIX system adapted to new hardware platforms as computer systems became more graphical, more interactive, more chatty, more roomy, and, of course, much faster. Other operating systems, built with less vision and less modularity, have had much more trouble adapting as new computing platforms have become popular.

A platform is an environment, a place where something can happen. To developers of application software, a platform is usually an operating system. Application developers talk about the UNIX platform, the DOS platform, the Windows platform, and so on. But from an operating system's perspective, which is the perspective in this chapter, a platform is the computer hardware that can run the operating system. For example, the Macintosh is a hardware platform; it is a range of machines from the primitive 128K Macs to today's powerful Quadras.

The Macintosh is a single-vendor platform, but most platforms are multi-vendor. For example, PCs have similar architectures and capabilities, and thus are a single platform, although they are manufactured by many different companies.

Evaluating a computer, like purchasing a car or a home, is an inexact process. The best you can do is to weigh the benefits and drawbacks of all the options, factor in the monetary aspects, and come to a decision. At the beginning of the process, it sometimes makes sense to examine a wide range of possibilities. But eventually, it helps to narrow the options so that you end up comparing, say, Florida oranges to California oranges.

The advice presented here will be helpful to you in the middle of the decision-making process. We're not going to start at the beginning of the process, where you try to decide whether the UNIX system is best for you. People who are reading this are likely to have already decided to use the UNIX system. But we're also not going to help you much with the end game, where you pick specific vendors, versions, and models. That sort of detailed, timely information isn't appropriate in a book, which has a relatively long production time, and a long shelf life, compared to the magazines and newsletters that specialize in detailed product reviews. What we are going to do is address the middle ground, so that you understand the criteria for evaluating UNIX systems, and so that you know the general strengths and weaknesses of the major UNIX platforms.

15.1 System Evaluation Criteria

Some aspects of system purchasing are quantifiable, such as speed or storage capacity. Other aspects are pass/fail, such as whether a system can run a certain application, whether it can use a specific flavor of networking, or whether the vendor is on an "approved vendors" list. And, of course, some criteria are very hard to measure, such as the prospects for continued support from the vendor or the reliability of the system.

15.1.1 The Herd Mentality

During the past few million years, many species survived because of the security offered by the herd. But today when people talk about a herd mentality, the implication is usually negative. Well, if you want to survive and prosper in the information age, you should consider joining the herd. If your peers all use Sun workstations, then there's very good reason to put Sun at the top of your list. If you're in a mostly Mac shop but you need a UNIX system, perhaps you should put AUX, Apple's UNIX-on-a-Mac product, at the top of your list.

Many people need to check out two herds. The first herd consists of your coworkers. These are the people you sit near, the people you have lunch with, and so on. The second herd consists of people who do the same thing you do, possibly in other departments or in other companies. If you're a financial analyst in a software development company, you may be better off with a PC version of UNIX (the platform of the same-job herd) even if most of your coworkers use workstations.

We deliberately placed the "herd mentality" criteria first in our list. For most people, compatibility with their peers is the most important consideration. But if you or your department is starting with a clean slate, or if you have specialized needs, then things are considerably more complex, as you'll see from the remainder of this chapter.

15.1.2 Communicating with Your Peers

The UNIX system is a communications hub; today few UNIX systems are truly stand-alone. If all you need to do is to communicate with other UNIX systems, then you're in luck, because UNIX systems from all major vendors support similar networking hardware and software. You obviously need to attend to the details, but in most cases the products and services that allow disparate UNIX systems to communicate are widely available.

If you need to communicate with non-UNIX systems, you need to be much more careful. In general, what you want is probably available, but it is probably not available for all flavors of UNIX. For example, if you need to access files stored on a NetWare file server, there are at least a half-dozen commercial solutions, ranging from Univel's version of UNIX, which supports both NetWare and UNIX protocols, to various third-party solutions, some of which run under NetWare and some of which run on certain UNIX versions.

15.1.3   Application Software

People buy UNIX systems because of the applications they can run. In the ancient past, people didn't worry much about what ran where because most software was delivered in source code form. When you have the source, most applications can be adapted by a programmer to work on a new UNIX system in a matter of hours or days.

But today most commercial UNIX software is delivered in executable form, and each application vendor supports a limited set of platforms. For example, if you need to use WordPerfect as your word processor, you should contact the WordPerfect Corporation to get a list of supported systems.

For demanding applications, there are well-supported platforms and then there often are barely supported platforms. If you're getting a system to run a specific high-octane application, like image analysis software, you should try to get performance figures for that application on the systems that you are considering. Applications vendors will rarely admit that their product runs poorly on a specific platform, but they will often do the next best thing, which is to tell you where their product runs really well.

15.1.4   Service, Support, and All That

Service, support, reliability, and longevity are intangibles. Yes, you can find out the cost of a service contract or the advertised mean time between failure (MTBF) of your system. But it is much harder to find out what happens if you have a repeated problem (i.e., a lemon), what happens if your model is discontinued soon after you buy it, or what happens if some key component, promised for delivery "real soon," ends up getting delayed or canceled.

When you're considering a system purchase, you should find out the cost of hardware and software support. For hardware support, there are often several options. The most expensive is usually a guaranteed response time, 24 hours, seven days a week. One notch down from that is usually 9-5 service on business days. The least expensive option usually allows you to return defective items for exchange. People often use the higher-cost service options early in a system's life, when failures and incompatibilities are common, and then switch to a lower-cost option when a system becomes stable and has proven its reliability.

Software support varies tremendously, but you should find out what it costs to get answers to your questions, and what it costs to get a steady stream of software upgrades and fixes (funny how we have to pay vendors to fix what was delivered broken).

The two clichés that experienced purchasers often mention in relation to service and support are that "big companies are big for a good reason" and "small companies try harder, so they can grow." We always keep in mind that every big company that we know has abandoned many products (and many users), and we have a lengthy personal list of small companies that we've bought from but that no longer exist. Perhaps a better cliché is that products that are popular are always well supported. If the original vendor isn't providing good service, second-tier vendors will step in and provide first-rate service. Unfortunately, my cliché only applies to popular products, which is another reason it's good to buy the same thing as the person in the next cubicle.

15.1.5 Graphics

Graphics is now a critical factor in computer system performance. Nearly all modern UNIX systems are running the X Window graphics system, which means that the responsiveness of your system is dependent on the power and speed of its graphics system. But more than responsiveness is at stake because there are big differences between the capabilities of different graphics hardware.

All Macintoshes, PCs, and graphics workstations allow graphics on the console screen. (Since about 1988, PCs have invariably included a graphics adapter. Prior to 1988, it was common for PCs to use an MDA display, which is similar in capabilities to CRT terminals that are connected to most minicomputers.) The details vary, but in all three of these platforms a region of memory is used to store the graphics image. Locations in the graphics memory, often called the *display buffer,* correspond to locations on the screen. A certain numeric value in the memory displays a specific color at the corresponding point on the screen (see Figure 15.1). Each separate point on the screen is called a *pixel,* which is a rough abbreviation of *picture element.*

You should pay attention to the following characteristics when you evaluate display options on computer systems:

- The spatial resolution, which means the number of addressable pixels in the X and Y directions. Typical resolutions range from 640x480 to about 1280x1024. Resolutions below 640x480 are difficult to use with graphical user interfaces. Resolutions above 1280x1024 are available but are most often used for specialized applications. High resolution is generally better than low, although systems with high resolution graphics work best with high-horsepower computers because there are more pixels to draw.

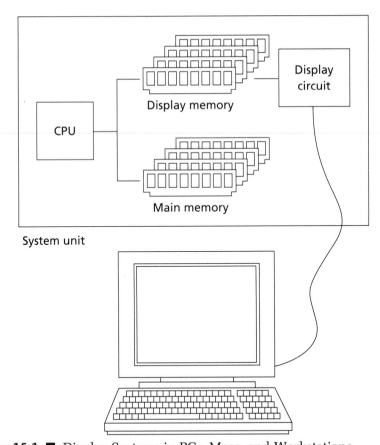

Figure 15.1 ■ Display Systems in PCs, Macs, and Workstations
Most computers with graphics use a similar architecture. The display memory, which stores the digital representation of the display image, is placed in the system unit, so that programs can access it as conveniently as main memory. The display circuit converts the data stored in the display memory into electronic signals that can be sent to a monitor, which displays the image.

■ The color resolution, which means how many distinct colors may be displayed. The color resolution is often implied by a closely related specification called the *number of bits per pixel*. Table 15.1 lists the common numbers of bits per pixel and the number of colors that is produced by each. Most people will be happy with 256-color systems, although people who are working with full-color images usually require higher color resolution. Higher color resolution is generally preferred, although higher color resolutions require more processing power to operate speedily.

■ Graphics accelerators. Modern computers are quick, but specialized graphics hardware is usually quicker. Computers that are used for modeling, image manipulation, and other graphically demanding tasks are often equipped with specialized graphics hardware that accelerates drawing operations.

Table 15.1 ■ Number of Colors that Can Be Displayed for Common Pixel Depths

Bits per pixel	Number of displayable colors
1	2
2	4
4	16
8	256
16	65 thousand
24	16.7 million

■ Three-dimensional graphics hardware. Computers used for modeling and other tasks that often render three-dimensional data on the screen often are equipped with specialized hardware that speeds the conversion of three-dimensional image representations into two-dimensional screen images.

If you are buying a complete system, then it's the vendor's responsibility to supply a suitable monitor. But if you are buying piecemeal or you're upgrading, you need to make sure that you choose a monitor whose characteristics match the characteristics of your computer's display system.

15.2 Performance

The first criterion for evaluating a machine is whether it will work for you, performing the tasks that are important to you. If it works, we move to the second criterion, which is how well those tasks are performed. Usually this means speed, because faster is lots better than slower. Of course a couple of weeks of evaluation on your desktop is one way to find the best system, but it's rarely practical, especially given the number of options today. So what's more often done for small purchases is to compare published performance numbers, with an eye to the criteria that are important to you.

When magazines evaluate computers, they sometimes reduce the whole evaluation to a single number for each system. This is generally a bad idea, because computer systems have a range of capabilities, each of which has its own performance. Depending on how you intend to use a system, you may be very interested in some aspects of performance but indifferent to others.

These are some of the common measures of computer performance:

■ Integer performance, which is the speed of the machine doing its bread-and-butter chores.

■ Floating point performance, which is the speed of performing floating point (real) arithmetic.

■ I/O performance, which is the speed at which information can be moved in and out of the system. Historically I/O performance was disk performance, but today it also includes network I/O performance.

■   Graphics performance, which is the speed of drawing operations.

You need to decide which of these measures of performance are most important and which are secondary, based on how you plan to use your computer. For example, if you are going to be running complex statistics on large data sets, the floating point performance may be the most important. However, if your statistics are done on more modest data sets, but you're constantly graphing and interacting with the results, then integer and graphics performance may be more important. If you're working with images, graphics performance is obviously important, as is I/O performance, because images are big. If you're primarily interested in office automation, then integer performance is most important, although good graphics will make life more pleasant. For most data base applications, integer and I/O performance are the obvious keys.

Computer advertisements often mention the computer's clock speed, typically expressed in megahertz (MHZ). For two otherwise similar machines, clock speed comparisons can give you a very crude idea of which machine is faster. For example, a 66 MHZ PC is likely faster than a 33 MHZ model. But is the 66 MHZ machine twice as fast? Perhaps for a few operations it might be. But for many other tasks, it would only be somewhat faster, and for still other tasks, like disk I/O, it would likely be the same speed.

When machines aren't otherwise similar, clock speed comparisons are meaningless. This is doubly true when machines have different processor architectures. For example, it makes no sense to compare clock speeds of a Silicon Graphics Iris Indigo, which is based on the MIPS 4000 processor, with a PC based on the Intel i486 processor. The Indigo, with a 50 MHZ clock speed, is three to five times faster, overall, than a typical 66 MHZ PC using an i486 processor.

15.2.1   Integer Performance

When you are evaluating computer systems, you will see many references to the machine's integer performance. What's meant by integer performance is not merely the speed of performing integer arithmetic but rather the speed of doing things that don't involve floating point arithmetic, input/output, or graphics. Integer performance is always important because it's a useful overall measure of a computer's speed.

There are several common tests that measure a computer's integer performance. One of the most notorious is the Sieve of Eratosthenes, which is a program that searches for prime numbers using a technique first outlined by the Greek mathematician Eratosthenes. Unfortunately, the sieve is a poor predictor of performance because it is a specialized task that only exercises a small fraction of what constitutes integer performance. Don't rely on sieve benchmark results.

Another common measure of integer performance is the dhrystone benchmark. The *dhrystone benchmark* performs a variety of tasks, and it was designed from the outset as a benchmark. The term dhrystone is a play on the term whetstone, which is an earlier benchmark for measuring floating point performance. Fast PC systems often have dhrystone ratings of about 50,000, while fast workstations often attain dhrystone ratings well beyond 100,000.

Another useful measure of integer speed is the SPECint92 benchmark. SPEC is the Systems Performance Evaluation Cooperative, which has developed several benchmarks. Don't confuse the SPECint92 benchmark with the older SPEC89 benchmark, which mingles both integer and floating point performance. Both dhrystone and SPECint92 are useful and accurate measures of a machine's integer performance.

15.2.2   Floating Point Performance

Floating point arithmetic is an inherently demanding task. The hardware and software for performing floating point arithmetic is far more complex than that for integer arithmetic. Today most computers contain specialized hardware for performing floating point operations, which is a big advance from the days of software-only floating point, but there are still vast differences in speed.

Some programs make little use of floating point arithmetic; others do little else. You need to think about your own tasks to decide if floating point performance is important to you. Of course faster is better, but how much are you willing to pay for faster if you will rarely if ever need it?

As mentioned earlier, the traditional measure of floating point performance is the whetstone benchmark. The *whetstone benchmark* is important because it is well standardized and because whetstone figures exist for most computers. The whetstone benchmark mimics the mix of floating point operations performed by scientific software.

There are two flavors of whetstone, single precision and double precision. Single-precision floating point numbers take less space and have a more limited numeric range than double-precision numbers. For most people, the double-precision measure is more important.

The SPECfp92 benchmark is a more modern floating point benchmark. It assigns the value 1 to the performance of the VAX 11/780 from Digital Equipment Corporation. Newer machines typically have SPECfp92 measures of 20 or more. Both whetstone and SPECfp92 are useful and reliable floating point benchmarks.

15.2.3   Graphics Performance

Even graphics performance isn't a simple issue. How fast can a computer draw on the screen? Well, is it two-dimensional operations, such as drawing text, lines, geometric figures, or images? Or is it calculating and displaying two-dimensional images, starting from a three-dimensional representation?

There are two common measures of two-dimensional graphics operations, grafstones and X11perf. The *grafstones benchmark,* whose name is yet another play on the term whetstone, is a generic measure of graphics performance. It can operate in the X Windows environment (see Chapter 16), or it can operate independently. If you're planning to run X Windows, the X version is probably most important. The *X11perf benchmark* is similar, but it's written specifically for the X Windows environment.

Any graphics benchmark running in the X Windows environment measures the performance of the whole environment, not just graphics performance. If you're going to be using X Windows, this is probably an advantage.

In comparing graphics performance, it's important to account for differing graphics capabilities. A high spatial resolution display will often draw images more slowly than a low-resolution display because it contains many more pixels. Similarly, a display with 24-bit color will usually operate more slowly than one with four-bit color, other things being equal, simply because it contains much more data.

15.3   Common UNIX Platforms

The major UNIX platforms today are minicomputers, Macintoshes, PCs, and workstations. UNIX is also available on many supercomputers, but that arena is very specialized and not discussed here. Similarly, there are some versions of the UNIX system that run on mainframes, but they are specialized, have met with limited success, and aren't discussed here.

15.3.1   Minicomputers

Minicomputers were the original home for UNIX. The traditional minicomputer system, shown in Figure 15.2, used terminals to access the computer. Today minicomputers are mostly legacy systems; systems that are working fine and doing their job, but that will one day be replaced with something better.

Most current purchases of minicomputers are for small business applications, in which access to shared data is important. Also, most minicomputers are sold by companies that also sell traditional big iron (mainframes), so minis often have excellent links to large systems. A minicomputer would be a poor choice for most scientific, office automation, or software development applications.

15.3.2   The Macintosh

Most Macintosh computers are used with Apple's own system software. But it is also possible to run Apple's version of the UNIX system, called A/UX, on most of the more powerful Macintoshes. When A/UX is running, you have seamless access to Macintosh applications and UNIX applications. A/UX comes with all the usual UNIX facilities, making it a best-of-both-worlds solution.

The Macintosh is a good UNIX platform only for those who also need compatibility with the Macintosh world.

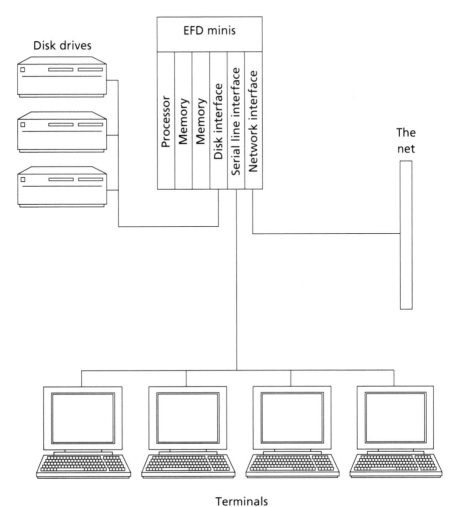

Terminals

Figure 15.2 ■ Minicomputers

Most minicomputers feature an expandable architecture that is optimized for multi-user operation. People traditionally accessed a minicomputer using terminals, although today minicomputers also support access via a network. Terminals are connected to the computer by serial-line interfaces, which typically transfer about 1,000 characters per second.

15.3.3   PCs

The UNIX system has been available for the PC architecture, starting with rudimentary versions of UNIX that worked reasonably well on the PC/XT in the early eighties. However, the immensely more powerful PCs of the late eighties and the nineties are far more comfortable UNIX hosts, which has increased the range of applications.

PC versions of UNIX have been used successfully for many small business applications. Usually, the system is applied to applications that today are called *group productivity applications,* in contrast to single-user productivity applications that operate well in the DOS and Windows environments. Many of these group productivity applications involve a data base that is shared by all the users of the system. We're starting to see a move to networked client-server data base applications that will replace some of these systems, but it's still cost-effective to have a single machine serve a group of people accessing a single pool of information.

PC versions of UNIX have also been used for training and education, and other applications where the "cost per seat" is a major concern. A UNIX system running on a PC, hooked up to a small group of terminals, is a very low-cost multiuser computing environment.

As PCs became more powerful, some people started to view them as workstation replacements. This has met with mixed success. Because the PC marketplace is vast compared to the workstation marketplace, prices are much lower. But compared to workstations, PCs generally have lower overall performance and much lower floating point and graphics performance.

PC floating point performance is lower than workstation floating point performance because floating point has never been a critical concern on the PC. Good floating point performance has been much more emphasized in the workstation world because workstations are often used by scientists and engineers who are keenly interested in floating point performance. PC graphics performance is lower because graphics is an afterthought on the PC. In contrast, graphics performance has always been a central feature of workstations. Both of these gaps are narrowing, but both remain.

Versions of UNIX on the PC usually allow you to run DOS and Windows applications using a software package called a DOS emulator. The DOS emulator provides an environment in which a copy of DOS can execute. Then the DOS software runs the DOS application. For many DOS applications, this process works fine. But some other DOS applications have been written to use certain features of the PC that are incompatible with running in a DOS emulation environment. Windows presents a similar set of difficulties and limitations. Many Windows programs operate well within an emulation environment, but some others rely on an operating mode of Windows that is not available within an emulator. Having access to many, if not all, Windows and DOS programs is indeed a boon, but if these programs are central to your work, you're probably better off running them in their intended manner, which means on a PC running DOS and Windows.

15.3.4   Workstations

During the eighties, the focus of UNIX activity switched from minicomputers to workstations. Supporting this transition were the networking enhancements to UNIX and the development of the X Window GUI software.

The role of a workstation is to provide a productive environment for an individual. The workstation architecture is both more encompassing and more elitist than the PC or Macintosh architecture. From the outset, workstations have embraced GUIs. But the goal on a workstation has emphasized

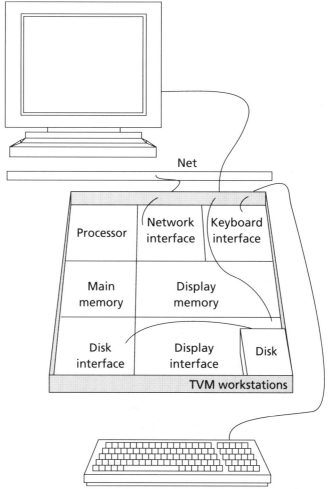

Figure 15.3 ■ Workstations

Most workstations place all the major subsystems, except for the monitor and keyboard, in a single box. The objectives are low cost and high performance.

the role of graphics in visualization and design, in contrast to the PC and Macintosh, where graphics was first used to improve ease of use.

Both workstations (see Figure 15.3) and Macintosh computers have based their hardware architectures on fast access to graphics memory. The visual result is obvious; both platforms enjoy speedy, responsive graphics systems. The PC was originally designed with very limited graphics capability, and until recently there was a hardware bottleneck that made it difficult to implement high performance graphics on PCs. Recently the hardware architecture of the PC has been expanded to eliminate the bottleneck, which will lead to an increasing level of graphics performance on the PC.

In some application areas, such as image editing and sophisticated drawing, the bounty of software for the DOS and Macintosh systems, which is usually available while running the UNIX system, may outweigh a workstation's generally higher graphics performance. In other areas, the workstation clearly is superior. For example, for graphically and computationally demanding tasks, such as scientific visualization and sophisticated 3-D graphics applications, the leading-edge software is written for UNIX workstations. Plus, workstations have inherently high performance, and they have specialized graphics accelerators that can have an impact on these high-end tasks.

Workstation vendors have always assumed that systems will be networked, in contrast to the PC and Macintosh worlds, which embraced networking much later, and which still see a smaller role for the network. However, when PCs and Macintoshes run versions of the UNIX system, they quickly attain standard UNIX communication prowess.

The same dichotomy of vision applies to floating point performance. The workstation makers' view has been that a variety of applications would be used, some of which would demand fast floating point performance. The PC and Macintosh view has been that floating point performance has little role in enhancing personal productivity. Consequently, floating point performance has received comparatively little attention on the PC and Macintosh platforms. People who need excellent floating point performance are usually best served by workstations.

The elitist aspect of workstations also has to do with both their price and their ease of use. The price has been high enough that workstations have been cost-effective only for a fraction of the work force. Similarly, the low emphasis on ease of use has narrowed UNIX's acceptance to those who are technically adept. Both of these problems are slowly disappearing, although there's much room for improvement.

16
Window Systems

The concept of a "window interface" is one of the greatest single advances in computer-user interaction in the history of computing. Using an ASCII terminal interface to UNIX, you can work on only one task at a time and are restricted to text only. A graphic window interface turns your computer screen into a virtual desktop; windows give you instant access to many tasks simultaneously. You can jump from one task to another simply by using the mouse to select another window and starting to work there. Use of both the keyboard and other hardware like a mouse or trackball lets you work with both text and graphics.

Most people, once they've worked with a window system, wouldn't think of going back to a dumb-terminal environment. The major reason is the convenience of the desktop metaphor. Having all your applications laid out in front of you, arranged as they suit you, and being able to jump from one application to another with the glide of a mouse, is a very intuitive and efficient way of working on a computer.

Another advantage is the user-friendly interface of programs written for a window environment. In the real world, everybody knows what a push button does and how to read a sliding indicator. Programmers use people's built-in knowledge about tools like these to create intuitive, usable human interfaces to very powerful, complex programs.

A third advantage is simply having multiple terminal windows available. Having what amounts to two (or more!) terminals on one screen makes jobs such as comparing files side by side a much easier proposition.

Another major advantage of a window system is the graphics capability. A bit-mapped graphics interface lets you see actual fonts in a word-processing program, on-screen graphics drawn as you watch, and so on. Spreadsheets, calendar programs, and network management packages are just a few examples of software that takes advantage of the graphics capabilities. Window systems have allowed UNIX to enter the office automation and business software marketplace and to compete with the microcomputer software that has always dominated there.

16.1   What Is a Window System?

The first commercially popular window systems were on personal computers. The best-known, and most influential on subsequent window systems, is probably that of the Apple Macintosh, but IBM's Presentation Manager and Microsoft Windows are well-known window systems for DOS machines.

A *window* is essentially just an area of the screen ("real estate") that is allocated to a given application program, which controls what is displayed within that window. Operations such as moving a window from one location to another on the screen, opening and closing a window, and layering windows on top of one another are some of the things that a window system does.

On personal computers such as a Macintosh or a DOS system, windows can simulate a multitasking environment; however, they don't increase the number of jobs which the computer can actually be doing "simultaneously." More recent operating systems such as OS/2 and Windows NT actually do support true multitasking. In either case, windows are a considerable time-saver for the user because they spare you the overhead of continually stopping and restarting applications. The context and environment of every task is retained along with the visual context of its window display; if you leave one window to work on a task in a different window, you can pick up exactly where you left off when you return.

Under UNIX, window systems allow you to interact with several tasks or processes at one time. As each process requires input or attention, you can easily switch to its window and provide what it needs. If a job doesn't require your input, it just runs in its window like a normal UNIX task.

In the early to mid 1980s, various UNIX vendors were working on proprietary window systems, such as Sun Microsystems' SunView and HP's Vue. By the mid 1980s, the X Window System, developed originally at MIT as part of Project Athena, had begun emerging as an industry standard. It was adopted and standardized by the X Consortium, a group of prominent hardware vendors, in 1987. If you're interested in reading more about its history and development, there are many books about X now on the market.

Today the X Window System has been ported to practically every UNIX platform, and it is the window system of choice for software developers because of its high availability. For this reason, our discussion of windowing systems will focus on X.

16.2   Window Interfaces: Some Basic Concepts

There are a few very basic concepts that are common to all window interfaces. They are the desktop or root window, application windows, the pointer (mouse), pointer focus, and menus.

The desktop, or *root window,* is the backdrop for all other windows; it generally takes up the entire physical monitor surface. Operations such as moving windows, closing them, and resizing them are all done within the context (and constraints) of the root window.

An application window is a region of the screen that is under the control of some application program. It's usually rectangular and may be "decorated" with a title bar, special controls for resizing, scroll bars, and so on, depending on the window manager being used (see more about window managers in the text that follows). The title bar, at the top of the window, usually also functions as a menu bar. Many applications also use windows or subwindows to display menus, dialog boxes, error messages, and so on (see Figure 16.1).

All window systems depend on the use of a pointer device, typically a mouse. The mouse pointer shows up on the screen as some kind of small symbol, most often an arrow. As you slide the physical mouse around on a mouse pad, the pointer moves correspondingly on the screen, allowing you to visit different windows. The button(s) on the mouse are used to interact with menus, push buttons, and other user-interface features of either an application window or the root window.

There is a standard terminology for mouse-button operations as well. *Click* means to depress a mouse button, then quickly release it. *Double-click* and *triple-click* mean to do two or three clicks in rapid succession. *Hold* means to press the mouse button down and hold it, often while doing something else such as moving the mouse around. Holding down a mouse button while moving the mouse is also called *dragging* it. *Release* means to let go of a mouse button that you have been holding down. *Shift-click* and *control-click* mean to hold down the Shift or Control key (yes, on the computer keyboard) while you click the mouse button.

Although it is possible for many windows to produce output at the same time, input from the user is a different story. Only one window at a time can receive what the user is typing (or mouse clicks and other events he may generate). The window that gets that input is said to have the *focus,* or *input focus;* it may also be referred to as the *active window.* The user is generally given a choice of how to move the focus from one window to another. The input focus can simply move around following the mouse pointer, or it may require a mouse click in a window to move the focus there; this second way is called *click-to-focus* or *click-to-type.* Most window managers distinguish the active window by darkening or highlighting its frame and/or title bar.

A menu is a list of items that can be selected. *Pop-up* menus can be called up at arbitrary points on the desktop or within a window by issuing a particular mouse-button sequence. *Pull-down* menus are anchored at a particular place on the screen, typically along a *menu bar* at the top of the window or screen.

Selection of a menu item can be done by dragging the mouse pointer down along the list until the desired item is highlighted, and then letting the mouse button up. Another style of item selection has the menu stay on the

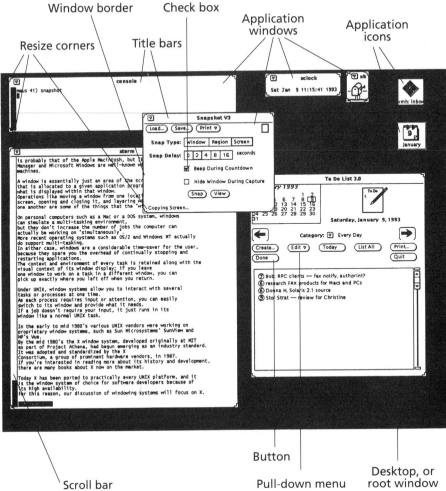

Figure 16.1 ■ A Desktop and Windows, Parts Labeled

screen (without you holding the mouse button down), with you then clicking on an item to select it.

Selecting a menu item usually causes some window operation to happen or a program to be invoked.

16.3   Window Operations

Window operations that are common to nearly all window systems include moving, overlapping, redrawing, resizing, closing or iconifying, and opening windows. Application programs should not be aware of, nor have to worry about, the way their windows are displayed or manipulated. In X, all these functions are performed by the window system and a special application called the window manager working together. In the following discussion, we use the term *window manager* to refer to this software partnership.

Normally a window manager provides a menu of window operations for each window it manages, allowing you to select any of the functions described here. However, it's very common for some or all of the operations also to be assigned to function keys (the special keys located in banks to the left and right of the normal typewriter keyboard or arrayed in a row across the top). If your window manager provides both a function key and a menu selection for a given operation, use whichever one is most convenient for you.

Moving a window is a three-step process. First, you tell the window manager that you want to move the window, and it prepares for the move by making the window track the mouse. Second, you move the mouse, and an outline of the window follows it around on the screen. Third, when the window is where you want it, you tell the window manager that you're through, typically with another mouse-button action. Then the window manager redraws the window in its new position. This is usually done entirely with the mouse: click in some appropriate part of the window's frame, drag the window to its new position, and release the mouse button. This process is easily learned and fairly intuitive, and it serves as a good example of why window systems are so popular.

When a window is moved, it may overlap another (note that some older, pre-X, window systems didn't allow windows to overlap; they supported *tiling,* where windows butt against one another). The window manager has to make sure that the overlapped windows are drawn correctly and that portions of a window that are covered up and then exposed are correctly redrawn. This means that it needs to maintain an accurate image of the window's contents at all times. Keeping this *backing store* can take up a considerable amount of memory and/or disk space.

A window that is partially or completely obscured by another window is said to be behind it. Most window managers support moving windows to the back and to the front on the screen. Under some window managers, giving a window the pointer focus also brings it to the front.

Making a window smaller or larger is called *resizing* it. All window managers allow you to resize windows, although some applications may not work correctly if the window is resized. An almost universal user interface for resizing is to have a resize corner on the window frame. When you click and hold the mouse button on that corner, the diagonally opposite corner remains anchored and an outline of the window changes shape according to where you move the resize corner. When you release the mouse button, the window is redrawn to the size of the outline at that time.

Finally, all window managers support *iconifying* a window, or reducing it to a small graphic image (an *icon*) that remains on the screen. Similarly, an iconified application can be opened back up to a full window. The purpose of iconifying windows is to reduce the clutter on a screen with many windows. Iconifying a window does not affect any application that may be running in that window.

16.4   Architecture of the X Window System

Although your own work may not require knowledge of X internals, there are some terms and concepts that will give you a basic understanding of its architecture. You should be conversant with X jargon if you will ever need to talk to a programmer to define requirements for an X-based application or read advertising literature in the course of evaluating or choosing commercial products. If you can speak and understand the same language the vendors and programmers use, it's much easier to know what you're getting, get what you need, and get the right kind of support.

The X Window System is a networked, device-independent system for windowing on bit-mapped displays. The overall architecture of X is a client-server model (see Figure 16.2). The X server is the program that provides the display capability, and it runs on a computer that has a bit-mapped display. (Some people also use the term "X server" to refer to the machine whose

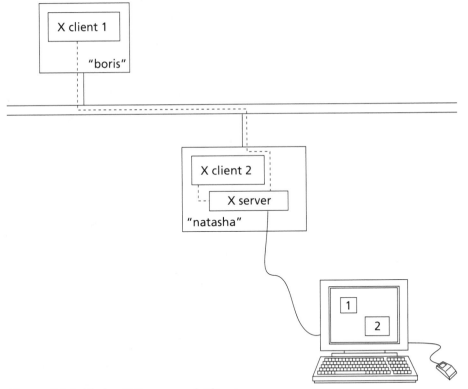

Figure 16.2 ■ An X Server and Clients

The X server program running on "natasha" manages its display hardware. Two X clients require a bit-mapped graphic display for their output. The X server accepts requests from X client 1, running on remote host "boris," and X client 2, running locally, and provides the display resource that each needs. Communication between X client 1 and the X server is done over a network connection, which most often is Ethernet.

video display is being used for X.) The X applications, or clients, are programs that may run on any host, but they need a bit-mapped display for their output. Although this client-server model sounds backward to many people, it makes sense once you realize what resource is being served: the display screen itself.

A word about hardware: the minimal requirements for running an X server are, generally, a bit-mapped monitor (which may be color, monochrome, or gray-scale), a keyboard, and a mouse (which typically has three buttons but may have as few as one or more than three buttons). Sometimes another device, such as a trackball or a graphics tablet, is used instead of a mouse; however, the basic function of all these devices is to control the position of the pointer (cursor, insertion point) on the monitor. More information about workstation hardware and configuration can be found in Chapter 15.

Most people think of workstations (machines with their own CPU) when they think of window systems, but there also exists a class of machines known as X terminals, which are kind of a windowing-system equivalent of dumb terminals. They have enough CPU power to manage a graphics display very well, and they function solely as servers to provide the display for X applications running on other hosts.

X client programs communicate with the X server exclusively through the X network protocol. A protocol is simply a detailed description of messages that can be sent between things (hardware or software) that need to communicate. There may be different implementations of a given protocol, but they should all be able to work together.

The X network protocol consists of two kinds of messages. Requests are things that the software asks the hardware to do, such as "draw a red line from point A to point B." Events report to the software about things that happen at the hardware level, such as a mouse movement or the user pressing a key. Every X protocol message is either a request or an event.

The X software architecture is multilayered (see Figure 16.3).

The first two pieces, the base X software and the X network protocol library, are used to build an X server. The remainder of the pieces may be used by X application developers.

The Base X Software

This software is the layer closest to the hardware, and it's responsible for several things. Most importantly, it does the actual communication with the display host's hardware devices or device drivers: the bit-mapped display, frame buffers, mouse, keyboard, and other I/O devices. Applications do not talk directly with the base X software; they may only communicate by sending X protocol messages to the X server (more about the X server later. See Figure 16.4). The base X software is device-dependent; it is reimplemented for each hardware platform and operating system on which X runs.

X Network Protocol Library

These routines essentially act as translators, translating X protocol requests into commands for the display hardware. They also turn signals from

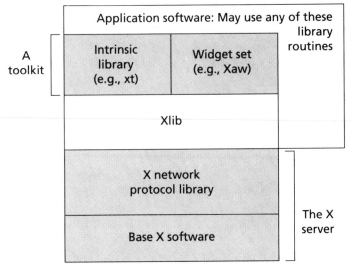

Figure 16.3 ■ X from the Programmer's Point of View

devices (key pushes, mouse clicks, and so on) into X protocol events, which the X server will send back to the application.

Xlib

This run-time library contains the lowest-level X functions that are callable by an application program. These routines translate client requests (in the form of high-level language data structures) into X protocol messages. In the other direction, they translate X protocol events into data structures, which can then be acted upon by the client. Xlib is part of the X Consortium's standard distribution.

Intrinsics Library

This is a set of object-oriented routines that implement basic functions; they are slightly higher level than Xlib. The most widely used intrinsics library is called Xt, which probably stands for "X toolkit" (compare this early use of the term toolkit with the definition of toolkit that follows). Xt is part of the X Consortium distribution.

Widget

This is a routine that implements a user-level entity such as a push button, a scroll bar, an editing window, or a pop-up menu. A widget is a high-level entity whose interface and behavior are very well defined and not subject to much, if any, modification by the programmer.

Widget Set

This is a collection of widget routines that are designed to work well together. Most widget sets are designed to help programmers easily produce

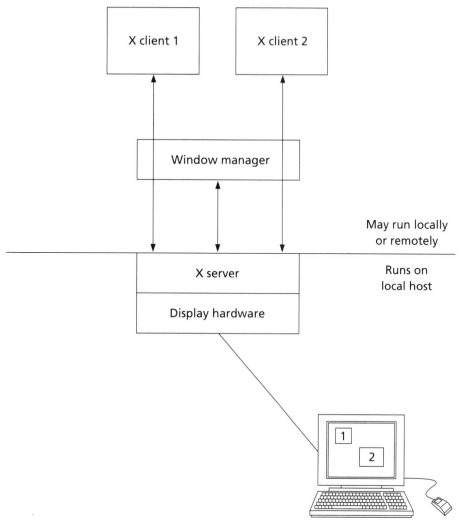

Figure 16.4 ■ X from the User's Point of View

The X server must run on the host with the display, since it communicates directly with the hardware. The window manager is normally run locally but, since it's just a special X client, it may run on another host. Other X clients may run anywhere on the network, or locally.

applications that adhere to a particular GUI, such as Motif or OPEN LOOK. One of the earliest widget sets, part of the X Consortium's distribution, is Xaw, the Athena widget set.

Toolkit

This is a high-level programming library, generally containing both low-level routines (such as Xt, or some other intrinsics library) and a widget set. Two well-known toolkits are Xm (Motif) and OLIT (OPEN LOOK). Writing applications with toolkit routines are less work for the programmer because they provide higher level functions than Xlib. However, they also impose a particular "look and feel" on the program and reduce the programmer's choices about the kind of interface presented to the user.

From the user's point of view, the X window system is considerably simpler to understand. It consists of the X server and X applications or *clients,* with one special type of client being the window manager (see Figure 16.4).

X Server

This is software that communicates with the display and other host hardware. It is built from the base X software and the X network protocol library. The X server must be running for X to work at all. The server acts as the clearinghouse for requests coming from all the applications displaying on its screens; it transmits and keeps straight the X protocol messages between each client and the hardware resources it is using at the moment. The X server also acts as a gatekeeper, permitting or denying access to the display by other hosts on the network. It caches certain heavily used resources (for example, font definitions and window structures), to cut down the amount of information that has to be passed over the network during an X session.

Window Manager

This is a special application program. The window manager is the program that most strongly influences the look and feel of an X session. Although applications have control of what is displayed within their windows, the window manager controls how client windows are decorated. Decorations include title bars, scroll bars, fonts, button shapes, and so on. For every GUI, there is at least one window manager that implements its look and feel.

Application (or Client)

This is software that produces output in the form of X protocol requests. For an X client to work, an X server must be running to service its display requests. Normally a window manager will be running as well.

16.4.1   X Fits Well with "Open Systems" Idea

One of the current trends in computing is that of "open systems." "Open" can mean one of several things. A product that runs on many platforms, or that coexists happily with other products, can be said to be "open" in a very general sense. More commonly, "open" refers to a product whose internal specification is made public so that others can develop products that use the same protocols or environment. Of all window systems in the UNIX world, X best fits the "open systems" paradigm.

The X window system has several important characteristics: it was designed to be policy-free, network-transparent, and device-independent.

Policy-free

The X network protocol defines a set of mechanisms or functions that a user might want in a workstation interface. However, X doesn't enforce any particular way in which these mechanisms are to be used; those "policy"-level decisions are left up to higher-level entities such as a window manager program or an application.

For the ordinary user, this means that X applications may vary widely in the way they expect you to interact with them (whether this is good or bad depends on how much you like variety versus consistency). For the software developer, it means that X provides a much more malleable set of tools and rules to work with than, for example, the Macintosh. The flip side of all this freedom is that the developer has to exercise good judgment to come up with a usable and efficient user interface.

Network-transparent

Because the X network protocol is equally well suited for use over a network connection or between processes running on the same machine, any X program can be used either locally or remotely (over the network) without reprogramming or even recompilation. This characteristic is called *network transparency,* and it's one of the keys to X's successful takeover as the de facto windowing standard.

Device-independent

This is a result of the design decision to restrict all X client-server communications to the X protocol. Since all X applications speak and understand the same X protocol, they can display on literally any machine that has an X server. Since the protocol is totally hardware- and OS-independent, it's possible (for instance) for an X client running on a UNIX machine to display on an X server running on a Macintosh or a DOS machine. Some capabilities may be supported in different ways on different platforms, but the X protocol itself is guaranteed to be robust and mutually understandable.

For the ordinary user, this property opens up a whole world of software possibilities. At an X workstation, you have access not only to applications on your own machine and other UNIX hosts but also to an ever-increasing array of Macintosh and PC programs with X interfaces. A side effect of this is that the CPU power available to a user sitting at an X workstation is practically unlimited. Windows displaying applications running all over the network can be at the user's fingertips.

All of these properties of X make it fit very nicely into the "open systems" paradigm, with the result that someone has written an X server for just about every hardware platform and operating system imaginable. In some ways this is comparable to the way (and the reasons) that UNIX itself became popular; however, in the case of X it happened much faster.

16.4.2   A Distributed Window System

X is a distributed window system, which means that the actual running of a program and the display of its output in an X window can be on two different machines. This flexible architecture is the key to X's dominance in the window market; it lends itself naturally to networked window applications as well as making it simple to create X applications that can work across a wide variety of hardware and operating systems.

Of course, the market has produced several competing flavors of X, where the distinguishing characteristics of each are expressed as a particular look and feel as well as separate programming libraries, or toolkits, unique to each. A term often used to refer to a windowing system's unique look and feel is *graphical user interface,* or GUI (sometimes pronounced "gooey").

The original implementation of X, from MIT, is sometimes called "vanilla X," or "Consortium X." The version discussed in this book is Version 11, Release 5 (known as X11R5). The most prominent GUIs available are the Open Software Foundation's Motif, and OPEN LOOK from SunSoft. The features of these two commercial GUIs and MIT X are discussed in this chapter.

16.4.3 The X Server and Display Connections

To use X on a workstation, a program called the X server must be running. This program initializes the display and input devices for use by an X window manager and applications and then continues running for the duration of the X session. Whenever an X client, or application, says it wants to use the local display, the X server does some validation and then opens a display connection for the client.

A *display connection,* which is a two-way communication channel for passing X network protocol messages, is established between an X client program and the X server that's running on the host where it wants to display its output (see Figure 16.5).

The protocol includes two basic kinds of messages. An application sends X protocol requests (such as "draw a red line from point A to point B") to the X server. The server sends X protocol events, such as mouse-button clicks, keystrokes, or mouse movements, to the application.

The other side of the X server acts as the intermediary to the display hardware. It translates the application's requests into hardware instructions and sends them to be carried out. In turn, hardware signals from keyboard and mouse events are passed to the X server, which generates the appropriate X protocol events.

16.4.4 Applications, or X Clients

Programs which do tasks in which ordinary people are interested (as opposed to internal operating-system functions) are called *applications.* Applications written with an X interface are also called *clients* because they are dependent on an X server to give them access to a display. One of the most basic X applications is a terminal emulator, a program that simulates a tty and allows you to work in the same way that you can from a real terminal. Such windows are sometimes called *virtual terminals.* You can have many virtual terminals on one display, running on the same or different hosts. The best-known vir-

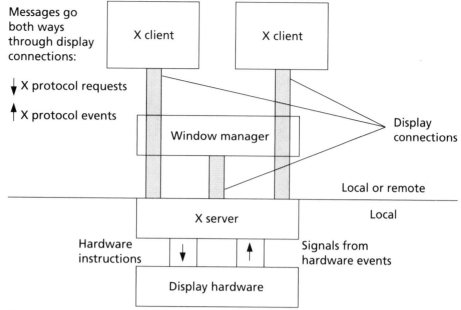

Figure 16.5 ■ The X Server and Display Connections

tual terminal X client, part of the MIT distribution, is called xterm; it emulates either a Tektronix 4014 or a VT-102 terminal.

16.4.5   Window Managers

A special kind of X client is the window manager. Its job is to manage the environment for all other (application) windows. In some sense, the window manager intervenes on behalf of the user: it intercepts X protocol requests and events that go back and forth on the display connection, modifying or augmenting them as necessary to reflect the GUI the user has chosen.

A window manager should always be invoked when an X session starts up. Running without a window manager is possible but not practical, since it's the window manager that provides you with the ability to move windows, pop up menus, and so on. The window manager is also primarily responsible for *decorations,* or the look and feel of the user interface: what window frames look like, what buttons look like, how scrolling of text is handled, what operations are supported on windows and icons, and how to perform them.

16.4.6   Compatibility: The ICCCM

Your choice of what X implementation to run can be influenced by what applications you want to use. Many applications are developed with the Motif look and feel, or with OPEN LOOK, and they certainly work best if you are running the appropriate window manager. However, even between different flavors of X there is a minimal standard of interoperability among X applications and window managers, so you can use, for example, the Motif window manager and run an OPEN LOOK application under it.

The protocol for communication between X clients and the X server is strictly codified in the X network protocol. However, clients also need to communicate among themselves (remember that a window manager is also an X client). For example, an application may need to tell the window manager that it has a preference for staying at least a certain minimum size. Another example is cut-and-paste operations between clients; this must be supported not only by both clients but also by the window manager, which acts as the agent for the operation.

The X Consortium has put out a standard called the ICCCM (Inter-Client Communication Conventions Manual), which gives a minimal-set guideline of the things clients must be able to communicate to one another and how to communicate them. Clients and window managers that are ICCCM-compliant are able to interoperate with respect to the functions covered by the standard.

A toolkit can support features not specified in the ICCCM, but programs written to take advantage of those enhancements will not be compatible with other ICCCM-compliant programs. A rule of thumb is that clients written to be totally ICCCM-compliant should work under any window manager. GUI-specific clients which use extra-ICCCM features may not work correctly under other window managers.

16.5   Starting X

When you're ready to start up an X session, the first step is to log in at the console of a workstation (or on an X terminal, but this discussion will be geared toward running X on a workstation). If you try to start X from an inappropriate configuration (for instance, if you are logged in on a dumb terminal or on a machine without a mouse), it will fail and print some error messages to your screen.

To get an X session going, several components need to be started: the X server, a window manager, and some initial set of X applications. On many UNIX systems, the program xinit is used to initialize the X server and start up your window manager and initial applications. Xinit provides a convenient and manageable handle on your own X environment. You specify which window manager to use and what applications to start in a configuration file called $HOME/.xinitrc. An example .xinitrc file is shown in Figure 16.6.

The .xinitrc file usually contains three kinds of commands: regular UNIX commands that adjust your environment for X; commands that invoke X applications, with appropriate arguments; and the command that invokes your window manager.

In Figure 16.6, the set path line adds the directory that contains the X client programs to the shell's search path. The xhost command tells the X

```
#!/bin/csh -f
set path=($path /usr/motif/bin)
xhost natasha boris rocky dudley
xterm -geometry 80x8+20+10 -fg red -C -title console -name console &
xterm -geometry 80x48+20+186 -title me -name me &
xbiff -geometry -221+5 &
/usr/openwin/bin/cm -geometry 920x550+20+100 &
xmh -geometry 740x760 &
xclock -geometry -277+7 -digital &
mwm
```

Figure 16.6 ■ A Sample .xinitrc File

server that client programs running on the four named machines have permission to use the local display. The next six lines start up various X applications. Xterm is a virtual terminal, or terminal emulator. The first xterm, as you can tell from the options, is started up as the console window; error messages and other system-level information will appear there. Xbiff is a mail notifier program (it beeps when new mail arrives). /usr/openwin/bin/cm is a calendar manager program that is written to Sun's OpenWindows GUI. Xmh is a mail handler, and xclock is an on-screen clock/date program. Notice that all the X applications are started in the background (as shown by the & at the end of each command line). This is the only way to start several processes that will run simultaneously. The Motif window manager mwm, started last, is not put into the background. When you exit the window manager, which is the only program running in the foreground, xinit takes care of terminating all the client applications and the X server.

16.5.1 If the X Server Is Started for You

At some sites, an MIT X11 program called xdm (X display manager) may automatically start the X server on every workstation. Xdm prompts for a user name and password, just as the standard UNIX login program would.

When you log into a workstation with an xdm-managed display, the X server reads a start-up file called $HOME/.xsession. It contains the same kinds of commands as the .xinitrc file, and it starts an X session with the window manager and applications you specify.

Only the superuser can set up a system to run xdm, since it is started at boot time. If xdm is running at your site and you have questions about how to use it, you should talk to your system administrator. If you are the system administrator, read the manual pages for X and xdm carefully; they are well written and should tell you what you need to know to configure your systems properly.

16.6 Customizing X

The application commands in Figure 16.6 are shown with relatively few options compared to what you might see in an actual .xinitrc file. The manual page for every X command will tell exactly what options it uses and what each one does. However, there are some common options that many X applications use. Table 16.1 lists some of the most important and universally supported.

The most important option is the one telling which display to use. The argument is a display specification as described in Section 16.7. If you set the DISPLAY environment variable, you need not provide this option; however, a -display option on the command line overrides $DISPLAY.

In the geometry examples in Table 16.1, 80x24 specifies a window size of 80 horizontally and 24 vertically. This is a common geometry specification for a virtual terminal window and is almost certainly in characters rather than pixels (the manual page for any application will tell how it interprets size specifications). 780x720 + 20 + 35 specifies a 780x720 (probably pixels) window, whose upper-left corner is 20 pixels from the left edge and 35 pixels from the top edge of the root window (desktop). Negative coordinates indicate distance from the right or bottom edge of the desktop, respectively, using the intuitively appropriate corner as the reference point. Thus, the 780x720-20 + 35 geometry places the window's upper-right corner 20 pixels from the right edge and 35 pixels from the top.

Foreground and background colors are frequently settable on the command line. The background is the basic color of the application window, not including the frame, title bar, and any other parts supplied by the window manager. The foreground is the text and any graphic designs rendered in the window. There are several standard ways for specifying colors: by name; as

Table 16.1 ■ Common Command-line Options for X Applications

Option	Example argument	Meaning
-display	unix:0	What display to use for this application's output and input
-geometry	80x24 780x720 + 20 + 35 780x720-20 + 35	Size, and possibly location coordinates, of a window. Sizes may either be pixels or characters; coordinates are always in pixels.
-foreground -fg -background -bg -font -fn	black black red red lucidasanstypewriter-bold-14 lucidasanstypewriter-bold-14	What color to use for the characters and graphics drawn in the window What color to use for the window background What text font to use
-name -title	console "My console window"	Name assigned to the window Title displayed in title bar of the window

a set of three numbers representing the red, green, and blue (RGB) values; or as a single hexadecimal RGB value. The command showrgb should show the list of X color names defined on your system and their RGB values. Warning: This list is likely to be quite long!

The font option tells what typeface and size to use for the text within a window. Fully-qualified font names can get very long and complicated, such as `-b&h-lucida-bold-r-normal-sans-0-0-75-75-p-0-iso8859-1`, or `-jis-fixed-medium-r-normal--16-110-100-100-c-160-jisx0208.19 83-0`. To find out what all of those numbers represent, read the chapter on fonts in any book on X. Some fonts have short names, like the one in Table 16.1. The command xlsfonts should list all X fonts available on your system. Warning: This list is also likely to be quite long!

The name option lets you assign a name to an individual window; the name can then be used to assign resources to that specific window (see Section 16.6.1).

The title option lets you specify a string to be displayed in the title bar of the window. The difference between this and the name option is that title is purely cosmetic, while name can be used to assign resources.

16.6.1 X Resources

You can customize practically everything about an X program's appearance and behavior by using X resources. A resource is a characteristic such as color, font, button shape, and so on. The naming of resources is hierarchical, so that you can set resources either broadly or very specifically. Each X program determines the structure and hierarchy of its own resource names, but most follow a common pattern. A well-written manual page for an X program should describe its resources, both their exact names and hierarchy, and the values each resource may have.

An example of a specific resource setting is Mwm*client*title* foreground=black. The first component of a resource name is either an application program name or the name of a particular window as assigned by the name option. In this example, it is an application name: mwm, the motif window manager. The second part says this resource applies only to mwm clients; the third component limits it further, to the title bars of client windows; and the last component nails it down to the foreground color. The value of this resource would be an X color, as described in the preceding text.

A similar resource specification but with a broader area of influence would be Mwm*foreground=black. This sets the foreground color for all mwm icons, client windows, window frames, and dialog boxes; that is, everything within mwm's purview that has a foreground color to set.

A specific resource setting will override a broader one; for example, the combination of Mwm*foreground=black and Mwm*client*title* foreground=blue would result in blue printing in client title bars but black printing in all other contexts.

Resources can be stored in one of several configuration files. Figure 16.7 shows a file called $HOME/.Xdefaults which is consulted by most X applications when they start up. You may store resource settings for any X program there too.

Resource settings for a particular X program can be stored in an application defaults file. Each file is named after its application, usually with the first letter capitalized; for example, Mwm. The defaults file delivered with an X program is usually kept in a well-known directory, such as /usr/lib/X11/app-defaults or /usr/openwin/lib/app-defaults. You can create your own app-defaults files and store them in a directory named in the environment variable XAPPLRESDIR (X application resources directory).

For example, you might have a directory named $HOME/app-defaults that contains app-defaults files Mwm and Xterm. In your .cshrc or .login file, you would type *setenv XAPPLRESDIR $HOME/app-defaults*. Whenever you start mwm, it will consult $XAPPLRESDIR/Mwm and use the resource definitions it finds there.

The X server can also maintain an internal resource data base, which is applied to every application program it starts. To load resource definitions directly into the running X server, use the command *xrdb -load $HOME/.Xdefaults*. Actually, you can put any file name after the -load option; see the xrdb manual page on your system for other options. A good place to run the xrdb command is in your .xinitrc file so that you won't have to remember to run it every time you start X.

Having the X server cache your resource data base is useful if you ever want to run an X client on a remote machine where you don't or can't have an .Xdefaults file, such as a Macintosh. The (locally running) X server can apply your resource preferences even though the client doesn't know anything about them.

With all these different ways and places for setting X resources, which ones take precedence? Here is the usual order in which resource data bases are searched, from first to last:

```
xterm*fullcursor:        true
xterm*vt100.geometry:    80x48
xterm*vt100.saveLines:   400
xterm*background:        MistyRose2
OpenWindows.IconLocation:        bottom
OpenWindows.Beep:        always
OpenWindows.SetInput:    followmouse
OpenWindows.ScrollbarPlacement: right
Scrollbar.JumpCursor:    True
*font:  lucidasanstypewriter-12
```

Figure 16.7 ■ Lines from an .Xdefaults File

- System Xdefaults file

- System app-defaults file for the particular program

- $HOME/.Xdefaults

- Your own app-defaults files ($XAPPLRESDIR/*)

- Resources specified through command-line options

If a resource is assigned values in more than one place, generally the more specific resource name wins; that is, the title-bar-specific Xterm*title *foreground = blue takes precedence over the more general Xterm* foreground = black. However, if the exact same resource is given different values in different places, the one found last is the winner.

16.6.2 Tools to Examine Resources

There are several programs that can give you information about the resources and properties of windows in your running X session. Programs designated (MIT/Motif/OL) are available for those flavors of X; (MIT/Motif; OL) indicates that OPEN LOOK has its own implementation of that tool.

Xwininfo (MIT/Motif; OL) lets you click in any visible window and then displays a lot of information about that window. An example of xwininfo output is shown in Figure 16.8.

Appres (APP-rez) (MIT/Motif; OL) is a command-line interface tool that displays the resource values that an X application will load, using your current X environment. The application name on the command line should be capitalized in the same way it would be when used as part of a resource name. For example, "appres Xterm" will show all the resources that would be set for xterm, using the combination of system resource files and your own personal ones. There are other options for using appres; read the manual page for more details. Sample appres output is shown in Figure 16.9.

In the sample output, note that there are two definitions for the font resource. Because Xmh*font is more specific than *font, its value is used for xmh windows.

Editres (MIT/Motif) is a graphical-interface tool for exploring the widget tree from which an application is built and reading and setting X resources. Its usefulness is limited to applications built with the Athena widget set, but there are many of those.

The xprop (MIT/Motif; OL) command is a command-line interface tool that displays information about a window from the window manager's point of view. Much of the information is of little interest to the average user, but it might be a helpful starting point in figuring out window manager or application mysteries. Sample xprop output is shown in Figure 16.10.

The easiest way to find out how these tools work is to start an X session, play with the tools and see what they tell you, and then read their manual pages to find out more about whatever looks interesting.

```
xwininfo: Window id: 0x1400006 "xbiff"

    Absolute upper-left X:   881
    Absolute upper-left Y:   7
    Relative upper-left X:   0
    Relative upper-left Y:   0
    Width: 48
    Height: 48
    Depth: 1
    Visual Class: StaticGray
    Border width: 0
    Class: InputOutput
    Colormap: 0x21 (installed)
    Bit Gravity State: NorthWestGravity
    Window Gravity State: NorthWestGravity
    Backing Store State: NotUseful
    Save Under State: no
    Map State: IsViewable
    Override Redirect State: no
    Corners:   +881+7   -223+7   -223-845   +881-845
    -geometry 48x48+0+0
```

Figure 16.8 ■ Xwininfo Output

16.7   The X Display

When you start an X application, you have to tell it where to display its output. "Where" in this case means a combination of which host, which station on that host, and possibly which screen at that station.

A station is defined as a complete monitor-keyboard-mouse configuration; the vast majority of hosts have only one station. A screen, in this context, is a display associated with a station. Most stations have only a single screen, but some may have two or even more; one of these will be the default screen for that station, and its ID will be 0. Also, some stations may have only a single physical monitor but two or more frame buffers that can be displayed on the monitor; these are also treated as separate screens.

A display specification looks like *hostname:station[.screen]*. In Figure 16.11, the first three examples use actual hostnames, and illustrate a host with one station, one with multiple stations, and one with a single station that has multiple screens. The final example uses the generic hostname "unix," which always refers to the local host. The conventional specification for the default local display is "unix:0." Completely omitting the hostname, for example, ":0," also refers to the local host.

The X architecture, and specifically its network transparency, provides enough flexibility to start an application on any machine on the network and have it display on any other host running an X server. In practice, there is

```
(many lines omitted)
Xmh*view.Accelerators:    #override\n\
        !:<Key>space:      next-page()\n\
        !:<Key>b:          previous-page()\n
Xmh*messageMenu.Accelerators:    #override\n\
        !:<Key>c:          XmhMarkCopy()\n\
        !:<Key>d:          XmhMarkDelete()\n\
        !:<Key>f:          XmhForward()\n\
        !:<Key>m:          XmhMarkMove()\n\
        !:<Key>Return:     XmhViewNextMessage()\n\
        !:<Key>n:          XmhViewNextMessage()\n\
        !:<Key>p:          XmhViewPreviousMessage()\n\
        !:<Key>q:          XmhClose()\n\
        !:<Key>u:          XmhUnmark()\n
Xmh*sendWidth:   65
Xmh*font:        lucidasanstypewriter-14
Xmh.geometry:    =740x740
Xmh*CompGeometry:        =740x500
Xmh*MailWaitingFlag:     false
*font:   lucidasanstypewriter-12
```

Figure 16.9 ■ Sample Appres Output

```
WM_STATE(WM_STATE):
        window state: Normal
        icon window: 0x0
__SWM_ROOT(WINDOW): window id # 0x80002e
_TWM_FLAGS(_TWM_FLAGS) = 0x2
WM_PROTOCOLS(ATOM): protocols  WM_DELETE_WINDOW
WM_CLASS(STRING) = "xbiff", "XBiff"
WM_HINTS(WM_HINTS):
        Client accepts input or input focus: True
        Initial state is Normal State.
WM_NORMAL_HINTS(WM_SIZE_HINTS):
        user specified location: 881, 5
        program specified size: 48 by 48
        window gravity: NorthEast
WM_CLIENT_MACHINE(STRING) = "maus"
WM_COMMAND(STRING) = { "xbiff", "-geometry", "-221+5" }
WM_ICON_NAME(STRING) = "xbiff"
WM_NAME(STRING) = "xbiff"
```

Figure 16.10 ■ Xprop Output

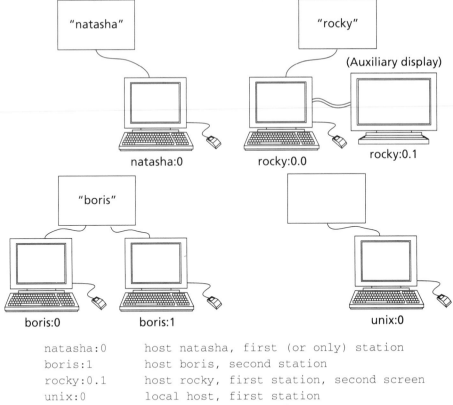

natasha:0	host natasha, first (or only) station
boris:1	host boris, second station
rocky:0.1	host rocky, first station, second screen
unix:0	local host, first station

Figure 16.11 ■ DISPLAY Specification Examples

almost never any reason (or sense!) in displaying anywhere other than to the screen where you are sitting. However, it is quite common to run applications on remote machines, so it is important to understand how and when you have to specify the display.

For most people, setting $DISPLAY to "unix:0" makes more sense than hard-wiring in a hostname, especially if you might find yourself working on different hosts from day to day. There are a couple of exceptions to this generalization. One would be for an application that requires a special display, such as a 24-bit color display, that only exists on one host. Another is when you are running an application on a remote host. You don't want to use the display that's "local" on the remote host; you have to provide a display specification that contains your hostname. For these cases, using the -display option on the individual command line is the way to override the $DISPLAY variable.

16.7.1 Display Permissions

When an X application is started, the display it will use is specified either by a -display option on the command line or by the $DISPLAY environment variable. The X server running on the display host has the task of establishing a display connection for each X application that will display there. Before doing that, it checks to see that the application is running on a host that has permission to use its display. You can't grant or deny access on a user-by-user basis; it's done solely by host.

In the simplest case, an X application running on a workstation will use the local display. A host always has permission to use its own display, but you have to tell the X server if any other hosts may use the display, using the xhost command. Xhost has to be run after the X server is started; the host list is maintained dynamically, only for the duration of an X session. You can either put an xhost command into your .xinitrc or other X start-up file, or issue it from a shell window once X is already running.

- **xhost** + *hostname,* or just **xhost** *hostname,* adds a host to your X server's access list.

- **xhost** –*hostname* takes that host off the list; and simply **xhost** displays all the hosts currently on the list.

- **xhost** + turns off access list checking altogether (which allows any X application on any host to display to your screen!).

- **xhost** – turns the access control back on, with the latest access list still in effect.

For example, say you want to run an X application (xtopmap) that displays topographical maps. This client can execute on only one host, rocky, which is licensed for the map images and the imaging software. From your host, natasha, you should start X and then execute the following command to allow rocky to access your display:

```
natasha% xhost +rocky
host rocky added to access display list
natasha% 
```

To verify that rocky has been added:

```
natasha% xhost
access control enabled, only authorized clients can connect
rocky
natasha% 
```

Now that rocky has permission to use the local display, you can use the standard UNIX rsh (remote shell) command to run xtopmap on rocky. Note the use of the -display option to specify that its output should be placed on natasha's screen, and the trailing ampersand that puts the rsh command in the background.

```
natasha% rsh rocky "xtopmap -display natasha:0" &
natasha% 
```

If there are applications that you use very frequently, you may want to personalize your X setup by adding menu items for those applications in your window manager configuration files.

16.8   Window Manager Configuration Files

Every flavor of X comes with a few default configuration files, which are usually installed in a system directory like /usr/lib/X11. Some of these configuration files are read by the window manager, some by the X server itself, or by a program that invokes the X server, like xinit. The easiest (and usual) way for a new user to create a personal configuration file is to copy the system default file to the correct location in his home directory, then modify it to taste.

Besides the .Xdefaults and .xinitrc files already described, each window manager has its own configuration file. Window manager configuration files let you specify your own personal menus or change the appearance or characteristics of windows or other objects under the control of the window manager. These files, as well as other special notes about each flavor of X, are briefly described in the following sections, devoted to Motif, OpenWindows, and MIT X.

16.8.1   Motif

Motif is an industry-wide standard for an X GUI. The Motif GUI specification was developed at the behest of the Open Software Foundation (OSF). Nearly all UNIX vendors, with the exception of Sun Microsystems, use Motif for their X products.

Motif was designed to look and feel very much like two microcomputer-based window standards, IBM's Presentation Manager and Microsoft's Windows. Motif tends toward an art deco look, with lots of 3-D effects on buttons, shading around boxes, and so on.

The Motif Window Manager, mwm, loads its X resources from a hierarchy of resource data base files, as described in Section 16.6.1. The default names of the resource data base files, and the mwm start-up files, are listed in Table 16.2. As with any UNIX product, these file names may be different on your system because of installation decisions made by your system administrator.

A sample of mwm menu specifications, and a picture of an mwm session using those specifications, is shown in Figures 16.12a and b.

Mwm has a number of built-in functions that you can use to customize your window setup. They are all named f.somefunction and are described in

Table 16.2 ■ Mwm Configuration and Resource Data Base Locations

	System default location	Personal location
mwm config file	/usr/motif/lib/system.mwmrc	$HOME/.mwmrc
Xdefaults	/usr/motif/lib/sys.Xdefault	$HOME/.Xdefaults
mwm resources	/usr/motif/lib/app-defaults/Mwm	$XAPPLRESDIR/Mwm
Application defaults files	/usr/motif/lib/app-defaults/*	$XAPPLRESDIR/*

```
Menu RootMenu
{
        "Root Menu"              f.title
        "Restart..."             f.restart
        "Quit"                   f.quit_mwm
}


Menu WeirdMenu
{
        "Weird Stuff"    f.title
        "Shell"          f.exec   "xterm -geometry 80x48 &"
        "To Do List"     f.exec   "xvtdl &"
        "Read News"      f.exec   "/usr/bin/X11/xrn &"
        "Mail-xmh"       f.exec   "xmh -geometry 740x760 &"
        no-label         f.separator
        "Calendar"       f.exec   "/usr/openwin/bin/cm -geometry 920x550+20+100 &"
        "Screen lock"    f.exec "xlock &"
        "Spider"         f.exec   "spider -geometry 910x840-168-3 &"
}


menu RlogMenu
{
    "Aux servers"        f.menu "Aux servers"
    "boris"              f.exec "xterm -title boris -e rlogin boris &"
    "natasha"            f.exec "xterm -title natasha -e rlogin natasha &"
    "moose"              f.exec "xterm -title moose -e rlogin moose &"
    "twain"              f.exec "rsh twain xterm -title twain -display 'hostname':0 &"
}


Buttons DefaultButtonBindings
{
        <Btn1Down>       icon|frame       f.raise
        <Btn1Down>       root             f.menu   RlogMenu
        <Btn2Down>       root             f.menu   WeirdMenu
        <Btn3Down>       root             f.menu   RootMenu
}
```

Figure 16.12a ■ Menu Specification in an .mwmrc File

detail in the mwm manual page. Some that are shown in Figure 16.12.a include f.menu to reference a submenu (which must be defined elsewhere in the file), f.exec to run a command (usually an X application), f.raise to bring a window or icon to the front, f.title and f.separator to add cosmetic text and lines to menus, and the intuitively named f.restart and f.quit_mwm.

Note the menu items for logging into remote systems, in the RlogMenu section of the config file. The example illustrates two ways of starting a remote UNIX session. The first way, seen in the boris entry, uses the standard UNIX rlogin command from a local xterm window. The -e option to xterm lets you specify a command to run in the xterm window: in this case, *rlogin boris.*

The second way (used for twain) takes advantage of X's ability to run a command remotely and display it on another system. In this case, an xterm

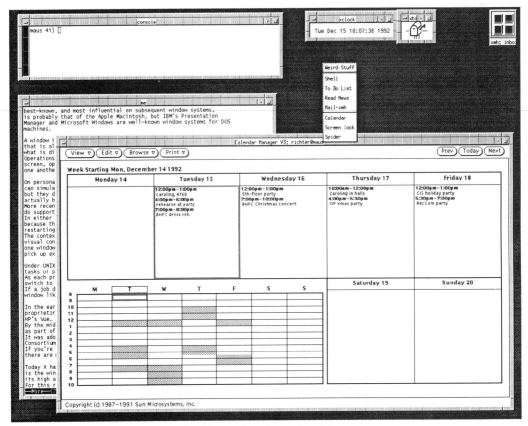

Figure 16.12b ■ An Mwm Session with Menu

is started on twain via the UNIX rsh command, and the -display option directs its output to the host running the X server. The *hostname* command in back quotes (or accent graves) returns the name of the local machine, and the :0 suffix specifies the default display for that host. Using '*hostname*' in the display specification makes a menu item portable, and is almost always preferable to hard-wiring a system's name. The example configuration files for olwm (Figure 16.13) and twm (Figure 16.14) show the syntax for both ways of starting remote sessions in those window managers.

In Motif, it is easy for you to customize what will happen when you press mouse buttons in different areas of the screen. This is called *binding* an action to a mouse button. The section of the sample .mwmrc file headed DefaultButtonBindings shows some simple examples. The physical mouse buttons are numbered 1, 2, and 3 from left to right. In the example, if you click the left button (button 1) while the cursor is positioned over an icon or a window frame, the action is f.raise. If you hold down button 1 while the cursor is over the root window, the menu called RlogMenu (defined in another part of the .mwmrc file) is displayed.

The Menu or menu keyword, followed by a title and a left curly brace, {, begins the definition of a custom menu; it's ended by the right brace, }. Similarly, button bindings are grouped using the Buttons or buttons keyword.

Motif's Microsoft Windows and OS/2 Presentation Manager heritage has led it to use slightly different terminology for some window operations. The terms *minimize* and *restore* are used to describe iconifying and de-iconifying windows, respectively. The somewhat related term *maximize* means to resize a window so it fills up the entire root window. The term *close,* which in most other window managers means to iconify the window, means to quit or terminate the application in Motif.

16.8.2 OPEN LOOK

The first thing to know about OPEN LOOK and the products that implement it is that the names (OPEN LOOK, OpenWindows, OPEN LOOK Window Manager) can be rather confusing. AT&T originally trademarked the OPEN LOOK GUI and then passed it on to UNIX System Laboratories (USL), an offshoot company devoted to UNIX. OPEN LOOK is not a product, a toolkit, or a window manager; it's just a look and feel. Sun Microsystems adopted OPEN LOOK as their X GUI and produced two different toolkits to implement that look and feel.

XView is a toolkit whose programmatic interface is very close to that of SunView, Sun's proprietary (and obsolete) window system. Sun developed XView to ease the task of converting existing SunView application programs to X. To further encourage that conversion, they donated the toolkit to the X Consortium to distribute as part of MIT X.

The second toolkit is OLIT (OPEN LOOK Interface Toolkit). It underlies Sun's flagship window system, OpenWindows, which is one of the five constituents of Solaris 2.0. The OPEN LOOK Window Manager (olwm) implements OPEN LOOK, which includes some inter-client communication enhancements (that is, features that are outside the ICCCM standard).

OpenWindows is Sun's name for their entire OLIT-based window package. It includes a start-up script called openwin, the olwm window manager, the xnews window server, and a set of applications called DeskSet™, that are written to the OPEN LOOK specification. All components of OpenWindows use the environment variable OPENWINHOME to find the libraries and other files they need. Users should set OPENWINHOME to the name of the directory at the top of the OpenWindows hierarchy (by default, /usr/openwin). This allows a system administrator to install OpenWindows in a different location without having to recompile everything; the users simply change OPENWINHOME to point to the new location.

Olwm loads its X resources from a hierarchy of resource data base files, as described in Section 16.6.1. It consults the environment variable OLWMMENU for the pathname of a root menu configuration file to use instead of the system default. The names of the resource data base files and olwm start-up files are listed in Table 16.3.

Table 16.3 ■ Olwm Configuration and Resource Data Base Locations

	System default location	Personal location
olwm root menu	`$OPENWINHOME/lib/openwin-menu`	`$OLWMMENU`
olwm config file	`$OPENWINHOME/lib/openwin-init`	`$HOME/.openwin-init`
Xdefaults file	`$OPENWINHOME/lib/Xdefaults`	`$HOME/.Xdefaults`
.xinitrc file	`$OPENWINHOME/lib/Xinitrc`	`$HOME/.xinitrc`
Application defaults files	`$OPENWINHOME/lib/app-defaults/*`	`$XAPPLRESDIR/*`

A sample of olwm menu specifications and a picture of an olwm session using those specifications are shown in Figures 16.13a and b.

Olwm defines the function of each mouse button; you can't bind them easily to other functions as you can in Motif. The only button that can call up menus is the right button. Auxiliary menus can be defined either in-line in the olwm root menu file ($OLWMMENU) or in separate files whose names are given after the MENU keyword.

OPEN LOOK has several built-in keywords, recognizable for being in all caps, for defining window manager and menu behavior. Some in the example include MENU for specifying a custom menu, END to mark the end of an in-line definition, PIN to make a menu pinnable to the screen (a pinned menu stays up even after you release the mouse button), TITLE and SEPARATOR to provide cosmetic text and lines on menus, and the intuitively-named RE-START and EXIT.

16.8.3   Twm Specifics

The window manager twm (tab, or tabbed, window manager) is part of the MIT X distribution. It can be considered a vanilla window manager since it doesn't conform to or enforce any particular GUI. With sufficient knowledge about the widgets used, the resources available on your system, and how to specify commands in the configuration files, you can make a twm session look pretty much any way you want it to look. For this reason, it is a fairly popular window manager among UNIX hackers and systems programmers.

Twm loads its X resources from a hierarchy of resource data base files, as described in Section 16.6.1. You'll notice that almost no default files are provided with twm, true to its nonadherence to a standard GUI. This makes it somewhat harder for novice users to customize it, since there is no easy template from which to start. The names of the resource data base files and twm start-up files are listed in Table 16.4.

The .twmrc file contains definitions for any custom menus that twm will display as well as many resource settings and twm-specific options. Menu specifications from a sample .twmrc file and a snapshot of a twm session using them are shown in Figures 16.14a and b.

The .twmrc file is basically similar to the Motif window manager's .mwmrc, but there are a couple of significant differences in syntax. One dif-

```
"Workspace" TITLE

"Remote Logins" MENU
    "Aux servers"         MENU $HOME/OLWMdir/menu.auxservers
    "boris"       exec xterm -title boris -e rlogin boris &
    "natasha"     exec xterm -title natasha -e rlogin natasha &
    "moose"       exec xterm -title moose -e rlogin moose &
    "twain"       exec rsh twain xterm -title twain -display 'hostname':0 &
"Remote Logins" END

"Weird Stuff" MENU
    "Weird Stuff"         TITLE
    "Shell"               exec    xterm -geometry 80x48 &
    "To Do List"          exec    xvtdl &
    "Read News"           exec    /usr/bin/X11/xrn &
    "Mail-xmh"            exec    xmh -geometry 740x760 &
    SEPARATOR
    "Calendar"            exec    cm -geometry 920x550+20+100 &
    "Screen lock"         exec    xlock &
    "Spider"              exec    spider -geometry  910x840-168-3 &
"Weird Stuff" END PIN

"Programs" MENU         $OPENWINHOME/lib/openwin-menu-programs

"Utilities" MENU        $OPENWINHOME/lib/openwin-menu-utilities

"Properties..."         PROPERTIES

SEPARATOR

"Restart"       RESTART

"Quit"          EXIT
```

Figure 16.13a ■ Menu Specification in an Openwin-menu File

ference is the way programs are run from menus: Instead of using the f.exec function, .twmrc uses an exclamation point followed by the quoted command line.

Another difference is the way button bindings are specified. Like Motif/mwm, twm allows you to bind mouse clicks in particular areas of the display to specific actions. The sample file in Figure 16.14a shows syntax for bindings to make mouse buttons 1, 2, and 3 call up the menus Rlogins, Weird Stuff, and WindowOps, respectively, when clicked and held while the cursor is in the root window.

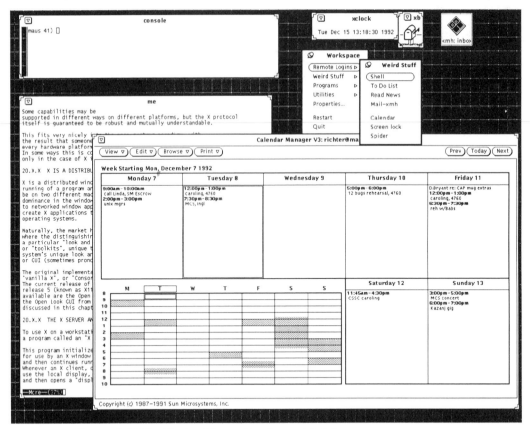

Figure 16.13b ■ An Olwm Session with Menu

The Keys section (between the = sign and the first colon) lets you specify different actions for mouse buttons combined with the control key, the meta key, and so on. Thus, the fourth and fifth button definitions say that pressing button 1 on a window's title bar will bring the window to the front, and pressing <CTRL>-button 1 will send it to the back.

16.9   Other Window Systems

Sun Microsystems developed suntools (later called Sunview), a proprietary window system that performed very well because it was optimized to run on the Sun hardware. Sunview had two serious limitations that contributed to its demise. First, since it was written specifically for the Sun hardware, it could not effectively be ported to any other UNIX platforms. Second, its architecture limited it to producing images on the local display. This made it useless for networked applications, where a user might want to run a program on some remote machine (e.g., a very powerful or special-purpose server) and have it display output on his own monitor.

Table 16.4 ■ Twm Configuration and Resource Data Base Locations

	System default location	**Personal location**
twm config file	/usr/lib/X11/twm/system.twmrc	$HOME/.twmrc
.xinitrc	(none)	$HOME/.xinitrc
Xdefaults	(none)	$HOME/.Xdefaults
Application defaults files	/usr/lib/X11/app-defaults/*	$XAPPLRESDIR/*

```
#Button = KEYS  : CONTEXT : FUNCTION
#--------------------------------
Button1 =       : root    : f.menu "Rlogins"
Button2 =       : root    : f.menu "Weird Stuff"
Button3 =       : root    : f.menu "WindowOps"
Button1 =       : title   : f.raise
Button1 = c     : title   : f.lower

menu "Weird Stuff"
  {
    "Weird Stuff"       f.title
    "Shell"             !"xterm -geometry 80x48 &"
    "To Do List"        !"xvtdl &"
    "Read News"         !"/usr/bin/X11/xrn &"
    "Mail-xmh"          !"/usr/bin/X11/xmh -geometry 740x760 &"
    "Calendar"          !"/usr/openwin/bin/cm -geometry 920x550+20+100 &"
    "Screen lock"       !"xlock &"
    "Spider"            !"spider -geometry 910x840-168-3 &"
  }

menu "Rlogins"
  {
    "Aux servers"       f.menu "Aux servers"
    "boris"             !"xterm -title boris -e rlogin boris &"
    "natasha"           !"xterm -title natasha -e rlogin natasha &"
    "moose"             !"xterm -title moose -e rlogin moose &"
    "twain"             !"rsh twain xterm -title twain -display 'hostname':0 &"
  }

menu "WindowOps"
  {
    "Refresh"           f.refresh
    "Restart"           f.twmrc
    "Exit"              f.quit
  }
```

Figure 16.14a ■ Menu Specification in a .twmrc File

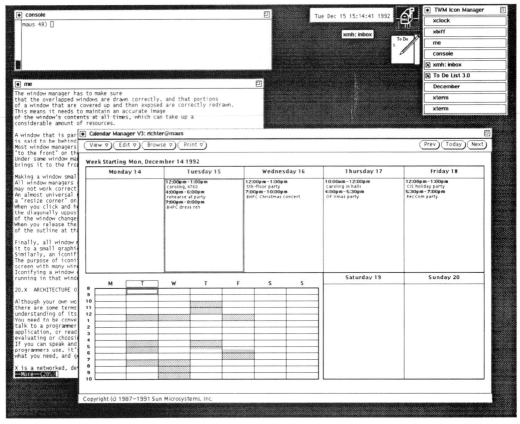

Figure 16.14b ■ A Twm Session

NeWS (Network Extensible Window System) was Sun's own invention. It used a PostScript™-based window protocol and was never picked up by any other vendor. Although it is still supported in Sun's xnews server (which supports both X11 and NeWS protocols), there doesn't seem to be much of a future for NeWS.

HP VUE has been Hewlett Packard's X/UNIX GUI since the mid 1980s. It looks very much like Motif because HP was a heavy contributor to the final Motif specification that was adopted by OSF.

The Macintosh look and feel, and the toolkits that implement it, come with a set of very rigid rules about how applications may use each component. Although programmers and designers like to complain about this hedge on their creativity, the Macintosh interface is one of the most uniform and well-known user interfaces in the world. The controls of a well-written Macintosh program should be intuitively understood by anyone who is familiar with other Mac programs. Such consistency is not a feature of most X GUIs.

16.10   Limitations of X

X is based on a two-dimensional imaging model, making it unsuited for use in applications like computer-aided design (CAD), which typically use three-dimensional modeling. The PEX (PHIGS Extensions to X) package addresses this limitation; PEX implementations are available for several flavors of X.

One of X's strengths, its hardware independence, has a down side. Because X client programs must work with any X server, they cannot be programmed to take advantage of any particular hardware's features. The trade-off is between blinding speed (on one platform) versus the portability to run on any platform.

17
Networking

A network is a group of similar individuals that work collectively and share information. Examples are cells, spies, and computer systems. Communication is the essential aspect of a computer network.

In today's data-oriented society, the ability of computers to share information is almost as important as the ability to process it. The catchphrase "the network is the computer" points out how vitally important connectivity is. Networking technology spans a broad spectrum of sophistication and power, from phone-line-based connections through state-of-the-art fiber optic links. Even computers at home can be networked, in a way; a modem lets you dial out to on-line data bases and information services such as Prodigy.

In this chapter, we introduce the concepts of UNIX networking, mention some of the most-used software and hardware technologies, and try to point out some practical concerns. We don't go into the nitty-gritty details of configuration file syntax or exhaustive descriptions of command options; in fact, some illustrative examples contain syntax which we will not explain. More detailed information about LAN networking utilities is presented in Chapter 18, and detailed information about UUCP networking utilities is presented in Chapter 19.

17.1 Uucp and IP Networking: Overview

There are two major families of networking software under UNIX: UUCP, which is serial-line-based or dial-up networking; and IP (Internet Protocol), which is high-speed, primarily Ethernet-based networking.

UUCP (which stands for UNIX-to-UNIX copy) is older and is implemented entirely outside the UNIX kernel; thus, it is available under any version of UNIX. It is an example of store-and-forward type networking. UUCP's advantage is that it can be used to network systems that are great distances apart and whose only networking hardware is a modem and a telephone line.

UUCP was written to work over serial lines, using either a direct connection (in the case of a machine in the same building) or a modem and phone line to connect to remote systems (see Figure 17.1). Very high-speed modems (56K baud or higher) may be used with dedicated or leased phone lines; the public telephone system can reliably support speeds only up to 9,600 or 14,400 baud at this time. Many sites operate with 1,200 or 2,400 baud dial-in lines.

IP networking, also often called TCP/IP networking, is a more recent addition to UNIX. It was originally developed as part of Berkeley UNIX, and the user-level programs are sometimes referred to as Berkeley networking commands. IP support is now available in every implementation of UNIX. IP networks are packet-switching networks; many hosts may use the same wire for transferring data, so there's no concept of a dedicated point-to-point connection from one site to another.

Berkeley-style networking requires an Ethernet transport system. The basic parts of an Ethernet network include segments of cable; various devices that either combine cable segments into a longer net, or connect one network to another; and *hosts,* the entities that communicate over the network (see Figure 17.2). Each host connected to the Ethernet must have an Ethernet interface, which is either built into the CPU board or added as a plug-in board. A transceiver cable plugs into the host interface at one end, and the other end attaches to the Ethernet cable with a device called a *tap.*

Ethernet is more expensive than serial-line networking and is limited in the physical distance it can cover, but it offers dramatically higher bandwidth. For example, a network disk on the Ethernet can achieve data transfer rates roughly comparable to a locally attached disk; this wouldn't be possible over even a fast serial line.

a. Two machines with a direct serial-line connection.
    Machines are in the same room.

b. Two machines with serial connection through modems and a phone system.
    May be anywhere in the world.

Figure 17.1 ■ Diagram of Modem Links, also of Direct Serial Connection

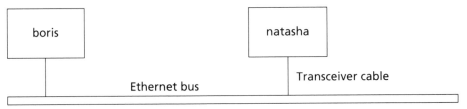

Figure 17.2 ■ Hosts on an Ethernet

After a period of several years during which uucp was the primary means of networking UNIX sites around the world, today it is considered a second-class alternative to the Internet, discussed in Section 17.20. UUCP connections are noninteractive and useful mainly for batch-mode activities such as electronic mail, file transfer, or remote job submission. For sites where money is a constraint, UUCP can be a very satisfactory networking solution.

Higher-speed IP networking offers interactive connections between remote hosts, with user programs such as rlogin, telnet, and ftp. IP and many of the higher-level protocols it supports are networking standards and are implemented on many platforms such as DOS machines, Macintoshes, and large mainframes. This makes it possible to set up IP-based networks in which hosts of completely different architectures and operating systems can exchange data easily.

17.2 Terminology

Many of the terms introduced in this chapter are defined in the text where they are first used. This section presents a few terms that need a bit more discussion or background than a simple definition. It is by no means an exhaustive glossary of the networking terms used throughout the chapter.

Asynchronous line: See serial line.

Bandwidth: Networking jargon that amounts to "how big is this pipe"; that is, what's the rate at which data can be transmitted? To give a real-world example, AM radio is a low-bandwidth medium and television is high bandwidth. A network with high bandwidth can support complex and I/O-intensive applications such as window systems, client-server shared data base systems, and file sharing across a network. Low-bandwidth connections are most suitable for applications such as file transfers or simple remote logins using an ASCII terminal.

Baud: The number of bits transmitted per second. Divide the baud rate by ten to get a rough estimate of the number of characters transmitted per second.

Heterogeneous: Made up of parts that are not all alike. A network that connects UNIX workstations, Macintoshes, and an IBM mainframe is heterogeneous. A network of all Sun workstations is homogeneous.

Internet: In general use, any network made up of other networks. When people refer to "the Internet," they mean the global network of networks that started out as ARPAnet and MILnet and that now includes hosts and networks all around the world. Communication over the Internet is IP-based; in fact, that's what the protocol is named after.

I/O: Input/output. I/O rates can be measured over any kind of communication interface, including serial, Ethernet, or to a local disk. In networking discussions, I/O usually refers to data being sent over the Ethernet.

Local-area network (LAN): A set of hosts, usually in the same building or on the same campus, that are connected by a high-speed medium such as Ethernet. A LAN may be a single IP network or a collection of networks or subnets that are connected through high-speed routers.

Metropolitan-area network (MAN): Like a WAN, with two primary differences. The geographical coverage is limited to a "metropolitan area," and the connection is over a high-speed medium such as a fiber-optic or microwave link.

Modem: Abbreviation of "modulator-demodulator." A device that allows digital computer signals to be transmitted over a phone line. The modem on the sending end modulates the computer signal into a transmittable form and puts it out onto the phone line, and the modem on the receiving end demodulates the signal back to a digital form and feeds it into the computer. An external modem has at least two data wires plugged into it: the cable connecting it to a serial port on the computer, and the wire going to the phone jack in the wall. Modems often have lights on the front to indicate the state of the connection, the baud rate, and so on. You may also be able to plug a telephone instrument into the back of the modem, so the same phone jack can support both voice and data. An internal modem, often found in personal computers, is on a board that plugs into the machine's I/O bus; it does not require a serial cable.

Packet: A group of bytes sent as a unit over a network connection. The bulk of a packet usually consists of addressing and protocol (header) information; the actual data portion can be as small as a single byte.

Packet-switching network: A network in which information going from one host to another is broken down into small packets. The packets are sent individually over the communication medium and then reassembled at the receiving end into the original file or byte stream.

Router: A device that provides high-speed connection between two or more packet-switching networks. The router examines each incoming packet to find its destination, and then sends the packet out on the right network interface. A UNIX host with two Ethernet interfaces can act as a router between two networks, but a dedicated router is much faster and more efficient.

Serial line: A communication line into a computer, most commonly used to support local terminals but also used to connect other devices such as modems. A cable runs between a serial port on the computer and the terminal or modem on the other end. Serial lines are capable of data transmission speeds from 300 to 9,600 baud, or even higher.

Store-and-forward network: A network in which files or messages destined for a remote site are batched up until a direct connection to the remote system is made. Then all the transfers are done, and the connection is terminated.

Wide-area network (WAN): A network that connects sites across long distances, via low-speed links such as leased telephone lines. The sites making up a WAN may be LANs or individual hosts.

17.3   The UUCP Family

UUCP is a suite of programs that was developed in the early days of UNIX, to help distribute software updates among a set of UNIX hosts. The idea was to use UUCP to transmit information over the phone lines rather than using the post office to transmit that information on computer tapes. The UUCP suite was rewritten in the late 1980s by Peter Honeyman, Dan Nowitz, and Brian Redman; their version, called HoneyDanBer UUCP, has considerably more utility and convenience features than the original.

UUCP provides the basis for creating a dial-up network. Two systems can communicate via UUCP if they are connected by a direct serial line or if they can call each other using the public phone system. The only hardware that a system needs for UUCP is a serial port and possibly a modem for accessing the phone system. UUCP doesn't require kernel modifications; thus it will run on any UNIX system. UUCP is discussed in detail in Chapter 19.

The original goal of UUCP was to manage unattended file transfers, using telephone connections to link one site with another. Unattended means that a person doesn't have to manually initiate the phone call, dial the number, log onto the remote computer, and perform the transfer. Rather, the user issues a request for a file transfer and then UUCP takes over, performing the necessary intermediate steps to carry out the request.

The term "UUCP" is used to describe the entire system, but uucp is actually just one user-level program that accepts and enqueues requests for inter-system file copies. The other major user-level program in the system is uux, which enqueues requests for command execution on remote systems.

HoneyDanBer UUCP has several other user-level commands that make it more convenient to do common tasks. Uuto allows you to send files to a user on a remote system, where they are placed into a specially-structured spool directory. The recipient then runs uupick, which traverses the spool directory and retrieves the files for that user. Uupick gives you several options for what to do with retrieved files, such as copying or moving them to your home directory. Uustat reports on the status of the jobs that have been submitted through any of the uucp commands. Uuname lists the names of all sites that this host knows how to call, to establish a direct UUCP connection.

Three internal programs are at the heart of the UUCP system. The most important of these is uucico (copy in, copy out; pronounced "you-you-cheeko"). It examines the queues of outgoing jobs, makes the necessary connections with remote systems, and supervises the transfer of information. A uucico process on your system dials up and logs into the remote system, where another uucico is started as its login shell. From that point forward the two uucico programs interact, passing data between the systems until the work is completed. The other two programs are uusched, which looks at the outgoing job queue and schedules calls to the necessary remote systems, and uuxqt, which executes jobs that have been sent from remote computers.

17.4 Sending Mail Through UUCP

The most widespread use of the UUCP system is for electronic mail, or e-mail (EE-mail). If your only networking need is e-mail connection with other UNIX machines, UUCP may be all you need. The UNIX mail program existed before UUCP was developed, but when UUCP provided inter-machine links, the mail program was enhanced to take advantage of this new capability. Sending mail to a user on another host requires an addressing scheme more sophisticated than simply "login name." You also need to specify to which host to send the mail, and it's possible that the destination machine is only reachable by making hops through several other hosts along the way. UUCP itself is limited to single-hop transfers, but an e-mail address can specify a chain of UNIX machines which make UUCP connections with one another.

A UUCP address consists of UNIX hostnames separated by exclamation points, with the final name in the chain being the login name of the intended recipient. This type of mail address is called "UUCP-style" or "bang" addressing (after the UNIX slang term for exclamation point). The first host in the chain is the one that is contacted directly. When it receives the message, it strips its own name from the front of the address and sends it to the next host in the chain, and so on.

```
To: boris!sscvax!jeanne
```

In this example of a To: line for an e-mail message, the local host only needs to know how to connect to host boris. Boris will then send the message on to sscvax, where it will be routed to the user named jeanne. Most mailer software also takes care of building up a return-address path somewhere in the mail header, so the recipient can see what machines were used to route the mail. Note that return addresses are not guaranteed to work, since UUCP connections are often made in one direction only.

There are several limitations to sending mail via UUCP. One is timeliness. Since delivery is accomplished in multiple hops, and each host along the way makes connections on its own schedule, it can take an unpredictable length of time for a message to get from point A to point B. Another limitation is connectivity. Establishing a working route can involve talking to the system administrators at many sites to find out who talks to whom. It's entirely up to the sender to keep up with the topology of the UUCP network and to figure out a route that works.

A third limitation is reliability. A route will stop working temporarily if one of the sites in the chain goes down, or permanently if it stops talking to the next. There's little that a sender can do about either problem. Finally, UUCP can't always return undeliverable mail or notify the user of the failure, because of the "invalid return address" problem mentioned previously.

17.5   UUCP Administration

UUCP's largest cost is its administration. The system administrator must manage a large set of configuration files. In HoneyDanBer UUCP, there are files that describe the dial-out lines available on your system (Devices), the characteristics of the modems you have (Dialers), and the information needed to connect to all remote systems to which you have access (Systems). These files normally live in the directory /usr/lib/uucp.

The most critical of these is the Systems file (in old-style UUCP, it was called L.sys), which contains an entry for every destination site that your system can reach. A few lines from a Systems file are shown in Figure 17.3.

Each entry specifies when the site can be called, the device and phone number to use, the login sequence for the site, and the password.

Many major UNIX installations support and accept UUCP connections from other UNIX sites; you have to contact the system administrator at a site you want to dial into for UUCP. If they agree to let you make UUCP connections, they assign you a special login name which has the uucico program as its login shell. When your machine calls theirs to make a connection, the uucico on your end has to supply this login name and its password. For this reason, the password has to be stored in clear text in your Systems file.

This approach, while necessary for a dial-up protocol such as UUCP, is a major violation of the UNIX approach to password maintenance. The UNIX password file /etc/passwd is readable by ordinary users, but the passwords it contains are encrypted. Since the passwords in the Systems file are kept in clear text, their only protection is through UNIX file permissions, which is a relatively weak mechanism.

Other sites' password security can be compromised, for example, simply by someone stealing a backup tape containing your Systems file and reading it on another system. Every site listed in the stolen Systems file now has at least one breached password, that of the UUCP login for your system. Turning this scenario around, the security of your system is at the mercy of the system

```
upeabody Any ACU 2400 12135551212 ogin:--ogin: uboris ssword: sherman
denver Any ACU 9600 13035551212 ogin:--ogin: uboris ssword: mtnhigh
```

Figure 17.3 ■ A Couple of Lines from boris's Systems File

administration practices of every machine to which you allow UUCP access (because their Systems files contain your password). Because UUCP passwords are so easy to discover, most system administrators severely restrict the commands and directories that UUCP accounts may access.

Although UUCP is no longer a state-of-the-art networking package, it must be recognized as one of the milestones in the history of UNIX. Its continued use and distribution more than a decade after its original development attest to its good design and usefulness.

17.6   Cu and Tip

There are two commands, cu (call UNIX) and tip, which can establish interactive connections to other UNIX machines using much the same hardware resources as UUCP. For more details about these commands, see the discussion in Section 19.2.

Cu is part of SysV UNIX. Like UUCP, it supports connections to remote systems over either a direct serial connection or a phone line. It also uses some of the UUCP configuration files (primarily the Devices file) to decide what lines to use. The difference is that cu connections are interactive; a person sitting at a terminal uses cu to log into another UNIX machine. Once a cu session is established, you can work on the remote machine as if it were local.

Cu supports a number of operations that allow you to give commands to your local UNIX machine, to transfer files, and to change the characteristics of your communication with the remote host. These operations are invoked by typing in lines starting with the tilde (~) character, and are often called *tilde escapes.* A tilde at the beginning of a line tells cu that what follows is a cu command, not just data to be passed through the connection. For example, typing ~! tells cu to start up an interactive shell on the local machine, allowing you to work there while still dialed into the remote host. Your remote session simply sits idle while you work locally.

Tip is another implementation of the functions of cu. It is very similar to cu from the user's point of view. Tip has a substantially extended set of tilde escapes, but its most basic commands (e.g., terminate the connection; start a shell on the local machine) are the same as cu's.

17.7   IP Networking

An IP network can have many different kinds of hosts attached to it.

Figure 17.4 shows a heterogeneous network, and the way various components of the network are connected. Starting at the top left and going clockwise around the net, these are the components:

- ■ A router (or gateway, or bridge): It connects one network to another. The other net may be local (same building) or remote (over phone lines).

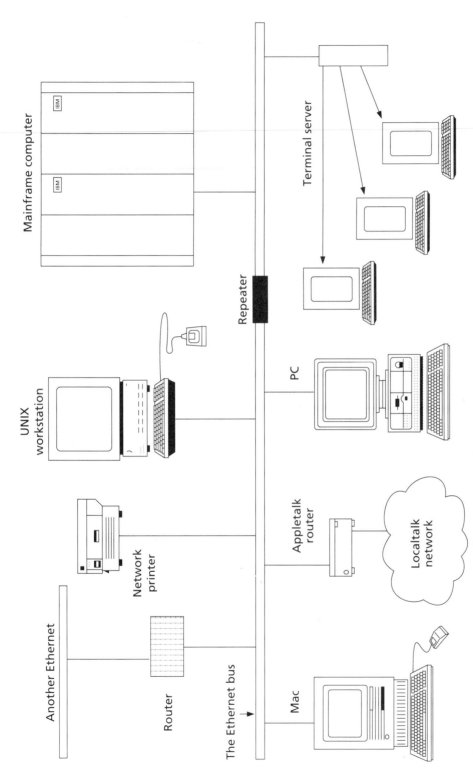

Figure 17.4 ■ A Heterogeneous Ethernet Network

- A network printer, or print server.

- A UNIX workstation.

- The black section on the net is a repeater, which simply connects two physical Ethernet segments to form one logical network and regenerates the packets going in either direction. It has no address and is, therefore, not a host on the net.

- A mainframe computer.

- A terminal server.

- A PC with an Ethernet interface.

- An AppleTalk router. Its function is to provide a connection between a LocalTalk (Macintosh) network and the Ethernet.

- A Macintosh with an Ethernet interface.

What we call "Berkeley networking" consists of three separate pieces: the physical hardware and protocols that support the connection (usually Ethernet), the software networking protocols (the most commonly used is TCP/IP), and the user-level commands.

A networking protocol is an exhaustive description of messages that are sent between levels of hardware and software to let hosts on a network communicate reliably. A protocol is neither hardware nor software, but a plan or description, like a blueprint. There may be more than one implementation of a given protocol. Depending on what layers of the network are involved, a protocol may be implemented in software drivers or in hardware or firmware. For a discussion of the seven-layer ISO/OSI network model, see *Internetworking with TCP/IP: Principles, Protocols, and Architectures,* by Douglas Comer (Prentice-Hall, 1988), or any other good book on computer networking.

17.8 The Ethernet

Ethernet is a standard hardware communications system that was jointly developed by Digital Equipment Corporation, Xerox, and Intel starting in 1980. The Ethernet protocol specifies the transmission and propagation of signals at a very low hardware level. Unlike telephone switching systems and other hardware designed for long-distance communication, Ethernet is a local communications system, spanning a maximum distance of 2.8 kilometers (most Ethernet networks are much smaller than that). Ethernet, being a hardware technology, can simultaneously support multiple software protocols.

If you are involved in setting up or maintaining a network of UNIX machines, you need to know what sort of network interface your computers come with and what kind of wiring your site will require. The original Ethernet implementation used heavy (approximately ½-inch in diameter) coaxial cable, commonly called *thick Ethernet.* There are newer implementations that use thinner media, including 10-base-T, which is unshielded twisted-pair wiring like that used in modern telephone wiring, and thin-net, which is thin coaxial cable. Computer manufacturers are increasingly using the latter two technologies because of market preference. The thinner wires and smaller connectors are much easier to work with and cheaper to manufacture and install.

17.9   How Ethernet Works

Ethernet is a high-bandwidth bus protocol, with collision detection. The raw transmission rate of Ethernet is ten million bits per second (10 Mbs), but various hardware and software operations lower the actual throughput significantly. "Bus" means that there is a single omni-directional medium for transmission of data; thus, every host attached to the bus has physical access to all data sent over the net.

Data is transmitted in formatted chunks called *packets;* it may take hundreds or thousands of packets to transfer all the data required for a single file transfer or other transaction, and each packet is sent independently of all others. Only one packet may be traveling across the bus at any time. A host that wants to transmit a packet checks to see whether the net is idle before transmitting.

Collision detection means that hosts that transmit simultaneously will notice the clash and withdraw to retry their transmissions. A pseudo-randomized delay period prevents hosts from repeatedly transmitting, colliding and then retrying at the exact same intervals. An Ethernet that has too many hosts, or hosts that can do extremely fast I/O, can become saturated, and the collision rate climbs. A substantial percentage of the traffic on the net then becomes retries, as hosts try again and again to send the same data. When your network reaches this state, it's time to think about splitting into multiple nets.

Although all network traffic travels over the same wire on the Ethernet, the normal behavior for a host is to listen for only those packets which are specifically addressed to it. There is also the concept of *broadcast* packets: these use a special host address (either all zeroes or all ones) as the destination. Packets with a broadcast address are intended to be readable by any host on the net.

A host can also be set to *promiscuous mode.* A host in promiscuous mode listens to all packets on the network, even those specifically addressed to other hosts. Network traffic monitoring programs, for example, use this capability to track the number of packets sent to and from particular hosts. UNIX restricts this behavior to the superuser, but because this monitoring capability exists, the Ethernet must be considered an inherently insecure networking medium.

Physical access to the net is a major vulnerability. Anyone with physical access to the Ethernet cable (and the proper tools) could attach his own host and become superuser on it. It could then, in promiscuous mode, spy on every packet that goes across the bus. Another physical security consideration is electromagnetic emissions. With sufficiently sensitive equipment, the electromagnetic radiation emitted from an unshielded Ethernet cable can be read over short to moderate distances through the air. To minimize the net's vulnerability to this kind of penetration, many sites run Ethernet cable through walls or ceilings and/or use metal or heavy plastic conduit to shield the cable between taps. See Chapter 22 for a more detailed discussion of security issues and some approaches to solving them.

17.10   Other Hardware Technologies

Other hardware technologies for computer networks also exist, and new ones are constantly being explored and developed. Two that are now being used for UNIX networks are Token-Ring and FDDI (fiber distributed data interface).

A Token-Ring network uses a single-directional transmission medium. There is a token which is passed from one host to the next around the network; only the host holding the token can transmit a packet. This prevents the collision problem. Some Token-Ring networks are capable of higher throughput than Ethernet, ranging up to 16 Mbs.

FDDI is a very high-speed network technology (up to 100 Mbs) based on fiber optics. An optical network can cover a much longer distance than a network based on transmission of electrical impulses, and it is not subject to electromagnetic interference. However, the cable and other hardware for optical networks cost considerably more than traditional equipment. Also, installation and maintenance are more difficult because of the precision work needed to make a clean optical connection.

A very new hardware networking technology is ATM (Asynchronous Transfer Mode), an offshoot of the switching technology used by the telephone company. In ATM, each host is not attached to a single common bus which transmits traffic for many other hosts. Rather, a host has an individual connection to a centralized switch, which routes data to the other hosts in the network. The switch is extremely high-speed, has very high bandwidth, and capacity can be added as needed. The benefit of ATM is that adding new hosts to the net has no effect on the network bandwidth of any other host, since each has an individual connection. At this time, it's unclear whether FDDI or ATM will emerge as the winning technology; ATM offers the promise of higher bandwidth and scalability, but FDDI is more established.

17.11   Software Networking Protocols

The most-used software networking protocol in the UNIX world is TCP/IP (Transmission Control Protocol/Internet Protocol). As the name implies, it is actually two protocols. IP is a low-level protocol, at the network layer of the

OSI model; it specifies how messages should be routed between systems. TCP is one level higher, at the transport layer, and it is concerned with the details of information transmission.

TCP and IP are actually only two members of a suite of protocols developed by the U. S. Government's Defense Advanced Research Projects Agency (DARPA). The suite includes many networking protocols that support communication over many types of links, both locally and over great distances. The suite is informally called TCP/IP because these two protocols are the most widely used.

Support for the TCP/IP protocols is provided in the UNIX kernel, as device drivers. TCP/IP drivers come with all modern UNIX and POSIX implementations, as well as many other operating systems. The standard IP driver for UNIX uses the Ethernet as its hardware medium. Another implementation of IP is SLIP (Serial Line Internet Protocol), which runs over serial lines. This allows you to run IP-based network applications on a host that is not attached to an Ethernet.

17.12   Network Addressing

Each host on an IP/Ethernet network has a hostname and two kinds of addresses: an ethernet address and an IP address. Each is made up of four or six eight-bit quantities, commonly called *octets*. (They're called octets instead of bytes because not all machine architectures have the same notion of a byte. Some have six-bit, nine-bit, or even larger bytes.)

You can think of the Ethernet address as being like a fingerprint for a particular piece of hardware. It is a six-octet number that is usually burned into a PROM (programmable read-only memory; a type of chip) at the time a device is manufactured, and it identifies that piece of hardware no matter where it goes. The first two octets generally identify the manufacturer of the device, and the remaining octets are assigned by the manufacturer to the devices they produce, like serial numbers. An Ethernet address is conventionally expressed as hexadecimal numbers separated by colons; for example, 20:81:0a:10:c4:93.

Like your fingerprint, the Ethernet address is not commonly used for identification. User-level programs never have to deal with it. If you are a system administrator, you may need to change a host's Ethernet address because of a hardware replacement. In many cases, the PROM containing the Ethernet address can be swapped onto the new board, and the host's address remains the same. Otherwise, you have to get the new Ethernet address (often, it's displayed on the screen during self-test, or appears at boot time) and change your Ethernet address table.

The hostname and IP address, on the other hand, are assigned to a host administratively. When a new host is added to a network, the system administrator gives it a hostname (e.g., natasha) and assigns it an IP address on the network to which it will be attached. If a host moves from one network to another, it is assigned a new IP address, but its hostname can remain the same.

A host may have more than one network interface; for example, a machine that is acting as a router between two networks needs to have one interface connecting it to each net. In this case, the host would have two Ethernet addresses and two IP addresses, one for each interface. Each interface would also have its own hostname.

An IP address is a four-octet number, conventionally written as decimal numbers separated by dots; for example, 192.15.28.173. The first portion of an IP address (the network part of the address) identifies the network to which the device is attached. The remainder (the host part) identifies the specific host within that network. Just how many bits of the address comprise the network part and the host part depends on the IP network class (discussed in the following text).

Most sites start out with one IP network, and many never outgrow that. Eventually, though, you may get so many hosts (or you may outdistance the physical limit of a single Ethernet) that you need to create a second network. At that point, your network has to include a type of host called a *router* to handle communications between your networks. A router may be as simple as a general-purpose computer with two Ethernet interfaces, each attached to a different net, or it may be a specialized piece of equipment designed to handle heavy traffic with great efficiency and speed.

17.13 The Network Information Center

IP network addresses, since they are used for communication between networks throughout the world, are controlled and administered on a global basis. The authorizing agency for IP network numbers is the Network Information Center (NIC, pronounced "nick"). It's necessary to register with the NIC and get an authorized network number if your site intends to communicate with anyone else in the outside world. Based on your site's anticipated requirements, the NIC will assign you a network number of a particular class.

As shown in Figure 17.5, the smallest IP network class is called class C. In a class C network, the first three octets, or 24 bits, are assigned by the NIC (e.g., 192.118.65). These define the network part of the address.

This leaves only eight bits for host addresses, for a total of 256 addresses; two of those 256 are reserved as possible broadcast addresses.

For a class B network (Figure 17.6), the NIC assigns only the first two octets (e.g., 145.30), which means there are 256 times more possible host addresses. The owner of a class B network number may choose to carve it up into *subnets* by allocating some or all of the third-octet bits as part of the network address. A very common configuration is to use all of the third octet for the network address, creating what amounts to 256 class-C-equivalent networks or subnets.

Use of subnets is a feature of IP networking that only became standard around 1985 or so. Some older networking software still in use doesn't un-

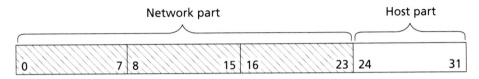

Network part   Host part

a. A class C IP address.

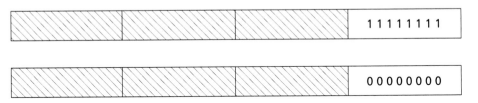

b. Broadcast addresses for a class C network.

Figure 17.5 ■ Diagram of Class C Address and of Broadcast Addresses

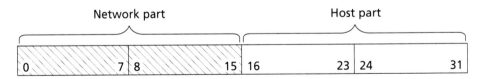

Network part   Host part

a. A class B IP address.

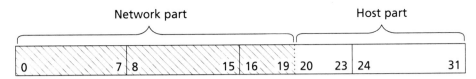

Network part   Host part

b. Subnetting to create 16 subnets.

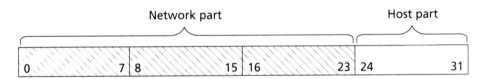

Network part   Host part

c. Subnetting to create 256 subnets.

Figure 17.6 ■ Diagram of Class B Address and Subnetting

derstand subnetting, and special hacks may have to be done to make it function in a network that uses subnets.

Because the set of network numbers is finite, and the number of computer networks in the world is growing explosively, the NIC is somewhat protective of the numbers it has left to assign. It is considerably harder to get a class B network than a class C. There is actually also a class A category, but only the very largest enterprises (like the U.S. government and the phone company) have class A network numbers.

The NIC also administers domain names, which are the Internet analog of hostnames. The Internet domain name system, or DNS, is a hierarchical scheme in which every site in the world has a unique name. There are several domains within the United States, and a separate domain for each country that requests one. Table 17.1 shows some of the top-level domains. There are over 100 international domain names, of which only a sampling are listed.

Within a top-level domain, sites or institutions are assigned names; they, in turn, assign hostnames within their domain. The example below shows the domain address to send mail to user pdq on the host okcorral at the University of Southern North Dakota at Hoople, which is an EDUcational institution.

```
To: pdq@okcorral.usndh.edu
```

Using domain addressing in e-mail solves a couple of problems. First, a fully qualified domain name is guaranteed unique in the world. Second, the address contains no routing information; how to route the mail to its destination is left to the DNS (or other) software, which can adjust dynamically to find the best route.

Table 17.1 ■ Internet Top-level Domain Names

Within the United States:

EDU	educational institution
COM	commercial enterprise
GOV	the government
MIL	the military
NET	network (large, commercial)
ORG	nonprofit organization

International:

AU	Australia	NL	Netherlands
CA	Canada	NZ	New Zealand
DE	Germany	PL	Poland
ES	Spain	SA	Saudi Arabia
FR	France	SE	Sweden
GB	Great Britain	UA	Ukraine
JP	Japan	UK	United Kingdom
MX	Mexico	US	United States

17.14   User-level Berkeley Networking Commands

Berkeley networking user commands include rlogin, to log into a remote machine; rsh, to execute a command on a remote machine; and rcp, to copy a file to/from (or between) remote machines. Besides these facilities specifically built for networking, some existing software, such as mail and lpr, has been modified to use the networking. Most commercial versions of UNIX, including System V, have now incorporated Berkeley-style networking. For more description of these commands, see Chapter 18.

17.15   Administration of Berkeley Networking

Berkeley networking is based on hostnames and addresses. The UNIX system administrator maintains a mapping of hostnames to Ethernet addresses, and another mapping of hostnames to IP addresses. These are stored in text files, usually named /etc/hosts and /etc/ethers, or in distributed data bases or *maps* (see Section 17.19). Whenever a host is added to the network, or a piece of hardware changes, the maps must be updated immediately so that the network will keep working.

The /etc/hosts file (see Figure 17.7) contains the IP address assigned to each Ethernet interface on the network, plus one or more hostnames associated with that interface. Multiple hostnames are synonymous. The names containing dots (e.g., moose.bullwinkle.com) are fully qualified domain names (see Section 17.13). In the example, moose is also given the hostname mailhost-sys. This kind of generic hostname is often used in system configuration files. If the mail host function moves to a different host, the only change needed is in /etc/hosts, rather than needing to ferret out all the scripts and files that might refer to the mail host by name.

The /etc/ethers file (see Figure 17.7) contains the Ethernet addresses of all the interfaces on the network, plus the primary hostname for each.

```
192.118.65.108   boris.bullwinkle.com boris
192.118.65.101   moose moose.bullwinkle.com mailhost-sys
192.118.65.154   rocky rocky.bullwinkle.com
192.118.65.93    natasha.bullwinkle.com natasha
```

a. A fragment of an /etc/hosts file.

```
8:0:20:7:d0:9a   boris
8:0:20:8:63:f3   moose
8:0:20:8:8a:2d   natasha
2:60:8c:b:7d:1   rocky
```

b. A fragment of an /etc/ethers file.

Figure 17.7 ■ /etc/hosts and /etc/ethers Files

There is a notion of trusted hosts in Berkeley networking (see Figure 17.8). If host boris trusts natasha, a user logged in on natasha can rlogin to boris without having to type his password again, but not vice versa. For the process to work in both directions, natasha would also have to trust boris. Trust applies to rcp and rsh as well as rlogin. Trust among hosts makes life more convenient for the user but weakens the security of the network as a whole.

The list of hosts trusted by a machine is kept in the file /etc/hosts.equiv. This file should be writable only by the superuser. At many sites, all the hosts on a network are kept in hosts.equiv to maximize the user's convenience in working across different machines. At other, more security-conscious sites, very few or no hosts are trusted by each machine. The system administrator needs to seek an appropriate balance between convenience and security for the users and the site.

An individual user can set up a trust relationship between hosts that applies only to herself as a user. The file $HOME/.rhosts contains a list of hosts and host-user pairs that the user trusts.

In Figure 17.9, the first two lines indicate that sue trusts remote requests from hosts dudley and natasha, if they are issued by user sue. The third line says that she also trusts requests from user susie on host snoopy.peanuts.com. This feature would normally only be used if you have a different login name

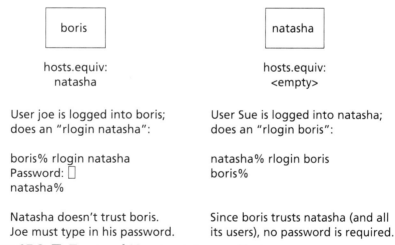

Figure 17.8 ■ Trust and Non-trust Among Hosts

```
dudley
natasha
snoopy.peanuts.com        susie
```

Figure 17.9 ■ .rhosts File for User sue

on some machine, and you want the convenience of being able to remotely log in without typing your password. It is a fairly large security loophole to trust login names that belong to other people, since that gives them unrestricted access to everything you own on the computer.

Berkeley's networking facilities provide a major improvement over the UUCP protocols for local networking. (Of course, Berkeley networking does not replace UUCP for communication between systems not on the same LAN or WAN.) The connections are much higher in bandwidth, and some facilities, such as remote login, are almost completely transparent. Security is generally better, partly because the user community on a LAN is more well-defined than the community of people who might dial in from a phone anywhere in the world.

17.16   Network File Systems

The Berkeley networking code doesn't do everything one might want. In particular, it doesn't provide much flexibility in accessing files. That is, new programs can be written to access files on remote machines, but Berkeley doesn't provide a mechanism to let existing software transparently access remote files. That brings us to network file systems.

The ordinary UNIX file system was designed to support the needs of a single, stand-alone machine. Physically, each disk is attached to a given host, and one might say that the files on that disk also reside on that machine. In a networking environment, a more flexible arrangement is preferred. The goal is to make file resources more generally available so that users on one host can access files from another host's disks, without having to log in to the other machine.

The first widely available network file system for UNIX, Network File System (NFS), was developed by Sun Microsystems. It provides file transparency by allowing a file system from one host (a server) to be mounted on other hosts (clients); see Figure 17.10a. As shown in Figure 17.10b, a host may be both an NFS server (if it has local file systems) and an NFS client, getting file systems from other hosts.

Only the superuser may mount a file system, whether local or remote (see Section 20.4.4 for a discussion of mounting file systems). Once a remote file system is mounted, users on the client can access its files as if they were local. Ordinary processes don't need to know that they are using files stored on a remote machine.

17.17   NFS Administration

Administratively, each host controls which of its file systems may be remotely mounted and what hosts mount them. When a file system is made available for remote mounting, it is said to be exported. The file /etc/exports

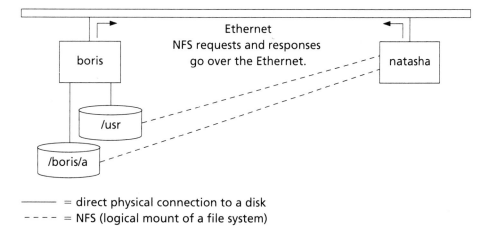

——— = direct physical connection to a disk
– – – – = NFS (logical mount of a file system)

Boris has disks containing the /usr and /boris/a file systems. Natasha has no disks, but can access boris's file systems through NFS. See configuration files in Figures 17.11 and 17.12.

Figure 17.10a. ■ Remote Mount Using NFS

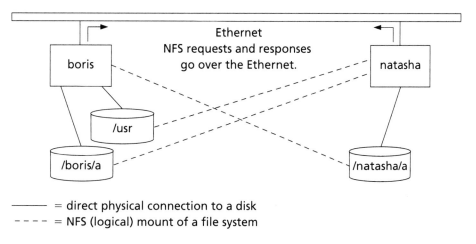

——— = direct physical connection to a disk
– – – – = NFS (logical) mount of a file system

Boris is a file server for /usr and /boris/a, and natasha is the client. But natasha is also the file server for /natasha/a, while boris is the client.

Figure 17.10b. ■ Dual Roles, Server and Client

lists all local file systems that are exported, along with an access list of the remote hosts that are allowed to use each.

In Figure 17.11, boris exports four different file systems. The colon-separated names following the access= keyword are the hosts allowed to remotely mount each file system. Hostnames following the root= keyword are allowed root permissions; that is, someone logged in as root on natasha is given superuser privileges on /boris/a even though it is a remote file system.

/usr	-access=natasha:rocky,root=natasha
/boris/a	-access=natasha:rocky:moose:dudley,root=natasha
/var/spool/mail	-access=natasha:rocky:moose:dudley
/var/spool/pcnfs	-access=snidely

Figure 17.11 ■ Slice of boris's /etc/exports File

In turn, each client host has a line in its /etc/fstab file that mounts each of the remote file systems from the appropriate host, as shown in Figure 17.12.

Using the /etc/fstab file, natasha mounts its root file system from a local disk, /dev/sd3a, as a 4.2 BSD file system. The other three file systems are NFS types, mounted from boris. Notice that the file system which boris calls /export/exec/sun4 is being mounted on /usr by natasha; a host is free to change the local name of a remote file system.

On a network where NFS is in use, it's important that all machines have the same idea of users' UID and GID mapping, if UNIX file permissions are to work reliably. One common way of doing this is to maintain the passwd and group data bases as NIS maps (see Section 17.19) and have all machines that share file systems be in the same NIS domain.

NFS makes it possible to operate a UNIX machine without an attached disk drive. Such a machine, called a *diskless workstation,* relies on other machines on the net to supply its operating system and other file systems.

There are pros and cons to diskless workstations. Among the advantages are economy and simplified system administration. It may be cheaper to buy a single large disk to serve several diskless workstations than to buy several smaller disks. As disk prices continue to drop, though, this becomes less of a concern. However, it is certainly easier to maintain and back up one disk than three or four.

Some disadvantages are increased network traffic and load on the file servers. Diskless workstations, by definition, do all their I/O over the network. A few busy, fast workstations can generate enough I/O to swamp an Ethernet. If many diskless workstations are dependent on one file server, its own performance may suffer because of having to provide NFS services.

Another network file system is the Remote File Sharing (RFS) system. It is similar to NFS in function, but with two big differences. RFS cannot be used to mount file systems that are necessary for a machine to boot; thus it

/dev/sd3a /		4.2 rw 1 1
boris:/export/exec/sun4 /usr		nfs ro 0 0
boris:/var/spool/mail /var/spool/mail		nfs rw 0 0
boris:/boris/a /boris/a		nfs rw 0 0

Figure 17.12 ■ Slice of natasha's /etc/fstab File

doesn't help with diskless workstations. However, RFS can mount special files (that is, devices such as tape drives) from remote hosts, which NFS cannot do. This is good economically, since it lets many hosts share relatively expensive pieces of equipment.

17.18   NFS and Automounting

File systems remotely mounted through NFS are still listed in each system's /etc/fstab file. As the number of disks and file systems grow, some problems arise with simply mounting every file system everywhere. It becomes difficult, or at least unwieldy, to keep up the list of file systems on every host. Cross-mounting of file systems increases the interdependence of machines. If a file server goes down, or has really bad response because of an overload, all hosts mounting a file system from there may also suffer. There are severe problems recovering from events like power outages; when all hosts are trying to boot at the same time, there may be deadlocks, or at least long delays, as they wait for each other's file systems to become available.

The concept of automounting NFS file systems essentially provides "on demand" mounting. When a host boots, only the file systems that are listed in /etc/fstab are mounted by default. When a user accesses a remote file system that isn't already mounted, the automounter establishes a connection and mounts that file system. It stays mounted as long as it's being used (i.e., a user is cd'ed to a directory there, or is actively using a file). After some period of inactivity (five minutes is a typical idle time-out period), the file system is silently unmounted.

In Figure 17.13, the file systems /boris/a, /natasha/a, /natasha/b, and /dudley/a are available for automount to all hosts. At the moment, a user on dudley is actually accessing a file on /natasha/b, so automount has mounted that file system on dudley. Some remote file systems, for example /usr on natasha and dudley, are not candidates for automounting, as they are required for the systems to boot.

Automounting does away with much of the interdependence and allows easier maintenance of NFS file systems across the network. An NIS map contains the list of file systems that may be automounted, along with information such as the host it lives on, what hosts may mount this file system, what directory it is to be mounted on, and so on. When a new file system is created, it can be added in a single place, instead of having to modify the /etc/fstab file on every host on the network.

Sun's automount program was the first implementation of automounting. A program called amd, available on the Internet, is a popular substitute.

17.19   Network Information Service

It's important for all hosts on a network to have the same mappings of hostnames, Ethernet addresses, IP addresses, and so on. One way to ensure this

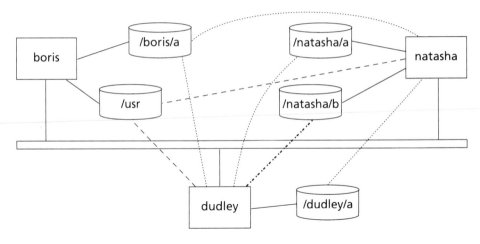

——— = direct physical access to disk
- - - - = regular NFS mounts
·············· = potential automounts
··—··—··· = automounted file systems in use

Figure 17.13 ■ Automounting File Systems

would be to manually keep copies of the administrative files in sync across all machines—a daunting task, especially when there are more than two machines!

To make this kind of task easier, the Network Information Service, or NIS, was developed by Sun Microsystems. NIS used to be called Yellow Pages, or YP, but this name was abandoned because of a trademark dispute over the name with a telephone company in Great Britain. Many people still refer to the maps as YP maps, and the software commands still have names like ypbind, ypmatch, ypcat, and so on.

NIS is a distributed information service, and it is built on a master-slave model. One host is the NIS master, and it maintains data bases of administrative information that are shared among the other machines on the net. All the hosts under one NIS master are said to be in the same NIS domain (or YP domain). There may be several domains on one network, but it's quite common for a site to have just one domain.

One very common use of NIS is to maintain the passwd and group data bases. When a user changes his password on any host, a modified passwd program passes the information on to the NIS master. The master updates its passwd map, which is then distributed to the rest of the machines on the network (the slaves). Both the master and the slaves have to be running special software for NIS to work.

Sites that use NIS typically use it for much more than the passwd and group data bases: It can also be used to maintain the maps of Ethernet addresses, IP addresses, and mail aliases, among others.

17.20   Networking the World: LANS, WANS, and Routers

A local area network (LAN) can be a single IP network connecting a handful of hosts over Ethernet or other high-speed medium, or a complex of networks and subnets interconnected through high-speed routers. The terms wide-area network (WAN) and metropolitan-area network (MAN) refer to a network that has sites in geographically separated locations, and these are traditionally connected using lower-speed media such as leased phone lines. As telecommunication technology advances, it's becoming more common to see WAN/MANs that are connected over megabit-per-second lines, and any practical distinction between LANs and WANs begins to blur.

What's commonly called the Internet is a worldwide network of networks; that is, it consists of a large number of LANs, regional networks, and other sites, all connected by high-speed long-haul links. The Internet is a diverse community that is not governed by any formal body. It is a more-or-less organic entity that has evolved, and continues to evolve, as its participants and the technology they use change.

The thing that allows one network to connect to another is called a *router,* or sometimes a *bridge* or a *gateway.* These terms mean different things to different people. In general, a router is any machine which has to decide which of several ways to send a packet so that it will reach its destination. A bridge selectively forwards packets from one segment of a network to another based on the location of the destination host. This can reduce the total traffic on each segment. A gateway can do anything a router or a bridge can do but has the added capability of translating packets from one format or protocol to another as needed. A gateway allows easy interconnection of diverse networks. All gateways are routers, but not vice versa.

In its simplest conceptual form, a router is just a node that has more than one network interface. It's not unusual for a dedicated router to have six or eight Ethernet interfaces and four or more serial interfaces. The Ethernet interfaces connect to local IP networks, and data transfer among those nets is made at Ethernet speed. The serial interfaces typically connect over modems and phone lines to distant networks (for example, across the city or across the country), and communication occurs at the speed of the phone-line link, commonly 56 kilobits per second (56 Kbps).

An example of a gateway is an AppleTalk router, which connects a LocalTalk network to an Ethernet. Since hosts on an IP Ethernet don't "speak" AppleTalk, and Macs on LocalTalk don't "speak" IP, one of the AppleTalk gateway's jobs is to fix up the packets going in either direction so they can be delivered properly. It does this by encapsulating LocalTalk packets inside IP packets for transmission over the Ethernet, and un-encapsulating the packets being sent back to the LocalTalk network. You can think of this as stuffing an AppleTalk packet inside an envelope (the IP header) and using an IP address to deliver it; the contents of the envelope are immaterial to the delivery mechanism.

A terminal server is an Ethernet host whose only purpose in life is to provide serial-line access to the Ethernet (see Figure 17.14). The async lines

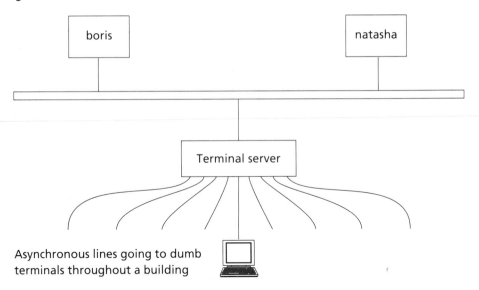

Asynchronous lines going to dumb
terminals throughout a building

A terminal server gives serial-line access to the Ethernet. The terminal server runs
a rudimentary operating system that supports user operations like rlogin and
telnet, but not much else except administrative and configuration commands.

Figure 17.14 ■ A Terminal Server

coming into the terminal server are identical to async lines on any time-
sharing computer; the difference is that once you've connected to it, you can't
do any computing. About the only thing a user can do from a terminal server
is remotely log in to another host on the Ethernet.

For sites with lots of UNIX hosts, a terminal server can be a practical and
economical way of allowing dumb-terminal users access to all of that computing power. Because the serial ports are a centralized resource, you don't
have to provide serial-port hardware for every UNIX host.

17.21   Packets

Just how is data transferred from one host to another over a network? On an
IP network, information is transferred in structures called *packets*. The general structure of an IP packet is shown in Figure 17.15.

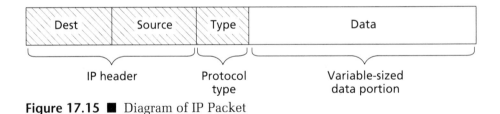

Figure 17.15 ■ Diagram of IP Packet

The source and destination addresses are IP addresses; another low-level network protocol (ARP, Address Resolution Protocol) translates the destination address into an Ethernet address to accomplish the delivery. The rest of the IP header holds information specific to the higher-level protocol being used.

The actual data portion of the packet may be very small, even as small as a single byte. In highly interactive applications like remote login, very high packet overhead is a reasonable price to pay for immediate response to user-generated keystrokes. In an application like file transfer, immediacy of response is not so critical. Data bytes are accumulated in a buffer until it is filled, and then a single packet transfers the whole buffer. This reduces the network overhead per byte sent.

Two of the most common higher-level protocols are TCP (Transmission Control Protocol) and UDP (User Datagram Protocol). TCP provides reliable end-to-end transport between two user processes; it's a connection-oriented protocol used for services like remote login.

UDP, by contrast, is an unreliable protocol that is used to provide various informational network services. An unreliable protocol is much easier and cheaper to implement than one that has to guarantee the arrival of data at the destination. It's suitable for services like broadcasting time of day or providing system performance statistics; if that information doesn't make it to some host, nothing is really lost.

17.22 Network Daemons

There are many operating system services that involve communication over a network. Many of these services are implemented through network daemons. A *daemon* is a background process that performs a single, fairly simple task. A daemon may be started at boot time and run forever, waiting for someone to make a request for its service; others are started only when needed. A network daemon listens on a particular TCP/IP port for a request and then sends off a response to the request.

A number of important services are under the control of a master daemon called inetd (eye-net-dee). Inetd services are generally those that are invoked by user-level commands; a few examples are rlogin, rsh, ftp, and telnet. A file called /etc/inetd.conf contains the list of services that inetd handles, along with some other information.

Inetd listens on all the ports assigned to the services listed in inetd.conf. When it receives a request for one of those services, it starts up a copy of the appropriate daemon to do the job, then allows it to die. For example, the finger daemon is started by inetd when a remote host requests user information from a system. The daemon sends the information, then exits. This scheme keeps the number of daemon processes down. There may be dozens of services that are available but are used only infrequently; it wouldn't make sense to keep a daemon for each one running all the time.

Another type of daemon provides services via the RPC (Remote Procedure Call) service. RPC, which is itself a service started up by inetd, allows a program running on one machine to make procedure calls on another machine. Each RPC program is identified by a name and a program number. Many RPC programs are daemons that are started up individually at boot time. Some important RPC daemons include the NFS daemons, NIS services (although they are called YP services), and rstatd, which gathers and reports performance statistics.

RPC programs also use port numbers to keep requests and responses going to the right places. A program called portmap reads a configuration file called /etc/rpc to get the list of supported RPC services and program numbers. When an RPC daemon is started, portmap creates a mapping of the program numbers the daemon can service and the IP port numbers it is using. When a process on a remote host needs to request an RPC service, it contacts the portmap program to find out what port to use.

It is important for all hosts on a network to agree on the port numbers used for each inetd service. When a host broadcasts a request for a particular service, say time of day, out onto the network, it is addressed to a particular port. If some host on the network has a different idea of which service that port maps to, it might respond instead with a login prompt or a system status report.

There is a set of "well known" or reserved port assignments that are universally agreed upon by all IP implementations, and another set that are well known within UNIX. These are listed in the file /etc/services (or the NIS map "services"). If you install third-party products that include inetd services, or if you write your own network daemon, it is important to assign it a port number that is not already in use by another service. Port numbers used by RPC daemons are automatically chosen from a range that is not reserved.

If you want to see some of the daemons that run on your UNIX host, run the ps command and look for processes whose process ID (PID) is a number less than 200 or so. PIDs are assigned sequentially from 0 starting at boot time, so many of the processes with low PIDs are likely to be daemons; they've been continuously present since the machine was booted. The daemons that are started up on demand by inetd, when you request a particular service, will not necessarily have low PIDs. Because they last only as long as it takes to provide the service, though, they can appear and disappear quickly, and thus are often hard to catch with ps.

17.23   Booting over the Network

An important benefit of having machines connected over a high-speed network is that not every host needs its own copy of the operating system. One machine with the operating system, which we will call a *boot server,* can share it with multiple other hosts on the net, called *clients.*

Three categories of clients are commonly used: diskless, dataless, and diskful. A *diskless client* is totally dependent on its boot server not only for the operating system but also for its root and swap partitions, and for any user data file systems. A *dataless client* has a local disk, but it contains only the root and swap partitions; no user data. A *diskful client*'s disk contains root, swap, and user file systems, but the operating system is still shared from its boot server. (See Figure 17.16).

Sharing the OS is advantageous primarily for two reasons: it usually takes up a lot of disk space, on the order of a couple of hundred megabytes; and keeping many copies of a large software system in sync over a network can be very difficult.

For a UNIX machine to boot, it needs several things: a boot image, which tells it where to find its root and swap partitions; a kernel; some swap space; and a copy of the operating system, which usually lives in the /usr directory. All of these things can either be on a locally attached disk or provided by some other host over the network. The more resources are local, the more independent the host will be, and the less network traffic it will generate as it's running. However, providing every client with its own hard disk is an expensive proposition, so diskless configurations are quite common in the real world.

When a diskless client starts to boot, the only thing it knows is its Ethernet address, because that's burned into its hardware. The client broadcasts a request to the network saying, "Here's my ether address; what's my IP address?" Any host on the net can reply to the booting client with its IP address. The protocol used to find out one's IP address from the network is called Reverse Address Resolution Protocol, or RARP.

Once it finds out its IP address, the booting client broadcasts another request saying, "Here's my IP address; who has the files I need to boot?" The client's boot server responds to its request by downloading its boot image across the network. Depending on what its boot image tells it to do, the client then downloads its kernel from the server. As with all UNIX machines, the entire kernel image stays resident in the client's physical memory as long as it is up.

When the boot process is finished, the client starts using the swap area set aside for it on its boot server (see Section 23.2.8 for a discussion of swapping). Swapping across the network is slower than to a local disk, and network bandwidth can be seriously chewed up if there are many clients using remote swap.

17.24   Networking UNIX with Other Kinds of Machines

The wonderful thing about standards is that sometimes they work, and people actually build products on different platforms that can work together. Networking seems to be an area where this is true. Writing software that allows people to interconnect the computers they already have, computers of various types, has proven to be a lucrative venture for many companies.

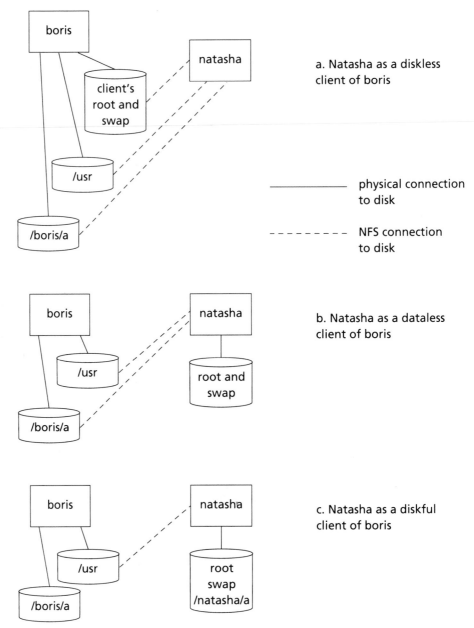

Figure 17.16 ■ Diagrams of a Few Possible Configurations of Clients

In particular, there are numerous implementations of TCP/IP for both DOS and the Macintosh operating system. This provides an infrastructure for PCs and Macintoshes to be networked with UNIX machines. Network applications such as telnet and ftp are built on a TCP/IP base.

Coming at heterogeneous networking from a different angle, several microcomputer networking protocols have been implemented under UNIX. UNIX systems can serve files to DOS machines using PC protocols. There are UNIX-based implementations of all the Novell NetWare protocols, as well as Microsoft's LanManager protocols.

There are also UNIX implementations of some of the Macintosh AppleTalk protocols. One public-domain package, available over the Internet, is Columbia University's CAP (Columbia AppleTalk Package). Some CAP applications include Aufs, a file-sharing package which lets Macintoshes mount UNIX directories as folders; papif, which lets UNIX hosts send print jobs to printers on a Macintosh LocalTalk network; and lwsrv, which lets Macs send print jobs to UNIX-attached LaserWriter printers.

NFS has also been ported to several non-UNIX platforms; for example, PC-NFS for DOS machines, and TOPS for both DOS and Macintosh. PC-NFS allows a PC client to remotely mount a file system from a UNIX server, as a DOS drive. Because DOS has no concept of user ID or permissions, a PC-NFS daemon runs on the UNIX host to validate all mount requests. It prompts the PC user for a UNIX login name and password and will only mount directories that are accessible to that user.

There are Macintosh and PC implementations of X servers. These allow a user sitting at a Mac or PC to have concurrent access to UNIX software and native applications. The UNIX software runs on a UNIX host and displays to the X server, which just runs as another application on the Mac or PC. There are also packages to make microcomputer applications use the X network protocol, which lets them display on X servers running on UNIX hosts.

18
LAN Networking Utilities

As discussed in Chapter 17, networking of one kind or another is universally available on UNIX systems. It is so intertwined in the workings of UNIX, and so necessary, that it's almost like air: We don't always think about it consciously, but without it, life would cease.

Some parts of networking are built into UNIX at a very low level and operate without the user's awareness. For example, to send e-mail to a remote machine, you just address the mail, and the mail system invisibly takes care of all the routing using the built-in networking knowledge. Or to manipulate files that are accessible through a network file system such as RFS or NFS, you simply act as if they are regular local files: the built-in networking facilities interpret your mv or cp commands and do the necessary work behind the scenes to execute those actions on files on a different machine.

Other uses of the network, though, require the user to be aware of the existence of different machines, and in some cases even of the topology in which they are connected. Commands have been specially written to provide the user with these kinds of functions: we call these user-level commands *networking utilities,* and they are the topic of Chapters 18 and 19.

Thus networking is an innate part of modern UNIX. It provides a natural and flexible way for you to connect to and combine forces with other UNIX hosts in your building or around the world. With the Internet and other global networking resources that have grown in the past few years, UNIX networking can literally put the world on your desktop.

18.1 User-level Networking Commands

The user-level commands used in networking fall into four major functional groups: logging into remote systems, executing commands on remote systems, transferring files, and informational or status-reporting commands. Crossing those function lines to form a matrix are the two big categories of networking we discussed earlier: UUCP or dial-up networking, and LAN/WAN based networking.

In this chapter, we will discuss the LAN/WAN commands. They fall into two groups: those that are part of "Berkeley networking," or the "r" commands; and those that aren't, including the programs telnet and ftp. As mentioned in Chapter 17, the networking code first developed at Berkeley is now available in every flavor of UNIX (including SVR4), so the name "Berkeley networking" is somewhat misleading. Since that's the common term for it, though, we use it cheerfully. Telnet and ftp are especially important because they are not UNIX-specific. The telnet and ftp protocols are almost universally known and implemented, so they can be used to transfer files or make connections to computers of all kinds, running any operating system. The commands described in this chapter are listed in Table 18.1.

System-level networking commands, many of which are daemons (daemons are described in Chapter 17), are of interest mainly to system administrators. Most can be run only by the superuser; for this reason, we don't talk about them here.

18.2   Connecting to Other Systems

One fundamental point you should understand is that you can only log into a remote system if you have a user account on that machine. Your site also needs to have the appropriate networking infrastructure and configuration files for any of the remote access commands described here in order to work. If you try some of these commands and have absolutely no luck, contact your system administrator to see whether your site even supports Berkeley networking or is running any TCP/IP software.

Rlogin and rsh, as part of the Berkeley networking suite, are used primarily among hosts on the same local IP network.

Although hosts that are "on the same IP network" generally are in the same building or site (often connected via an Ethernet cable), some LANs also include long-haul telephone or leased-line links, so distance is not really the issue. Hosts that are in the same IP network must all be able to reach each other over high-bandwidth connections (no disjoint network segments), and they all have IP addresses in the same network (see the discussion of IP

Table 18.1 ■ User-level Commands for LAN Networking

	Remote login	Execution	File transfer	Information
Berkeley	rlogin	rsh	rcp	rwho, ruptime
	rsh	remsh	—	rup
Other	telnet	—	ftp	ping

network classes in Section 17.13). This almost always means they are administered by the same organization or person.

Telnet establishes a TCP connection between hosts, which may be either on the same local Ethernet or quite distant. Although we discuss it here primarily in the context of remote login, it can also be used to contact any TCP service (e.g., the sendmail daemon) on the remote host.

18.2.1   Rlogin

Rlogin can be used to log into a UNIX host on the same IP network. The syntax for rlogin is simple:

rlogin [*options*] *hostname*

Common rlogin command-line options are described in Table 18.2.

Sometimes when you use rlogin to connect to a remote host, you will be asked to type your password before getting on. Other times, you will get right in. This is because Berkeley networking has the concept of hosts "trusting" one another (see Section 17.15). The network or system administrator has the ability to specify which hosts on an IP network will trust each other. If you use rlogin to connect to a remote system from a host it trusts, you will not be required to give your password to complete the login process. You can also individually specify a set of hosts (and, optionally, user names on that host) to trust in a file called $HOME/.rhosts.

If you use the -l flag with a user name, you will be required to give that user's password to log into the remote system (barring an entry in their $HOME/.rhosts file that allows you unrestricted access; this is strongly not recommended, for security reasons!). Without the -l flag, you will be logged in with the same user name you are assigned on the local system.

Rlogin is a very powerful command; because of the "trusted host" concept, it can give you access to any host on a network once you've logged into any one host. If you try to rlogin to a host that doesn't trust your current host, it simply prompts you for your password, just as if you were logging in from a regular terminal. If you type in the right password, you are logged in successfully and can work without any further constraint.

When you rlogin to a system, your dot files on the remote system are processed just as for a regular login at a terminal or workstation. That is, your login shell's start-up file (e.g., .cshrc) is sourced, then your .login file.

Table 18.2 ■ Common Rlogin Command-line Options

-l *username*	Log into the remote system as *username.* The default is to log in as yourself.
-8	Enable transfer of eight-bit data across the network. The default is seven-bit data.
-ec	Use the character *c* as the escape character. The default escape character is tilde (~).

Bear in mind that when you rlogin from one host to another, the UNIX session on the original host is still there; in fact, every keystroke you type is processed first by the local host, then sent to the remote host. If you continue remotely logging in from one host to another, you can quickly get several layers deep and start seeing performance degradation. Not only that, you are liable to get somewhat confused about exactly where you are and how you got there (and how to get out!).

If you are using a shell that supports job control (such as the C-shell), you can escape back to the UNIX session on your local host by typing the rlogin escape character (usually tilde, ~) followed by the shell's SUSPEND character (usually Ctrl-Z, ^Z). If you are multiple layers deep, you can use multiple tildes to send the escape sequence to successively newer rlogin sessions. For example, ~~^Z escapes to the second-deepest rlogin, ~~~^Z to the third-deepest, and so on, as illustrated in Figure 18.1. Other tilde escapes (see Table 18.3) can similarly be directed to a specific rlogin session by using multiple tildes.

One fairly common practice among system administrators is to create a set of scripts or links to rlogin in the directory /usr/hosts. Each link is named for a particular host in the local network. By mentioning /usr/hosts in your $PATH, you can then rlogin to a host just by using its name as a command. On a system with such a setup, the following two commands are equivalent:

```
% rlogin boris
% boris
```

18.2.2   Telnet

Telnet is similar to rlogin in that it lets you log in to a remote host that's reachable over an IP network. Note that the remote host need not be in the same IP network, as is true for rlogin. In fact, it doesn't even have to be a UNIX system. You can use telnet to connect to almost any kind of system such as PCs, mainframes, VMS machines, or any other system that's on a TCP/IP network and can accept telnet connections.

Telnet is one of the most widely-implemented networking protocols, so it's somewhat the lingua franca for connecting to remote systems of any kind (heterogeneous networks). Telnet implementations on UNIX generally don't include any kind of terminal emulation (you just use the characteristics of the physical terminal you're using), but PC and Mac versions of telnet usually do include terminal emulators. Common terminal choices for these emulators are vt100 or vt220, or sometimes Tektronix terminals.

The syntax for telnet is:

```
% telnet hostname
```

where the hostname is usually a fully qualified Internet domain name. Sometimes you may want to telnet to some remote host whose name is not in your system's hosts data base. If this is the case, your system will respond with the error message *hostname:* unknown host. If you know the remote system's IP address, you can use that directly on the command line: telnet *IP_address.*

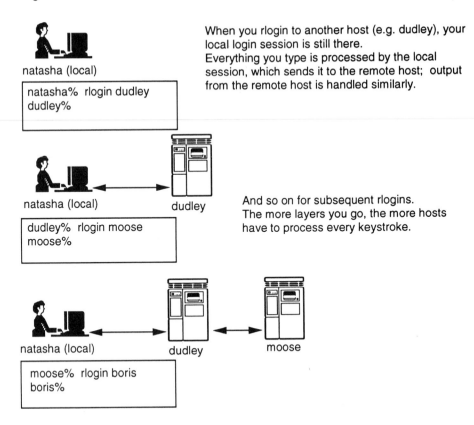

natasha (local)

natasha% rlogin dudley
dudley%

When you rlogin to another host (e.g. dudley), your local login session is still there.
Everything you type is processed by the local session, which sends it to the remote host; output from the remote host is handled similarly.

natasha (local)   dudley

dudley% rlogin moose
moose%

And so on for subsequent rlogins. The more layers you go, the more hosts have to process every keystroke.

natasha (local)   dudley   moose

moose% rlogin boris
boris%

From an rlogin session, you can use tilde escapes to get back to your local session or any intermediate rlogin, but you must have a good mental map of the levels. Each additional tilde takes you to a more recent (newer) rlogin session, as illustrated in the examples below.

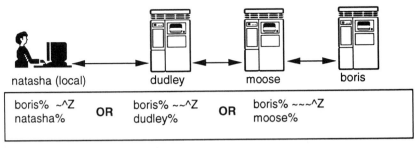

natasha (local)   dudley   moose   boris

| boris% ~^Z | OR | boris% ~~^Z | OR | boris% ~~~^Z |
| natasha% | | dudley% | | moose% |

Figure 18.1 ■ Chained Rlogin Sessions

Table 18.3 ■ Common Rlogin Tilde Escapes

~.	Close the connection. This does not guarantee a clean shutdown of any remote processes and should not be considered as a substitute for properly logging out.
~*susp*	Suspend the remote connection and return temporarily to the local session. *susp* is your UNIX suspend character (job control), often set to Ctrl-Z. In the C-shell, typing fg (foreground) in the local session will resume the rlogin connection.
~*dsusp*	Like ~*susp,* but allow output from the remote session to continue coming to your screen. The *dsusp* or deferred suspend character is often set to Ctrl-Y.
~~	Pass a tilde character on to the remote UNIX session. Multiple tildes are needed to communicate with the different layers of rlogin when you have a chain of them connecting several machines. See Figure 18.1.

This bypasses the host-to-IP address translation normally done by the local host.

Because it can be used among so many different kinds of hosts, telnet makes no pretense of trusting other hosts or knowing who is trying to log in. It makes you provide your login name as well as your password.

```
natasha% telnet boris
Trying 111.222.33.44 ...
Connected to boris.bigcorp.com.
Escape character is '^]'.
SunOS UNIX (boris.bigcorp.com)
login: richter
Password:
Last login: Mon Jan 11 16:25:23 from natasha
Tuesday, January 12, 1993
    boris will be down at 17:30 PST for 15 minutes for hardware
    reconfiguration.
boris%
```

Telnet is quite versatile. Although its default behavior is to start up a login session, you can also provide a port number argument, and it will try to connect to the system service assigned that port number. A common use of this feature is **telnet** *hostname* **25**, to talk to a remote host's sendmail daemon. One might do this to verify the existence of an e-mail address or mail alias on that system (of course, you have to know how to talk to send-mail!).

A relatively innocuous port number to experiment with is 13, which is the "daytime" service. Many systems allow anyone to connect to this port to get the current date and time, then they immediately close the connection.

```
natasha% telnet boris 13
Trying 111.222.33.44 ...
Connected to boris.bigcorp.com.
Escape character is '^]'.
```

```
Sat Mar 20 07:55:14 1993
Connection closed by foreign host.
natasha%
```

When you are in a telnet login session, you can escape back to the inter-active mode by typing the telnet escape sequence (usually Ctrl-[, ^[). In in-teractive mode, you can issue commands to telnet (see Table 18.4) to manip-ulate the current session, open new connections, and so on.

18.3   Executing Commands on Remote Systems— Rsh/Remsh

The rsh command allows you to execute a command on another host that is on the same IP network. On some SysV UNIX systems, this command is called remsh to avoid confusion with another rsh command. The other rsh is a restricted shell, one which allows users only a limited set of commands and is intended for use in turnkey applications.

The rsh (remote shell) syntax is

```
% rsh hostname command
```

On the remote machine, the current directory is set to your home direc-tory, and a copy of your login shell is spawned to execute the command you gave. The shell reads your dot files to set up its environment. However, C-shell users should note that it does not process the .login file; only .cshrc is read. If you omit the *command* argument from the rsh command line, it actually does an rlogin. In this case, all the dot files normally used for a login are processed.

The stdin, stdout, and stderr files of the remote command are attached to your terminal by default, just as if it were a local command. You can use I/O redirection, but you have to be careful that the input or output files you specify are really on the system where you want them to be.

```
natasha% rsh boris who > /tmp/userlist
```

In the preceding example, the who command will list all the users cur-rently on boris, and the output will be stored in the file /tmp/userlist—but in natasha's /tmp directory, not boris's! To redirect output on the remote machine, you must quote the command string as described in the following text.

There are two important "gotchas" about rsh, which can be avoided by quoting the command string correctly. First, the command that is sent for remote execution ends at the first symbol that the shell sees as an end-of-command character. These include the semicolon (;), pipe (|), ampersand (&), and any redirection (<, >, or >>), as well as the logical tests (|| and &&). Second, shell variables and backquoted commands are interpreted or executed on the local system, before the command string is sent to the remote system. (C-shell users: ~username references are expanded to the user's home directory on the local machine.)

Table 18.4 ■ Telnet Interactive Commands

`close`	Close the current connection. This is useful if, for some reason, you cannot log out from a remote host by normal means.
`display`	Display operating parameters, including flow control and interrupt character processing, special character settings, and debugging status. Here's an example of display output:

```
will flush output when sending interrupt characters.
won't send interrupt characters in urgent mode.
won't map carriage return on output.
won't recognize certain control characters.
won't process ^S/^Q locally.
won't turn on socket level debugging.
won't print hexadecimal representation of network traffic.
won't show option processing.
        [^E]   echo.
        [^]]   escape.
        [^H]   erase.
        [^O]   flushoutput.
        [^C]   interrupt.
        [^U]   kill.
        [^\]   quit.
        [^D]   eof.
```

`mode [line|character]`	Enter line-by-line or character-at-a-time mode.
`open` *name*	Try to establish a connection to the named site.
`quit`	Exit telnet, terminating any open connections.
`send`	Transmit special characters. Telnet lets you use symbolic representations of special characters, instead of having to know exactly what control characters are required by the connection. Typing send ? displays the names of special characters known to your telnet.
`set`	Set values of special characters used to communicate with telnet during information transfers. Typing set ? shows you the names of all the special characters that can be set in your telnet.
`status`	Print a summary of telnet's current status. An example is:

```
Connected to boris.bigcorp.com.
Operating in line-by-line mode.
Catching signals locally.
Escape character is '^]'.
```

`toggle` *parameter*	Toggle operating parameters. These are on/off variables which control things like low-level debugging, flow control, translation and filtering of control characters, and so on. Typing toggle ? displays the list of all parameters known to your telnet. There is no way to find out what state a toggle variable is in except by toggling it (then you can immediately toggle it back if need be).
`z`	Suspend telnet. Return to your shell, but leave the telnet session connected. This only works on systems that support Berkeley-style job control. From the C-shell, you can resume telnet by bringing it to the foreground (using the fg command).
`?`	Print help information.

If you want to send a command string that contains multiple commands, I/O redirection, or shell variable references, you must enclose it in quotes. Single quotes are safest, since they prevent the shell from interpreting anything locally; double quotes allow shell variable interpretation but protect all the end-of-command characters. You can also escape the meaning of each special shell character by preceding it with a backslash, \, but quoting the entire string is much easier both to type and to read.

```
natasha% rsh boris 'who > /tmp/userlist'
```

In this example, the list of users on boris will be stored in /tmp/userlist on boris. Note that the only difference from the previous example is the quotes: compare the results of the two commands.

Rsh will fail if the remote host doesn't trust the host you're on. Unlike rlogin, rsh will not ask for a password to verify that you are who you claim to be; it simply refuses to do the command.

Using rsh instead of rlogging in can be a considerable timesaver if you have to do one or two commands on a lot of different systems (see Figure 18.2).

18.4   File Transfer Between Hosts

Files can be transferred from one host to another by using any of several commands, depending on how the hosts are connected. For hosts on the same Ethernet LAN, rcp is used (unless a network file system such as NFS or RFS is in use, in which case no special command is required). For hosts connected to a long-haul IP network (such as the Internet), the ftp command is used.

18.4.1   Remote Copy, Rcp

The rcp (remote copy) command copies files between the local host and a remote host, or between two remote hosts (referred to as *third-party remote copy*). The command syntax is

rcp [*hostname:*]*srcfile* [*hostname:*]*destfile*

Like regular cp, the destination on an rcp command may be a directory; in this case, multiple source files can be specified. If either host doesn't trust the other, the copy operation fails. Like rsh (and unlike rlogin), rcp will not prompt for a password to verify the user's identity from a nontrusted host; the copy is simply refused.

The default current working directory on the remote machine is the user's home directory; you may start at an arbitrary location by giving an absolute pathname. File permissions on the remote machine are checked according to your user and group identities there.

Rcp is unnecessary when files on a remote machine are mounted through NFS (or any other network file system, such as RFS). Then, the regular cp command is used to copy files between hosts. Similarly, mv and rm are used

```
natasha% foreach host (boris moose squirrel)
? echo Users on ${host}: ========== >> userlist
? rsh $host "date; w" >> userlist
? echo " " >> userlist
? end
natasha% ▓
```

The preceding C-shell loop might produce the following output in the local file user list:

```
Users on boris: =============
Sat Mar 20 12:53:49 PST 1993
12:53pm  up 9 days, 12:53,  2 users,  load average: 1.46, 1.12, 0.74
User      tty        login@   idle   JCPU   PCPU   what
bob       console    11Mar93  19:49  6:43   11     -sh

Users on moose: =============
Sat Mar 20 12:53:54 PST 1993
12:53pm  up 3 days, 3:10,   7 users,  load average: 0.67, 0.67, 0.50
User      tty        login@   idle   JCPU   PCPU   what
oper      console    Wed 8pm  34     10     2      rlogin natasha
herb      ttyh1      9:18am   3:19   42     15     -csh
richter   ttyi1      Fri 8am  1:23   10     2      -csh
root      ttyp3      Wed 3pm  22     3             -csh
oper      ttyp6      Fri12am  14:25  29     5      telnet vcx

Users on squirrel: =============
Sat Mar 20 12:54:12 PST 1993
12:54pm  up 3 days, 3:16,   4 users,  load average: 3.70, 2.74, 2.74
User      tty        login@   idle   JCPU   PCPU   what
oper      ttyh2      Fri12am  14:26  21     10     -csh
kc        ttyi3      11:49am  21:25  3:18   1:32   -csh
oper      ttyp0      12:10pm  34     12     5      -csh
```

Figure 18.2 ■ Use of Rsh in a Foreach Loop

to move and delete NFS-mounted files, respectively. The NFS code in the UNIX kernel takes care of implementing the file operations on the proper remote host. If your site has NFS and people are still constantly using rcp, you should find out what file system they are accessing and think about adding it to your NFS configuration (or educate the users so that they know they don't have to use rcp).

18.4.2   Ftp and Anonymous Ftp

Ftp, which stands for *file transfer protocol,* is a standard mechanism for transferring files between UNIX and non-UNIX machines alike. The name is used both for the protocol and for the user-level program. Ftp is a reliable file transfer protocol; that is, if it works at all, it makes sure that the file gets to the other end intact.

On the Internet, ftp is virtually universally available. It is by far the most widely used tool for dispersing documents, source code, and other information throughout the Internet community. Many sites act as repositories for public-domain software and other on-line materials, and they allow anonymous ftp access so that anyone whose machine supports ftp can get these materials simply by dialing in. Because it is interactive, it is fairly intuitive to use.

The syntax for ftp is

```
% ftp hostname
```

where the *hostname* is usually a fully qualified Internet domain name. Sometimes you may want to make an ftp connection with a remote host whose name is not in your system's hosts data base. If this is the case, your system will respond with the error message "*hostname:* unknown host". If you know the remote system's IP address, you can use that directly on the command line: "ftp *IP_address*". This bypasses the host-to-IP address translation normally done by the local host.

Chunks of a sample ftp dialog are shown in the sections below, interspersed with explanations of what's going on at each step. The interactive ftp commands are summarized in Table 18.5, at the end of the dialog samples.

18.4.2.1 Making the Ftp Connection

```
dudley% ftp boris.bigcorp.com
Connected to boris.bigcorp.com.

Welcome to the FTP service of Bigcorp Inc.  We are running 4.3BSD-
Reno FTP.  Please note that some files archived here are copyrighted
or "copylefted" by their authors.  Their presence in a publicly
accessible archive service such as this does not affect the
validity of such copyrights, and you are urged to respect them.

220 boris.bigcorp.com FTP server (Version 5.75) ready.
Name (boris.bigcorp.com:richter): anonymous
331 Guest login ok, send ident as password.
Password:
230 Guest login ok, access restrictions apply.
```

In the portion of the preceding dialog, an ftp connection was initiated with the host boris.bigcorp.com. I logged in as "anonymous." When it prompted for my password, I typed my Internet user ID (username@host), richter@rand.org. This is the standard Internet convention for anonymous ftp sign-on. Note that, just like log-in, ftp does not echo your password as you're typing it in.

It's also possible to make an ftp connection as a recognized user (rather than as "anonymous"). You must make arrangements with the administrator

Table 18.5 ■ The Most Commonly Used Interactive Ftp Commands

ascii	Set up to transfer an ASCII (plain text) file.
binary	Set up to transfer a binary (data or executable) file.
cd *dir*	Change directories within the remote ftp directory.
close	Terminate the connection with the current host.
delete *file*	Delete a file (not allowed by many ftp sites).
dir [*files*]	Get a long format listing, like ls -l. Often more useful than ls, especially for finding out how big files are before retrieving them.
get *file*	Retrieve a file to your local system.
mget *files*	Retrieve multiple files.
glob	Toggle ability to use wildcard file name matching in the remote ftp directory.
help [*cmd*]	List the ftp commands. "Help *command*" gives a brief description of *command*'s function.
lcd *dir*	Change directory on your local system. Useful when you are retrieving files and they need to go into different directories.
ls [*files*]	List the names of files in the current (remote) directory.
open *host*	Open a connection to another host.
put *file*	Upload a file to the remote system (not allowed by many ftp sites).
mput *files*	Upload multiple files.
pwd	Print working directory on ftp host.
quit	Terminate the current connection and exit ftp.
rename *file*	Rename a file (not allowed by many ftp sites).
status	Display connection parameters of current session, including ascii/binary, glob off/on, and so on.

There are also numerous commands to toggle debugging status, communication modes, and so on.

of the remote system to do that, just as if you wanted to log in to the system. By far the most prevalent use of ftp on the Internet is anonymous, to retrieve files made available for public use.

Just about every time ftp gives a response to one of your commands, it starts the line with a number such as 220 or 331. Although they make the dialog look cluttered and somewhat threatening (they look like error codes to some people), you can ignore them; they refer to parts of the ftp protocol and are there mostly for debugging (and for historical reasons).

18.4.2.2   Ftp On-line Help

```
ftp> ?
Commands may be abbreviated.  Commands are:
!          cr          macdef     proxy      send
$          delete      mdelete    sendport   status
account    debug       mdir       put        struct
append     dir         mget       pwd        sunique
ascii      disconnect  mkdir      quit       tenex
bell       form        mls        quote      trace
```

binary	get	mode	recv	type
bye	glob	mput	remotehelp	user
case	hash	nmap	rename	verbose
cd	help	ntrans	reset	?
cdup	lcd	open	rmdir	
close	ls	prompt	runique	

I typed ? to get a list of the ftp commands; this trick works in nearly all interactive UNIX applications. Either ? or help will almost always produce a list of commands.

18.4.2.3   Ftp's View of the World

```
ftp> pwd
257 "/" is current directory.
ftp> ls
200 PORT command successful.
150 Opening ASCII mode data connection for file list.
lost+found
pub
bin
etc
dev
README
226 Transfer complete.
34 bytes received in 0.13 seconds (30 Kbytes/s)
ftp> cd pub
250 CWD command successful.
ftp> ls
200 PORT command successful.
150 Opening ASCII mode data connection for file list.
ACKNOWL.TXT
CPYRIGHT.TXT
DOC
INDEX.TXT
MAIL
README.TXT
SRC
226 Transfer complete.
59 bytes received in 0.0069 seconds (21 Kbytes/s)
```

Ftp's view of the world is based on the UNIX file system. When you connect to a site using anonymous ftp, you are set down in a subdirectory specified by that site's administrator, and you can only look at files within that directory. In fact, as far as you can tell, there is no other part of the file system; as you can see, pwd says I am in the root ("/") directory.

Ftp has many of the common UNIX file and directory commands, such as pwd, cd, and ls, although you can't specify any options. This is because they aren't really the UNIX commands of the same names; they're ftp built-in commands.

18.4.2.4 Retrieving a File

```
ftp> get INDEX.TXT
200 PORT command successful.
150 Opening ASCII mode data connection for INDEX.TXT (3259 bytes).
226 Transfer complete.
local: INDEX.TXT remote: INDEX.TXT
3345 bytes received in 0.29 seconds (11 Kbytes/s)
ftp> quit
221 Goodbye.
dudley% ls -l INDEX.TXT
-rw-r--r-- 1 richter   3259    Mar 27 16:11   INDEX.TXT
dudley%
```

Since ftp's purpose in life is to transfer files from one system to another, it has easy-to-use commands for accomplishing that task. The get command pulls a file from the remote system to your local system, and the put command would transfer a file in the opposite direction (although many systems do not allow incoming file transfers).

Another somewhat confusing aspect of ftp's view of the world is its idea of "local" and "remote": files on the ftp system (which you would think of as the remote system) are referred to as "local," and files on your system (which you think of as local) are called "remote." It makes sense, but it takes some getting used to. Once back in the UNIX shell, an ls command shows that the file was indeed transferred to the local system. Note that the file name is identical with the original file name, including being stated in uppercase.

18.4.2.5 Retrieving Multiple Files and Globbing

```
ftp> ls xvt-*
200 PORT command successful.
150 Opening data connection for /bin/ls (ascii mode) (0 bytes).
xvt-1.0.README
xvt-1.0.tar.Z
226 Transfer complete.
remote: xvt-*
31 bytes received in 0.0042 seconds (7.3 Kbytes/s)
ftp> mget xvt-*
mget xvt-1.0.README? y
200 PORT command successful.
150 Opening data connection for xvt-1.0.README (ascii mode) (4185 bytes).
226 Transfer complete.
local: xvt-1.0.README remote: xvt-1.0.README
4306 bytes received in 0.67 seconds (6.3 Kbytes/s)
mget xvt-1.0.tar.Z? y
200 PORT command successful.
150 Opening data connection for xvt-1.0.tar.Z (ascii mode) (59445 bytes).
226 Transfer complete.
local: xvt-1.0.tar.Z remote: xvt-1.0.tar.Z
59711 bytes received in 2.8 seconds (20 Kbytes/s)
ftp> glob
```

```
Globbing off.
ftp> mget xvt-*
mget xvt-*? n
ftp> glob
Globbing on.
ftp> quit
221 Goodbye.
```

One thing that often causes confusion among ftp users is retrieval of multiple files. First of all, you must use the mget command, not get. Normally, you will be retrieving several files that have similar file names (like a C source file and a README file that are for the same piece of software). The simplest way to specify these files, and the way that works best with mget, is to use wildcard matching. In ftp, use of wildcards in file names is called *globbing*. When you give mget a globbed file name specification, ftp expands it on the remote system and then asks you, for each file, whether you want to retrieve the file. Answer with a simple y or n.

Beware: Mget does not work with multiple individual file names that do not use globbing! If you have to retrieve files with totally dissimilar names, just use multiple get commands.

You can also use globbing to limit the files that are listed by the ls or dir commands, as shown in the first ls command in the dialog above. If globbing doesn't seem to be working for you (that is, you get a message like 550 I*: No such file or directory.), it might be turned off. You can check the state of globbing with the status command, and toggle it off or on with the glob command.

18.4.2.6   Binary or ASCII Mode?

By default, ftp is prepared to deal with plain ASCII text. Using ftp jargon to describe this, you would say that the representation type is set to ASCII, or that the session is using ASCII mode. This is suitable for retrieving any normal text file, such as C language or other source code, electronic mail, documents, and so on. Quite often you may need to transfer executable programs or other binary data, and for this kind of copy you need to change the representation type using the binary command. (Some versions of ftp may tell you they're going into image mode rather than binary, but the command to get there is the same.)

There are many file formats (for example, compressed files and tar images) that, although they are not executable program images, still may need to be transferred using binary mode. If you are in doubt about a file's format, it's always safe to transfer it using binary mode. Beware that if you use ASCII mode to transfer a file that requires binary mode, the file may arrive looking like it's okay—it will be the right size—but it will be corrupted. Usually when someone makes a file available for anonymous ftp, he will indicate if it needs binary mode transfer.

18.4.2.7   Transferring Directory Hierarchies

By itself, ftp doesn't handle directory hierarchies. If you have to put a directory full of files into an ftp repository, you should bundle them together first using an archival program like tar or cpio. The most common practice is to use tar, and convention says you should name the resulting file with a .tar suffix; for example, myprog.tar. If the resulting file is very large, you should also compress it before putting it out for ftp access; if you do, the final file name will be myprog.tar.Z. Looking in a typical ftp directory on the Internet, you will see many files with names of this form.

18.4.2.8 Ftp versus Electronic Mail

When you need to send a file to someone on a remote system, your first idea may be just to send it in e-mail. This often works, but there are some trade-offs in capability between ftp and e-mail of which you should be aware. First, most e-mail systems have a size limitation on what you can send in a single message. In older systems, it was often 64K bytes; more modern mail systems may have larger limits, but there is still some limit. Ftp can handle files of any size, up to the disk capacity of the systems on either end. Also, you can't send binary or image data through e-mail; you must first uuencode any data, which increases the size of the file.

On the plus side for e-mail, it works more or less automatically. You compose the mail message, put the right address on, send it off, and everything else is done for you. Ftp requires a bit more in the way of establishing a connection, setting parameters, babysitting a file transfer, and so on. But for large files or binary data, ftp is the only choice.

18.5   What's Going on on the Network?

The ruptime and rwho commands are useful for getting status information about other hosts on an IP network. One disadvantage, and a reason many sites do not support these commands, is that every host that participates must run the rwhod (ar-who-dee) daemon, which broadcasts status information periodically (usually once a minute). If a network has a large number of hosts, running rwhod on all of them can represent a significant amount of network traffic. If you run rwho or ruptime on your system and get no results, that means your site is not running the rwhod daemon.

Rup queries hosts for their status, similar to ruptime. The difference is that rup's information gathering is done only on request, while with ruptime the information is continuously generated whether or not anyone asks for it. Ping is a utility to check the responsiveness and accessibility of a host across the network.

18.5.1   Rwho

The rwho command produces a list of all users currently logged into any system on the local IP network (see Table 18.6 for a command-line option). The output is very similar to that of the who command, plus it reports each user's idle time. By default, users who have been idle for an hour or more are not reported.

18.5.2 Ruptime

The ruptime command reports the status of every host on the local network that is alive. Along with the hostname, ruptime reports how long each host has been up, how many users are logged in, and the load average. By default, systems are listed in alphabetical order by hostname. There are several options to ruptime (see Table 18.7), most controlling how the output is sorted.

18.5.3 Rup

The rup command, which is otherwise somewhat similar to ruptime, does not depend on the rwhod daemon. Instead, it broadcasts a query and listens for answers (which are generated by another daemon, rstatd). Thus, network traffic is generated only when someone executes the rup command, rather than continuously, no matter whether anyone is paying attention or not. The syntax is

```
% rup [options] [hostname ... ]
```

The options (see Table 18.8) are similar to ruptime's and they control how the output is sorted (normally, output is displayed in the order responses are received over the network). Rup doesn't report the number of users logged into a system.

If you specify no hostnames, rup asks for information from any host on the net and gathers the results as they come back in. It times out after a reasonable period of time, typically one to three minutes. If you do give one or more hostnames, rup contacts those hosts individually and in order, asking

Table 18.6 ■ Rwho Command-line Option

-a	Include even those users who have been idle.

Table 18.7 ■ Ruptime Command-line Options

-a	Count even users who have been idle for an hour or more.
-l	Sort the systems by load average.
-r	Reverse the sorting order (can be combined with another sort order flag).
-t	Sort by length of time the system has been up.
-u	Sort by number of users.

Table 18.8 ■ Rup Command-line Options

-h	Sort alphabetically by hostname.
-l	Sort by load average.
-t	Sort by up-time.

for their status. Rup waits through the time-out period before giving up on a host and going to the next, so if several specified hosts are down, rup may take a long time to complete. Sample rup output is shown in the following:

```
moose         up 24 days, 15:25,      load average: 0.26, 0.29, 0.01
iguana        up  3 days, 16:03,      load average: 0.82, 0.76, 0.50
boris         up 19 days,  9:59,      load average: 0.40, 0.39, 0.43
natasha       up  6 days, 16:57,      load average: 0.34, 0.06, 0.02
rocky         up 10 days, 17:14,      load average: 0.03, 0.00, 0.00
```

18.5.4   Ping

The ping command is a simpleminded program that simply sends a small IP packet to a host and waits for it to ping or reflect back. There are several versions of ping floating around (read the manual page on your local system for details), but the lowest-common-denominator syntax is:

```
% ping hostname
```

Although very simple, ping tells you whether the remote system is known, reachable, and alive—valuable information for tracking down network connectivity problems. If ping returns an error about unknown host, there is a problem with your system's hosts file. If it says "destination unreachable," there may be something wrong with the way network routing is set up. If it says "no response from *host*," then the remote system is probably down. As a user, you can't do much about these problems other than report them to your system administrator, but it can be nice to have some idea where the problems lie.

It's important to understand that ping works at a very low level, so that a machine which is powered on but not running UNIX, or in the process of booting up, might still respond. If, for any reason, you're not sure about the status of a machine, it's best to first try ping, followed by rup or rwho.

The ping command often lives in the /etc or /usr/etc directory, since it is used by system administrators.

19
UUCP Networking Utilities

The UUCP suite of programs was the first attempt to bring network power to the UNIX community. It was originally developed in the late 1970s to distribute source code among UNIX hosts at then-Bell Telephone Laboratories. From those modest beginnings, UUCP spread rapidly, somewhat like UNIX itself, to encompass a far wider role. By the early eighties, most UNIX sites were linked by UUCP to other UNIX sites, forming a worldwide network of UNIX systems. This network was primarily used for electronic mail and news. By the mid 1980s, Berkeley had introduced the UNIX community to the ease and power of LAN/WAN networking, and the Internet rapidly grew in both size and utility. This reduced the importance of uucp connections among UNIX hosts.

Though its role is diminished, UUCP remains an important aspect of UNIX communications. For example, if you have a UNIX workstation or notebook computer at home, you may use UUCP to transfer files between that system and UNIX systems at your workplace. Similarly, sites that aren't large enough to warrant (or afford) a direct connection to the Internet are often connected via UUCP to an Internet-connected site. Many sites use both kinds of networking. It's very common for sites that have a TCP/IP network also to have UUCP connections to neighboring sites. Some of the ancillary programs in the UUCP suite are also important. For example, many people use tip or cu from a UNIX system to connect to remote information utilities, other UNIX systems, or BBS services.

19.1 UUCP User-level Commands

User-level networking commands fall into four major functional groups: logging into remote systems, executing commands on remote systems, transferring files, and informational or status-reporting commands. In this chapter, we discuss the UUCP-based commands, listed in Table 19.1.

System-level networking commands, many of which can only be run by the superuser, are of interest mainly to system administrators. The configuration files needed to set up UUCP networking are writable only by the superuser. Therefore, we don't talk about them here. Brief descriptions of some system-level networking commands are found in Chapters 20 and 21.

19.2   Connecting to Other Systems

Just as in LAN networking, you can only log into a remote system if you have a user account on that machine. Your site also needs to have the appropriate networking infrastructure and configuration files for any of the remote access commands described here in order to work. If these commands don't work for you, contact your system administrator to see whether your site even supports UUCP networking.

In the UUCP networking family, cu is the command used to log in to other systems. The tip command, which is similar in function to cu, was actually written at Berkeley. It's not considered part of Berkeley networking, though, because it works through serial lines. All implementations of UNIX have cu; many also include tip. Tip is newer, and its design gives you, the user, more power and flexibility than does cu.

The cu and tip commands work primarily over dial-up lines (a serial line → modem → telephone jack setup), although they can also deal with systems or peripheral devices such as terminals or printers directly connected to a serial line.

19.2.1   Cu, Call UNIX

The basic syntax of the cu command is

```
% cu [options] sysname
```

There are numerous options for setting communication parameters as well as debugging. The SVR4 cu command-line options are listed in Table 19.2.

There are many slight variants of UUCP and cu in existence; it's always best to consult the manual page on your own system for the exact options available.

Table 19.1 ■ User-level Commands for UUCP Networking

Remote login	Execution	File transfer	Information
cu	uux	uucp	uustat
tip	—	uuto	uuname
		uupick	uulog

Table 19.2 ■ Cu Command-line Options (SVR4)

`-s`*speed*	Specify the speed, or baud rate, of the connection.
`-l`*device*	Specify the device (e.g., /dev/tty01) to use, in case more than one dial-out line is available.
`-b`*n*	Use n-bit characters.
`-d`	Print diagnostics.
`-h`	Half-duplex mode; do local echoing.
`-e`	Use even parity.
`-o`	Use odd parity.
`-t`	Map carriage returns (CR) to CR/linefeed pairs as appropriate.
`-n`	Prompt user for the phone number to dial.

The sysname can be either the phone number of a remote system's dial-in modem or the name of an entry in your host's Systems file. Using a phone number gives you the flexibility to call up an arbitrary site that you might need to connect to only once. The Systems file makes it convenient to set up calling for frequently-called sites; you refer to them by name, and the entry contains not only the phone number (or direct line to use), but other connection parameters. The uuname command lists all the Systems entries; only the system administrator may modify that file.

When you're starting a cu session, you should be prepared to wait through some possibly lengthy delays as the various components in the end-to-end telephone circuit get acquainted with one another. Dialing and tone negotiation can take many seconds, and it's easy to think things have gone awry. A good rule of thumb is to give it a full minute (and use a watch—a minute is longer than you might think!); if nothing has happened by then, break off the attempt and start trying to find out what is wrong.

Once a cu connection is established, you log into the remote host and work just as if you were on a local system. Let's say you are sitting at a terminal connected to minicomputer alfie, which is running UNIX. You use cu to log in to another UNIX host, betty, which is in a different time zone:

```
alfie% date
Wed Feb 17 07:16:19 PDT 1993
alfie% cu betty
Login: richter
Password:
Welcome to betty!
betty% date
Wed Feb 17 10:17:43 EDT 1993
betty%
```

At this point, you're still sitting at alfie's terminal, and the keys you hit as you type are still transmitting their electrical signals to alfie, but the cu software running on alfie transparently passes them on to the betty system. When you type the date command at the betty% prompt, the five keystrokes (d, a, t, e, <CR>) are each individually intercepted by the cu software and passed on to betty; they cause nothing to happen on alfie.

Let's be more specific about how input and output are handled by cu. Two separate cu processes run on your local system during a cu session: transmit and receive. Once you've established a cu connection, characters you type are intercepted by the transmit process, which passes them on to the remote system.

The software running on the remote system (usually a login shell, plus whatever commands you start up in the course of your login session) isn't aware that you are using cu. It's just reading stdin and writing stdout to the terminal—which in this case is you using cu! It's worth pointing out here that the remote system isn't necessarily running UNIX: you can use cu to connect to any kind of system that has the concept of "logging in." Many people use cu to connect to bulletin board systems (BBSs), commercial information systems, and so on.

Now, returning to our "story": characters coming back from betty (for example, the characters d, a, etc., that must be echoed on your terminal screen) are sent back over the cu connection to alfie and intercepted by the receive process, which echoes them to your screen.

Occasionally, you need to communicate with the cu process itself, rather than with the machine at the other end of the connection. If you type a line starting with a tilde (~), the transmit process recognizes this as the beginning of a cu command and does not pass it to the remote system. These commands are called *tilde escapes*.

Here's an example of a tilde escape. The ~! escape says to perform the following command on the local system. For example:

```
betty% date
Wed Feb 17 10:17:43 EDT 1993
betty% ~!date
Wed Feb 17 07:17:39 PDT 1993
betty% 
```

The second date command was executed on alfie, not betty. Note that the betty session is still active; it's betty that will see your next command (unless you use another tilde escape).

The most important cu tilde escapes are listed in Table 19.3. The two marked "UNIX only," ~%put and ~%take, are dependent on finding various UNIX-specific features on both the local and remote systems to work properly. Although it's possible to transfer reasonably large files using the ~%put and ~%take mechanisms, there are a couple of important limitations you should know about. First, transmission is artificially slowed to avoid buffering problems across slow links, so file transfers can take much longer than you might expect if you calculate a time based on the connection's baud rate. Second, only plain text files can be transferred; if you need to transfer a binary or data file, you should first turn it into plain text with uuencode.

As shown in Figure 19.1, if you are on local machine natasha, connected via cu to dudley, and then connected from there to host moose, you would type ~~. to terminate the dudley-to-moose connection (and end up at the dudley command prompt). Typing ~. would have terminated the natasha-to-

Table 19.3 ■ The Most Important Cu Tilde Escapes

~.	Terminate the connection immediately. This does not give the remote system any warning and should not be considered the equivalent of logging out. When you log out from the remote system, the cu session should be terminated cleanly for you.
~!	Start an interactive shell on the local system. This lets you do local commands while keeping the remote connection alive. Exiting the shell puts you back into the remote connection.
~!*cmd*	Run *cmd* on the local system, and send output to the screen. Good for doing a single command, such as listing a directory.

~$*cmd*	Run *cmd* on the local system, and send output to the remote system. Note that if you issue this escape while at the remote system's command prompt, the output will be interpreted as command lines, and they will try to execute. This escape is most useful within a sequence such as:
	
	`% cat > myfiles.ls`
	`~$ls -l`
	`( output from the local ls command )`
	`^D`
	`%`

~%take *remfile* [*locfile*]	Copy *remfile* from the remote system to *locfile* on the local host. If you omit *locfile*, *remfile* is used as the target file name on the local host. If it's not an absolute pathname, it is relative to the current directory on the local host. UNIX only.
~%put *locfile* [*remfile*]	Copy *locfile* from the local system to *remfile* on the remote host. If *remfile* is not specified, *locfile* is used as the target file name on the remote system. UNIX only.
~%b	Send a BREAK signal to the remote host. This can be useful for communicating with devices such as terminal multiplexors or modems between you and the remote system.
~%cd [*dir*]	Change directory on the local system to *dir*. If no argument is given, change to your home directory.
~%d	Turn debugging on or off (toggle switch). Turning on debugging can generate a lot of messages you wouldn't want to see in normal operation but can be invaluable in tracking down connection or other problems.
~~...	Two or more tildes at the beginning of a line allow you to pass a cu command line through the transmit process (it eats up one tilde on the way). This is necessary if you have a chain of cu's connecting several machines and you want to send a cu command to any but the local machine.

From a cu session, you can use tilde escapes to get back to your local host. If you have a chain of cu connections, multiple tildes can be used to send commands back to any intermediate host, as illustrated in the figure.

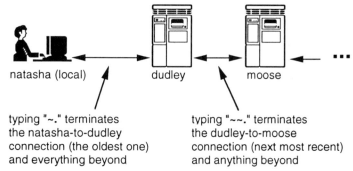

natasha (local)   dudley   moose

typing "~." terminates   typing "~~." terminates
the natasha-to-dudley   the dudley-to-moose
connection (the oldest one)   connection (next most recent)
and everything beyond   and anything beyond

Figure 19.1 ■ Chained Cu Sessions

dudley connection and should terminate all connections beyond dudley as well. However, it's possible that dudley doesn't know to end other connections when you log out, so it's safest to take care of terminating them yourself.

19.2.2 Tip

The tip command is functionally similar to cu, but it uses different underlying software and administrative files. Tip is not part of SVR4, but it is widely available in the UNIX world. Tip supports not only log-in to remote systems (which do not necessarily have to be UNIX systems) but also file transfers. One big advantage of tip over cu is that the user has the power to do his own administration, supplying private lists of calling destinations. Another advantage is the large number of tip's internal variables, which allow you to customize the behavior and characteristics of connections on a call-by-call basis.

The primary tip configuration file (roughly equivalent to the Systems file) is called /etc/remote (see Figure 19.2). It contains named entries for calling

```
cual:dv=/dev/cual:br#1200:
dialup1|Dial-up system:pn=2015551212%:tc=UNIX-1200:
mmouse:pn=@:tc=cual:
hardwire:\
:dv=/dev/ttyhardwire:br#9600:el=^C^S^Q^U^D:ie=%$:oe=^D:
UNIX-300:\
:el=^D^U^C^S^Q^O@:du:at=ventel:ie=#$%:oe=^D:br#300:tc=dialers:
UNIX-1200:\
:el=^D^U^C^S^Q^O@:du:at=ventel:ie=#$%:oe=^D:br#1200:tc=dialers:
```

Figure 19.2 ■ Fragment of an /etc/remote File

destinations, along with the phone number or direct line to use, and any settings needed to communicate properly. Only the system administrator or superuser is usually allowed to modify the /etc/remote file. To keep your own list of sites to call, define them in a configuration file and then set the environment variable REMOTE to point to it.

The syntax of /etc/remote is similar to that of /etc/printcap. The remote(5) manual page (this notation means "the manual page for the 'remote' file, to be found in Section 5 of the manual") describes the syntax of a calling entry in detail.

A second configuration file is /etc/phones (see Figure 19.3), which contains just a list of destination host names and their phone numbers. This file is consulted if the phone number field in an /etc/remote entry is set to the at sign, @. Only the superuser may modify the /etc/phones file. The environment variable PHONES can point to your own list of phone numbers. The phones(5) manual page describes the syntax for a phones file.

If you are faced with the task of writing your own remote or phones file, the easiest way to start (according to time-honored UNIX tradition) is to copy an entry from the system file and then modify it. If your system file doesn't have anything close to what you need, another resource is the Internet news groups. If you have access to a machine with a netnews feed, you could post a query to the news group comp.unix.questions, and it's very likely you'll receive at least one reply within a matter of a day or two.

Since it was written at Berkeley, and considerably later than cu, tip has a lot of bells and whistles that cu lacks, such as internal variables and a user-specific configuration file, $HOME/.tiprc.

Its basic syntax is:

```
tip [-v] [-speed-entry] name
```

Tip has very few command-line options (see Table 19.4), because settings can be specified in the .tiprc configuration file.

Like cu, tip also uses tilde escapes for commands during a session. The common tilde escapes recognized by tip are listed in Table 19.5. Note that many of them are similar to cu's.

The .tiprc file can contain a multitude of options, which are settings of internal tip variables (see Table 19.6). Many of these variables correspond to

---

```
mmouse      909-987-6543
esuvax      345-6789
```

Figure 19.3 ■ Fragment of an /etc/phones File

Table 19.4 ■ Tip Command-line Options

-v	Verbose; display the commands from .tiprc as they are executed.
-speed-entry	Specify the baud rate at which to connect.

Table 19.5 ■ Commonly Used Tilde Escapes in Tip

~^D or ~.	Terminate the connection immediately. As in cu, this is not the equivalent of logging out; you may still be logged in on the remote machine.
~c [name]	Change directory on the local system to *name*. If no argument is given, change to your home directory.
~!	Start an interactive shell on the local system. This lets you do local commands while keeping the remote connection alive. Exiting the shell returns you to the tip connection.
~>	Copy file from local to remote system (may be used when connecting to non-UNIX hosts). Tip prompts for a file name and sends it to stdout. If you have started up some command on the remote system which is listening over the connection (a UNIX example would be cat > remfile), it will receive the file as it is transferred.
~<	Copy file from remote to local system. Like ~<, only in the opposite direction.
~p locfile [remfile]	Copy *locfile* to a remote host running the UNIX system. If you omit *remfile*, *locfile* is used as the target file name on the remote host. This is actually a UNIX system-specific version of the '~>' command; it runs the necessary "cat" command on the remote host.
~t remfile [locfile]	Take *remfile* from a remote host running the UNIX system. If you omit *locfile*, *remfile* is used as the target file name on the local host. This is actually a UNIX system specific version of the ~< command.
~#	Send a BREAK to the remote system.
~s	Set a tip internal variable (see discussion of .tiprc file).
~^Z	Stop tip (only available when run under a shell that supports job control, such as the C-shell).
~?	Get a summary of the tilde escapes.
~~	To actually send a tilde to the remote system, use two tildes.

attributes that can be specified in a configuration entry in the /etc/remote file. Settings in a user's .tiprc file override any specifications in /etc/remote.

Some variables are simply on-off settings (Boolean); these are set by mentioning the variable name and unset by preceding the name with an exclamation point, !. The rest take either a numeric or a string argument and are set by mentioning the variable name, an equal sign, =, and the desired value (white space around the = sign is not allowed). In Table 19.6, the type of each variable and its abbreviation are shown in parentheses after the variable name.

19.3   File Transfer Between Hosts

File transfer between hosts is one of the most basic needs in setting up a "network," and it was one of the first functions implemented. It was the

Table 19.6 ■ Tip Internal Variables

beautify	(bool, be) Discard unprintable characters when a session is being scripted (default on).
baudrate	(num, ba) The baud rate at which the connection was established (default 300, settable only by superuser once connection is made).
dialtimout	(num, dial) When dialing a phone number, the time (in seconds) to wait for a connection to be established (default 60 seconds).
disconnect	(str, di) The string to send to the remote host to drop the connection (default the null string "").
echocheck	(bool, ec) Synchronize with the remote host during file transfer by waiting for the echo of the last character transmitted (default off).
eofread	(str, eofr) The set of characters which signify an end-of-transmission during a ~< file transfer command (default the null string "").
eofwrite	(str, eofw) The string sent to indicate end-of-transmission during a ~> file transfer command (default the null string "").
eol	(str, eol) The set of characters which indicate an end-of-line (default the null string "").
escape	(char, es) The command prefix (escape) character (default tilde ~).
etimeout	(num, et) The amount of time, in seconds, that tip should wait for the echo-check response when echocheck is set (default ten seconds).
exceptions	(str, ex) The set of characters which should not be discarded due to the beautification switch (default '\t\n\f\b').
force	(char, fo) The character used to force literal data transmission (default is octal \377, which disables it).
framesize	(num, fr) The amount of data (in bytes) to buffer between file system writes when receiving files (default 1024).
halfduplex	(bool, hdx) Do local echoing because the host is half-duplex (default off).
hardwareflow	(bool, hf) Do hardware flow control (default off).
host	(str, ho) The name of the host to which you are connected (set to the name given on the command line or the value of $HOST).
localecho	(bool, le) Synonym for half-duplex.
log	(str, log) The name of the file to which to log information about outgoing phone calls (can only be inspected or changed by the superuser).
parity	(str, par) The parity to be generated and checked when talking to the remote host (default none). Possible values are none, zero, one, even or odd. For zero and one, input parity is not checked.
phones	(str, phones) The file in which to find hidden phone numbers (set to value of $PHONES or /etc/phones; cannot be changed from within tip).
prompt	(char, pr) The character which indicates an end-of-line on the remote host (default newline \n).
raise	(bool, ra) Uppercase mapping mode, meaning all lowercase letters will be mapped to uppercase by tip for transmission to the remote machine (default off).
raisechar	(char, rc) The input character used to toggle uppercase mapping mode (default is octal \377, which disables it).
rawftp	(bool, raw) Send all characters during file transfers, meaning do not filter nonprintable characters and do not do translations like \n (newline) to \r (carriage return) (default off).

Table 19.6 ■ Tip Internal Variables (*continued*)

record	(str, rec) The name of the file in which a session script is recorded (default tip.record).
remote	(str, remote) The file in which to find descriptions of remote systems (set to value of $REMOTE or /etc/remote; cannot be changed from within tip).
script	(bool, sc) Session scripting mode, meaning tip will record everything transmitted by the remote machine in the file specified in record (default off).
tabexpand	(bool, tab) Expand each TAB character to 8 SPACE characters during file transfers (default off).
tandem	(bool, ta) Use XON/XOFF flow control to limit the rate that data is sent by the remote host (default off).
verbose	(bool, verb) Verbose mode, meaning tip prints messages while dialing, shows the current number of lines transferred during a file transfer operation, and so on (default off).

"UNIX-to-UNIX copy" program from which the entire UUCP system, with all the functionality added later, got its name.

For dial-up connections, the uucp command is the primary file-copying utility. It guarantees reliable, perfect transmission of a file from one host to another. Note, though, that cu and tip also have file transfer capabilities. Because tip and cu are interactive, many people find them more convenient for doing file transfers. However, neither tip nor cu has any mechanism for checking to guarantee correct transmission of files; you are responsible for noticing any interruption or errors due to line noise during a transmission. Also, uucp can transfer binary files whereas tip and cu are limited to text files.

19.3.1   UUCP

The uucp command transfers files between the local host and any other machine accessible via UUCP connections.

When you issue a uucp command, the file transfer is not instantly done. Rather, your request is saved in a queue along with other uucp and uux jobs and waits until the appropriate remote system is called. The UUCP queueing system is based on the concept of polling, which means that remote systems are each called on a regular schedule. The schedule may be (and usually is) different for each remote site and is set based on how much traffic is expected between the local system and that site. Some important sites may be polled hourly or even more frequently, while others may only get daily or even weekly attention.

What this means is that, especially if you are transferring large files through uucp, you may need to wait a long (and unpredictable) amount of time for a file transfer to be completed. Uucp has numerous options (see Table 19.7) that let you specify how you are to be notified of your job's status.

Table 19.7 ■ Some Useful Uucp Options

-C	Copy files to the spool directory for transfer. You might want to do this if you are working on the files, or want to delete them, and you want to make sure they get transferred in their current state.
-c	Don't copy files to the spool directory (the default).
-d	Create directories as needed at the destination (the default).
-f	Do not make directories if they don't exist.
-gpriority	Submit job at *priority*, which can be a digit 0-9 or an alpha character A-Z or a-z. 0 is the highest priority, z is the lowest. A higher priority job is done earlier during a connection, but doesn't cause the connection to be made any earlier (that is, it doesn't affect the polling interval or schedule).
-j	Output the uucp job ID, which can be used with uustat to check the status of your job.
-m	Send mail to the person who issued the uucp command, when the copy is completed.
-nuser	Send notification mail to *user*. Often used to send mail to the intended recipient of the files, on the destination system.
-sfile	When the copy is complete, write its status into *file* rather than sending mail to anyone. Useful for keeping a log file.
-xlevel	Produce debugging output at *level*, which can be from 0 (no debugging) to 9 (most extensive).

When a site is polled, any jobs waiting to go to that system are transferred across the connection. Then any jobs waiting on the remote site for your system are transferred. Normally jobs are transferred or executed in the order they were queued, but there are options to bump up the priority of a particular job.

The uucp syntax is similar to the normal cp command:

```
uucp sourcefile destfile
uucp sourcefile ... destdir
```

Any of the file specifications can be preceded with a system designator, which is one or more hostnames each followed by an exclamation point:

```
host1!filename
host1!host2!host3!...!filename
```

The system designator defines the set of hosts that must contact one another (in sequence) to do the file transfer. The first hostname must be accessible directly from the local host, and the last hostname (closest to the file name) is where the file actually lives.

For file names on remote systems, the prefix ''~username/'' is interpreted as ''username's home directory'' and ''~/'' as the public UUCP directory on the specified system. If you give a relative pathname, it is prefixed with the pathname of the current directory. Note that the ''current directory'' on the local system may not exist on a remote system.

If the destination is a directory name, there can be multiple source files. You force the destination to be considered a directory by adding a trailing slash to its name. By default, uucp will create any directories necessary to make the destination directory; that is, you can specify "~/richter/junk/", and uucp will create the directories richter and richter/junk within the public UUCP directory, if they don't already exist.

UNIX file permissions are enforced for both reading and writing. Also, it's quite common for sites to restrict uucp so that files can be read or written only in the public UUCP directory, for security reasons.

19.3.2   Uuto and Uupick

To streamline the UUCP process somewhat and eliminate much of the confusion about where files may be copied, how pathnames are expressed, and so on, the HoneyDanBer version of UUCP has two commands called uuto and uupick (see Chapter 17 for more about HoneyDanBer UUCP, a standard part of SVR4 UNIX). You should note that the uuto program is really just a pretty face on top of uucp. It frees you from having to know so many details about public directory names and hierarchical tree structures, but it's still the same program.

The uuto command copies one or more files to a remote destination, but that is expressed simply as a hostname and a user name (see Table 19.8 for command-line options). The files are automatically copied into the public spool area on the remote system, into a subdirectory that belongs to that particular user. The syntax is:

```
uuto sourcefile ... hostname!user
```

When the files are copied to the remote machine, mail is sent to the recipient notifying him of their arrival.

The complementary command is uupick, which is used for receiving files sent with uuto. Uupick looks in the public spool directory, in the subdirectory that belongs to you—the same place uuto writes files sent from remote systems. By default, it displays all the files it finds (see Table 19.9 for a command-line option). You can choose what to do with each file by giving interactive commands (see Table 19.10).

Table 19.8 ■ Uuto Command-line Options

-m	Send mail to the sender when the transfer is completed.
-p	Copy files to the spool directory for transfer (same as uucp's -C flag).

Table 19.9 ■ Uupick Command-line Option

-ssystem	Display only the files sent from remote host *system*.

Table 19.10 ■ Uupick Interactive Commands

`<CR>`	Move down to the next file in the list.
`d`	Delete this file.
`mdir`	Move this file to the named directory.
`p`	Print this file.
`adir`	Move all the files sent from *system* to the named directory.
`q or Ctrl-D`	Quit uupick.
`!cmd` (shell escape)	Execute the shell command *cmd,* then return to the uupick session. You might want to use this to list the contents of some directory you're thinking of moving files to, for example.
`*`	Print a summary of the commands available.

19.4 Executing Commands on Remote Systems—Uux

Uux is the UUCP-style command for remote execution of commands. Besides executing commands on a remote host, uux can also gather files from multiple remote hosts to be used in the execution of that command.

Uux was quite impressive when it was first developed, in the days before the Internet. Today it seems very clumsy and difficult to use, and few people use it for anything except transfer of electronic mail, using canned scripts.

There are a number of limitations to consider when using uux. First, it is a batch command facility. You can't do anything through uux that requires user interaction, and commands aren't necessarily executed in a timely fashion. Finally, the entire concept rests on the robustness and cooperation of other hosts who may be down at any time or decide to stop serving as UUCP hosts.

When you issue a uux command, that command is not instantly sent off to the remote system and executed. Rather, it is saved in a queue along with other uucp and uux jobs and waits until the appropriate remote system is called (see the description of polling in Section 19.3.1).

The uux syntax is:

```
uux [options] [command line]
```

The command line looks much like an ordinary shell command line, but it isn't simply handed off to a shell on the remote machine for execution. Uux actually has built-in implementations of many shell functions, such as I/O redirection. For that reason, not all shell functions are supported in uux. Simple I/O redirection (< and >) and pipes are implemented. Uux command-line options are listed in Table 19.11.

The command name may be preceded by a system designator, which is an optional hostname followed by an exclamation point, !. (C-shell users, note that the exclamation must be escaped with a backslash, \!, to prevent the shell from interpreting it as a history event.) The hostname has to be one that is recognized by UUCP; the uuname command lists the hosts reachable via UUCP from your system. You can also specify a chain of hostnames that make UUCP connections with one another. In this case, each host passes the

Table 19.11 ■ Some Useful Uux Command-line Options

`-auser`	Send notification of success to *user*.
`-C`	Copy files to the spool directory for transfer. You might want to do this if you are working on the files, or want to delete them, and you want to make sure they get transferred in their current state.
`-c`	Don't copy files to the spool directory (the default).
`-d`	Create directories as needed at the destination (the default).
`-f`	Do not make directories if they don't exist.
`-gpriority`	Submit job at *priority,* which can be a digit 0-9 or an alpha character A-Z or a-z. 0 is the highest priority, z is the lowest. A higher priority job is done earlier during a connection but doesn't cause the connection to be made any earlier (that is, it doesn't affect the polling interval or schedule).
`-j`	Output the uux job ID, which can be used with uustat to check the status of your job.
`-n`	Do not send notification mail to the user even if the job fails.
`- or -p`	Use uux as a filter; that is, read the standard input of uux and send it as the standard input to the command line.
`-xlevel`	Produce debugging output at *level,* which can be from 0 (no debugging) to 9 (most extensive).
`-z`	Send notification mail to the user even if the job succeeds (default is to notify only of failure).

uux request to the next, and the last hostname in the chain specifies where the command will actually be executed.

Here are examples of commands with host designators:

`boris!ls`   Execute the ls command on host boris.
`!diff`   Execute the diff command on the local host.

Within a uux request, all commands must be executed on the same host. That is, you can't give a command pipeline with the first command to be executed on one host and the second on a different host. Also, it's quite common for sites to severely restrict the set of commands that can be executed by uux, for security reasons.

File names may also be preceded by a system designator. For file names on remote systems, the prefix "~username/" is interpreted as "username's home directory" and "~/" as the public UUCP directory, on the specified system. If you give a relative pathname, it is prefixed with the pathname of the current directory. Note that the "current directory" on the local system may not exist on a remote system.

File name examples include:

`!~richter/p.data`	On the local system, the file p.data in richter's home directory.
`dudley!neptune!~/OPEN/daily.stat`	On host neptune, which is reachable from dudley, the file daily.stat in the OPEN subdirectory of the public UUCP directory.

19.5   UUCP Status Commands

There is a handful of commands which can provide useful information as you use the UUCP system to do tasks. Uustat and uulog tell you the status of your uucp or uux requests, and uuname gives information about how your site's UUCP network is configured.

19.5.1   Uustat

The uustat command (see Table 19.12 for command-line options) shows the status of uucp and uux jobs that are queued for execution and the latest accessibility status for each remote site, and it allows the user to cancel his own jobs.

19.5.2   Uulog

The uulog command (see Table 19.13 for command-line options) command displays log messages about uucp commands already executed or attempted. Every destination has its own log file; by default, the logs for all systems are shown.

Table 19.12 ■ Common Uustat Command-line Options

`-a`	Report on all queued jobs. By default, uustat shows only jobs owned by the invoking user.
`-kjobid`	Cancel the job identified by *jobid*. Only the owner or the superuser can cancel a job.
`-m`	Show the accessibility of all machines (based on the success or failure of the last attempted connection).
`-p`	Show ps(1) for all currently active connections.
`-q`	List the jobs queued for each remote system, as well as the status of the last connection attempt, time of next scheduled connection, and other administrative information.
`-ssystem`	Report on jobs queued for remote host *system*.
`-uuser`	Report on queued jobs owned by *user,* including the job ID of each request.

Table 19.13 ■ Uulog Command-line Options

`-x`	Report on uux jobs (default is uucp jobs).
`-ssystem`	Report on jobs involving remote host *system*.
`-fsystem`	Tail the log file for *system,* and keep displaying lines as they are added. To exit, you must strike your interrupt character (often Ctrl-C).
`-n`	Show only the last *n* lines of each specified log file.

Table 19.14 ■ Uuname Command-line Options

-c	List hosts that are available for cu(1) connection (usually the same as those available for UUCP).
-l	Output the local host's name.

19.5.3 Uuname

The uuname command (see Table 19.14 for command-line options) lists all the hosts with which your system can establish a direct UUCP connection. Bear in mind that many other hosts may be accessible through UUCP, by going through a chain of intermediate hosts.

20
System Management

Managing a computer system involves more than just turning on the power before the users start logging in each morning. The system manager or system administrator (sysadmin) is responsible for maintaining the integrity of the system, installing new software, adapting software to local conditions, performing periodic backups of users' files, recovering lost data, and informing the users of new services and features. At some installations these responsibilities are widely distributed; at other installations there is a single person who accepts these responsibilities.

UNIX system administration is an important aspect of routine operations for many because of the increasing use of UNIX on single-user workstations and personal computers. The chores described in this chapter are usually performed by professional computer system managers on large minicomputer systems, but they must be performed by relatively inexperienced users on many smaller systems.

The goal of this chapter is to provide an introduction to some of the procedures and issues that must be understood by anyone who manages a UNIX system. The number of important subsystems that must be set up and administered to make a UNIX system truly functional is staggering. It would take several whole books to cover them in detail, and this is only a single chapter. We chose to stick to the very basic tasks of overall system configuration, handling disks and file systems, managing user accounts, and doing backups to secure the data. Along the way, we try to explain some of the incidental lore of UNIX. This chapter does not explain how to fix every conceivable file system problem or how to set up a comprehensive backup policy. You must learn by a combination of trial and error, improvisation, and adaptation of the tried and true to your environment.

This chapter omits such important areas as printer administration, electronic mail, and UUCP and TCP/IP network administration. These areas are quite complex; if you need to understand any of them in sufficient depth to set it up, turn to one of the books on the market that specialize in that topic.

In the first six sections of this chapter, the role of the superuser is explored, and several of the most important sysadmin tasks are examined at an overview level. When specific file names are mentioned in those sections, they are taken from Sun's Solaris 2.0 UNIX implementation, which is based on System V Release 4. Chapter 21 presents some of the utility programs used to accomplish those tasks. The materials in Chapter 21 cover the syntax and options of the actual commands without getting into background explanations or tying things together at a high level. Read this chapter for an overall understanding of how things work and Chapter 21 for specific details of command usage.

Starting with Section 20.7, we cover some miscellaneous features of UNIX that are primarily of interest to sysadmins, including swapping, special file modes, symbolic links, and fifo files.

20.1   The Superuser

Many of the operations performed by a sysadmin should be inaccessible to ordinary users. In the UNIX system this is accomplished by providing a special privilege level called *superuser.*

The UNIX superuser, who uses the login name root, is the most privileged user. The superuser is able to perform many operations that are denied to ordinary users. Most of the operations discussed in the remainder of this chapter must be invoked by the superuser. In addition, several of the commands mentioned in other parts of this book function differently when invoked by the superuser. For example, ordinary users can use the date command to display the date and time, but the superuser can also use the date command to set the date and time.

Ordinary users are constrained by UNIX's file access mode protection system. However, the superuser is not constrained by the protection system. The superuser can change the mode of any file or access any file in any way. One exception is on remotely mounted file systems. For better security, many sites deny root's special access privileges on remote file systems. In this case, the superuser is granted blanket permissions of the "other" user; that is, unless a file is world-readable, root can't read it either. This scheme means that an intruder who breaks into one system as root doesn't have the entire network at his fingertips.

Inadvertent superuser commands can do great damage because the normal constraints don't apply. The superuser password should be entrusted only to responsible and experienced users, and the number of people with this privilege should be kept as small as possible.

There are two ways to acquire the superuser privilege. One way is to log in using the special name root. The other method is to log in using your normal login name and then execute the su (superuser) command. For security's sake, using the su command is preferred (see Section 22.5). In either case, the system will ask you to enter the superuser password. If you enter the correct password, the system will display a different prompt (usually a sharp, #) while you are operating with superuser privilege. At the conclusion of the operations requiring the superuser privilege, you should strike Ctrl-D. If you logged in as root, then you will be logged out; if you used the su command, you will be returned to your normal identity and your original prompt will be shown.

Don't do ordinary work while logged in as root. Simple mistakes can cause disasters. The su command makes it easy to log in as yourself and then elevate your privilege temporarily to root, as often as necessary.

20.2   System Configuration

Although some UNIX systems are stable over a period of years, it is much more common for configurations to change. It's also common for a site to have several different configurations of machines, each with a different mix of peripherals. Rapid advances in the speed and capacity of hardware, both CPUs and storage media, mean that people are constantly upgrading their equipment. If you are adding a new peripheral device to your UNIX system, you need to know some basics about making it fit in and work properly.

One of the things to consider when purchasing new equipment is its degree of support under UNIX. Many vendors provide equipment that conforms to some established interface. For example, many third parties produce disk and tape devices that use the SCSI (Small Computer Systems Interface) standards. Most versions of UNIX include a host-side SCSI driver and generic device-side SCSI disk and tape drivers. When you are considering buying a third-party SCSI tape or disk drive, you should find out (either from the vendor or by asking the Internet community) whether it requires a special device driver. If it does, you'll need to find out where to get the driver.

Some vendors provide excellent UNIX support for their products, providing and updating their own device drivers and making sure to keep up with the latest release of the UNIX operating system. Others seem to be totally disinterested in providing software support; however, if their product is sufficiently good (and if the specifications are available), someone in the UNIX community is likely to write a device driver and make it available on the Internet.

Once you've acquired your new peripheral and its software support, you have to install them into the UNIX system. You should be able to do the following two steps, hardware installation and software installation, in either order. The UNIX kernel generally works just fine even if unsupported hardware is installed (it just won't see those devices). Likewise, you should be able to run a version of UNIX into which you have added new device support even if that device is not yet present. The exception to this rule is installation of devices necessary for booting, such as the root disk or the system console. To replace one of these devices, you must arrange to boot the system in some alternate way so the device of interest is not used, and then replace it.

One of the most common procedures, adding a new disk, is fairly simple. Some other changes, such as replacing one disk with another, can be trickier, mostly because of the need to preserve existing data. Adding tape drives, serial port adaptors, CD-ROM drives, and other peripherals is usually less hassle than changing a disk configuration, because there is no data to preserve. If you have to move a file system from one disk to another, the process would be something like this:

- Unmount the file system so users can't change any of its data during the move.

- Dump the file system, either to tape or to another disk if it has enough room.

- Shut the system down, remove the old disk and install the new one.

- Format and partition the new disk.

- Restore the dump of the file system to the new disk.

- Mount the file system to allow user access.

If you are installing a new disk for the root partition, or if you are moving only one file system from a disk that contains several, even more elaborate steps must be taken. In all such operations, the most important thing you can do is to make a detailed plan before taking action. It can be somewhat like a puzzle; it's much easier to make everything fit together when all the pieces are clearly laid out in front of you.

The SCSI standard has become so prevalent in the last three to five years that nearly all types of peripherals are now available in a SCSI interface version. This greatly simplifies integration, since you don't have to install a new device driver for every peripheral you add. An adequate host-side SCSI driver should work well with almost every SCSI device. Unusual devices such as film recorders, scanners, and so on are likely to need special drivers.

20.2.1 Adding Device Drivers

Adding new device support to a pre-SVR4 UNIX system is fairly straightforward. In this traditional model, support for all devices has to be compiled into the kernel (/vmunix or /unix) statically. To add a device, you have to edit the kernel config file to specify the support configuration for the new device, move the device driver files into the proper directories, and then rebuild the kernel. The actual kernel-building process is controlled by special scripts and Makefiles supplied as part of the UNIX distribution. From the sysadmin's point of view, it is a matter of editing the config file and then typing two or three simple commands. It's not difficult, but it can be time-consuming.

SVR4 supports loadable device drivers. The kernel doesn't need to be recompiled for routine device changes; rather, it reads a configuration file called /etc/system at boot time to determine what devices it will support. Both the kernel and the device driver modules are kept in the /kernel directory. The kernel is called /kernel/unix, and the device driver modules are organized in subdirectories of /kernel. For every device mentioned in /etc/system, the kernel looks for a loadable module containing the code for that driver. To install a new device, you need only copy its loadable driver module to the appropriate /kernel subdirectory, mention it in the /etc/system file, and reboot.

The SVR4 "loadable modules" concept also extends to other kernel-level code such as support for new file system types, executable formats, system calls, and STREAMS modules for I/O processing. It provides immense flexibility and expandability for the UNIX kernel, with very little trouble for the system administrator.

20.2.2 Special Device Files

UNIX special device files are the link between the peripheral I/O devices and the operating system. For a more detailed discussion of special device files, see Chapter 23. Each special device has a major and minor device number, which are printed in a long format file listing as a pair of comma-separated numbers. The major device number tells what kind of device it is (for example, a tty line), and the minor number is used to identify the individual instances of each device type.

Under SVR4, with its loadable device drivers, there is no need to manually create special device files. Each driver creates the special files it needs when it is loaded by the kernel at boot time. In pre-SVR4 UNIX, though, the special files in /dev have to be created before a peripheral device can be used. Most UNIX systems come with a script in /dev called MAKEDEV which contains instructions for creating the special files for all but the most unusual peripherals. For example, to create the special files for a SCSI tape drive, you would cd to /dev and use the command MAKEDEV sd0. Since MAKEDEV is a shell script, you can read through it to see what device files it can create.

There may still be cases when you have to create a special file by hand, using the mknod command. One kind of special file that must be created with mknod is the fifo, or named pipe (see Section 20.9).

20.3 User Account Administration

One of the tasks of a sysadmin is user administration: adding new users to the system and deleting them when they are gone. The specific programs provided to do these tasks are as varied as the versions of UNIX available. Most UNIX vendors supply a menu-oriented or graphical user administration program to simplify the process and minimize the incidence of bookkeeping error.

When you are faced with this task, you should look up the recommended procedures for your system. In this book, we won't even attempt to describe an actual adduser or sysadm program, since they are so varied. Rather, we explain the various elements of adding users to a UNIX system so you will be able to make informed use of the tools you are given.

20.3.1   The Passwd and Group Files

The two key files for user administration in a standard UNIX system are /etc/passwd and /etc/group (a third file, /etc/shadow, is used to provide more secure passwords; see the discussion in Chapter 22). The passwd file has an entry for each user of the system, containing the following information:

- User's login name

- User's encrypted password

- UNIX user ID number, or UID

- UNIX group ID number, or GID, for this user

- User's full name, or description (traditionally called gecos field)

- User's home directory

- User's login shell

These components are individually discussed in the following sections. Here are a few lines from a hypothetical passwd file:

```
root:FcXB6m3BeTTsI:0:0:System Superuser:/:/bin/csh
bin:*:3:3:,u0000:/bin:
uucp:*:4:8:,u0000:/usr/spool/uucppublic:/usr/lib/uucp/uucico
porter:IKlIEt/nSzVKI:196:50:Laura Porter:/home/u/porter:/usr/bin/tcsh
loril:HxjEpjpJoFF.U:407:45:Lori Lewis:/home/u/loril:/bin/sh
jdp:ZFMoZEJQnEnAK:765:50:Jon Patton:/home/u2/jdp:/bin/csh
richter:wT445tfvfmBsw:826:10:Susan Richter:/home/u2/richter:/bin/csh
```

The /etc/group file contains an entry for each UNIX group on the system, with the following information:

- Group name

- Group's encrypted password, if any (usually none)

- Group ID or GID

- Comma-separated list of all the login names belonging to this group

Here are a few entries from a group file:

```
wheel:*:0:
daemon:*:1:uucp,daemon
kmem:*:2:
bin:*:3:bin
uucp:*:8:uucp,oper
```

```
staff:*:10:maint,porter,richter,ron
ppp:*:40:loril,ron
dbgroup:*:45:porter
corpmgr:*:50:sjohns,porter,jdp
```

When you add a new user, there are a few commonsense rules to follow
that will make the job easier. Some are actual limitations imposed by UNIX,
while others are simple rules of thumb.

20.3.2   Login Name

First, choose a user name that is not already in use. If you are administering
several machines at one site, they may be sharing a common passwd file
(through NIS or other means). Even if they are not, it's still a good idea to
choose a name that is not in use on any of the other machines, which means
you may need to do some checking. A user name can be a maximum of eight
characters long. It's good practice to make the login name identifiable as the
person; common conventions are to assign last name, or first initial plus last
name, or three initials. The examples in the first column of the following
would be good login name choices for Susan Richter; the second column
contains bad choices, because they don't have any clear association with
Susan.

```
richter     ir2rZk81
srichter    sss
sdr         booboo
```

20.3.3   User ID

UNIX user ID numbers (UIDs) range from 0, defined as the superuser, through
65535. It's common UNIX practice to reserve low UIDs for system use and to
not use them for ordinary users. The definition of low varies, but at least the
first 20 (often the first 100) are sacrosanct. Your system's administration program will probably offer to use the next available UID but allow you to override it. Some sysadmins like to use ranges of UIDs to group certain users
together while others simply add users willy-nilly as they come up.

20.3.4   Group ID

Group ID numbers (GIDs), like UIDs, range from 0 through 65535. The GID
that appears in a user's password entry is her default group. You can also
add the user to other groups, which means her name is added to the list of
members of that group in the /etc/group file. The way UNIX file permissions
work, a user has the privileges of all groups of which she is a member, all
the time.

One group affiliation is considered active during a login session; by default it's the GID mentioned in the passwd entry. The user can change the
active group by running the newgrp command. The active group affects the

group ownership of files created during that login session, except for files created in a directory that has the setgid bit set. In that case, all files created within that directory inherit the group ownership of the directory.

20.3.5 Initial Password

Every user must be assigned an initial password. User administration programs may allow you to skip this and add a user who has no password, but this is very dangerous from a security standpoint (see the discussion in Chapter 22). A password may be up to eight characters in length; some administration programs will impose other restrictions such as "must be at least six characters long," "must contain at least one nonalphabetic character," or "may not be a word found in the dictionary." All such restrictions are aimed toward improving password security, and it's in your best interest to go along with them.

If the password field in the /etc/passwd file is set to * (or to any string that is not a 13-character encrypted password), it is impossible for that user to log in. Some sysadmins like to keep the password entries for deleted users in /etc/passwd but alter the password field, to prevent that UID from being reused. Pseudo-users such as bin and dev, which are used exclusively for permissions, are always given a password string of *. It would be very insecure to allow anyone to log in as bin or dev, since those accounts own many critical system files.

By contrast, a password string of * in the /etc/group file means that there is no password for that group. Group passwords are almost never used, and this is typified by the entries shown in the example in Section 20.3.1.

20.3.6 Home Directory

You will have to assign a home directory for each new user. If your system has only one file system for user directories, say /home/u, the choice is simple. The name of the upper-level directory plus the login name are combined to form the user's home directory name; for example, /home/u/richter.

If there are several user file systems, it's a good idea to balance the load by adding a new user to the file system with the most available space (use the df command to check disk space). Another possibility is to put a new user's home directory in a file system shared by other members of his work group.

20.3.7 Login Shells and /etc/shells

Finally, you must choose a login shell for the new user. At most sites, one shell predominates in the culture, whether it be /bin/csh (the C-shell), /bin/sh (the Bourne shell), or /bin/ksh (the Korn shell). Unless they request otherwise, new users should probably be assigned the same login shell as that used by the majority of users at your site. The list of acceptable login shells is kept in the file /etc/shells, and most user administration programs will not allow any other programs to be used. This is another security precaution, to prevent a cracker from specifying a tampered program as his login shell and thereby gain access he should not have.

The program provided for user administration on your system will take care of putting the information about each user in the correct file and in the correct format. All you have to do is provide the correct information. Most of these programs also create the home directory and furnish skeletal dot files for new users.

20.3.8   Deleting a User Account

When a user's login account is removed from the system, the /etc/passwd entry and all references to that user in the /etc/group file should be removed. In addition to removing the user from the /etc/passwd and /etc/group files, you need to dispose of his files. It's a common practice to make an archival copy of a departing user's home directory. If the user ever comes back, it's very convenient to have his old files with which to start. Once the archive copy is made, delete the entire directory to free up the disk space. Most user administration programs offer to dispose of a deleted user's home directory and its contents.

The passwd file is used to map user ID numbers to user names. Once a user's passwd entry is gone, any file owned by that user will show up as belonging to a numeric user ID, since UNIX no longer has a way to map the UID to a login name. For example, if user kc has an entry in the /etc/passwd file, a long listing of some of his files might look like this:

```
$ ls -l
total 66
-rw-r--r--  1 kc          25142 Jul 22  1992 chadm1.t
-rw-r--r--  1 kc          30025 Jul 22  1992 chadm2.t
-rw-r--r--  1 kc          10839 Jul 22  1992 chnet.t
$
```

But if the user's passwd file entry is not there, ls -l will show the UID number as the owner of the files. Here's what the list of the previous files looks like, after kc is removed from /etc/passwd:

```
$ ls -l
total 66
-rw-r--r--  1 2485        25142 Jul 22  1992 chadm1.t
-rw-r--r--  1 2485        30025 Jul 22  1992 chadm2.t
-rw-r--r--  1 2485        10839 Jul 22  1992 chnet.t
$
```

If these files are not deleted from the system and another user account (say, richter) is later added with the same UID number, the files will "magically" be owned by that user. (This is one good reason to avoid reusing UIDs.)

```
$ ls -l
total 66
-rw-r--r--  1 richter     25142 Jul 22  1992 chadm1.t
```

```
-rw-r--r--  1 richter     30025 Jul 22  1992 chadm2.t
-rw-r--r--  1 richter     10839 Jul 22  1992 chnet.t
$ ▓
```

It's important to realize that through all of these "changes," nothing about the files themselves was touched. The apparent changes in ownership just point out that, in the UNIX file system, file ownership is recorded by numeric user ID. The mapping of UID to login name is done completely outside the file system.

A user may own files that aren't within his home directory (for example, if he has been collaborating on a project with other users). You can use the find command to search for files that belong to a particular user, with the -user *username* option. Once you have the names of those files, they can be deleted or transferred (using the chown command) to some other user, or archived.

```
$ find /home/u -user kc -print
```

If the user's passwd entry has already been removed, you can use the same find command by just substituting the numeric UID for the user name.

```
$ find /home/u -user 2485 -print
```

To discover files that belong to any user who is not in the passwd file (for example, if you have removed several users from the /etc/passwd file at one time), use the -nouser option.

```
$ find /home/u -nouser -print
```

Some other cleanup considerations have to do with electronic mail. You should delete the user's mail spool file to free up that disk space. It's also a good idea to make arrangements for forwarding electronic mail, if possible. This is done by creating a mail alias for the user in the system aliases file (normally /etc/aliases or /usr/lib/aliases). For example, the entry

```
richter:  richter@bigcorp.com
```

would ensure that any mail addressed to local user richter will be sent on to the Internet domain address richter@bigcorp.com.

20.4 File Systems

A file system is a collection of files and directories on a disk or tape in standard UNIX file system format. Low capacity disks (such as floppy disks) usually contain a single file system. Large disks usually are divided into several regions, each containing one file system.

There are several motivations for partitioning a disk into several file systems. In the early days of UNIX, partitioning of very large disks was necessary because the kernel data structures for managing and accessing the physical blocks of data couldn't address the total number of blocks on a disk. Also, the commands used for backing up file systems in pre-SVR4 System V UNIX were restricted to a single volume of the medium (e.g., a single reel of tape), so a file system had to be small enough to fit your backup media.

In modern UNIX, a single file potentially can be as large as 2 gigabytes (2,000 megabytes), and a file system can be as large as a terabyte (1,000,000 megabytes). No disks made today approach this size, so partitioning is a matter of choice rather than necessity. The SVR4 backup command, ufsrestore, is capable of spanning multiple volumes, so fitting a file system onto a single backup tape is no longer a concern.

One reason for partitioning disks is modularity: partitions allow you to control the amount of disk storage that is allocated to a given activity or type of use. Partitions also allow finer control over chores such as backups. Read-only files and temporary workspace can be backed up infrequently or not at all, while user data should be backed up frequently. If these kinds of files are all on the same file system, the backup process gets all or nothing; putting them on separate partitions lets you tune the backup schedule to deal with each type of file appropriately.

Creation of a file system is a multistep process that is complicated and version-specific enough that we will give only the broadest overview here.

20.4.1   Disk Partitions (Pre-SVR4)

First, the physical disk is formatted to divide it into *partitions.* In pre-SVR4 UNIX, a disk can have a maximum of eight partitions, and they are designated by the letters a through h (see Figure 20.1). Conventionally, the a partition is used only for the root partition (and therefore is used only on the root disk), and the b partition is used for swapping. The c partition is traditionally configured to be the whole disk. Partitions d through h may be allocated according to the whim of the sysadmin.

It is acceptable for a disk's partition table to define partitions that overlap, as long as you are very careful not to use overlapping ones at the same time. For example, on a disk with 500 cylinders, you could make partitions d and e be cylinders 1-100 and 101-500, while partitions f, g, and h could be 101-200, 201-350, and 351-500 respectively. With these definitions, you could choose to build either two file systems on d and e, or four smaller file systems using d, f, g, and h. This gives some flexibility in the sizes of the file systems you choose to use.

20.4.2   Disk Slices (SVR4)

System V Release 4 UNIX has the same general notion of dividing a physical disk into separate parts for various uses, but the terminology and functions are different from the traditional UNIX partition scheme. The parts of the disk are called *slices,* there is still a maximum of eight slices, and they are numbered from 0 through 7. SVR4 assigns a particular use to each of the eight slices, unlike the somewhat random functions of most partitions in the earlier UNIX systems.

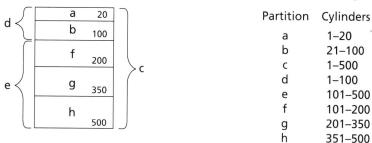

Hypothetical partitioning of a disk

Partition	Cylinders
a	1–20
b	21–100
c	1–500
d	1–100
e	101–500
f	101–200
g	201–350
h	351–500

Partitions whose cylinder definitions overlap cannot be used (with the newfs command, to build a file system) at the same time. A few possible combinations are shown below.

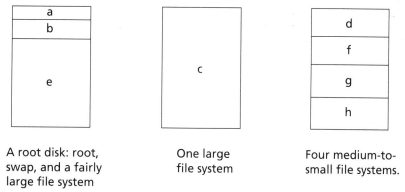

A root disk: root, swap, and a fairly large file system

One large file system

Four medium-to-small file systems.

Figure 20.1 ■ Partitions on a Disk (Pre-SVR4)

Slices 0, 1, and 2 correspond to partitions a, b, and c; that is, they are used for the system's root file system, swap, and the whole disk. Slices 3 through 6 are used for other operating system files, including those for supporting clients and machines of other architectures; slice 7 is the only one designated for holding user files.

20.4.3   Building a File System

The newfs (new file system) command is used to build a file system on a partition or slice. It clears any existing data on that portion of the disk, creates the skeleton of a directory structure including a special directory called lost+found, sets aside space for i-nodes and configures several other file system parameters. Once newfs has been run, the partition is ready to be mounted as a file system, and files and directories can be created there (see Figure 20.2). Newfs is actually a user-friendly front-end to another command called mkfs (make file system).

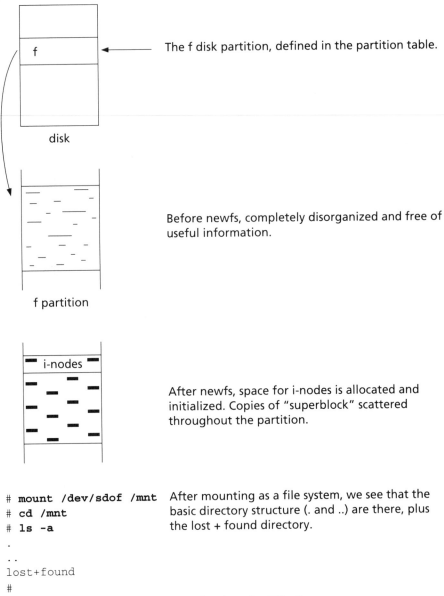

The f disk partition, defined in the partition table.

disk

Before newfs, completely disorganized and free of useful information.

f partition

i-nodes

After newfs, space for i-nodes is allocated and initialized. Copies of "superblock" scattered throughout the partition.

```
# mount /dev/sdof /mnt
# cd /mnt
# ls -a
.
..
lost+found
#
```

After mounting as a file system, we see that the basic directory structure (. and ..) are there, plus the lost + found directory.

Figure 20.2 ■ A Disk Partition (Slice) and a File System

20.4.4   Mounting a File System

The information on a disk slice or partition becomes available for use only after the kernel has been notified of its existence through the mount command. A file system that exists but is not incorporated into the accessible file system structure is said to be *unmounted*. One that is incorporated into the accessible structure is said to be *mounted*. Mounting a file system logically attaches the information stored in that file system to a specific directory that already exists (see Figure 20.3).

Usually the directory, called the *mount point* for the file system, is empty and provided specially for mounting the file system. If you mount a file system on a nonempty directory, its contents are completely inaccessible (even to the superuser) until the file system is unmounted. This behavior can cause some baffling problems, so use empty directories as mount points.

Each file system is itself a tree, with a root directory. It can be attached or mounted on any directory in the UNIX tree. Mounting it on one directory versus another changes the pathname of the files down to the root of the file system but has no effect on the structure of the files and directories within the file system. A file system may be mounted from a local disk or across the network from another UNIX host, or even from a PC or other computer.

It is possible to mount a file system so that it can be read but not written. This capability is useful when you are backing up a file system, and you want

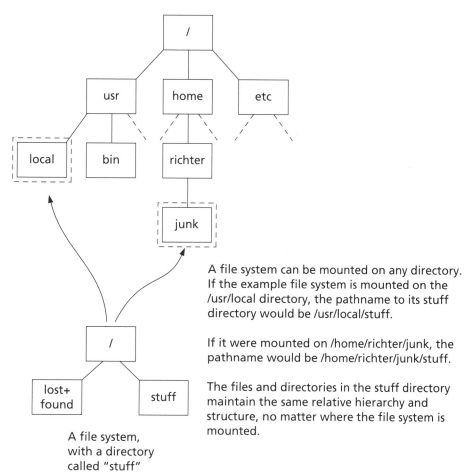

A file system can be mounted on any directory. If the example file system is mounted on the /usr/local directory, the pathname to its stuff directory would be /usr/local/stuff.

If it were mounted on /home/richter/junk, the pathname would be /home/richter/junk/stuff.

The files and directories in the stuff directory maintain the same relative hierarchy and structure, no matter where the file system is mounted.

A file system, with a directory called "stuff"

Figure 20.3 ■ A File System Mounted at Two Different Points

to be sure that the data on the file system does not change while the backup tape is being written. When a file system is mounted read/write, the access dates of the files are modified whenever the files are accessed even if the files are not explicitly written. Mounting a file system read-only prevents this update, hence a file system should be mounted read-only when you don't want to disturb the access dates of the files.

The UNIX kernel usually is unaware of any write-protect switches on the disk or tape drives. If you logically mount a file system as read/write and then use the switches on the disk drive to write-protect the media, a flood of errors will occur each time a file is accessed. This is because the write-protect feature of the hardware prevents the operating system from updating the access dates of the files. The media won't be corrupted, but the voluminous console error messages may impact the operation of your system. If you use the write-protect switches on a disk drive, you should also logically mount the file system read-only.

20.4.5   Unmounting a File System

Once a file system is mounted, users can access the information stored on its files and directories (subject to UNIX access permissions, of course). Sometimes it's necessary to prevent all access to a file system for some reason, such as to repair file system damage. To make a file system inaccessible, it must be unmounted using the umount (pronounced "you-mount") command.

When you have mounted a file system, you must be extremely careful that the physical disk remains powered on and attached to the computer (or in the case of removable media, in the drive) while the file system is mounted. When a file system is mounted, certain vital information about the locations of files on that file system is kept in memory with the kernel. Removing the physical media without performing the unmount may cause the memory resident information about the file system to be lost. One purpose of the unmount operation is to flush all of the memory resident information out to the physical media so that everything is consistent. Failure to logically unmount prior to physical removal is one of the major causes of corrupt (inconsistent) UNIX file systems.

If any part of a file system is being used (which can be as innocuous as someone having a directory in that file system as their current directory), UNIX will not unmount it, giving an error message such as "device busy." In SVR4, the fuser command can track down the processes that are keeping a file system tied up and even kill those processes if necessary.

In pre-SVR4 UNIX, it can be difficult to track down what has a file system tied up; a public-domain program called ofiles, available from the Internet, can help identify the files or directories that are in use, as well as the process that is holding them open. For the file system to be unmountable, the process has to release the file (in the case of cd, the user must cd to a directory not in that file system). If the user responsible for the offending process can't be contacted, it may be necessary to kill the process. If you can't kill the process, the only remedy is to halt the system (performing all the customary shutdown tasks) and then reboot.

20.4.6 Checking File System Consistency

A file system is a fairly complicated data structure; there are many things to keep track of, such as data blocks for each file, the list of free blocks, and all the information within directories and i-nodes that keep the directory structure glued together (see the discussion in Chapter 23 for more details). From time to time, some of these pointers and counters get scrambled or damaged in some way. This particularly happens when the UNIX system crashes or is shut down in a less-than-orderly way. If a disk was not synced (see the sync command in Section 21.3.1) before UNIX halted, it's very likely to have some inconsistencies in its structural elements.

When a file system is damaged or corrupted, it's very important to repair it as quickly as possible, or data will certainly be lost. Occasionally a file system is so corrupt that it must be discarded and recovered entirely from a backup, but usually only a file or two is lost and sometimes nothing is lost.

A program called fsck (for file system consistency check) is used to traverse a file system and report any anomalies it finds, and ask you whether to repair it. Common parlance uses the name of the program, spelled out, as a verb: "Did you eff-ess-cee-kay the root file system, too?" Fsck is ordinarily run on all local file systems whenever a machine is booted. Fsck should always be run on an unmounted file system if possible; the root file system cannot be unmounted, so it requires special handling (read the following).

An fsck of a large file system can take as much as ten minutes. If several file systems are on the same disk, they should be checked in different fsck passes to minimize disk thrashing (fsck is quite disk-intensive). Simultaneous fsck processes can run on different disks with little additional impact. Modern versions of UNIX have a mechanism for marking a file system as clean when UNIX is shut down, thereby avoiding the need for fsck on the next start-up.

Fsck goes through several phases of checking. It looks at each i-node to see what data blocks it references, and then compares the number of blocks it finds with the i-node's own idea of the file size. It notes whether any data blocks are referenced by more than one file, which would be an error. It traverses the directory structure of the file system, making sure that the . (dot) and .. (dot dot) references all hook together properly, and that each file is referenced by some directory. It compares the number of references found for each file with the i-node's own idea of its reference count (a file that has hard links would have a reference count greater than one).

Finally, it checks the *free list*. Every file system contains a list of free blocks. When a file is created, the blocks of data in the file are gathered from the list of free blocks. Occasionally the list of free blocks is damaged; sometimes blocks that are free aren't in the list, or blocks that are used in an existing file are also mentioned in the free list. Usually when fsck discovers errors in the course of checking a file system, it will ask for your permission to rebuild the free list. The following example shows the five phases of an fsck run against a clean file system:

```
# fsck /u1
** Phase 1 - Check Blocks and Sizes
** Phase 2 - Check Pathnames
** Phase 3 - Check Connectivity
** Phase 4 - Check Reference Counts
** Phase 5 - Check Free List
1185 files 11782 blocks 14620 free
#
```

When you rebuild the free list of a mounted file system (usually the root file system), you must halt the system immediately after the rebuild and then boot from scratch. Halting the computer without the usual sync operation prevents the UNIX kernel from writing the old (bad) free list out to disk.

Occasionally files and their names become separated. This is possible in the UNIX system because the name of a file is stored in a directory while the rest of the information about the file (like the addresses of the physical disk blocks that hold the file's data) is stored in an i-node. Files without names are called *orphaned files,* and fsck will place them in a directory called lost+found, created by newfs. In the lost+found directory, fsck will use a number as the name of the file. You should attempt to determine the real name of the file based on its contents and either restore the file to its rightful owner or remove it.

20.4.7   The Root File System

The root file system can never be unmounted because it contains the programs and files that are necessary for basic system operation. It contains the binary file containing the kernel code, plus the /etc, /dev, and /bin directories. The dev directory contains all of the special files for the special I/O device files, the bin directory contains the most frequently used commands, and the etc directory contains files for system initialization and system management.

The root file system can never be mounted read-only.

20.4.8   Network File Systems

Network file systems, or remote file systems, are those which are physically attached to one UNIX host (the fileserver) and which are made available for mounting on other systems (clients). File systems are not automatically available for remote mounting; a server has to *export* each file system that is to be mounted over the network. A file called /etc/exports lists the file systems to be exported and the list of hosts that can mount it. If no hosts are named, it is available for mounting by any system. When changes are made to the exports file on a server, the exportfs command should be run to activate the new configuration.

From the client system's point of view, network file systems are manipulated using the same mount and umount commands as local file systems, but the underlying mechanism is different. For NFS or any other remote file system to work, the UNIX kernel has to be modified to support it. In pre-SVR4 UNIX, the NFS subroutines had to be compiled into the kernel. Under SVR4, this support comes in the form of loadable file system support modules. For more information about network file systems, see Chapter 23. For a description of automounting file systems, see the discussion in Chapter 17.

20.4.9   File System Tables

A file called /etc/vfstab (/etc/fstab in pre-SVR4 UNIX releases) lists all the file systems that should be automatically mounted when the system is booted multiuser. The table includes the name of the special device where the file system is located (or in the case of a network file system, the name of its host and the file system's name there), the name of the directory it should be mounted on, the file system type, and some parameters telling whether the file system should be checked with fsck, and on which pass.

The kernel maintains a list of all the file systems it knows are mounted, in a file called /etc/mnttab. This file is consulted and updated by the mount and umount commands.

Mount commands are contained in the /etc/rc files (pre-SVR4) or in the run-level specific boot files (SVR4) to mount the appropriate file systems for each boot state. For single-user operation, normally only the root and /usr file systems are mounted.

20.4.10   File System Types

In classic UNIX, the only file system type was what is now called ufs (UNIX file system), which was built to deal with files on a locally attached disk drive. File and directory commands were built to work with it. When other file system types such as NFS came along, the same commands were rewritten to work with them, or the operating system had to be modified to make the commands work appropriately.

Under SVR4, multiple file system types are supported, and many commands take options to make them work with various file system types. Other commands are specifically designed to work with only one type of file system (e.g., ufsdump and ufsrestore). New file system types can be added to the SVR4 kernel as loadable modules (see Section 20.2.1).

- ■ vfs: Virtual file system (supports all file system abstractions, and underlies all other file system types)

- ■ ufs: UNIX file system (the standard traditional file system type)

- ■ nfs: Network file system

- ■ hsfs: High Sierra file system (the earliest standard CD ROM file system format)

- lofs: Loopback file system

- pcfs: DOS file system mountable on UNIX

20.5   booting

The term *booting* refers to the process a computer system goes through between the time it is turned on and the time it is ready for use. Booting a UNIX system typically includes stages such as hardware diagnostics, loading the kernel into memory, checking and mounting file systems, starting various background or daemon tasks, and establishing connectivity to a network.

The details of the booting procedure vary from one computer to another but in all systems, the result is that the UNIX kernel is loaded into memory from the root file system. The root file system contains the most essential UNIX utilities and files.

20.5.1   Traditional Boot Process

In pre-SVR4 UNIX versions, booting the system from a disk is a fairly monolithic process. A boot program, which is very small and simple, lives in a known place on the root file system. It takes the name of a kernel file to load into memory; the default file is /vmunix (or /unix, in some versions). Being able to specify a file name means you can test an experimental version of the kernel, which might be named /vmunix.new, without disturbing the real kernel. In fact, you need not even boot a UNIX kernel; many UNIX systems come with a hardware diagnostic program to boot when extensive testing of the hardware is required.

The boot process for a diskless system is similar, except that the system can't look for a boot program on its root disk. Instead, it broadcasts its Ethernet address to the network and waits for someone to supply its IP address. Then it broadcasts a request for a boot program and engages its boot server in a dialog to obtain the necessary files over the network (see Chapter 17).

Once the UNIX kernel is loaded, the remainder of the boot process is controlled by commands stored in a file called /etc/rc (and sometimes in auxiliary files with similar names such as /etc/rc.local). All commands executed from /etc/rc run as root, so it is important to control the contents of that file and any auxiliary files it may execute. /etc/rc should be owned by root and writable only by the owner.

There are a couple of ways to boot the UNIX kernel. Booting multiuser is the standard procedure, and it brings the system up fully ready for users; all file systems are mounted, and terminal access is enabled. Booting single-user (with the -s option) loads the kernel and mounts the /usr file system but doesn't mount any user file systems. When a UNIX system is in single-user mode, the system console is logged on as the superuser, and no other access is allowed. This is typically used for system administration, file system repair, or other maintenance activities. When single-user mode is terminated, the default action is to continue booting to multiuser mode. There is no way to go from multiuser back to single-user mode other than by rebooting the system.

20.5.2 SVR4 Booting and Init States

The SVR4 boot model is more sophisticated. It has the concept of *init states* (also called *run levels, system states,* or *run states*), which define different levels of operation. SVR4 defines eight init states, designated as numbers 0-6 and s or S (for single-user) but not all are of general interest. Init state 0 halts UNIX. Run level 1 is roughly equivalent to single-user mode but is called administrative state; file systems needed for multiuser login are mounted. Init states 2 and 3 are multiuser modes; at level 2, no file systems are exported, while at level 3 they are. Run level 6 reboots the system to its default state.

The default run state is defined in the /etc/inittab file, which is consulted every time the system boots. /etc/inittab also contains a set of start-up commands that are common to all run levels. Each run level has its own set of configuration files, similar to the /etc/rc file, that tell what processes and services should be started for that state. The run-level specific files are kept in directories named /etc/rc#.d, where # represents the run level.

The SVR4 run-level model allows flexible and fine-grained control of the services and access allowed by UNIX. It also supports moving from one run state to another (for example, from multiuser to single-user mode) without having to reboot the system. This is done with the init # command, where # represents the run state.

20.5.3 Shutting Down the System

Shutting down a UNIX system in an orderly fashion requires numerous activities prior to turning the power switch off. At a high level, users who are busily working on the system would appreciate a warning that it is about to halt, particularly if they are given enough time to finish or save their work. At a lower level, system daemons should be terminated in a graceful manner, and data that is waiting in buffers needs to be written to a disk so that it is not lost, a process known as syncing the disks.

In both SVR4 and pre-SVR4 UNIX versions, the shutdown command is used to schedule an impending shutdown, notify the users with a broadcast message, and take care of terminating daemons and syncing the disks. This is the preferred method for halting UNIX. Only the superuser can run shutdown.

If for some reason shutdown is not appropriate, more drastic measures can be taken. In pre-SVR4 UNIX, the superuser can manually sync the disks and then terminate UNIX with the halt command. No warning is given to users. Under SVR4, the equivalent commands are sync and init 0.

20.6   Backups

There is more than one road to securing the data on a UNIX system. If you have excellent backups, damage to a file system need not spell catastrophe. If you can patch even the most corrupt file system, your need for comprehensive backups is diminished. Most people find it easier to stick to a good backup schedule than to perform the wizardry necessary to retrieve data from a mangled disk, and sometimes no amount of wizardry will work. Thus, the strongest defense against lost data is to keep good backups and to understand the procedure for restoring a file (or files) or an entire file system.

20.6.1   Backup and Restore Basics

There are two fundamental types of backup (the term "dump" is synonymous with backup and is often used): full and incremental. A *full backup* records a copy of all the files and directories on a file system. An *incremental backup* records only those files that have changed since some earlier backup and is said to be based on that earlier backup. An incremental can be based either on a full backup or on an incremental of a higher level.

To restore a file, especially if you can't discover when it was last modified, you may need to look through several backups. The set of possible backups to look through is obtained by starting with the last incremental dump before the file was lost, then going back through all the dumps that dump was based on, back to the full dump. The restore program will produce the most recent version of the file that existed while a backup was being made; obviously, it can't restore a file that was created and destroyed between backup runs.

When a file system is being backed up, it is best if it can be unmounted so none of the files are changed during the backup process. At most sites, file systems are left mounted during backup to minimize the inconvenience to the users; this is called *backing up a live file system*. It can cause inconsistencies in the backup image, but this is a glitch most sites are willing to live with. Some sites, such as financial institutions, have real-time data processing needs. Such sites are usually not willing to risk inconsistent backups, nor to live without their data for the minutes to hours needed to back it up; they may use special methods of backup involving redundant copies of live data.

Many sites schedule backups to be run during the night. This reduces the chance that files will be changing during backup. Backing up file systems can also cause a noticeable drop in a system's responsiveness; scheduling them at night keeps the users from having to suffer through that lag.

20.6.2   Backup Levels

Under UNIX, there are different levels of backups, ranging from 0 through 9. A full backup is level 0; levels 1 through 9 are incrementals, with 1 being the highest level. As a simple illustrative example of how levels work, consider a file system that has a level 0 dump taken on Sunday. On Monday evening, a level 1 dump will record all data that has changed since the full backup. On Tuesday, a level 2 dump would record everything changed since the level 1 dump; it is based on that higher-level incremental. On Wednesday, another level 1 dump would record everything changed since the full dump. It goes back to the full rather than to the previous level 1, since a backup must be based on a higher-level dump. The one exception to this rule is level 9 incrementals. Consecutive level 9 backups record only the files changed since the previous level 9.

UNIX backups are scheduled and performed on a file system basis, but the unit of data recorded is the file. If only a single byte of data in a file changes, the entire file is recorded on the next incremental backup. This is because the backup program, dump, compares the file's modification date (from its i-node) with the date of the last backup, to decide whether or not it needs to be backed up. Dump doesn't know or care to what extent a file was changed, only that its modification time is recent. In fact, you can force files to be dumped by changing their modification times with the touch command.

20.6.3   Backup Schedule

A backup schedule has to be designed to fit the needs of an individual site. The goals of a backup scheme include:

- Getting accurate backups of the files on the system.

- Minimizing the amount of work lost if a disaster occurs.

- Minimizing inconvenience to the users during the backup process.

- Making the restore process relatively easy and straightforward.

As with so many other administrative tasks, there are trade-offs to be made. The most secure kind of backup might be to take a full dump of every file system every day. If you are talking about only one or two moderate-sized file systems, this is certainly the way to go as it enormously simplifies backup administration. Restoring files would be trivial: just go to the previous day's full dump, and the file is guaranteed to be there. With more than a few file systems, the amount of time taken by full dumps can be onerous, and the amount of backup media required would be quite large.

The opposite approach would be to schedule a full dump only very infrequently, say once a month, and have only level 9 incrementals in between. This would require very little backup time, and the amount of media needed would be almost negligible. There are disadvantages: keeping track of all those tiny incremental backups can be a real nightmare, and file restores are harder. Restoring a file lost late in the month would require going through all the incrementals, a laborious and time-consuming process.

Most sites end up with a compromise between these two extremes. A quite common backup schedule is a full dump weekly (perhaps on a weekend), with incrementals daily (nightly) throughout the week. The following would enable you to restore a file at any time during the week, using only the Saturday full backup and the latest level 5 incremental.

Sat	Sun	Mon	Tue	Wed	Thu	Fri
0	—	5	5	5	5	5

Using that schedule, the incrementals could get fairly large by Friday, since they are all based on the Saturday full dump. A scheme such as the following breaks up the week with a higher-level incremental so that the Thursday and Friday incrementals will be smaller. The trade-off is that restores done past Thursday may require looking at three backups instead of just two: the level 0, the Wednesday level 3, and the latest level 5.

Sat	Sun	Mon	Tue	Wed	Thu	Fri
0	—	5	5	3	5	5

20.6.4   Backup Media

The traditional backup medium for UNIX has been nine-track or half-inch tape. These are the tapes on big round reels; you see them in science fiction movies, whirring around on the computers. Half-inch tape drives come in various densities, the most common of which today is 6,250 bpi (bits per inch). A standard 2,400-foot reel of tape holds about 140 to 150 megabytes of data at 6,250 bpi. A backup of a large file system could easily fill eight to ten reels of tape.

Rapidly eclipsing half-inch tape, not only for backups but for all tape applications, is 8mm or Exabyte™ tape. A single tape, identical in size with those used in 8mm video cameras, holds over 2 gigabytes of data (see Table 20.1 for capacities of various media). High-density drives can store up to 5 gigabytes on a single tape, and new technology that does data compression in the drive can pack almost twice that much data onto a tape. With the continuing explosive growth in the amount of data people want to store on computer systems, the 8mm technology comes as a godsend to sysadmins managing backups. The data that would previously have filled ten to 40 bulky reels of tape now fits on a single small cartridge, and the hassles of dealing with multireel backup sets are almost eliminated.

Table 20.1 ■ Backup Media and Approximate Capacities

Media type	Density	Capacity
9-track tape (2400′)	1,600 bpi	35 mb
9-track tape (2400′)	6,250 bpi	140 mb
8mm tape	standard	2.2 gb
8mm tape	high	5 gb
DAT (digital audio tape)	—	4 gb

With large media, you can stack multiple backup images on the same tape. You have to use the nonrewind tape device to make this work, and you must keep careful records of which backup images (file system and level) are on each tape and in what order. By backing up systems over a network, you can use one tape drive and one piece of media to back up an entire group of workstations. This makes unattended backups a possibility.

20.6.5   Rotation of Media

Any backup scheme is based on having enough tape media to keep previous backups around until they are superseded. As an absolute minimum, you should have enough tapes for two full backups plus enough for all of their incrementals (the tapes for a full backup plus all the incrementals based on it is called a *set*). This allows you to restore files from the previous cycle while you're using the second set of media for the current cycle. If you want to be able to restore files from farther back, you need to allocate more sets.

If you wanted to establish a four-week restore window, you would need to rotate among five sets of media; the current set is always out of the picture, since once you overwrite the tapes of a full backup, you also cancel the usefulness of all incrementals upon which it is based.

To maintain sanity and order, label your backup sets and keep a written schedule of when to use which set. The best way to keep to a backup schedule is to make it a part of the daily routine. Do not treat backups as a task to be done when there's spare time.

20.7   Swapping and Sticky Mode

Ordinary files are not stored contiguously on the disk. The information in a file is divided into blocks, and the blocks assigned to a given file may be scattered throughout the disk. If you are displaying a file to your terminal screen, the system's overhead in retrieving the file from the various places on the disk is low because humans don't read very fast: your requests to read the file are interleaved with other user I/O requests. However, if the system is loading the file for execution, the overhead of retrieving from noncontiguous disk storage can be very high. The sticky mode helps to reduce this undesirable overhead by causing the binary image of a file to remain in memory once it is read in.

When a running program is temporarily suspended from execution, the system may copy the process's memory image to temporary storage on disk. This use of disk to mimic physical memory is called *virtual memory;* the process is called *swapping,* and the disk area used for the virtual memory is called *swap space* or the *swap partition*. The swap partition is organized contiguously so that it can be accessed rapidly. In the UNIX system, a special mode can be assigned to a file so that once the program is executed for the first time its executable image stays in the swap space even when the program is not being executed. Since the program gets stuck in the swap space, the mode is called the *sticky mode,* and the bit in the i-node that controls this trait is called the *sticky bit.*

Relatively few programs are assigned the sticky mode, because swap space has traditionally been a precious commodity that would be rapidly exhausted if the sticky mode was overused. Frequently used programs (e.g., the editor, ls, cat) are often assigned the sticky mode. On small systems where swap space is at a premium, the sticky mode seldom is used. On systems where more swap space is available, more programs are likely to have the sticky mode. If a system has gigantic amounts of swap space, use of the sticky mode is not really necessary.

The sticky mode can be assigned to a file only by the superuser, using the chmod command. Users cannot assign the sticky mode to their own files. The sticky mode is indicated by a t in the last position of the permissions in a long format ls output.

20.8   Setuid and Setgid Modes

Occasionally the sophisticated UNIX system access protection scheme gets in the way of valid access requirements. The classic example is the requirement posed by games programs. Many games want to keep an auxiliary file that contains scores or information for the game. For example, in an adventure program the list of messages in an auxiliary file should be hidden from inquisitive adventurers. The normal UNIX system mechanism to protect this sort of information would be to make the auxiliary file owned by the creator of the game and restrict access to the file so it is readable only by the owner. However, when someone is playing the game, the messages from the auxiliary file need to be readable.

The problem is simple: when you are not playing the game, you should be prohibited from accessing the private game information. However, when you are playing the game you should, within the structure imposed by the game, be allowed access to that information.

The set user ID, or setuid, mode solves this problem. If an executable program file has the setuid mode, that program "runs as" the owner of the executable file, no matter who invokes it. That is, anyone who runs that program acquires all the privileges of the program's owner, while the program is running. The setgid mode is very similar, except that it grants the access privileges of the file's group ownership, rather than the user.

Needless to say, it's important to limit what a setuid or setgid program does, in order to prevent people from abusing the privileges it gives. The classic example of a security loophole is a setuid program that allows a shell escape; anyone who uses that program can run an interactive shell as the program's owner. If the owner is root, the security implications are enormous.

Many of the programs that ordinary users use to find out about the system or to issue system requests, such as print requests, are setuid or setgid. For example, many people use the df program to print a list of the free space on various file systems. The df program needs to access two key files, /etc/vfstab and /etc/mnttab, and it needs to access the disk special file for each filesystem.

```
$ ls -l /etc/mnttab /etc/vfstab /dev/rdsk/c0t0d2s0 /bin/df
-rws--x--x   1 root    bin    12802 Apr 13  1990 /bin/df
crw-------   1 root    wheel  4, 0  Aug 23  1992 /dev/rdsk/c0t0d2s0
-rw-r--r--   1 root    bin    331   Jun  3 20:48 /etc/vfstab
-rw-r--r--   1 root    bin    612   Nov 27 16:23 /etc/mnttab
$ █
```

The preceding listing shows that the files in /etc could be read without df's setuid mode but root privileges are needed to access the raw disk interface special file /dev/rdsk/c0t0d2s0.

The owner of a file can set the setuid or setgid mode on his own files, using the chmod command. The setuid mode is indicated by an s in the owner execute (x) position:

```
-rwsr-xr-x   1 root     workers   12288 Nov 29 20:51 phonels
```

Setgid is shown by an s in the group execute (x) position:

```
-rwxr-sr-x   1 bin      wheel     37842 Nov 17 13:19 zprint
```

There is no "set other ID" mode because it would accomplish nothing.

20.9 Fifo Files

Fifo (pronounced "fie-foe") files are a mechanism for one program to transfer information to another program. Fifo is an acronym for "first in, first out," and it is a standard description for one type of queue. Typically one program writes into a fifo and another program reads from it. Information is stored in the fifo file only during the short period between when one program writes it and the second program reads it; once the information is read, it is cleared from the fifo.

Fifo files obviously are similar to UNIX pipes. The advantage of using a fifo is that any two unrelated programs can use it to communicate. Pipes can only be set up between programs that are children of the same parent process. Often this parent is the UNIX system shell. A fifo is used when it is not possible or convenient for the communicating processes to have the same parent.

Fifos can be created using the mknod (make node) command (discussed in Section 21.4). Fifos, like ordinary files, are owned by some user, and access to them is governed by the usual three-tiered UNIX permissions scheme.

You have to create a fifo before you can use it. For instance, the following command reads data from the communication line /dev/term/99 and then writes it out to a fifo file named fifo1.tel:

```
$ cat < /dev/term/99 > fifo1.tel
```

If the fifo file fifo1.tel didn't exist when the command was entered, the shell would have created an ordinary file named fifo1.tel to receive the output of the cat command.

A command could pick up information from the fifo using input redirection:

```
$ sh < fifo1.tel
```

In these two examples, we have used the shell's I/O redirection to access the fifo.

20.10   Links and Symbolic Links

Both symbolic links and ordinary links provide pseudonyms for files. Ordinary links, or *hard links,* are available on all versions of UNIX. A hard link to a file is simply a second (or subsequent) directory entry that references that file's i-node. All references have equal weight; one can't say that one name for a file is its real name and that the other names are aliases. Thus, if you access a file through any of its hard links and modify it (i.e., with an editor), the modification time and contents of the file are also changed when you reference it through any other link. If you remove one of a file's hard links, the other links are still there. Two major limitations of hard links are that they cannot bridge across file systems, and you cannot create a hard link to a directory.

The *symbolic link* (symlink), which was originally available only on Berkeley systems, now exists in SVR4 UNIX as well. It is more powerful than an ordinary link because a symlink on one file system can reference a file or directory on another file system. Hard links are restricted to file names within the same file system because they are based on i-nodes, and i-nodes are specific to a single file system. Symbolic links are based on pathnames, which are by definition unique across an entire UNIX file system hierarchy. They work by embedding a pathname into an ordinary file, whose i-node is then modified to mark it as a symbolic link. Thus an attempt to access the file will actually access whatever file the link references.

One consequence of the Berkeley symbolic link design is that one file actually is the original, while any symlink references to that file are mere aliases. If you remove the original, the file is really gone, although the symlinks to that pathname will remain. Such pointers to nothingness are called *dangling symlinks.*

Although symlinks can be used wherever ordinary links are used, they are slightly more expensive (less efficient) because the kernel must fetch the symbolic link file, read its text, and then chase down the new pathname. Although this overhead is acceptable wherever the facilities of symlinks are necessary, it is much more than the (nonexistent) overhead of ordinary links.

Symbolic links are often used to provide system-wide aliases. For example, most UNIX programmers have grown accustomed to looking in the /usr/include/sys directory for system-dependent C language include files. On many systems, the natural home for those include files is on the same file system that contains system source, which is often different from the /usr file system. The solution is to make /usr/include/sys a symbolic link to wherever the system include files are actually stored.

Another common use for symlinks is to provide a uniform file name space for UNIX systems of different machine architectures. For example, the operating system binaries for Sun3 and Sun4 workstations ordinarily are stored in separate directories that are identified by machine type, such as /export/exec/sun3/bin and /export/exec/sun4/bin. To make life easier for users, a sysadmin might create a symlink called /usr/bin that would point to /export/exec/sun3/bin on Sun3 machines, but to /export/exec/sun4/bin on Sun4s.

Programs can determine that a file is a symbolic link, although few programs need that capability. One program that does is ls. It "follows" symlinks while producing a short format output, but it describes the link itself in the long format output. An l (letter ell) in the first column of an ls listing indicates a symlink, and the target of the link is printed after the file name. The ^C characters in the following example show the very long listing being truncated by the interrupt character:

```
$ ls /usr/include/sys
acct.h      file.h        param.h       text.h        user.h
bk.h        fs.h          param.h.org   time.h        vadvise.h
^C
$ ls -l /usr/include/sys
lrwxrwxrwx   1   root    6    Jan 29  1991   /usr/include/sys -> /sys/
h
$ ls /sys/h
acct.h      file.h        param.h       text.h        user.h
bk.h        fs.h          param.h.org   time.h        vadvise.h
buf.h       gprof.h       proc.h        timeb.h       vcmd.h
^C
$ ▓
```

Notice that the length of this particular symbolic link is 6, which is just enough to store the text /sys/h. Symbolic links are created using the -s option of the ln command, which is covered in Chapter 6.

20.11 Device Names

The naming of the special files in the /dev directory changed dramatically in SVR4. In older versions of UNIX, /dev was a "flat" directory; that is, all the special files were immediately under the /dev directory. With potentially hundreds of devices on a system, this arrangement made /dev hard to scan or manage. In the SVR4 scheme, devices are grouped into subdirectories of /dev, based on the device type. Table 20.2 shows examples of the old and new names for several device types.

In the following discussion, the parenthesized characters refer to the examples in Table 20.2.

Table 20.2 ■ Device Naming Changes in SVR4

What	Pre-SVR4	Under SVR4
disk partition (block)	/dev/sd0c	/dev/dsk/c0t0d0s2
raw disk partition (character)	/dev/rsd0c	/dev/rdsk/c0t0d0s2
tape	/dev/rmt8	/dev/rmt/0h
tape (nonrewind)	/dev/rmt12	/dev/rmt/0hn
serial ports	/dev/ttyj4	/dev/term/j4

The disk partition names require a bit of interpretation. Under the old system, a disk partition name had three parts: the device type (sd), the unit number (0) and the partition name (c). In the SVR4 scheme, a name has four parts, and includes mnemonic letters to identify each part: the controller (c0), the target or logical unit number (t0), the disk number (d0), and the slice (s2).

Tape device names are simpler to understand in the SVR4 scheme. In pre-SVR4 UNIX, tape device names contained numbers that were calculated from the unit number, density, and rewind/nonrewind characteristics of that device. Under SVR4, a tape device name has three parts: the unit number (0), a letter indicating low, medium, or high density (h), and an optional n indicating a nonrewind device. If the n is omitted, the tape rewinds at the end of an operation.

21
System Management Utilities

This chapter describes some of the programs used to accomplish the tasks described in Chapter 20. System administrators also use many ordinary UNIX utilities in their daily work, but the programs in this chapter are an indispensable part of the sysadmin toolbox.

Unless otherwise noted, all of the programs described here require the superuser privilege to operate. Ordinary users should not be able to mount or unmount file systems, boot the system, and so on. At the end of the chapter, we present a handful of programs that are sysadmin-like in nature but that any user can execute.

21.1   Su—Become Superuser

The su (pronounced by spelling "ess-you") program allows a logged-in user to assume the identity of another user, as long as she knows the password for the desired new identity. Anyone can use su, although it is most often used by system administrators to assume the identity of the superuser. The syntax of su is:

```
su [-] [login_name]
```

If a login name is specified, su prompts for that user's password. If no login name is specified, it's assumed you want to become superuser. If you type in the correct password, su starts a new shell running as that user, using the new user's login shell. When you exit that shell, you are back in your original login session.

When you su, the shell that is started is initialized with the new user's .profile commands (for C-shell users, the .cshrc commands). The current di-

431

rectory remains the same as it was before you issued the su command. Su has but a single command-line option, the –. With this option, the .login file is also processed, and the shell starts out in the new user's home directory.

During an su session, you assume all the privileges and permissions of the other user with respect to both user and group identities. In UNIX parlance, your "effective user ID" has been changed. UNIX also remembers the identity you had in the underlying login session; that's called your "real user ID." Most programs use the effective user ID to determine permissions, but a few insist on using the real user ID. Thus, sometimes running a program while su'ed will not give you the same results as doing it while logged in as that user.

21.2   Mount and Unmount File Systems

The mount and umount (pronounced "you mount") commands are used to control the logical connection of files and directories stored on a disk to the file system. Mountall is a variant of the mount command.

21.2.1   Mount

The mount command has many options, some of which are specific to a file system type. Under SVR4, the general syntax of the mount command is:

```
# mount [-F fs_type] [options] [-o soptions] special    directory
```

The *special* argument is either the name of a special device file or a remote directory name in the form *hostname:directory*. The *directory* argument is the mount point for the file system. With no options or arguments, mount prints the list of all file systems currently mounted. It consults the file /etc/mnttab (/etc/mtab in earlier UNIX versions) for that list.

The mount command is used much more often in system boot scripts than interactively. A superuser needs to manually mount and unmount file systems in a few situations: when file system damage is being repaired or when file systems are being moved, dumped, or restored. Here are two examples of interactive mount commands. In the first example, the file system on the /dev/dsk/c0t0d1s4 device is mounted on an empty directory called /mnt:

```
# mkdir   /mnt
# mount   /dev/dsk/c0t0d1s4   /mnt
#
```

In the second example, the /tmp file system from a remote machine is mounted on a local directory called /scratch to provide temporary workspace:

```
# mount   -F nfs   -o soft,bg,intr,rw   natasha:/tmp   /scratch
#
```

The file /etc/vfstab contains information about the file systems that are to be mounted whenever a UNIX system boots. In older versions of UNIX, this file was called /etc/fstab, and it contained slightly different information. Every file system has a one-line entry in /etc/vfstab containing the following information:

- The device to mount (a block special device for ufs file systems, or a *host:directory* name for nfs file systems)

- The device to fsck (a character or raw special device name)

- The mount point (a directory name)

- The file system type (e.g., ufs, nfs, hsfs, swap)

- Which pass to run fsck (an integer, or – to skip fsck)

- Whether to mount the file system automatically at boot time (yes or no)

- Mount options

Under SVR4, the mount command actually is a front-end for several different programs, one for each file system type. The options described in Table 21.1 are common to all file system types.

Each file system type has its own peculiar set of mount options. The -F *fs_type* mount option directs the mount command to use the program specific to that file system type. We describe only the ufs and nfs options, since these are the most commonly used file system types. The UFS-specific options are described in Table 21.2.

NFS file systems have many more mount options (see Table 21.3) than any other file system type. Because they are mounted over a network, it's important to be able to tune factors such as the block size for data transfers, the amount of time to wait for network response, the number of retries to attempt, and so on.

Table 21.1 ■ Mount Command-line Options, Generic

-F *fs_type*	Specify a file system type. The default is ufs.
-p	Print a list of all currently mounted file systems in a format suitable for putting into the /etc/vfstab file.
-v	Print a list of all currently mounted file systems in a verbose format.
-V	Given a command, expand it to include all default settings and echo the resulting command line but do not actually execute it. Useful for verifying a mount command when the set of system defaults (not all discussed in this chapter) are complicated.
-m	Mount the file system, but don't list it in /etc/mnttab.
-r	Mount the file system read-only.
-o	Any arguments following the -o flag are options specific to the file system type mentioned after the -F flag. Multiple specific options may be put in a comma-separated list.

Table 21.2 ■ UFS-specific Mount Options

f	Fake a mount; record it in /etc/mnttab but do not actually mount a file system.
n	Mount the file system but do not record it in /etc/mnttab.
rw|ro	Mount the file system read-write (default) or read-only.
nosuid	Do not allow setuid programs in this file system to run (default is to allow such programs to execute).
remount	For a file system mounted read-only, override it temporarily by remounting it for read-write access.
intr|nointr	Allow (do not allow) users to give keyboard interrupts to processes waiting for a mount to complete. Default is intr.

Table 21.3 ■ Some Commonly Used NFS-specific Mount Options

rw|ro	Mount the file system read/write (default) or read-only.
suid|nosuid	Allow (do not allow) setuid programs in this file system to run. Default is suid.
remount	For a file system mounted read-only, override it temporarily by remounting it for read/write access.
intr|nointr	Allow (do not allow) users to give keyboard interrupts to processes waiting for a mount to complete. Default is intr.
soft|hard	Soft means return an error if the NFS server does not respond; hard means keep retrying until the server responds.
fg|bg	If the first mount attempt fails, do retries in the foreground (background). Default is fg.
retry=n	Number of retries if the mount operation fails. Default is 10000.
rsize=n	Use a read buffer of n bytes.
wsize=n	Use a write buffer of n bytes.
timeo=n	Set the NFS time-out interval to n tenths of a second.
retrans=n	Retry each NFS transmission a maximum of n times.

21.2.2   Mountall

The mountall command is used to mount all the file systems listed as "mount automatically" either in /etc/vfstab or in the optional *fs_table* file argument, which must be in vfstab format. Each file system is checked by fsck before mounting, if its file system table entry so specifies.

The syntax is:

```
# mountall [-l] [-r] [-F fs_type] [fs_table]
```

The mountall command corresponds roughly to the pre-SVR4 command "mount -a." Mountall can be used safely even if some file systems are already mounted; it will simply tell you that those file systems are already mounted. Command-line options are listed in Table 21.4.

21.2.3   Umount, Umountall

A mounted file system can be unmounted with the umount command. The syntax of the umount command is:

Table 21.4 ■ Mountall Command-line Options

`-l`	Mount only local file systems marked for automatic mounting.
`-r`	Mount only remote file systems marked for automatic mounting.
`-F fs_type`	Mount only file systems of the specified file system type that are marked for automatic mounting.

```
# umount  [-V]  special|directory
```

You may specify either the directory on which the file system is mounted or the name of the special device file. If umount cannot find the specified file system in /etc/mnttab, it returns an error message. The command-line options are shown in Table 21.5.

```
# umount /dev/dsk/c0t0d1s4
#
```

The umountall command is similar to the mountall command in that it allows unmounting of file systems en masse. See the command-line options in Table 21.6. The syntax is:

```
# umountall [-l] [-r] [-F fs_type]
```

21.3   Shutting Down the System

21.3.1   Sync—Synchronize Disk Information

The sync command, which takes no arguments, flushes buffered information about the file systems out to the physical media, synchronizing the disk with the latest in-memory information. You should always execute the sync command before you halt the system (the shutdown command does this for you). UNIX system lore dictates that you should sync twice just to be sure.

Table 21.5 ■ Umount Command-line Option

`-V`	Given a umount command, expand it to include all default settings and echo the resulting command line but do not actually execute it. Useful for verifying a command's effect before doing it.

Table 21.6 ■ Umountall Command-line Options

`-l`	Unmount all local file systems.
`-r`	Unmount all remote file systems.
`-F fs_type`	Unmount all file systems of the specified file system type, except the file systems such as / and /usr which cannot be unmounted.

There is one exception to the rule that you should run the sync command before halting the computer. When you repair a mounted file system (usually the root file system) using the fsck program, the information on the disk is more timely than the information in memory. In this one instance, you should not sync before you halt.

21.3.2   Init

The init command is used to change the system's operational state (see the brief discussion of init states in Chapter 20. A full discussion of the SVR4 init state scheme is beyond the scope of this book). The syntax is simple:

```
# init    state
```

The state is a single digit, which can be any of the run levels 0-6, s, or S. When init is run, the command files needed to enter run state # are looked up in the /etc/rc#.d directory. The three most common uses of init are probably:

1. init 0

    to bring the system to a halt;

2. init s

    to bring the system to single-user state from any other state; and

3. init 3

    to take the system to multiuser state with all resources (most importantly, file systems) exported.

21.3.3   Shutdown

The shutdown command is used to halt UNIX, or bring the system to another init state, in an orderly manner. Its function is basically the same as that of init, with a couple of frills thrown in to make it friendlier (see command-line options in Table 21.7). Shutdown asks the superuser for confirmation before it starts to kill processes; it also gives users a warning message 60 seconds before the system shuts down. The syntax of the SVR4 shutdown command is:

```
# shutdown   [-y]   [-g n]   [-i state]
```

Table 21.7 ■ Shutdown Command-line Options

-y	Automatically answer 'yes' to the confirmation query. This lets shutdown be run noninteractively; that is, from a command script or a crontab file.
-g n	Give users a grace period of *n* seconds (default is 60).
-i state	Go to init level *state* (default is s).

(In pre-SVR4 UNIX versions, the shutdown command's syntax was quite different.)

21.3.4 Halt

The halt command is equivalent to init 0, but it offers a few options (see Table 21.8). By default, halt does a sync of the disks and then terminates UNIX. It will actually power down the machine if the hardware supports it. The halt syntax is:

```
# halt [-l] [-n] [-q] [-y]
```

21.4 Mknod—Create Special Files

Mknod creates special device files and named pipes, or fifos. The syntax of mknod is:

```
# mknod filename type major minor
```

where *filename* is the name in the /dev directory (under SVR4, in one of the subdirectories of /dev, such as /dev/dsk or /dev/term). The *type* may be either b (block), c (character), or p (named pipe or fifo). The *major* and *minor* device numbers for a particular device may be found in one of the kernel configuration files, often in a file called conf.c. The p type (fifo) does not require either a major or minor device number, and an ordinary user can create a fifo. Only the superuser can create a special device file.

Let's suppose that you are creating the character special file for a paper tape device, hardly a standard UNIX peripheral. Examining the system generation files reveals that the major device number is 17, and the minor device number for the first such device is ordinarily zero. Here's how you can use mknod to create the character special file /dev/pt for the paper tape device:

```
# /etc/mknod  /dev/pt  c  17  0
# ls -l /dev/pt
crw--w--w-  1 root     sys     17,  0    Apr 9 14:30   pt
#
```

Here is an example of a mknod command used to create a fifo file:

Table 21.8 ■ Halt Command-line Options

-l	Suppress log messages about the halt. Normally, halt logs the identity of the user who executed it.
-n	Do not sync the disks before halting.
-q	Quick halt; do not try for a graceful shutdown, just halt immediately.
-y	Force a halt, even if the user is executing the command from a dial-up terminal. Normally halt needs to be run from the system console or another secure terminal.

```
$ /etc/mknod fifo1 p
$ ls -l fifo1
prw-r--r--  1  kc    staff    0   Jun 8 16:20  fifo1
$
```

21.5   Backups

The primary utilities for backing up and restoring ufs file systems under SVR4 UNIX are ufsdump and ufsrestore. Both programs, since they are specific to one file system type, live in the directory /usr/lib/fs/ufs rather than in one of the usual directories such as /bin or /usr/bin. The volcopy and labelit programs are used to make bit-image copies of file systems, either to another disk or to tape.

21.5.1   Ufsdump

The ufsdump program makes either full or incremental backups of ufs file systems, or full backups of individual files and directories. We describe only the file-system-based backup aspect. Its syntax is:

ufsdump [*options*] [*arguments*] *file_system*

The options (see Table 21.9), which are all single letters or digits, modify the behavior of the ufsdump command. All the options are lumped together into a single string, not preceded by the UNIX-standard hyphen. Some options require an argument; if any of those are specified, their arguments follow the option string in the same order that the options appear in the string. The last argument must be the name of the file system to be dumped.

Ufsdump can create multivolume backups if a file system is too large to fit on a single piece of media. When it needs a new volume to be mounted, it sends a message to the operator console to that effect. If problems arise during a dump, it may send messages to the console that require a yes or no answer. Thus, don't assume that ufsdump can run unattended.

When a dump is successfully completed, ufsdump writes a record into the file /etc/dumpdates. It includes the name of the file system, the date, and the dump level.

If no options are given, the default is to do a level 9 backup, write a record into /etc/dumpdates, and use /dev/rmt/0 as the dump device.

21.5.2   Ufsrestore

The ufsrestore command reads backup images (on tapes or files) created by ufsdump and restores individual files or entire file systems. The syntax is similar to that of ufsdump:

ufsrestore [*function*] [*options*] [*arguments*] [*files*]

Table 21.9 ■ Commonly Used Ufsdump Options and Arguments

digit	A digit 0-9 defines the dump level, as described in Section 20.6.2. If no dump level is specified, the default is 9.
a *archive*	Create a dump table of contents in the argument file *archive*. This file can be searched to determine whether a given file is in the dump, without having to invoke ufsrestore.
b *factor*	Blocking factor for writing to tapes, in 512-byte blocks. The default varies with media type: 800 or 1600 bpi 9-track tape, 20; 6250 bpi 9-track tape, 64; 8mm and other cartridge tapes, 126.
d *bpi*	Density of the backup tape, in bits per inch. Estimated values to use for various media: 9-track tape, 1600 or 6250; 8mm (high or normal density), 54000; ¼″ cartridge, 1000.
D	Dump to diskette.
f *dump_file*	Write the backup image to *dump_file*. The default is /dev/rmt/0. *dump_file* can be a tape device, a file, or – for standard output. You may also specify a tape device on a remote machine, using the hostname:device notation. This is the mechanism by which multiple systems can dump to a single tape drive across the network. Note that the ufsdump process runs on each machine with a local disk and writes to a remote tape device; there is no provision for dumping a remote file system to a local tape drive. The /.rhosts or /etc/hosts.equiv file on the remote machine must allow root access by the local machine.
s *size*	Size of the backup media, in feet. Not normally required, since ufsdump can detect end of media. Estimated values to use for various media: 9-track tape, 2300; 8mm normal density, 6000; 8mm high density, 13000; QIC-150 ¼″ cartridge, 700; diskette, 1422 (interpreted as blocks rather than feet).
S	Estimate the size of the backup according to the options given, but do not actually back up anything. Useful for determining how much media needs to be available before starting a backup.
u	Record the backup in /etc/dumpdates.
v	Verify (file system must be unmounted). After the dump, compare the contents of the backup with the source file system. If there are differences, repeat the dump with fresh media each time until there are no discrepancies.
w	Warn of file systems that need to be backed up. Every ufs file system in /etc/vfstab that has not been backed up within the last day (according to /etc/dumpdates) is listed.

The options (see Table 21.10) are all single letters, which are lumped together into one string. There is a small set of options from which you must choose exactly one; we have called this the function, but it is specified in the same string as the rest of the options. As in ufsdump, some options require an argument; if any of those are specified, their arguments follow the option string in the same order that the options appear in the string. The list of files to be restored, if needed, follows all other arguments on the command line.

Files restored by ufsrestore retain their original ownership, mode, and modification time, if the program is run by the superuser. Ufsrestore can be run by an ordinary user but the files may only be restored into directories

Table 21.10 ■ Most-used Ufsrestore Command-line Options

The function options (choose exactly one):

i	Interactive restore. We do not describe interactive mode in detail. The interface is similar to browsing through the UNIX file system, and commands are provided to select files to restore and to actually extract them. There is a help command in interactive mode.
r	Full restore. This is used to restore an entire file system hierarchy. You must be at the root of an empty file system before invoking restore with this option since files from the backup image will overwrite any existing files by the same name. To completely restore a file system from backups, use the r option with the latest full dump, and then again with each incremental that follows it.
R	Resume a full restore. Used to pick up when a full restore has had to be interrupted.
t	List the table of contents of a backup. If file or directory names are specified on the command line, only those files are listed if found in the backup; otherwise, every file in the backup is listed. If an archive file is specified, the table of contents is taken from there; otherwise, the backup tape must be mounted and the table of contents is taken directly from there.
x	Extract and restore specified files or directories. If no files are specified, the entire contents of the backup are extracted and restored.

Other options:

a *archive*	Read the dump table of contents from the argument file *archive*. This lets you determine whether a given file is in the dump, without having to mount the backup media.
b *factor*	Blocking factor for reading tapes, in 512-byte blocks. Ordinarily, ufsrestore is able to figure out the blocking factor from the tape.
d	Debug mode.
f *dump_file*	Read the backup image from *dump_file*. The default is /dev/rmt/0. *dump_file* can be a tape device, a file, or – for standard input. You may also specify a tape device on a remote machine, using the *hostname:device* notation. See the discussion under ufsdump.
h	If a directory is specified, restore only the directory and not the files it contains. Default behavior is to restore directories and their contents recursively.
s *n*	Skip to the *n*th file on the tape. Used when there are multiple backup files on one tape.
v	Verbose. Ufsrestore prints a line for each file it restores, listing the file type, i-node number, and file name.

where the user has write permission, and all restored files will be owned by the user and have the current date and time.

21.5.3 Volcopy and Labelit

The volcopy program copies an exact image of a whole file system from one disk to another disk, or to tape. The labelit program writes a short user-assigned label into the superblock of a file system to identify it for subsequent operations. When volcopy is told to make a copy of a file system, it scrupulously checks its label to make sure that the correct volumes are mounted.

Since volcopy makes a bit-for-bit copy, it can only be used to back up an entire file system; there is no "incremental" volcopy. Volcopy is usually used for fast, disk-to-disk, "snapshot" copies. Doing volcopy to tape can be very slow because of the difficulty in keeping the tape device streaming. If you have many file systems to back up and you want to use volcopy to make disk copies, you essentially have to buy twice as many disks as you actually need to hold your data.

The big advantage of volcopy is that it is extremely easy to recover lost data. Since an entire file system is saved, it is possible to mount the saved file system to recover a single file, or to copy the file system back from the backup medium, in order to recover an entire file system. Volcopy backups from disk to tape are good for long-term archival storage of data, but they are inconvenient for day-to-day work because it is hard to remove a single file from a backup tape.

The minimal syntax of labelit for ufs file systems is:

```
# labelit  -F ufs  dev  fsname  vol
```

The -F ufs option specifies the ufs file system type. *Dev* is the raw disk device being labeled. *Fsname* is an arbitrary nickname that identifies the mount point for the file system on this device; for example, usr or home1. *Vol* is an arbitrary identifier for the physical media. Both *fsname* and *vol* may be a maximum of six characters long.

The minimal syntax of volcopy for ufs file systems is:

```
# volcopy  -F ufs  fsname  srcdev  vol1  destdev  vol2
```

The -F ufs option specifies the ufs file system type. *Fsname* is the name of the mount point for the file system being copied; for example, home1. *srcdev* and *destdev* are the raw disk devices for the file system being copied and the device to which it's being copied, respectively. *Vol1* and *vol2* are the labels that are expected to be found on the source and destination devices, respectively. If the specified labels do not match what's found on the physical media, volcopy will not make the copy.

21.6 Newfs—Create a File System

The newfs command turns a raw disk partition into a UNIX file system by creating the directory infrastructure and bookkeeping data structures in a portion of the disk space. Running newfs on a disk partition destroys any data that might have been stored there in a previously created file system. In fact, running newfs is a very fast way to completely clear a file system.

Newfs is actually a friendly front-end to the mkfs program. Newfs only works for ufs file systems. The newfs command syntax is:

```
# newfs [-N] [-v] [options] special
```

Table 21.11 ■ Commonly Used Newfs Command-line Options

-N	Print out the parameters that newfs will use, but do not actually create a file system.
-v	Verbose; newfs prints messages explaining everything it does, including echoing all the parameters it passes to mkfs.
-b *n*	Block size of the new file system, in bytes. Can be either 4096 or 8192; 8192 is the default.
-c *n*	Number of cylinders per cylinder group. Default is 16.
-d *n*	Rotational delay in milliseconds. Used to determine how far apart to space consecutive blocks of a file, to maximize reading/writing efficiency. Value is disk-type dependent.
-f *n*	Fragment size in bytes. The smallest amount of disk space that can be allocated to a file. Default is 1024, maximum is the block size (see the -b option).
-i *n*	Number of bytes per i-node; a larger number means fewer files can exist on the file system but less space is taken up by the i-node structures. Default is 2048.
-m *free*	"Minfree," percentage of space to reserve as a pad in the file system. Once the file system is within minfree percent of being full, no one but the superuser is able to write more data there. This is to allow efficient utilization of disk blocks and to provide maneuvering room for getting out of tight disk-space situations.
-o *opt*	Optimize disk usage for "space" or "time." If a file system is configured to optimize for space, UNIX will spend time trying to find the best fit for each data block, to squeeze the most data into the available space. If optimized for time, blocks will be written into the first space that fits, and the available disk space may be broken into little unusable fragments.
-r *n*	Rpm of the disk. Default is 3600, but the value to use is disk-type dependent.
-t *n*	Number of tracks per cylinder; the default is read from the disk's label.

Many of the newfs options (see Table 21.11) specify very technical parameters used to fine-tune the layout and performance of a file system on a particular kind of disk. Choosing newfs options wisely is an art that we can't explain in this book. Fortunately, there are default values for nearly all the options that will produce a fairly efficient and usable file system.

21.7 Fsck—Check and Repair File Systems

With no arguments, fsck checks all file systems whose /etc/vfstab entries say they are to be checked. You can check one or more individual file systems by giving their names on the command line. See Section 20.4.6 for a complete discussion of what fsck does.

The fsck syntax for checking ufs file systems is:

```
# fsck -F ufs [options] [special ...]
```

Special is a raw disk device name. The command-line options are listed in Table 21.12. The file system should be unmounted before fsck is run. If it cannot be unmounted (for example, the root file system), the system should

Table 21.12 ■ Fsck Command-line Options

-V	Given a command, expand it to include all default settings and echo the resulting command line but do not actually execute it.
-m	Check but don't repair anything. This is used on file systems that are expected to be clean; it's a sanity check. If problems are found, you need to run fsck again with serious options.
-o *options*	Multiple ufs-specific options are specified as a comma-separated list. Common options include f, force a check even if the file system's flag indicates it is clean; p, preen the file system noninteractively, and exit on the first error; w, check writable file systems only.

be as inactive as possible during the fsck, and it should be rebooted immediately afterwards.

21.8   Dd—Convert Files

Dd is a general purpose data conversion and transfer program. It is often used to perform general data transfers between disk and tape, or from tape to tape. It, like volcopy, is an efficient way to copy an entire file system image from one place to another. Unlike volcopy, dd doesn't perform any label checking but it offers many more options than volcopy for managing the transfer.

Another task that dd often performs is data conversion, such as ASCII to EBCDIC character set, blocking or unblocking of fixed-length format data from mainframe computers, and so on. The dd command-line syntax is rather skewed from the UNIX norm; it is one of the oldest UNIX utilities, and its quirky option style (see Table 21.13) has been left alone to preserve some semblance of backward compatibility.

Table 21.13 ■ Common Dd Command-line Options

if=*name* of=*name*	Name of the input and output files, respectively; either may be a tape device or an ordinary file. If none is specified, standard input/output is the default.
ibs=*n* obs=*n*	Input and output block size, respectively, in bytes. Default is 512.
bs=*n*	Set both input and output block size, overriding ibs and obs.
cbs=*n*	Conversion buffer size (logical record length), for example, for reading fixed-length records and turning them into null-terminated UNIX strings.
count=*n*	Read only *n* input blocks.
conv=*ctype*	Perform conversion *ctype* on the input. Common conversion types are ascii, turn EBCDIC into ASCII; ebcdic, turn ASCII into EBCDIC; ibm, turn ASCII into the IBM flavor of EBCDIC; block, turn null-terminated strings into fixed-length records; unblock, to do the opposite; swab, swap bytes pair-wise; lcase and ucase, turn alphabetic input to lowercase or uppercase respectively; sync, pad each input block to ibs. Several conversions can be given by separating them with commas.

You need not be superuser to run dd. The syntax is:

```
% dd [option=value] ...
```

21.9   Df—Disk Free Space

The df (disk free) command with no arguments prints a summary of the free space on all the mounted file systems. You need not be superuser to run df; anyone can do it. The summary under SVR4 includes the number of free blocks and the number of free i-nodes, plus the percentage of disk space still available in the file system.

Df also allows you to specify which file systems to examine by specifying either a disk special device name, a directory, or the name of a remotely mounted resource. There are many options to control just what statistics df will report and to qualify what type of file systems on which it will report.

The basic syntax of df is:

```
% df [options] [directory|special]
```

When you specify a directory, df determines on which local disk or remote resource that directory actually resides and reports the free space on that disk or resource. This can be a useful way of cutting through a morass of symlinks, mount points, and so on, to find out where a directory actually lives.

The system manager should run df routinely to monitor the free space on all of the file systems. Some systems need 20 or 30 percent free space, other systems only need 5 or 10 percent; experience is your best guide.

21.10   Cron, Crontab—Run Programs at Specified Times

The cron program, a daemon, is used to execute programs at specified times. The cron program usually is started shortly after the system is booted, and there should only be one cron process running in a system.

Cron reads commands from crontab files which are stored in the directory /var/spool/cron/crontabs. Any user on a system can create a crontab file by using the crontab command; a user's crontab file is named with his login name and is owned by him. The spool directory is local to each UNIX system; there is no way for a single crontab file to cause commands to be executed on multiple systems except by placing rsh (remsh) commands into the crontab.

Each line in a crontab file specifies a command and the time or times when it should be executed. Every command cron executes from a user's crontab file is run with the privileges of that user (like a setuid program) and with that user's shell environment.

An entry in the crontab file consists of five fields that specify when a command should be run, followed by the command. From left to right, the five fields represent minutes (0-59), hours (0-23), day of the month (1-31),

Table 21.14 ■ Crontab Command-line Options

-e	Edit the crontab file. If the environment variable EDITOR is set, that editor is used. The default editor is ed.
-r	Remove the crontab file from the spool directory.
-l	List the contents of the crontab file.

month of the year (1-12), and day of the week (0-6, with Sunday as zero). The fields are separated by spaces or tabs.

The following line in a crontab file causes the date to be printed on the console every ten minutes:

```
0,10,20,30,40,50 * * * * date > /dev/console
```

The numbers representing the time can either be a single number in the range mentioned above, a list of numbers separated by commas (as in the example), or two numbers separated by a hyphen to indicate a range of times, or an asterisk to indicate all legal values.

The crontab program is used to create, edit, list, and remove individuals' crontab files in the spool directory (see Table 21.14 for a list of command-line options). Every time a change is made to a crontab file, the cron daemon is notified with a signal. The syntax of the crontab program is:

```
% crontab [-e] [-r] [-l] [username]
```

An ordinary user can manipulate only his own crontab file. The super-user may specify a *username,* to affect any user's crontab.

22
Security

Computer security is a phrase with at least two distinct meanings. In a more or less general sense, it means making sure that the data stored on a computer, or computer network, is accessible only to people who are authorized to see it, and that the data is safeguarded against corruption or loss.

A second, more technical definition has to do with government- or industry-mandated classification levels. It's sometimes referred to as "Orange Book" security, after the cover of the (U.S. government-produced) document that describes the special measures necessary to safeguard computing facilities used for national security. Orange Book security defines strict procedures that govern exactly what operations can be done by any given user, or upon any given piece of information, and is organized into various levels ranging from C-2 (minimal security) up through A-1 (absolutely unimpeachable, not yet implemented on any computing system).

Any Orange Book security is also accompanied by elaborate logging and monitoring schemes; at high security levels, these features can take so much of a computer system's resources that there's little left for end-user computing. Nonetheless, such security is required by some sites. If you work at such a site, you will certainly be given careful instruction about how to administer or work within such security regulations by your organization's security office.

In this chapter, we talk about computer security only in the first, more general sense. The security of a system is its reliability in the face of adversity. If a system unexpectedly crashes, loses files, or allows unauthorized access to files, then it is insecure. A secure system works reliably and maintains and protects users' files.

There are two major goals of security: protecting the data against loss and securing the system against intrusion and unauthorized use. The first goal is relatively straightforward to do, with backup procedures: it's covered in the first section of this chapter. The second goal is one of the thorniest problems facing any UNIX system administrator or user, and the problems and solutions we present in the remaining sections of this chapter just barely scratch the surface.

22.1   Data Protection

An important aspect of UNIX security is the protection of the data on your system against loss. It isn't just malicious crackers that are a threat; users are perfectly capable of deleting or destroying their own files through a slip of the fingers, and unexpected system crashes and hardware failures can also cause catastrophic loss of data.

There are three basic reasons computer systems lose files: the hardware malfunctions, the operating system software malfunctions, or the computer user makes mistakes. Hardware malfunctions are inevitable, operating system bugs are likely, and computer user mistakes are assured. The goal of computer manufacturers and operating system designers is to minimize the data loss caused by hardware and software; at the very least these losses should be small compared to accidental file erasures by users.

22.1.1   Irrecoverable Data Loss

There are a few situations in which data loss cannot be prevented or recovered by backup software. One paradox of the UNIX system is that from a user's point of view all I/O transactions are synchronous (that is, they happen immediately), whereas from the system's point of view all I/O is buffered and asynchronous. Because the kernel holds data in buffers and only writes it out to disk periodically (on the order of every 15 seconds or so, usually), some irrecoverable data loss is likely whenever the computer stops unexpectedly.

Another implication of buffering is that a process may have exited before the buffers containing its data are written out to the disk. If a write failure occurs at that point, it would be impossible for the kernel to report that failure back to the process. These problems, undesirable as they may seem, are an unavoidable result of biasing the UNIX system's I/O design toward quick interactive response.

In reality, the incidence of such problems is vanishingly small. The reliability of the UNIX system (its crash resistance) is high. UNIX systems generated from standard software modules often run for months without a crash. This record compares favorably with the reliability of most computer and network hardware. UNIX systems that have been augmented with locally modified or imported software sometimes are less reliable.

Another reason for loss of data is simply catastrophic failure of a disk drive. Although modern disk technology is quite reliable, there will always be a small percentage of below-standard hardware that makes it to market, and it may fail at any time. There seems to be an "infant mortality" period for disk hardware: If a disk makes it through the first few months of use, it will usually run smoothly for several years. If a disk fails in a spectacular way (e.g., a "head crash," where one of the read/write heads actually skims the disk surface, leaving a long spiral gouge), the data on the disk can be completely irrecoverable. In this case, the only recourse is backups.

22.1.2 Backup Security

In the normal case, assuming no system crashes, the most important way to protect your users' data is to back up the system regularly, using UNIX system utilities such as dump (ufsdump, under SVR4) or cpio. Some fundamental principles for backing up data reliably are discussed in Section 20.6, and the actual procedures for implementing a backup scheme are discussed in Section 21.5.

The very act of making backups of your data creates another potential security vulnerability, though. One simple, brute-force way that a cracker can steal data from your system is by getting a copy of your backup media. It is critical to safeguard your backup media, both against theft or unauthorized access and against disaster such as fire. One way to do this is to keep one copy of the backups locked in a secure room at your facility and to store a duplicate set at a secure off-site facility. There are companies that provide this kind of storage service.

22.2 Protection Against Intruders

Security is a relative term; there is no such thing as an absolutely secure computer system. Even a stand-alone computer is subject to tampering by anyone who has physical access to it. Also, intelligence agencies have explored the possiblity of snooping without physical access, using the electrical emissions of computers. Computers that are connected to a network or a dial-in modem are subject to unauthorized access by anyone who has access to any host on the network, or to a telephone. However, the ultimate weakness in many systems' security is the human element. A would-be cracker who gains the trust of a system administrator often has little trouble discovering how to get into the computer.

(NOTE: The terms *hacker* and *cracker* are often blurred together, and indeed not everyone agrees on their meanings. In this book, we use cracker to mean someone who tries to gain unauthorized access to a computer system, whether or not for personal gain or destructive purposes. A hacker is someone who's very knowledgeable about computing and computers.)

For most people, the goal isn't absolute security, which is very difficult to attain. Rather the goals are more modest: to make it hard for the intruder; to detect intrusions when they occur; and to make sure that if there is an intrusion, backups are able to compensate for any damage done by the intruder. It's this reasonable and attainable goal that is the focus of this chapter.

Military and other people who have more stringent goals need more information than we can provide in this book.

The primary watchwords for making your system secure are common sense, alertness, knowledge of your system, and careful, thorough administrative policies and procedures.

22.2.1 Physical Security

Good physical security is the hardest for a potential intruder to foil, but it also can cause the most inconvenience for legitimate users of a system. Complete physical security means that no part of the computer or network is physically accessible to anyone who is not "trusted," however the administrators of the system define that term.

The most obvious way to achieve physical security is to keep all computer equipment in a secure room. There would be no network, and only trusted, authorized people could enter the room to use the equipment. For most sites whose work relies on computers, this is too restrictive and inflexible to be a real solution, at least for everyday work. There are special situations that may make it worthwhile to put up with this kind of inconvenience. For example, a company may be developing a new product line that has to be kept secret from its competitors. (In the real world, industrial spying is far more intense than anything carried out in the Cold War!)

Another approach to security is to shut a system down whenever it is not specifically needed. When the computer is running, it should be attended by someone who is trusted. This is not a practical arrangement for many sites, but it does effectively prevent unwanted access.

One fact of life is that when you have computers attached to a network, there is no such thing as physical security unless you have the entire network contained and protected. If any workstation on a network is open to physical access, the entire network is vulnerable.

Thus, users of workstations on a network need to observe many of the same rules of behavior that applied to system operators in the old, pre-network days. Some of those rules are: limit access to the system console; don't leave your workstation unattended with an open login session; be especially careful never to leave a superuser login session unattended.

Some security-conscious sites have policies that require workstation owners to lock their offices at the end of the day. There are a couple of big loopholes in this "solution." First, nearly all workstations are attached to a network. A workstation that's left running, even behind a locked door, is still vulnerable to attack over the network.

Second, most companies entrust at least a few people with master keys, including custodial staff and security people. With some UNIX workstations it is trivially easy, given access to the console, to halt the computer and reboot to single-user mode, which comes up as the superuser. Under SVR4, the single-user boot process prompts for the root password, so this is not a problem.

22.2.2 Terminal Line Security

The next most secure approach is to keep the computer itself in a secure facility but to allow one or more (serial-line) terminals in external locations. The cables that connect a terminal to the host may be shielded or enclosed in the walls or ceiling to prevent anyone from tapping in to intercept the signals going in either direction. To further increase security, you can avoid putting terminals in public access areas, even including private offices if they are left unlocked.

Each terminal can connect to a specific tty port on the computer, as opposed to using a rotary that assigns an arbitrary free tty port to any terminal as it becomes active. This way, if a security breach occurs, you know exactly which terminal the cracker used to get access. The cost is that you need to have one dedicated tty port for every terminal; with a rotary or serial-line multiplexer, you can get by with fewer tty ports, because not everyone will be logged in at once.

On-site serial-line security is not as important as it once was. Most sites running UNIX now consider the workstation as the basic unit of computing equipment rather than a computer terminal which is used to access a central computer server. With networked systems, a whole new set of security problems comes into play. However, dial-in lines are serial, and they have historically proved the most fruitful area for crackers to ply their trade.

22.2.3 Telephone Access

Telephone access to the computer is inherently insecure. Anyone with a modem and the phone number to your system can dial in and start hacking away. With luck, persistence, or the help of carelessness on the system administrator's part, a cracker might gain access in a matter of weeks—or minutes!

A system that does "dial-back" can increase security. With a dial-back system, the incoming caller has to provide a phone number for the computer to call back. This means that the caller also has to have a modem that can answer incoming calls. You can keep a list of approved numbers that your system will dial back. You should log any unknown numbers that are provided by callers; if a cracker is gullible enough to leave his own number in hopes of getting a call-back, you may be able to trace the number to a person.

SVR4 UNIX has another security feature called dial-up passwords. When this feature is enabled, anyone who logs in through a dial-in port must type in a password just to get to the regular login: prompt. One weakness of this system is that all users with the same login shell (which is usually almost everyone—every site generally has one predominant login shell) share the same dial-in password.

When many people share a password in this way, it tends to become public knowledge very quickly. Even if it doesn't quite reach the point where the dial-up password is scrawled on the bathroom wall, people are willing to give out information they figure is generally available. If someone asks in a sort of embarrassed tone of voice, "Hey, can you tell me the dial-up password for boris? I've forgotten it again," a user might be inclined to be helpful and provide the information. Crackers love to exploit these "social engineering" cracks in system security. Passwords, whether personal or dial-up, only work to the extent that they are guarded by their legitimate users.

22.3 Security Procedures and Education

Probably the most effective ways to improve security at a site are through education and procedures. Educate yourself and your users about the security concerns at your site, what they must do to help, and why. Then establish and enforce a consistent and thorough set of security procedures for both users and system administrators to follow.

22.3.1 Know Your System

If you are the administrator of a UNIX system, the first step toward keeping it secure is becoming familiar with its normal behavior. If you know all the system software that is supposed to be running and how it behaves, you will notice if your login program, for example, doesn't react in quite the right way. If you know all the regular users on your system, you will notice when an inactive account suddenly starts seeing a lot of activity, or when you see a burst of nighttime logins from someone who is normally a "day person."

These are all clues that someone may be tampering with your system, just as noticing that a light is on isn't alarming in itself, but (if you're sure you turned it off) it may be an indication that someone else has been in your house.

How would you notice that someone has been logging in at night unless you were watching the system 24 hours a day? A file called /etc/wtmp keeps a binary-format record of every login made to the system: the name of the user, the tty port to which he connected, and the date and time and duration of the login. The "last" command displays this information in a human-readable format. On many systems, this file is rotated on a regular basis so the record may not go back as far as you would like. Older versions of the file can be recovered from backup tapes, and some sites keep the last few weeks or months worth of files on line before deleting them. The last command has an -f option to read from a specified file.

Another interesting source of information is the record of su attempts (only when someone tries to su to root, not to an ordinary user) written into the system messages file, /var/adm/messages. The date and time, name of the user trying to become root, and serial port used are logged, as shown here:

```
May 12 09:22:07 maus su: 'su root' failed for richter on /dev/ttyp0
May 12 09:22:37 maus su: 'su root' succeeded for richter on /dev/ttyp0
```

The contents of wtmp and the su log messages can be valuable in investigating an earlier break-in. If someone's files mysteriously disappear or are altered, for example, you may find from wtmp that he logged in during a time when he was actually out of town and not logging in at all. This shows that someone else had the user's password and used it to access his account. Further detective work is left to the reader's imagination.

In the same way, all the users at a site should be encouraged to report any anomalies in system behavior (such as, "login always misses my password the first time, and I have to type it again") to the administrator. Many users are quite sensitive to even small changes in program behavior, especially if they use the same small set of programs day in and day out. If they understand that they can help safeguard the system by noting and reporting any unexplained changes, they can be of great help in catching software sabotage at an early stage.

The attitude of the system support staff can have a great effect on users' willingness to report things. If user feedback is to be of any help, the people who talk to users must be open to such feedback. Some computer support people, when told that passwords are always rejected the first time, will subtly or not so subtly blame the user. A typical response is, "You must have typed it wrong. Be more careful and it won't happen again" (sometimes accompanied by an implied roll of the eyes). When a user is dismissed in this way a time or two, you're not likely to hear about any future problems from that user. A much better response to the user's report would be, "Most often, passwords are rejected because they are typed wrong, but sometimes they are rejected because of a security problem. Please let me know if the problem continues, and in the meantime I'll look into it and see if we have a problem."

22.3.2   The Human Dimension

It's just as important to know the users of the system. A system administrator should always be apprised of personnel situations such as dismissal, layoff, or disciplinary action. It's not unheard of for a disgruntled employee to take revenge by sabotaging computer files. If the system administrator has some advance notice of such actions, she can protect the system by inactivating the user's account or making extra backups of vulnerable files.

22.3.3   The (Friendly) Cracker

Crackers use any method available in their attempts to get into a computer system. One of the easiest ways is to get friendly with a legitimate user (or system administrator!) and cajole information out of her, often in the guise of asking a favor. People like to be helpful, and it may not seem like such a big deal to let someone who doesn't have an account on your system use your computer account for a few minutes to read netnews, especially when they seem so reasonable and knowledgeable about UNIX! The danger is that even a few minutes of access as a regular user can be enough for a very knowledgeable hacker to exploit security holes and provide himself a permanent entry to the system.

Another method of attack, which works particularly well in large anonymous computing environments such as a university, is for the cracker to pose as a system or network authority via e-mail. One actual episode involved a cracker who sent e-mail to numerous users explaining that there was a potential security problem on the system. He asked them to aid his investigation of it by changing their password to a certain string (which was included in the message). Only a very naive user would believe such a story and actually change his password, but it only takes one to get the cracker onto the system.

The protection against this kind of attack is user awareness and education. Users should be made to realize that computer access is a valuable asset: it's something to be protected and used wisely, and not to be shared with anyone.

22.4 Passwords and Accounts

Some very basic security procedures have to do with passwords and user accounts. All UNIX file permissions are based on user identity, or account. The key to gaining the privileges and permissions of any user is his password. These two resources, a user account and its password, are valuable and should be administered wisely and protected.

A UNIX system is like an apartment building whose many occupants each have a key that fits the front door. Any of them can get into the building, and once inside, it becomes easier to discover how to get into someone else's apartment. Similarly, once an intruder has any access at all to a UNIX system, it is much easier to expand that access. Anyone who is lax about password security can enable an intruder to enter. Someone who chooses a weak password, or writes it on the screen or keyboard, or posts it on the bulletin board, endangers everyone's files and work, not just his or her own.

22.4.1 Who Gets an Account

First, be careful in giving out computer accounts; only people who really have a need to access the computer should be allowed to log in. Granted, as electronic mail and word processing become more and more widely used, lots of companies find that almost everyone needs a computer account. Be a good housekeeper: remove the accounts of people who no longer need access to the system or people who have left the company.

Every person should have his or her own individual account. While it may seem convenient to have one login for all secretaries or for all the people working on a particular project, it is very bad from a security point of view. When multiple users use the same account, there is no accountability of individual actions; that is, you can't tell who created (or destroyed, or changed) a particular file. The users also lose the capability of easily tailoring their own work environment (one of UNIX's strengths), because an account has only one set of dot files.

22.4.2   Basic Rules and Initial Password

Every user account must have a password. When you create a new user account, assign an initial password. Give this password to the user (it's known only to you and the user) with instructions to change it immediately upon logging in the first time. It's desirable for the user to change the password so that no one else knows it, not even the system administrator.

It is possible to set up an account with no initial password. Why not just do this, and let the user pick a password when he logs in? It seems convenient but it is actually fraught with peril. First, if an account has no password, literally anyone can log into that account and then set the password, possibly locking out the real user. Second, even though the policy is for the user to set a password upon first login, the temptation to leave his account unprotected can be great. It's very convenient not to have to type a password. If an account is initially assigned a password, though, the user can change the password, but he cannot make the account have "no password." Only the superuser can do that.

22.4.3   How Passwords Work

In an ordinary UNIX system, the /etc/passwd file contains the actual password for each user account, in an encrypted form. As shown in Figure 22.1, the encrypted password is the second colon-separated field in an ordinary UNIX /etc/passwd file.

The encryption algorithm is a good one, and there is no easy way to decrypt a password (as you will see, though, crackers take a brute-force approach rather than trying decryption). The encrypted string is always 13 characters long, and the first two characters are the "salt": these are characters that are fed into the encryption algorithm along with the clear-text password to produce the 13-character encrypted string.

For example, if we were to use the password "HitoWtgi" (the first letters of the phrase "Here is the only Way to get in," with a couple of key words capitalized), UNIX might encrypt it as g7dMg1ormG3OY. The two characters g7 are the salt, which are chosen randomly by the passwd program. The remainder of the string is the encrypted representation of HitoWtgi.

How does UNIX check your password when you log in, if the string is impossible to decrypt? Simple: it reads what you type in at the Password: prompt, looks up your encrypted password in the /etc/passwd file, and encrypts what you just typed in with the same salt that was used for the stored

---

```
person:o1FXt4poIH7eQ:154:11:Dorothy Person:/boris/a/person:/bin/csh
sharman:mueNjfCg.CqdI:170:83:Steven Harman:/boris/a/sharman:/bin/sh
dmcmahon:IJpb5S59vpveQ:218:51:Don McMahon:/natasha/a/dmcmahon:/bin/ksh
sawtelle:h2BTwZCqdRZgY:109:68:Ann Sawtelle:/boris/c/sawtelle:/bin/csh
```

Figure 22.1 ■ Some Lines from an /etc/passwd File

password. If the resulting string matches what is stored in /etc/passwd, you're in.

22.4.4   How They Are Cracked

What crackers do to break passwords is a permutation of that, although it's a much more arduous task. A cracker would take each individual password from a stolen /etc/passwd file and, using the salt from that string, encrypt every word in the on-line dictionary /usr/dict/words. By comparing each of those encrypted strings with the stolen password, he might get a hit. Most crackers have figured out other sources that people commonly use for passwords, such as their own names or names of family members, local geographic names, license plate numbers, and so on.

You should see why it is very important to choose a password that is nonobvious. Something as simple as inserting a punctuation character or a number into an otherwise normal word, or capitalizing some of the letters, will make a password encrypt differently—and might slip you through the cracker's sieve.

Clearly, it makes a lot of sense for a cracker to write a program to do the encryptions and comparisons. Although this may be surprising, elaborate password cracking programs have been propagated through the Internet community by the "good guys." Why? It's actually a good system administration practice to run a password cracker on your own site's passwd file to detect easily broken passwords. If you can get the user to change her password before a real cracker gets there, you have closed a potential security hole.

22.4.5   Password Filtering

If possible, use a password filtering program to prevent people from choosing easily guessable passwords. Bad choices for passwords include the user's login name (spelled backwards or forwards), words found in a dictionary, the user's name, phone number, or license plate number, and any other piece of information that a cracker would be likely to discover and try. A password that fails the filtering test is rejected, and the user has to propose another password.

One balancing act that a system administrator has to do is decide how strict a password filter program should be. There are some password filters that will reject a password if it contains any three-character string that appears in any English word! That pretty much eliminates pronounceable passwords, and therein is the problem: if users are forced to choose completely incomprehensible, nonrememberable passwords, they are very likely to write them down. That's a very serious security problem, and one that arguably makes your system more vulnerable to break-ins than more lax password filtering standards.

A password filtering program compares a password against many of the same sources that a cracker's password-breaking program would, except that it doesn't have to do the time-consuming encryption. The difference is that it's done ahead of time, to prevent the user from setting a vulnerable password in the first place. This is an example of the same idea being applied to both good and bad purposes, depending on who's using it.

Most standard UNIX passwd programs check that a password is at least a minimum length (typically six characters), and that it contains at least one nonalphabetic character. There are numerous more sophisticated programs available over the Internet or from CERT (discussed later in this chapter) to do password filtering as previously described.

22.4.6   Password Aging

Password aging, a feature included in SVR4 UNIX, is a way to force users to change their passwords periodically. Why is this desirable? The idea of password aging is to present a moving target to crackers. A cracker who steals a copy of the /etc/passwd file can then try to break the passwords at his leisure, using software running on his own machine. The password-cracking process can take a long time, though. If a cracker takes a month to process a passwd file, and users are required to change their passwords every six weeks, there is limited time for him to actually get into the system.

The SVR4 password aging scheme lets the system administrator specify how often each user must change his password on a user-by-user basis. When a password is about to expire, the user is warned each time he logs in. When it actually does expire, the user is prompted to choose a new password the next time he tries to log in. If he doesn't change it, he doesn't get onto the system. The system administrator can also force an immediate password expiration for a user.

22.4.7   Shadow Passwords

Realistically, a cracker with a very powerful computer at his disposal might get through a password file in a matter of days or hours. To protect against this kind of threat, System V UNIX provides a security feature called *shadow passwords.* In the normal UNIX scheme, the /etc/passwd file contains the actual encrypted password for each user as well as other information that is used by lots of programs.

With SVR4 shadow passwords, only the innocuous information such as login name, user's real name, and so on, is stored in /etc/passwd. The encrypted passwords are stored in a completely different file, /etc/shadow, which is readable only by root, the superuser. Although this makes it much harder for an intruder to get a copy of the encrypted passwords in the first place, once he has them he can apply the regular methods of cracking them.

22.4.8   The Root Password

An especially sensitive security consideration on UNIX systems is the superuser password. Anyone who manages to obtain this piece of information has complete control of the system, so it's essential to safeguard it very carefully.

The list of people with the root password should be as small as possible, and they should be both trustworthy and knowledgeable. A well-intentioned but ignorant (or half-informed!) superuser can cause as much damage to a system as the most malicious cracker. It's not good to have only one superuser because of the possibility of sudden death or unavailability. It's fairly difficult to recover from not having the root password. For safety's sake, it may be a good idea to write down the root password and lock it up in a secure place.

22.5   Superuser Precautions

It's a standard UNIX security practice to discourage or disable direct logins as root. The preferred procedure for becoming superuser is to log in as a regular user, then type /bin/su to become root. The reason for using su rather than login is that su attempts are logged. Every su attempt, successful or failed, is written to a log file along with the name of the user who issued the su command. This provides a paper trail of superuser access. The reason for typing /bin/su rather than just su is to make sure you are using the standard su program and not a trojan horse (see Section 22.7.3).

When you are logged in as root, extra care (approaching paranoia) is required as you run utility programs. Any program executed by root can do anything, so it is very important to use the root privilege minimally. If root should execute a tampered program, security is gone from that point forward.

Therefore the search path for the superuser is critically important. It should never reference the current directory, and it should never reference directories that contain user-contributed software. The typical root $PATH is:

```
# echo $PATH
/bin:/etc:/usr/bin
#
```

Note that the $PATH shown does not reference ., the current directory. Including . in the path is a dangerous mistake. It's easy to accidentally include the current directory; a leading or trailing colon in the $PATH list implies the . entry at the beginning or end of the path. Each of the following paths contains an implied reference to the current directory:

```
:/bin:/etc:/usr/bin
/bin:/etc:/usr/bin:
/bin::/etc:/usr/bin
```

The first one is at the beginning of the path; the second one is at the end; and the third is between /bin and /etc.

22.6   Unix File Permissions and Security

The file and directory permissions built into the UNIX file system offer an easy-to-use but not particularly flexible way of protecting files from unauthorized use. Individual users are free to assign permissions to protect their own files, however they see fit. The system administrator has a particular responsibility to make sure that system files are protected against tampering or unwanted use.

The following discussions assume you know about setuid and setgid programs; these are explained in Section 20.8.

22.6.1   Protection of System Directories

Maintaining the correct access permissions for system files and directories is a good first line of defense. Many standard cracker attacks rely on lax permission monitoring. As a minimum, the directories mentioned in root's search path should be as secure as possible:

■ Owned by root

■ Write permission denied for the directory, for all except the owner

■ Write permission denied for executable files in those directories

In fact, all directories containing system software, even those containing user-contributed software, should be protected from write access by everyone except root. If they are writable by anyone else, a cracker can easily compromise the system by installing his own tampered version of a system utility, configuration file, or shell script.

A very simple way of scanning for tampered programs is to do a long format listing of the files in each system directory. If any files have a too-recent modification date, you should investigate more carefully. A more sophisticated way of checking would be to use the find command to find files that have been modified within the last few days.

```
% find /bin -mtime -7 -print
```

will print the names of all files in the /bin directory that have been modified within the last seven days. Of course, you should choose the time period that makes sense at your installation.

The permissions for the special files in the /dev directory must also be carefully controlled. If a raw disk interface (in the /dev/rdsk directory under SVR4) is writable, the permissions granted through the UNIX file system interface are moot: a knowledgeable user can patch the file system to grant whatever access is desired. If it is merely readable, any information stored on that disk is readable by anyone. Raw disk devices should be owned and readable only by root.

The memory special files (/dev/mem and /dev/kmem) should be owned by root and accessible only by root and a special group, usually called kmem (for kernel memory). Programs such as ps need to read kernel memory, so they are given the setgid kmem permission; this is safer than running setuid root. The terminal special files need to be writable by everyone, to allow programs such as write and wall to work, but they should have read privilege only for the owner. This prevents spying on someone's terminal session by reading from the terminal device.

You can use a simple set of UNIX shell commands to systematically monitor the permissions of system files. When you are confident that all the files and directories are in good order, make and keep a recursive long listing of the contents of each top-level directory:

```
% ls -lR /bin > /var/adm/bin.master
% ls -lR /usr/bin > /var/adm/usrbin.master
% ls -lR /etc > /var/adm/etc.master
```

and so on.

Then periodically make a similar listing of each directory into another file and compare the two listings with the diff command. In the following example, the new listing's file name includes a date stamp; this makes it much easier to pick out the listing of interest from a directory full of similar files.

```
% ls -lR /bin > /tmp/bin.930412
% diff /var/adm/bin.master /tmp/bin.930412 > /tmp/bin.diffs
```

There will very likely be some differences from week to week, but you should be able to explain them. For example, if you install a new version of an existing program, its date and time would change. If you delete a program, not only would its listing disappear, but the date and time on its parent directory would change as well. If you are satisfied that the changes you see are explainable and the files and directories are still in order, it's a good idea to replace the master list with the latest information, although you may want to keep the historical listings for tracking purposes later on:

```
% mv /var/adm/bin.master /var/adm/bin.930329
% mv /tmp/bin.930412 /var/adm/bin.master
```

Some full-blown and much more sophisticated security monitoring programs are available from the Internet. One such program in widespread use is called COPS. If you'd like to experiment with security programs, the CERT office (see the end of this chapter) would be a good place to find out how and where to acquire them.

22.6.2 Setuid and Setgid Programs

To increase the security of your system, you should keep the number of programs that run in privileged mode, or with the setuid bit on, to a minimum. Programs owned by root that run in setuid mode (su, mail, etc.) are dangerous. These programs' executable files should have write privilege denied so that they cannot be altered by an ordinary user.

In the early days of UNIX, making a program setuid was seen as a convenient way to sidestep the inconvenience of permissions. Many a print utility, mail program, or other system program was made setuid to enable writing to "protected" spool directories, and so on. The problem is that clever hackers can often find a way to make a setuid program spawn off another process, giving them a shell process running as root.

You should be particularly careful about installing third-party software that insists on being setuid root. Many vendors of third-party software, especially office automation and productivity software, are used to a DOS or Mac world where there is no concept of user IDs or file permissions. When they port a product for the UNIX market, they often take the path of least resistance to make their products run smoothly, and that means having them run as root. In many cases, appropriate use of user and group permissions can enable a product to work just as well as making it setuid root.

The find program can be used to locate all of the programs in a file system that have the setuid mode.

```
$ find /usr/bin -perm -4000 -exec ls -l {} \;
---s--s--x  1 uucp      11264 Feb 14  1991 /usr/bin/uuname
---s--s--x  2 uucp      15360 Feb 14  1991 /usr/bin/uusend
---s--s--x  1 uucp      26624 Feb 14  1991 /usr/bin/uucp
---s--s--x  1 uucp      26624 Feb 14  1991 /usr/bin/uux
---s--s--x  1 uucp      12288 Feb 14  1991 /usr/bin/uulog
-rws--s--x  2 uucp      46080 Jun  1  1992 /usr/bin/tip
^C
$ ▮
```

The octal mask 4000 shown above finds setuid programs. You can alternatively use the mask 2000 to find setgid programs.

22.7 Security of Installed Software

Most UNIX systems have at least some software installed that didn't come as part of the purchased UNIX distribution. It might be user-contributed software, local modifications to standard programs, or software from the Internet. Each of these categories has its own security risks. It's a very good idea to put such externally sourced programs in a separate directory, so the standard /bin, /etc, and /usr/bin directories contain only known safe programs. Many sites put such software in directories called /local/bin or /usr/local.

All software in public directories should go through a superuser for installation; it is irresponsible to allow users to install software unchecked (obviously, one can't control what a user installs in her own home directory). The superuser is the only one who can install software with the correct (writable only by root) permissions, but she should also at least cursorily inspect each program for antisocial tendencies and security holes before installation.

You should also prevent users who mount their own disks or diskettes from running programs in privileged mode. One of the easiest ways to break UNIX security is to import a version of su (which runs setuid root) that has been altered so that no password is required to become superuser. If you do allow people to mount file systems from their own media, make sure the "nosuid" option to mount is enforced.

22.7.1 Outside Software

Another class of outside software is that freely available from the Internet or other parties, usually in source form. This is sometimes called *public-domain software, shareware,* or *freeware.* Shareware is named after the practice of the author asking users to send him some small amount of money if they find the program useful or fun.

Much public-domain software is written by high-school or college students, or by other hackers who just like to share their creativity with the world. Some is created and distributed by organizations whose purpose in life is improving the state of software in the world, such as the Free Software Foundation and its Gnu products. Richard Stallman, the founder of the FSF, believes in the open and free propagation of software and programming ideas. He wrote a rather famous document called the Gnu Manifesto to explain his ideas, and the Gnu "copyleft" agreement is distributed along with all Gnu software. A copyleft is an agreement that anyone may use the software as long as they don't claim to have written it, and that the copyleft stays in any copies of the software that are distributed.

Some questions you should consider before uploading software from an outside source are:

- Is the distribution site itself reliable and probably free from tampering? If you get the software from a well-known Internet ftp site, or directly from the author, the answer is probably yes.

- Have other people used the software without major problems? You may be able to get a reference list of other users, and some software is so widely used and discussed on the Internet that you can assume it is good.

- Is the author a known quantity? If he or she is affiliated with some known organization or institution, it will be easier to get in touch later if you do have problems or concerns.

- Are you considering using this software for a critical system application, such as networking, e-mail, or security? If so, you should be doubly careful to check out the quality of the software and the experience of other users, and make sure to test the software thoroughly before entrusting your system to it.

If (when) you pull freeware or PD software off the net and are ready to try it out, take care. First, look through the source code and the Makefile for obvious, blatant attempts to compromise your system; for example, a Makefile that removes or replaces a standard system utility. If you don't feel you can examine C or another programming language source and be confident that you know what it does, you're probably better off not installing software from untrusted sources.

If you decide to go ahead and try it out, don't log in as root to do the initial compilation. Any hidden traps in the build process can cause much more damage when run as root than as an ordinary, unprivileged user. If a Makefile is provided (as it usually is), you should run "make -n" first. This echoes the commands that would be done to make the software, but doesn't actually do anything. If you see anything suspicious, investigate more closely. When you first try the software, too, do not run it as root.

22.7.2   Viruses and Worms

It's worth pointing out that UNIX systems are not as subject to computer virus infection as are microcomputers (Macs and PCs). The biggest reason is that microcomputer shareware is usually distributed in binary format, which makes it impossible for the user to tell exactly what a program really does. UNIX shareware, on the other hand, is almost always distributed in source form, because of the huge number of different UNIX platforms. Since the user can examine the source code and find obvious security breaches, few crackers even try to tamper with programs distributed in source code form.

UNIX's vulnerability lies in its well-known, trusted daemon programs, many of which run as root. These programs have been dissected and studied by crackers the world over, and many of them contain subtle security loopholes that can be exploited by a sufficiently clever and knowledgeable programmer. Programs that wiggle in through such holes are known as *worms;* the most notorious is the Internet worm of 1988.

Most of the really gaping holes in the standard UNIX daemons (sendmail, fingerd, and so on) have been found and patched by this time, thanks to the efforts of CERT and other security organizations. Recent software is being designed with much more attention to security issues, as one would hope.

22.7.3   Trojan Horse Programs

One way a cracker can break system security is by installing a trojan horse program. A trojan horse is outwardly a facsimile of a legitimate program, but its real purpose is to compromise the security of a system. A trojan horse "login" program might ape the login dialog, squirrel away the user's password in a secret file after he types it in, issue a "Login incorrect" message so the user will try again, and then turn over control to the real login program.

Malicious users can also plant trojan horses in source code. For example, a user might modify the on-line source code of a standard program to provide a security hole, and then complain to the administrator about a trivial (but easy to fix) bug in that program. When the administrator makes the fix and installs the updated program, it also includes the user's security hole. This technique has been applied successfully to ordinary programs and to the kernel.

The way to keep trojan horses out of your system is to protect all system directories so they are not writable by anyone except root. Source code files and the directories where they are stored must be protected as well as binary directories and files.

22.7.4 User-provided Security Holes

Users can do things to make a system vulnerable to unwanted access. For example, a user on a system that supports Berkeley networking may create a $HOME/.rhosts file that allows unrestricted access from an insecure host like a terminal server. This would allow anyone who connected to that terminal server, perhaps through a dial-in modem, to log in to the UNIX system as that user without ever giving a password. This is a fairly serious security hole.

Most people would agree that no one should be allowed to examine or change someone else's files without their permission. As networked systems become the norm, though, many sites are adopting policies that allow system administrators to monitor user files for potentially disastrous setups like that described above, and to disable or change them without prior warning. If your site allows such monitoring, be sure to let the users know ahead of time (i.e, when they get an account) so that nobody is surprised.

This is a gray area because it's hard to draw a clear line where the system administrator's privilege stops and the user's absolute privacy begins.

22.8 Security for the Individual User

Most of what has been covered so far could be classed as "site security" measures: things that a system administrator does to make sure the machines under her control are adequately protected. There are also things an individual can do to protect his computer account and the information it holds.

22.8.1 E-mail

First, be circumspect when using electronic mail. It should not be considered a secure channel, especially for information that is sensitive in any way. E-mail that goes out across public carriers (that is, outside the confines of your own local area net) could be subject to all kinds of illicit scrutiny. It's even rumored that e-mail is routinely monitored by national security agencies for the occurrence of sensitive keywords such as "nuclear weapons."

Besides, addressing errors and other delivery problems with e-mail are generally handled by routing the mail to the "postmaster" (one of the system administrators) on the originating machine. That person is usually busy enough not to be interested in reading all through the body of your message—his concern is finding out what's wrong with the mail header that kept it from being delivered properly—but if you wrote anything embarrassing or potentially damaging, it's there for him to see.

A rule of thumb for e-mail is don't send anything in e-mail that you wouldn't leave lying around on your desk for anyone to read. If it's more sensitive than that, don't send it in e-mail (unless you encrypt it first).

22.8.2   Protection of Files

"Why should I worry about my files? I've used chmod to set everything to mode 600, and my umask is 077; I'm the only one who can read them." The UNIX file permission system is intentionally porous; it certainly affords protection against ordinary users, but the superuser can read anything. This is not to suggest that system administrators or superusers are in the habit of perusing users' files. Life is much too busy for most of them to have the time for that. Still, you need to be aware that your files are always readable by someone, no matter what permissions you assign.

More than that, many employers feel that it is within their rights to monitor any activities and information that is stored on a computer system they own. It may not be ethical, but people have been disciplined or fired because "someone" discovered an updated resume and job-search letters on the computer. When an employee is fired or leaves under bad circumstances, it's also fairly common practice to have someone go through his or her files, both to reassign company or project files to someone else and to make sure there is no sabotage.

A couple of rules of thumb for how to safely store information under your UNIX account are: Don't store personal or private files on a business computer system; and don't expect complete privacy and respect for privacy in the workplace—your employer has concerns about appropriate use of his equipment (and your time!).

22.8.3   Encryption

What else can you do? You can encrypt especially sensitive files. The UNIX crypt command allows you to specify a keyword to encrypt a file. Giving the same keyword will decrypt the file back to its original state. Crypt lets you specify the keyword as a command-line option, but that exposes it to anyone monitoring your activities with the w command, or by snooping in your .history file if you're a C-shell user. It's far better to let the command prompt for the keyword, and enter it interactively (note that the keyword is not echoed to the screen as you type it):

```
boris% cat myfile
This is a file with plain text.
boris% ls -l myfile
-rw-r--r--  1 richter        32 May 11 07:23 myfile
boris% crypt < myfile > myfile.cr
Enter key:
boris% rm myfile
boris% cat myfile.cr
Tg$4Tb_]O=J^E^HKH4>Di?^H}pzJW=
boris% crypt < myfile.cr
Enter key:
This is a file with plain text.
boris% ls -l myfile*
-rw-r--r--  1 richter        32 May 11 07:28 myfile.cr
boris% 
```

Another way of encrypting files is by using the -x option of the vi editor. With this option, the editor prompts for a keyword before starting the edit session. You edit the file as usual, in plain text, but whenever the file is written out to the disk, it is encrypted with that keyword. No one snooping around through your files will be able to read it.

22.9   Network Security Considerations

From the system administrator's view, UUCP can be a dangerous program, particularly because the UUCP password for your system might be stored on multiple foreign systems. A security breach on any of those systems can yield the UUCP password for your system, so you're really at the mercy of your neighboring systems' security procedures. UUCP should be installed conservatively in most environments. You should limit the number of commands that foreign systems can execute.

If your site allows anonymous ftp, it should be carefully set up so that incoming users cannot freely roam through your entire file system hierarchy. If you allow anonymous writes (that is, users can put files onto your system as well as retrieve files), it is wise to isolate the ftp directory in a file system of its own. That way, a very prolific ftp user who fills up the file system will only affect other ftp users, not the regular users of the system.

In the IP network world, a fundamental trade-off is security versus convenience. You can make things very convenient for the users by having all hosts trust each other (see the discussion of Berkeley networking, trust, and the /etc/hosts.equiv and $HOME/.rhosts file in Chapter 20) and by cross-mounting all file systems on all hosts—but that reduces the security of all the systems. If you make a network very secure by having no hosts trust each other and not cross-mounting any file systems, you may as well not have a network—you lose much of the convenience and synergy gained by linking computer resources together for sharing.

Many sites have a double standard for security; they trust their own employees more than they trust people from the outside world. For the sake of convenience, they would like to run their internal networks with minimal security measures. They would also like to provide their employees with access to the Internet and other "dangerous" outside resources. One common solution to this dilemma is to set up a "firewall" system to act as a gateway between the company-internal network and the outside world (see Figure 22.2). A typical firewall configuration might allow anything to pass through to the outside, but only electronic mail can pass through from the outside to the internal network.

There are a couple of well-known software packages that provide additional security for UNIX networks. One, called Kerberos, was developed at MIT. It uses a scheme whereby a central authentication service verifies the identity of a user who wants to do something on a computer and grants him a time-stamped "ticket" for that service. Kerberos is in use at some universities but has not come into widespread use in the commercial world.

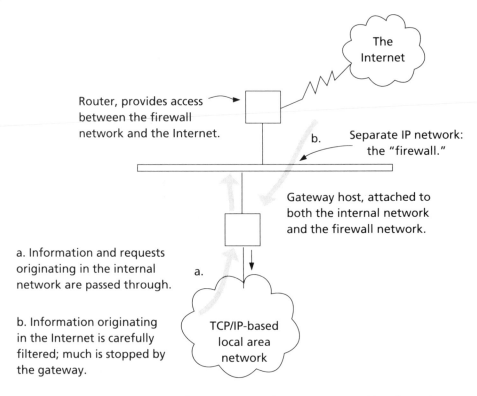

Router, provides access
between the firewall
network and the Internet.

The
Internet

b.   Separate IP network:
the "firewall."

Gateway host, attached to
both the internal network
and the firewall network.

a. Information and requests
originating in the internal
network are passed through.

a.

b. Information originating
in the Internet is carefully
filtered; much is stopped by
the gateway.

TCP/IP-based
local area
network

The gateway host has 2 IP interfaces and is configured to allow all outbound
traffic but to filter incoming packets to prevent outsiders from free access to
the internal net. Often e-mail is the only traffic allowed in.

Figure 22.2 ■ A network "firewall" configuration

The second is secure RPC (remote procedure call). The NFS (network file
system) protocol is based on RPC, and in its original incarnation RPC is insecure. Secure RPC adds some authentication to the protocol, which makes
it possible to implement a secure NFS.

22.10   Security Discussions

Many people in the UNIX community are very interested in security, so naturally there are several news groups and mailing lists on the topic. Some
groups to look at are comp.security and subdiscussions such as
comp.security.misc, comp.risks (which deals with all kinds of risks, but includes much discussion of computer-related risks), and misc.security.

Security groups often get into quite explicit discussions of security holes
and how to exploit them. There is disagreement on whether it's wise to put
everything in the open this way. One side asks, "Why put ideas into people's
heads? Why point right at the most glaring weaknesses of the system? You're

inviting trouble." This point of view is sometimes called "security through obscurity": just don't advertise the holes in your system, and people are not likely to find them.

On the other side are people who believe that open security discussions are the only way to stay ahead of the bad guys. Dedicated crackers are often brighter and more knowledgeable about computers than average users, they are very focused on their aims, and they are busily learning everything they can about the same security holes that the good guys are trying to plug. Having security discussions that are open to the network community is a good way of trying to level the playing field. Law-abiding system administrators may not have time to fool around with obscure system security loopholes, but they should be given the chance to benefit from someone else's experiences.

22.11 CERT—Computer Emergency Response Team

The Computer Emergency Response Team, or CERT, is an organization of computer security experts chartered by DARPA in response to the Internet worm incident of 1988. They are set up to assist anyone who suspects a computer security breach or break-in attempt, as well as to answer general security questions. There is no charge for using CERT; it's provided more or less as a public service. You can contact CERT at:

Computer Emergency Response Team (CERT)
Software Engineering Institute
Carnegie Mellon University
Pittsburgh, PA 15213-3890
Internet: cert@cert.org
Telephone: (412) 268-7090   24-hour hotline
Fax: (412) 268-6989

CERT issues advisories from time to time as security holes in various commercial software packages come to light. These advisories are sent out to news groups and also to people on CERT's mailing list. CERT also maintains a repository of computer-security documentation, which you can access by doing anonymous FTP to cert.org. When you get onto the system, cd to the pub directory and 'get' the file called cert.faq. It contains a list of Frequently-Asked Questions about CERT (along with the answers) and is a good introduction to the organization.

23
The UNIX System Kernel

The UNIX system kernel is the master organizer of UNIX. The kernel schedules processes, allocates memory and disk storage, supervises the transmission of data between the main storage and the peripheral devices, and honors the processes' requests for service. This chapter looks under the hood to partially answer the question, "How does the UNIX system really work?"

Much of the information in this chapter has direct practical applications for UNIX system managers, programmers, and users. For example, understanding a little about virtual memory can help you decide whether a workstation version of UNIX or a PC implementation is better for running your solid modeling software. Knowing how file systems are organized can help you install a new release of the UNIX system or repair the file system of a working system.

This chapter is not intended to be a programmer's guide to the kernel. If you're planning to modify your kernel, you need more information than we're presenting in this chapter. Much of this chapter is relevant to any version of the UNIX system, although details usually vary from one implementation to another.

The kernel is the memory resident portion of the UNIX system. Compared to most mainframe operating systems, the UNIX kernel provides a relatively small repertoire of services. However, compared to microcomputer operating systems such as MS-DOS, the UNIX kernel has a large repertoire of services. The kernel never does anything directly for a user; rather the basic kernel services are provided by utility programs, which provide the interface between users and the kernel. This has worked out extremely well, because utility programs are easier to create, maintain, and customize than the kernel itself.

The UNIX Version 7 kernel contained about 10,000 lines of C code and about 1,000 lines of assembly code. The more modern System V kernel is larger but still small compared to many other operating systems. Historically, many UNIX systems were distributed with the source code for both the kernel and the utilities. This policy, coupled with the modest size of the system, allowed programmers to study and tinker with their own system. Today, distribution of full source code is much less common, and it usually costs a lot of money. Plus, the complexity of modern UNIX makes the source much harder to understand and modify, even if you do have it.

23.1   Overview

The traditional UNIX system kernel, which to most longtime UNIX users is probably the Version 7 kernel, addressed three major tasks:

- Process management: starting processes, scheduling processes, swapping processes to disk, allocating resources such as memory, and honoring processes' requests for service.

- Device management: supervising the transmission of data between the main memory and the peripheral devices. The device management part of the kernel typically contains a software module for every hardware device that is attached to a computer. This is the most hardware-dependent part of the UNIX kernel.

- File management: storing files on disks. In the past, each kernel supported a single type of file system, but modern kernels can support multiple file system types.

These three traditional concerns remain central, but dramatic advances in hardware and continuing advances in software have expanded the role of the kernel. Today's kernels usually provide these additional basic services:

- Virtual memory. The kernel pretends that it has more memory than is actually present, using disk storage to fill in for the missing main memory. When references are made to data that's not present in main memory, the kernel automatically brings it in from disk. Virtual memory provides similar advantages to swapping because it allows a computer to run more processes than will fit in memory, but is more fine-grained and more efficient. Virtual memory was first supported by Berkeley UNIX systems but is now supported on most versions of the UNIX system, including System V.4.

- Networking. The kernel implements the hardware and software protocols that are necessary for computer-to-computer high-speed communication. Local area networking was first a standard feature of Berkeley UNIX systems but is now supported on most versions of the UNIX system.

■ Network file systems. The kernel implements the protocols that allow one computer to mount, over the network, the files that are stored on another computer. This technology was first commercialized by Sun Microsystems but is now widely available.

The kernel part of networking has been in place since the mid- to late-eighties and operates well. Now that computers can easily communicate, what's still missing is a comprehensive approach to the broader networking issues. How can security be provided in a networked environment? How can distributed systems be managed? These important topics are not addressed by the kernel so they are not discussed here.

You might be surprised that we haven't mentioned any kernel enhancements to support the increased use of graphics displays on both workstations and PCs. The reason is quite simple: There is little support in the kernel for graphics displays, other than a device driver to access the video display hardware. The X Window System has dramatically revolutionized how UNIX systems are used, but it operates on top of UNIX, requiring no changes to the kernel.

There's a third category of kernel features: experimental. These features are often discussed, and they exist in some versions of the UNIX system, but they aren't universally available:

■ Multiprocessor support. The ability of a UNIX system to take advantage of a computer containing multiple processors. Modern computer hardware has increasing support for multiple processor configurations, and they are expected to become widely used in time.

■ Lightweight process support (also called threads). The ability to have separate processes sharing a single address space. Each lightweight process usually has its own stack. Lightweight processes make it easier to develop software that attends to several chores at once.

These experimental features are found in some versions of the UNIX system, but they will not be discussed here.

Typical applications programs have a beginning, a middle, and an end, somewhat like a good novel. The UNIX system is more like a woven tapestry than a novel. The UNIX system does not have a single plot that runs from beginning to end; instead it has a number of interrelated threads that are woven in response to the needs of the moment. The fact that the kernel is not a simple sequential program makes it inherently more difficult to understand than most programs.

23.2 Processes

A process is a program that is being executed. For a given program, such as vi, there may be any number of active processes running at a particular time. For example, if vi is being executed by a single person, we would say that there is one vi process in the system. If a second vi command is issued, there may be two active vi processes at once. Thus when we speak of a process, we're interested in something active, something that is executing. The term program refers to static characteristics, such as what task it performs, its arguments, and so on. In this book we will confine the term process to entities that are cataloged in the UNIX system kernel's process table. Hence the activity of the UNIX system kernel is generally excluded as a process.

The UNIX system supports two powerful illusions: that the file system has "places" and that processes have "life." The strong visceral connection of directories with "places" makes it easier for people to master the file system. Similarly, the illusion that processes have "life" and can perform useful work makes it easy to think about and control processes. A computer scientist might describe a process as the execution of an abstract data structure. The energy in a computer is in the hardware, but the intelligence is in the programs, so it is reasonable to bestow the life force on the software.

The process is the fundamental unit of organization in the UNIX system. Even though the instructions are executed by the CPU and stored in memory, even though the disks and tapes may be spinning furiously, we talk about what process is executing and we ignore the obvious fact: the computer hardware is actually doing the work.

The UNIX kernel exists to support the needs of processes. From a process's point of view, the kernel's operations are a sort of overhead that must be endured. The view from within the kernel is rather different; processes are just cataloged data structures that are manipulated according to a set of rules. The following description of processes is the view from within; processes are just data, more like an accountant's worksheet than a vital force.

23.2.1 The Process Table and the User Table

The kernel stores vital information for processes in two places: the process table and the user table. There is a single process table for the entire system. It contains one entry for each process. Each entry details the most important information about the state of a process. This information includes the location of the process (memory address or swapped address), its size in memory, its process ID number or PID, and the user ID number of the user running the process. The user table is sometimes called the *per process data segment* because there is one for each process, stored as part of each process's data segment.

Each UNIX system is generated with a certain number of entries in the process table and each process consumes one entry in the table. It is impossible to have more processes than there are entries in the process table. If you try to start a new process when the table is full, the kernel simply refuses, and you will see a message like "system process table full."

The process table is referenced during all of the life stages of processes. Creating a process involves initializing an entry in the process table, initializing a user table, and loading the actual text and data for the process. When a process changes its state (running, waiting, swapped out, swapped in, etc.) or receives a signal, the interaction focuses on the process table. When a process terminates, its entry in the process table is freed so that it can be used by future processes.

The process table must always be in memory so that the kernel can manage the life crises of a process even while the process is inactive. Many of the events in the life of a process occur while the process is inactive. For instance, a process may be sleeping while waiting for I/O. The I/O completion causes the process to be awakened and marked as ready to resume execution. The information necessary to manage the wake-up of a sleeping process is contained in the process table.

The kernel allocates one user table or user structure for each active process (see Figure 23.1a). The user table contains information that must be accessible while the process is executing, but that is not usually needed when the process is inactive. While a process is suspended, its user table ordinarily is not accessed or modified. The user table is part of the process's own data region. When the process is swapped out to disk, the user table is swapped with the rest of the process image.

Most of the user structure contains current information about the process. For example, the user table contains the user and group identification numbers for determining file access privileges, pointers into the system's file table

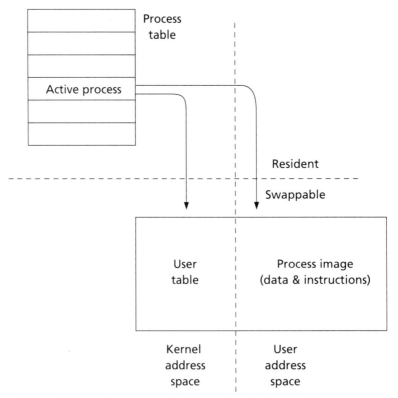

Figure 23.1a ■ Data Structures for Managing Ordinary Processes

(see Section 23.5.3) for all of the process's open files, a pointer to the i-node of the current directory (see Section 23.5.2) in the i-node table, and pointers to the routines that should be executed for each type of signal that the process might receive.

The current information about a process is manipulated very simply. If the process executes the chdir system call, then the value of the pointer to the current directory i-node is changed. If a process elects to ignore a certain signal or elects to install a custom signal handler, then the appropriate entry in the table of signal responses is modified. Most of the manipulations of information in the user table are so simple that you might expect the program to perform the manipulation itself, rather than have them performed by the kernel. In part, these simple manipulations are performed by the kernel for the sake of uniformity; however, the important reason is system integrity. On a computer with memory protection, which today means almost all computers, the user table is inaccessible to a process (except via system calls) even though it is part of the process image.

23.2.2 Sharing Program Text and Software Libraries

Many programs, such as the shell, are often being executed by several users simultaneously. Each process must have its own copy of the variable part of the process image but the fixed part, the program text, can be shared. In order to be shared, a program must be compiled using a special option that arranges the process image so that the variable part and the text part are cleanly separated (see Figure 23.1b). Sharing program text allows the UNIX system to use the main memory of the computer more effectively. In order to keep track of the program text segments, the UNIX system maintains a text table. When a program uses shared text, the process table entry contains a pointer into the text table and the text table actually points to the location of the process text.

An extension to the idea of sharing text is sharing libraries. In a system without shared libraries, all the executing programs contain their own copies of the software found in standard software development libraries. For example, nearly all UNIX programs use a set of subroutines called the Standard I/O library. Without shared libraries, each process will have its own copy in memory of the Standard I/O library. With shared libraries, only one copy needs to be in memory for all of the active processes. Besides using memory more efficiently, shared libraries make it easier to distribute software updates, since updating a single shared library automatically updates all the programs using that library.

23.2.3 System Calls

When a process needs to access a UNIX system service, it makes a system call. For example, if a process needs to know the time, it will execute the time() system call. When a system call occurs, the kernel takes over. It per-

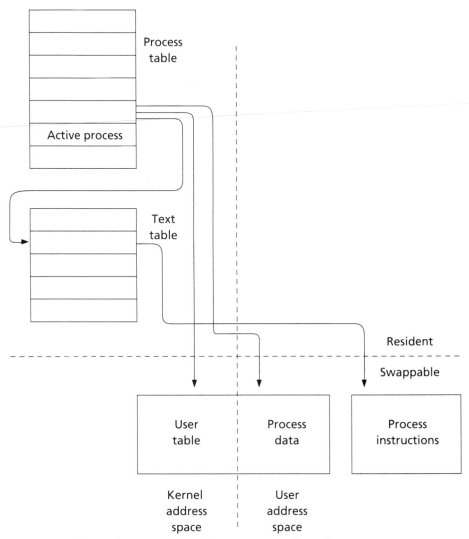

Figure 23.1b ■ Data Structures for Managing Shared Text Processes

forms the requested service, and then it resumes the process that issued the system calls.

Some system calls, like the time() system call, can be accomplished almost instantly. Other system calls, especially those that request input or output operations, can take a relatively long time.

23.2.4 User Mode and Kernel Mode

At any given instant a computer running the UNIX system is either executing a process or the kernel itself is running. We say that the computer is in user mode when it is executing instructions in a user process and it is in kernel mode when it is executing instructions in the kernel. While most modern processors have distinct hardware privileges for kernel mode, the distinction is the source of the instructions, not the privilege level of the hardware.

Several things can prompt a switch from user mode to kernel mode. Perhaps the most important from the point of view of system integrity is the system clock. The system clock periodically interrupts (usually 50 or 60 times per second) whatever is going on. (An interrupt is a hardware signal that can divert the computer to a special software routine.) Each time the system clock interrupt occurs, the kernel switches to a service routine that reevaluates the processes' priorities. Often the reevaluation prompts the kernel to suspend the current process and switch to some other process. The system clock is an important part of the basic time-slicing that enables a computer to attend to many tasks.

System calls are the second reason that the kernel computer switches from user mode to kernel mode. System calls that perform I/O operations often lead to a suspension of the calling process while the data are being transferred. A different user process will be executed in the interim if possible. Thus the natural I/O requirements of programs often drive the time-slicing mechanism.

The service requirements of the I/O peripherals is the third mechanism that causes a switch from user mode to kernel mode. I/O peripherals typically have a response time that is much longer than the normal instruction execution time of a computer. The details vary greatly from one computer architecture to another, but on most UNIX systems an interrupt occurs each time a transfer is complete. (At various times a transfer is either 512 bytes, a single byte, or a variable-length string of bytes.) The transfer completion interrupt usually updates various status elements in certain tables and then possibly initiates another transfer. If a process has been suspended while waiting for an I/O operation, the "I/O done" interrupt will usually mark that process as ready to run but won't directly cause it to resume.

23.2.5   The Fork, Exec, and Wait System Calls

There are two fundamental system calls that shape the UNIX environment. The first, the fork() system call, is used by a process to create a copy of itself. Forking is the traditional mechanism in the UNIX system for increasing the number of processes. After a fork there are two nearly identical processes, the parent and the child (see Figure 23.2a). The major difference between the two subsequent processes is the fact that the two processes have different process ID numbers and different parent process ID numbers. The two processes share open files and each process is able to determine whether it is the parent or the child.

The second major system call for managing processes is exec() (see Figure 23.2b). The exec() system call is used to transform the calling process into a new process. The total number of processes in the system isn't changed, only the character of the calling process changes. After an exec system call, the process ID number is unchanged and open files remain open. The exec sys-

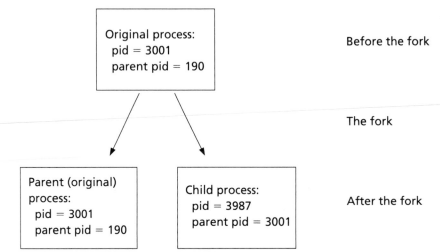

Figure 23.2a ■ The Fork System Call

The fork system call duplicates a process. After the fork, the two processes are nearly identical, and they share open files. The only differences are that the two processes have different PIDs and parent PIDs, and that they receive a different return value from the fork system call.

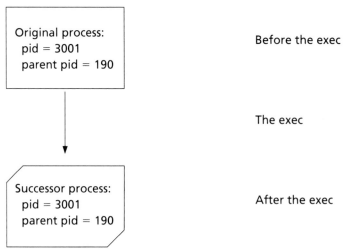

Figure 23.2b ■ The Exec System Call

The exec system call transforms one process into another. Only the process PID and the parent PID stay the same.

tem call is similar to the chaining feature in other operating systems, which allows a process to choose its successor.

A fork followed by an exec is commonly used by a parent process to spawn a child process with a new identity (see Figure 23.2c). For example, the shell forks and then execs each time it runs a program for you. Fork/exec is powerful because it makes it easy for programmers to manage processes, and it is relatively fast and efficient, compared to other operating systems.

The traditional problem with fork/exec is that there is a lot of extra data copying performed during the fork that is immediately discarded when the exec occurs. Modern versions of the UNIX system avoid most of this extra work by implementing copy on write. With copy on write, when something is "copied" it isn't initially moved to the new location, which makes the "copy" extremely efficient. However, if the process attempts to write to the copied data, then the kernel automatically moves the data before the write, honoring its promise to have two copies. In the case of a fork/exec, copy on write greatly increases efficiency because little of the new process created by the fork is modified prior to the exec.

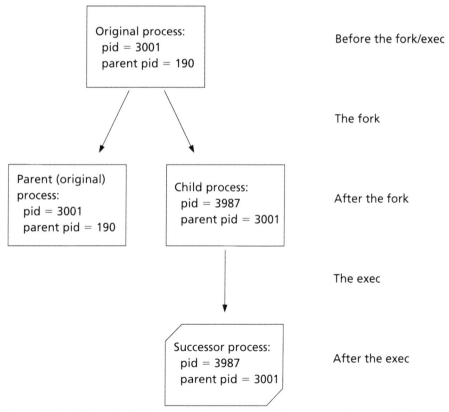

Figure 23.2c ■ A Fork System Call, Followed by an Exec System Call
A fork followed by an exec is used to create a child process with a new identity. It is the standard procedure followed by the shell to execute your commands.

The wait() system call is commonly used in conjunction with fork() and exec(). The wait() system call allows a parent process to wait for the demise of a child process. This is used by the shell when you execute a program in the foreground. First the shell forks, then the shell's child execs the child process, and then the parent shell uses the wait system call to wait for the demise of the child. When the child dies, the parent shell resumes and prompts you to enter another command. The shell runs processes in the background simply by omitting the wait for the demise for the child process.

23.2.6   Handling Signals

From its earliest days, UNIX has contained a simple yet effective signaling system. A signal is a message from one process to another. There are different signal numbers with different meanings that are well defined and uniform. Unlike messages that have content, like the apocryphal message in a bottle, UNIX signals are content-free. The only thing that can be said about a signal is "it has arrived" or "it has not arrived."

There are predefined meanings to most signals. For example, the sighup (hangup) signal is sent to a process if the telephone connection is lost (hangs up). Other examples are sigint, which politely asks a process to terminate; sigquit, which asks a process to terminate and produce a core dump; sigfpe, which informs a process of a floating point error; and sigkill, which forces a process to terminate.

Some signals may be caught or ignored by a process. For example, when you strike the Interrupt key on your keyboard, which is usually <CTRL-C> or <DEL>, the current process receives the sigint signal. By default the process will terminate when sigint arrives, but a process can alternatively arrange to ignore the signal or to activate a special signal handler routine.

Other signals cannot be caught. For example, the sigkill signal is guaranteed to terminate a process that is still able to respond to signals. A process may not receive a signal for some time, or ever, if it is hung up waiting for a kernel service, such as I/O from a disk that has gone off line.

Two kernel data structures, the process table and the user table, are the key to understanding the kernel implementation of signals. The user table contains a list with one entry per signal. If the value in the entry for a particular signal is zero, the default action will occur if the signal arrives. If the entry contains a one, the signal will be ignored. Any other value is presumed to be the address of a signal handler routine. Processes manage their responses to signals using the signal() system call.

When a process sends a signal, by using the poorly named kill() system call, it specifies the process ID number of the target process and the number of the signal. The kernel records the signal in the process table. Other possibly useful information, such as the sending process ID, the time of arrival, the number of times the signal has arrived, and so on, are not recorded.

When the target process gets its next chance to execute, the kernel checks its slot in the process table to see if any new signals have arrived. If there are new arrivals, the kernel decides how to handle them. For some signals, such as sigkill, the action is predetermined. However, for catchable signals the kernel checks the user table to see if the process has arranged to catch or ignore the signal. If a signal handler has been installed by the process, the kernel starts the execution of the process with a call to the signal handler. When the signal handler is done, the process resumes where it was last suspended. Alternatively, the signal handler can call the exit() system call to terminate the program.

The fork system call doesn't alter the list of signal actions in the user table. However, the exec call is forced to deal with the signal dispositions in the user table. When an exec occurs, caught signals are reset to their default state because the new process doesn't contain the same handler as the original process. However, ignored signals remain ignored when an exec occurs. If ignored signals were reset during an exec, programs such as nohup wouldn't be able to leave a signal-ignoring legacy for their offspring.

23.2.7 Scheduling Processes

In a time-sharing computer system, processes compete for execution time slices. Scheduling is the series of actions that decides which of the current user processes will execute next. Obviously scheduling is one of the key elements of a time-sharing system. The fundamental act of time-sharing is suspending a process and then restarting it at some later time. In most time-sharing systems, including the UNIX system, the suspension/resumption of active processes occurs many times each second to create the impression that the computer is performing several tasks simultaneously.

On a traditional single-CPU computer, at most one user process is active at a time. All of the other user processes are suspended. We can divide the set of suspended processes into two groups: those that are ready to run and those that are blocked. Blocked processes are often waiting for the completion of an I/O request, although processes can also wait for their children to die, for a specified time interval, or for a signal from another process. When the event occurs, the blocked process is marked as ready to run, although being ready doesn't mean that a process will immediately start to execute.

The traditional scheduling approach dynamically calculated a priority for each ready-to-run process. In the original scheme, the lowest priority process was selected for execution. The base priority was a characteristic of each process, and then the priority was decreased each time the process was passed over. Because each process's priority decreased over time, each would eventually get its chance.

Processes can influence this system by setting their baseline priority to a positive number so that they will execute less often. This is called "running nice" or "nicing" the process, because it is performed by calling the nice() system call. In addition, processes running with superuser privilege can specify a negative baseline priority, so they are able to execute more often.

The net effect of this procedure is that I/O-intensive processes tend to execute until they have to wait on the result of an I/O operation. Computation-intensive processes tend to fill the gaps while the I/O processes are waiting for their I/O to complete. Ideally the system balances itself to keep the processor busy and give all the processes some execution time.

There are two consequences to this simple system. One is that any process that's ready to run will eventually do so because over time its priority will drop low enough to move to the head of the queue. This means that there's no way to write a program that only soaks up unused time. Similarly, there's no way to specify that a process should always run, if it's ready. This makes it hard to write programs that provide guaranteed response, which means they need to move to the head of the list when they are ready to go.

In System V the original scheduling system has been expanded to accommodate process classes. Most processes are in the time-sharing class, which behaves similarly to the traditional scheduling approach. The second standard scheduling class in System V is the real-time class, which accommodates processes that need guaranteed response times. When a real-time process is ready to run, its priority exceeds that of all the time-sharing processes.

In the UNIX system there is extremely little overhead for a suspended process. This crucial fact has had a profound impact on the nature of the system. The low overhead of suspended processes has enabled many "operating system" functions to be exported from the UNIX system kernel and placed in ordinary programs. Consider the getty program. The getty program prints a login message on a communication line and then waits for a user to start logging in. There is a (usually suspended) getty process for every communication line in a UNIX system that can be used for logging in but is not presently in use. Many systems have 50 to 100 such getty processes. This design wouldn't be possible if suspended processes required significant overhead.

23.2.8   Swapping and Paging

Ideally, all of a system's processes reside in memory, and the role of the scheduler is simply to choose the active process from the group of memory resident processes. Unfortunately, the memory on modern computers, while large, is often not large enough to store all the processes that are active in a UNIX system. The solution is to store some of the suspended processes on disk, a procedure known as *swapping* (Figure 23.3). A process stored on disk must be reloaded into memory before it can resume execution.

Paging, which is available on systems that support virtual memory, is a similar capability (Figure 23.4). Paging requires specialized hardware, and is not available on all versions of the UNIX system. The basic idea of paging is to allow small parts of a process to be temporarily stored on disk. Whenever the process tries to reference a location that isn't resident in memory, the operating system kernel automatically steps in, suspends the process, pages in the missing information, and then restarts the process.

Paging requires hardware support for two reasons. First, it's necessary to generate an interrupt when the process attempts to use nonresident information. The interrupt notifies the kernel that something needs to be paged in. It suspends the process, and starts the I/O operation to retrieve the missing

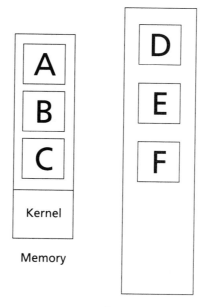

Swap space on disk.

Figure 23.3 ■ Swapping Copies Entire Process Images Out to Disk

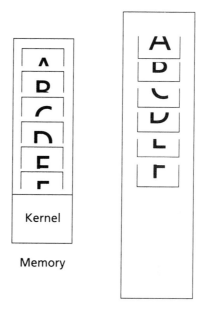

Swap space on disk.

Figure 23.4 ■ Paging Copies Infrequently Used Parts of Processes Out to Disk

information. Second, and usually much harder, it's necessary to restart the instruction that tried to access the nonresident information. Computers that support virtual memory must be designed from the outset to provide instruction restart.

Paging is preferable to swapping for several reasons. One reason is that it is more efficient than swapping. Swapping in a large process is much more work and takes more time than paging in a few blocks of memory. Another advantage is that paging allows one to run processes that are larger than physical memory because the entire process need not be present in memory at once. With swapping, the maximum process size is limited by the size of free memory.

23.2.9   Zombie Processes

A zombie is a process that persists forever because it is waiting for an event that will never happen. The most common reason for a zombie is that a process has tried to exit but it has a living parent that has not issued the wait system call. This problem occurred with some regularity in the past because so much software was home-brewed, but in today's more polished world it's unusual to encounter software that fosters zombie processes.

The other major possibility is that a process is stuck waiting for an I/O that will never happen. This can occur because of a hardware fault or because of a software fault in a device driver. The relatively high reliability of today's hardware and software makes such occurrences unlikely but not impossible.

Zombies are bad because they waste a slot in the process table. A single zombie doesn't matter much, but if they start to accumulate, they will inevitably cause the computer to fail because the process table will become full.

23.3   Networking

Networking allows computers to communicate. It helps people collaborate and has become an integral part of what we expect from a computer. The UNIX system was developed before networking hardware and protocols were commonplace, so networking support is a relatively recent development. But because the UNIX system is supported by many manufacturers, and because it has been enhanced and extended by many groups, UNIX's network support is diverse. Most UNIX vendors support standard protocols, such as the ubiquitous TCP/IP, and standard transports, such as Ethernet. Vendors who have a stake in alternate technologies usually provide additional support. For example, IBM is committed to the Token-Ring transport technology, which it supports in its workstation version of the UNIX system. Similarly, Novell is committed to its own IPX/SPX network protocols, which are supported in its versions of the UNIX system.

Network support means different things to different people. Most PC and Macintosh users mention accessing files and sharing printers when they are asked about networking. However, many UNIX users mention remote login when they are asked about networking. But to a system administrator or to a software developer, networking usually means protocols.

A protocol is a specification that dictates how systems will communicate. At the lowest level, the messages are relatively simple. One field of the message might specify the sender, another the recipient, a third might be a checksum to guard against transmission errors, and the fourth might be the body of the message. But low-level protocols are just a part of what's required. Users want services such as remote booting of diskless workstations, file sharing, file transfer, remote login, convenient electronic mail, printer sharing, and myriad other high-level services.

Integrating networking into the UNIX system required many choices, but two choices were paramount:

■ What protocols should be managed by the kernel, and which should be handled by user-level processes?

■ How should networking be added to the kernel?

The consensus on the first design decision is clear: only the very low-level protocols are handled within the kernel. Wherever possible, the higher-level protocols are managed by daemons, which are processes that run continuously in the background. These daemon processes wait for something to happen, and then provide the response. Thus a part of the description of how the kernel manages networking is very simple: it hands many tasks off to user-level processes for them to manage.

The second design decision has proven to be much thornier. The problem with adding networking to the UNIX kernel is that it doesn't fit the model established by earlier UNIX services. For example, the UNIX system manages files by providing low-level driver to access the disk drive, a set of routines for organizing the storage, and a small number of system calls for accessing files. This simple system works because the idea of a file itself is simple yet powerful; there are only a few basic file operations so it's relatively easy to provide a complete set of services. The problem with networking is that there is so much more complexity, and networking has nothing comparable to the file abstraction to provide a unifying model.

The solution adopted by Berkeley was to relate networking services to an abstraction called a *socket*. A socket is a communication endpoint. Programs that need to communicate open a socket and then specify how they want the socket to operate. For example, a program can ask to use a given protocol to send messages to a remote system, or to be notified whenever a certain type of network event occurs. Sockets are discussed in Section 23.7.1.

A separate solution was subsequently developed at AT&T by Dennis Ritchie, who originally co-invented UNIX with Ken Thompson. The AT&T solution is Streams, which are configurable kernel processing routines. Streams provide a flexible way to add intelligent processing to the kernel. They are used primarily to implement network protocols and to provide a better way to manage serial communications with terminals. Streams are discussed in Section 23.7.2.

The key aspect of stream processing modules is that they can be connected to each other dynamically. Each stream processing module performs a single task and then passes data along to the next module in the chain. User-level programs can dynamically add and subtract stream processing modules, as necessary. Streams are the basis of networking facilities in System V, although sockets are emulated so that socket-based utilities are easily supported.

23.4 Booting

Now that some of the basic ideas of the UNIX system kernel have been introduced, we can turn our attention to what happens when the kernel is first started. Several unique actions must be performed early in the course of execution in order to progress to the steady-state condition. Starting the system, which is often called *booting*, is a two-phase process:

1. In the first stage, which is called *kernel initialization,* the kernel is loaded into memory, I/O hardware and software drivers are initialized, and the system process structure is initialized.

2. In the second stage, which is called *system initialization,* the UNIX system runs initialization scripts that initiate standard system utilities.

The remainder of this section will cover these two phases in greater detail.

The UNIX kernel, like other executable programs, is stored in an ordinary file. Usually this file is named unix and it is stored in the root directory (/), or the /root directory.

On a computer with its own disk drive, the following process is usually followed:

1. Whenever the computer is powered on or rebooted, a short built-in program reads the first block or two of the disk into memory. These blocks contain a loader program, which was placed on the disk when the disk was formatted.

2. Next, the loader is started. The loader searches the root directory for the /unix or /root/unix file, and loads that file into memory.

3. The kernel starts to execute.

Loading the kernel into memory occurs somewhat differently on a diskless workstation:

1. When a diskless workstation is powered on or rebooted, a built-in network communication program takes over.

2. This program performs a basic initialization of the network hardware and then broadcasts a request over the network asking for boot assistance from a file server. The request for help includes an ID number of the workstation so that the servers can tell which workstation is trying to boot.

3. The server that is configured to provide that workstation's root and swap disk regions responds, and then the server downloads the workstation's kernel to the workstation. Usually the download is performed using the trivial file transfer (tftp) protocol.

4. The kernel starts to execute.

Once the kernel is in memory and executing, the initialization process is the same on both diskless and ordinary (with disk) systems. The first thing that the kernel does is initialize the hardware interfaces. The kernel goes through its list of device drivers and calls each driver's initialization routine. As a byproduct, this part of the process determines which peripheral devices are present.

Of particular importance are the memory management hardware and the system clock. In its first few moments of life, the kernel also initializes its data structures, including the block buffers, the character lists, and the i-node buffers. The kernel always stays in memory; it's never swapped out. This explains the need to keep it relatively small.

23.4.1 The First Processes

Following these rather mundane initializations, the kernel begins to initialize the process structure. Its first task is to create the first process, which is often called *process 0*. Processes ordinarily are created via the fork system call, which instructs the system to make a copy of the calling process. Obviously this method is not feasible for creating the first process; so instead, the kernel handcrafts process 0, which is called the *scheduler*, by allocating a per-user data structure and installing pointers to the data structure in the first slot of the process table.

Process 0 is unique for several reasons. First, there is no code segment for process 0: its entire being is a per-user data structure. All other processes contain code that is executed to perform some function; they are images resulting from the compilation and subsequent execution of a program. Second, process 0 is created anomalously and persists for the life of the system. Finally, process 0 is truly a system process; it is active exclusively while the processor is in kernel mode.

After process 0 is created and initialized, the system creates process 1 by making a copy of process 0. The copy of process 0 is made by following essentially the same procedure that is followed when a user program executes the fork system call. Although process 1 is handcrafted, now the handcrafting is beginning to resemble the ordinary process creation scheme.

Initially process 1 is an exact copy of process 0; it has no code region. The first event that occurs after process 1 is created is that it is expanded in size. The size of process 1 is increased by executing the same code that would be executed if the process had issued the break (increase memory allocation) system call. Once again process 1 is acted on anomalously but in imitation of the procedure that is followed by an ordinary program executing a system call.

The third event in the creation of a viable process 1 is the copying of a very simple program into its newly created code region. The program that is copied into process 1's code region essentially contains the machine instructions to perform the exec system call to execute a program called /etc/init.

Process 0 is a per-user data structure that is used by the kernel during the scheduling and process management operations. Process 1 is a viable program image that might have resulted from the compilation of a program, although it actually was hand-installed by the kernel.

On traditional UNIX systems, creation of processes 0 and 1 is the full story of process initialization because after that, all processes are created normally. But on most modern UNIX systems, a few additional processes are created by the kernel, as a way of regularizing its own internal actions.

At this point the initialization of the kernel is complete. However, the initialization of the system is just beginning and we will conclude this section with a brief description of the first few events in the life of the system. The scheduler is responsible for deciding what processes to run and which processes to swap in or swap out. This first time that the scheduler is called, the decision-making is very easy: there are no processes to swap, and there is only one process that is anxious to run, process 1. Executing process 1 immediately leads to the exec system call which replaces the original code in process 1 with the code contained in the file /etc/init. Now that process 1 has attained its final form, we can call it by its usual name: the init process.

23.4.2   The Init Process

The *init process* isn't a part of the UNIX kernel, but it's a key part of how UNIX operates because it is responsible for setting up the process structure of the UNIX system. In traditional UNIX systems, init created two distinct process structures, the single-user mode and multiuser mode. On System V, init can create more than two distinct process environments. Usually init starts by attaching a shell to the system console and giving this shell superuser privilege. This is commonly called *single-user mode.* In single-user mode, the console is automatically logged in with root privileges and none of the other communication lines will accept logins. Single-user mode often is used to check and repair file systems and to perform basic system testing functions and other activities that require exclusive use of the computer.

At the conclusion of single-user mode, the init process sets up the multiuser process structure. Init does this by creating a getty process for every active communication line, and on a machine with a graphic display, init usually creates an X Windows display management process to manage the display. Init also creates a shell process to execute the start-up command file. Traditionally the system's start-up commands were placed in the file /etc/rc, but on most modern systems there are multiple rc scripts. These rc scripts (rc stands for run commands) usually contain commands to mount file systems, start daemons, remove outdated temporary files, and start accounting programs.

Init continues to have an important role throughout the life of the system. Many of the programs that init starts during system initialization run once and are through. For example, the shell that processes the rc scripts runs once and is done. But other processes operate cyclically. For example, a program called getty is used to initiate the login process on serial lines. Getty execs login to validate passwords, and login execs a shell if the login is successful (see Figure 23.5). When the user logs off, the shell terminates, which wakes up init. Then init completes the cycle by starting another getty on that communication line.

23.5   The File System

A file system is a region of a disk in which a certain set of rules specify how information is stored. At the lowest level, disks are divided into blocks, which usually store 512 eight-bit bytes. The file system is a scheme or a plan which specifies how the blocks are used.

The most basic function of any file system is to organize the storage on disks and tapes into named units that we call files. In many systems there are several types of files with distinct access methods for each type. In the UNIX system, all ordinary files are a simple sequence of bytes. Sometimes files are referred to as text files or binary files but the distinction is the content of the file (text files contain ASCII values only), not the structure of the file or the access method.

Every UNIX disk-based file system (see Figure 23.6) contains four major parts:

1. The boot block. The boot block, which may actually be several blocks, is the first block (or blocks) on the disk. The boot block contains a short loader program on file systems that may be used for booting; it is blank on other file systems.

2. The superblock. The superblock contains key information about a file system, including the list of free blocks. On early file systems, the superblock was the second block on the file system, but on modern file systems, copies of the superblock are often stored in many places in the file system for redundancy.

3. The i-node table. I-nodes store information about files, such as the file's size, its location on the disk, its creation date, and so on. There is one i-node for each file on the disk, and i-node numbers are (only) unique within a file system.

4. The file storage. After space is set aside for the boot block, superblock, and i-node table, all the remaining blocks on the file system are used for file storage.

Most large disks are partitioned into several chunks, and individual chunks, which are usually called *partitions* or *slices,* may contain a file sys-

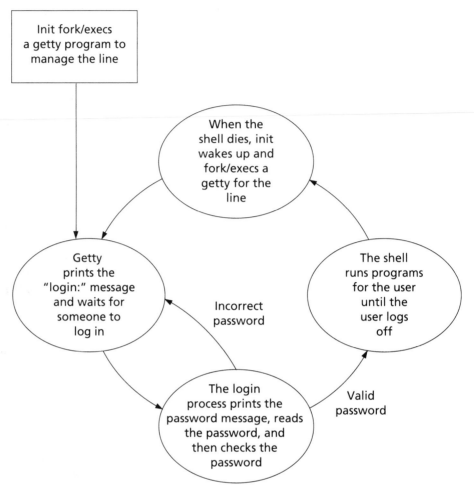

Figure 23.5 ■ The Cycle of Events on Communication Lines

Communication lines used for login operate cyclically, under init's supervision. The cycle is started by init, which fork/execs a getty process for each communication line. Getty then waits patiently for someone to log in on a particular communication line. When someone does start to log in, the getty program performs a few basic adjustments to the communication protocol, such as setting the communication speed, and then it execs the login program to check the password. If the password is entered correctly, the login program execs a login shell program to accept commands from the user. A login shell is a shell whose parent is process 1, init. When a login shell program exits, the init program (its parent), awakens and fork/execs a new getty program to monitor the line and wait for the next login.

tem (see Figure 23.7). Partitions that contain UNIX file systems can be mounted, which means they can be attached to an already-mounted part of the file system, making their files part of the already-available collection of files. The root file system needn't be mounted; it's made accessible during system boot-up.

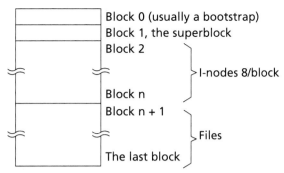

Figure 23.6 ■ File Systems Traditionally Used This Simple Layout

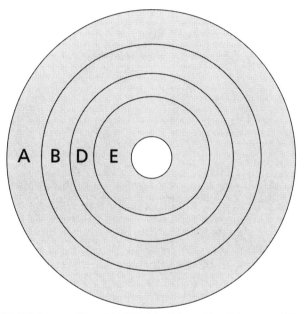

Figure 23.7 ■ Disks are Usually Divided into Partitions or Slices

Partition A (or zero) often contains the root file system, and partition B (or one) is often the swap partition. Partition C (or three), which is not shown, often encompasses the whole disk.

Disks may contain partitions that don't contain UNIX file systems. For example, it is common to use the second partition on a disk for swap space. Some applications have unique storage requirements, which leads them to implement their own filing systems. For example, some data base and transaction processing programs prefer to implement their own file storage systems to gain performance.

In the past, versions of the UNIX system supported a single type of file system. Today, however, most versions of UNIX support several file system types, often including:

- UFS, the standard UNIX file system

- NFS, Sun's network file system

- RFS, AT&T's network file system

- AFS, project Andrew's file system

- HSFS, the High-Sierra file system which is used on CD-ROM drives

Multiple file system support lets system administrators choose a file system that best meets their needs, it lets UNIX users easily work with file systems from "foreign" operating systems, such as OS/2, it provides compatibility with past file systems, and it lets people access file systems via a network.

23.5.1   Directories

The UNIX system uses directories to implement a hierarchical file system. A directory is a file that contains a list of files. The files in a directory may be ordinary files, any of the special file types (see Section 23.6.1), or a directory file. Inclusion of directories within directories is what makes the system hierarchical; the structure resembles a tree. Directories are places; they are the metaphor that makes it easy to organize your files.

For each file, the system must keep track of where it is stored on the disk, when it was last modified, its size, and so on. Somewhat surprisingly, this information isn't stored in directories. Instead, directories only contain two pieces of information for each file: its name and the number of its i-node. I-nodes, the master ledger of the file system, are discussed in the next section.

The first two entries in every directory are for . and .. . The . entry lists the i-node number of the directory itself and the .. entry lists the i-node number of the parent directory. (This rule is slightly modified for the root directory of a file system, in which both . and .. reference the root directory because the root directory has no parent.) These two canonical entries are automatically placed in a directory when the directory is created by the system and they cannot be removed by a user. A directory is considered empty when it contains only the . and the .. entries.

A path through the file system as viewed from the UNIX system kernel is actually a ricochet between directories and i-nodes. Consider the path ../a/b. The path leads from the current directory, to the parent of the current directory, to the parent's subdirectory a, and finally to the file named b in the directory a. In order to follow this path, the UNIX kernel follows the following steps:

1.   It fetches the i-node for the current directory. (The i-node pointer for the current directory is in the user structure.)

2.   It uses the information in the i-node for the current directory to fetch and search the current directory for the name .. and retrieve its i-node number.

3. It fetches the i-node for .. .

4. It uses the information in the .. i-node to fetch the parent directory, search for the file a, and retrieve its i-node number.

5. It fetches the i-node for a.

6. It uses the information in the a i-node to fetch and search the a directory for the file named b and retrieve its i-node number.

7. It fetches the i-node for b.

8. It uses the information in the b i-node to access the file b.

This is a lot of work just to fetch a file (see Figure 23.8.), but following pathnames is a relatively rare event; accessing the files that have already been located is much more common.

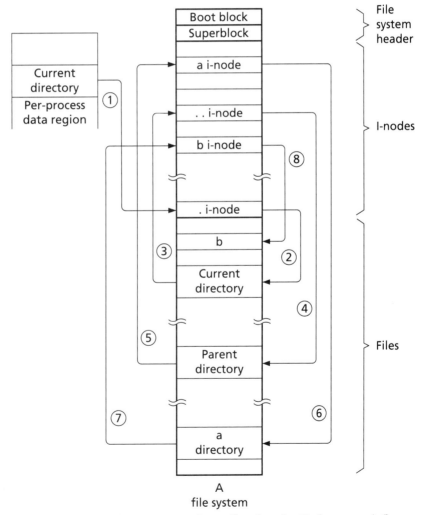

Figure 23.8 ■ Kernel Operations for Following the Pathname ../a/b

23.5.2   I-nodes

I-nodes store the important information about files. Unlike directories, i-nodes are hidden from users but they are a central part of how the UNIX system manages files. I-nodes are the center of the action in the UNIX file system. There is one i-node for each file.

Each i-node stores the following information about a file:

■   The type of the file. On System V there are the following types of files: ordinary files, directory files, block special device files, character special device files, fifo files, and symbolic link files.

■   The length, in bytes.

■   The list of blocks used by the file.

■   The access modes of a file (read, write, and execute for owner, group, and other).

■   The relevant dates (creation time, modification time, access time).

■   The owner and group affiliation.

Notice that the i-node does not contain the name of a file; the name is stored in the file's directory, along with the file's i-node number. Most UNIX users are well insulated from i-nodes, at least until the i-node structures become inconsistent and need repair.

The location information stored in an i-node is used to locate the blocks that contain the file's data (see Figure 23.9). The i-node itself contains a list of the first few, often ten or 12, blocks of the file. (A block is typically 512 bytes.) This is fine for short files, but for longer files a more capacious scheme is required. So for larger files, the i-node contains the disk address of a block-full of block numbers. Such a block is called an *indirect block* because it is used indirectly by the kernel to access the blocks in the file.

Having an indirect block increases the length of the block list from about ten (stored in the i-node) to about 140 (ten or so in the i-node and 128 in the indirect block). This is nice as far as it goes, but it doesn't go nearly far enough, because a 140-block file would only be about 70,000 bytes long.

To increase capacity further, the i-node contains the address of both a double indirect block and a triple indirect block. The *double indirect block* is a block that contains addresses of indirect blocks, and the *triple indirect block* contains addresses of double indirect blocks. Using these techniques, the UNIX system can handle files of about 2 gigabytes in size. The 2-gigabyte limit comes more from the size of 32-bit integers than from limitations in the i-node's addressing scheme.

Fetching information from very large files is harder than fetching information from small files because the indirect blocks need to be fetched in order to determine the addresses of the actual blocks in the file. This overhead is a small price to pay for the ability to accommodate very large files. For example, to entirely read a 10,000-block file (about 5 megabytes), the

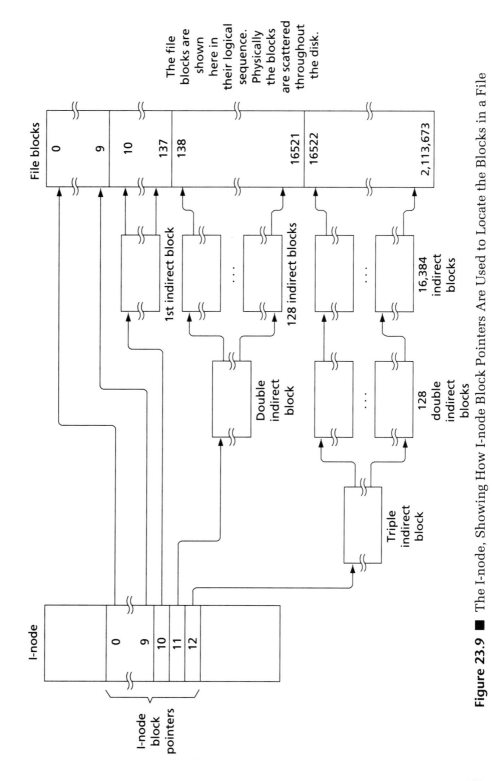

Figure 23.9 ■ The I-node, Showing How I-node Block Pointers Are Used to Locate the Blocks in a File

system has to fetch the 10,000 blocks in the file, one double indirect block, and 79 indirect blocks.

23.5.3 The File Table

There is one remaining table that the kernel keeps in memory for accessing files, the file table. Each entry in the file table contains a pointer to a particular entry in the i-node table, plus it contains the read/write pointer for the file. The per-user data area for each process contains a pointer into the file table for each open file, the file table points at the i-node table, and the i-node table actually points at the file (see Figure 23.10).

This seems somewhat complicated; you might think that the per-process data area would contain pointers directly into the i-node table. Storing the read/write pointer for the file is the real reason for the file table. When a process forks, the two subsequent processes share a single pointer to the current read/write position within each of the original process's open files. The pointer to the read/write position is stored in the file table.

This feature often is used in the shell. Whenever the shell runs a program, it fork/execs the new process, and then waits for the termination of the new process. Meanwhile, the new process reads from its standard input and writes to its standard output. The fact that the shell and the child process share the pointers to the read/write position causes the shell's subsequent I/O operations to be positioned correctly, just past where the child process last performed I/O.

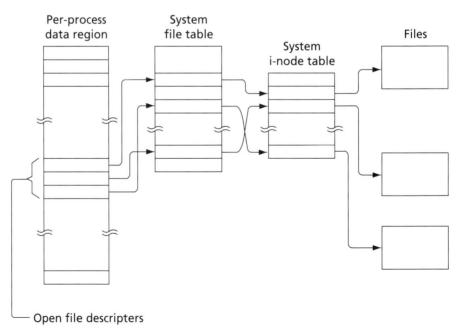

Figure 23.10 ■ The Kernel Data Structure for Accessing Files

23.5.4 Pipes

A pipe is an I/O connection between two related processes. At the user level, a pipe is established when a process performs the following sequence of events:

1. The process executes the pipe system call, which returns two file descriptors: one for reading and one for writing.

2. The process forks (often followed immediately by an exec in the child, the parent, or both). At this point there are two processes sharing the pipe connections set up by the original pipe call.

3. Each of the two resultant processes closes one of the pipe file descriptors. If the pipe is to be from process A to process B, then A must close the read descriptor and process B must close the write descriptor.

Notice that a pipe connection relies on the fact that open files remain open across forks and execs. Notice also that the use of a fork to create the two processes involved in a pipe forces pipes to work only between closely related processes, usually between parent and child although more distant relationships are possible. To remedy this shortcoming, System V has fifo files, which are locations in the file system that allow unrelated processes to have a pipe connection.

In the kernel, pipes have been implemented in several different ways. Traditionally the pipe system call was implemented by allocating an in-core i-node. Then special code in the kernel regulated the flow of data through the pipe, using the in-core i-node and block buffers. In Berkeley UNIX, pipes were implemented using sockets, and in some versions of System V, pipes are implemented using streams.

23.5.5 Network File Systems

Once basic networking was installed in the kernel, the next logical step was to build advanced facilities on top of the low-level networking facilities. The first and perhaps the most important networking extension was the network file system.

A network file system is a means of mounting machine B's files on machine A. This makes B's files look the same, to a user or a program running on A, as files that are stored on A's local disks. It also makes it possible to have diskless computers, which use the network for all file access.

The first commercially successful network file system is Sun Microsystem's Network File System, which is commonly called NFS. Today NFS is supported on most versions of the UNIX system, including System V, and it is also supported by PCs and a few other non-UNIX operating systems.

NFS consists of three parts:

1. The NFS protocol. The protocol was first developed on TCP/IP networks, but other underlying network protocols can be supported. The NFS pro-

tocol uses Sun's Remote Procedure Call (RPC) facility, which allows a program on one machine to execute a subroutine on another machine.

2. The client side. The client implementation of NFS enables a machine to redirect file operations onto the network and to a remote host machine.

3. The server side. The server NFS implementation enables a machine to make its file resources available over the network.

The client and server parts of NFS required some changes to the UNIX kernel. The major change was to divide the file access code into two layers, a virtual layer and a low-level layer. The virtual layer addresses common aspects of any supported file system, and the low-level layer implements a specific file system, which in Sun systems is usually either the native file system or NFS. This dual layer approach is now the standard way to implement UNIX file systems because it allows for multiple types of file systems.

The NFS protocol is a stateless protocol, which means the file server doesn't keep track of what it has been doing on behalf of its clients. It doesn't remember what files are open, or what blocks have been read from those files. This seemingly curious design puts all the recordkeeping burden onto the client systems. Because the servers are stateless, they can crash and then reboot, without causing crashes on the client systems. Surely a server crash will cause a delay from the client's point of view, but often a delay is much less disruptive than a crash, which is what usually happens to a client when there's a crash of a server that maintains state information.

23.6 Device Drivers

A peripheral is something that is attached to a computer, usually for performing input or output (or both). Disks, tapes, communication lines, graphical display adapters, mouse interfaces, and printer interfaces are typical peripherals.

The UNIX system includes two strategies for managing I/O peripherals:

1. The block I/O system. The block model usually is used for devices that can be addressed as a sequence of blocks of 512 bytes. Usually the block model is applied to disks and tapes.

2. The character I/O system. The character model is usually used for devices that transfer a stream of characters, such as a terminal. Most block devices also have a character interface, which is used for special functions.

The block model is used for disks and tapes, which usually allocate space and transfer data in chunks, usually chunks of 512 bytes. The block I/O system uses a pool of in-core block buffers to store data that has been recently read or that is about to be written. Whenever a program requests data from a file, the kernel searches the pool of block buffers to see if the data is already in memory. If the requested block is not in memory, the kernel will free one of the block buffers and transfer the requested block between the block buffer and the I/O device. Frequently used blocks tend to stay in memory, thereby reducing I/O traffic. A second benefit of using a buffer pool is that it allows the kernel to perform I/O operations in an optimal order, based on the physical characteristics of the disk drive. For example, a block scheduled to be written to the disk may have its write delayed until there happens to be a read operation of a nearby block, to minimize the travel of the relatively slow-moving read/write head.

The character model is used for I/O to devices that don't fit the block model. Usually, the character model is used for communication lines, printers, and so on. Most devices that have a block structured interface also have a character interface, so the device can be read or written without using the kernel's block buffering facilities. Accesses to character devices which transfer a character at a time, such as a terminal, usually are buffered by the kernel in character lists (*clists,* pronounced "see-lists"; see Section 23.6.3) while accesses to character devices which transfer chunks (usually blocks) of data are usually not buffered at all by the kernel.

There are two major difficulties in developing the I/O portion of an operating system. The first difficulty is the fact that each peripheral requires slightly different management techniques. All of these different techniques need to be programmed into the operating system. The second problem is the fact that the peripherals of many computers are constantly being rearranged. The operating system's behavior needs to be modified each time a peripheral device is added or deleted. These two problems are solved in the UNIX system by using individual software modules to control each different type of peripheral and using a set of tables to logically connect the kernel to different device drivers.

A device driver is a set of subroutines that works within the operating system to supervise the transmission of data between the computer and a particular type of peripheral device. Each version of the UNIX system is distributed with the drivers for all of the common peripherals on that particular machine. Drivers for more unusual peripherals are usually available from the device manufacturer or from the UNIX system community.

Getting the correct drivers incorporated into the operating system is the major operation during a system configuration (see Section 20.2). Operating systems utilize many different approaches to the problem of reconfiguration. The traditional method for reconfiguration is to modify several text files that specify the system's configuration, and then recompile. However, some versions of the UNIX system use a menu-based program that lets you specify a configuration interactively, and some have dynamically loadable device drivers that add additional flexibility to the system.

23.6.1 Special Device Files and the Cdevsw and Bdevsw Tables

Inside the kernel, the connection between I/O devices and specific device drivers is made by a pair of data structures called bdevsw and cdevsw. Bdevsw is a table that lists the device driver entry points for block devices, and cdevsw lists entry points for character devices. A program can access an I/O device by opening a special device file. A special device file doesn't store data, rather it acts as a passageway to a specific I/O peripheral. I/O operations performed on a special device file actually access the associated I/O peripheral.

But which device is associated with each special device file? The answer is given by the type of the special device file, which is either character special or block special, and by the special device file's major device number, which selects a driver from either the bdevsw table or the cdevsw table. For example, suppose that the serial port driver is entry number one in the cdevsw table. Then a character special device file whose major device file is one can be used to access the serial port driver (see Figure 23.11).

But most machines don't have just one serial port, they have several. How does a special device file indicate which serial port? The answer is the minor device number. The minor device number is passed to the driver when a special device file is opened. It is interpreted by the driver however the driver wishes, but it usually conveys the meaning "which one." For example, if a machine has eight serial ports, then they will likely be accessed using minor device numbers 0 through 7.

For some devices, individual bits of the minor device number are assigned meanings. For example, on a PC running the UNIX system, the minor device numbers for the floppy diskette often reserve one bit to specify which of the two floppies, and use additional bits to specify what density, and how many tracks, and so on.

Special device files are usually stored in the /dev directory, or sometimes in subdirectories of /dev (see Section 20.11). They can be created using the mknod program, but you rarely need to create them manually because they are usually created during system generation.

You can display the major and minor device numbers for special files using the ls program. Because special files don't have a "size," the size field of the ls long format listing instead contains the major and minor device numbers:

```
$ ls -l /dev/tty0[0123]
crw--w--w-  1 root    root    3,    0 Feb 13 14:21 /dev/tty00
crw--w--w-  1 root    root    3,    1 Feb 13 14:21 /dev/tty01
crw-rw-rw-  1 root    root    3,    2 Feb  5 11:38 /dev/tty02
crw--w--w-  1 root    root    3,    3 Feb 14 11:44 /dev/tty03
$
```

When you use the mknod command to create a special file, you may need to examine the conf.c file, found in the directory that contains kernel configuration files, to determine the major device number for the device. The four ttys shown in the preceding list have major device number 3, and minor device numbers 0 through 3.

Each entry in the cdevsw table defines the addresses of the driver routines for opening, closing, reading, writing, and controlling the transmission mode for a particular device. The open and close routines perform any spe-

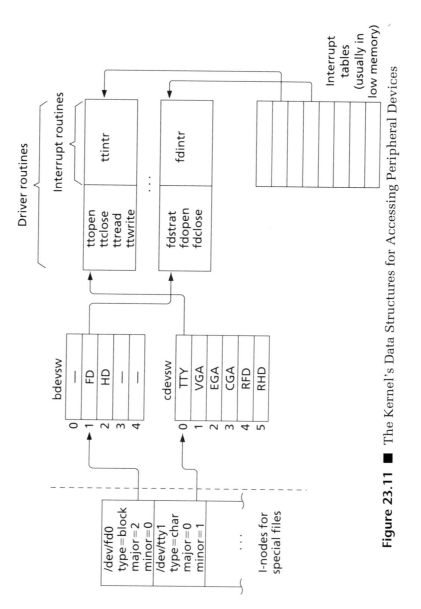

Figure 23.11 ■ The Kernel's Data Structures for Accessing Peripheral Devices

499

cial processing that is required before and after data transfers. For example, the open on a telephone communication line might wait for the line to ring and then answer before completing; the close routine on the same line would probably hang up the line. The read and write routines are called from within the kernel to transfer data to and from the device. The read and write routines usually are used in conjunction with interrupt service routines which actually supervise the data transmission. The transmission mode routine is used on communication line devices to adapt the channel to a particular terminal or line protocol. The transmission mode routine is only used for character devices which are sending characters to computer terminals.

Each entry in the bdevsw table contains the address of open and close routines, the address of a strategy routine, and the address of a device table. The open and close routines perform any processing that is necessary when the device is first opened and they are often unused for block devices. The strategy routine is called to perform block reads and writes. The reason that a single routine is called is that the overall access time often can be optimized by rearranging the order in which blocks are fetched.

23.6.2   Interrupts

Many of the peripheral devices that are attached to UNIX systems use interrupt techniques for transferring data. A hardware interrupt is an electrical signal that is generated by an I/O peripheral when it needs attention. The hardware interrupt causes the processor to stop whatever it is doing and go to an interrupt service routine. The interrupt service routine usually tends to the immediate needs of the peripheral device and then returns control to the interrupted program. Character-oriented devices often interrupt once per character, or occasionally once per line or once per block of data; block-oriented devices usually interrupt once per block of data.

An interrupt handler is the part of a device driver that actually supervises the transmission of data to and from interrupt-driven peripherals. These routines are activated when the I/O interface hardware generates an interrupt. In many computer systems, such as the IBM PC, the addresses of the interrupt service programs must be stored in low memory at specified locations. The address locations are determined by options that are enabled on the interface circuit card.

23.6.3   Traditional Character Handling

Character I/O is deceptive. The overall mandate is clear; transfer character data between processes and terminals with maximum efficiency. However, there are a raft of details which follow immediately. Certain input characters, such as the ubiquitous erase, kill, and interrupt characters, are special. They cause things to happen other than simple data transfer from keyboard to process. Another difficulty is device management. Each I/O device has its own control sequence and timing requirements. Yet another difficulty is the large number of modes that are available. Just examine your stty manual page to see how many different character I/O states are available.

In the broadest sense, the UNIX kernel divides the problem into two parts: generic management of character I/O data, and specific management of I/O devices. Generic character I/O management is performed by the tty driver. It handles erase/kill processing, most tty modes, and so on. Character I/O device drivers, which are accessed via the cdevsw table, handle the hardware-dependent aspects of character transmission. They catch the hardware interrupts, manage the device-dependent details, and so on. There is one character I/O device driver for each type of communications hardware.

Character I/O drivers for terminals are written to automatically call the generic tty handler as necessary. For example, when a device's open routine is called, it performs any necessary hardware management functions and then calls the generic open routine in the tty handler. The generic tty open routine performs some routine initialization plus one key initialization for init's offspring; it records the tty device in the user table and starts a new process group (see Section 23.6.4).

The major data element for managing a communications line is the tty structure. There is one tty structure for every communication line. It contains the key information about the state of the line, such as whether echoing is enabled, whether the line is in raw mode, the assignments for the special characters, and so on. It also contains pointers to three clists: the raw queue, the canonical queue, and the output queue. A clist is a buffering mechanism for character data. Each clist contains a small buffer plus forward and backward pointers to other buffers in the chain. Although the capacity of each clist is just a few dozen characters, a linked list of clists can store a considerable quantity of data.

The raw clist contains information that is received from the communication line. Each time a character is received, the device driver performs standard error checking, and so on, and then calls the tty handler's input routine to deposit the character into the raw clist. The tty handler then performs all of the input processing and eventually deposits the character into the raw clist. In line-oriented operation, when the tty handler is passed a line termination character, it copies the raw clist to the canonical clist and makes it available for reading by the user process. In raw (or Berkeley's cbreak) mode, each character is made available immediately to the user process.

The output queue collects characters from process's write requests, and it also receives "echo" characters from the character input routines. Characters are processed as they are placed into the output queue. The processing often includes mapping of tabs to spaces, mapping lowercase to uppercase, and adding delays to accommodate hardware limitations.

The various operational modes of the tty character-handling system are controlled using the ioctl (sometimes spelled out, sometimes pronounced i-o-cuttle) system call. (In older systems, the ioctl functions were handled using stty and gtty, but today both System V and Berkeley use ioctl.) When a device driver gets an ioctl request, it first calls the tty handler's ioctl routine. The tty handler gets first chance to handle the request. If the request is not in the tty handler's domain, then the device driver tries to handle the request. Only if both fail is an error returned to the calling process.

There's a long-standing pseudo device called /dev/tty. This special device file doesn't correspond to any specific I/O peripheral but rather is a generic way to access the controlling terminal. A process that wants to read or write the controlling terminal, regardless of I/O redirection that has been supplied by the shell, can always do so by opening the /dev/tty special file. The device driver associated with the /dev/tty special file knows how to use the tty device information in the user table to call the appropriate routine in the actual device driver.

23.6.4   Process Groups

The character-handling system is directly involved in UNIX's process group mechanism. A process group is a set of processes that all receive certain signals, such as hang-up signals. As previously mentioned, when an offspring of init opens a tty device driver, the generic tty handler creates a new process group. The new process group ID is set to the PID number of the process. All offspring of this process, which is usually getty, will inherit that group affiliation. You can send a signal to all of the processes in your process group using the special PID number zero instead of an actual PID number.

It is possible for a process to resign from its current process group and instead create and enroll in a new process group. This is often done by background daemons, so that they don't get signals that are sent to their parent processes.

23.7   Communication Extensions

In the original UNIX system, communication meant sending characters to a serial port. And even in that simpler world, a significant fraction of the code in the kernel addressed this need. Over time, the definition of communication has broadened significantly. Modern UNIX systems support a host of communication protocols that didn't exist when the kernel was first designed.

Two separate strategies were developed to meet this need. One solution was sockets, which were developed at Berkeley to implement networking. The second solution was streams, developed by Dennis Ritchie at AT&T.

23.7.1   Sockets

Sockets are a general-purpose communication facility that is present in Berkeley UNIX, and in versions of UNIX derived from Berkeley UNIX, such as Sun UNIX. A socket is a communication endpoint. When a socket is opened, the process specifies a particular communication domain. The two original communication domains are the UNIX domain, for sockets used as interprocess communication endpoints on a single machine, and the Internet domain, for sockets used to communicate with processes on remote machines.

A socket is opened and initialized by a sequence of system calls. Each system call further specifies exactly how the socket is going to be used. Once a socket has been created and initialized, data can be sent to/from the socket using the standard read and write system calls, although the more flexible socket I/O system calls sendto and recvfrom are also available.

The Berkeley kernel contains a socket data structure for each active socket. It details the state of the socket, contains pointers to data storage, and pointers to processing routines. Essentially, the socket data structure is the kernel's way of keeping track of where the data is going and how it is going to get there. This additional layer isolates a user process from the data source/destination, thereby allowing much greater flexibility in routing data. Remember that in the traditional kernel a process's I/O connections are rigidly tied to buffers, which are in turn rigidly committed to specific I/O devices (or to other processes in the case of pipes).

23.7.2 Streams

Streams are modular, full-duplex character processing elements. They were designed by Dennis Ritchie, one of the two original UNIX architects, to replace the traditional character-handling system in the kernel. Ritchie first described streams in "A Stream Input-Output System" in the October 1984 issue of *AT&T Bell Laboratories Technical Journal.* They are also described in a booklet from AT&T titled *UNIX System V Streams Primer,* and in AT&T's *UNIX System V Streams Programmer's Guide.* Streams are available starting in System V.3.

There were several problems with UNIX's traditional character-handling system that Ritchie sought to eliminate with streams. The most important improvement is modularity. The traditional character-handling system is complicated and interconnected, but streams achieve the same facilities within a simpler and more modular framework. The second improvement is efficiency; characters are traditionally passed from one kernel routine to another individually, while in streams entire blocks of characters are passed.

A streams processing module is a kernel routine that performs some processing on a stream. Typical streams processing modules perform chores such as the traditional tty character management (character echo, erase, and so on), networking protocols, and so on.

Streams processing modules are bidirectional. Each can handle data traveling in two directions. Data traveling from the user process to the hardware device (or to the pseudo device) are said to be flowing downstream; data traveling the other way are said to be flowing upstream.

A user process can reconfigure the modules that process data flowing between it and a device (or pseudo device). The standard ioctl mechanism is used to request specific streams modules. For example, while a networking protocol is being developed, it can reside in a user process, and a minimal streams module can connect the process to the hardware device driver. When the protocol is working, it can be transported to a streams module, thereby allowing a user process to access the protocol service simply by asking the kernel to insert the protocol module in the process-to-device data path.

Streams processing modules have a standard interface to other kernel routines. Thus a network protocol module can work with any appropriate hardware drivers. If you are familiar with the ISO seven-layer protocol model, you may have noticed that streams make it easy to write kernel software that corresponds to the standard layers.

APPENDIX I
Vi Visual Command Reference

The ex/vi family of text editors has two major user interfaces: ex, which is a line-oriented interface, and vi, which is a full-screen interface. This appendix primarily discusses the visual, full-screen aspects of the editor; the line-editing ex aspect of the editor is discussed in Appendix III. Appendix II has a list of the options that can be set to alter vi's behavior.

Command-line Options

-t *tag*   The editor commences at the tagged location in the appropriate file. This option usually replaces a command-line file name. Tag must be a tag name that is found in a tags file. The default tags files are the files named tags in the current directory and the file /usr/lib/tags. Alternate tags files can be specified in the .exrc editor start-up script. (The .exrc file is discussed in the "Environment Variables" section of this appendix.)

-r *file*   When vi is terminated by a hang-up or a system crash, it saves the current edit buffer, and then sends you mail that says that an edit buffer has been saved. The -r option tells vi to recover that file from the recovery area. Usually you must specify the full pathname to recover the file.

-L   List the files that have been saved in the recovery area. (On some versions of vi, this function is activated by using the -r option without mentioning a file name.)

-x	Vi will prompt for a key, which will then be used to de-crypt all files that are read in and encrypt all files that are written out.
-C	Same as -x, except that vi assumes that all text read in has been encrypted.
-R	The input file will be considered read-only. All write com-mands will fail unless you use the w! form of the write command to override the write protection. You can unset the read-only mode by setting the noreadonly option from inside vi. If you invoke the editor using the name view instead of vi, then the read-only option will be set auto-matically.
-c *excmd*	The editing session will commence by executing the given ex editor command. The most common uses of this option are specifying a search target (e.g., -c /Jones to move the cursor to the first occurrence of Jones in the file) or line number (e.g., -c 50 to start the editing session with the cursor on line 50). The editor will be positioned on the last line of the buffer prior to executing the command.
	On older versions of vi, this option was specified +excmd; e.g., the command-line option +/Jones would start the editing session with the cursor on the first line containing the text *Jones*, or +50 would start the session with the cursor on line 50.
-l	Sets the showmatch and lisp options so that it is easier to edit lisp programs.
-w*n*	Sets the window size to *n*. This option overrides the size implied by the $TERM environment variable and is usu-ally used to shrink the size of the window when using a slow communication line, so that less time is spent re-drawing the (smaller) screen.
-s	Sets the noautoprint mode. This makes ex less chatty, which is useful when processing edit scripts. (On older versions of vi, this option was - instead of -s.)

Overview

Vi attempts to portray on the screen of your terminal, or on a window of your workstation, the current appearance of the text file being edited. Changes are shown immediately, as you type and edit the file. This is a big improvement over line editors such as ed and ex, which show on the screen a record of the edits that you've made. But vi is far less supportive than word processors, which usually offer menus and help systems and other aids that make work easier. Vi is extensively used in the UNIX system for programming, for mod-ifying system configuration files, and other chores related to text files.

There are two major vi modes: visual command mode and text entry mode. (There are also several ex specific modes, but they are not discussed here.) During visual command mode, everything that you type is interpreted as a command. Visual commands are not echoed on the screen; just their effect is visible. The second mode is text entry mode, in which everything that you type (with a few exceptions) is added to the text of the file. Entering a Text Entry Command (Section 5 of Table A.1.1) changes from visual command mode to text entry mode; pressing <ESC> terminates text entry mode and resumes visual command mode. You need to remember which mode you are using.

While you are editing a file with vi, you are actually working with a copy of that file, which is stored in the edit buffer. Changes made to the edit buffer don't alter the original file until you issue a write command. You should periodically write out the edit buffer to the disk file so that your work will be safe from computer crashes or your own mistakes. If you make a disastrous alteration to the edit buffer, do not write out the buffer to the original file (although you might want to write it out to another file, just in case). Vi will warn you if you try to exit without saving a modified edit buffer.

Before using vi, you must properly set the environment variable $TERM to indicate the type of terminal that you are using. If $TERM is unset, or, even worse, if it is set incorrectly, vi will not be able to function properly. The $TERM variable is often set in your .profile (or .login for C-shell users) login script. Some users also need to initialize their terminals, usually by calling tput (tset on some systems).

Commands in visual command mode are typically one or a few keystrokes long. You do not have to enter a final <CR> for most commands. They are executed as you type the keys. Because visual mode commands are not echoed on the screen and they are executed immediately, it is easy to enter commands incorrectly. It is especially important to strike the correct keys because there is no way to take back a keystroke (or to even see what you have typed). You can always cancel a partially entered multikeystroke command by striking <ESC>.

Since vi has several modes, it is possible for the novice to move unintentionally from one to the other. All of the commands in this reference assume that you are in vi visual command mode. That's where you want to be unless you care to learn the powerful ex line-editing commands.

Commands that start with a : or a ! are displayed on the bottom line of the screen as they are entered. For these commands, you can use the backspace to make corrections as you enter the command, you can abort the command by striking the interrupt character (usually ^C or <DEL>), and you must hit <CR> (carriage return) when the command has been completely entered.

Numeric Prefixes

Many vi commands accept an optional numeric prefix. Usually a numeric prefix means execute the command that many times; otherwise the command will be executed once. Occasionally a numeric prefix has a different meaning. The exact meaning of the numeric prefix is detailed below only when it does something other than repeat the command. Commands that accept a numeric prefix are indicated in Table A.1.1, with a • in front of the citation. As you enter a numeric prefix, vi does not echo its value on the screen, so type carefully.

Operators

The commands c, y, d, <, >, and ! (change, yank, delete, shift left, shift right, and filter the buffer) are called *operators* because they operate on regions of text. An operator must be followed by a suffix, symbolized by § in Table A.1.1, that indicates the text region. The actual suffix may be any of the Cursor Movement Commands, any of the Text Search Commands, or either of the Goto Marked Text Commands. (The suffix need not be a single keystroke.) The <, >, and ! operators always affect whole lines; thus, they allow only suffixes that specify line positions; the c, y, and d operators accept any suffix. When an operator is doubled, it affects entire lines. Thus, cc will change the current line, and 5yy will yank five lines starting with the current line.

Many people who use vi extensively over long periods of time don't take advantage of vi's operators. That's unfortunate because the operators are relatively easy to use, powerful, and flexible. The most important part of using an operator is knowing the cursor movement commands well enough to know exactly how to specify a given region of text. Once you've mastered cursor movement, you've nearly mastered operators.

For example, *d$* will delete from the current cursor position to the end of the line, *d^* will delete from the current cursor position to the beginning of the line, *dfq* will delete from the current cursor position to the next letter *q* on the line, *dG* will delete from the current line to the end of the file, and *d100G* will delete from the current line to line 100. Take some time to learn to use vi operators; they are often useful.

Returning to Visual Command Mode

- If you are in visual text insert mode, all the text that you type will appear on the screen and will be added to the file. If you're in visual text insert mode, you should strike <ESC> to return to visual command mode.

- If you are in ex command-line mode, a : will be printed each time you hit <CR>, and <ESC> will be echoed as ^[. If you're in ex command mode, enter the command vi<CR> to reenter visual mode. (If that doesn't work, try <CR>.<CR>vi<CR>.)

■ If you are in open-line editing mode, the *j* and *k* cursor movement commands will constantly redraw the bottom line of the screen. If you're in open-line editing mode, enter the command Q (or <ESC>Q) to move to ex command-line mode, and then enter the command vi<CR> to return to visual mode.

Environment Variables

Before using vi, the environment variable $TERM must be correctly set for your terminal. If $TERM isn't set, then vi will complain when it starts to run, and you will be put in ex command-line mode. If $TERM is set incorrectly, then when vi starts it is likely that your screen display will be garbled. If either of these two problems arises, you should probably enter the command :q<CR> and get help. Since there are several families of similar terminals, it is possible for $TERM to be wrong even if everything appears correct for a while. Get help from an expert if your screen doesn't seem to behave as expected.

The environment variable $EXINIT may contain the name of a file containing ex commands that will be executed each time vi starts. If $EXINIT doesn't exist, vi will read commands from the file .exrc in your home directory. Then in either case, the editor will read any commands in the file .exrc in the current directory. .exrc start-up files typically contain set commands to set desired vi options, abbreviation commands to specify abbreviations, and map commands to specify macros.

Visual Commands

Table A.1.1 lists all of the vi commands using 12 categories.

1. Cursor Movement
2. Marked Text
3. Text Searches
4. Screen Management
5. Text Entry
6. During an Insertion
7. Text Deletion
8. Buffers
9. Shell Escapes
10. Status
11. Macros
12. File Manipulation

Ordinarily you will want to find out how to accomplish a given task by examining the commands in one of the categories. You can also do the opposite, decipher a keystroke sequence by looking up each keystroke in the alphabetically organized Visual Commands Index that follows Table A.1.1.

Several conventions are used in Table A.1.1:

^X	Ctrl-*X*, where *X* may be any character.
<CR>	Carriage return (often labeled Enter on the keyboard).
<DEL>	Delete key (often labeled DEL).
<ESC>	Escape key (often labeled ESC).
<SP>	Spacebar key.
<BS>	Backspace key.
text	In the Text Entry Commands, *text* refers to any printable characters; any escaped (using ^V) control characters; or tabs, spaces, or carriage returns.
•	Indicates a command that can take an optional numeric prefix.
§	Symbolizes any position specifier suffix for an operator.

While you are entering text during a Text Entry Command, only those commands described under "Commands Used During an Insertion" are available. You must terminate the insertion (by striking <ESC>) before using the full visual command set.

Table A.1.1 ■ Visual Commands Reference Table

1. Cursor Movement Commands

h j k l	• Cursor left, down, up, right.
◀ ▼ ▲ ▶	• Cursor left, down, up, right.
^H ^N ^P <SP>	• Cursor left, down, up, right.
^J	• Cursor down.
+ <CR>	• Cursor to first nonblank on following line.
-	• Cursor to first nonblank on previous line.
G	• Go to line. (Without preceding count, go to end of file.)
w b e	• Move forward word, backward word, or to end of word. (A word is a sequence of letters and digits, or group of punctuation symbols.)
W B E	• Move forward word, backward word, or to end of word. (A word is any text delimited by white space.)
0	Cursor to beginning of line (zero).
^	Cursor to first nonblank on line.
|	• Cursor to column 1, or column specified by count.
$	• Cursor to end of line, or if count is supplied, then cursor to end of count-th following line.
( )	• Cursor moves backward or forward to beginning of sentence. A sentence is any text followed by . or ! which is followed by at least two spaces.
{ }	• Cursor moves backward or forward to beginning of paragraph. A paragraph is any region of the file followed by a blank line, or followed by one of the paragraph markers from nroff/troff and their macro packages, listed in the paragraphs option of Appendix II.

[[ ]]	● Cursor moves backward or forward to beginning of section. A section is a region of text followed by one of the section markers, listed in the sections option of Appendix II.
H M L	● Move cursor to home (top line of screen), middle line, or lowest line. For H, a count means move to that many lines from top of screen; for L, a count means move to that many lines from bottom.

2. Marked Text Commands

m*a*	Mark location with mark named *a*, where *a* may be any lowercase letter.
' '	Go to the cursor's previous line.
'*a*	Go to line marked by *a*.
` `	Go to the cursor's previous character position.
`*a*	Go to character position marked by *a*.

3. Text Search Commands

f*c* F*c*	● Move cursor forward (f) or backward (F) to find character *c* on current line.
t*c* T*c*	● Move cursor forward (t) or backward (T) to position left of character *c* on current line.
; ,	● Repeat last intra-line search forwards (;) or backwards (,).
/*pat*<CR>	Forward search for pattern *pat*.
?*pat*<CR>	Reverse search for pattern *pat*.
n N	Repeat last search in same (n) or opposite (N) direction.
%	Search for balancing parenthesis ( ) or brace { }. The % command works only when the cursor is initially positioned on a parenthesis or brace.

4. Screen Management Commands

^F ^B	● Scroll forward (^F) or backward (^B) one screenful.
^U ^D	● Scroll up (^U) or down (^D) one-half screenful. A preceding count specifies how many lines to scroll, and it redefines the scroll amount for subsequent ^U and ^D commands.
^Y ^E	● Scroll up (^Y) or down (^E) one line.
z<CR>	● Scroll so that the current line is at the top, middle,
z.	or bottom of the screen. A numeric prefix to z
z-	specifies which line; a numeric suffix to z specifies a new window size.
^R	Minimally redraw screen by closing up empty screen lines created during editing on dumb terminals.
^L	Completely redraw the screen. (Needed after a phone-line transmission error, or after some other program writes to the screen.)

(continued)

5. Text Entry Commands

r *c*	• Replace character under cursor with *c*.
a *text* <ESC>	• Append *text* following current cursor position.
A *text* <ESC>	• Append *text* at the end of the line.
i *text* <ESC>	• Insert *text* before the current cursor position.
I *text* <ESC>	Insert *text* at the beginning of the current line.
o *text* <ESC>	Open up a new line following the current line and add *text* there.
O *text* <ESC>	Open up a new line in front of the current line and add *text* there.
s *text* <ESC>	• Substitute *text* for character under cursor.
c§ *text* <ESC>	• Change the given object to *text*. § is any cursor movement command that specifies a character position. For example, the command *cwBob*<ESC> will change the next word to *Bob*.
C *text* <ESC>	• A synonym for c$. Replaces from cursor position to end of line with *text*.
S *text* <ESC>	• A synonym for cc. Replaces lines with *text*.
R *text* <ESC>	• Replace the original material with *text*.
>§	• Shift lines right (>) or left (<). § is a cursor
<§	movement command that specifies a line. Cursor movement commands that operate within the current line, such as h, l, ^H, <SP>, w, W, b, B, e, E, 0, ^, |, $, f, F, t, T, ; and , (comma) are not allowed.
=	• Reindent line according to lisp conventions.
J	• Join the current line to the next, replacing the intervening <CR> and any white space with a single space.
!§ *unixcmd* <CR>	• Filter lines of text through a UNIX pipeline. The pipeline's output replaces the original text. § is a line specifier, as described in the < and > command citations.
~	• Change the case of the character under the cursor and move right one position.
.	Repeat the last change.
&	Repeat the last ex substitute command. A synonym for :&<CR>.
u	Undo last change. This command can only undo changes to the edit buffer; changes to external files cannot be undone.
U	Restore line; undo all changes to the current line since the cursor was most recently moved to the current line.

6. Commands Used During an Insertion

^V	Quote the next character. For example, in text insert mode ^V^L will put a linefeed (^L) in the text.
\	Quote a following ^H, erase, or kill.
^W	Erase last entered word.

^H		Erase last entered character.
<CR>		Start a new line.
^T		In autoindent mode, indent shiftwidth at beginning of line.
^I	<TAB>	Insert a tab character.
^D		In autoindent mode, move back one tab from beginning of line.
0^D		In autoindent mode, move to left margin and reset autoindent amount to zero.
^ ^D		In autoindent mode, move to left margin, but don't change autoindent amount (Caret, Ctrl-D).
<ESC>		Terminate insertion.
<DEL>		Abnormally terminate insertion.

7. Text Deletion Commands

d§	• Delete the given object. § is any position specifier.
x	• A synonym for d<SP>. Delete character under cursor. (Preceding count repeats, but only on current line.)
X	• A synonym for d<BS>. Delete character to left of the cursor. (Count repeats, but only on current line.)
D	A synonym for d$. Deletes from the cursor to the end of the line.

8. Buffer Commands

y§		• Yank text into buffer. § is any position specifier.
Y		• A synonym for yy. Yanks lines of text into a buffer.
p	P	Put back text from buffer and place it after (p) or before (P) current line or character position.
"a		A prefix to yank (y), delete (d), put (p), or change (c) to indicate that the buffer named *a* should be used (*a* is any lowercase letter).
"A		A prefix to yank (y), delete (d), or change (c) to indicate that the selected text should be appended to the buffer named *A* (*A* is any uppercase letter).

9. Shell Escape Commands

:!cmd<CR>	Escape to perform one UNIX command. The output of the command appears on the screen, but the file that you are editing is not altered.
:sh<CR>	Start a subshell. You may enter commands, then exit from the subshell to return to vi.

10. Status Commands

^G	Display file name, modified status, line number, and relative location in file.
^Z	On UNIX systems that support job suspension, ^Z will suspend vi.
Q	Change from vi mode to ex mode. The Q command can also be used in open-line editing mode to return to ex command-line mode.

(continued)

`<DEL>`	Striking the interrupt character returns to vi command mode from a search or from inserting text. Many people prefer to use `<CTRL-C>` as their interrupt character.
`<ESC>`	Terminate insertion if in insert mode; otherwise, sound the terminal's bell.
`:set<CR>`	List settings of options that are set differently than the default.
`:set all`	List settings of all options.
`:set opt[=val]`	If *val* is present, set string-valued option named *opt* to *val*; otherwise, show the current setting of *opt*. (Vi options are discussed in Appendix II.)
`:set [no]opt`	Set the Boolean-valued option named *opt*, or unset the option if *no* is specified. (Vi options are discussed in Appendix II.)

11. Macro Commands

`@ b`	Execute the commands stored in the buffer named *b*.
`:map key repl<CR>`	Create a command macro that will be invoked when you press *key*. *Key* is either a single keystroke, the escape code generated by a function key, or #*n*, which means function key *n*. When you hit the key, the commands stored in *repl* will be executed. Use ^V to escape special characters (e.g., `<ESC>`, `<CR>`) in *repl*.
`:map<CR>`	List the current command macros.
`:unmap key<CR>`	Delete a command macro.
`:map! key repl<CR>`	Create an insertion macro that will be invoked when you hit *key* in insert mode. *Key* is coded as detailed previously for map. *Key* becomes a single keystroke abbreviation for *repl*.
`:map!<CR>`	List the current insertion macros.
`:unmap! key<CR>`	Delete an insertion macro.
`:ab word repl<CR>`	Create an abbreviation for *word*. During a text insertion, whenever you type *word* surrounded by white space or new lines, it will be replaced with *repl*. *Word* can be more than one character. Use ^V in *repl* to escape special characters.
`:ab<CR>`	List the current abbreviations.
`:unab word<CR>`	Delete an abbreviation.
`#n`	Manually simulate a function key on a terminal that lacks function keys. (#n will literally insert the characters #*n* into the edit buffer on terminals that do have function keys.)

12. File Manipulation Commands

`:w<CR>`	Write the edit buffer to the original file.
`:w filename<CR>`	Write the edit buffer to *filename*. The write will not occur if *filename* exists and is not the current file.

`:w! filename<CR>`	Write the edit buffer to *filename*, overwriting the existing file unconditionally.
`:wq<CR>`	Write the edit buffer to original file and then quit.
`:e filename<CR>`	Start editing a new file. A warning will be printed if edit buffer has been modified but not yet saved.
`:e! filename<CR>`	Start editing a new file regardless of whether the buffer has been saved since it was last modified.
`:e #<CR>`	Edit alternate file. The alternate file is the previous file that you were editing, or the last file mentioned in an unsuccessful :e command.
`:n<CR>`	Edit the next file in the list of files to edit. The list is either created by specifying the files on the command line or by using the :n *filelist* command.
`:n filelist<CR>`	Specify a list of files to edit, as if they had been mentioned on the command line.
`:r filename<CR>`	Read in a file to the edit buffer following the current line. The :r command does not change the remembered filename.
`:n r filename<CR>`	Read in a file, placing it after line *n*. The command `:0r filename` is particularly useful; it places the file's contents in front of existing text.
`:r !cmd<CR>`	Read in the output of the UNIX command *cmd* to the buffer following the current line.
`:n r !cmd<CR>`	Read in the output of the UNIX command *cmd* to the buffer following line *n*.
`:q<CR>`	Quit. (A warning is printed, and you will remain in the editor if the edit buffer has been modified but not yet saved.)
`:q!<CR>`	Forced quit, even if the current buffer is modified. (No warning.)
`ZZ`	Save edit buffer and quit. Equivalent to :x<CR> or :wq<CR>.
`:cd dir<CR>`	Change directory to *dir*. A warning will be printed, and the move will not occur if the buffer has been modified but not yet saved.
`:cd! dir<CR>`	Change directory to *dir*, even if the buffer has been modified but not yet saved.

Visual Commands Index

Char.	Sect.	Char.	Sect.	Char.	Sect.	Char.	Sect.
^@		\<SP\>	1.	@	11.	'	2.
^A		!	5.	A	5.	a	5.
^B	4.	"	8.	B	1.	b	1.
^C		#	11.	C	5.	c	5.
^D	4. 6.	$	1.	D	7.	d	7.
^E	4.	%	3.	E	1.	e	1.
^F	4.	&	5.	F	3.	f	3.
^G	10.	'	2.	G	1.	g	
^H	1. 6.	(	1.	H	1.	h	1.
^I	6.	)	1.	I	5.	i	5.
^J	1.	*		J	5.	j	1.
^K		+	1.	K		k	1.
^L	4.	,	3.	L	1.	l	1.
^M	1.	-	1.	M	1.	m	2.
^N	1.	.	5.	N	3.	n	3.
^O		/	3.	O	5.	o	5.
^P	1.	0	1.	P	8.	p	8.
^Q		1		Q	10.	q	
^R	4.	2		R	5.	r	5.
^S		3		S	5.	s	5.
^T	6.	4		T	3.	t	3.
^U	4.	5		U	7.	u	7.
^V	6.	6		V		v	
^W	6.	7		W	1.	w	1.
^X	4.	8		X	7.	x	7.
^Y	4.	9		Y	8.	y	8.
^Z	10.	:	9-12.	Z	12.	z	4.
\<ESC\>	5. 6. 10.	;	3.	[	1.	{	1.
		\<	5.	\\	6.	|	1.
		=	5.	]	1.	}	1.
		\>	5.	^	1.	~	5.
		?	3.	_		\<del\>	10.

APPENDIX II
Vi Options Reference

The ex/vi text editor has various options that are used to customize its operation. The set command lets you display or change these option settings. Set can be used interactively, or set commands can be placed into an .exrc script so that they will be set automatically each time vi or ex starts to execute. Vi looks for an .exrc script in the current directory, in your home directory, and in a location specified by the $EXINIT environment variable.

Many options are Boolean, which means they are either on or off. For example, if the errorbells option is set, vi will ring the terminal's bell when it encounters an error; otherwise, it will refrain from making noises. On/off options are set using the vi command

```
:set opt
```

to set the option and

```
:set noopt
```

to turn the option off. Boolean options are identified by a • in Table A.2.1.

Other options have values, such as the term option, whose value is the name of the terminal that you are using. Options with values are set using the command

```
:set opt=val
```

You can see a list of all of the option settings if you enter the command

```
:set all
```

Alternatively you can see a list of the options that are set differently from the default by entering the vi command

```
:set
```

Several options can be set from the ex/vi command line:

-R   Sets the readonly option.
-l   Sets the showmatch and lisp options for lisp editing.
-w   Sets the default window size.

See Appendix I for a complete list of ex/vi command-line options.

There is some variation in the options supported by the various versions of vi. Some of the options in Table A.2.1 may not be supported on all versions of vi, and some versions of vi have additional options.

Table A.2.1 ■ Vi Options Reference Table

Option	Abb.	Meaning
autoindent	ai	• Autoindent makes vi automatically indent each new line to the same level as the previous, or to the same level as the one the cursor was on when a new line was opened. ^T will increase the indentation one shiftwidth. ^D at the beginning of a line will cause the indent to retreat left one stop. ^^D will retreat to the left margin. The default is noai.
autoprint	ap	• When autoprint is set, lines are printed after being modified by one of the following ex commands: d, c, J, m, t, u, <, or >. This option applies only in line-editing mode, and the effect is as if a trailing p were added to each of the preceding ex commands. The default is ap.
autowrite	aw	• When autowrite is set, vi will automatically write out the current file before executing commands that might switch to another file, or before executing a shell escape command. The default is noaw.
beautify	bf	• Beautify tells vi to discard all control characters (other than tab, newline, and form-feed) from the input. The default is nobf.
directory	dir	Directory tells vi where to place its temporary files. The default is /tmp.
edcompatible		• Edcompatible makes the ex substitute command more closely resemble ed's. The default is noedcompatible.
errorbells	eb	• Errorbells tells vi to ring the terminal's bell for a larger set of errors. The default is noeb.
exrc		When exrc is set, vi is allowed to read the .exrc file in the current directory. If it is not set, vi will only read the .exrc file in your home directory. This option is usually set either in the file specified by the $EXINIT environment variable or in $HOME/.exrc.
flash		• Flash the screen instead of ringing the bell, on those terminals that are capable of flashing the screen. (Only available on newer versions of vi.) The default is flash.
hardtabs	ht	Hardtabs defines the hardware tab stops for your terminal. The default is eight spaces.
ignorecase	ic	• Ignorecase tells vi to ignore case distinctions in searches and substitutions. The default is noic.
lisp		• Lisp alters the indent strategy in indent mode for lisp programs. The default is nolisp.

Option	Abb.	Meaning
list	li	• List mode displays tabs and linefeeds explicitly. Tabs are displayed as ^I, and linefeeds are displayed as $. The default is noli.
magic		• In magic mode all regular expression characters are active. In nomagic mode only ^, $, and \ are metacharacters. In nomagic mode a metacharacter (e.g., ?) can be restored its power by preceding it with a backslash (e.g.,). The default is magic.
mesg		• Mesg allows messages to be written on your screen during vi sessions. The default is nomesg.
modelines		• Modelines allows you to place mode setting commands in individual files that you are editing. If modelines is set, then each time you edit a file, vi will look for ex:*cmd*: or vi:*cmd*: in the first and last five lines of the file. The specified commands, if found, will be executed. The default is nomodelines.
number	nu	• Number numbers lines on the display. The default is nonu.
novice		• Novice prevents switches to open-line editing so that editing is less confusing. The default is nonovice.
open		• Open mode allows you to issue the open or visual commands from ex-line editing mode. Noopen prevents these commands so that novices will be less confused by modes (called novice on System V). The default is open.
optimize	opt	• Optimize uses cursor positioning escape sequences at the end of each line to move to the beginning of the next line. This is more efficient on many terminals. The default is opt.
paragraphs	para	Paragraphs tells vi the names of the nroff/troff paragraph macros. When you move to the beginning or end of a paragraph (using the { or } commands), vi searches for the closest paragraph marker in the paragraphs list, or for a blank line. In the list, pairs of characters are macro names (e.g., IP). The default is:
		`IPLPPPQPP LIpplpipnpbp`
		The default covers standard -ms and -mm paragraphs, -mm list items, and manual page breaks of the -ms and -mm troff macro packages.
prompt		• Prompt tells vi to print the : prompt when it is waiting for line-editing commands. The default is prompt.
readonly	ro	• When readonly is set, the editor will refuse to write to a file (unless you use the w! command). Readonly can be set like any other option, or it can be set by invoking vi with the -R command-line option. The default is noreadonly.
redraw		• Redraw tells vi to constantly keep the screen display up to date, even on dumb terminals. This option generates much output on a dumb terminal. The default is noredraw.
remap		• Remap makes vi repeatedly scan the text of macros to see if any further macros are invoked. Noremap scans each only once, thus making it impossible for one macro to invoke another. The default is remap.
report		When a command modifies more than report lines, vi prints a message. The default is 5.

(continued)

Option	Abb.	Meaning
scroll		Scroll is the number of lines the display scrolls in ex mode when you type the EOF character. The default is one-half the number of lines in the window.
sections		Sections is a list of nroff/troff macro names that vi searches for when you enter the [[and]] commands to move to the beginning and end of the section. In the sections list, pairs of characters denote macro names (e.g., SH). The default is NHSHH HUuhsh The default covers the heading start commands of the -ms and -mm troff macro packages.
shell	sh	Shell contains the name of the default shell. When vi starts to execute, shell is copied from the $SHELL environment variable.
shiftwidth	sw	Shiftwidth is the size of the software tab stop. The default is 8.
showmatch	sm	• When showmatch is set, vi will automatically move the cursor to the matching (or { for one second each time you type a) or }. This is useful for programmers, especially for lisp programmers. The default is nosm.
showmode		• Showmode displays the current edit mode on the status line. When terse is set, the mode is represented by a single character. (Only available on newer versions of vi.) The default is noshowmode.
slowopen	slow	• The slowopen mode is an alternate output strategy for open or visual mode. It improves vi on dumb terminals by reducing the amount of screen updating during text inputs. Its value and default depend on terminal type.
tabstop	ts	Tab characters in the input file produce movement to the next tabstop boundary. Reducing tabstop to 2 or 4 often makes it easier to view heavily indented material, such as C programs. The default is 8.
taglength	tl	Taglength is the number of significant characters in a tag. Zero means the entire tag is significant. The default is 0.
tags		Tags is a list of files containing tags. The default list is /usr/lib/tags.
term		Term is the name of the output terminal. Its initial value comes from the $TERM environment variable. Term must be correct or vi will not run correctly.
terse		• Terse makes vi produce shorter error messages. The default is noterse.
timeout		• When timeout is set, the complete character sequence invoking a macro must be entered within one second. The default is timeout.
warn		• When warn is set, vi will warn you if you enter a ! (shell) command without first saving your text. The default is warn.
window		Window is the size of the text display in visual mode. The default varies according to the baud rate. It is eight lines at speeds less than 1,200 baud, 16 lines at 1,200 baud, and the full screen at more than 1,200 baud.
w300		W300 is a synonym for window, but it is effective only if the baud rate is less than 1,200. The default is 8.

Option	Abb.	Meaning
w1200		W1200 is a synonym for window, but it is effective only if the baud rate is 1,200. The default is 16.
w9600		W9600 is a synonym for window, but it is effective only if the baud rate is higher than 1,200. The default is full screen.
wrapmargin	wm	When you are entering text and the cursor position gets to within wrapmargin characters of the right margin, vi will automatically insert a line break (between two words). This allows you to type continuously without striking return to form each line. Wrapmargin applies only to text entry in visual mode, not in line-editing mode. The value 0 disables automatic line break insertion. The default is 0.
wrapscan	ws	• Wrapscan makes vi search the entire file every time. Searches always start from the current line and proceed to the end (or beginning) of the file. When wrapscan is set and a vi search reaches the end (or beginning) of the file, the search continues from the beginning (or end) to the current line. The default is ws.
writeany	wa	• When writeany is set, vi will allow you to overwrite existing files without warning you. The default is nowa.

Note: When you assign a value to an option, there can't be any white space on either side of the equal sign. The command
`:set wm=10`
will work, but the command
`:set wm = 10`
will complain `=: No such option`.

APPENDIX III
Ex Command Reference

Ex is the line-editing version of the ex/vi text editor. Ex is strongly reminiscent of the older ed editor because it was originally developed from ed's source code. Although ex does improve significantly upon ed, the major improvement of ex/vi is visual editing, which is described in Chapters 9 and 10, and which is detailed in Appendixes I and II. Ex's command-line options are identical to those of vi; thus they are described at the beginning of Appendix I. The ex/vi family of editors has various operational modes that can be controlled using the editor's set command; they are described in Appendix II.

For most users the vi interface is more convenient. Vi requires a terminal with an addressable cursor, but such terminals are commonplace. Ex is best when you want more power and speed than the visual interface can provide, when you want ex to perform commands stored in an editing script, or when a video terminal is not available.

Overview

Ex is a program that lets you modify text files. You can enter your editing commands interactively or provide them in a supplied script. Commands are typically entered one per line. Most commands operate on a region of the text, which is specified as a line or a range of lines. For convenience, ex keeps track of the current line, which is the default region for many commands. For most other commands, the default region is the entire text.

When you are editing a file with ex, you are actually working with a copy of that file, which is stored in an ex buffer. Changes made to the buffer don't alter the original file until you issue a write command. Once understood, this aspect of ex becomes a feature because mistaken alterations of the buffer's contents needn't destroy the original file. However, novices sometimes have trouble with this concept and forget to write out the buffer contents at the end of the edit session, thereby losing their work. (Ex prints a warning and refuses to quit if the buffer has not been saved, but there is a "forced quit" command that will always quit.)

Ex is a multimode editor. This means that the interpretation of what you type depends on ex's mode. The two native ex modes are command-line mode and text entry mode. In command-line entry mode, ex prints a : prompt at the beginning of each line; each of your input lines is presumed to be ex commands. In text entry mode, there isn't an explicit prompt; each of your input lines is presumed to be text that is added to the file. Ex has several commands that initiate text entry mode, and you can change from text entry mode to command-line mode by entering a period alone on a line. Note that this differs from vi, which expects you to hit the <ESC> key to switch from text entry mode to visual command mode. Ex also has the vi command, which leads to the vi side of the editor, where the vi specific modes (discussed in Appendix I) apply. In our experience, ex's modes are its most difficult feature.

You can usually return to ex command-line mode from within the ex portion of the editor by typing a line that consists of a single period. This code will return you to command-line mode if you are in text entry mode, or it will print the current line if you are already in command-line mode. Returning to a known mode (state) is somewhat harder if you wander into the visual or open-line editing portion of the editor. To return to ex command-line mode from visual or open-line editing, you should press the escape key and then type an uppercase Q.

Line Specifiers

Ex contains multiple ways to identify lines in a file. The easiest way is to just type a line number, but how often do we keep track of line numbers while editing a file? You can also refer to lines by their relative address, their content, or by using marks. The following paragraphs discuss each of these strategies in more detail.

Line Numbers are the easiest way to specify a line, and they are also the least ambiguous method. In ex you can always discover the line number of the current line by entering the command

```
:  .=
```

You can also determine line numbers by using the number command, which is an alternate form of the print command. (The number option applies only to vi.) The first line in the buffer is numbered 1, although the fictitious line 0 can be mentioned to make it easier to place text in front of line 1.

Relative Line Numbers are used when you want to address lines in the immediate vicinity of the current line. For example, -3 is the line three in front of the current, and $+5$ is the fifth line past the current. You can also write relative line numbers with sequences of $+$ and $-$. For example, $- - -$ is the line three in front of the current and $+ + + + +$ is the fifth line past the current. $+ + + - - -$ is a wanton way to address the current line.

Marked Lines are referred to by 'x (apostrophe, x) where *x* is any lowercase letter. Before you can reference a mark, you must set it using the mark command. Your location in the buffer previous to your last nonrelative movement is named ' ' (two single quotes). You can add an offset to a mark; for example, 'x-3 indicates a line three in front of the line marked *x*.

Patterns are used to refer to a line containing a given text pattern. You can surround a pattern with slashes /pat/ to indicate a forward search to the next line that contains the pattern, or you can surround the pattern with question marks ?pat? to indicate a reverse search. You can add an offset to a pattern; for example, the pattern ?Sam?-2 indicates a line two in front of the preceding line containing the text *Sam*.

There are also three symbols that refer to specific lines in the buffer:

.	is shorthand notation for the current line in the buffer.
$	is shorthand notation for the last line in the buffer.
%	is shorthand notation for the entire buffer.

The following example illustrates each of these address forms. It also demonstrates the print, mark, and quit commands. When the print command is supplied with one address, it prints that line and then makes that line the current line; when it is supplied with two addresses, it prints from the first specified line to the second, and then makes the last line printed the current line. The mark command takes a single-character argument, which can subsequently be used to reference the current line.

You can abbreviate most ex commands, often down to the command's first letter. For example, the abbreviation for the print command is p, and the abbreviation for quit is q. Both full names and abbreviations are shown in the following dialog. When two commands have the same first letter, such as append and abbreviate, the command with the stronger ed heritage is usually the one with the single-character abbreviation.

Here is an example that shows some of the ways you can specify lines using ex:

```
$ cat fivelines
This is one
and two,
three,
four,
and five.
$ ex fivelines
"fivelines" 5 lines, 44 characters
: .=
5
: . print
and five.
```

```
: 3 print
three,
: -2 p
This is one
: /ou/
four,
: 2 p
and two,
: mark c
: 'c+,$ p
three,
four,
and five.
: quit
$ ▓
```

The beginning of this example shows that you are initially positioned at the end of the file when you start to edit it with ex, which is the normal ed behavior. In vi you are initially positioned at the beginning of the file.

Command Syntax Summary

Ex commands can be broadly divided into two classes—those that take addresses, such as delete, and those that don't, such as quit. The general form of commands that take addresses is

```
n1 cmd
n2,n3 cmd
```

N1, n2 and n3 are line specifiers, as previously discussed.

Commands that operate on a range of lines, such as delete, take either one or two line specifiers, while commands that do something before or after a given line, such as append, take only one line specifier. Some commands take optional parameters following the command name. These commands are idiosyncratic and will be discussed individually.

Commands generally appear one per line, although several separate commands can be entered on a single line by separating them with a | (vertical bar). You can correct typing mistakes by using your usual erase character (often backspace or delete). All command lines must be followed by a carriage return, which isn't shown in the examples in this appendix.

From within the vi realms of the editor you can access ex line commands by prefacing them with a colon. Native ex (but not ed) also allows a colon (do nothing) preface to all commands, to accommodate fingers accustomed to vi.

Some commands have a variant form that is activated by placing a ! after the command. For many commands, the variant form tells ex that you know what you're doing. For example, quit! tells ex to quit, even if there are unsaved changes in the buffer. Most other variants are relatively obscure. For example, the global command usually does something on lines that match a pattern, but the ! variant of the global commands means "do the following on lines that don't match." In the insert command the ! means "toggle autoindent mode." You should try to avoid confusing !'s role in forcing variant forms of commands, with its use as a command name, where it means execute a UNIX command. (Fortunately, the ! command doesn't have a variant.)

Ed Compatibility

Today most UNIX systems contain both ed and ex. For historical reasons, ed is often used in shell scripts for simple automated editing tasks. Ed is also required knowledge for systems programmers because on many systems ex/vi is not available in single-user mode without mounting additional file systems. Thus, even today there is occasional use of ed for system repair and troubleshooting.

Some ed commands have variants, which are usually accessed by capitalizing the command letter. For example, the Q command means you really want to quit, even if the buffer has been modified but not yet saved. This system is different from ex and its ! suffix for accessing variant behavior.

Ex is a straightforward extension of ed. If you already know ed, you can use almost all of that knowledge with ex, because ex is mostly upwardly compatible with ed. However, if you only know ex, you may be surprised when you use ed, because ed doesn't contain many of the ex commands. When one of your favorite ex commands doesn't work in ed, simplify.

If you're native line-editing tongue is ex, keep the following in mind while using ed:

- Don't use the : command prefix.

- Don't use buffers.

- Remember to write the closing / when using the substitute command.

- Remember that ed and ex use different ways of specifying variants.

In the detailed command reference section of this appendix, the ed-like subset of ex is identified by the **ED** symbol at the end of the citation. (Most commands with a single-character abbreviation are native ed commands. Those without a single-character abbreviation definitely don't appear in ed because ed command names are all single characters.)

Commands

In this section, the left column shows the major forms that each command takes, and the right column describes the commands. When a command has both an abbreviation and a full name, the abbreviation appears in the left column and the full name appears at the start of the description in the right column. Commands that take addresses have the default addresses shown in parentheses. If you don't explicitly specify an address (or address range), the command uses the default addresses. Commands shown with two addresses also accept just one address, to operate on a single line.

The **ED** mark indicates that the given ex command also exists in the latest System V version of ed. Some of the details vary slightly for ed, and ed commands that don't have an ex analog aren't listed. If someday you're forced to use ed, the information in this section will be more than enough to get by.

Text Display Commands

^D   Striking the end-of-file character makes the editor scroll through the file. The number of lines that are printed depends on the scroll option, which is set by default to a half screenful.

(+,+)   Specifying lines without mentioning a command prints those lines. Simply hitting carriage return will print the next line in the file.

($)=   The line number of the specified line will be printed. By default, the number of the last line in the buffer will be printed, but the most common form of this command is probably .= to print the line number of the current line. **ED**

(.,.)l   list   Display the specified lines on the terminal, showing ^I for each tab, and showing $ for each newlines. This lets you distinguish between tabs and spaces, and it lets you identify white space at the end of a line. **ED**

(.,.)nu   number   Print the specified lines, each preceded by its line number. The ed version of this command is the n command (but the n command in ex has a totally different meaning). The # command is another name in ex for the number command. **ED**

(.,.)p   print   The specified lines are displayed on the terminal. **ED**

(.+1)z   Display a block of text. The default block length is specified by the window option, although the block can be specified to be *n* lines using the second form of the command. By default, the block of text starts with the line after the current line, so you can page through a file by repeatedly entering the z command.

(.,+1)z *n*   Same as z, but the displayed block will be *n* lines long.

(.)z-   Display the block, with the specified line at the bottom of the block.

(.)z=   Display a block of text, with the specified line in the middle of the block. The specified line will be highlighted (on some versions of vi) by placing a line of dashes above and below it.

(.)z^   Display the block of text that starts windowsize lines in front of the specified line.

Here is a short example of some text display commands:

```
$ ex fivelines
"fivelines" 5 lines, 44 characters
: 1,3 list
This is^Ione$
and two, $
three,$
: 1,$nu
     1  This is one
     2  and two,
     3  three,
     4  four,
     5  and five.
: --,.p
three,
four,
and five.
: quit
$ ▊
```

Notice on line 1 of the fivelines file that what appears to be simply a space is actually a tab, shown as ^I. Notice also that the second line contains a trailing blank at the end of the line.

Text Entry Commands

The following text entry commands change the mode of the editor from command-line mode to text entry mode. In text entry mode, each line of input is added to the file, until a line containing a single period is entered. Unlike the format of the rest of the command citations, the format of the left column here sketches the ex text entry dialog comand line, (multi) line text entry, and then termination of text entry by a line consisting of a period.

(.)a

text

.

append   The given *text* is added to the buffer following the specified line. Text entry mode ceases when a line consisting of a single period is entered. The variant version of this command, a!, toggles the autoindent mode during the text entry. **ED**

(.,.)c

text

.

change   The specified lines are changes to the given *text*. Text entry mode ceases when a line consisting of a single period is entered. The variant version of this command, c!, toggles the autoindent mode during the text entry. **ED**

(.)i

text

.

insert   The given text is added to the buffer in front of the given line. Text entry mode ceases when a line consisting of a single period is entered. The variant version of this command, i!, toggles the autoindent mode during the text entry. **ED**

u

undo   The last alteration to the buffer is undone. The global, visual, and open commands are considered a single change. Undo works with the ex buffer; commands such as w that interact with the file system cannot be undone. **ED**

The following example demonstrates the text entry commands:

```
$ ex fivelines
"fivelines" 5 lines, 44 characters
: 0 append
The new line one.
.
: 2,4c
This line replaces the old lines 1-3.
.
: 3p
four,
: i
Make this three, please.
.
: 1,$p
The new line one.
This line replaces the old lines 1-3.
Make this three, please.
four,
and five.
: write
"fivelines" 5 lines, 97 characters
: quit
$
```

Cut and Paste Commands

(. , .)co *line*

copy   Take a copy of the addressed lines and place it after the specified line. You may specify that the lines should be placed after line zero, if you want the copy placed at the beginning of the buffer.

(. , .)t *line*

      t is a synonym for co in ex, and it is the primary command name in ed.

(. , .)d

delete   Delete the specified lines and save them in the unnamed buffer. **ED**

(. , .)d *buf*

delete   You can specify *buf* to store the deleted text in a named buffer. If the buffer name is a single uppercase character, the text will be appended to the buffer, but if it is a single lowercase character, the deleted text will overwrite the buffer's current contents.

(. , .)d *n*

delete   You can specify a count to delete that number of lines.

(.,.)d *buf n*	delete	You can specify both a buffer and a count to delete *n* lines into the buffer.
(.,+)j	join	The specified lines will be joined to form a single line. At each joint the original white space will be replaced by two spaces if there was a period at the end of the line, no white space if there was a) at the start of the next line, or one space otherwise. The j! variant form of this command doesn't perform any special processing on the white space at the beginning and end of the original lines. **ED**
(.,.)m *line*	move	The specified lines will be moved from their original place in the buffer to just after the specified line. You may specify line 0, if you want the text moved to the beginning of the buffer. **ED**
(.)put	put	The previously deleted or yanked lines stored in the unnamed buffer will be put into the file after the specified line.
(.)put *buf*	put	The previously deleted or yanked lines stored in *buf* will be put into the file after the specified line.
(.,.)ya	yank	The specified lines will be yanked from the file and saved in an unnamed buffer. The file isn't altered by a yank.
(.,.)ya *buf*	yank	The specified lines will be yanked from the file and saved in *buf*. The file isn't altered by a yank.

Here is an example of several cut and paste commands:

```
$ ex girls
"girls" 5 lines, 32 characters
: 1,$nu
     1  everything
     2  spice
     3  sugar
     4  nice
     5  and
: 3m0
sugar
: $m1
and
: y
: put
and
: 1,$nu
     1  sugar
     2  and
     3  and
     4  everything
     5  spice
     6  nice
: 3,4d
spice
```

```
: put
everything
: 1,$p
sugar
and
spice
and
everything
nice
: 1,4join
sugar and spice and
: 2,3j
everything nice
: w
"girls" 2 lines, 36 characters
: q
$ cat girls
sugar and spice and
everything nice
$ ▓
```

Modifying Lines

(. , .) s/*pat*/*repl*/   substitute   Substitute *repl* for *pat* on the specified lines. *Pat* may be a regular expression, as explained in the "Regular Expressions" section of this appendix. *Repl* is ordinary text, except for a few characters that are described in the "Replacement Text" section of this appendix. The replacement text may consist of multiple lines, although each new line in *repl* must be escaped with a backslash. Although the / character is shown separating s from *pat* and *pat* from *repl*, any character may be used. (The separator should be escaped with a backslash if it appears in *pat* or *repl*.) You may place a g after the command if you want all instances of *pat* replaced with *repl*; ordinarily only the first *pat* on each line will be replaced. You may place a c after the command if you want to confirm each substitution by typing in y or n when requested. ED

(. , .) s   substitute   If *pat* and *repl* are omitted, the substitute command will repeat the most recent substitution.

(. , .) &   The & command will repeat the most recent substitution.

(. , .) >   The specified lines will be shifted to the right. You can shift more than one shiftwidth unit (usually a tab) at a time by repeating the >. Thus, the command >>> will shift the current line three shiftwidths to the right.

(. , .) <   Like >, but shifts left. Left shifts never discard text other than white space.

Global Commands

(1,$)g/*pat*/*cmds*   global   The global command initiates a two-step operation. During phase one, the specified lines (by default the entire file) are examined to see if they match the given *pat*, which may contain the regular expression features discussed in the "Regular Expressions" section of this appendix. Those lines that match *pat* are marked. During phase two, the given editor *cmds* are performed at each marked line. The *cmds* may be any ex command other than undo or global. You can escape newlines with a backslash if your list of *cmds* must appear on multiple lines. If *cmds* contains append, insert, or change commands, then each line of added text must have a trailing backslash to escape the new line. If *cmds* is omitted, then each of the matched lines will be printed. The undo command can undo all of the changes made by a single global command. **ED**

(1,$)g!/*pat*/*cmds*   g! is the same as g, except that *cmds* are executed on each line that does not match the specified *pat*.

(1,$)v/*pat*/*cmds*   v is the same as g, except that *cmds* are executed on each line that does not match the specified *pat*. **ED**

(.)mark *x*   mark   The specified line will be marked for later identification with the letter *x*. Marks aren't visible in the file; rather they are ways for ex to remember locations so that you can refer to them by name. You can refer to a marked line using the ' feature; for example 't refers to the line marked as t. (The ed name for the mark command is k.) **ED**

Macros and Abbreviations

ab *word repl*   abbreviate   The *repl* text, which may consist of several words, is stored as an abbreviation for *word*. During a text insertion in visual mode, each time you enter the given *word* surrounded by white space (or new lines), it will be replaced by its abbreviation. Abbreviations don't have any effect on the operation of text insertions during ex line-editing mode.

ab   abbreviate   The ab command, when used without *word* and *repl*, will list the current abbreviations.

unab *word*   The unab command will remove an abbreviation for *word*.

map key repl   map   The *repl* text, which may consist of several words, will be stored and used as a replacement whenever *key* is pressed in visual command mode. *key* should be a single character, or the multicharacter sequence produced by a single keystroke (usually a function key sequence), or #*n*, meaning the code produced by function key *n*.

map   map   When used without *key* and *repl*, the map command lists the current maps.

map! *key repl*	map!	The map! variant command creates a map that is active during visual insert mode instead of during visual command mode.
map!	map!	When used without *key* and *repl*, the map! command lists the current insert-mode maps.
unmap *key*	unmap	The unmap command removes the map for *key*.
unmap! *key*	unmap!	The unmap! command removes the insert-mode map for *key*.

Operation Commands

(.)o	open	Leave ex line-editing mode and enter open-line editing mode. In open line mode, the bottom line of the screen acts as a one-line window into the file, and you can use the native vi commands to operate within this one-line window. You can return to line-editing mode by typing an uppercase Q while in command mode or by striking <ESC>Q during open line text entry. Open-line editing works acceptably on most video terminals, even if their type is unknown or if the terminal type is set incorrectly.
q	quit	Leave the editor and return to the shell. Quit will print an error and refuse to quit if the buffer has been modified since it was last saved. **ED**
q!		You can use the ex variant q! (or the ed variant Q) to leave while unconditionally discarding any buffer modifications. **ED**
set *option*	set	The set command allows you to set *option*. The meanings of each option are detailed in Appendix II.
set no*option*	set	Turn off *option*.
set option=value	set	Set *option* to *value*.
set option ?	set	Print the value of *option*.
set	set	Print the value of all options that are set to nondefault values.
set all	set	Print the value of all options.
sh	shell	Spawn a secondary shell to execute UNIX commands. Note that this shell will be different from your original login shell. When you have completed executing shell commands, you can resume editing by exiting from the shell, either by entering the exit command or by striking ^D to force end of file.
source file	source	Read ex commands from the given file. The file may not contain another source command.

stop	stop	On systems that support job control, the stop command will suspend the editor and return to the shell command interpreter. When you have finished executing shell commands, you can resume your editing session by entering the fg (C-shell or Bourne) shell command. If the autowrite option is set, the editor will save a changed buffer before suspending itself, unless the variant form of the command is specified.
stop!		The variant stop commands suspend the current editing session without saving, even if the autowrite option is set.
ta *tag*	tag	A tags file is a small data base that records the locations of various items in a text file. In practice, most tags files are created by the ctags program, which records the locations of all of the subroutines in a group of C language files. When you enter the ex editor's tag command, the current line moves to the specified tag, even if it is in another file. For example, the command *ta xputs* will move to the location specified for *xputs* in the tags file. By default, the tags file is named tags, although the tags option can be set to the names of additional tags files.
ve	version	The version command prints the editor's version number and last modification date.
vi	visual	The visual command enters the vi realms of the editor. You can return to line-editing mode by typing an uppercase Q while in visual command mode, or by striking <ESC>Q during visual mode text entry. You can also specify a file name if you want to enter visual command mode to edit that file.
vi *file*	visual	If you specify a file when you enter the visual command, you will commence visual editing of that file.
x	xit	If the buffer has been modified since it was last saved, save it, and then leave the editor. (Ed also has an x command, but it relates to encryption, not to exiting from the editor.)
! *cmd*		Execute the given UNIX command. When the command completes, the editor will print a ! alone on a line to delimit the end of *cmd*'s output and then the editing session will resume. Within the text of *cmd*, a % will be replaced by the current file name, # will be replaced by the alternate (usually the previous) file name, and ! will be replaced by the entire previous command. Note that this command doesn't alter the buffer; it is simply a convenient way to enter a UNIX command from within the editor. (Older versions of ed don't allow typical shell syntax for *cmd*.) **ED**
adr,adr! *cmd*		Send the specified lines of the buffer to the given UNIX command, and then use the output of that UNIX command as a replacement for the given lines. This is the only command that operates on a region of the buffer but does not have a default region. You must specify the address (or addresses) explicitly.

File Commands

args   args   Print the list of files to be edited. Multiple files can be mentioned on the ex/vi command line, and this list is displayed using the args command. The file being edited is surrounded by square brackets.

e *file*   edit   Edit *file*. The editor will refuse to perform this command if the buffer has been modified but not yet saved. Within the text of the file name, the character % will be replaced by the current file name and the character # will be replaced by the alternate (usually the previous) file name. **ED**

e! *file*   edit   Edit *file*, even if there are unsaved changes, which will be lost, to the current file. This variant is E in **ED**.

e   edit   Restart editing the current file. **ED**

e +*n* *file*   edit   Start editing *file* at line *n*.

e +/*pat* *file* edit   Start editing *file* at the first line that matches *pat*.

f   file   Print the name and status of the current file. **ED**

f *file*   file   Change the file name associated with the buffer, and change the status of the buffer to modified. **ED**

n   next   Start editing the next file in the list of files to be edited. You will get an error message if the current buffer has been modified but not yet saved. You can also specify a line number or a context pattern if you want to start editing at that place in the file.

n!   next   The n! variant command starts editing the next file in the list of files to be edited, even if the buffer has been modified.

n *filelist* next   Specify a list of files, which will then be used as the editor's file list, and then start editing the first file in the list.

n +*n*   next   Start editing the next file in the list of files to edit, at line *n*.

n +/*pat*   next   Start editing the next file in the list of files to edit, starting at the first line that matches *pat*.

preserve   preserve   The edit buffer will be saved in a special preservation area. This command is useful if you are having trouble saving your work. Typical problems that preserve can circumvent are write-protected files, write-protected directories, and full file systems. Use recover to retrieve your preserved file. (Or you can recover your work by starting a fresh editing session using the -r command-line option of ex or vi.)

(.)r *file*   read   The contents of *file* will be added to the current buffer following the specified line. Unlike the edit command, which effectively starts a new editing session, read simply adds text to the current buffer. If the buffer has not yet been named, the file name used in the read command will become the file name associated with the buffer. If the buffer is empty, the read command is equivalent to the edit command. Specify 0 as the line number if you want the material to be added in front of existing text. **ED**

`(.)r ! `*`cmd`*	read	Add the output of *cmd* to the buffer, following the given line. Note the space between r and !. **ED**
`recover `*`file`*	recover	Recover the file that was preserved in the special file preservation area. This command is useful after a crash, to recover a file that was saved automatically, or after using the preserve command.
`rew`	rewind	Start editing the first file in the list of files to edit. This command will issue an error message if the buffer has been modified but not yet saved.
`rew!`	rewind	The variant rewind command will start editing the first file in the list of files to edit, even if the buffer has been modified.
`(1,$)w`	write	The specified lines (by default the entire buffer) will be written to the file associated with the buffer. Error checking is performed to warn you if you try to write a buffer to an existing file other than the original file. Use the w! variant to force the write. **ED**
`(1,$)w>>`	write	The symbol >> after the write command specifies that you want to append the buffer to the end of the file.
`(1,$)w>> `*`file`*	write	The symbol >> after the write command specifies that you want to append the buffer to the end of *file*. **ED**
`(1,$)w!`	write	The w! variant forces the write. The variant is W in **ED.**
`(1,$)w !`*`cmd`*	write	You can also write the buffer into a UNIX pipeline by replacing the file name with !*cmd*, where *cmd* is any command, preferably one that reads its standard input. Note the difference between `w!` which forces a write, and `w !`*`cmd`* which sends the buffer to that command. **ED**
`(1,$)wq`	write	Write the buffer and then quit. **ED**
`(1,$)wq!`	write	Write the buffer and then quit, even if the buffer has been modified but not saved.

Regular Expressions

A regular expression is a text pattern that can match other text patterns. Ordinary characters stand for themselves, so a text pattern consisting solely of ordinary characters will simply match itself. However, matching gets more interesting when metacharacters are involved. A metacharacter is a character that is treated specially. For example, ^ (discussed in the following) is a metacharacter that anchors a pattern to the beginning of a line; it guarantees that a match will succeed only if the target is the first text on a line. Skillful use of metacharacters lets you work more productively.

Regular expressions have two roles in the editor:

1. contextual line specifiers

2. the *pat* in the substitute command

When used as a line specifier, the regular expression is enclosed in // (for a forward search) or ?? (for a reverse search). For example, the line specifier /fort/ specifies the next line containing the text *fort*. The substitute command replaces one chunk of text with another. The original text, which is often called the pattern, is specified as a regular expression; the replacement text is just ordinary text. (However, a few characters in the replacement are treated specially; see the "Replacement Text" section of this appendix.)

^	A caret anchors a search target to the beginning of a line. Thus, the pattern ^*the* will match the letters *the* only when they occur at the beginning of a line. The caret is magic only when used as the first character of a target (or when used in a character set, where it has a different meaning).
$	A currency symbol anchors a search target to the end of a line. Thus, the pattern *PP$* will match the letters *PP* only when they occur at the end of a line.
.	A period matches any single character. Thus, the pattern *b.d* will match *bed*, *bid*, *bad*, and any other three letters that begin with *b* and end with *d*.
[set]	A left square bracket introduces a character set. The end of the set is indicated by a right bracket. A character set matches any one of the characters in the set; for example, *[aeiou]* matches any single vowel. A hyphen may separate two characters to indicate that range of characters; for example, *[0-9]* indicates any one of the numerals. A caret as the first character of a character set means "the character set consists of all characters not explicitly mentioned." Thus, the character set *[^A-Z]* matches anything other than a capital letter.
*	An asterisk matches zero or more repetitions of the previous single-character matching expression. The asterisk is often used after a period to match anything, or after a character set to match any number of occurrences of that set. Thus, the pattern *[aeiou][aeiou]** will match any sequence of one or more vowels.
\<	The pair of characters, backslash, less than, anchors a pattern to the beginning of a word.
\>	The pair of characters, backslash, greater than, anchors a pattern to the end of a word.
\(	A backslash followed by a left parenthesis introduces a subexpression, which is terminated by \). Subexpressions have no effect on the regular expression matching, but they are useful when you want parts of the regular expression to appear in the replacement text.
\	A backslash is used to escape the following character.

The ex/vi editor has several option settings that affect pattern matching:

- The ignorecase option controls case sensitivity. When ignorecase is set, upper- and lowercase distinctions are ignored; when noignorecase is set, matches must be exact: *abc* won't match *Abc*.

- The magic mode dicates whether metacharacters are active. When magic is set, all of the metacharacters discussed are active; when nomagic is set, only the ^ and $ metacharacters are active.

See Appendix II for more information on these options.

Replacement Text

Although the replacement text of a substitute command is not a regular expression, it can contain several special characters.

&	An ampersand in the replacement text will be replaced by the text matched by the regular expression.
~	A tilde in the replacement text will be replaced by the previous replacement text.
\n	A backslash followed by a numeric digit will match the *n*th subexpression of the regular expression.
\u	The following single character will be converted to uppercase.
\l	The following single character will be converted to lowercase.
\U	The following text will be converted to uppercase, until a \e or \E is encountered.
\L	The following text will be converted to lowercase, until a \e or \E is encountered.

The following example demonstrates several aspects of regular expressions and some of the special characters in the replacement text:

```
$ ex Abe
"Abe" 4 lines, 138 characters
: 1,$p
four scor and SEVEN yeaars ago
hour four fathers brought for the anew
nation, dedicated to the proposition that
allmen are kreated equal.
: 1s/f/F
Four scor and SEVEN yeaars ago
: s/ a/e a/
Four score and SEVEN yeaars ago
: s/S.*N/\L&/
Four score and seven yeaars ago
: s/aa/a/
Four score and seven years ago
: s/ //
Fourscore and seven years ago
: +s/h//
our four fathers brought for the anew
```

```
: s/four //
our fathers brought for the anew
: s/for .*/forth a new/
our fathers brought forth a new
: +
nation, dedicated to the proposition that
: s/, / conceived in liberty and\
/
dedicated to the proposition that
: -,+
nation conceived in liberty and
dedicated to the proposition that
allmen are kreated equal.
: s/ll/& /
all men are kreated equal.
: s/k/c/
all men are created equal.
: w
"Abe" 5 lines, 155 characters
: q
$ cat Abe
Fourscore and seven years ago
our fathers brought forth a new
nation conceived in liberty and
dedicated to the proposition that
all men are created equal.
$
```

Index